Course	Managerial Accounting
Course Number	**ACCT 2301**
	Northeastern University
	College of Business Administration

http://create.mcgraw-hill.com

ISBN-10: 0697798631   ISBN-13: 9780697798633

Contents

Credits

CHAPTER 1

Management Accounting and Corporate Governance

LEARNING OBJECTIVES

After you have mastered the material in this chapter, you will be able to:

1 Distinguish between managerial and financial accounting.

2 Identify the cost components of a product made by a manufacturing company: the cost of materials, labor, and overhead.

3 Explain the effects on financial statements of product costs versus general, selling, and administrative costs.

4 Distinguish product costs from upstream and downstream costs.

5 Explain how product costing differs in service, merchandising, and manufacturing companies.

6 Show how just-in-time inventory can increase profitability.

7 Identify the key components of corporate governance.

8 Identify emerging trends in accounting (Appendix A).

CHAPTER OPENING

Andy Grove, Senior Advisor to Executive Management of Intel Corporation, is credited with the motto "Only the paranoid survive." Mr. Grove describes a wide variety of concerns that make him paranoid. Specifically, he declares:

I worry about products getting screwed up, and I worry about products getting introduced prematurely. I worry about factories not performing well, and I worry about having too many factories. I worry about hiring the right people, and I worry about morale slacking off. And, of course, I worry about competitors. I worry about other people figuring out how to do what we do better or cheaper, and displacing us with our customers.

Do Intel's historically-based financial statements contain the information Mr. Grove needs? No. **Financial accounting** is not designed to satisfy all the information needs of business managers. Its scope is limited to the needs of external users such as investors and creditors. The field of accounting designed to meet the needs of internal users is called **managerial accounting.**

The Curious Accountant

In the first course of accounting, you learned how retailers, such as Sears, account for the cost of equipment that lasts more than one year. Recall that the equipment was recorded as an asset when purchased, and then it was depreciated over its expected useful life. The depreciation charge reduced the company's assets and increased its expenses. This approach was justified under the matching principle, which seeks to recognize costs as expenses in the same period that the cost (resource) is used to generate revenue.

Is depreciation always shown as an expense on the income statement? The answer may surprise you. Consider the following scenario. Schwinn manufactures the bicycles that it sells to Sears. In order to produce the bicycles, Schwinn had to purchase a robotic machine that it expects can be used to produce 50,000 bicycles.

Do you think Schwinn should account for depreciation on its manufacturing equipment the same way Sears accounts for depreciation on its registers at the checkout counters? If not, how should Schwinn account for its depreciation? Remember the matching principle when thinking of your answer. (Answer on page 12.)

DIFFERENCES BETWEEN MANAGERIAL AND FINANCIAL ACCOUNTING

Distinguish between managerial and financial accounting.

While the information needs of internal and external users overlap, the needs of managers generally differ from those of investors or creditors. Some distinguishing characteristics are discussed in the following section.

Users and Types of Information

Financial accounting provides information used primarily by investors, creditors, and others *outside* a business. In contrast, managerial accounting focuses on information used by executives, managers, and employees who work *inside* the business. These two user groups need different types of information.

Internal users need information to *plan, direct,* and *control* business operations. The nature of information needed is related to an employee's job level. Lower level employees use nonfinancial information such as work schedules, store hours, and customer service policies. Moving up the organizational ladder, financial information becomes increasingly important. Middle managers use a blend of financial and nonfinancial information, while senior executives concentrate on financial data. To a lesser degree, senior executives also use general economic data and nonfinancial operating information. For example, an executive may consider the growth rate of the economy before deciding to expand the company's workforce.

External users (investors and creditors) have greater needs for general economic information than do internal users. For example, an investor debating whether to purchase stock versus bond securities might be more interested in government tax policy than financial statement data. Exhibit 1.1 summarizes the information needs of different user groups.

Level of Aggregation

External users generally desire *global information* that reflects the performance of a company as a whole. For example, an investor is not so much interested in the performance of a particular Sears store as she is in the performance of Sears Roebuck Company versus that of JC Penney Company. In contrast, internal users focus on detailed information about specific subunits of the company. To meet the needs of the different user groups, financial accounting data are more aggregated than managerial accounting data.

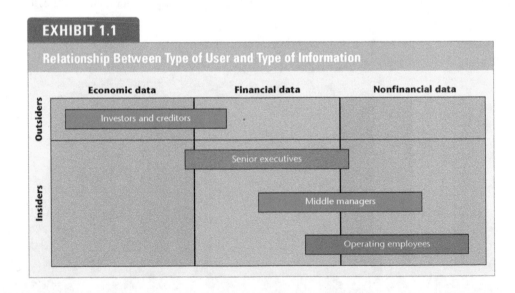

EXHIBIT 1.1

Relationship Between Type of User and Type of Information

Regulation

Financial accounting is designed to generate information for the general public. In an effort to protect the public interest, Congress established the **Securities and Exchange Commission (SEC)** and gave it authority to regulate public financial reporting practices. The SEC has delegated much of its authority for developing accounting rules to the private sector **Financial Accounting Standards Board (FASB),** thereby allowing the accounting profession considerable influence over financial accounting reports. The FASB supports a broad base of pronouncements and practices known as **generally accepted accounting principles (GAAP).** GAAP severely restricts the accounting procedures and practices permitted in published financial statements.

Beyond financial statement data, much of the information generated by management accounting systems is proprietary information not available to the public. Since this information is not distributed to the public, it need not be regulated to protect the public interest. Management accounting is restricted only by the **value-added principle.** Management accountants are free to engage in any information gathering and reporting activity so long as the activity adds value in excess of its cost. For example, management accountants are free to provide forecasted information to internal users. In contrast, financial accounting as prescribed by GAAP does not permit forecasting.

Information Characteristics

While financial accounting is characterized by its objectivity, reliability, consistency, and historical nature, managerial accounting is more concerned with relevance and timeliness. Managerial accounting uses more estimates and fewer facts than financial accounting. Financial accounting reports what happened yesterday; managerial accounting reports what is expected to happen tomorrow.

Time Horizon and Reporting Frequency

Financial accounting information is reported periodically, normally at the end of a year. Management cannot wait until the end of the year to discover problems. Planning, controlling, and directing require immediate attention. Managerial accounting information is delivered on a continuous basis.

Exhibit 1.2 summarizes significant differences between financial and managerial accounting.

PRODUCT COSTING IN MANUFACTURING COMPANIES

A major focus for managerial accountants is determining **product cost.**[1] Managers need to know the cost of their products for a variety of reasons. For example, **cost-plus pricing** is a common business practice.[2] **Product costing** is also used to control business operations. It is useful in answering questions such as: Are costs higher or lower than expected? Who is responsible for the variances between expected and actual costs? What actions can be taken to control the variances?

LO 2

Identify the cost components of a product made by a manufacturing company: the cost of materials, labor, and overhead.

Components of Product Cost

A company normally incurs three types of costs when making products. Specifically, the company must pay for (1) the *materials* used to make the products, (2) the *labor*

---

[1]This text uses the term *product* in a generic sense to mean both goods and services.
[2]Other pricing strategies will be introduced in subsequent chapters.

EXHIBIT 1.2

Comparative Features of Managerial versus Financial Accounting Information

Features	Managerial Accounting	Financial Accounting
Users	Insiders including executives, managers, and operators	Outsiders including investors, creditors, government agencies, analysts, and reporters
Information type	Economic and physical data as well as financial data	Financial data
Level of aggregation	Local information on subunits of the organization	Global information on the company as a whole
Regulation	No regulation, limited only by the value-added principle	Regulation by SEC, FASB, and other determiners of GAAP
Information characteristics	Estimates that promote relevance and enable timeliness	Factual information that is characterized by objectivity, reliability, consistency, and accuracy
Time horizon	Past, present, and future	Past only, historically based
Reporting frequency	Continuous reporting	Delayed with emphasis on annual reports

expended by the employees who transform the materials into products, and (3) the *overhead* (other resources such as utilities and equipment consumed in the process of making the products). If the company stores its products, the costs of the materials, labor, and overhead used in making the products are maintained in an inventory account until the products are sold. For a detailed explanation of how product costs flow through the financial statements, refer to the following example of Tabor Manufacturing Company.

Tabor Manufacturing Company

Tabor Manufacturing Company makes wooden tables. The company spent $1,000 cash to build four tables: $390 for materials, $470 for a carpenter's labor, and $140 for tools used in making the tables. How much is Tabor's expense? The answer is zero. The $1,000 cash has been converted into products (four tables). The cash payments for materials, labor, and tools (overhead) were *asset exchange* transactions. One asset (cash) decreased while another asset (tables) increased. Tabor will not recognize any expense until the tables are sold; in the meantime, the cost of the tables is held in an asset account called **Finished Goods Inventory.** Exhibit 1.3 illustrates how cash is transformed into inventory.

Average Cost per Unit

How much did each table made by Tabor cost? The *actual* cost of each of the four tables likely differs. The carpenter probably spent a little more time on some of the tables than others. Material and tool usage probably varied from table to table. Determining the exact cost of each table is virtually impossible. Minute details such as a second of labor time cannot be effectively measured. Even if Tabor could determine the exact cost of each table, the information would be of little use. Minor differences in the cost per table would make no difference in pricing or other decisions management needs to make. Accountants therefore normally calculate cost per unit as an *average*. In the case of Tabor Manufacturing, the **average cost** per table is $250 ($1,000 ÷ 4 units). Unless otherwise stated, assume *cost per unit* means *average cost per unit*.

EXHIBIT 1.3

Transforming the Asset Cash Into the Asset Finished Goods Inventory

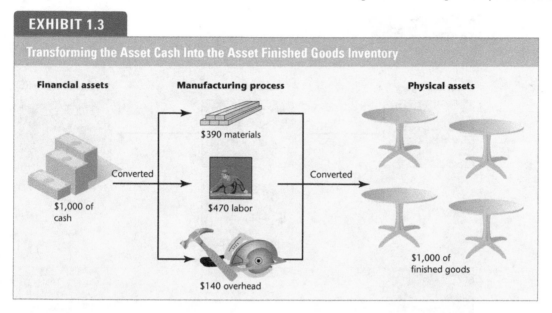

Financial assets

$1,000 of
cash

Converted

Manufacturing process

$390 materials

$470 labor

$140 overhead

Converted

Physical assets

$1,000 of
finished goods

✓ CHECK YOURSELF 1.1

All boxes of General Mills' Total Raisin Bran cereal are priced at exactly the same amount in your local grocery store. Does this mean that the actual cost of making each box of cereal was exactly the same?

Answer No, making each box would not cost exactly the same amount. For example, some boxes contain slightly more or less cereal than other boxes. Accordingly, some boxes cost slightly more or less to make than others do. General Mills uses average cost rather than actual cost to develop its pricing strategy.

Costs Can Be Assets or Expenses

It might seem odd that wages paid to production workers are recorded as inventory instead of being expensed. Remember, however, that expenses are assets used in the process of *earning revenue*. The cash paid to production workers is not used to produce revenue. Instead, the cash is used to produce inventory. Revenue will be earned when the inventory is used (sold). So long as the inventory remains on hand, all product costs (materials, labor, and overhead) remain in an inventory account.

When a table is sold, the average cost of the table is transferred from the Inventory account to the Cost of Goods Sold (expense) account. If some tables remain unsold at the end of the accounting period, part of the *product costs* is reported as an asset (inventory) on the balance sheet while the other part is reported as an expense (cost of goods sold) on the income statement.

Costs that are not classified as product costs are normally expensed in the period in which they are incurred. These costs include *general operating costs, selling and administrative costs, interest costs,* and the *cost of income taxes.*

To illustrate, return to the Tabor Manufacturing example. Recall that Tabor made four tables at an average cost per unit of $250. Assume Tabor pays an employee who sells three of the tables a $200 sales commission. The sales commission is expensed immediately. The total product cost for the three tables (3 tables × $250 each = $750) is expensed on the income statement as cost of goods sold. The portion of the total

EXHIBIT 1.4

Cost Classification for Tabor Manufacturing Company

product cost remaining in inventory is $250 (1 table × $250). Exhibit 1.4 shows the relationship between the costs incurred and the expenses recognized for Tabor Manufacturing Company.

Effect of Product Costs on Financial Statements

LO 3

Explain the effects on financial statements of product costs versus general, selling, and administrative costs.

We illustrate accounting for product costs in manufacturing companies with Patillo Manufacturing Company, a producer of ceramic pottery. Patillo, started on January 1, 2013, experienced the following accounting events during its first year of operations.[3] *Assume that all transactions except 6, 8, and 10 are cash transactions.*

1. Acquired $15,000 cash by issuing common stock.
2. Paid $2,000 for materials that were used to make products. All products started were completed during the period.
3. Paid $1,200 for salaries of selling and administrative employees.
4. Paid $3,000 for wages of production workers.
5. Paid $2,800 for furniture used in selling and administrative offices.
6. Recognized depreciation on the office furniture purchased in Event 5. The furniture was acquired on January 1, had a $400 estimated salvage value, and a four-year useful life. The annual depreciation charge is $600 [($2,800 − $400) ÷ 4].
7. Paid $4,500 for manufacturing equipment.
8. Recognized depreciation on the equipment purchased in Event 7. The equipment was acquired on January 1, had a $1,500 estimated salvage value, and a three-year useful life. The annual depreciation charge is $1,000 [($4,500 − $1,500) ÷ 3].
9. Sold inventory to customers for $7,500 cash.
10. The inventory sold in Event 9 cost $4,000 to make.

[3]This illustration assumes that all inventory started during the period was completed during the period. Patillo therefore uses only one inventory account, Finished Goods Inventory. Many manufacturing companies normally have three categories of inventory on hand at the end of an accounting period: Raw Materials Inventory, Work in Process Inventory (inventory of partially completed units), and Finished Goods Inventory. Chapter 11 discusses these inventories in greater detail.

EXHIBIT 1.5

Effect of Product versus Selling and Administrative Costs on Financial Statements

Event No.	Assets							Equity			Rev.	–	Exp.	=	Net Inc.
	Cash	+	Inventory	+	Office Furn.*	+	Manuf. Equip.*	=	Com. Stk.	+	Ret. Earn.					
1	15,000							=	15,000							
2	(2,000)	+	2,000													
3	(1,200)							=			(1,200)		–	1,200	=	(1,200)
4	(3,000)	+	3,000													
5	(2,800)	+			2,800											
6					(600)			=			(600)		–	600	=	(600)
7	(4,500)	+					4,500									
8			1,000	+			(1,000)									
9	7,500							=			7,500	7,500			=	7,500
10			(4,000)					=			(4,000)		–	4,000	=	(4,000)
Totals	9,000	+	2,000	+	2,200	+	3,500	=	15,000	+	1,700	7,500	–	5,800	=	1,700

*Negative amounts in these columns represent accumulated depreciation.

The effects of these transactions on the balance sheet and income statement are shown in Exhibit 1.5. Study each row in this exhibit, paying particular attention to how similar costs such as salaries for selling and administrative personnel and wages for production workers have radically different effects on the financial statements. The example illustrates the three elements of product costs, materials (Event 2), labor (Event 4), and overhead (Event 8). These events are discussed in more detail below.

Materials Costs (Event 2)

Materials used to make products are usually called **raw materials.** The cost of raw materials is first recorded in an asset account (Inventory). The cost is then transferred from the Inventory account to the Cost of Goods Sold account at the time the goods are sold. Remember that materials cost is only one component of total manufacturing costs. When inventory is sold, the combined cost of materials, labor, and overhead is expensed as *cost of goods sold*. The costs of materials that can be easily and conveniently traced to products are called **direct raw materials** costs.

Labor Costs (Event 4)

The salaries paid to selling and administrative employees (Event 3) and the wages paid to production workers (Event 4) are accounted for differently. Salaries paid to selling and administrative employees are expensed immediately, but the cost of production wages is added to inventory. Production wages are expensed as part of cost of goods sold at the time the inventory is sold. Labor costs that can be easily and conveniently traced to products are called **direct labor** costs. The cost flow of wages for production employees versus salaries for selling and administrative personnel is shown in Exhibit 1.6.

Overhead Costs (Event 8)

Although depreciation cost totaled $1,600 ($600 on office furniture and $1,000 on manufacturing equipment), only the $600 of depreciation on the office furniture is expensed directly on the income statement. The depreciation on the manufacturing equipment is split between the income statement (cost of goods sold) and the balance sheet (inventory). The depreciation cost flow for the manufacturing equipment versus the office furniture is shown in Exhibit 1.7.

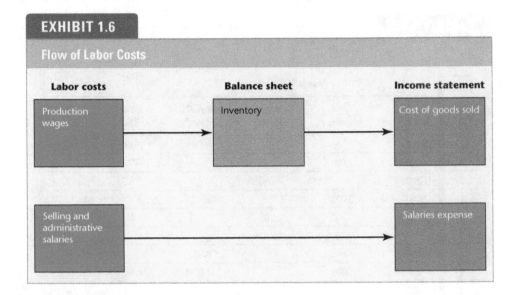

EXHIBIT 1.6

Flow of Labor Costs

EXHIBIT 1.7

Flow of Depreciation Costs

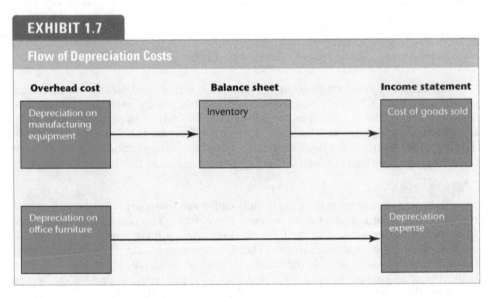

Total Product Cost.   A summary of Patillo Manufacturing's total product cost is shown in Exhibit 1.8.

Financial Statements

The income statement and balance sheet for Patillo Manufacturing are displayed in Exhibit 1.9.

Product Costs.   The $4,000 cost of goods sold reported on the income statement includes a portion of the materials, labor, and overhead costs incurred by Patillo during the year. Similarly, the $2,000 of finished goods inventory on the balance sheet includes materials, labor, and overhead costs. These product costs will be recognized as expense in the next accounting period when the goods are sold. Initially classifying a cost as a product cost delays, but does not eliminate, its recognition as an expense. All product costs are ultimately recognized as expense (cost of goods sold).

Selling, General, and Administrative Costs.   Selling, general, and administrative costs (SG&A) are normally expensed *in the period* in which they are incurred. Because of this recognition pattern, nonproduct expenses are sometimes called **period costs.** In Patillo's

EXHIBIT 1.8

Schedule of Inventory Costs

Materials	$2,000
Labor	3,000
Manufacturing overhead*	1,000
Total product costs	6,000
Less: Cost of goods sold	(4,000)
Ending inventory balance	$2,000

*Depreciation [($4,500 − $1,500) ÷ 3]

EXHIBIT 1.9

PATILLO MANUFACTURING COMPANY
Financial Statements

Income Statement for 2013

Sales revenue	$ 7,500
Cost of goods sold	(4,000)
Gross margin	3,500
SG&A expenses	
Salaries expense	(1,200)
Depreciation expense—office furniture	(600)
Net income	$ 1,700

Balance Sheet as of December 31, 2013

Cash		$ 9,000
Finished goods inventory		2,000
Office furniture	$2,800	
Accumulated depreciation	(600)	
Book value		2,200
Manufacturing equipment	4,500	
Accumulated depreciation	(1,000)	
Book value		3,500
Total assets		$16,700
Stockholders' equity		
Common stock		$15,000
Retained earnings		1,700
Total stockholders' equity		$16,700

case, the salaries expense for selling and administrative employees and the depreciation on office furniture are period costs reported directly on the income statement.

Overhead Costs: A Closer Look

Costs such as depreciation on manufacturing equipment cannot be easily traced to products. Suppose that Patillo Manufacturing makes both tables and chairs. What part of the depreciation is caused by manufacturing tables versus manufacturing chairs? Similarly, suppose a production supervisor oversees employees who work on both tables and chairs. How much of the supervisor's salary relates to tables and how much to chairs? Likewise, the cost of glue used in the production department would be difficult to trace to tables versus chairs. You could count the drops of glue used on each product, but the information would not be useful enough to merit the time and money spent collecting the data.

Costs that cannot be traced to products and services in a *cost-effective* manner are called **indirect costs.** The indirect costs incurred to make products are called **manufacturing overhead.** Some of the items commonly included in manufacturing overhead are indirect materials, indirect labor, factory utilities, rent of manufacturing facilities, and depreciation on manufacturing assets.

✓ **CHECK YOURSELF 1.2**

Lawson Manufacturing Company paid production workers wages of $100,000. It incurred materials costs of $120,000 and manufacturing overhead costs of $160,000. Selling and administrative salaries were $80,000. Lawson started and completed 1,000 units of product and sold 800 of these units. The company sets sales prices at $220 above the average per unit production cost. Based on this information alone, determine the amount of gross margin and net income. What is Lawson's pricing strategy called?

Answer Total product cost is $380,000 ($100,000 labor + $120,000 materials + $160,000 overhead). Cost per unit is $380 ($380,000 ÷ 1,000 units). The sales price per unit is $600 ($380 + $220). Cost of goods sold is $304,000 ($380 × 800 units). Sales revenue is $480,000 ($600 × 800 units). Gross margin is $176,000 ($480,000 revenue − $304,000 cost of goods sold). Net income is $96,000 ($176,000 gross margin − $80,000 selling and administrative salaries). Lawson's pricing strategy is called *cost-plus* pricing.

EXHIBIT 1.10

Cost Allocation

Since indirect costs cannot be effectively traced to products, they are normally assigned to products using **cost allocation**, a process of dividing a total cost into parts and assigning the parts to relevant cost objects. To illustrate, suppose that production workers spend an eight-hour day making a chair and a table. The chair requires two hours to complete and the table requires six hours. Now suppose that $120 of utilities cost is consumed during the day. How much of the $120 should be assigned to each piece of furniture? The utility cost cannot be directly traced to each specific piece of furniture, but the piece of furniture that required more labor also likely consumed more of the utility cost. Using this line of reasoning, it is rational to allocate the utility cost to the two pieces of furniture based on *direct labor hours* at a rate of $15 per hour ($120 ÷ 8 hours). The chair would be assigned $30 ($15 per hour × 2 hours) of the utility cost and the table would be assigned the remaining $90 ($15 × 6 hours) of utility cost. The allocation of the utility cost is shown in Exhibit 1.10.

We discuss the details of cost allocation in a later chapter. For now, recognize that overhead costs are normally allocated to products rather than traced directly to them.

Manufacturing Product Cost Summary

As explained, the cost of a product made by a manufacturing company is normally composed of three categories: direct materials, direct labor, and manufacturing overhead. Relevant information about these three cost components is summarized in Exhibit 1.11.

Answers to **The Curious Accountant**

As you have seen, accounting for depreciation related to manufacturing assets is different from accounting for depreciation for nonmanufacturing assets. Depreciation on the checkout equipment at Sears is recorded as depreciation expense. Depreciation on manufacturing equipment at Schwinn is considered a product cost. It is included first as a part of the cost of inventory and eventually as a part of the expense, cost of goods sold. Recording depreciation on manufacturing equipment as an inventory cost is simply another example of the matching principle, because the cost does not become an expense until revenue from the product sale is recognized.

Components of Manufacturing Product Cost

Component 1—Direct Raw Materials
Sometimes called *raw materials*. In addition to basic resources such as wood or metals, it can include manufactured parts. For example, engines, glass, and car tires can be considered as raw materials for an automotive manufacturer. If the amount of a material in a product is known, it can usually be classified as a direct material. The cost of direct materials can be easily traced to specific products.

Component 2—Direct Labor
The cost of wages paid to factory workers involved in hands-on contact with the products being manufactured. If the amount of time employees worked on a product can be determined, this cost can usually be classified as direct labor. Like direct materials, labor costs must be easily traced to a specific product in order to be classified as a direct cost.

Component 3—Manufacturing Overhead
Costs that cannot be easily traced to specific products. Accordingly, these costs are called indirect costs. They can include but are not limited to the following:

1. Indirect materials such as glue, nails, paper, and oil. Indeed, note that indirect materials used in the production process may not appear in the finished product. An example is a chemical solvent used to clean products during the production process but not a component material found in the final product.

2. Indirect labor such as the cost of salaries paid to production supervisors, inspectors, and maintenance personnel.

3. Rental cost for manufacturing facilities and equipment.

4. Utility costs.

5. Depreciation.

6. Security.

7. The cost of preparing equipment for the manufacturing process (i.e., setup costs).

8. Maintenance cost for the manufacturing facility and equipment.

UPSTREAM AND DOWNSTREAM COSTS

Most companies incur product-related costs before and after, as well as during, the manufacturing process. For example, Ford Motor Company incurs significant research and development costs prior to mass producing a new car model. These **upstream costs** occur before the manufacturing process begins. Similarly, companies normally incur significant costs after the manufacturing process is complete. Examples of **downstream costs** include transportation, advertising, sales commissions, and bad debts. While upstream and downstream costs are not considered to be product costs for financial reporting purposes, profitability analysis requires that they be considered in cost-plus pricing decisions. To be profitable, a company must recover the total cost of developing, producing, and delivering its products to customers.

Distinguish product costs from upstream and downstream costs.

PRODUCT COSTING IN SERVICE AND MERCHANDISING COMPANIES

Companies are frequently classified as being service, merchandising, or manufacturing businesses. As the name implies, service organizations provide services, rather than physical products, to consumers. For example, St. Jude Children's Hospital provides treatment programs aimed at healing patient diseases. Other common service providers include public accountants, lawyers, restaurants, dry cleaning establishments, and lawn care companies. Merchandising businesses are sometimes called retail or wholesale companies; they sell goods other companies make. The Home Depot, Inc., Costco Wholesale Corporation,

Explain how product costing differs in service, merchandising, and manufacturing companies.

and Best Buy Co., Inc., are merchandising companies. Manufacturing companies make the goods they sell to their customers. Toyota Motor Corporation, Texaco, Inc., and American Standard Companies, Inc., are manufacturing businesses.

How do manufacturing companies differ from service and merchandising businesses? Do service and merchandising companies incur materials, labor, and overhead costs? Yes. For example, Ernst & Young, a large accounting firm, must pay employees (labor costs), use office supplies (material costs), and incur utilities, depreciation, and so on (overhead costs) in the process of conducting audits. *The primary difference between manufacturing entities and service companies is that the products provided by service companies are consumed immediately.* In contrast, products made by manufacturing companies can be held in the form of inventory until they are sold to consumers. Similarly, most labor and overhead costs incurred by merchandising companies result from providing assistance to customers. These costs are normally treated as selling, general, and administrative expenses rather than accumulated in inventory accounts. Indeed, merchandising companies are often viewed as service companies rather than considered a separate business category.

The important point to remember is that all business managers are expected to control costs, improve quality, and increase productivity. Like managers of manufacturing companies, managers of service and merchandising businesses can benefit from the analysis of the cost of satisfying their customers. For example, Wendy's, a service company, can benefit from knowing how much a hamburger costs in the same manner that Bayer Corporation, a manufacturing company, benefits from knowing the cost of a bottle of aspirin.

✓ CHECK YOURSELF 1.3

The cost of making a Burger King hamburger includes the cost of materials, labor, and overhead. Does this mean that Burger King is a manufacturing company?

Answer   No, Burger King is not a manufacturing company. It is a service company because its products are consumed immediately. In contrast, there may be a considerable delay between the time the product of a manufacturing company is made and the time it is consumed. For example, it could be several months between the time Ford Motor Company makes an Explorer and the time the Explorer is ultimately sold to a customer. The primary difference between service and manufacturing companies is that manufacturing companies have inventories of products and service companies do not.

JUST-IN-TIME INVENTORY

Show how just-in-time inventory can increase profitability.

Companies attempt to minimize the amount of inventory they maintain because of the high cost of holding it. Many **inventory holding costs** are obvious: financing, warehouse space, supervision, theft, damage, and obsolescence. Other costs are hidden: diminished motivation, sloppy work, inattentive attitudes, and increased production time.

Many businesses have been able to simultaneously reduce their inventory holding costs and increase customer satisfaction by making products available **just in time (JIT)** for customer consumption. For example, hamburgers that are cooked to order are fresher and more individualized than those that are prepared in advance and stored until a customer orders one. Many fast-food restaurants have discovered that JIT systems lead not only to greater customer satisfaction but also to lower costs through reduced waste.

Just-in-Time Illustration

To illustrate the benefits of a JIT system, consider Paula Elliot, a student at a large urban university. She helps support herself by selling flowers. Three days each week,

Paula drives to a florist, purchases 25 single-stem roses, returns to the school, and sells the flowers to individuals from a location on a local street corner. She pays $2 per rose and sells each one for $3. Some days she does not have enough flowers to meet customer demand. Other days, she must discard one or two unsold flowers; she believes quality is important and refuses to sell flowers that are not fresh. During May, she purchased 300 roses and sold 280. She calculated her driving cost to be $45. Exhibit 1.12 displays Paula's May income statement.

After studying just-in-time inventory systems in her managerial accounting class, Paula decided to apply the concepts to her small business. She *reengineered* her distribution system by purchasing her flowers from a florist within walking distance of her sales location. She had considered purchasing from this florist earlier but had rejected the idea because the florist's regular selling price of $2.25 per rose was too high. After learning about *most-favored customer status,* she developed a strategy to get a price reduction. By guaranteeing that she would buy at least

At **Ford Motor Company**'s plant in Valencia, Spain, suppliers feed parts such as these bumpers just in time and in the right order directly to the assembly line.

30 roses per week, she was able to convince the local florist to match her current cost of $2.00 per rose. The local florist agreed that she could make purchases in batches of any size so long as the total amounted to at least 30 per week. Under this arrangement, Paula was able to buy roses *just in time* to meet customer demand. Each day she purchased a small number of flowers. When she ran out, she simply returned to the florist for additional ones.

The JIT system also enabled Paula to eliminate the cost of the *nonvalue-added activity* of driving to her former florist. Customer satisfaction actually improved because no one was ever turned away because of the lack of inventory. In June, Paula was able to buy and sell 310 roses with no waste and no driving expense. The June income statement is shown in Exhibit 1.13.

Paula was ecstatic about her $115 increase in profitability ($310 in June − $195 in May = $115 increase), but she was puzzled about the exact reasons for the change. She had saved $40 (20 flowers × $2 each) by avoiding waste and eliminated $45 of driving expenses. These two factors explained only $85 ($40 waste + $45 driving expense) of the $115 increase. What had caused the remaining $30 ($115 − $85) increase in profitability? Paula asked her accounting professor to help her identify the remaining $30 difference.

The professor explained that May sales had suffered from *lost opportunities.* Recall that under the earlier inventory system, Paula had to turn away some prospective customers because she sold out of flowers before all customers were served. Sales increased from 280 roses in May to 310 roses in June. A likely explanation for the 30 unit difference (310 − 280) is that customers who would have purchased flowers in May were unable to do so because of a lack of availability. May's sales suffered from the lost opportunity to earn a gross margin of $1 per flower on 30 roses, a $30 **opportunity cost.** This opportunity cost is the missing link in explaining the profitability difference between May and June. The total $115 difference consists of (1) $40 savings from waste elimination, (2) $45 savings from eliminating driving expense, and (3) opportunity cost of $30. The subject of opportunity cost has widespread application and is discussed in more depth in subsequent chapters of the text.

EXHIBIT 1.12

Income Statement for May

Sales revenue (280 units × $3 per unit)	$840
Cost of goods sold (280 units × $2 per unit)	(560)
Gross margin	280
Driving expense	(45)
Excess inventory waste (20 units × 2)	(40)
Net income	$195

EXHIBIT 1.13

Income Statement for June

Sales revenue (310 units × $3 per unit)	$930
Cost of goods sold (310 units × $2 per unit)	(620)
Gross margin	310
Driving expense	0
Net income	$310

✓ **CHECK YOURSELF 1.4**

A strike at a General Motors brake plant caused an almost immediate shutdown of many of the company's assembly plants. What could have caused such a rapid and widespread shutdown?

Answer   A rapid and widespread shutdown could have occurred because General Motors uses a just-in-time inventory system. With a just-in-time inventory system, there is no stockpile of inventory to draw on when strikes or other forces disrupt inventory deliveries. This illustrates a potential negative effect of using a just-in-time inventory system.

CORPORATE GOVERNANCE

LO 7

Identify the key components of corporate governance.

Corporate governance is the set of relationships between the board of directors, management, shareholders, auditors, and other stakeholders that determine how a company is operated. Until recently, corporations were generally free to govern themselves. However, several high-profile scandals have motivated governmental authorities to enact legislation designed to influence corporate governance. This section of the chapter examines the factors affecting corporate governance. We examine the motives and means of management corruption. Further, we introduce the mechanisms for self control including codes of ethics and internal controls. Finally, we discuss recent legislation designed to influence managerial responsibility for financial reporting.

Management accountants are at the forefront of corporate governance. They are the guardians of the information used to report on the financial condition of their companies. The information they prepare and analyze is used by the board of directors and company executives to formulate the company's operating strategy. Indeed, management accountants constitute the intelligence function of corporate governance. Scandals usually begin with schemes to manipulate a company's financial reports and end when the falsification is so great it becomes obvious the reports no longer represent reality. The appropriate management of the information function is a highly effective force against corrupt governance. It is little wonder why recent legislation requires the chief financial officer along with the chief executive officer to personally certify that the company's annual report does not contain false statements nor omit significant facts.

The Motive to Manipulate

Many managers are judged on their company's financial statements or the company's stock price which is determined, in part, by the financial statements. Managers are rewarded for strong financial statements with promotions, pay raises, bonuses, and stock options. Weak financials can result in a manager being passed over for promotions, demoted, or even fired. It is little wonder that some executives are tempted to manipulate financial statements.

To illustrate implications of statement manipulation, consider the events experienced by Marion Manufacturing Company (MMC) during its first year of operations. All transactions are cash transactions.

1. MMC was started when it acquired $12,000 from issuing common stock.
2. MMC incurred $4,000 of costs to design its product and plan the manufacturing process.
3. MMC incurred specifically identifiable product costs (materials, labor, and overhead) of $8,000 to make 1,000 units of product, resulting in a cost per unit of $8 ($8,000 ÷ 1,000 units).
4. MMC sold 700 units of inventory for $18 each.

EXHIBIT 1.14

Financial Statements Under Alternative Cost Classification Scenarios

Income Statements	Scenario 1	Scenario 2
Sales revenue (700 × $18)	$12,600	$12,600
Cost of goods sold	(5,600)[1]	(8,400)[3]
Gross margin	7,000	4,200
Selling and administrative expense	(4,000)	0
Net income	$ 3,000	$ 4,200

Balance Sheets		
Assets		
Cash	$12,600	$12,600
Inventory	2,400[2]	3,600[4]
Total assets	$15,000	$16,200
Stockholders' equity		
Common stock	$12,000	$12,000
Retained earnings	3,000	4,200
Total stockholders' equity	$15,000	$16,200

[1] 700 units × $8 per unit = $5,600
[2] 300 units × $8 per unit = $2,400
[3] [$5,600 + ($4,000 × .70)] = $8,400
[4] [$2,400 + ($4,000 × .30)] = $3,600

Exhibit 1.14 displays a balance sheet and income statement prepared under the following two scenarios.

Scenario 1: The $4,000 of design and planning costs are classified as selling and administrative expenses.

Scenario 2: The $4,000 of design and planning costs are classified as product costs, meaning they are first accumulated in the Inventory account and then expensed when the goods are sold. Given that MMC made 1,000 units and sold 700 units of inventory, 70% (700 ÷ 1,000) of the design cost has passed through the Inventory account into the Cost of Goods Sold account, leaving 30% (300 ÷ 1,000) remaining in the Inventory account.

Statement Differences

Comparing the financial statements prepared under Scenario 1 with those prepared under Scenario 2 reveals the following.

1. There are no selling and administrative expenses under Scenario 2. The design cost was treated as a product cost and placed into the Inventory account rather than being expensed.
2. Cost of goods sold is $2,800 ($4,000 design cost × .70) higher under Scenario 2.
3. Net income is $1,200 higher under Scenario 2 ($4,000 understated expense − $2,800 overstated cost of goods sold).
4. Ending inventory is $1,200 ($4,000 design cost × .30) higher under Scenario 2.

Practical Implications

The financial statement differences shown in Exhibit 1.14 are *timing differences*. When MMC sells the remaining 300 units of inventory, the $1,200 of design and planning costs included in inventory under Scenario 2 will be expensed through cost of goods sold. In other words, once the entire inventory is sold, total expenses and retained earnings will be the same under both scenarios. Initially recording cost in an inventory account only delays eventual expense recognition. However, the temporary effects on the financial statements can influence the (1) availability of financing, (2) motivations of management, and (3) timing of income tax payments.

Availability of Financing.   The willingness of creditors and investors to provide capital to a business is influenced by their expectations of the business's future financial performance. In general, more favorable financial statements enhance a company's ability to obtain financing from creditors or investors.

Management Motivation.   Financial statement results might affect executive compensation. For example, assume that Marion Manufacturing adopted a management incentive plan that provides a bonus pool equal to 10 percent of net income. In Scenario 1, managers would receive $300 ($3,000 × 0.10). In Scenario 2, however, managers would receive $420 ($4,200 × 0.10). Do not be deceived by the small numbers used for convenience in the example. We could illustrate with millions of dollars just as well as with hundreds of dollars. Managers would clearly favor Scenario 2. In fact, managers might be tempted to misclassify costs to manipulate the content of financial statements.

Income Tax Considerations.   Since income tax expense is calculated as a designated percentage of taxable income, managers seek to minimize taxes by reporting the minimum amount of taxable income. Scenario 1 in Exhibit 1.14 depicts the most favorable tax condition. In other words, with respect to taxes, managers prefer to classify costs as expenses rather than assets. The Internal Revenue Service is responsible for enforcing the proper classification of costs. Disagreements between the Internal Revenue Service and taxpayers are ultimately settled in federal courts.

Statement of Ethical Professional Practice

The preceding discussion provides some insight into conflicts of interest management accountants might face. It is tempting to misclassify a cost if doing so will significantly increase a manager's bonus. Management accountants must be prepared not only to make difficult choices between legitimate alternatives but also to face conflicts of a more troubling nature, such as pressure to:

1. Undertake duties they have not been trained to perform competently.
2. Disclose confidential information.
3. Compromise their integrity through falsification, embezzlement, bribery, and so on.
4. Issue biased, misleading, or incomplete reports.

To provide management accountants with guidance for ethical conduct the Institute of Management Accountants (IMA) issued a *Statement of Ethical Professional Practice,* which is shown in Exhibit 1.15. Management accountants are also frequently required to abide by organizational codes of ethics. Failure to adhere to professional and organizational ethical standards can lead to personal disgrace, loss of employment, or imprisonment.

The Fraud Triangle

Unfortunately, it takes more than a code of conduct to stop fraud. People frequently engage in activities that they know are unethical or even criminal. The auditing profession has determined that the following three elements are typically present when fraud occurs:

1. The availability of an *opportunity.*
2. The existence of some form of *pressure* leading to an incentive.
3. The capacity to *rationalize.*

EXHIBIT 1.15

Statement of Ethical Professional Practice

Members of IMA shall behave ethically. A commitment to ethical professional practice includes overarching principles that express our values, and standards that guide our conduct. IMA's overarching ethical principles include: Honesty, Fairness, Objectivity, and Responsibility. Members shall act in accordance with these principles and shall encourage others within their organizations to adhere to them. A member's failure to comply with the following standards may result in disciplinary action.

Competence Each member has a responsibility to
- Maintain an appropriate level of professional expertise by continually developing knowledge and skills.
- Perform professional duties in accordance with relevant laws, regulations, and technical standards.
- Provide decision support information and recommendations that are accurate, clear, concise, and timely.
- Recognize and communicate professional limitations or other constraints that would preclude responsible judgment or successful performance of an activity.

Confidentiality Each member has a responsibility to
- Keep information confidential except when disclosure is authorized or legally required.
- Inform all relevant parties regarding appropriate use of confidential information. Monitor subordinates' activities to ensure compliance.
- Refrain from using confidential information for unethical or illegal advantage.

Integrity Each member has a responsibility to
- Mitigate actual conflicts of interest and avoid apparent conflicts of interest. Advise all parties of any potential conflicts.
- Refrain from engaging in any conduct that would prejudice carrying out duties ethically.
- Abstain from engaging in or supporting any activity that might discredit the profession.

Credibility Each member has a responsibility to
- Communicate information fairly and objectively.
- Disclose all relevant information that could reasonably be expected to influence an intended user's understanding of the reports, analyses, or recommendations.
- Disclose delays or deficiencies in information, timeliness, processing, or internal controls in conformance with organization policy and/or applicable law.

Resolution of Ethical Conflict In applying these standards, you may encounter problems identifying unethical behavior or resolving an ethical conflict. When faced with ethical issues, follow your organization's established policies on the resolution of such conflict. If these policies do not resolve the ethical conflict, consider the following courses of action:
- Discuss the issue with your immediate supervisor except when it appears that the supervisor is involved. In that case, present the issue to the next level. If you cannot achieve a satisfactory resolution, submit the issue to the next management level. Communication of such problems to authorities or individuals not employed or engaged by the organization is not considered appropriate, unless you believe there is a clear violation of the law.
- Clarify relevant ethical issues by initiating a confidential discussion with an IMA Ethics Counselor or other impartial advisor to obtain a better understanding of possible courses of action.
- Consult your own attorney as to legal obligations and rights concerning the ethical conflict.

The three elements are frequently arranged in the shape of a triangle as shown in Exhibit 1.16.

Opportunity is shown at the head of the triangle because without opportunity fraud could not exist. The most effective way to reduce opportunities for ethical or criminal misconduct is to implement an effective set of internal controls. *Internal controls* are policies and procedures that a business implements to reduce opportunities for fraud and to ensure that its objectives will be accomplished. Specific controls are tailored to meet the individual needs of particular businesses. For example, banks use elaborate vaults to protect cash and safety deposit boxes, but universities have little use for this type of equipment. Even so, many of the same procedures are used by a wide variety of businesses.

EXHIBIT 1.16

REALITY BYTES

Unethical behavior occurs in all types of organizations. In its **2007 National Government Ethics Survey,** the Ethics Resource Center reported its findings on the occurrences and reporting of unethical behavior in local, state, and federal governments.

Fifty-seven percent of those surveyed reported having observed unethical conduct during the past year. Unethical conduct was reported most often by those in local governments (63%) and least often at the federal level (52%). The definition of ethical misconduct used in the study was quite broad, ranging from behavior such as an individual putting his or her personal interest ahead of the interest of the organization, to sexual harassment, to taking bribes. The more egregious offences, such as discrimination or taking bribes, were reported much less often than activities such as lying to customers, vendors, or the public.

Once observed, unethical behavior often was not reported. For example, only 25 percent of observed incidents of the alteration of financial records were reported to supervisors or whistleblower hotlines, and only 54 percent of observed bribes were reported.

The survey also found that only 18 percent of government entities have ethics and compliance programs in place that could be considered well-implemented. However, where well-implemented programs do exist, observed unethical misconduct is less likely to occur and more likely to be reported. In these entities only 36 percent of respondents said they had observed misconduct (compared to 57 percent overall), and when they did observe misconduct, 75 percent said they reported it.

For the complete *2007 National Government Ethics Survey,* go to www.ethics.org.

Exhibit 1.17 contains a summary of many of the internal control policies and procedures that have gained widespread acceptance.

Only a few employees turn to the dark side even when internal control is weak and opportunities abound. So, what causes one person to commit fraud and another to remain honest? The second element of the fraud triangle recognizes *pressure* as a key ingredient of misconduct. A manager who is told to either make the numbers or be fired is more likely to cheat than one who is told to tell it like it is. Pressure can come from a variety of sources, including:

- Personal vices such as drug addiction, gambling, and promiscuity.
- Intimidation from superiors.
- Personal debt from credit cards, consumer loans, mortgage loans or, poor investments.
- Family expectations to provide a standard of living that is beyond one's capabilities.
- Business failure caused by poor decision making or temporary factors such as a poor economy.
- Loyalty or trying to be agreeable.

The third and final element of the fraud triangle is *rationalization*. Few individuals think of themselves as evil. They develop rationalizations to justify their misconduct. Common rationalizations include the following:

- Everybody does it.
- They are not paying me enough. I'm only taking what I deserve.
- I'm only borrowing the money. I'll pay it back.
- The company can afford it. Look what they are paying the officers.
- I'm taking what my family needs to live like everyone else.

EXHIBIT 1.17

Common Internal Control Practices

Internal Control Practice	Explanation
Separating duties	Separating the duties necessary to complete a task and assigning the separated duties to two or more employees reduces the opportunity for either employee to defraud the company. It would require collusion between the two employees in order to make payment for a fabricated expense.
Hiring competent personnel	Cheap labor is not a bargain if the employees are incompetent. Employees should be properly trained and have a record that attests to personal integrity.
Bonding employees	Employees in positions of trust should be bonded through insurance policies that protect a company from losses caused by employee dishonesty.
Requiring extended absences	Forcing extended absences (such as vacations) creates an opportunity for the temporary replacement employee to check the work of the absent employees. Fraud is difficult to cover up if you are not present to do so.
Establishing clear lines of authority and responsibility	Employees tend to be more zealous in supporting company policies when they have clear authority to exercise enforcement. Further, they take their work more seriously when they realize that they cannot shirk responsibility.
Using prenumbered documents	Missing documents become apparent when there are gaps in a recorded sequence of numbers. For example, a stolen check would become apparent if a check register omits a check number.
Establishing physical controls	Keeping money in a safe; holding inventory in locked warehouses; and bolting computers to a desk are examples of using physical controls designed to protect assets.
Performing evaluations at regular intervals	Knowing that inventory will be counted on a regular basis encourages the inventory control manager to maintain documents that support the actual balance of inventory on hand. Similarly verifying the mileage on a car will encourage employees to use company-owned vehicles for legitimate business purposes. Regular evaluations and examinations are strong deterrents to the inappropriate utilization of company-owned assets.

Most people are able to resist pressure and the tendency to rationalize ethical or legal misconduct. However, some people will yield to temptation. What can companies do to protect themselves from unscrupulous characters? The answer lies in personal integrity. The best indicator of personal integrity is past performance. Accordingly companies must exercise due care in performing appropriate background investigations before hiring people to fill positions of trust.

Sarbanes-Oxley Act of 2002

In spite of ethics training and accounting controls, fraud and its devastating consequences persist. Enron, WorldCom, and HealthSouth are examples of massive scandals that destroyed or crippled major U.S. corporations in recent years. These high-profile cases led government officials to conclude that the force of law would be necessary to restore and maintain confidence in the capital markets. The **Sarbanes-Oxley (SOX) Act,** which became effective July 30, 2002, provides the muscle that Congress hopes will deter future fiascos. SOX affects four groups including: management, boards of directors, external auditors, and the Public Company Accounting Oversight Board (PCAOB). In

FOCUS ON INTERNATIONAL ISSUES

FINANCIAL ACCOUNTING VERSUS MANAGERIAL ACCOUNTING—AN INTERNATIONAL PERSPECTIVE

This chapter has already explained some of the conceptual differences between financial and managerial accounting, but these differences have implications for international businesses as well. With respect to financial accounting, publicly traded companies in most countries must follow the generally accepted accounting principles (GAAP) for their country, but these rules can vary from country to country. Generally, companies that are audited under the auditing standards of the United States follow the standards established by the Financial Accounting Standards Board. Most companies located outside of the United States follow the standards established by the International Accounting Standards Board. For example, the United States is one of very few countries whose GAAP allow the use of the LIFO inventory cost flow assumption.

Conversely, most of the managerial accounting concepts introduced in this course can be used by businesses in any country. For example, *activity-based costing (ABC)* is a topic addressed in Chapter 6 and is used by many companies in the United States. Meanwhile, a study published in *Accountancy Ireland** found that approximately one-third of the companies surveyed in Ireland, the United Kingdom, and New Zealand were also either using ABC, or were considering adopting it.

*Bernard Pierce, "Activity-Based Costing; the Irish Experience: True Innovation or Passing Fad?" *Accountancy Ireland,* October 2004, pp. 28–31.

this text, we focus on how SOX affects corporate management. While extensive coverage of SOX is beyond the scope of this text, all management accountants should be aware of the following:

- SOX holds the chief executive officer (CEO) and the chief financial officer (CFO) responsible for the establishment and enforcement of a strong set of internal controls. Along with its annual report, companies are required to report on the effectiveness of their internal controls. Also, the company's external auditors are required to attest to the accuracy of the internal controls report.

- SOX charges the CEO and the CFO with the ultimate responsibility for the accuracy of the company's financial statements and the accompanying notes. Even though lower-level managers will likely prepare the annual report, the CEO and CFO are required to certify that they have reviewed the report and that, to their knowledge, the report does not contain false statements or significant omissions. An intentional misrepresentation is punishable by a fine of up to $5 million and imprisonment of up to 20 years.

- SOX requires management to establish a code of ethics and to file reports on the code in the company's annual 10K report filed with the Securities and Exchange Commission.

- SOX demands that management establish a hotline and other mechanisms for the anonymous reporting of fraudulent activities. Further, SOX prohibits companies from punishing whistleblowers, employees who legally report corporate misconduct.

The accounting profession and government authorities are becoming increasingly intolerant of unethical conduct and illegal activity. A single mistake can jeopardize an accountant's career. A person guilty of white-collar crime loses the opportunity for white-collar employment. Second chances are rarely granted.

A Look Back

Managerial accounting focuses on the information needs of *internal* users, while *financial accounting* focuses on the information needs of *external* users. Managerial accounting uses economic, operating, and nonfinancial, as well as financial, data. Managerial accounting information is local (pertains to the company's subunits), is limited by cost/benefit considerations, is more concerned with relevance and timeliness, and is future oriented. Financial accounting information, on the other hand, is more global than managerial accounting information. It supplies information that applies to the whole company. Financial accounting is regulated by numerous authorities, is characterized by objectivity, is focused on reliability and accuracy, and is historical in nature.

Both managerial and financial accounting are concerned with product costing. Financial accountants need product cost information to determine the amount of inventory reported on the balance sheet and the amount of cost of goods sold reported on the income statement. Managerial accountants need to know the cost of products for pricing decisions and for control and evaluation purposes. When determining unit product costs, managers use the average cost per unit. Determining the actual cost of each product requires an unreasonable amount of time and record keeping and it makes no difference in product pricing and product cost control decisions.

Product costs are the costs incurred to make products: the costs of direct materials, direct labor, and overhead. *Overhead costs* are product costs that cannot be cost effectively traced to a product; therefore, they are assigned to products using *cost allocation*. Overhead costs include indirect materials, indirect labor, depreciation, rent, and utilities for manufacturing facilities. Product costs are first accumulated in an asset account (Inventory). They are expensed as cost of goods sold in the period the inventory is sold. The difference between sales revenue and cost of goods sold is called *gross margin*.

Selling, general, and administrative costs are classified separately from product costs. They are subtracted from gross margin to determine net income. Selling, general, and administrative costs can be divided into two categories. Costs incurred before the manufacturing process begins (research and development costs) are *upstream costs*. Costs incurred after manufacturing is complete (transportation) are *downstream costs*.

Service companies, like manufacturing companies, incur materials, labor, and overhead costs, but the products provided by service companies are consumed immediately. Therefore, service company product costs are not accumulated in an Inventory account.

A *code of ethical conduct* is needed in the accounting profession because accountants hold positions of trust and face conflicts of interest. In recognition of the temptations that accountants face, the IMA has issued a *Statement of Ethical Professional Practice,* which provides accountants guidance in resisting temptations and in making difficult decisions.

Emerging trends such as *just-in-time inventory* and *activity-based management* are methods that many companies have used to reengineer their production and delivery systems to eliminate waste, reduce errors, and minimize costs. Activity-based management seeks to eliminate or reduce *nonvalue-added activities* and to create new *value-added activities.* Just-in-time inventory seeks to reduce inventory holding costs and to lower prices for customers by making inventory available just in time for customer consumption.

A Look Forward

In addition to distinguishing costs by product versus SG&A classification, other classifications can be used to facilitate managerial decision making. In the next chapter, costs are classified according to the *behavior* they exhibit when the number of units of product increases or decreases (volume of activity changes). You will learn to distinguish between costs that vary with activity volume changes versus costs that remain fixed with activity volume changes. You will learn not only to recognize *cost behavior* but also how to use such recognition to evaluate business risk and opportunity.

APPENDIX A

Emerging Trends in Managerial Accounting

Identify emerging trends in accounting.

Global competition has forced many companies to reengineer their production and delivery systems to eliminate waste, reduce errors, and minimize costs. A key ingredient of successful **reengineering** is benchmarking. **Benchmarking** involves identifying the **best practices** used by world-class competitors. By studying and mimicking these practices, a company uses benchmarking to implement highly effective and efficient operating methods. Best practices employed by world-class companies include total quality management (TQM), activity-based management (ABM), and value-added assessment.

Total Quality Management

To promote effective and efficient operations, many companies practice **total quality management (TQM).** TQM is a two-dimensional management philosophy using (1) a systematic problem-solving philosophy that encourages frontline workers to achieve *zero defects* and (2) an organizational commitment to achieving *customer satisfaction*. A key component of TQM is **continuous improvement,** an ongoing process through which employees strive to eliminate waste, reduce response time, minimize defects, and simplify the design and delivery of products and services to customers.

Activity-Based Management

Simple changes in perspective can have dramatic results. For example, imagine how realizing the world is round instead of flat changed the nature of travel. A recent change in perspective developing in management accounting is the realization that an organization cannot manage *costs*. Instead, it manages the *activities* that cause costs to be incurred. **Activities** represent the measures an organization takes to accomplish its goals.

The primary goal of all organizations is to provide products (goods and services) their customers *value*. The sequence of activities used to provide products is called a **value chain. Activity-based management** assesses the value chain to create new or refine existing **value-added activities** and to eliminate or reduce *nonvalue-added activities*. A value-added activity is any unit of work that contributes to a product's ability to satisfy customer needs. For example, cooking is an activity that adds value to food served to a hungry customer. **Nonvalue-added activities** are tasks undertaken that do not contribute to a product's ability to satisfy customer needs. Waiting for the oven to preheat so that food can be cooked does not add value. Most customers value cooked food, but they do not value waiting for it.

To illustrate, consider the value-added activities undertaken by a pizza restaurant. Begin with a customer who is hungry for pizza; certain activities must occur to satisfy that hunger. These activities are pictured in Exhibit 1.18. At a minimum, the restaurant must conduct research and development (devise a recipe), obtain raw materials (acquire the ingredients), manufacture the product (combine and bake the ingredients), market the product (advertise its availability), and deliver the product (transfer the pizza to the customer).

EXHIBIT 1.18

Value Chain

Conducting research and development → Obtaining materials → Manufacturing → Marketing → Delivering

Businesses gain competitive advantages by adding activities that satisfy customer needs. For example, Domino's Pizza grew briskly by recognizing the value customers placed on the convenience of home pizza delivery. Alternatively, Little Caesar's has been highly successful by satisfying customers who value low prices. Other restaurants capitalize on customer values pertaining to taste, ambience, or location. Businesses can also gain competitive advantages by identifying and eliminating nonvalue-added activities, providing products of comparable quality at lower cost than competitors.

Value Chain Analysis Across Companies

Comprehensive value chain analysis extends from obtaining raw materials to the ultimate disposition of finished products. It encompasses the activities performed not only by a particular organization but also by that organization's suppliers and those who service its finished products. For example, PepsiCo must be concerned with the activities of the company that supplies the containers for its soft drinks as well as the retail companies that sell its products. If cans of Pepsi fail to open properly, the customer is more likely to blame PepsiCo than the supplier of the cans. Comprehensive value chain analysis can lead to identifying and eliminating nonvalue-added activities that occur between companies. For example, container producers could be encouraged to build manufacturing facilities near Pepsi's bottling factories, eliminating the nonvalue-added activity of transporting empty containers from the manufacturer to the bottling facility. The resulting cost savings benefits customers by reducing costs without affecting quality.

A step-by-step audio-narrated series of slides is provided on the text website at www.mhhe.com/edmonds2011.

SELF-STUDY REVIEW PROBLEM

Tuscan Manufacturing Company makes a unique headset for use with mobile phones. During 2012, its first year of operations, Tuscan experienced the following accounting events. Other than the adjusting entries for depreciation, assume that all transactions are cash transactions.

1. Acquired $850,000 cash from the issue of common stock.
2. Paid $50,000 of research and development costs to develop the headset.
3. Paid $140,000 for the materials used to make headsets, all of which were started and completed during the year.
4. Paid salaries of $82,200 to selling and administrative employees.
5. Paid wages of $224,000 to production workers.
6. Paid $48,000 to purchase furniture used in selling and administrative offices.
7. Recognized depreciation on the office furniture. The furniture, acquired January 1, had an $8,000 estimated salvage value and a four-year useful life. The amount of depreciation is computed as [(cost − salvage) ÷ useful life]. Specifically, [($48,000 − $8,000) ÷ 4 = $10,000].
8. Paid $65,000 to purchase manufacturing equipment.
9. Recognized depreciation on the manufacturing equipment. The equipment, acquired January 1, had a $5,000 estimated salvage value and a three-year useful life. The amount of depreciation is computed as [(cost − salvage) ÷ useful life]. Specifically, [($65,000 − $5,000) ÷ 3 = $20,000].
10. Paid $136,000 for rent and utility costs on the manufacturing facility.
11. Paid $41,000 for inventory holding expenses for completed headsets (rental of warehouse space, salaries of warehouse personnel, and other general storage costs).
12. Tuscan started and completed 20,000 headset units during 2012. The company sold 18,400 headsets at a price of $38 per unit.
13. Compute the average product cost per unit and recognize the appropriate amount of cost of goods sold.

Required

a. Show how these events affect the balance sheet and income statement by recording them in a horizontal financial statements model.

b. Prepare a formal income statement for the year.

c. Distinguish between the product costs and the upstream and downstream costs that Tuscan incurred.

d. The company president believes that Tuscan could save money by buying the inventory that it currently makes. The warehouse supervisor said that would not be possible because the purchase price of $27 per unit was above the $26 average cost per unit of making the product. Assuming that the purchased inventory would be available on demand, explain how the company president could be correct and why the warehouse supervisor could be biased in his assessment of the option to buy the inventory.

Solution to Requirement a

Event No.	Cash	Inventory +	Office Furn.* +	Manuf. Equip.* =	Com. Stk. +	Ret. Earn.	Rev. −	Exp. =	Net Inc.
	Assets				**=**	**Equity**			
1	850,000				850,000				
2	(50,000)					(50,000)	−	50,000	(50,000)
3	(140,000)	140,000							
4	(82,200)					(82,200)	−	82,200	(82,200)
5	(224,000)	224,000							
6	(48,000)		48,000						
7			(10,000)			(10,000)	−	10,000	(10,000)
8	(65,000)			65,000					
9		20,000		(20,000)					
10	(136,000)	136,000							
11	(41,000)					(41,000)	−	41,000	(41,000)
12	699,200					699,200	699,200		699,200
13		(478,400)				(478,400)	−	478,400	(478,400)
Totals	763,000 +	41,600 +	38,000 +	45,000 =	850,000 +	37,600	699,200 −	661,600 =	37,600

*Negative amounts in these columns represent accumulated depreciation.

The average cost per unit of product is determined by dividing the total product cost by the number of headsets produced. Specifically, ($140,000 + $224,000 + $20,000 + $136,000) ÷ 20,000 = $26. Cost of goods sold is $478,400 ($26 × 18,400).

Solution to Requirement b

TUSCAN MANUFACTURING COMPANY
Income Statement
For the Year Ended December 31, 2012

Sales revenue (18,400 units × $38)	$699,200
Cost of goods sold (18,400 × $26)	(478,400)
Gross margin	220,800
R&D expenses	(50,000)
Selling and admin. salaries expense	(82,200)
Admin. depreciation expense	(10,000)
Inventory holding expense	(41,000)
Net income	$ 37,600

Solution to Requirement c

Inventory product costs for manufacturing companies focus on the costs necessary to make the product. The cost of research and development (Event 2) occurs before the inventory is made and is therefore an upstream cost, not an inventory (product) cost. The inventory holding costs (Event 11) are incurred after the inventory has been made and are therefore downstream costs, not product costs. Selling costs (included in Events 4 and 7) are normally incurred after products have been made and are therefore usually classified as downstream costs. Administrative costs (also included in Events 4 and 7) are not related to making products and are therefore not classified as product costs. Administrative costs may be incurred before, during, or after products are made, so they may be classified as either upstream or downstream costs. Only the costs of materials, labor, and overhead that are actually incurred for the purpose of making goods (Events 3, 5, 9, and 10) are classified as product costs.

Solution to Requirement d

Since the merchandise would be available on demand, Tuscan could operate a just-in-time inventory system thereby eliminating the inventory holding expense. Since the additional cost to purchase is $1 per unit ($27 − $26), it would cost Tuscan an additional $20,000 ($1 × 20,000 units) to purchase its product. However, the company would save $41,000 of inventory holding expense. The warehouse supervisor could be biased by the fact that his job would be lost if the company purchased its products and thereby could eliminate the need for warehousing inventory. If Tuscan does not maintain inventory, it would not need a warehouse supervisor.

KEY TERMS

Activities 24	Finished Goods Inventory 6	Raw materials 9
Activity-based management (ABM) 23	Generally accepted accounting principles (GAAP) 5	Reengineering 24
Average cost 26	Indirect costs 11	Sarbanes-Oxley Act of 2002 21
Benchmarking 24	Inventory holding costs 14	Securities and Exchange
Best practices 24	Just in time (JIT) 14	Commission (SEC) 5
Continuous improvement 24	Managerial accounting 2	Selling, general, and
Cost allocation 12	Manufacturing	administrative costs
Cost-plus pricing 5	overhead 11	(SG&A) 10
Direct labor 9	Nonvalue-added	Total quality management
Direct raw materials 9	activities 15	(TQM) 24
Downstream costs 14	Opportunity cost 15	Upstream costs 13
Financial accounting 2	Overhead 6	Value-added activity 24
Financial Accounting	Period costs 10	Value-added principle 5
Standards Board	Product costs 5	Value chain 24
(FASB) 5	Product costing 5	

QUESTIONS

1. What are some differences between financial and managerial accounting?

2. What does the value-added principle mean as it applies to managerial accounting information? Give an example of value-added information that may be included in managerial accounting reports but is not shown in publicly reported financial statements.

3. What are the two dimensions of a total quality management (TQM) program? Why is TQM being used in business practice? (Appendix A)

4. How does product costing used in financial accounting differ from product costing used in managerial accounting?

5. What does the statement "costs can be assets or expenses" mean?

6. Why are the salaries of production workers accumulated in an inventory account instead of being expensed on the income statement?

7. How do product costs affect the financial statements? How does the classification of product cost (as an asset vs. an expense) affect net income?

8. What is an indirect cost? Provide examples of product costs that would be classified as indirect.

9. How does a product cost differ from a selling, general, and administrative cost? Give examples of each.

10. Why is cost classification important to managers?

11. What is cost allocation? Give an example of a cost that needs to be allocated.

12. How has the Institute of Management Accountants responded to the need for high standards of ethical conduct in the accounting profession?

13. What are some of the common ethical conflicts that accountants encounter?

14. What costs should be considered in determining the sales price of a product?

15. What is a just-in-time (JIT) inventory system? Name some inventory costs that can be eliminated or reduced by its use.

16. What does the term *reengineering* mean? Name some reengineering practices. (Appendix A)

17. What does the term *activity-based management* mean? (Appendix A)

18. What is a value chain? (Appendix A)

19. What do the terms *value-added activity* and *nonvalue-added activity* mean? Provide an example of each type of activity. (Appendix A)

MULTIPLE-CHOICE QUESTIONS

Multiple-choice questions are provided on the text website at www.mhhe.com/edmonds2011.

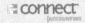
www.mhhe.com/edmonds2011

EXERCISES—SERIES A

All applicable Exercises in Series A are available with McGraw-Hill's *Connect Accounting*.

LO 1

Exercise 1-1A *Identifying financial versus managerial accounting items*

Required

Indicate whether each of the following items is representative of managerial or of financial accounting.

a. Information is provided to outsiders including investors, creditors, government agencies, analysts, and reporters.

b. Information is regulated by the SEC, FASB, and other sources of GAAP.

c. Information is based on estimates that are bounded by relevance and timeliness.

d. Information is historically based and usually reported annually.

e. Information is local and pertains to subunits of the organization.

f. Information includes economic and nonfinancial data as well as financial data.

g. Information is global and pertains to the company as a whole.

h. Information is provided to insiders including executives, managers, and employees.

i. Information is factual and is characterized by objectivity, reliability, consistency, and accuracy.

j. Information is reported continuously and has a current or future orientation.

LO 2, 3

Exercise 1-2A *Identifying product versus general, selling, and administrative costs*

Required

Indicate whether each of the following costs should be classified as a product cost or as a selling, general, and administrative cost.

a. Salaries of employees working in the accounting department.

b. Commissions paid to sales staff.

c. Interest on the mortgage for the company's corporate headquarters.

d. Indirect labor used to manufacture inventory.

e. Attorney's fees paid to protect the company from frivolous lawsuits.

f. Research and development costs incurred to create new drugs for a pharmaceutical company.

g. The cost of secretarial supplies used in a doctor's office.

h. Depreciation on the office furniture of the company president.

i. Direct materials used in a manufacturing company.

j. Indirect materials used in a manufacturing company.

Exercise 1-3A   *Classifying Costs: Product or SG&A/Asset or Expense*   LO 2, 3

Required

Use the following format to classify each cost as a product cost or a selling, general, and administrative (SG&A) cost. Also indicate whether the cost would be recorded as an asset or an expense. The first item is shown as an example.

Cost Category	Product/SG&A	Asset/Expense
Research and development costs	SG&A	Expense
Cost to set up manufacturing equipment		
Utilities used in manufacturing facility		
Cars for sales staff		
Distributions to stockholders		
General office supplies		
Raw materials used in the manufacturing process		
Cost to rent office equipment		
Wages of production workers		
Advertising costs		
Promotion costs		
Production supplies		
Depreciation on administration building		
Depreciation on manufacturing equipment		

Exercise 1-4A   *Identifying effect of product versus selling, general, and administrative costs on financial statements*   LO 3

Required

Nailry Corporation recognized accrued compensation cost. Use the following model to show how this event would affect the company's financial statement under the following two assumptions: (1) the compensation is for office personnel and (2) the compensation is for production workers. Use pluses or minuses to show the effect on each element. If an element is not affected, indicate so by placing the letters NA under the appropriate heading.

	Assets	=	Liab.	+	Equity	Rev.	−	Exp.	=	Net Inc.
1.										
2.										

Exercise 1-5A   *Identify effect of product versus selling, general, and administrative costs on financial statements*   LO 3

Required

Engle Industries recognized the annual cost of depreciation on its December 31, 2012, financial statements. Using the following horizontal financial statements model, indicate how this event affected the company's financial statements under the following two assumptions: (1) the depreciation was on office furniture and (2) the depreciation was on manufacturing equipment. Indicate whether the event increases (I), decreases (D), or has no affect (NA) on each element of the financial statements. (Note: Show accumulated depreciation as a decrease in the book value of the appropriate asset account.)

	Assets				Equity				
Event No.	Cash	+ Inventory	+ Manuf. Equip.	+ Office Furn.	= Com. Stk.	+ Ret. Ear.	Rev.	− Exp.	= Net Inc.
1.									
2.									

LO 2

Exercise 1-6A *Identifying product costs in a manufacturing company*

Tiffany Crissler was talking to another accounting student, Bill Tyrone. Upon discovering that the accounting department offered an upper-level course in cost measurement, Tiffany remarked to Bill, "How difficult can it be? My parents own a toy store. All you have to do to figure out how much something costs is look at the invoice. Surely you don't need an entire course to teach you how to read an invoice."

Required

a. Identify the three main components of product cost for a manufacturing entity.

b. Explain why measuring product cost for a manufacturing entity is more complex than measuring product cost for a retail toy store.

c. Assume that Tiffany's parents rent a store for $7,500 per month. Different types of toys use different amounts of store space. For example, displaying a bicycle requires more store space than displaying a deck of cards. Also, some toys remain on the shelf longer than others. Fad toys sell rapidly, but traditional toys sell more slowly. Under these circumstances, how would you determine the amount of rental cost required to display each type of toy? Identify two other costs incurred by a toy store that may be difficult to allocate to individual toys.

LO 3

Exercise 1-7A *Identifying product versus selling, general, and administrative costs*

A review of the accounting records of Rayford Manufacturing indicated that the company incurred the following payroll costs during the month of September.

1. Salary of the company president—$32,000.
2. Salary of the vice president of manufacturing—$16,000.
3. Salary of the chief financial officer—$18,800.
4. Salary of the vice president of marketing—$15,600.
5. Salaries of middle managers (department heads, production supervisors) in manufacturing plant—$196,000.
6. Wages of production workers—$938,000.
7. Salaries of administrative secretaries—$112,000.
8. Salaries of engineers and other personnel responsible for maintaining production equipment—$178,000.
9. Commissions paid to sales staff—$252,000.

Required

a. What amount of payroll cost would be classified as selling, general, and administrative expense?

b. Assuming that Rayford made 4,000 units of product and sold 3,600 of them during the month of September, determine the amount of payroll cost that would be included in cost of goods sold.

LO 2, 3

Exercise 1-8A *Recording product versus selling, general, and administrative costs in a financial statements model*

Pappas Manufacturing experienced the following events during its first accounting period.

1. Recognized depreciation on manufacturing equipment.
2. Recognized depreciation on office furniture.

3. Recognized revenue from cash sale of products.
4. Recognized cost of goods sold from sale referenced in Event 3.
5. Acquired cash by issuing common stock.
6. Paid cash to purchase raw materials that were used to make products.
7. Paid wages to production workers.
8. Paid salaries to administrative staff.

Required

Use the following horizontal financial statements model to show how each event affects the balance sheet and income statement. Indicate whether the event increases (I), decreases (D), or has no effect (NA) on each element of the financial statements. The first transaction has been recorded as an example. (*Note:* Show accumulated depreciation as a decrease in the book value of the appropriate asset account.)

Event No.	Assets				Equity		Rev.	− Exp.	= Net Inc.
	Cash	+ Inventory +	Manuf. Equip. +	Office Furn. =	Com. Stk. +	Ret. Ear.	Rev.	− Exp.	= Net Inc.
1.	NA	I	D	NA	NA	NA	NA	NA	NA

Exercise 1-9A *Allocating product costs between ending inventory and cost of goods sold*   LO 2

Howle Manufacturing Company began operations on January 1. During the year, it started and completed 1,700 units of product. The company incurred the following costs.

1. Raw materials purchased and used—$3,150.
2. Wages of production workers—$3,530.
3. Salaries of administrative and sales personnel—$1,995.
4. Depreciation on manufacturing equipment—$4,370.
5. Depreciation on administrative equipment—$1,835.

Howle sold 1,020 units of product.

Required

a. Determine the total product cost for the year.
b. Determine the total cost of the ending inventory.
c. Determine the total of cost of goods sold.

Exercise 1-10A *Financial statement effects for manufacturing versus service organizations*   LO 3

The following financial statements model shows the effects of recognizing depreciation in two different circumstances. One circumstance represents recognizing depreciation on a machine used in a factory. The other circumstance recognizes depreciation on computers used in a consulting firm. The effects of each event have been recorded using the letter (I) to represent increase, (D) for decrease, and (NA) for no effect.

Event No.	Assets			Equity		Rev.	− Exp.	= Net Inc.
	Cash +	Inventory +	Equip. =	Com. Stk. +	Ret. Ear.	Rev.	− Exp.	= Net Inc.
1.	NA	NA	D	NA	D	NA	I	D
2.	NA	I	D	NA	NA	NA	NA	NA

Required

a. Identify the event that represents depreciation on the computers.

b. Explain why recognizing depreciation on equipment used in a manufacturing company affects financial statements differently from recognizing depreciation on equipment used in a service organization.

LO 3

Exercise 1-11A *Identifying the effect of product versus selling, general, and administrative cost on the income statement*

Each of the following events describes acquiring an asset that requires a year-end adjusting entry.

1. Paid $14,000 cash on January 1 to purchase computer equipment to be used for administrative purposes. The equipment had an estimated expected useful life of four years and a $2,000 salvage value.

2. Paid $14,000 cash on January 1 to purchase manufacturing equipment. The equipment had an estimated expected useful life of four years and a $2,000 salvage value.

3. Paid $12,000 cash in advance on May 1 for a one-year rental contract on administrative offices.

4. Paid $12,000 cash in advance on May 1 for a one-year rental contract on manufacturing facilities.

5. Paid $2,000 cash to purchase supplies to be used by the marketing department. At the end of the year, $400 of supplies was still on hand.

6. Paid $2,000 cash to purchase supplies to be used in the manufacturing process. At the end of the year, $400 of supplies was still on hand.

Required

Explain how the adjusting entry affects the amount of net income shown on the year-end financial statements. Assume a December 31 annual closing date. The first event has been recorded as an example. Assume that any products that have been made have not been sold.

	Net Income
Event No.	**Amount of Change**
1. Adjusting entry	$(3,000)

LO 4

Exercise 1-12A *Upstream and downstream costs*

During 2011, Gallo Manufacturing Company incurred $90,000,000 of research and development (R&D) costs to create a long-life battery to use in computers. In accordance with FASB standards, the entire R&D cost was recognized as an expense in 2011. Manufacturing costs (direct materials, direct labor, and overhead) are expected to be $260 per unit. Packaging, shipping, and sales commissions are expected to be $50 per unit. Gallo expects to sell 2,000,000 batteries before new research renders the battery design technologically obsolete. During 2011, Gallo made 440,000 batteries and sold 400,000 of them.

Required

a. Identify the upstream and downstream costs.

b. Determine the 2011 amount of cost of goods sold and the ending inventory balance.

c. Determine the sales price assuming that Gallo desires to earn a profit margin that is equal to 25 percent of the *total cost* of developing, making, and distributing the batteries.

d. Prepare an income statement for 2011. Use the sales price developed in Requirement *c*.

e. Why would Gallo price the batteries at a level that would generate a loss for the 2011 accounting period?

LO 6

Exercise 1-13A *Identify the effect of a just-in-time inventory system on financial statements*

After reviewing the financial statements of Bearden Company, Todd Howard concluded that the company was a service company. Mr. Howard based his conclusion on the fact that Bearden's financial statements displayed no inventory accounts.

Required

Explain how Bearden's implementation of a 100 percent effective just-in-time inventory system could have led Mr. Howard to a false conclusion regarding the nature of Bearden's business.

Exercise 1-14A   *Using JIT to minimize waste and lost opportunity*

LO 6

Anne Kyser, a teacher at Hewitt Middle School, is in charge of ordering the T-shirts to be sold for the school's annual fund-raising project. The T-shirts are printed with a special Hewitt School logo. In some years, the supply of T-shirts has been insufficient to satisfy the number of sales orders. In other years, T-shirts have been left over. Excess T-shirts are normally donated to some charitable organization. T-shirts cost the school $8 each and are normally sold for $14 each. Ms. Kyser has decided to order 800 shirts.

Required

a. If the school receives actual sales orders for 725 shirts, what amount of profit will the school earn? What is the cost of waste due to excess inventory?
b. If the school receives actual sales orders for 825 shirts, what amount of profit will the school earn? What amount of opportunity cost will the school incur?
c. Explain how a JIT inventory system could maximize profitability by eliminating waste and opportunity cost.

Exercise 1-15A   *Using JIT to minimize holding costs*

LO 6

Lee Pet Supplies purchases its inventory from a variety of suppliers, some of which require a six-week lead time before delivering the goods. To ensure that she has a sufficient supply of goods on hand, Ms. Polk, the owner, must maintain a large supply of inventory. The cost of this inventory averages $21,000. She usually finances the purchase of inventory and pays a 9 percent annual finance charge. Ms. Polk's accountant has suggested that she establish a relationship with a single large distributor who can satisfy all of her orders within a two-week time period. Given this quick turnaround time, she will be able to reduce her average inventory balance to $4,000. Ms. Polk also believes that she could save $2,500 per year by reducing phone bills, insurance, and warehouse rental space costs associated with ordering and maintaining the larger level of inventory.

Required

a. Is the new inventory system available to Ms. Polk a pure or approximate just-in-time system?
b. Based on the information provided, how much of Ms. Polk's inventory holding cost could be eliminated by taking the accountant's advice?

Exercise 1-16A   *Applications of the Sarbanes-Oxley Act*

LO 7

The CFO of the Rigney Microscope Corporation intentionally misclassified a downstream transportation expense in the amount of $67,500,000 as a product cost in an accounting period when the company made 12,000 microscopes and sold 7,000 microscopes. Rigney rewards its officers with bonuses that are based on net earnings.

Required

a. Indicate whether the elements on the financial statements (i.e., assets, liabilities, equity, revenue, expense, and net income) would be overstated or understated as a result of the misclassification of the upstream research and development expense. Determine the amount of the overstatement or understatement for each element.
b. Based on the provisions of the Sarbanes-Oxley Act, what is the maximum penalty that the CFO could face for deliberately missrepresenting the financial statements?

Exercise 1-17A   *Professional conduct and code of ethics*

LO 7

In February 2006 former senator Warren Rudman of New Hampshire completed a 17-month investigation of an $11 billion accounting scandal at Fannie Mae (a major enterprise involved in home mortgage financing), The Rudman investigation concluded that Fannie Mae's CFO and controller used an accounting gimmick to manipulate financial statements in order to meet earnings-per-share (EPS) targets. Meeting the EPS targets triggered bonus payments for the executives. Fannie Mae's problems continued after 2006, and on September 8, 2008, it went into conservatorship under the control of the Federal Housing Financing Agency. The primary executives at the time of the Rudman investigation were replaced, and the enterprise reported a $59.8 billion loss in 2008.

Required

Review the principles of ethical professional practice shown in Exhibit 1.15. Identify and comment on which of the ethical principles the CFO and controller violated.

LO 8

Exercise 1-18A   *Value chain analysis (Appendix)*

Sonic Company manufactures and sells high-quality audio speakers. The speakers are encased in solid walnut cabinets supplied by Moore Cabinet, Inc. Moore packages the speakers in durable moisture-proof boxes and ships them by truck to Sonic manufacturing facility, which is located 50 miles from the cabinet factory.

Required

Identify the nonvalue-added activities that occur between the companies described in the preceding scenario. Provide a logical explanation as to how these nonvalue-added activities could be eliminated.

PROBLEMS—SERIES A

connect
ʲACCOUNTING

All applicable Problems in Series A are available with McGraw-Hill's *Connect Accounting*.

LO 2, 3

CHECK FIGURES
a. Average Cost per Unit: $8.40
f. $90,400

Problem 1-19A   *Product versus selling, general, and administrative costs*

Jolly Manufacturing Company was started on January 1, 2011, when it acquired $90,000 cash by issuing common stock. Jolly immediately purchased office furniture and manufacturing equipment costing $10,000 and $28,000, respectively. The office furniture had a five-year useful life and a zero salvage value. The manufacturing equipment had a $4,000 salvage value and an expected useful life of three years. The company paid $12,000 for salaries of administrative personnel and $16,000 for wages to production personnel. Finally, the company paid $18,000 for raw materials that were used to make inventory. All inventory was started and completed during the year. Jolly completed production on 5,000 units of product and sold 4,000 units at a price of $15 each in 2011. (Assume that all transactions are cash transactions.)

Required

a. Determine the total product cost and the average cost per unit of the inventory produced in 2011.
b. Determine the amount of cost of goods sold that would appear on the 2011 income statement.
c. Determine the amount of the ending inventory balance that would appear on the December 31, 2011, balance sheet.
d. Determine the amount of net income that would appear on the 2011 income statement.
e. Determine the amount of retained earnings that would appear on the December 31, 2011, balance sheet.
f. Determine the amount of total assets that would appear on the December 31, 2011, balance sheet.

LO 3

eXcel

CHECK FIGURES
Cash balance: $33,000
Net income: $4,600

Problem 1-20A   *Effect of product versus period costs on financial statements*

Hoehn Manufacturing Company experienced the following accounting events during its first year of operation. With the exception of the adjusting entries for depreciation, assume that all transactions are cash transactions.

1. Acquired $50,000 cash by issuing common stock.
2. Paid $8,000 for the materials used to make its products, all of which were started and completed during the year.
3. Paid salaries of $4,400 to selling and administrative employees.
4. Paid wages of $7,000 to production workers.
5. Paid $9,600 for furniture used in selling and administrative offices. The furniture was acquired on January 1. It had a $1,600 estimated salvage value and a four-year useful life.

6. Paid $13,000 for manufacturing equipment. The equipment was acquired on January 1. It had a $1,000 estimated salvage value and a three-year useful life.

7. Sold inventory to customers for $25,000 that had cost $14,000 to make.

Required

Explain how these events would affect the balance sheet and income statement by recording them in a horizontal financial statements model as indicated here. The first event is recorded as an example.

	Financial Statements Model								
	Assets				**Equity**				
Event No.	**Cash**	**+ Inventory**	**Manuf. + Equip.***	**Office + Furn.***	**= Com. Stk.**	**Ret. + Ear.**	**Rev.**	**− Exp.**	**= Net Inc.**
1.	50,000				50,000				

*Record accumulated depreciation as negative amounts in these columns.

Problem 1-21A *Product versus selling, general, and administrative costs*

LO 2, 3

The following transactions pertain to 2012, the first-year operations of Hall Company. All inventory was started and completed during 2012. Assume that all transactions are cash transactions.

1. Acquired $4,000 cash by issuing common stock.
2. Paid $720 for materials used to produce inventory.
3. Paid $1,800 to production workers.
4. Paid $540 rental fee for production equipment.
5. Paid $180 to administrative employees.
6. Paid $144 rental fee for administrative office equipment.
7. Produced 300 units of inventory of which 200 units were sold at a price of $12 each.

Required

Prepare an income statement and a balance sheet.

Problem 1-22A *Service versus manufacturing companies*

LO 2, 3, 5

Goree Company began operations on January 1, 2011, by issuing common stock for $30,000 cash. During 2011, Goree received $40,000 cash from revenue and incurred costs that required $60,000 of cash payments.

Required

Prepare an income statement and a balance sheet for Goree Company for 2011, under each of the following independent scenarios.

a. Goree is a promoter of rock concerts. The $60,000 was paid to provide a rock concert that produced the revenue.

b. Goree is in the car rental business. The $60,000 was paid to purchase automobiles. The automobiles were purchased on January 1, 2011, have four-year useful lives, with no expected salvage value. Goree uses straight-line depreciation. The revenue was generated by leasing the automobiles.

c. Goree is a manufacturing company. The $60,000 was paid to purchase the following items:

   (1) Paid $8,000 cash to purchase materials that were used to make products during the year.

   (2) Paid $20,000 cash for wages of factory workers who made products during the year.

   (3) Paid $2,000 cash for salaries of sales and administrative employees.

   (4) Paid $30,000 cash to purchase manufacturing equipment. The equipment was used solely to make products. It had a three-year life and a $6,000 salvage value. The company uses straightline depreciation.

   (5) During 2011, Goree started and completed 2,000 units of product. The revenue was earned when Goree sold 1,500 units of product to its customers.

d. Refer to Requirement *c*. Could Goree determine the actual cost of making the 907th unit of product? How likely is it that the actual cost of the 907th unit of product was exactly the same as the cost of producing the 908th unit of product? Explain why management may be more interested in average cost than in actual cost.

LO 3, 7

CHECK FIGURES
a. Option 1: NI = $38,000
   Option 2: Total
   Assets = $82,000

Problem 1-23A   *Importance of cost classification*

Cooke Manufacturing Company (CMC) was started when it acquired $40,000 by issuing common stock. During the first year of operations, the company incurred specifically identifiable product costs (materials, labor, and overhead) amounting to $24,000. CMC also incurred $16,000 of engineering design and planning costs. There was a debate regarding how the design and planning costs should be classified. Advocates of Option 1 believe that the costs should be classified as general, selling, and administrative costs. Advocates of Option 2 believe it is more appropriate to classify the design and planning costs as product costs. During the year, CMC made 4,000 units of product and sold 3,000 units at a price of $24 each. All transactions were cash transactions.

Required

a. Prepare an income statement and a balance sheet under each of the two options.

b. Identify the option that results in financial statements that are more likely to leave a favorable impression on investors and creditors.

c. Assume that CMC provides an incentive bonus to the company president equal to 13 percent of net income. Compute the amount of the bonus under each of the two options. Identify the option that provides the president with the higher bonus.

d. Assume a 35 percent income tax rate. Determine the amount of income tax expense under each of the two options. Identify the option that minimizes the amount of the company's income tax expense.

e. Comment on the conflict of interest between the company president as determined in Requirement *c* and the owners of the company as indicated in Requirement *d*. Describe an incentive compensation plan that would avoid a conflict of interest between the president and the owners.

LO 6

Problem 1-24A   *Using JIT to reduce inventory holding costs*

Burt Manufacturing Company obtains its raw materials from a variety of suppliers. Burt's strategy is to obtain the best price by letting the suppliers know that it buys from the lowest bidder. Approximately four years ago, unexpected increased demand resulted in materials shortages. Burt was unable to find the materials it needed even though it was willing to pay premium prices. Because of the lack of raw materials, Burt was forced to close its manufacturing facility for two weeks. Its president vowed that her company would never again be at the mercy of its suppliers. She immediately ordered her purchasing agent to perpetually maintain a one-month supply of raw materials. Compliance with the president's orders resulted in a raw materials inventory amounting to approximately $1,600,000. Warehouse rental and personnel costs to maintain the inventory amounted to $8,000 per month. Burt has a line of credit with a local bank that calls for a 12 percent annual rate of interest. Assume that Burt finances the raw materials inventory with the line of credit.

CHECK FIGURE
a. $288,000

Required

a. Based on the information provided, determine the annual holding cost of the raw materials inventory.

b. Explain how a JIT system could reduce Burt's inventory holding cost.

c. Explain how most-favored customer status could enable Burt to establish a JIT inventory system without risking the raw materials shortages experienced in the past.

LO 6

Problem 1-25A   *Using JIT to minimize waste and lost opportunity*

CMA Review, Inc., provides review courses twice each year for students studying to take the CMA exam. The cost of textbooks is included in the registration fee. Text material requires constant updating and is useful for only one course. To minimize printing costs and ensure availability of books on the first day of class, CMA Review has books printed and delivered to its offices two weeks in advance of the first class. To ensure that enough books are available, CMA Review normally orders 10 percent more than expected enrollment. Usually there is an oversupply and books are thrown away. However, demand occasionally exceeds expectations by more than 10 percent and there are too few books available for student use. CMA Review has been forced to turn away students because of a lack of textbooks. CMA Review expects to enroll approximately 100 students per course. The tuition fee is $800 per student. The cost of teachers is $25,000 per course, textbooks cost $60 each, and other operating expenses are estimated to be $35,000 per course.

Required

a. Prepare an income statement, assuming that 95 students enroll in a course. Determine the cost of waste associated with unused books.

b. Prepare an income statement, assuming that 115 students attempt to enroll in the course. Note that five students are turned away because of too few textbooks. Determine the amount of lost profit resulting from the inability to serve the five additional students.

c. Suppose that textbooks can be produced through a high-speed copying process that permits delivery *just in time* for class to start. The cost of books made using this process, however, is $65 each. Assume that all books must be made using the same production process. In other words, CMA Review cannot order some of the books using the regular copy process and the rest using the high-speed process. Prepare an income statement under the JIT system assuming that 95 students enroll in a course. Compare the income statement under JIT with the income statement prepared in Requirement *a*. Comment on how the JIT system would affect profitability.

d. Assume the same facts as in Requirement *c* with respect to a JIT system that enables immediate delivery of books at a cost of $65 each. Prepare an income statement under the JIT system, assuming that 115 students enroll in a course. Compare the income statement under JIT with the income statement prepared in Requirement *b*. Comment on how the JIT system would affect profitability.

e. Discuss the possible effect of the JIT system on the level of customer satisfaction.

Problem 1-26A *Internal control procedures*

LO 7

Adam Kimble is a model employee. He has not missed a day of work in the last five years. He even forfeits his vacation time to make sure that things run smoothly. Adam literally does the work of two people. He started out working as the purchasing agent in charge of buying raw materials for a small manufacturing company. Approximately five years ago the inventory control agent in the receiving department resigned. Adam agreed to assume the duties of the control agent until a replacement could be hired. After all, Adam said that he knew what was supposed to be delivered to the company because as the purchasing agent he had been the person who placed orders for the inventory purchases. Adam did such a good job that the company never got around to hiring a replacement. Adam received the employee of the year award five out of the last six years. Adam is also very active in his community. He works with underprivileged children. His weekends are always filled with community service. Indeed, his commitment to social consciousness is described by some people as bordering on fanatical.

Adam recently had a serious heart attack. People said that he had overworked himself. His hospital room was filled with flowers and a steady stream of friends visited him. So, people were in shock when Adam was charged with embezzlement. Ultimately, it was revealed that while Adam was in the hospital his replacement discovered that Adam had been purchasing excess quantities of raw materials. He then sold the extra materials and kept the money for himself. This became apparent when the companies to whom Adam had been selling the excess materials called to place new orders. It was difficult to determine the extent of the embezzlement. After the accounting department paid for Adam's excess purchases, he would remove the paid voucher forms from the accounting files and destroy them. Since the forms were not numbered, it was impossible to determine how many of the paid forms were missing. At his trial, Adam's only explanation was: "I did it for the children. They needed the money far more than the company needed it."

Required

a. If the internal control procedures shown in Exhibit 1.17 had been followed, this embezzlement could have been avoided. Name the internal control procedures that were violated in this case.

b. Identify the specific components of the fraud triangle that were present in this case.

LO 8

Problem 1-27A   *Value chain analysis (Appendix)*

Jensen Company invented a new process for manufacturing ice cream. The ingredients are mixed in high-tech machinery that forms the product into small round beads. Like a bag of balls, the ice cream beads are surrounded by air pockets in packages. This design has numerous advantages. First, each bite of ice cream melts rapidly when placed in a person's mouth, creating a more flavorful sensation when compared to ordinary ice cream. Also, the air pockets mean that a typical serving includes a smaller amount of ice cream. This not only reduces materials cost but also provides the consumer with a low-calorie snack. A cup appears full of ice cream, but it is really half full of air. The consumer eats only half the ingredients that are contained in a typical cup of blended ice cream. Finally, the texture of the ice cream makes scooping it out of a large container a very easy task. The frustration of trying to get a spoon into a rock-solid package of blended ice cream has been eliminated. Jensen Company named the new product Sonic Cream.

Like many other ice cream producers, Jensen Company purchases its raw materials from a food wholesaler. The ingredients are mixed in Jensen's manufacturing plant. The packages of finished product are distributed to privately owned franchise ice cream shops that sell Sonic Cream directly to the public.

Jensen provides national advertising and is responsible for all research and development costs associated with making new flavors of Sonic Cream.

Required

a. Based on the information provided, draw a comprehensive value chain for Jensen Company that includes its suppliers and customers.
b. Identify the place in the chain where Jensen Company is exercising its opportunity to create added value beyond that currently being provided by its competitors.

EXERCISES—SERIES B

LO 1

Exercise 1-1B   *Financial versus managerial accounting items*

Required

Indicate whether each of the following items is representative of financial or managerial accounting.

a. Condensed financial information sent to current investors at the end of each quarter.
b. Audited financial statements submitted to bankers when applying for a line of credit.
c. A weekly cash budget used by the treasurer to determine whether cash on hand is excessive.
d. Monthly sales reports used by the vice president of marketing to help allocate funds.
e. Divisional profit reports used by the company president to determine bonuses for divisional vice presidents.
f. Financial results used by stockbrokers to evaluate a company's profitability.
g. Quarterly budgets used by management to determine future borrowing needs.
h. Financial statements prepared in accordance with generally accepted accounting principles.
i. Annual financial reports submitted to the SEC in compliance with federal securities laws.
j. Projected budget information used to make logistical decisions.

LO 2, 3

Exercise 1-2B   *Identifying product versus selling, general, and administrative costs*

Required

Indicate whether each of the following costs should be classified as a product cost or as a general, selling, and administrative cost.

a. The salary of the cell phone manufacturing plant manager.
b. The depreciation on administrative buildings.
c. The depreciation on the company treasurer's computer.
d. The fabric used in making a customized sofa for a customer.
e. The salary of an engineer who maintains all manufacturing plant equipment.
f. Wages paid to workers in a manufacturing plant.

g. The salary of the receptionist working in the sales department.

h. Supplies used in the sales department.

i. Wages of janitors who clean the factory floor.

j. The salary of the company president.

Exercise 1-3B *Classifying costs: product or period / asset or expense*

LO 2, 3

Required

Use the following format to classify each cost as a product cost or a selling, general, and administrative (SG&A) cost. Also indicate whether the cost would be recorded as an asset or an expense. The first cost item is shown as an example.

Cost Category	Product/ SG&A	Asset/ Expense
Supplies used in the plant manager's office	Product	Asset
Purchase of computers for the accounting department		
Depreciation on computers used in factory		
Natural gas used in the factory		
Cost of television commercials		
Wages of factory workers		
Paper and ink cartridges used in the cashier's office		
Raw material used to make products		
Lubricant used to maintain factory equipment		
Cost of a delivery truck		
Cash dividend to stockholders		
Cost of merchandise shipped to customers		
Depreciation on vehicles used by salespeople		
Wages of administrative building security guards		

Exercise 1-4B *Effect of product versus selling, general, and administrative costs on financial statements*

LO 3

Required

Pedigo Plastics Company accrued a tax liability for $4,000. Use the following horizontal financial statements model to show the effect of this accrual under the following two assumptions: (1) the tax is on administrative buildings, or (2) the tax is on production equipment. Use plus signs and/or minus signs to show the effect on each element. If an element is not affected, indicate so by placing the letters NA under the appropriate heading.

	Assets	=	Liab.	+	Equity	Rev.	−	Exp.	=	Net Inc.
1.										
2.										

Exercise 1-5B *Effect of product versus selling, general, and administrative cost on financial statements*

LO 3

Required

Stanley Corporation recognized the annual expiration of insurance on December 31, 2012. Using the following horizontal financial statements model shown, indicate how this event affected the company's financial statements under the following two assumptions: (1) the insurance was for office equipment, or (2) the insurance was for manufacturing equipment. Indicate whether the event increases (I), decreases (D), or does not affect (NA) each element of the financial statements.

Event No.	Assets				Equity					
	Cash	+ Prepaid Insurance	+ Inventory	=	Com. Stk.	+ Ret. Ear.		Rev.	− Exp.	= Net Inc.
1.										
2.										

LO 2

Exercise 1-6B *Product costs in a manufacturing company*

Because friends and neighbors frequently praise her baking skills, Martha Plott plans to start a new business baking cakes for customers. She wonders how to determine the cost of her cakes.

Required

a. Identify and give examples of the three components of product cost incurred in producing cakes.

b. Explain why measuring product cost for a bakery is more complex than measuring product cost for a retail store.

c. Assume that Martha decides to bake cakes for her customers at her home. Consequently, she will avoid the cost of renting a bakery. However, her home utility bills will increase. She also plans to offer different types of cakes for which baking time will vary. Cakes mixed with ice cream will require freezing, and other cakes will need refrigeration. Some can cool at room temperature. Under these circumstances, how can Martha estimate the amount of utility cost required to produce a given cake? Identify two costs other than utility cost that she will incur that could be difficult to measure.

LO 3

Exercise 1-7B *Product versus selling, general, and administrative costs*

In reviewing Laxton Company's September accounting records, Mitchell Hinz, the chief accountant, noted the following depreciation costs.

1. Factory buildings—$25,000.
2. Computers used in manufacturing—$4,000.
3. A building used to display finished products—$8,000.
4. Trucks used to deliver merchandise to customers—$14,000.
5. Forklifts used in the factory—$22,000.
6. Furniture used in the president's office—$9,000.
7. Elevators in administrative buildings—$6,000.
8. Factory machinery—$9,000.

Required

a. What amount of depreciation cost would be classified as selling, general, and administrative expense?

b. Assume that Laxton manufactured 3,000 units of product and sold 2,000 units of product during the month of September. Determine the amount of depreciation cost that would be included in cost of goods sold.

LO 2, 3

Exercise 1-8B *Recording product versus selling, general, and administrative costs in a financial statements model*

Reid Electronics Company experienced the following events during its first accounting period.

1. Received $120,000 cash by issuing common stock.
2. Paid $18,000 cash for wages to production workers.
3. Paid $9,000 for salaries to administrative staff.
4. Purchased for cash and used $9,000 of raw materials.
5. Recognized $1,000 of depreciation on administrative offices.
6. Recognized $1,500 of depreciation on manufacturing equipment.

7. Recognized $48,000 of sales revenue from cash sales of products.

8. Recognized $30,000 of cost of goods sold from the sale referenced in Event 7.

Required

Use a horizontal financial statements model to show how each event affects the balance sheet and income statement. Indicate whether the event increases (I), decreases (D), or does not affect (NA) each element of the financial statements. The first transaction is shown as an example. (*Note:* Show accumulated depreciation as a decrease in the book value of the appropriate asset account.)

Event No.	Assets				Equity					
	Cash	+ Inventory	+ Manuf. Equip.	+ Adm. Offices	= Com. Stk.	+ Ret. Ear.	Rev.	− Exp.	= Net Inc.
1.	I	NA	NA	NA	I	NA	NA	NA	NA

Exercise 1-9B *Allocating product costs between ending inventory and cost of goods sold*   LO 2

Ryan Manufacturing Company began operations on January 1. During January, it started and completed 3,000 units of product. The company incurred the following costs:

1. Raw materials purchased and used—$5,000.
2. Wages of production workers—$4,000.
3. Salaries of administrative and sales personnel—$2,000.
4. Depreciation on manufacturing equipment—$3,000.
5. Depreciation on administrative equipment—$2,400.

Ryan sold 2,500 units of product.

Required

a. Determine the total product cost.
b. Determine the total cost of the ending inventory.
c. Determine the total of cost of goods sold.

Exercise 1-10B *Financial statement effects for manufacturing versus service organizations*   LO 3

The following horizontal financial statements model shows the effects of recording the expiration of insurance in two different circumstances. One circumstance represents the expiration of insurance on a factory building. The other circumstance represents the expiration of insurance on an administrative building. The effects of each event have been recorded using the letters (I) for increase, (D) for decrease, and (NA) for no effect.

Event No.	Assets			Equity					
	Cash	+ Prepaid Insurance	+ Inventory	= Com. Stk.	+ Ret. Ear.	Rev.	− Exp.	= Net Inc.
1.	NA	D	I	NA	NA	NA	NA	NA
2.	NA	D	NA	NA	D	NA	I	D

Required

a. Identify the event that represents the expiration of insurance on the factory building.

b. Explain why recognizing the expiration of insurance on a factory building affects financial statements differently than recognizing the expiration of insurance on an administrative building.

LO 3

Exercise 1-11B   *Effect of product versus selling, general, and administrative cost on the income statement*

Each of the following asset acquisitions requires a year-end adjusting entry.

1. Paid $80,000 cash on January 1 to purchase a hamburger franchise that had an estimated expected useful life of 10 years and no salvage value.
2. Paid $80,000 cash on January 1 to purchase a patent to manufacture a special product. The patent had an estimated expected useful life of 10 years.
3. Paid $10,000 cash on April 1 for a one-year insurance policy on the administrative building.
4. Paid $10,000 cash on April 1 for a one-year insurance policy on the manufacturing building.
5. Paid $5,400 cash to purchase office supplies for the accounting department. At the end of the year, $1,000 of office supplies was still on hand.
6. Paid $5,400 cash to purchase factory supplies. At the end of the year, $500 of factory supplies was still on hand.

Required

Explain how the adjusting entry affects the amount of net income reported in the annual financial statements. The first event is shown as an example. Assume that any products that have been made have not been sold.

	Net Income
Event No.	Amount of Change
1. Adjusting Entry	(8,000)

LO 4

Exercise 1-12B   *Upstream and downstream costs*

During 2011 Jada Pharmaceutical Company incurred $50,000,000 of research and development (R&D) costs to develop a new hay fever drug called Allergone. In accordance with FASB standards, the entire R&D cost was recognized as expense in 2011. Manufacturing costs (direct materials, direct labor, and overhead) to produce Allergone are expected to be $40 per unit. Packaging, shipping, and sales commissions are expected to be $5 per unit. Jada expects to sell 5,000,000 units of Allergone before developing a new drug to replace it in the market. During 2011, Jada produced 800,000 units of Allergone and sold 500,000 of them.

Required

a. Identify the upstream and downstream costs.
b. Determine the 2011 amount of cost of goods sold and the December 31, 2011, ending inventory balance.
c. Determine the unit sales price Jada should establish assuming it desires to earn a profit margin equal to 40 percent of the *total cost* of developing, manufacturing, and distributing Allergone.
d. Prepare an income statement for 2011 using the sales price from Requirement *c*.
e. Why would Jada price Allergone at a level that would generate a loss for 2011?

LO 6

Exercise 1-13B   *Effect of a just-in-time inventory system on financial statements*

In reviewing Kopplin Company's financial statements for the past two years, Nancy Martin, a bank loan officer, noticed that the company's inventory level had increased significantly while sales revenue had remained constant. Such a trend typically indicates increasing inventory carrying costs and slowing cash inflows. Ms. Martin concluded that the bank should deny Kopplin's credit line application.

Required

Explain how implementing an effective just-in-time inventory system would affect Kopplin's financial statements and possibly reverse Ms. Martin's decision about its credit line application.

Exercise 1-14B *Using JIT to minimize waste and lost opportunity*

LO 6

May Motz is the editor-in-chief of her school's yearbook. The school has 1,000 students and 60 faculty and staff members. The firm engaged to print copies of the yearbook charges the school $13 per book and requires a 10-day lead time for delivery. May and her editors plan to order 800 copies to sell at the school fair for $20 each.

Required

a. If the school sells 700 yearbooks, what amount of profit will it earn? What is the cost of waste due to excess inventory?

b. If 150 buyers are turned away after all yearbooks have been sold, what amount of profit will the school earn? What amount of opportunity cost will the school incur?

c. How could May use a JIT inventory system to maximize profits by eliminating waste and opportunity cost?

Exercise 1-15B *Using JIT to minimize holding costs*

LO 6

Olivia's Beauty Salon purchases inventory supplies from a variety of vendors, some of which require a four-week lead time before delivering inventory purchases. To ensure that she will not run out of supplies, Olivia Stear, the owner, maintains a large inventory. The average cost of inventory on hand is $9,000. Ms. Stear usually finances inventory purchases with a line of credit that has a 12 percent annual interest charge. Her accountant has suggested that she purchase all inventory from a single large distributor that can satisfy all of her orders within a three-day period. With such prompt delivery, Ms. Stear would be able to reduce her average inventory balance to $2,000. She also believes that she could save $1,000 per year through reduced phone bills, insurance costs, and warehouse rental costs associated with ordering and maintaining the higher level of inventory.

Required

a. Is the inventory system the accountant suggested to Ms. Stear a pure or approximate just-in-time system?

b. Based on the information provided, how much inventory holding cost could Ms. Stear eliminate by taking the accountant's advice?

Exercise 1-16B *The fraud triangle*

LO 7

The accounting records of Rice Manufacturing Company (RMC) revealed that the company incurred $3 million of materials, $5 million of production labor, $4 million of manufacturing overhead, and $6 million of selling, general, and administrative expense during 2011. It was discovered that RMC's chief financial officer (CFO) included $2.6 million dollars of upstream research and development expense in the manufacturing overhead account when it should have been classified as selling, general, and administrative expense. RMC made 5,000 units of product and sold 4,000 units of product in 2011.

Required

a. Indicate whether the elements on the 2011 financial statements (i.e., assets, liabilities, equity, revenue, expense, and net income) would be overstated or understated as a result of the misclassification of the upstream research and development expense. Determine the amount of the overstatement or understatement for each element.

b. Speculate as to what would cause the CFO to intentionally misclassify the research and development expense. (Hint: Review the chapter material regarding the fraud triangle.)

Exercise 1-17B *Applications of the Sarbanes-Oxley Act*

LO 7

Greg Madrid, a HealthSouth billing clerk, filed a suit under the False Claims Act charging that HealthSouth purchased computer equipment from a company owned by Richard Scrushy's parents at prices two and three times the normal price. At the time, Richard Scrushy was the CEO of HealthSouth. The overcharges inflated HealthSouth's expense ratios that the government used when calculating a Medicare reimbursement rate. As a result, the government was overcharged for services provided by HealthSouth. While refusing to recognize any wrongdoing, HealthSouth agreed to pay an $8 million settlement related to the lawsuit brought by the whistleblower.

Required

Explain how the provisions of Sarbanes-Oxley would provide protection to a whistleblower such as Greg Madrid.

LO 10

Exercise 1-18B   *Value chain analysis (Appendix)*

Fastidious Vincent washed his hair at home and then went to a barbershop for a haircut. The barber explained that shop policy is to shampoo each customer's hair before cutting, regardless of how recently it had been washed. Somewhat annoyed, Vincent submitted to the shampoo, after which the barber cut his hair with great skill. After the haircut, the barber dried his hair and complimented Vincent on his appearance. He added, "That will be $18; $3 for the shampoo and $15 for the cut and dry." Vincent did not tip the barber.

Required

Identify the nonvalue-added activity described. How could the barber modify this nonvalue-added activity?

PROBLEMS—SERIES B

LO 2, 3

Problem 1-19B   *Product versus selling, general, and administrative costs*

Garcin Manufacturing Company was started on January 1, 2011, when it acquired $180,000 cash by issuing common stock. Garcin immediately purchased office furniture and manufacturing equipment costing $20,000 and $38,000, respectively. The office furniture had a four-year useful life and a zero salvage value. The manufacturing equipment had a $2,000 salvage value and an expected useful life of six years. The company paid $14,000 for salaries of administrative personnel and $18,000 for wages of production personnel. Finally, the company paid $24,000 for raw materials that were used to make inventory. All inventory was started and completed during the year. Garcin completed production on 8,000 units of product and sold 6,000 units at a price of $14 each in 2011. (Assume that all transactions are cash transactions.)

Required

a. Determine the total product cost and the average cost per unit of the inventory produced in 2011.

b. Determine the amount of cost of goods sold that would appear on the 2011 income statement.

c. Determine the amount of the ending inventory balance that would appear on the December 31, 2011, balance sheet.

d. Determine the amount of net income that would appear on the 2011 income statement.

e. Determine the amount of retained earnings that would appear on the December 31, 2011, balance sheet.

f. Determine the amount of total assets that would appear on the December 31, 2011, balance sheet.

LO 2, 3

Problem 1-20B   *Effect of product versus selling, general, and administrative costs on financial statements*

Windsor Company experienced the following accounting events during its first year of operation. With the exception of the adjusting entries for depreciation, all transactions were cash transactions.

1. Acquired $80,000 cash by issuing common stock.

2. Paid $15,000 for the materials used to make its products. All products started were completed during the period.

3. Paid salaries of $6,000 to selling and administrative employees.

4. Paid wages of $9,000 to production workers.

5. Paid $12,000 for furniture used in selling and administrative offices. The furniture was acquired on January 1. It had a $1,500 estimated salvage value and a seven-year useful life.

6. Paid $22,000 for manufacturing equipment. The equipment was acquired on January 1. It had a $2,000 estimated salvage value and a five-year useful life.

7. Sold inventory to customers for $43,000 that had cost $25,000 to make.

Required

Explain how these events would affect the balance sheet and income statement by recording them in a horizontal financial statements model as indicated here. The first event is recorded as an example.

Financial Statements Model										
	Assets					**Equity**				
Event No.	**Cash**	**+ Inventory**	**Manuf. + Equip.***	**Office + Furn.***	**=**	**Com. Stk.**	**Ret. + Ear.**	**Rev.**	**− Exp.**	**= Net Inc.**
1.	80,000					80,000				

*Record accumulated depreciation as negative amounts in these columns.

Problem 1-21B *Product versus selling, general, and administrative costs*   LO 2, 3

The following transactions pertain to 2012, the first year of operations of Jardine Company. All inventory was started and completed during the accounting period. All transactions were cash transactions.

1. Acquired $56,000 of contributed capital from its owners.
2. Paid $9,600 for materials used to produce inventory.
3. Paid $4,400 to production workers.
4. Paid $5,000 rental fee for production equipment.
5. Paid $1,500 to administrative employees.
6. Paid $3,200 rental fee for administrative office equipment.
7. Produced 1,900 units of inventory of which 1,500 units were sold at a price of $17.40 each.

Required

Prepare an income statement and a balance sheet.

Problem 1-22B *Service versus manufacturing companies*   LO 2, 3, 5

Knoll Company began operations on January 1, 2012, by issuing common stock for $94,000 cash. During 2012, Knoll received $77,000 cash from revenue and incurred costs that required $90,000 of cash payments.

Required

Prepare an income statement and a balance sheet for Knoll Company for 2012, under each of the following independent scenarios.

a. Knoll is an employment agency. The $90,000 was paid for employee salaries and advertising.

b. Knoll is a trucking company. The $90,000 was paid to purchase two trucks. The trucks were purchased on January 1, 2012, had five-year useful lives and no expected salvage value. Knoll uses straight-line depreciation.

c. Knoll is a manufacturing company. The $90,000 was paid to purchase the following items:

(1) Paid $18,000 cash to purchase materials used to make products during the year.

(2) Paid $28,000 cash for wages to production workers who make products during the year.

(3) Paid $4,000 cash for salaries of sales and administrative employees.

(4) Paid $40,000 cash to purchase manufacturing equipment. The equipment was used solely for the purpose of making products. It had a six-year life and a $4,000 salvage value. The company uses straight-line depreciation.

(5) During 2012, Knoll started and completed 2,600 units of product. The revenue was earned when Knoll sold 2,200 units of product to its customers.

d. Refer to Requirement *c.* Could Knoll determine the actual cost of making the 500th unit of product? How likely is it that the actual cost of the 500th unit of product was exactly the same as the cost of producing the 501st unit of product? Explain why management may be more interested in average cost than in actual cost.

LO 2, 3, 7

Problem 1-23B   *Importance of cost classification*

Livy Company was started when it acquired $70,000 by issuing common stock. During the first year of operations, the company incurred specifically identifiable product costs (materials, labor, and overhead) amounting to $40,000. Livy also incurred $20,000 of product development costs. There was a debate regarding how the product development costs should be classified. Advocates of Option 1 believed that the costs should be included in the selling, general, and administrative cost category. Advocates of Option 2 believed it would be more appropriate to classify the product development costs as product costs. During the first year, Livy made 10,000 units of product and sold 8,000 units at a price of $14 each. All transactions were cash transactions.

Required

a. Prepare an income statement and a balance sheet under each of the two options.

b. Identify the option that results in financial statements that are more likely to leave a favorable impression on investors and creditors.

c. Assume that Livy provides an incentive bonus to the company president that is equal to 8 percent of net income. Compute the amount of the bonus under each of the two options. Identify the option that provides the president with the higher bonus.

d. Assume a 35 percent income tax rate. Determine the amount of income tax expense under each of the two options. Identify the option that minimizes the amount of the company's income tax expense.

e. Comment on the conflict of interest between the company president as determined in Requirement *c* and the stockholders of the company as indicated in Requirement *d.* Describe an incentive compensation plan that would avoid conflicts between the interests of the president and the owners.

LO 6

Problem 1-24B   *Using JIT to reduce inventory holding costs*

Olsen Automobile Dealership, Inc. (OAD), buys and sells a variety of cars made by Great Motor Corporation. OAD maintains about 30 new cars in its parking lot for customers' selection; the cost of this inventory is approximately $400,000. Additionally, OAD hires security guards to protect the inventory from theft and a maintenance crew to keep the facilities attractive. The total payroll cost for the guards and maintenance crew amounts to $75,000 per year. OAD has a line of credit with a local bank that calls for a 15 percent annual rate of interest. Recently, Neil Tanner, the president of OAD, learned that a competitor in town, Pardoe Dealership, has been attracting some of OAD's usual customers because Pardoe could offer them lower prices. Mr. Tanner also discovered that Pardoe carries no inventory at all but shows customers a catalog of cars as well as pertinent information from online computer databases. Pardoe promises to deliver any car that a customer identifies within three working days.

Required

a. Based on the information provided, determine OAD's annual inventory holding cost.

b. Name the inventory system that Pardoe uses and explain how the system enables Pardoe to sell at reduced prices.

LO 6

Problem 1-25B   *Using JIT to minimize waste and lost opportunity*

Mark's Hamburger is a small fast-food shop in a busy shopping center that operates only during lunch hours. Mark Haygood, the owner and manager of the shop, is confused. On some days, he does not have enough hamburgers to satisfy customer demand. On other days, he has more hamburgers than he can sell. When he has excess hamburgers, he has no choice but to dump them. Usually, Mr. Haygood prepares about 160 hamburgers before the busy lunch hour. The product cost per hamburger is approximately $0.75; the sales price is $3.00 each. Mr. Haygood pays general, selling, and administrative expenses that include daily rent of $60 and daily wages of $40.

Required

a. Prepare an income statement based on sales of 100 hamburgers per day. Determine the cost of wasted hamburgers if 160 hamburgers were prepared in advance.

b. Prepare an income statement assuming that 200 customers attempt to buy a hamburger. Since Mr. Haygood has prepared only 160 hamburgers, he must reject 40 customer orders because of insufficient supply. Determine the amount of lost profit.

c. Suppose that hamburgers can be prepared quickly after each customer orders. However, Mr. Haygood must hire an additional part-time employee at a cost of approximately $20 per day. The per unit cost of each hamburger remains at $0.75. Prepare an income statement under the JIT system assuming that 100 hamburgers are sold. Compare the income statement under JIT with the income statement prepared in Requirement *a*. Comment on how the JIT system would affect profitability.

d. Assume the same facts as in Requirement *c* with respect to a JIT system that requires additional labor costing $20 per day. Prepare an income statement under the JIT system, assuming that 200 hamburgers are sold. Compare the income statement under JIT with the income statement prepared in Requirement *b*. Comment on how the JIT system would affect profitability.

e. Explain how the JIT system might be able to improve customer satisfaction as well as profitability.

Problem 1-26B *The fraud triangle, ethics, and the Sarbanes-Oxley Act*

LO 7

The CEO and the CFO of Automation Company were both aware that the company's controller was reporting fraudulent revenues. Upper level executives are paid very large bonuses when the company meets the earnings goals established in the company's budgets. While the CEO had pushed the CFO and controller to "make the numbers," he had not told him to "make up the numbers." Besides, he could plead ignorance if the fraud was ever discovered. The CFO knew he should prohibit the fraudulent reporting but also knew the importance of making the numbers established in the budget. He told himself that it wasn't just for his bonus but for the stockholders as well. If the actual earnings were below the budgeted target numbers, the stock price would drop and the shareholders would suffer. Besides, he believed that the actual revenues would increase dramatically in the near future and they could cover for the fraudulent revenue by underreporting these future revenues. He concluded that no one would get hurt and everything would be straightened out in the near future.

Required

a. Explain why the internal control practice of separation of duties failed to prevent the fraudulent reporting.

b. Identify and discuss the elements of the fraud triangle that motivated the fraud.

c. Explain how the provisions of the Sarbanes-Oxley Act would serve to deter this type of fraudulent reporting.

d. Review the statement of ethical professional practice shown in Exhibit 1.15. Identify and comment on which of the ethical principles were violated by the CFO.

Problem 1-27B *Value chain analysis (Appendix)*

LO 8

Ellen Milan visited her personal physician for treatment of flu symptoms. She was greeted by the receptionist, who gave her personal history and insurance forms to complete. She needed no instructions; she completed these same forms every time she visited the doctor. After completing the forms, Ms. Milan waited for 30 minutes before being ushered into the patient room. After waiting there for an additional 15 minutes, Dr. Heape entered the room. The doctor ushered Ms. Milan into the hallway where he weighed her and called her weight out to the nurse for recording. Ms. Milan had gained 10 pounds since her last visit, and the doctor suggested that she consider going on a diet. Dr. Heape then took her temperature and asked her to return to the patient room. Ten minutes later, he returned to take a throat culture and draw blood. She waited another 15 minutes for the test results. Finally, the doctor returned and told Ms. Milan that she had strep throat and bronchitis. Dr. Heape prescribed an antibiotic and told her to get at least two days of bed rest. Ms. Milan was then ushered to the accounting department to settle her bill. The accounting clerk asked her several questions; the answers to most of them were on the forms that she had completed when she first arrived at the office. Finally, Ms. Milan paid her required copayment and left the office. Three weeks later, she received a bill indicating that she had not paid the copayment. She called the accounting department, and after a search of the records, the clerk verified that the bill had, in fact, been paid. The clerk apologized for the inconvenience and inquired as to whether Ms. Milan's health had improved.

Required

a. Identify at least three value-added and three nonvalue-added activities suggested in this scenario.

b. Provide logical suggestions for how to eliminate the nonvalue-added activities.

ANALYZE, THINK, COMMUNICATE

ATC 1-1   Business Applications Case   *Financial versus managerial accounting*

The following information was taken from the 2008 and 2009 Form 10-Ks for Dell, Inc.

	Fiscal Year Ended	
	January 30, 2009	February 1, 2008
Number of regular employees	76,500	82,700
Number of temporary employees	2,400	5,500
Revenues (in millions)	$61,101	$61,133
Properties owned or leased in the U.S.	7.4 million square feet	8.2 million square feet
Properties owned or leased outside the U.S.	9.4 million square feet	9.7 million square feet
Total assets (in millions)	$26,500	$27,561
Cross margin (in millions)	$10,957	$11,671

Required

a. Explain whether each line of information in the table above would best be described as being primarily financial accounting or managerial accounting in nature.

b. Provide some additional examples of managerial and financial accounting information that could apply to Dell.

c. If you analyze only the data you identified as financial in nature, does it appear that Dell's 2009 fiscal year was better or worse than its 2008 fiscal year? Explain.

d. If you analyze only the data you identified as managerial in nature, does it appear that Dell's 2009 fiscal year was better or worse than its 2008 fiscal year? Explain.

ATC 1-2   Group Assignment   *Product versus upstream and downstream costs*

Victor Holt, the accounting manager of Sexton, Inc., gathered the following information for 2011. Some of it can be used to construct an income statement for 2011. Ignore items that do not appear on an income statement. Some computation may be required. For example, the cost of manufacturing equipment would not appear on the income statement. However, the cost of manufacturing equipment is needed to compute the amount of depreciation. All units of product were started and completed in 2011.

1. Issued $864,000 of common stock.
2. Paid engineers in the product design department $10,000 for salaries that were accrued at the end of the previous year.
3. Incurred advertising expenses of $70,000.
4. Paid $720,000 for materials used to manufacture the company's product.
5. Incurred utility costs of $160,000. These costs were allocated to different departments on the basis of square footage of floor space. Mr. Holt identified three departments and determined the square footage of floor space for each department to be as shown in the table below.

Department	Square Footage
Research and development	10,000
Manufacturing	60,000
Selling and administrative	30,000
Total	100,000

6. Paid $880,000 for wages of production workers.

7. Paid cash of $658,000 for salaries of administrative personnel. There was $16,000 of accrued salaries owed to administrative personnel at the end of 2011. There was no beginning balance in the Salaries Payable account for administrative personnel.

8. Purchased manufacturing equipment two years ago at a cost of $10,000,000. The equipment had an eight-year useful life and a $2,000,000 salvage value.

9. Paid $390,000 cash to engineers in the product design department.

10. Paid a $258,000 cash dividend to owners.

11. Paid $80,000 to set up manufacturing equipment for production.

12. Paid a one-time $186,000 restructuring cost to redesign the production process to implement a just-in-time inventory system.

13. Prepaid the premium on a new insurance policy covering nonmanufacturing employees. The policy cost $72,000 and had a one-year term with an effective starting date of May 1. Four employees work in the research and development department and eight employees in the selling and administrative department. Assume a December 31 closing date.

14. Made 69,400 units of product and sold 60,000 units at a price of $70 each.

Required

a. Divide the class into groups of four or five students per group, and then organize the groups into three sections. Assign Task 1 to the first section of groups, Task 2 to the second section of groups, and Task 3 to the third section of groups.

Group Tasks

(1) Identify the items that are classified as product costs and determine the amount of cost of goods sold reported on the 2011 income statement.

(2) Identify the items that are classified as upstream costs and determine the amount of upstream cost expensed on the 2011 income statement.

(3) Identify the items that are classified as downstream costs and determine the amount of downstream cost expensed on the 2011 income statement.

b. Have the class construct an income statement in the following manner. Select a member of one of the groups assigned the first group task identifying the product costs. Have that person go to the board and list the costs included in the determination of cost of goods sold. Anyone in the other groups who disagrees with one of the classifications provided by the person at the board should voice an objection and explain why the item should be classified differently. The instructor should lead the class to a consensus on the disputed items. After the amount of cost of goods sold is determined, the student at the board constructs the part of the income statement showing the determination of gross margin. The exercise continues in a similar fashion with representatives from the other sections explaining the composition of the upstream and downstream costs. These items are added to the income statement started by the first group representative. The final result is a completed income statement.

ATC 1-3 Research Assignment *Identifying product costs at Snap-on Inc.*

Use the 2008 Form 10-K for Snap-on Inc. to complete the requirements below. To obtain the Form 10-K you can use either use the EDGAR system following the instructions in Appendix A, or it can be found under "Corporate Information" on the company's corporate website; www.snapon.com. Read carefully the following portions of the document:

■ "Products and Services" on page 5.
"Consolidated Statement of Earnings" on page 55.
The following parts of Note 1 on page 60:
  • "Shipping and handling"
  • "Advertising and promotion"
■ "Note 4: Inventories" on page 66.
■ "Note 5: Property and equipment" on page 67.

Required

a. Does the level of detail that Snap-on provides regarding costs incurred to manufacture its products suggests the company's financial statements are designed primarily to meet the needs of external or internal users?

b. Does Snap-on treat shipping and handling costs as product or period costs?

c. Does Snap-on treat advertising and promotion costs as product or period costs?

d. In the first accounting course you learned about a class of inventory called merchandise inventory. What categories of inventory does Snap-on report in its annual report?

e. What is the cost of the land owned by Snap-on? What is the cost of its machinery and equipment?

ATC 1-4   Writing Assignment   *Emerging practices in managerial accounting*

An annual report of the Maytag Corporation contained the following excerpt:

> *The Company announced the restructuring of its major appliance operations in an effort to strengthen its position in the industry and to deliver improved performance to both customers and shareowners. This included the consolidation of two separate organizational units into a single operation responsible for all activities associated with the manufacture and distribution of the Company's brands of major appliances and the closing of a cooking products plant in Indianapolis, Indiana, with transfer of that production to an existing plant in Cleveland, Tennessee.*

The restructuring cost Maytag $40 million and disrupted the lives of many of the company's employees.

Required

Assume that you are Maytag's vice president of human relations. Write a letter to the employees who are affected by the restructuring. The letter should explain why it was necessary for the company to undertake the restructuring. Your explanation should refer to the ideas discussed in the section "Emerging Trends in Managerial Accounting" of this chapter (see Appendix A).

ATC 1-5   Ethical Dilemma   *Product cost versus selling and administrative expense*

Emma Emerson is a proud woman with a problem. Her daughter has been accepted into a prestigious law school. While Ms. Emerson beams with pride, she is worried sick about how to pay for the school; she is a single parent who has worked hard to support herself and her three children. She had to go heavily into debt to finance her own education. Even though she now has a good job, family needs have continued to outpace her income and her debt burden is staggering. She knows she will be unable to borrow the money needed for her daughter's law school.

Ms. Emerson is the chief financial officer (CFO) of a small manufacturing company. She has just accepted a new job offer. Indeed, she has not yet told her employer that she will be leaving in a month. She is concerned that her year-end incentive bonus may be affected if her boss learns of her plans to leave. She plans to inform the company immediately after receiving the bonus. She knows her behavior is less than honorable, but she believes that she has been underpaid for a long time. Her boss, a relative of the company's owner, makes twice what she makes and does half the work. Why should she care about leaving with a little extra cash? Indeed, she is considering an opportunity to boost the bonus.

Ms. Emerson's bonus is based on a percentage of net income. Her company recently introduced a new product line that required substantial production start-up costs. Ms. Emerson is fully aware that GAAP requires these costs to be expensed in the current accounting period, but no one else in the company has the technical expertise to know exactly how the costs should be treated. She is considering misclassifying the start-up costs as product costs. If the costs are misclassified, net income will be significantly higher, resulting in a nice boost in her incentive bonus. By the time the auditors discover the misclassification, Ms. Emerson will have moved on to her new job. If the matter is brought to the attention of her new employer, she will simply plead ignorance. Considering her daughter's needs, Ms. Emerson decides to classify the start-up costs as product costs.

Required

a. Based on this information, indicate whether Ms. Emerson believes the number of units of product sold will be equal to, less than, or greater than, the number of units made. Write a brief paragraph explaining the logic that supports your answer.

b. Explain how the misclassification could mislead an investor or creditor regarding the company's financial condition.

c. Explain how the misclassification could affect income taxes.

d. Identify the specific components of the fraud triangle that were present in this case.

e. Review the Statement of Ethical Professional Practice shown in Exhibit 1.15 and identify at least two ethical principles that Ms. Emerson's misclassification of the start-up costs violated.

f. Describe the maximum penalty that could be imposed under the Sarbanes-Oxley Act for the actions Ms. Emerson has taken.

g. Comment on how proper internal controls could have prevented fraudulent reporting in this case.

ATC 1-6   Spreadsheet Assignment   *Using Excel*

The following transactions pertain to 2011, the first year of operations of the Barlett Company. All inventory was started and completed during 2011. Assume that all transactions are cash transactions.

1. Acquired $2,000 cash by issuing common stock.
2. Paid $400 for materials used to produce inventory.
3. Paid $600 to production workers.
4. Paid $200 rental fee for production equipment.
5. Paid $160 to administrative employees.
6. Paid $80 rental fee for administrative office equipment.
7. Produced 300 units of inventory of which 200 units were sold at a price of $7.00 each.

Required

Construct a spreadsheet that includes the income statement and balance sheet.

ATC 1-7   Spreadsheet Assignment   *Mastering Excel*

Mantooth Manufacturing Company experienced the following accounting events during its first year of operation. With the exception of the adjusting entries for depreciation, assume that all transactions are cash transactions.

1. Acquired $50,000 by issuing common stock.
2. Paid $8,000 for the materials used to make its products, all of which were started and completed during the year.
3. Paid salaries of $4,400 to selling and administrative employees.
4. Paid wages of $7,000 to production workers.
5. Paid $9,600 for furniture used in selling and administrative offices. The furniture was acquired on January 1. It had a $1,600 estimated salvage value and a four-year useful life.
6. Paid $13,000 for manufacturing equipment. The equipment was acquired on January 1. It had a $1,000 estimated salvage value and a three-year useful life.
7. Sold inventory to customers for $25,000 that had cost $14,000 to make.

Construct a spreadsheet of the financial statements model as shown here:

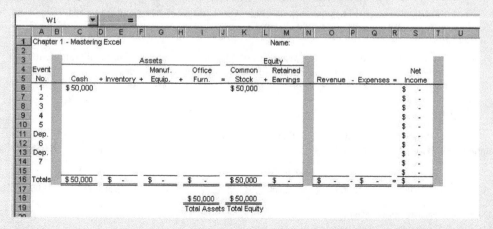

Required

Place formulas in row 16 to automatically add the columns. Also add formulas in column S to calculate net income after each event, and add formulas in row 18 to compute total assets and equity. Notice that you must enter the events since only the first one is shown as an example.

Spreadsheet Tips

1. The column widths are set by choosing Format, then Column, and then Width.
2. The shading in columns B, N, and T is added by highlighting a column and choosing Format, then Cells, and then clicking on the tab titled Patterns and choosing a color.
3. The sum function is an easy way to add a column or row. For example, the formula in cell C16 is =SUM(C6:C15).
4. As an example of the formulas in column S (net income), the formula in cell S7 is =O7−Q7.
5. If you find that some of the columns are too far to the right to appear on your screen, you can set the zoom level to show the entire spreadsheet. The zoom is set by choosing View, then Zoom, and then clicking on Custom and typing 100 percent in the box. The shortcut method to set the zoom is to click in the box on the right side of the top tool bar that appears immediately below the menu.

COMPREHENSIVE PROBLEM

Magnificent Modems, Inc., makes modem cards that are used in notebook computers. The company completed the following transactions during 2010. All purchases and sales were made with cash.

1. Acquired $750,000 of cash from the owners.
2. Purchased $270,000 of manufacturing equipment. The equipment has a $30,000 salvage value and a four-year useful life. Label the purchase of the equipment as **Event 2a** and the recognition of depreciation as **Event 2b.**
3. The company started and completed 5,000 modems. Direct materials purchased and used amounted to $40 per unit.
4. Direct labor costs amounted to $25 per unit.
5. The cost of manufacturing supplies used amounted to $4 per unit.
6. The company paid $50,000 to rent the manufacturing facility.
7. Magnificent sold all 5,000 units at a cash price of $120 per unit. Label the recognition of the sale as **Event 7a** and the cost of goods sold as **Event 7b.** (Hint: It will be necessary to determine the manufacturing costs in order to record the cost of goods sold.)
8. The sales staff was paid a $6 per unit sales commission.
9. Paid $39,000 to purchase equipment for administrative offices. The equipment was expected to have a $3,000 salvage value and a three-year useful life. Label the purchase of the equipment as **Event 9a** and the recognition of depreciation as **Event 9b.**
10. Administrative expenses consisting of office rental and salaries amounted to $71,950.

Required

a. Record the transaction data for Magnificent Modems, Inc., in the financial statements like the one shown below. The first transaction is recorded as an example.

Event No.		Assets						=		Equity							
	Cash	+	Inventory	+	Manuf. Equip.*	+	Office Equip.*	=	Com. Sock.	+	Ret. Ear.		Rev.	−	Exp.	=	Net Inc.
1.	750,000								750,000								
Ck. Fig.	544,050	+	0	+	210,000	+	27,000	=	750,000	+	31,050		600,000	−	568,950	=	31,050

*Negative amounts in these columns represent accumulated depreciation.

b. Use the following forms to prepare an income statement and balance sheet.

MAGNIFICENT MODEMS, INC.
Income Statement
For the Period Ended December 31, 2011

Sales	
Cost of goods sold	
Gross margin	
Sales commission	
Depreciation expense	
Administrative expense	
Net income	$31,050

MAGNIFICENT MODEMS, INC.
Balance Sheet
As of December 31, 2011

Assets:	
Cash	
Manufacturing equipment, net of acc. depreciation	
Office equipment, net of acc. depreciation	
Finished goods inventory	
Total assets	$781,050
Equity	
Common stock	
Retained earnings	
Total stockholder's equity	$781,050

CHAPTER 2

Cost Behavior, Operating Leverage, and Profitability Analysis

LEARNING OBJECTIVES

After you have mastered the material in this chapter, you will be able to:

1 Identify and describe fixed, variable, and mixed cost behavior.

2 Demonstrate the effects of operating leverage on profitability.

3 Prepare an income statement using the contribution margin approach.

4 Calculate the magnitude of operating leverage.

5 Demonstrate how the relevant range and decision context affect cost behavior.

6 Select an appropriate time period for calculating the average cost per unit.

7 Use the high-low method, scattergraphs, and regression analysis to estimate fixed and variable costs.

CHAPTER OPENING

Three college students are planning a vacation. One of them suggests inviting a fourth person along, remarking that four can travel for the same cost as three. Certainly, some costs will be the same whether three or four people go on the trip. For example, the hotel room costs $800 per week, regardless of whether three or four people stay in the room. In accounting terms the cost of the hotel room is a **fixed cost**. The total amount of a fixed cost does not change when volume changes. The total hotel room cost is $800 whether 1, 2, 3, or 4 people use the room. In contrast, some costs vary in direct proportion with changes in volume. When volume increases, total variable cost increases; when volume decreases, total variable cost decreases. For example, the cost of tickets to a theme park is a **variable cost**. The total cost of tickets increases proportionately with each vacationer who goes to the theme park. Cost behavior (fixed versus variable) can significantly impact profitability. This chapter explains cost behavior and ways it can be used to increase profitability.

The Curious Accountant

News flash! On April 29, 2009, Eastman Kodak, Inc., announced that its first quarter's revenues decreased 29 percent compared to the same quarter in 2008, yet its earnings had decreased by 213 percent. On May 4, 2009, Walt Disney announced that a decrease in revenue of 7 percent for the just-ended quarter would cause its earnings to decrease 46 percent compared to the same quarter in 2008. On April 12, 2009, Apple computer reported that its revenue for the quarter had increased by 9 percent compared to the previous year, but its earnings increased by 15 percent.

Can you explain why such relatively small changes in these companies' revenues resulted in such relatively large changes in their earnings or losses? In other words, if a company's sales increase 10 percent, why do its earnings not also increase 10 percent? (Answer on page 60.)

Identify and describe fixed, variable, and mixed cost behavior.

FIXED COST BEHAVIOR

How much more will it cost to send one additional employee to a sales meeting? If more people buy our products, can we charge less? If sales increase by 10 percent, how will profits be affected? Managers seeking answers to such questions must consider **cost behavior.** Knowing how costs behave relative to the level of business activity enables managers to more effectively plan and control costs. To illustrate, consider the entertainment company Star Productions, Inc. (SPI).

SPI specializes in promoting rock concerts. It is considering paying a band $48,000 to play a concert. Obviously, SPI must sell enough tickets to cover this cost. In this example, the relevant activity base is the number of tickets sold. The cost of the band is a fixed cost because it does not change regardless of the number of tickets sold. Exhibit 2.1 illustrates the fixed cost behavior pattern, showing the *total cost* and the *cost per unit* at three different levels of activity.

Total versus *per-unit* fixed costs behave differently. The total cost for the band remains constant (fixed) at $48,000. In contrast, fixed cost per unit decreases as volume (number of tickets sold) increases. The term *fixed cost* is consistent with the behavior of *total cost.* Total fixed cost remains constant (fixed) when activity changes. However, there is a contradiction between the term *fixed cost per unit* and the *per-unit behavior pattern of a fixed cost.* Fixed cost per unit is *not* fixed. It changes with the number of tickets sold. This contradiction in terminology can cause untold confusion. Study carefully the fixed cost behavior patterns in Exhibit 2.2.

EXHIBIT 2.1

Fixed Cost Behavior

Number of tickets sold (a)	2,700	3,000	3,300
Total cost of band (b)	$48,000	$48,000	$48,000
Cost per ticket sold (b ÷ a)	$17.78	$16.00	$14.55

EXHIBIT 2.2

Fixed Cost Behavior

	When Activity Increases	When Activity Decreases
Total fixed cost	Remains constant	Remains constant
Fixed cost **per unit**	Decreases	Increases

The fixed cost data in Exhibit 2.1 help SPI's management decide whether to sponsor the concert. For example, the information influences potential pricing choices. The per-unit costs represent the minimum ticket prices required to cover the fixed cost at various levels of activity. SPI could compare these per-unit costs to the prices of competing entertainment events (such as the prices of movies, sporting events, or theater tickets). If the price is not competitive, tickets will not sell and the concert will lose money. Management must also consider the number of tickets to be sold. The volume data in Exhibit 2.1 can be compared to the band's track record of ticket sales at previous concerts. A proper analysis of these data can reduce the risk of undertaking an unprofitable venture.

OPERATING LEVERAGE

Heavy objects can be moved with little effort using *physical* leverage. Business managers apply **operating leverage** to magnify small changes in revenue into dramatic changes in profitability. The *lever* managers use to achieve disproportionate changes between revenue and profitability is fixed costs. The leverage relationships between revenue, fixed costs, and profitability are displayed in Exhibit 2.3.

When all costs are fixed, every sales dollar contributes one dollar toward the potential profitability of a project. Once sales dollars cover fixed costs, each

Demonstrate the effects of operating leverage on profitability.

EXHIBIT 2.3

Operating Leverage

FOCUS ON INTERNATIONAL ISSUES

FIXED COSTS BRING INTERNATIONAL INTRIGUE INTO THE AUTOMOBILE INDUSTRY

The major advantage of fixed costs is that as output increases, cost per unit decreases. Of course fixed costs can be a disadvantage if output is falling. Due to the nature of the industry automobile manufacturers have high fixed costs. It takes a lot of land, buildings, and machinery to mass produce cars and trucks.

In 2007 the worldwide production of autos was 73.3 million units;* in 2008 it had fallen to 70.5 million units due to the global recession. Not surprisingly, this had an adverse effect on companies that were already struggling, such as GM, Ford, and Chrysler, but it also affected the strongest company in the industry, Toyota. In its fiscal year ended March 31, 2008, Toyota produced 8.5 million vehicles and had a profit of $17.1 billion. In its fiscal year ended March 31, 2009, the company's output had fallen to 7.1 million vehicles, and it had a *net loss* of $4.0 billion.

A company with high fixed costs suffers on two fronts during a recession. First, the lower production causes its cost per unit to rise. Second, the weak economy puts pressure on it, and its competitors, to lower prices, or at least not to raise them. In Toyota's case, this meant that a company that had been reporting growing profits for many years suddenly had a significant loss.

*Sources of data: International Organization of Motor Vehicle Manufactures and Toyota's annual reports.

---

additional sales dollar represents pure profit. As a result, a small change in sales volume can significantly affect profitability. To illustrate, assume SPI estimates it will sell 3,000 tickets for $18 each. A 10 percent difference in actual sales volume will produce a 90 percent difference in profitability. Examine the data in Exhibit 2.4 to verify this result.[1]

EXHIBIT 2.4

Effect of Operating Leverage on Profitability

Number of tickets sold	2,700	⇐ −10% ⇐	3,000	⇒ +10% ⇒	3,300
Sales revenue ($18 per ticket)	$48,600		$54,000		$59,400
Cost of band (fixed cost)	(48,000)		(48,000)		(48,000)
Gross margin	$ 600	⇐ −90% ⇐	$ 6,000	⇒ +90% ⇒	$11,400

Calculating Percentage Change

The percentages in Exhibit 2.4 are computed as follows:

$$(\text{Alternative measure} - \text{Base measure}) \div \text{Base measure} = \%\text{ change}$$

The base measure is the starting point. To illustrate, compute the percentage change in gross margin when moving from 3,000 units (base measure) to 3,300 units (the alternative measure).

$$(\text{Alternative measure} - \text{Base measure}) \div \text{Base measure} = \%\text{ change}$$

$$(\$11,400 - \$6,000) \div \$6,000 = 90\%$$

---

[1]Do not confuse operating leverage with financial leverage. Companies employ *financial leverage* when they use debt to profit from investing money at a higher rate of return than the rate they pay on borrowed money. Companies employ *operating leverage* when they use proportionately more fixed costs than variable costs to magnify the effect on earnings of changes in revenues.

The percentage *decline* in profitability is similarly computed:

$$(\text{Alternative measure} - \text{Base measure}) \div \text{Base measure} = \% \text{ change}$$

$$(\$600 - \$6{,}000) \div \$6{,}000 = (90\%)$$

Risk and Reward Assessment

Risk refers to the possibility that sacrifices may exceed benefits. A fixed cost represents a commitment to an economic sacrifice. It represents the ultimate risk of undertaking a particular business project. If SPI pays the band but nobody buys a ticket, the company will lose $48,000. SPI can avoid this risk by substituting *variable costs* for the *fixed cost.*

VARIABLE COST BEHAVIOR

Identify and describe fixed, variable, and mixed cost behavior.

To illustrate variable cost behavior, assume SPI arranges to pay the band $16 per ticket sold instead of a fixed $48,000. Exhibit 2.5 shows the total cost of the band and the cost per ticket sold at three different levels of activity.

EXHIBIT 2.5

Variable Cost Behavior

Number of tickets sold (a)	2,700	3,000	3,300
Total cost of band (b)	$43,200	$48,000	$52,800
Cost per ticket sold (b ÷ a)	$16	$16	$16

Since SPI will pay the band $16 for each ticket sold, the *total* variable cost increases in direct proportion to the number of tickets sold. If SPI sells one ticket, total band cost will be $16 (1 × $16); if SPI sells two tickets, total band cost will be $32 (2 × $16); and so on. The total cost of the band increases proportionately as ticket sales move from 2,700 to 3,000 to 3,300. The variable cost *per ticket* remains $16, however, regardless of whether the number of tickets sold is 1, 2, 3, or 3,000. The behavior of variable cost *per unit* is contradictory to the word *variable*. Variable cost per unit remains *constant* regardless of how many tickets are sold. Study carefully the variable cost behavior patterns in Exhibit 2.6.

EXHIBIT 2.6

Variable Cost Behavior

	When Activity Increases	When Activity Decreases
Total variable cost	Increases proportionately	Decreases proportionately
Variable cost **per unit**	Remains constant	Remains constant

Risk and Reward Assessment

Demonstrate the effects of operating leverage on profitability.

Shifting the cost structure from fixed to variable enables SPI to avoid the fixed-cost risk. Recall that under the fixed cost structure, SPI was locked into a $48,000 cost for the band regardless of how many tickets are sold. If no tickets are sold, SPI will have to report a $48,000 loss on its income statement. The risk of incurring this loss is eliminated by the variable cost structure that requires SPI to only pay the band $16 per ticket sold. If SPI sells zero tickets then the cost of the band is zero. For each ticket sold, SPI earns a $2 profit ($18 ticket sales price − $16 fee paid to band).

Shifting the cost structure from fixed to variable reduces not only the level of risk but also the potential for profits. Managers cannot avoid the risk of fixed costs without also sacrificing the benefits. Variable costs do not offer operating leverage. Exhibit 2.7 shows

EXHIBIT 2.7						
Variable Cost Eliminates Operating Leverage						
Number of tickets sold	2,700	⇐ −10% ⇐	3,000	⇒ +10% ⇒	3,300
Sales revenue ($18 per ticket)	$48,600		$54,000		$59,400
Cost of band ($16 variable cost)	(43,200)		(48,000)		(52,800)
Gross margin	$ 5,400	⇐ −10% ⇐	$ 6,000	⇒ +10% ⇒	$ 6,600

that a variable cost structure produces a proportional relationship between sales and profitability. A 10 percent increase or decrease in sales results in a corresponding 10 percent increase or decrease in profitability. While the variable cost structure reduces risk, Exhibit 2.7 demonstrates that it also limits the opportunity to benefit from operating leverage.

The risk versus reward trade-off of cost structure is widespread in business practice. For example, borrowing money to buy an office building may require a company to commit to a fixed monthly principal and interest payment. If the company's revenue stream unexpectedly declines, the company still has to make its monthly payment. Indeed, many companies are forced into bankruptcy because they cannot satisfy their fixed debt commitments. Many companies avoid these fixed cost risks by renting their office space instead of purchasing buildings. If revenue dips, the company simply reduces the amount of office space it rents, thereby reducing its rental cost. Other real-world examples of fixed-cost risk avoidance include using temporary employees instead of hiring for permanent positions and paying a variable retainer fee to an independent law firm instead of creating a legal department within the company. These examples demonstrate the widespread applicability of the trade-offs associated with cost structure. Managers continually apply professional judgment to assess the risks of locking in costs with the opportunities provided by operating leverage.

✓ CHECK YOURSELF 2.1

Suppose that you are sponsoring a political rally at which Ralph Nader will speak. You estimate that approximately 2,000 people will buy tickets to hear Mr. Nader's speech. The tickets are expected to be priced at $12 each. Would you prefer a contract that agrees to pay Mr. Nader $10,000 or one that agrees to pay him $5 per ticket purchased?

Answer　Your answer would depend on how certain you are that 2,000 people will purchase tickets. If it were likely that many more than 2,000 tickets would be sold, you would be better off with a fixed cost structure, agreeing to pay Mr. Nader a flat fee of $10,000. If attendance numbers are highly uncertain, you would be better off with a variable cost structure thereby guaranteeing a lower cost if fewer people buy tickets.

EFFECT OF COST STRUCTURE ON PROFIT STABILITY

The preceding discussion suggests that companies with higher levels of fixed costs are more likely to experience earnings volatility. To illustrate, suppose three companies produce and sell the same product. Each company sells 10 units for $10 each. Furthermore, each company incurs costs of $60 in the process of making and selling its products. However, the companies operate under radically different **cost structures.** The entire $60 of cost incurred by Company A is fixed. Company B incurs $30 of fixed cost and $30 of variable cost ($3 per unit). All $60 of cost incurred by Company C is variable ($6 per unit). Exhibit 2.8 displays income statements for the three companies.

LO 2

Demonstrate the effects of operating leverage on profitability.

EXHIBIT 2.8

Income Statements

	Company Name		
	A	B	C
Variable cost per unit (a)	$ 0	$ 3	$ 6
Sales revenue (10 units × $10)	$100	$100	$100
Variable cost (10 units × a)	0	(30)	(60)
Fixed cost	(60)	(30)	0
Net income	$ 40	$ 40	$ 40

EXHIBIT 2.9

Income Statements

	Company Name		
	A	B	C
Variable cost per unit (a)	$ 0	$ 3	$ 6
Sales revenue (11 units × $10)	$110	$110	$110
Variable cost (11 units × a)	0	(33)	(66)
Fixed cost	(60)	(30)	0
Net income	$ 50	$ 47	$ 44

When sales change, the amount of the corresponding change in net income is directly influenced by the company's cost structure. The more fixed cost, the greater the fluctuation in net income. To illustrate, assume sales increase by one unit; the resulting income statements are displayed in Exhibit 2.9.

Company A, with the highest level of fixed costs, experienced a $10 ($50 − $40) increase in profitability; Company C, with the lowest level of fixed cost (zero), had only a $4 ($44 − $40) increase in profitability. Company B, with a 50/50 mix of fixed and variable cost, had a mid-range $7 ($47 − $40) increase in net income. The effect of fixed cost on volatility applies to decreases as well as increases in sales volume. To illustrate, assume sales decrease by one unit (from 10 to 9 units). The resulting income statements are displayed in Exhibit 2.10.

EXHIBIT 2.10

Income Statements

	Company Name		
	A	B	C
Variable cost per unit (a)	$ 0	$ 3	$ 6
Sales revenue (9 units × $10)	$90	$90	$90
Variable cost (9 units × a)	0	(27)	(54)
Fixed cost	(60)	(30)	0
Net income	$30	$33	$36

Company A again experiences the largest variance in earnings ($10 decrease). Company B had a moderate decline of $7, and Company C had the least volatility with only a $4 decline.

What cost structure is the best? Should a manager use fixed or variable costs? The answer depends on sales volume expectations. A manager who expects revenues to increase should use a fixed cost structure. On the other hand, if future sales growth is uncertain or if the manager believes revenue is likely to decline, a variable cost structure makes more sense.

Answers to The Curious Accountant

The explanation for how a company's earnings can rise faster, as a percentage, than its revenue rises is operating leverage, and operating leverage is due entirely to fixed costs. As the chapter explains, when a company's output goes up, its fixed cost per unit goes down. As long as it can keep prices about the same, this lower unit cost will result in higher profit per unit sold. In real-world companies, the relationship between changing sales levels and changing earnings levels can be very complex, but the existence of fixed costs helps to explain why a 9 percent rise in revenue can cause a 15 percent rise in net earnings. Chapter 3 will investigate the relationships among an entity's cost structure, output level, pricing strategy, and profits earned in more depth.

✓ CHECK YOURSELF 2.2

If both Kroger Food Stores and Delta Airlines were to experience a 5 percent increase in revenues, which company would be more likely to experience a higher percentage increase in net income?

Answer Delta would be more likely to experience a higher percentage increase in net income because a large portion of its cost (e.g., employee salaries and depreciation) is fixed, while a large portion of Kroger's cost is variable (e.g., cost of goods sold).

AN INCOME STATEMENT UNDER THE CONTRIBUTION MARGIN APPROACH

The impact of cost structure on profitability is so significant that managerial accountants frequently construct income statements that classify costs according to their behavior patterns. Such income statements first subtract variable costs from revenue; the resulting subtotal is called the **contribution margin.** The contribution margin represents the amount available to cover fixed expenses and thereafter to provide company profits. Net income is computed by subtracting the fixed costs from the contribution margin. A contribution margin style income statement cannot be used for public reporting (GAAP prohibits its use in external financial reports), but it is widely used for internal reporting purposes. Exhibit 2.11 illustrates income statements prepared using the contribution margin approach.

LO 3

Prepare an income statement using the contribution margin approach.

EXHIBIT 2.11

Income Statements

	Company Name	
	Bragg	**Biltmore**
Variable cost per unit (a)	$ 6	$ 12
Sales revenue (10 units × $20)	$200	$200
Variable cost (10 units × a)	(60)	(120)
Contribution margin	140	80
Fixed cost	(120)	(60)
Net income	$ 20	$ 20

USING FIXED COST TO PROVIDE A COMPETITIVE OPERATING ADVANTAGE

Mary MaHall and John Strike have established tutoring companies to support themselves while they attend college. Both Ms. MaHall and Mr. Strike function as owner/managers; they each hire other students to actually provide the tutoring services. Ms. MaHall pays her tutors salaries; her labor costs are fixed at $16,000 per year regardless of the number of hours of tutoring performed. Mr. Strike pays his employees $8 per hour; his labor is therefore a variable cost. Both businesses currently provide 2,000 hours of tutoring services at a price of $11 per hour. As shown in Exhibit 2.12, both companies currently produce the same profit.

Suppose Ms. MaHall adopts a strategy to win over Mr. Strike's customers by reducing the price of tutoring services from $11 per hour to $7 per hour. If Ms. MaHall

LO 2

Demonstrate the effects of operating leverage on profitability.

EXHIBIT 2.12

Comparative Profitability at 2,000 Hours of Tutoring

		MaHall		Strike
Number of hours of tutoring provided		2,000		2,000
Service revenue ($11 per hour)		$22,000		$22,000
Cost of tutors	Fixed	(16,000)	Variable ($8 × 2,000)	(16,000)
Net income		$ 6,000		$ 6,000

succeeds, her company's income will double as shown in Exhibit 2.13. Mr. Strike is in a vulnerable position because if he matches MaHall's price cut he will lose $1 ($7 new per-hour price − $8 cost per hour for tutor) for each hour of tutoring service that his company provides.

EXHIBIT 2.13

MaHall's Profitability at 4,000 Hours of Tutoring

		MaHall
Number of hours of tutoring provided		4,000
Service revenue ($7 per hour)		$28,000
Cost of tutors	Fixed	(16,000)
Net income (loss)		$12,000

Is Mr. Strike's business doomed? Not necessarily; Ms. MaHall's operating leverage strategy only works if volume increases. If Mr. Strike matches Ms. MaHall's price, thereby maintaining the existing sales volume levels between the two companies, both companies incur losses. Exhibit 2.14 verifies this conclusion. Under these circumstances, Ms. MaHall would be forced to raise her price or to face the same negative consequences that she is attempting to force on Mr. Strike.

EXHIBIT 2.14

Comparative Profitability at 2,000 Hours of Tutoring

		MaHall		Strike
Number of hours of tutoring provided		2,000		2,000
Service revenue ($7 per hour)		$14,000		$14,000
Cost of tutors	Fixed	(16,000)	Variable ($8 × 2,000)	(16,000)
Net income (loss)		$(2,000)		$(2,000)

MEASURING OPERATING LEVERAGE USING CONTRIBUTION MARGIN

LO 4

Calculate the magnitude of operating leverage.

A contribution margin income statement allows managers to easily measure operating leverage. The magnitude of operating leverage can be determined as follows:

$$\text{Magnitude of operating leverage} = \frac{\text{Contribution margin}}{\text{Net income}}$$

Applying this formula to the income statement data reported for Bragg Company and Biltmore Company in Exhibit 2.11 produces the following measures.

Bragg Company:

$$\text{Magnitude of operating leverage} = \frac{\$140}{\$20} = 7$$

Biltmore Company:

$$\text{Magnitude of operating leverage} = \frac{\$80}{\$20} = 4$$

The computations show that Bragg is more highly leveraged than Biltmore. Bragg's change in profitability will be seven times greater than a given percentage change in revenue. In contrast, Biltmore's profits change by only four times the percentage change in revenue. For example, a 10 percent increase in revenue produces a 70 percent increase (10 percent × 7) in profitability for Bragg Company and a 40 percent increase (10 percent × 4) in profitability for Biltmore Company. The income statements in Exhibits 2.15 and 2.16 confirm these expectations.

EXHIBIT 2.15

Comparative Income Statements for Bragg Company

Units (a)	10		11
Sales revenue ($20 × a)	$200	⇒ +10% ⇒	$220
Variable cost ($6 × a)	(60)		(66)
Contribution margin	140		154
Fixed cost	(120)		(120)
Net income	$ 20	⇒ +70% ⇒	$ 34

EXHIBIT 2.16

Comparative Income Statements for Biltmore Company

Units (a)	10		11
Sales revenue ($20 × a)	$200	⇒ +10% ⇒	$220
Variable cost ($12 × a)	(120)		(132)
Contribution margin	80		88
Fixed cost	(60)		(60)
Net income	$ 20	⇒ +40% ⇒	$ 28

Operating leverage itself is neither good nor bad; it represents a strategy that can work to a company's advantage or disadvantage, depending on how it is used. The next section explains how managers can use operating leverage to create a competitive business advantage.

✓ CHECK YOURSELF 2.3

Boeing Company's 2001 10K annual report filed with the Securities and Exchange Commission refers to "higher commercial airlines segment margins." Is Boeing referring to gross margins or contribution margins?

Answer   Since the data come from the company's external annual report, the reference must be to gross margins (revenue − cost of goods sold), a product cost measure. The contribution margin (revenue − variable cost) is a measure used in internal reporting.

COST BEHAVIOR SUMMARIZED

The term *fixed* refers to the behavior of *total* fixed cost. The cost *per unit* of a fixed cost *varies inversely* with changes in the level of activity. As activity increases, fixed cost per unit decreases. As activity decreases, fixed cost per unit increases. These relationships are graphed in Exhibit 2.17.

LO I

Identify and describe fixed, variable, and mixed cost behavior.

EXHIBIT 2.17

Graphical Presentation of Fixed Cost Behavior

Total Fixed Cost | Fixed Cost per Unit

EXHIBIT 2.18

Graphical Presentation of Variable Cost Behavior

Total Variable Cost | Variable Cost per Unit

EXHIBIT 2.19

Fixed and Variable Cost Behavior

When Activity Level Changes	Total Cost	Cost per Unit
Fixed costs	Remains constant	Changes *inversely*
Variable costs	Changes in direct proportion	Remains constant

The term *variable* refers to the behavior of *total* variable cost. Total variable cost increases or decreases proportionately with changes in the volume of activity. In contrast, variable cost *per unit* remains *fixed* at all levels of activity. These relationships are graphed in Exhibit 2.18.

The relationships between fixed and variable costs are summarized in the chart in Exhibit 2.19. Study these relationships thoroughly.

Mixed Costs (Semivariable Costs)

Mixed costs (semivariable costs) include both fixed and variable components. For example, suppose Star Productions, Inc., has to pay for janitorial services. The charge for these services includes a base fee of $1,000 plus $20 per hour required to do a cleanup. The $1,000 base fee is fixed. It is the same no matter how many hours it takes to accomplish the cleanup. In contrast, the $20 hourly cost is a variable cost because the total cost increases with each additional hour it takes to complete the cleanup. Since the total janitorial cost is composed of fixed and variable components, it is frequently called a mixed cost. It may also be called a semivariable cost.

Given the $1,000 base plus $20 per hour cost components, the total janitorial cost for any cleanup can be easily computed as shown below:

$$\text{Total cost} = \text{Fixed cost} + (\text{Variable cost per hour} \times \text{Number of hours})$$

If 60 hours are required to accomplish a cleanup, the total mixed cost is:

$$\text{Total cost} = \$1,000 + (\$20 \times 60) = \$2,200$$

If 90 hours are required to accomplish a cleanup, the total mixed cost is:

$$\text{Total cost} = \$1,000 + (\$20 \times 90) = \$2,800$$

Exhibit 2.20 illustrates a variety of mixed costs businesses commonly encounter.

EXHIBIT 2.20

Examples of Mixed Costs

Type of Cost	Fixed Cost Component(s)	Variable Cost Component(s)
Cost of sales staff	Monthly salary	Bonus based on sales volume
Truck rental	Monthly rental fee	Cost of gas, tires, and maintenance
Legal fees	Monthly retainer	Reimbursements to attorney for out-of-pocket costs (copying, postage, travel, filing fees)
Outpatient service cost	Salaries of doctors and nurses, depreciation of facility, utilities	Medical supplies such as bandages, sterilization solution, and paper products
Phone services	Monthly connection fee	Per-minute usage fee
LP gas utility cost	Container rental fee	Cost of gas consumed
Cable TV services	Monthly fee	Pay-per-view charges
Training cost	Instructor salary, facility cost	Textbooks, supplies
Shipping and handling	Salaries of employees who process packages	Boxes, packing supplies, tape, and other shipping supplies, postage
Inventory holding cost	Depreciation on inventory warehouse, salaries of employees managing inventory	Delivery costs, interest on funds borrowed to finance inventory, cost of supplies

The Relevant Range

Suppose SPI, the rock concert promoter mentioned earlier, must pay $5,000 to rent a concert hall with a seating capacity of 4,000 people. Is the cost of the concert hall fixed or variable? Since total cost remains unchanged regardless of whether one ticket, 4,000 tickets, or any number in between is sold, the cost is fixed relative to ticket sales. However, what if demand for tickets is significantly more than 4,000? In that case, SPI might rent a larger concert hall at a higher cost. In other words, *the cost is fixed only for a designated range of activity (1 to 4,000).*

A similar circumstance affects many variable costs. For example, a supplier may offer a volume discount to buyers who purchase more than a specified number of products. The point is that descriptions of cost behavior pertain to a specified range of activity. The range of activity over which the definitions of fixed and variable costs are valid is commonly called the **relevant range.**

Context-Sensitive Definitions of Fixed and Variable

The behavior pattern of a particular cost may be either fixed or variable, depending on the context. For example, the cost of the band was fixed at $48,000 when SPI was considering hiring it to play a single concert. Regardless of how many tickets SPI sold, the total band cost was $48,000. However, the band cost becomes variable if SPI decides to hire it to perform at a series of concerts. The total cost and the cost per concert for one, two, three, four, or five concerts are shown in Exhibit 2.21.

In this context, the total cost of hiring the band increases proportionately with the number of concerts while cost per concert remains constant. The band cost is therefore variable. The same cost can behave as either a fixed cost or a variable cost, depending on the **activity base.** When identifying a cost as fixed or variable, first ask, fixed or variable *relative to what activity base?* The cost of the band is fixed relative to *the number of tickets sold for a specific concert;* it is variable relative to *the number of concerts produced.*

LO 5

Demonstrate how the relevant range and decision context affect cost behavior.

EXHIBIT 2.21

Cost Behavior Relative to Number of Concerts

Number of concerts (a)	1	2	3	4	5
Cost per concert (b)	$48,000	$48,000	$ 48,000	$ 48,000	$ 48,000
Total cost (a × b)	$48,000	$96,000	$144,000	$192,000	$240,000

✓ CHECK YOURSELF 2.4

Is the compensation cost for managers of Pizza Hut Restaurants a fixed cost or a variable cost?

Answer   The answer depends on the context. For example, since a store manager's salary remains unchanged regardless of how many customers enter a particular restaurant, it can be classified as a fixed cost relative to the number of customers at a particular restaurant. However, the more restaurants that Pizza Hut operates, the higher the total managers' compensation cost will be. Accordingly, managers' salary cost would be classified as a variable cost relative to the number of restaurants opened.

COST AVERAGING

Select an appropriate time period for calculating the average cost per unit.

Lake Resorts, Inc. (LRI), offers water skiing lessons for guests. Since the demand for lessons is seasonal (guests buy more lessons in July than in December), LRI has chosen to rent (rather than own) the necessary equipment (boats, skis, ropes, life jackets) only when it is needed. LRI's accountant has collected the following data pertaining to providing ski lessons:

1. The daily fee to rent equipment is $80.
2. Instructors are paid $15 per lesson hour.
3. Fuel costs are $2 per lesson hour.
4. Lessons take one hour each.
5. LRI can provide up to 20 lessons in one day.

During a recent weekend, LRI provided 2 lessons on Friday, 10 on Saturday, and 20 on Sunday. Exhibit 2.22 shows the total cost per day and average cost per lesson for each of the three days. Since equipment rental cost is fixed relative to the number of lessons provided, the cost per lesson declines as the number of lessons increases. This explains why the cost per lesson is significantly lower on Sunday than Friday.

Assume LRI uses a cost-plus pricing strategy. The cost per lesson figures shown in Exhibit 2.22 are not useful in determining the price to charge customers. For example, it makes no sense to charge more for lessons on days like Friday when demand is low. Indeed, many businesses lower prices on days when demand is low in order to stimulate business.

The pricing problem can be solved by averaging the costs over a longer span of time. To illustrate, assume LRI uses the

EXHIBIT 2.22

Analysis of Total and Unit Cost

Number of Lessons (a)	2	10	20
Cost of equipment rental	$ 80	$ 80	$ 80
Cost of instruction (a × $15)	30	150	300
Cost of fuel (a × $2)	4	20	40
Total cost (b)	$114	$250	$420
Cost per lesson (b ÷ a)	$ 57	$ 25	$ 21

REALITY BYTES

Alice is a business student who works part time at Costco Wholesale Corporation to help pay for her college expenses. She is currently taking a managerial accounting course and has heard her instructor refer to depreciation as a fixed cost. However, as a requirement for her first accounting course, Alice reviewed Costco's financial statements for 2006, 2007, and 2008. The depreciation expense increased about 21 percent over these three years. She is not sure why depreciation expense would be considered a fixed cost.

Alice's accounting instructor reminded her that when an accountant says a cost is fixed, he or she means the cost is fixed in relation to one particular factor. A cost that is fixed in relation to one factor can be variable when compared to some other factor. For example, the depreciation for a retailer may be fixed relative to the number of customers who visit a particular store, but variable relative to the number of stores the company opens. In fact, Costco's depreciation increased from 2006 to 2008 mainly because the company built and opened additional stores.

Alice's instructor suggested that Costco's depreciation expense would be more stable if analyzed on a per store basis, rather than in total. Being curious, Alice prepared the following table, where costs are in thousands. Over the three years, she noted that total depreciation expense increased 21.1 percent, while depreciation per store increased only 11.8 percent. Although the costs on a per store basis were more stable than the total depreciation costs, they still were not fixed, so she asked her instructor for further explanation.

Fiscal year	Total Depreciation Expense	Average Depreciation Expense per Store
2006	$515,285	$1,125.1
2007	566,385	1,160.6
2008	653,082	1,275.6

The instructor suggested Costco's average per store depreciation costs were increasing because the equipment and buildings purchased for the new stores (opened from 2006 to 2008) probably cost more than those purchased for the older stores and Costco's new stores are often bigger than its older stores. This would raise the average depreciation expense per store. The instructor also reminded her that in the real world very few costs are perfectly fixed or perfectly variable.

weekly average instead of a daily average. Further, assume that the costs for the week include the following:

Equipment rental (7 days × $80 per day)	$ 560
Cost of instruction ($15 × 50 lessons)	750
Cost of fuel ($2 × 50 lessons)	100
Total	$1,410
Average cost per lesson	$1,410/50 lessons = $28.20

If LRI desires to earn a profit of $10 per lesson, the company will set the price at $38.20 ($28.20 weekly average cost per lesson + $10.00 profit) per lesson regardless of the day of the week that a lesson is administered. On slow days the daily profit margin is less than $10 per lesson. Indeed, on Friday, when only two lessons are provided, LRI incurs a loss of $18.80 per lesson ($38.20 price per lesson − $57 daily average cost per lesson). This loss is offset on busy days when the daily profit margin exceeds the $10 weekly average. For example, on Sunday, when 20 lessons are administered, the profit margin is $17.20 per lesson ($38.20 price per lesson − $21 daily average cost per lesson). The differences in the daily profit margins average out over the course of the week. As a result, LRI is able to charge the same price per lesson regardless of the daily demand and still attain an average profit margin of $10 per lesson for the week.

The need for a weekly average occurs because the number of lessons per day fluctuates radically, thereby causing significant differences in the cost per lesson when calculated on a daily basis. A similar problem occurs if the number of lessons per week fluctuates radically from week to week. For example, the demand for skiing lessons may increase significantly during the week of July 4th or other holidays. Similarly, the demand for lessons may taper off toward the end of the summer. In this case, it will be necessary to expand the time frame for which the average is calculated, perhaps over the summer months or even several seasons.

Distortions can occur when the time period is too long as well as too short. For example, the price of fuel and equipment rental changes over time. If older costs are mixed with newer costs, the average does not represent current conditions. Choosing the best time frame for calculating the average cost of a product or service requires thoughtful analysis and judgment.

USE OF ESTIMATES IN REAL-WORLD PROBLEMS

LO 7

Use the high-low method, scattergraphs, and regression analysis to estimate fixed and variable costs.

Imagine trying to classify as fixed or variable all the different costs incurred by a large company such as Delta Airlines. Record keeping would be horrendous. Further complications would arise because some costs are mixed costs. Consider the cost Delta incurs to use airport facilities. An airport may charge Delta a flat annual rental fee for terminal space plus a charge each time a plane takes off or lands. The flat rental fee is a fixed cost while the charge per flight is variable. The total facilities cost is mixed.

To minimize the record-keeping difficulties involved in identifying actual fixed and variable costs, many companies make decisions using estimated rather than actual costs. Several techniques exist to divide total cost into estimated fixed and variable components.

High-Low Method of Estimating Fixed and Variable Costs

The management of Rainy Day Books (RDB) wants to expand operations. To help evaluate the risks involved in opening an additional store, the company president wants to know the amount of fixed cost a new store will likely incur. Suppose RDB's accountant decides to use the **high-low method** to supply the president with the requested information. The estimated amount of fixed cost for the new store would be developed in the following four steps.

EXHIBIT 2.23

Cost Data

Month	Units Sold	Total Cost
January	30,000	$450,000
February	14,000	300,000
March	12,000	150,000
April	25,000	440,000
May	10,000	180,000
June	11,000	240,000
July	20,000	350,000
August	18,000	400,000
September	17,000	360,000
October	16,000	320,000
November	27,000	490,000
December	34,000	540,000

Step 1   *Assemble sales volume and cost history for an existing store.* Assuming the new store would operate with roughly the same cost structure, the accountant can use the historical data to estimate the fixed cost likely to be incurred by the new store. To illustrate, assume the accounting data set for the existing store is displayed in Exhibit 2.23.

Step 2   *Select the high and low points in the data set.* In this example, the month with the lowest number of units sold does not correspond to the month with the lowest total cost. The lowest point in units sold occurred in May; the lowest total cost occurred in March. Because the total cost depends on the *number of units sold,* May should be classified as the low point. The high point in sales volume occurred in December. The units sold and cost data for the December and May high and low points follow:

	Units Sold	Total Cost
High (December)	34,000	$540,000
Low (May)	10,000	$180,000

Step 3   *Determine the estimated variable cost per unit.* The variable cost per unit is determined by dividing the difference in the total cost by the difference in the number of units sold. In this case, the variable cost per unit is as follows:

$$\frac{\text{Variable}}{\text{cost per unit}} = \frac{\text{Difference in total cost}}{\text{Difference in volume}} = \frac{(\$540{,}000 - \$180{,}000)}{(34{,}000 - 10{,}000)} = \frac{\$360{,}000}{24{,}000} = \$15$$

Step 4   *Determine the estimated total fixed cost.* The total fixed cost can now be determined by subtracting the variable cost from the total cost using either the high point or the low point. Either point yields the same result. Computations using the high point follow:

$$\text{Fixed cost} + \text{Variable cost} = \text{Total cost}$$

$$\text{Fixed cost} = \text{Total cost} - \text{Variable cost}$$

$$\text{Fixed cost} = \$540{,}000 - (\$15 \times 34{,}000 \text{ units})$$

$$\text{Fixed cost} = \$30{,}000$$

Once determined, the *total* fixed cost and variable cost *per unit* estimates can be used to predict expected total cost at any volume of activity as follows:

$$\text{Total cost} = \text{Fixed cost} + (\text{Variable cost per unit} \times \text{Number of units})$$

If 22,000 books are sold, the total estimated cost is:

$$\text{Total cost} = \$30{,}000 + (\$15 \times 22{,}000) = \$360{,}000$$

If 32,000 books are sold, the total estimated cost is:

$$\text{Total cost} = \$30{,}000 + (\$15 \times 32{,}000) = \$510{,}000$$

Although 12 data points are available, the high-low method uses only 2 of them to estimate the amounts of fixed and variable costs. If either or both of these points is not representative of the true relationship between fixed and variable costs, the estimates produced by the high-low method will be inaccurate. *The chief advantage of the high-low method is its simplicity; the chief disadvantage is its vulnerability to inaccuracy.* RDB's accountant decides to test the accuracy of the high-low method results.

Scattergraph Method of Estimating Fixed and Variable Costs

Scattergraphs are sometimes used as an estimation technique for dividing total cost into fixed and variable cost components. To assess the accuracy of the high-low estimate of fixed cost, RDB's accountant constructs a **scattergraph.** The horizontal axis is labeled with the number of books sold and the vertical axis with total costs. The 12 data points are plotted on the graph, and a line is drawn through the high and low points in the data set. The result is shown in Exhibit 2.24.

After studying the scattergraph in Exhibit 2.24, the accountant is certain that the high and low points are not representative of the data set. Most of the data points are above the high-low line. As shown in the second scattergraph in Exhibit 2.25, the line should be shifted upward to reflect the influence of the other data points.

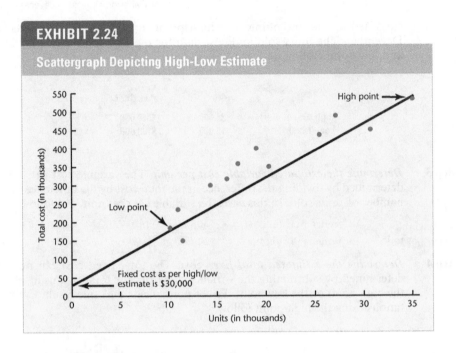

EXHIBIT 2.24

Scattergraph Depicting High-Low Estimate

High point

Low point

Fixed cost as per high/low estimate is $30,000

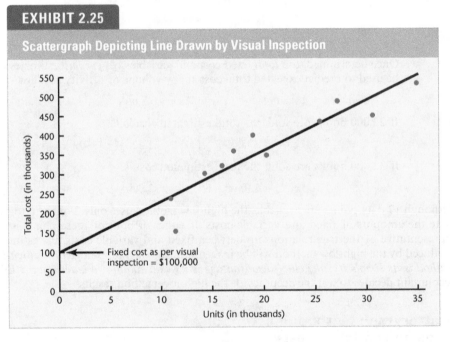

EXHIBIT 2.25

Scattergraph Depicting Line Drawn by Visual Inspection

Fixed cost as per visual inspection = $100,000

The graph in Exhibit 2.25 is identical to the graph in Exhibit 2.24 except the straight line is plotted through the center of the entire data set rather than just the high and low points. The new line, a **visual fit line,** is drawn to visually minimize the total distance between the data points and the line. Usually, half of the data points are above and half below a visual fit line. The estimated variable cost per unit is measured by the slope (steepness) of the visual fit line. The fixed cost is the point (the *intercept*) where the visual fit line intersects the vertical axis (the total cost line).

The intercept in Exhibit 2.25 provides a fixed cost estimate of $100,000. Although RDB's president had only asked for the amount of fixed cost, the variable cost can be easily determined by subtracting the fixed cost from the total cost at any point along

FOCUS ON INTERNATIONAL ISSUES

ANOTHER REASON FIXED COSTS AREN'T ALWAYS FIXED

Suppose that a company is renting a facility at an annual rental rate that does not change for the next five years *no matter what*. Is this a fixed cost? By now, you are aware that the proper response is to ask fixed in relation to what? Is the rental cost of this facility fixed in relation to the activity at this facility? The answer seems to be yes, but it might be "not necessarily."

Consider the Exxon Mobil Corporation. If Exxon Mobil rents facilities in a country in the eastern hemisphere, Malaysia for example, the annual rental fee may be stated and paid in the local currency. In Malaysia, this is the ringgit. Even though Exxon Mobil may be paying the same number of ringgit in rent each year, Exxon Mobil's rental cost in U.S. dollars could vary greatly over time. Such potential foreign currency exchange fluctuations cause companies to enter very complex hedging arrangements to add stability to transactions that must be paid in foreign currencies.

Exxon Mobil was founded and has its headquarters in the United States. It does much business in the United States. Furthermore, it is listed on the New York Stock Exchange and prepares its financial statements in U.S. dollars. However, it does much more business and has many more assets in countries outside the United States. Consider the following table from Exxon Mobil's 2008 financial statements. Before a multinational company can determine whether a cost is fixed, it must determine the applicable currency.

Geographical Area	Earnings*	Percentage of Total	Total Assets*	Percentage of Total
United States	$ 8,616	19%	$ 46,240	25%
Non-United States	37,894	81	139,094	75
Totals	$46,510	100%	$185,334	100%

*Amounts in millions.

the visual fit line. For example, at 15,000 units, total cost is $300,000. Variable cost is determined as follows:

$$\text{Fixed cost} + \text{Variable cost} = \text{Total cost}$$

$$\text{Variable cost} = \text{Total cost} - \text{Fixed cost}$$

$$\text{Variable cost} = \$300,000 - \$100,000$$

$$\text{Variable cost} = \$200,000$$

Variable cost per unit is $13.3333, calculated by dividing the total variable cost by the number of units ($200,000 ÷ 15,000 units = $13.3333 per unit).

As with the high-low method these *total* fixed cost and variable cost *per unit* estimates can be used to predict expected total cost at any volume of activity as follows:

$$\text{Total cost} = \text{Fixed cost} + (\text{Variable cost per unit} \times \text{Number of units})$$

If 22,000 books are sold, the total estimated cost is:

$$\text{Total cost} = \$100,000 + (\$13.3333 \times 22,000) = \$393,333$$

If 32,000 books are sold, the total estimated cost is:

$$\text{Total cost} = \$100,000 + (\$13.3333 \times 32,000) = \$526,666$$

Clearly, the visual fit scattergraph approach produces different estimates of total cost than the high-low method provides. Remember, both approaches produce estimates about anticipated future costs. Accuracy cannot be determined until actual costs are incurred. Accountants must exercise judgment in deciding which method is the best approach for the particular circumstances under consideration.

Regression Method of Cost Estimation

Since the scattergraph is drawn by simple visual inspection, it is subject to human error. A better fit can be obtained using a statistical procedure known as **least-squares regression**.[2] Many of today's spreadsheet programs include a regression procedure. For example, the regression estimates shown in Exhibit 2.26 were generated in an *Excel* spreadsheet by performing the following functions.

EXHIBIT 2.26

Excel Spreadsheet Showing the Results of Least-Squares Regression

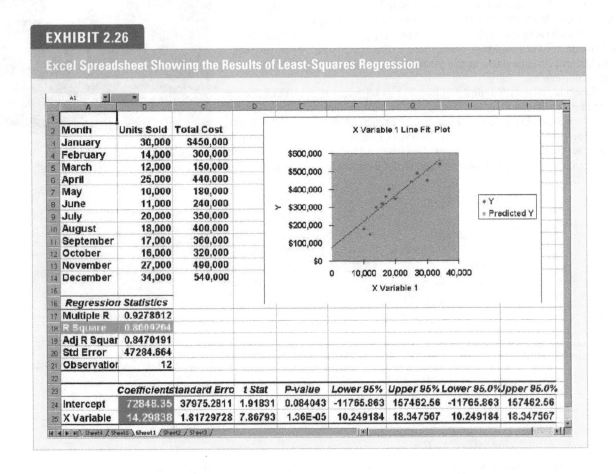

Month	Units Sold	Total Cost
January	30,000	$450,000
February	14,000	300,000
March	12,000	150,000
April	25,000	440,000
May	10,000	180,000
June	11,000	240,000
July	20,000	350,000
August	18,000	400,000
September	17,000	360,000
October	16,000	320,000
November	27,000	490,000
December	34,000	540,000

Regression Statistics	
Multiple R	0.9278612
R Square	0.8609264
Adj R Squar	0.8470191
Std Error	47284.664
Observation	12

	Coefficient	Standard Erro	t Stat	P-value	Lower 95%	Upper 95%	Lower 95.0%	Upper 95.0%
Intercept	72848.35	37975.2811	1.91831	0.084043	-11765.863	157462.56	-11765.863	157462.56
X Variable	14.29838	1.81729728	7.86793	1.36E-05	10.249184	18.347567	10.249184	18.347567

[2]Although the least-squares regression is a more accurate method than the high-low method and the visual scattergraph method, the three methods follow the same logical reasoning. Basically, the procedure locates a straight line on a coordinate with the *Y* axis representing the cost in dollars and the *X* axis representing the cost driver. In the examples shown in this chapter, the measurement of production in units is used as the cost driver and appears on the *X* axis. The basic regression model can be explained in the following equation:

$$Y = a + bX$$

Where

a = total fixed cost, or the *Y* intercept of the regression line
b = variable cost per unit of *X*, or the slope of the regression line
X = independent variable
Y = dependent variable

1. Enter the data in spreadsheet columns[3] (see columns B and C, rows 3 through 14 in Exhibit 2.26).
2. Click the *Data* tab.
3. Click *Data Analysis.*[4]
4. Click *Regression* and then *OK.*
5. Define data ranges and click *Line Fit Plot.*
6. Click *OK.*

Cost Estimates

The regression function returns a fixed cost estimate of $72,848 and a variable cost estimate of $14.30 per unit. These estimates are highlighted in blue in the spreadsheet shown in Exhibit 2.26. As with the high-low and visual fit scattergraph methods, the *total* fixed cost and variable cost *per unit* estimates computed using regression can be used to predict expected total cost at any volume of activity as follows:

$$\text{Total cost} = \text{Fixed cost} + (\text{Variable cost per unit} \times \text{Number of units})$$

If 22,000 books are sold, the total estimated cost is:

$$\text{Total cost} = \$72,848 + (\$14.30 \times 22,000) = \$387,448$$

If 32,000 books are sold, the total estimated cost is:

$$\text{Total cost} = \$72,848 + (\$14.30 \times 32,000) = \$530,448$$

As with the high-low method, **regression analysis** can be skewed by data points that are not representative of the complete data set. Here also, such outliers can be identified using visual fit scattergraphs. Again, management accountants must use common sense when interpreting the cost estimates. Choosing among the high-low method, visual fit scattergraphs, or regression analysis requires judgment. All three methods may be used to evaluate the consistency of the results.

Regression Statistics

An advantage of the regression method is that it provides statistics that give insight as to the reliability of the cost estimates. The R Square (R^2), highlighted in red in Exhibit 2.26, is the most commonly used measure of reliability. The **R^2 statistic** represents the percentage of change in the dependent variable (total cost) that is explained by a change in the independent variable (units sold). In the case of Rainy Day Books, the R^2 suggests that 86% of the change in the total monthly cost of operating a new store is caused by a change in the number of books sold. In other words, some factors other than the number of books sold also affect total costs. For example, the weight and size of the books, as well as the number sold, may affect shipping costs.

The R^2 values vary between zero and 100 percent. Higher R^2 values suggest that the independent variable more strongly influences the dependent variable. For Rainy Day Books, the relatively high R^2 of 86% suggests that the number of books sold will significantly affect the total cost of operating a new store.

Multiple Regression Analysis

As discussed above, Rainy Day Books' dependent variable (total cost) is influenced by more factors than the single independent variable (units sold). **Multiple regression analysis** is a statistical tool that permits analysis of how a number of independent variables

---

[3]Statistical reliability requires an information set that includes more than 30 data points. The illustration shown here has been limited in size to simplify the demonstration.

[4]If the data tab does not contain a data analysis option, it is likely that the statistical functions have not been activated in your program. You will need to consult the *Excel* user manual or help routine for instructions to activate the statistical functions.

simultaneously affect a dependent variable. Multiple regression analysis can improve the accuracy of fixed and variable cost estimates. A trial and error process using multiple regression analysis is frequently used to assess the relative importance of a variety of independent variables. The regression analysis is performed repeatedly, dropping and adding independent variables, until an acceptable level of accuracy is achieved.

<< A Look Back

To plan and control business operations effectively, managers need to understand how different costs behave in relation to changes in the volume of activity. Total *fixed cost* remains constant when activity changes. Fixed cost per unit decreases with increases in activity and increases with decreases in activity. In contrast, total *variable cost* increases proportionately with increases in activity and decreases proportionately with decreases in activity. Variable cost per unit remains constant regardless of activity levels. The definitions of fixed and variable costs have meaning only within the context of a specified range of activity (the relevant range) for a defined period of time. In addition, cost behavior depends on the relevant volume measure (a store manager's salary is fixed relative to the number of customers visiting a particular store but is variable relative to the number of stores operated). A mixed cost has both fixed and variable cost components.

Fixed costs allow companies to take advantage of *operating leverage*. With operating leverage, each additional sale decreases the cost per unit. This principle allows a small percentage change in volume of revenue to cause a significantly larger percentage change in profits. The *magnitude of operating leverage* can be determined by dividing the contribution margin by net income. When all costs are fixed and revenues have covered fixed costs, each additional dollar of revenue represents pure profit. Having a fixed cost structure (employing operating leverage) offers a company both risks and rewards. If sales volume increases, costs do not increase, allowing profits to soar. Alternatively, if sales volume decreases, costs do not decrease and profits decline significantly more than revenues. Companies with high variable costs in relation to fixed costs do not experience as great a level of operating leverage. Their costs increase or decrease in proportion to changes in revenue. These companies face less risk but fail to reap disproportionately higher profits when volume soars.

Under the contribution margin approach, variable costs are subtracted from revenue to determine the *contribution margin*. Fixed costs are then subtracted from the contribution margin to determine net income. The contribution margin represents the amount available to pay fixed costs and provide a profit. Although not permitted by GAAP for external reporting, many companies use the contribution margin format for internal reporting purposes.

Cost per unit is an average cost that is easier to compute than the actual cost of each unit and is more relevant to decision making than actual cost. Accountants must use judgment when choosing the time span from which to draw data for computing the average cost per unit. Distortions can result from using either too long or too short a time span.

Fixed and variable costs can be estimated using such tools as the *high-low method, scattergraphs* and regression analysis. The high-low method and scattergraphs are easy to use. Regression analysis is more accurate.

>> A Look Forward

The next chapter will show you how changes in cost, volume, and pricing affect profitability. You will learn to determine the number of units of product that must be produced and sold in order to break even (the number of units that will produce an amount of revenue that is exactly equal to total cost). You will learn to establish the price of a product using a cost-plus pricing approach and to establish the cost of a product using a target-pricing approach. Finally, the chapter will show you how to use a break-even chart to examine potential profitability over a range of operating activity and how to use a technique known as *sensitivity analysis* to examine how simultaneous changes in sales price, volume, fixed costs, and variable costs affect profitability.

A step-by-step audio-narrated series of slides is provided on the text website at www.mhhe.com/edmonds2011.

   SELF-STUDY REVIEW PROBLEM

Mensa Mountaineering Company (MMC) provides guided mountain climbing expeditions in the Rocky Mountains. Its only major expense is guide salaries; it pays each guide $4,800 per climbing expedition. MMC charges its customers $1,500 per expedition and expects to take five climbers on each expedition.

Part 1

Base your answers on the preceding information.

Required

a. Determine the total cost of guide salaries and the cost of guide salaries per climber assuming that four, five, or six climbers are included in a trip. Relative to the number of climbers in a single expedition, is the cost of guides a fixed or a variable cost?

b. Relative to the number of expeditions, is the cost of guides a fixed or a variable cost?

c. Determine the profit of an expedition assuming that five climbers are included in the trip.

d. Determine the profit assuming a 20 percent increase (six climbers total) in expedition revenue. What is the percentage change in profitability?

e. Determine the profit assuming a 20 percent decrease (four climbers total) in expedition revenue. What is the percentage change in profitability?

f. Explain why a 20 percent shift in revenue produces more than a 20 percent shift in profitability. What term describes this phenomenon?

Part 2

Assume that the guides offer to make the climbs for a percentage of expedition fees. Specifically, MMC will pay guides $960 per climber on the expedition. Assume also that the expedition fee charged to climbers remains at $1,500 per climber.

Required

g. Determine the total cost of guide salaries and the cost of guide salaries per climber assuming that four, five, or six climbers are included in a trip. Relative to the number of climbers in a single expedition, is the cost of guides a fixed or a variable cost?

h. Relative to the number of expeditions, is the cost of guides a fixed or a variable cost?

i. Determine the profit of an expedition assuming that five climbers are included in the trip.

j. Determine the profit assuming a 20 percent increase (six climbers total) in expedition revenue. What is the percentage change in profitability?

k. Determine the profit assuming a 20 percent decrease (four climbers total) in expedition revenue. What is the percentage change in profitability?

l. Explain why a 20 percent shift in revenue does not produce more than a 20 percent shift in profitability.

Solution to Part 1, Requirement a

Number of climbers (a)	4	5	6
Total cost of guide salaries (b)	$4,800	$4,800	$4,800
Cost per climber (b ÷ a)	1,200	960	800

Since the total cost remains constant (fixed) regardless of the number of climbers on a particular expedition, the cost is classified as fixed. Note that the cost per climber decreases as the number of climbers increases. This is the *per-unit* behavior pattern of a fixed cost.

Solution to Part 1, Requirement b

Since the total cost of guide salaries changes proportionately each time the number of expeditions increases or decreases, the cost of salaries is variable relative to the number of expeditions.

Solution to Part 1, Requirements c, d, and e

Number of Climbers	4	Percentage Change	5	Percentage Change	6
Revenue ($1,500 per climber)	$6,000	⇐ (20%) ⇐	$7,500	⇒ +20% ⇒	$9,000
Cost of guide salaries (fixed)	4,800		4,800		4,800
Net income	$1,200	⇐ (55.6%) ⇐	$2,700	⇒ +55.6% ⇒	$4,200

Percentage change in revenue: ±$1,500 ÷ $7,500 = ±20%
Percentage change in profit: ±$1,500 ÷ $2,700 = ±55.6%

Solution to Part 1, Requirement f

Since the cost of guide salaries remains fixed while volume (number of climbers) changes, the change in net income, measured in absolute dollars, exactly matches the change in revenue. More specifically, each time MMC increases the number of climbers by one, revenue and net income increase by $1,500. Since the base figure for net income ($2,700) is lower than the base figure for revenue ($7,500), the percentage change in net income ($1,500 ÷ $2,700 = 55.6%) is higher than percentage change in revenue ($1,500 ÷ $7,500). This phenomenon is called *operating leverage*.

Solution for Part 2, Requirement g

	4	5	6
Number of climbers (a)	4	5	6
Per climber cost of guide salaries (b)	$ 960	$ 960	$ 960
Cost per climber (b × a)	3,840	4,800	5,760

Since the total cost changes in proportion to changes in the number of climbers, the cost is classified as variable. Note that the cost per climber remains constant (stays the same) as the number of climbers increases or decreases. This is the *per-unit* behavior pattern of a variable cost.

Solution for Part 2, Requirement h

Since the total cost of guide salaries changes proportionately with changes in the number of expeditions, the cost of salaries is also variable relative to the number of expeditions.

Solution for Part 2, Requirements i, j, and k

Number of Climbers	4	Percentage Change	5	Percentage Change	6
Revenue ($1,500 per climber)	$6,000	⇐ (20%) ⇐	$7,500	⇒ +20% ⇒	$9,000
Cost of guide salaries (variable)	3,840		4,800		5,760
Net income	$2,160	⇐ (20%) ⇐	$2,700	⇒ +20% ⇒	$3,240

Percentage change in revenue: ±$1,500 ÷ $7,500 = ±20%
Percentage change in profit: ±$540 ÷ $2,700 = ±20%

Solution for Part 2, Requirement l

Since the cost of guide salaries changes when volume (number of climbers) changes, the change in net income is proportionate to the change in revenue. More specifically, each time the number of climbers increases by one, revenue increases by $1,500 and net income increases by $540 ($1,500 − $960). Accordingly, the percentage change in net income will always equal the percentage change in revenue. This means that there is no operating leverage when all costs are variable.

KEY TERMS

QUESTIONS

1. Define *fixed cost* and *variable cost* and give an example of each.

2. How can knowing cost behavior relative to volume fluctuations affect decision making?

3. Define the term *operating leverage* and explain how it affects profits.

4. How is operating leverage calculated?

5. Explain the limitations of using operating leverage to predict profitability.

6. If volume is increasing, would a company benefit more from a pure variable or a pure fixed cost structure? Which cost structure would be advantageous if volume is decreasing?

7. When are economies of scale possible? In what types of businesses would you most likely find economies of scale?

8. Explain the risk and rewards to a company that result from having fixed costs.

9. Are companies with predominately fixed cost structures likely to be more profitable?

10. How is the relevant range of activity related to fixed and variable cost? Give an example of how the definitions of these costs become invalid when volume is outside the relevant range.

11. Sam's Garage is trying to determine the cost of providing an oil change. Why would the average cost of this service be more relevant information than the actual cost for each customer?

12. When would the high-low method be appropriate for estimating variable and fixed costs? When would least-squares regression be the most desirable?

13. Which cost structure has the greater risk? Explain.

14. The president of Bright Corporation tells you that he sees a dim future for his company. He feels that his hands are tied because fixed costs are too high. He says that fixed costs do not change and therefore the situation is hopeless. Do you agree? Explain.

15. All costs are variable because if a business ceases operations, its costs fall to zero. Do you agree with the statement? Explain.

16. Because of seasonal fluctuations, Norel Corporation has a problem determining the unit cost of the products it produces. For example, high heating costs during the winter months causes per-unit cost to be higher than per-unit cost in the summer months even when the same number of units of product is produced. Suggest several ways that Norel can improve the computation of per-unit costs.

17. Verna Salsbury tells you that she thinks the terms fixed cost and variable cost are confusing. She notes that fixed cost per unit changes when the number of units changes. Furthermore, variable cost per unit remains fixed regardless of how many units are produced. She concludes that the terminology seems to be backward. Explain why the terminology appears to be contradictory.

MULTIPLE-CHOICE QUESTIONS

Multiple-choice questions are provided on the text website at www.mhhe.com/edmonds2011.

EXERCISES—SERIES A

All applicable Exercises in Series A are available with McGraw-Hill's *Connect Accounting*.

Exercise 2-1A *Identifying cost behavior*

LO 1

Deer Valley Kitchen, a fast-food restaurant company, operates a chain of restaurants across the nation. Each restaurant employs eight people; one is a manager paid a salary plus a bonus equal to 3 percent of sales. Other employees, two cooks, one dishwasher, and four waitresses, are paid salaries. Each manager is budgeted $3,000 per month for advertising costs.

Required

Classify each of the following costs incurred by Deer Valley Kitchen as fixed, variable, or mixed:

a. Cooks' salaries at a particular location relative to the number of customers.
b. Cost of supplies (cups, plates, spoons, etc.) relative to the number of customers.
c. Manager's compensation relative to the number of customers.
d. Waitresses' salaries relative to the number of restaurants.
e. Advertising costs relative to the number of customers for a particular restaurant.
f. Rental costs relative to the number of restaurants.

LO 1

Exercise 2-2A *Identifying cost behavior*

At the various activity levels shown, Ambrose Company incurred the following costs:

	Units sold	20	40	60	80	100
a.	Depreciation cost per unit	$ 240.00	$ 120.00	$ 80.00	$ 60.00	$ 48.00
b.	Total rent cost	3,200.00	3,200.00	3,200.00	3,200.00	3,200.00
c.	Total cost of shopping bags	2.00	4.00	6.00	8.00	10.00
d.	Cost per unit of merchandise sold	90.00	90.00	90.00	90.00	90.00
e.	Rental cost per unit of merchandise sold	36.00	18.00	12.00	9.00	7.20
f.	Total phone expense	80.00	100.00	120.00	140.00	160.00
g.	Cost per unit of supplies	1.00	1.00	1.00	1.00	1.00
h.	Total insurance cost	480.00	480.00	480.00	480.00	480.00
i.	Total salary cost	1,200.00	1,600.00	2,000.00	2,400.00	2,800.00
j.	Total cost of goods sold	1,800.00	3,600.00	5,400.00	7,200.00	9,000.00

Required

Identify each of these costs as fixed, variable, or mixed.

LO 1

Exercise 2-3A *Determining fixed cost per unit*

Henke Corporation incurs the following annual fixed costs:

Item	Cost
Depreciation	$ 50,000
Officers' salaries	120,000
Long-term lease	51,000
Property taxes	9,000

Required

Determine the total fixed cost per unit of production, assuming that Henke produces 4,000, 4,500, or 5,000 units.

LO 1

Exercise 2-4A *Determining total variable cost*

The following variable production costs apply to goods made by Watson Manufacturing Corporation:

Item	Cost per Unit
Materials	$5.00
Labor	2.50
Variable overhead	0.25
Total	$7.75

Required

Determine the total variable production cost, assuming that Watson makes 5,000, 15,000, or 25,000 units.

Exercise 2-5A   *Fixed versus variable cost behavior*

Robbins Company's cost and production data for two recent months included the following:

	March	April
Production (units)	100	250
Rent	$1,500	$1,500
Utilities	$ 450	$1,125

Required

a. Separately calculate the rental cost per unit and the utilities cost per unit for both March and April.

b. Identify which cost is variable and which is fixed. Explain your answer.

Exercise 2-6A   *Fixed versus variable cost behavior*

Lovvern Trophies makes and sells trophies it distributes to little league ballplayers. The company normally produces and sells between 8,000 and 14,000 trophies per year. The following cost data apply to various activity levels:

Number of trophies	8,000	10,000	12,000	14,000
Total costs incurred				
Fixed	$42,000			
Variable	42,000			
Total costs	$84,000			
Cost per unit				
Fixed	$ 6.00			
Variable	6.00			
Total cost per trophy	$ 12.00			

Required

a. Complete the preceding table by filling in the missing amounts for the levels of activity shown in the first row of the table. Round all cost per unit figures to the nearest whole penny.

b. Explain why the total cost per trophy decreases as the number of trophies increases.

Exercise 2-7A   *Fixed versus variable cost behavior*

Harrell Entertainment sponsors rock concerts. The company is considering a contract to hire a band at a cost of $75,000 per concert.

Required

a. What are the total band cost and the cost per person if concert attendance is 2,000, 2,500, 3,000, 3,500, or 4,000?

b. Is the cost of hiring the band a fixed or a variable cost?

c. Draw a graph and plot total cost and cost per unit if attendance is 2,000, 2,500, 3,000, 3,500, or 4,000.

d. Identify Harrell's major business risks and explain how they can be minimized.

Exercise 2-8A   *Fixed versus variable cost behavior*

Harrell Entertainment sells souvenir T-shirts at each rock concert that it sponsors. The shirts cost $9 each. Any excess shirts can be returned to the manufacturer for a full refund of the purchase price. The sales price is $15 per shirt.

Required

a. What are the total cost of shirts and cost per shirt if sales amount to 2,000, 2,500, 3,000, 3,500, or 4,000?
b. Is the cost of T-shirts a fixed or a variable cost?
c. Draw a graph and plot total cost and cost per shirt if sales amount to 2,000, 2,500, 3,000, 3,500, or 4,000.
d. Comment on Harrell's likelihood of incurring a loss due to its operating activities.

LO 1

Exercise 2-9A   *Graphing fixed cost behavior*

The following graph setups depict the dollar amount of fixed cost on the vertical axes and the level of activity on the horizontal axes:

Required

a. Draw a line that depicts the relationship between total fixed cost and the level of activity.
b. Draw a line that depicts the relationship between fixed cost per unit and the level of activity.

LO 1

Exercise 2-10A   *Graphing variable cost behavior*

The following graph setups depict the dollar amount of variable cost on the vertical axes and the level of activity on the horizontal axes:

Required

a. Draw a line that depicts the relationship between total variable cost and the level of activity.
b. Draw a line that depicts the relationship between variable cost per unit and the level of activity.

LO 1

Exercise 2-11A   *Mixed cost at different levels of activity*

Omar Corporation paid one of its sales representatives $4,300 during the month of March. The rep is paid a base salary plus $15 per unit of product sold. During March, the rep sold 200 units.

Required

Calculate the total monthly cost of the sales representative's salary for each of the following months:

Month	April	May	June	July
Number of units sold	240	150	250	160
Total variable cost				
Total fixed cost				
Total salary cost				

Exercise 2-12A   *Using fixed cost as a competitive business strategy*   LO 1, 2, 3

The following income statements illustrate different cost structures for two competing companies:

Income Statements		
	Company Name	
	Hank	Rank
Number of customers (a)	80	80
Sales revenue (a × $250)	$20,000	$20,000
Variable cost (a × $175)	N/A	(14,000)
Variable cost (a × $0)	0	N/A
Contribution margin	20,000	6,000
Fixed cost	(14,000)	0
Net income	$ 6,000	$ 6,000

Required

a. Reconstruct Hank's income statement, assuming that it serves 160 customers when it lures 80 customers away from Rank by lowering the sales price to $150 per customer.

b. Reconstruct Rank's income statement, assuming that it serves 160 customers when it lures 80 customers away from Hank by lowering the sales price to $150 per customer.

c. Explain why the price-cutting strategy increased Hank Company's profits but caused a net loss for Rank Company.

Exercise 2-13A   *Using contribution margin format income statement to measure the*   LO 3, 4
**   *magnitude of operating leverage***

The following income statement was drawn from the records of Ulrich Company, a merchandising firm:

ULRICH COMPANY	
Income Statement	
For the Year Ended December 31, 2011	
Sales revenue (4,000 units × $150)	$600,000
Cost of goods sold (4,000 units × $80)	(320,000)
Gross margin	280,000
Sales commissions (10% of sales)	(60,000)
Administrative salaries expense	(90,000)
Advertising expense	(40,000)
Depreciation expense	(50,000)
Shipping and handling expenses (4,000 units × $1)	(4,000)
Net income	$ 36,000

Required

a. Reconstruct the income statement using the contribution margin format.
b. Calculate the magnitude of operating leverage.
c. Use the measure of operating leverage to determine the amount of net income Ulrich will earn if sales increase by 10 percent.

LO 4

Exercise 2-14A   *Assessing the magnitude of operating leverage*

The following income statement applies to Stuart Company for the current year:

Income Statement	
Sales revenue (400 units × $25)	$10,000
Variable cost (400 units × $10)	(4,000)
Contribution margin	6,000
Fixed costs	(3,500)
Net income	$ 2,500

Required

a. Use the contribution margin approach to calculate the magnitude of operating leverage.
b. Use the operating leverage measure computed in Requirement *a* to determine the amount of net income that Stuart Company will earn if it experiences a 10 percent increase in revenue. The sales price per unit is not affected.
c. Verify your answer to Requirement *b* by constructing an income statement based on a 10 percent increase in sales revenue. The sales price is not affected. Calculate the percentage change in net income for the two income statements.

LO 6

Exercise 2-15A   *Averaging costs*

Getaway Camps, Inc., leases the land on which it builds camp sites. Getaway is considering opening a new site on land that requires $3,000 of rental payment per month. The variable cost of providing service is expected to be $7 per camper. The following chart shows the number of campers Getaway expects for the first year of operation of the new site:

Jan.	Feb.	Mar.	Apr.	May	June	July	Aug.	Sept.	Oct.	Nov.	Dec.	Total
120	250	200	200	300	500	650	650	350	380	100	300	4,000

Required

Assuming that Getaway wants to earn $8 per camper, determine the price it should charge for a camp site in February and August.

LO 7

Exercise 2-16A   *Estimating fixed and variable costs using the high-low method*

Knox Boat Company makes inexpensive aluminum fishing boats. Production is seasonal, with considerable activity occurring in the spring and summer. Sales and production tend to decline in the fall and winter months. During 2011, the high point in activity occurred in June when it produced 200 boats at a total cost of $140,000. The low point in production occurred in January when it produced 40 boats at a total cost of $44,000.

Required

a. Use the high-low method to estimate the amount of fixed cost incurred each month by Knox Boat Company.
b. Determine the total estimated cost if 100 boats are made.
c. Comment on the strengths and weaknesses of the high-low method.
d. Explain how a visual fit scattergraph could be used to improve accuracy.

PROBLEMS—SERIES A

All applicable Problems in Series A are available with McGraw-Hill's
Connect Accounting.

Problem 2-17A   *Identifying cost behavior*

LO 1

Required

Identify the following costs as fixed or variable:

Costs related to plane trips between Seattle, Washington, and Orlando, Florida, follow. Pilots are paid on a per-trip basis.

a. Pilots' salaries relative to the number of trips flown.
b. Depreciation relative to the number of planes in service.
c. Cost of refreshments relative to the number of passengers.
d. Pilots' salaries relative to the number of passengers on a particular trip.
e. Cost of a maintenance check relative to the number of passengers on a particular trip.
f. Fuel costs relative to the number of trips.

First Federal Bank operates several branch offices in grocery stores. Each branch employs a supervisor and two tellers.

g. Tellers' salaries relative to the number of tellers in a particular district.
h. Supplies cost relative to the number of transactions processed in a particular branch.
i. Tellers' salaries relative to the number of customers served at a particular branch.
j. Supervisors' salaries relative to the number of branches operated.
k. Supervisors' salaries relative to the number of customers served in a particular branch.
l. Facility rental costs relative to the size of customer deposits.

Costs related to operating a fast-food restaurant follow.

m. Depreciation of equipment relative to the number of restaurants.
n. Building rental cost relative to the number of customers served in a particular restaurant.
o. Manager's salary of a particular store relative to the number of employees.
p. Food cost relative to the number of customers.
q. Utility cost relative to the number of restaurants in operation.
r. Company president's salary relative to the number of restaurants in operation.
s. Land costs relative to the number of hamburgers sold at a particular restaurant.
t. Depreciation of equipment relative to the number of customers served at a particular restaurant.

Problem 2-18A   *Cost behavior and averaging*

LO 1, 6

Carlia Weaver has decided to start Carlia Cleaning, a residential housecleaning service company. She is able to rent cleaning equipment at a cost of $750 per month. Labor costs are expected to be $75 per house cleaned and supplies are expected to cost $6 per house.

Required

a. Determine the total expected cost of equipment rental and the average expected cost of equipment rental per house cleaned, assuming that Carlia Cleaning cleans 10, 20, or 30 houses during one month. Is the cost of equipment a fixed or a variable cost?
b. Determine the total expected cost of labor and the average expected cost of labor per house cleaned, assuming that Carlia Cleaning cleans 10, 20, or 30 houses during one month. Is the cost of labor a fixed or a variable cost?
c. Determine the total expected cost of supplies and the average expected cost of supplies per house cleaned, assuming that Carlia Cleaning cleans 10, 20, or 30 houses during one month. Is the cost of supplies a fixed or a variable cost?
d. Determine the total expected cost of cleaning houses, assuming that Carlia Cleaning cleans 10, 20, or 30 houses during one month.

e. Determine the average expected cost per house, assuming that Carlia Cleaning cleans 10, 20, or 30 houses during one month. Why does the cost per unit decrease as the number of houses increases?

f. If Ms. Weaver tells you that she prices her services at 25 percent above cost, would you assume that she means average or actual cost? Why?

LO 1

CHECK FIGURE

b. Average teller cost for 60,000 transactions: $1.50

Problem 2-19A   *Context-sensitive nature of cost behavior classifications*

Pacific Bank's start-up division establishes new branch banks. Each branch opens with three tellers. Total teller cost per branch is $90,000 per year. The three tellers combined can process up to 90,000 customer transactions per year. If a branch does not attain a volume of at least 60,000 transactions during its first year of operations, it is closed. If the demand for services exceeds 90,000 transactions, an additional teller is hired, and the branch is transferred from the start-up division to regular operations.

Required

a. What is the relevant range of activity for new branch banks?

b. Determine the amount of teller cost in total and the average teller cost per transaction for a branch that processes 60,000, 70,000, 80,000, or 90,000 transactions. In this case (the activity base is the number of transactions for a specific branch), is the teller cost a fixed or a variable cost?

c. Determine the amount of teller cost in total and the average teller cost per branch for Pacific Bank, assuming that the start-up division operates 10, 15, or 25 branches. In this case (the activity base is the number of branches), is the teller cost a fixed or a variable cost?

LO 1

CHECK FIGURES

a. Average cost at 400 units: $200

b. Average price at 250 units: $265

Problem 2-20A   *Context-sensitive nature of cost behavior classifications*

Susan Hicks operates a sales booth in computer software trade shows, selling an accounting software package, *Dollar System*. She purchases the package from a software manufacturer for $175 each. Booth space at the convention hall costs $10,000 per show.

Required

a. Sales at past trade shows have ranged between 200 and 400 software packages per show. Determine the average cost of sales per unit if Ms. Hicks sells 200, 250, 300, 350, or 400 units of *Dollar System* at a trade show. Use the following chart to organize your answer. Is the cost of booth space fixed or variable?

	Sales Volume in Units (a)				
	200	250	300	350	400
Total cost of software (a × $175)	$35,000				
Total cost of booth rental	10,000				
Total cost of sales (b)	$45,000				
Average cost per unit (b ÷ a)	$225.00				

b. If Ms. Hicks wants to earn a $50 profit on each package of software she sells at a trade show, what price must she charge at sales volumes of 200, 250, 300, 350, or 400 units?

c. Record the total cost of booth space if Ms. Hicks attends one, two, three, four, or five trade shows. Record your answers in the following chart. Is the cost of booth space fixed or variable relative to the number of shows attended?

	Number of Trade Shows Attended				
	1	2	3	4	5
Total cost of booth rental	$10,000				

d. Ms. Hicks provides decorative shopping bags to customers who purchase software packages. Some customers take the bags; others do not. Some customers stuff more than one software package into a single bag. The number of bags varies in relation to the number of units sold, but the relationship is not proportional. Assume that Ms. Hicks uses $30 of bags for every 50 software packages sold. What is the additional cost per unit sold? Is the cost fixed or variable?

Problem 2-21A *Effects of operating leverage on profitability*

Webster Training Services (WTS) provides instruction on the use of computer software for the employees of its corporate clients. It offers courses in the clients' offices on the clients' equipment. The only major expense WTS incurs is instructor salaries; it pays instructors $5,000 per course taught. WTS recently agreed to offer a course of instruction to the employees of Chambers Incorporated at a price of $400 per student. Chambers estimated that 20 students would attend the course.

Base your answers on the preceding information.

LO 1, 2

CHECK FIGURES
Part 1, b: $2,200
Part 2, h: $3,000 & 10%
Part 3, k: cost per student for 22 students: $25

Part 1:

Required

a. Relative to the number of students in a single course, is the cost of instruction a fixed or a variable cost?

b. Determine the profit, assuming that 20 students attend the course.

c. Determine the profit, assuming a 10 percent increase in enrollment (i.e., enrollment increases to 22 students). What is the percentage change in profitability?

d. Determine the profit, assuming a 10 percent decrease in enrollment (i.e., enrollment decreases to 18 students). What is the percentage change in profitability?

e. Explain why a 10 percent shift in enrollment produces more than a 10 percent shift in profitability. Use the term that identifies this phenomenon.

Part 2:

The instructor has offered to teach the course for a percentage of tuition fees. Specifically, she wants $250 per person attending the class. Assume that the tuition fee remains at $400 per student.

Required

f. Is the cost of instruction a fixed or a variable cost?

g. Determine the profit, assuming that 20 students take the course.

h. Determine the profit, assuming a 10 percent increase in enrollment (i.e., enrollment increases to 22 students). What is the percentage change in profitability?

i. Determine the profit, assuming a 10 percent decrease in enrollment (i.e., enrollment decreases to 18 students). What is the percentage change in profitability?

j. Explain why a 10 percent shift in enrollment produces a proportional 20 percent shift in profitability.

Part 3:

WTS sells a workbook with printed material unique to each course to each student who attends the course. Any workbooks that are not sold must be destroyed. Prior to the first class, WTS printed 20 copies of the books based on the client's estimate of the number of people who would attend the course. Each workbook costs $25 and is sold to course participants for $40. This cost includes a royalty fee paid to the author and the cost of duplication.

Required

k. Calculate the workbook cost in total and per student, assuming that 18, 20, or 22 students attempt to attend the course.

l. Classify the cost of workbooks as fixed or variable relative to the number of students attending the course.

m. Discuss the risk of holding inventory as it applies to the workbooks.

n. Explain how a just-in-time inventory system can reduce the cost and risk of holding inventory.

LO 2

CHECK FIGURES
a. Eastern NI: $810
b. NI: $2,610

Problem 2-22A *Effects of fixed and variable cost behavior on the risk and rewards of business opportunities*

Eastern and Western Universities offer executive training courses to corporate clients. Eastern pays its instructors $5,310 per course taught. Western pays its instructors $295 per student enrolled in the class. Both universities charge executives a $340 tuition fee per course attended.

Required

a. Prepare income statements for Eastern and Western, assuming that 18 students attend a course.

b. Eastern University embarks on a strategy to entice students from Western University by lowering its tuition to $220 per course. Prepare an income statement for Eastern assuming that the university is successful and enrolls 36 students in its course.

c. Western University embarks on a strategy to entice students from Eastern University by lowering its tuition to $220 per course. Prepare an income statement for Western, assuming that the university is successful and enrolls 36 students in its course.

d. Explain why the strategy described in Requirement *b* produced a profit but the same strategy described in Requirement *c* produced a loss.

e. Prepare income statements for Eastern and Western Universities, assuming that 15 students attend a course, and assuming that both universities charge executives a $340 tuition fee per course attended.

f. It is always better to have fixed rather than variable cost. Explain why this statement is false.

g. It is always better to have variable rather than fixed cost. Explain why this statement is false.

LO 4

Problem 2-23A *Analyzing operating leverage*

Justin Zinder is a venture capitalist facing two alternative investment opportunities. He intends to invest $1 million in a start-up firm. He is nervous, however, about future economic volatility. He asks you to analyze the following financial data for the past year's operations of the two firms he is considering and give him some business advice.

	Company Name	
	Ensley	Kelley
Variable cost per unit (a)	$ 21.00	$ 10.50
Sales revenue (8,000 units × $28)	$224,000	$224,000
Variable cost (8,000 units × a)	(168,000)	(84,000)
Contribution margin	$ 56,000	$140,000
Fixed cost	(25,000)	(109,000)
Net income	$ 31,000	$ 31,000

CHECK FIGURES
b. % of change for Kelley: 45.16
c. % of change for Ensley: (18.06)

Required

a. Use the contribution margin approach to compute the operating leverage for each firm.

b. If the economy expands in coming years, Ensley and Kelley will both enjoy a 10 percent per year increase in sales, assuming that the selling price remains unchanged. Compute the change in net income for each firm in dollar amount and in percentage. (*Note:* Since the number of units increases, both revenue and variable cost will increase.)

c. If the economy contracts in coming years, Ensley and Kelley will both suffer a 10 percent decrease in sales volume, assuming that the selling price remains unchanged. Compute the change in net income for each firm in dollar amount and in percentage. (*Note:* Since the number of units decreases, both total revenue and total variable cost will decrease.)

d. Write a memo to Justin Zinder with your analyses and advice.

LO 6

Problem 2-24A *Selecting the appropriate time period for cost averaging*

Trinkle Cinemas is considering a contract to rent a movie for $1,800 per day. The contract requires a minimum one-week rental period. Estimated attendance is as follows:

Monday	Tuesday	Wednesday	Thursday	Friday	Saturday	Sunday
450	300	200	550	1,000	1,000	500

Required

a. Determine the average cost per person of the movie rental contract separately for each day.
b. Suppose that Trinkle chooses to price movie tickets at cost as computed in Requirement *a* plus $2.50. What price would it charge per ticket on each day of the week?
c. Use weekly averaging to determine a reasonable price to charge for movie tickets.
d. Comment on why weekly averaging may be more useful to business managers than daily averaging.

Problem 2-25A *Identifying relevant issues for cost averaging*

Cliff Corporation, offers mountain-climbing expeditions for its customers, providing food, equipment, and guides. Climbs normally require one week to complete. The company's accountant is reviewing historical cost data to establish a pricing strategy for the coming year. The accountant has prepared the following table showing cost data for the most recent climb, the company's average cost per year, and the five-year average cost.

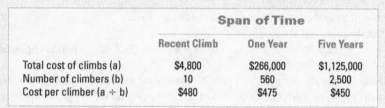

	Span of Time		
	Recent Climb	**One Year**	**Five Years**
Total cost of climbs (a)	$4,800	$266,000	$1,125,000
Number of climbers (b)	10	560	2,500
Cost per climber (a ÷ b)	$480	$475	$450

Required

Write a memo that explains the potential advantages and disadvantages of using each of the per-unit cost figures as a basis for establishing a price to charge climbers during the coming year. What other factors must be considered in developing a pricing strategy?

Problem 2-26A *Estimating fixed and variable cost*

Newteh Computer Services, Inc., has been in business for six months. The following are basic operating data for that period.

	Month					
	July	Aug.	Sept.	Oct.	Nov.	Dec.
Service hours	120	136	260	420	320	330
Revenue	$6,000	$6,800	$13,000	$21,000	$16,000	$16,500
Operating costs	$4,300	$5,300	$ 7,100	$11,200	$ 9,100	$10,600

Required

a. What is the average service revenue per hour for the six-month time period?
b. Use the high-low method to estimate the total monthly fixed cost and the variable cost per hour.
c. Determine the average contribution margin per hour.
d. Use the scattergraph method to estimate the total monthly fixed cost and the variable cost per hour.
e. Compare the results of the two methods and comment on the difference.

Problem 2-27A *Estimating fixed and variable cost*

Nabil Woodcraft Company (NWC) manufactures "antique" wooden cabinets to house modern radio and CD players. NWC began operations in January of last year. Paul Nabil, the owner, asks for your assistance. He believes that he needs to better understand the cost of the cabinets for pricing purposes. You have collected the following data concerning actual production over the past year:

Month	Number of Cabinets Produced	Total Cost
January	800	$21,000
February	3,600	32,500
March	1,960	29,500
April	600	18,600
May	1,600	29,000
June	1,300	27,000
July	1,100	25,600
August	1,800	31,000
September	2,280	32,000
October	2,940	31,500
November	3,280	32,000
December	400	16,500

Required

a. To understand the department's cost behavior, you decide to plot the points on graph paper and sketch a total cost line.

    (1) Enter the number of units and their costs in increasing order.

    (2) Plot the points on the graph.

    (3) Sketch a graph so the line "splits" all of the points (half of the points appear above and half below the line).

    (4) Using the line you just sketched, visually estimate the total cost to produce 2,000 units.

b. Using the high-low method, compute the total cost equation for the preceding data.

    (1) Compute the variable cost per unit.

    (2) Compute total fixed costs.

    (3) Sketch a line between the high and low points on your graph.

    (4) Calculate the total cost assuming 2,000 cabinets are made.

c. Comment on which method you believe is better.

LO 7

CHECK FIGURES
b. VC/hr: $15.19
   FC: $1,142

Problem 2-28A   Estimating fixed and variable cost using the regression method

Latif and Koehler Tax Services Company has 31 branch offices in the nation. Each office has about three to six professional accountants and one to two secretaries. In a busy season, the office manager, who is also a professional accountant, can hire temporary employees for support work such as document filing and typing. Josh Lane, the president, is wondering whether he should expand his business by opening more offices. One of the factors that he is considering is how to estimate office support costs. Vineeta Riley, the accountant, collected the following cost data for all 31 offices:

Branch	Professional Hours	Support Costs	Branch	Professional Hours	Support Costs
A1	225	$4,241	F2	165	$3,856
A2	113	3,435	G1	358	5,936
A3	387	6,398	G2	471	8,615
A4	412	6,502	G3	492	9,639
B1	258	4,140	G4	328	5,968
B2	146	3,368	G5	359	7,115
B3	275	3,820	G6	174	3,287
D1	364	6,396	H1	394	7,515
D2	190	3,946	H2	386	7,374
D3	484	8,189	I2	279	5,376
D4	251	4,506	I5	314	5,784
D5	377	6,744	J2	283	5,426
E1	264	4,645	J3	198	4,418
E2	169	6,073	J4	226	4,506
E3	338	6,290	J5	341	6,488
F1	437	9,113			

Required

a. The company uses the number of professional hours as the cost driver for office support costs. Use an algebraic equation to describe how total office support costs can be estimated.

b. Use a spreadsheet program to perform a regression analysis. Use office support costs as the dependent variable (Y) and the professional hours as the independent variable (X). Determine the total fixed cost per office and variable cost per professional hour.

c. Identify the R^2 statistic provided by the Excel program and explain what it means.

d. Mr. Lane plans to open a new branch office in a Chicago suburb. He expects that the monthly professional hours will be 3,000. Estimate the total office support cost for Mr. Lane. What portion of the total cost is fixed and what portion is variable?

e. Explain how multiple regression analysis could be used to improve the accuracy of the cost estimates.

EXERCISES—SERIES B

Exercise 2-1B   *Identifying cost behavior*   LO 1

Parker Copies Company provides professional copying services to customers through the 35 copy stores it operates in the southwestern United States. Each store employs a manager and four assistants. The manager earns $4,000 per month plus a bonus of 3 percent of sales. The assistants earn hourly wages. Each copy store costs $3,000 per month to lease. The company spends $5,000 per month on corporate-level advertising and promotion.

Required

Classify each of the following costs incurred by Parker Copies as fixed, variable, or mixed:

a. Lease cost relative to the number of stores.

b. Advertising and promotion costs relative to the number of copies a particular store makes.

c. Lease cost relative to the number of copies made for customers.

d. Assistants' wages relative to the number of copies made for customers.

e. Store manager's salary relative to the number of copies made for customers.

f. Cost of paper relative to the number of copies made for customers.

Exercise 2-2B   *Identifying cost behavior*   LO 1

At the various sales levels shown, Kukreja Company incurred the following costs:

	Units sold	50	100	150	200	250
a.	Total insurance cost	$ 500.00	$ 500.00	$ 500.00	$ 500.00	$ 500.00
b.	Total salary cost	1,500.00	2,000.00	2,500.00	3,000.00	3,500.00
c.	Cost per unit of merchandise sold	8.00	8.00	8.00	8.00	8.00
d.	Total cost of goods sold	4,000.00	8,000.00	12,000.00	16,000.00	20,000.00
e.	Depreciation cost per unit	30.00	15.00	10.00	7.50	6.00
f.	Total rent cost	600.00	600.00	600.00	600.00	600.00
g.	Total shipping cost	40.00	80.00	120.00	160.00	200.00
h.	Rent cost per unit of merchandise sold	12.00	6.00	4.00	3.00	2.40
i.	Total utility cost	200.00	300.00	400.00	500.00	600.00
j.	Supplies cost per unit	4.00	4.00	4.00	4.00	4.00

Required

Identify each of these costs as fixed, variable, or mixed.

LO 1

Exercise 2-3B   *Determining fixed cost per unit*

Miranda Corporation incurs the following annual fixed production costs:

Item	Cost
Insurance cost	$ 50,000
Patent amortization cost	400,000
Depreciation cost	250,000
Property tax cost	100,000

Required

Determine the total fixed production cost per unit if Miranda produces 10,000, 20,000, or 50,000 units.

LO 1

Exercise 2-4B   *Determining total variable cost*

The following variable manufacturing costs apply to goods produced by King Manufacturing Corporation:

Item	Cost per Unit
Materials	$2.80
Labor	2.40
Variable overhead	2.00
Total	$7.20

Required

Determine the total variable manufacturing cost if King produces 4,000, 6,000, or 8,000 units.

LO 1

Exercise 2-5B   *Fixed versus variable cost behavior*

Griffin Company's production and total cost data for two recent months follow:

	January	February
Units produced	1,000	500
Total depreciation cost	$4,000	$4,000
Total factory supplies cost	$2,000	$1,000

Required

a. Separately calculate the depreciation cost per unit and the factory supplies cost per unit for both January and February.
b. Identify which cost is variable and which is fixed. Explain your answer.

LO 1

Exercise 2-6B   *Fixed versus variable cost behavior*

Satcher Chairs Corporation produces ergonomically designed chairs favored by architects. The company normally produces and sells from 4,000 to 10,000 chairs per year. The following cost data apply to various production activity levels:

Number of Chairs	4,000	6,000	8,000	10,000
Total costs incurred				
Fixed	$ 84,000			
Variable	60,000			
Total costs	$144,000			
Per-unit chair cost				
Fixed	$ 21.00			
Variable	15.00			
Total cost per chair	$ 36.00			

Required

a. Complete the preceding table by filling in the missing amounts for the levels of activity shown in the first row of the table.

b. Explain why the total cost per chair decreases as the number of chairs increases.

Exercise 2-7B *Fixed versus variable cost behavior*   LO 1, 2

Dennis Owen needs extra money quickly to help cover some unexpected school expenses. Mr. Owen has learned fortune-telling skills through his long friendship with Joel Allman, who tells fortunes during the day at the city market. Mr. Allman has agreed to let Mr. Owen use his booth to tell fortunes during the evening for a rent of $50 per night.

Required

a. What is the booth rental cost both in total and per customer if the number of customers is 5, 10, 15, 20, or 25?

b. Is the cost of renting the fortune-telling booth fixed or variable relative to the number of customers?

c. Draw two graphs. On one, plot total booth rental cost for 5, 10, 15, 20, and 25 customers; on the other, plot booth rental cost per customer for 5, 10, 15, 20, or 25 customers.

d. Mr. Owen has little money. What major business risks would he take by renting the fortune-telling booth? How could he minimize those risks?

Exercise 2-8B *Fixed versus variable cost behavior*   LO 1, 2

In the evenings, Dennis Owen works telling fortunes using his friend Joel Allman's booth at the city market. Mr. Allman pays the booth rental, so Mr. Owen has no rental cost. As a courtesy, Mr. Owen provides each customer a soft drink. The drinks cost him $0.50 per customer.

Required

a. What is the soft drink cost both in total and per customer if the number of customers is 5, 10, 15, 20, or 25?

b. Is the soft drink cost fixed or variable?

c. Draw two graphs. On one, plot total soft drink cost for 5, 10, 15, 20, and 25 customers; on the other, plot soft drink cost per customer for 5, 10, 15, 20, and 25 customers.

d. Comment on the likelihood that Mr. Owen will incur a loss on this business venture.

Exercise 2-9B *Graphing fixed cost behavior*   LO 1

Saeed Computers leases space in a mall at a monthly rental cost of $3,000. The following graph setups depict rental cost on the vertical axes and activity level on the horizontal axes:

Required

a. Draw a line that depicts the relationship between the total monthly rental cost and the number of computers sold.

b. Draw a line that depicts the relationship between rental cost per computer and the number of computers sold.

LO 1

Exercise 2-10B   *Graphing variable cost behavior*

Dubovsky Computers purchases computers from a manufacturer for $500 per computer. The following graph setups depict product cost on the vertical axes and activity level on the horizontal axes:

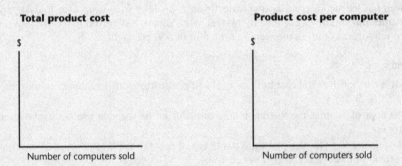

Required

a. Draw a line that depicts the relationship between total product cost and the number of computers sold.

b. Draw a line that depicts the relationship between cost per computer and the number of computers sold.

LO 1

Exercise 2-11B   *Mixed cost at different levels of activity*

Blackwell Hats Corporation uses workers in Indonesia to manually weave straw hats. The company pays the workers a daily base wage plus $0.25 per completed hat. On Monday, workers produced 100 hats for which the company paid wages of $70.

Required

Calculate the total cost of the workers' wages for each of the following days:

Day	Monday	Tuesday	Wednesday	Thursday
Number of hats woven	100	120	160	80
Total variable cost				
Total fixed cost				
Total wages cost				

Exercise 2-12B   *Effect of cost structure on projected profits*   LO 1, 2

Bland and Strand compete in the same market. The following budgeted income statements illustrate their cost structures:

Income Statements		
	Company	
	Bland	Strand
Number of customers (a)	100	100
Sales revenue (a × $100)	$10,000	$10,000
Variable cost (a × $64)	NA	(6,400)
Contribution margin	10,000	3,600
Fixed costs	(6,400)	N/A
Net income	$ 3,600	$ 3,600

Required

a. Assume that Bland can lure all 100 customers away from Strand by lowering its sales price to $60 per customer. Reconstruct Bland's income statement based on 200 customers.

b. Assume that Strand can lure all 100 customers away from Bland by lowering its sales price to $60 per customer. Reconstruct Strand's income statement based on 200 customers.

c. Why does the price-cutting strategy increase Bland's profits but result in a net loss for Strand?

Exercise 2-13B   *Using a contribution margin format income statement to measure*   LO 3, 4
                          the magnitude of operating leverage

Willig Company, a merchandising firm, reported the following operating results:

Income Statements	
Sales revenue (4,000 units × $75)	$ 300,000
Cost of goods sold (4,000 units × $45)	(180,000)
Gross margin	120,000
Sales commissions (10% of sales revenue)	(30,000)
Administrative salaries expense	(25,000)
Advertising expense	(31,000)
Depreciation expense	(24,000)
Shipping and handling expense (4,000 units × $1)	(4,000)
Net income	$ 6,000

Required

a. Reconstruct the income statement using the contribution margin format.

b. Calculate the magnitude of operating leverage.

c. Use the measure of operating leverage to determine the amount of net income that Willig will earn if sales revenue increases by 10 percent.

Exercise 2-14B   *Assessing the magnitude of operating leverage*   LO 4

The following budgeted income statement applies to Biggio Company:

Income Statement	
Sales Revenue (1,000 units × $90)	$ 90,000
Variable Cost (1,000 units × $50)	(50,000)
Contribution margin	40,000
Fixed Costs	(30,000)
Net Income	$ 10,000

Required

a. Use the contribution margin approach to calculate the magnitude of operating leverage.

b. Use the operating leverage measure computed in Requirement *a* to determine the amount of net income that Biggio Company will earn if sales volume increases by 10 percent. Assume the sales price per unit remains unchanged at $90.

c. Verify your answer to Requirement *b* by constructing an alternative income statement based on a 10 percent increase in sales volume. The sales price per unit remains unchanged at $90. Calculate the percentage change in net income for the two income statements.

LO 6

Exercise 2-15B   *Averaging costs*

Nuttall Entertainment Company operates a movie theater that has monthly fixed expenses of $5,000. In addition, the company pays film distributors $1.00 per ticket sold. The following chart shows the number of tickets Nuttall expects to sell in the coming year:

Jan.	Feb.	Mar.	Apr.	May	June	July	Aug.	Sept.	Oct.	Nov.	Dec.	Total
2,000	1,600	3,200	3,400	3,200	4,200	4,700	4,000	5,000	3,100	3,000	2,600	40,000

Required

Assume that Nuttall wants to earn $3.00 per movie patron. What price should it charge for a ticket in January and in September?

LO 7

Exercise 2-16B   *Estimating fixed and variable costs using the high-low method*

Conry Ice Cream Company produces various ice cream products for which demand is highly seasonal. The company sells more ice cream in warmer months and less in colder ones. Last year, the high point in production activity occurred in August when Conry produced 50,000 gallons of ice cream at a total cost of $42,000. The low point in production activity occurred in February when the company produced 20,000 gallons of ice cream at a total cost of $33,000.

Required

a. Use the high-low method to estimate the amount of fixed cost per month incurred by Conry Ice Cream Company.

b. Determine the total estimated monthly cost when 40,000 gallons of ice cream are produced.

c. What factors could cause the estimate determined in Requirement *b* to be inaccurate?

d. Explain how regression analysis could be used to improve accuracy. Your explanation should include a discussion of the R^2 statistic as well as the potential impact of multiple regression analysis.

PROBLEMS—SERIES B

LO 1

Problem 2-17B   *Identifying cost behavior*

Required

Identify the following costs as fixed or variable:

Costs related to operating a retail gasoline company.

a. Depreciation of equipment relative to the number of stations.

b. Cashiers' wages relative to the number of customers served in a station.

c. Salary of a manager of a particular station relative to the number of employees.

d. Gasoline cost relative to the number of customers.

e. Utility cost relative to the number of stations in operation.

f. The company's cost of national TV commercials relative to the number of stations in operation.

g. Depreciation of equipment relative to the number of customers served at a station.

h. Property and real estate taxes relative to the amount of gasoline sold at a particular station.

Costs related to shuttle bus trips between John F. Kennedy International Airport and downtown New York. Each bus driver receives a specific salary per month. A manager schedules bus trips and supervises drivers, and a secretary receives phone calls.

i. Fuel costs relative to the number of passengers on a particular trip.

j. Drivers' salaries relative to the number of trips driven.

k. Office staff salaries relative to the number of passengers on a particular trip.

l. Depreciation relative to the number of buses in service.

m. A driver's salary relative to the number of passengers on a particular trip.

n. Fuel costs relative to the number of trips.

Suzy's Barbershop operates several stores in shopping centers. Each store employs a supervisor and three barbers. Each barber receives a specific salary per month plus a 10 percent commission based on the service revenues he or she has generated.

o. Store rental costs relative to the number of customers.

p. Barbers' commissions relative to the number of customers.

q. Supervisory salaries relative to the number of customers served in a particular store.

r. Barbers' salaries relative to the number of barbers in a particular district.

s. Supplies cost relative to the number of hair services provided in a particular store.

t. Barbers' salaries relative to the number of customers served at a particular store.

Problem 2-18B   *Cost behavior and averaging*   LO 1, 6

Andy Posey asks you to analyze the operating cost of his lawn services business. He has bought the needed equipment with a cash payment of $45,000. Upon your recommendation, he agrees to adopt straight-line depreciation. The equipment has an expected life of three years and no salvage value. Mr. Posey pays his workers $30 per lawn service. Material costs, including fertilizer, pesticide, and supplies, are expected to be $6 per lawn service.

Required

a. Determine the total cost of equipment depreciation and the average cost of equipment depreciation per lawn service, assuming that Mr. Posey provides 20, 25, or 30 lawn services during one month. Is the cost of equipment a fixed or a variable cost?

b. Determine the total expected cost of labor and the average expected cost of labor per lawn service, assuming that Mr. Posey provides 20, 25, or 30 lawn services during one month. Is the cost of labor a fixed or a variable cost?

c. Determine the total expected cost of materials and the average expected cost of materials per lawn service, assuming that Mr. Posey provides 20, 25, or 30 lawn services during one month. Is the cost of fertilizer, pesticide, and supplies a fixed or a variable cost?

d. Determine the total expected cost per lawn service, assuming that Mr. Posey provides 20, 25, or 30 lawn services during one month.

e. Determine the average expected cost per lawn service, assuming that Mr. Posey provides 20, 25, or 30 lawn services during one month. Why does the cost per unit decrease as the number of lawn services increases?

f. If Mr. Posey tells you that he prices his services at 30 percent above cost, would you assume that he means average or actual cost? Why?

Problem 2-19B   *Context-sensitive nature of cost behavior classifications*   LO 1

Warren and Carter Tax Services' Development Department is responsible for establishing new community branches. Each branch opens with two tax accountants. Total cost of payroll per branch is $108,000 per year. Together the two accountants can process up to 2,500 simple tax returns per year. The firm's policy requires closing branches that do not reach the quota of 1,500 tax returns per year. On the other hand, the firm hires an additional accountant for a branch and elevates it to the status of a regular operation if the customer demand for services exceeds 2,500 tax returns.

Required

a. What is the relevant range of activity for a new branch established by the Development Department?

b. Determine the amount of payroll cost in total and the average payroll cost per transaction for a branch that processes 1,500, 2,000, or 2,500 tax returns. In this case (the activity base is the number of tax returns for a specific branch), is the payroll cost a fixed or a variable cost?

c. Determine the amount of payroll cost in total and the average payroll cost per branch for Warren and Carter Tax Services, assuming that the Development Department operates 20, 30, or 40 branches. In this case (the activity base is the number of branches), is the payroll cost a fixed or a variable cost?

LO 1

Problem 2-20B   *Context-sensitive nature of cost behavior classifications*

Kevin Munden sells a newly developed camera, Sharp Vision. He purchases the cameras from the manufacturer for $70 each and rents a store in a shopping mall for $5,000 per month.

Required

a. Determine the average cost of sales per unit if Mr. Munden sells 100, 200, 300, 400, or 500 units of Sharp Vision per month. Use the following chart to organize your answer.

	Sales Volume in Units (a)				
	100	200	300	400	500
Total cost of cameras (a × $70)	$ 7,000				
Total cost of store rental	5,000				
Total cost of sales (b)	$12,000				
Average cost per unit (b ÷ a)	$120.00				

b. If Mr. Munden wants to make a gross profit of $20 on each camera he sells, what price should he charge at sales volumes of 100, 200, 300, 400, or 500 units?

c. Record the total cost of store rental if Mr. Munden opens a camera store at one, two, three, four, or five shopping malls. Record your answers in the following chart. Is the cost of store rental fixed or variable relative to the number of stores opened?

	Shopping Malls				
	1	2	3	4	5
Total cost of store rental	$5,000				

d. Mr. Munden provides decorative ornaments to customers who purchase cameras. Some customers take the ornaments, others do not, and some take more than one. The number of ornaments varies in relation to the number of cameras sold, but the relationship is not proportional. Assume that, on average, Mr. Munden gives away $150 worth of ornaments for every 100 cameras sold. What is the additional cost per camera sold? Is the cost fixed or variable?

LO 1, 2

Problem 2-21B   *Effects of operating leverage on profitability*

CPAs R Us conducts CPA review courses. Public universities that permit free use of a classroom support the classes. The only major expense incurred by CPAs R Us is the salary of instructors, which is $6,000 per course taught. The company recently planned to offer a review course in Houston for $320 per candidate; it estimated that 50 candidates would attend the course.

Complete these requirements based on the preceding information.

Part 1:

Required

a. Relative to the number of CPA candidates in a single course, is the cost of instruction a fixed or a variable cost?

b. Determine the profit, assuming that 50 candidates attend the course.

c. Determine the profit, assuming a 10 percent increase in enrollment (i.e., enrollment increases to 55 students). What is the percentage change in profitability?

d. Determine the profit, assuming a 10 percent decrease in enrollment (i.e., enrollment decreases to 45 students). What is the percentage change in profitability?

e. Explain why a 10 percent shift in enrollment produces more than a 10 percent shift in profitability. Use the term that identifies this phenomenon.

Part 2:

The instructor has offered to teach the course for a percentage of tuition fees. Specifically, he wants $120 per candidate attending the class. Assume that the tuition fee remains at $320 per candidate.

Required

f. Is the cost of instruction a fixed or a variable cost?

g. Determine the profit, assuming that 50 candidates take the course.

h. Determine the profit, assuming a 10 percent increase in enrollment (i.e., enrollment increases to 55 students). What is the percentage change in profitability?

i. Determine the profit, assuming a 10 percent decrease in enrollment (i.e., enrollment decreases to 45 students). What is the percentage change in profitability?

j. Explain why a 10 percent shift in enrollment produces a proportional 10 percent shift in profitability.

Part 3:

CPAs R Us sells a workbook to each student who attends the course. The workbook contains printed material unique to each course. Workbooks that are not sold must be destroyed. Prior to the first class, CPAs R Us printed 50 copies of the books based on the estimated number of people who would attend the course. Each workbook costs $40 and is sold for $50. This cost includes a royalty fee paid to the author and the cost of duplication.

Required

k. Calculate the total cost and the cost per candidate of the workbooks, assuming that 45, 50, or 55 candidates attempt to attend the course.

l. Classify the cost of workbooks as fixed or variable relative to the number of candidates attending the course.

m. Discuss the risk of holding inventory as it applies to the workbooks.

n. Explain how a just-in-time inventory system can reduce the cost and risk of holding inventory.

Problem 2-22B *Effects of fixed and variable cost behavior on the risk and rewards of business opportunities*

LO 2

Beach Club and Mountain Club are competing health and recreation clubs in Chicago. They both offer tennis training clinics to adults. Beach pays its coaches $9,000 per season. Mountain pays its coaches $300 per student enrolled in the clinic per season. Both clubs charge a tuition fee of $432 per season.

Required

a. Prepare income statements for Beach and Mountain, assuming that 30 students per season attend each clinic.

b. The ambitious new director of Beach Club tries to increase his market share by reducing the club's tuition per student to $250 per clinic. Prepare an income statement for Beach, assuming that the club attracts all of Mountain's customers and therefore is able to enroll 60 students in its clinics.

c. Independent of Requirement *b,* Mountain Club tries to lure Beach's students by lowering its price to $210 per student. Prepare an income statement for Mountain, assuming that the club succeeds in enrolling 60 students in its clinics.

d. Explain why the strategy described in Requirement *b* produced a profit while the same strategy described in Requirement *c* produced a loss.

e. Prepare an income statement for Beach Club and Mountain Club, assuming that 18 students attend a clinic at the original $432 tuition price.

f. It is always better to have fixed rather than variable cost. Explain why this statement is false.

g. It is always better to have variable rather than fixed cost. Explain why this statement is false.

LO 5, 6

Problem 2-23B *Analysis of operating leverage*

Rachel Geer has invested in two start-up companies. At the end of the first year, she asks you to evaluate their operating performance. The following operating data apply to the first year:

	Company Name	
	Ander	Sander
Variable cost per unit (a)	$12	$6
Sales revenue (25,000 units × $16)	$400,000	$400,000
Variable cost (25,000 units × a)	(300,000)	(150,000)
Contribution margin	100,000	250,000
Fixed cost	(50,000)	(200,000)
Net income	$ 50,000	$ 50,000

Required

a. Use the contribution margin approach to compute the operating leverage for each firm.

b. If the economy expands in the coming year, Ander and Sander will both enjoy a 10 percent per year increase in sales volume, assuming that the selling price remains unchanged. (*Note:* Since the number of units increases, both revenue and variable cost will increase.) Compute the change in net income for each firm in dollar amount and in percentage.

c. If the economy contracts in the following year, Ander and Sander will both suffer a 10 percent decrease in sales volume, assuming that the selling price remains unchanged. (*Note:* Since the number of units decreases, both revenue and variable cost decrease.) Compute the change in net income for each firm in both dollar amount and percentage.

d. Write a memo to Rachel Geer with your evaluation and recommendations.

LO 6

Problem 2-24B *Selecting the appropriate time period for cost averaging*

The Vaughan Amusement Park is considering signing a contract to hire a circus at a cost of $2,400 per day. The contract requires a minimum performance period of one week. Estimated circus attendance is as follows:

Monday	Tuesday	Wednesday	Thursday	Friday	Saturday	Sunday
500	450	450	600	950	1,500	1,400

Required

a. For each day, determine the average cost of the circus contract per person attending.

b. Suppose that the park prices circus tickets at cost as computed in Requirement *a* plus $1.60. What would be the price per ticket charged on each day of the week?

c. Use weekly averaging to determine a reasonable price to charge for the circus tickets.

d. Comment on why weekly averaging may be more useful to business managers than daily averaging.

LO 5

Problem 2-25B *Identifying relevant issues for cost averaging*

Sahara Tours, Inc., organizes adventure tours for people interested in visiting a desert environment. A desert tour generally lasts three days. Sahara provides food, equipment, and guides. Larry Jobaria, the president of Sahara Tours, needs to set prices for the coming year. He has available the company's past cost data in the following table:

	Span of Time		
	Recent Tour	One Year	Ten Years
Total cost of tours (a)	$8,000	$390,000	$2,700,000
Number of tourists (b)	32	1,500	12,000
Cost per tourist (a ÷ b)	$ 250	$ 260	$ 225

Required

Write a memo to Mr. Jobaria explaining the potential advantages and disadvantages of using each of the different per-tourist cost figures as a basis for establishing a price to charge tourists during the coming year. What other factors must Mr. Jobaria consider in developing a pricing strategy?

Problem 2-26B   *Estimating fixed and variable costs*   LO 7

Hanno Legal Services provides legal advice to clients. The following data apply to the first six months of operation:

	Month					
	Jan.	Feb.	Mar.	Apr.	May	June
Service hours	60	80	120	160	180	200
Revenue	$4,800	$6,400	$9,600	$12,800	$14,400	$16,000
Operating costs	6,200	7,100	8,380	8,500	8,761	9,700

Required

a. What is the average service revenue per hour for the six-month time period?
b. Use the high-low method to estimate the total monthly fixed cost and the variable cost per hour.
c. Determine the average contribution margin per hour.
d. Use the scattergraph method to estimate the total monthly fixed cost and the variable cost per hour.
e. Compare the results of the two methods and comment on any differences.

Problem 2-27B   *Estimating fixed and variable cost*   LO 7

Vicardo Frames Company, which manufactures ornate frames for original art work, began operations in January 2011. Sam Waits, the owner, asks for your assistance. He believes that he needs to better understand the cost of the frames for pricing purposes. You have collected the following data concerning actual production over the past year:

Month	Number of Frames Produced	Total Cost
January	1,600	$42,000
February	7,200	65,000
March	3,920	59,000
April	1,200	37,200
May	3,200	58,000
June	2,600	54,000
July	2,200	51,200
August	3,600	62,000
September	4,560	64,000
October	5,880	63,000
November	6,560	64,000
December	800	33,000

Required

a. To understand the department's cost behavior, you decide to plot the points on graph paper and sketch a total cost line.

  (1) Enter the number of units and their costs in increasing order.

  (2) Plot the points on the graph.

  (3) Sketch a graph so the line "splits" all of the points (half of the points appear above and half appear below the line).

  (4) Using the line you just sketched, visually estimate the total cost to produce 4,000 units.

b. Using the high-low method, compute the total cost equation for the preceding data.

  (1) Compute the variable cost per unit.

  (2) Compute total fixed costs.

  (3) Sketch a line between the high and low points on your graph.

  (4) Using the high-low method, estimate the total cost to produce 4,000 units.

c. Name a third method that could be used to determine the fixed and variable cost estimate and comment on the advantages of your suggested approach.

LO 7

Problem 2-28B *Estimating fixed and variable cost using the regression method*

Ray Rogers, the production manager of Martin Construction Components, is trying to figure out the cost behavior of his factory supplies cost. The company uses machine hours as the cost driver. Victor Hoover, the assistant manager, collected the following cost data for the last 32 weeks:

Week No.	Machine Hours	Supplies Costs	Week No.	Machine Hours	Supplies Costs
1	86	$3,819	17	64	$3,856
2	72	3,610	18	88	4,279
3	79	3,916	19	129	5,633
4	62	2,915	20	137	5,298
5	91	4,327	21	144	6,721
6	42	2,214	22	37	2,448
7	37	2,106	23	56	3,528
8	33	2,390	24	49	2,837
9	23	2,107	25	12	1,359
10	96	4,868	26	57	3,296
11	94	5,021	27	54	3,472
12	91	4,811	28	65	3,264
13	72	3,580	29	77	3,925
14	60	2,800	30	85	4,002
15	48	2,269	31	92	4,583
16	53	2,748	32	82	3,523

Required

a. The company uses the number of machine hours as the cost driver for factory supplies costs. Use an algebraic equation to describe how total factory supplies costs can be estimated.

b. Use a spreadsheet program to perform a regression analysis. Use factory supplies costs as the dependent variable (Y) and the machine hours as the independent variable (X). Determine the total fixed cost per week and variable cost per machine hour.

c. Identify the R^2 statistic provided by the Excel program and explain what it means.

d. Identify a potential weakness of regression analysis and explain what can be done to minimize it.

e. Determine the estimated total cost of factory supplies, if machine hour usage amounts to 100 hours for the next week. What portion of the total cost is fixed and what portion is variable?

ANALYZE, THINK, COMMUNICATE

ATC 2-1 Business Applications *Operating leverage*

Description of Business for Amazon.com, Inc.

Amazon.com opened its virtual doors on the World Wide Web in July 1995 and we offer Earth's Biggest Selection. We seek to be Earth's most customer-centric company for three primary customer sets: consumer customers, seller customers and developer customers. In addition, we generate revenue through co-branded credit card agreements and other marketing and promotional services, such as online advertising.

Amazon.com	2008	2007
Operating revenue	$19,166	$14,835
Operating earnings	842	655

Description of Business for CSX, Inc.

CSX Corporations ("CSX") together with its subsidiaries (the "Company"), based in Jacksonville, Florida, is one of the nation's leading transportation suppliers. The Company's rail and intermodal businesses provide rail-based transportation services including traditional rail service and the transport of intermodal containers and trailers.

CSX, Inc.	2008	2007
Operating revenue	$11,255	$10,030
Operating earnings	2,768	2,260

Required

a. Determine which company appears to have the higher operating leverage.

b. Write a paragraph or two explaining why the company you identified in Requirement *a* might be expected to have the higher operating leverage.

c. If revenues for both companies declined, which company do you think would likely experience the greater decline in operating earnings? Explain your answer.

ATC 2-2 Group Assignment *Operating leverage*

The Parent Teacher Association (PTA) of Meadow High School is planning a fund-raising campaign. The PTA is considering the possibility of hiring Eric Logan, a world-renowned investment counselor, to address the public. Tickets would sell for $28 each. The school has agreed to let the PTA use Harville Auditorium at no cost. Mr. Logan is willing to accept one of two compensation arrangements. He will sign an agreement to receive a fixed fee of $10,000 regardless of the number of tickets sold. Alternatively, he will accept payment of $20 per ticket sold. In communities similar to that in which Meadow is located, Mr. Logan has drawn an audience of approximately 500 people.

Required

a. In front of the class, present a statement showing the expected net income assuming 500 people buy tickets.

b. The instructor will divide the class into groups and then organize the groups into four sections. The instructor will assign one of the following tasks to each section of groups.

Group Tasks

(1) Assume the PTA pays Mr. Logan a fixed fee of $10,000. Determine the amount of net income that the PTA will earn if ticket sales are 10 percent higher than expected. Calculate the percentage change in net income.

(2) Assume that the PTA pays Mr. Logan a fixed fee of $10,000. Determine the amount of net income that the PTA will earn if ticket sales are 10 percent lower than expected. Calculate the percentage change in net income.

(3) Assume that the PTA pays Mr. Logan $20 per ticket sold. Determine the amount of net income that the PTA will earn if ticket sales are 10 percent higher than expected. Calculate the percentage change in net income.

(4) Assume that the PTA pays Mr. Logan $20 per ticket sold. Determine the amount of net income that the PTA will earn if ticket sales are 10 percent lower than expected. Calculate the percentage change in net income.

c. Have each group select a spokesperson. Have one of the spokespersons in each section of groups go to the board and present the results of the analysis conducted in Requirement *b.* Resolve any discrepancies in the computations presented at the board and those developed by the other groups.

d. Draw conclusions regarding the risks and rewards associated with operating leverage. At a minimum, answer the following questions:

(1) Which type of cost structure (fixed or variable) produces the higher growth potential in profitability for a company?

(2) Which type of cost structure (fixed or variable) faces the higher risk of declining profitability for a company?

(3) Under what circumstances should a company seek to establish a fixed cost structure?

(4) Under what circumstances should a company seek to establish a variable cost structure?

ATC 2-3   Research Assignment   *Fixed versus variable cost*

Use the 2008 Form 10-K for Black & Decker Corp. (B&D) (not StanleyBlack & Decker) to complete the requirements below. To obtain the Form 10-K you can use either use the EDGAR system following the instructions in Appendix A, or it can be found under "Investor Relations" on the company's corporate website at www.bdk.com. Be sure to read carefully the following portions of the document:

- "General Development of the Business" on page 1.
- "Consolidated Statement of Earnings" on page 36.

Required

a. Calculate the percentage decrease in B&D's sales and its "operating income" from 2007 to 2008.

b. Would fixed costs or variable costs be more likely to explain why B&D's operating earnings decreased by a bigger percentage than its sales?

c. On page 42, B&D reported that it incurred product development costs of $146.0 million in 2008. If this cost is thought of in the context of the number of units of products sold, should it be considered as primarily fixed or variable in nature?

d. If the product development costs are thought of in the context of the number of new products developed, should they be considered as primarily fixed or variable in nature?

ATC 2-4   Writing Assignment   *Cost averaging*

Candice Sterling is a veterinarian. She has always been concerned for the pets of low-income families. These families love their pets but frequently do not have the means to provide them proper veterinary care. Dr. Sterling decides to open a part-time veterinary practice in a low-income neighborhood. She plans to volunteer her services free of charge two days per week. Clients will be charged only for the actual costs of materials and overhead. Dr. Sterling leases a small space for $300 per month. Utilities and other miscellaneous costs are expected to be approximately $180 per month. She estimates the variable cost of materials to be approximately $10 per pet served. A friend of Dr. Sterling who runs a similar type of clinic in another area of town indicates that she should expect to treat the following number of pets during her first year of operation.

Jan.	Feb.	Mar.	Apr.	May	June	July	Aug.	Sept.	Oct.	Nov.	Dec.
18	26	28	36	42	54	63	82	42	24	20	15

Dr. Sterling's friend has noticed that visits increase significantly in the summer because children who are out of school tend to bring their pets to the vet more often. Business tapers off during the winter and reaches a low point in December when people spend what little money they have on Christmas presents for their children. After looking at the data, Dr. Sterling becomes concerned that the people in the neighborhood will not be able to afford pet care during some months of operation even if it is offered at cost. For example, the cost of providing services in December would be approximately $42 per pet treated ($480 overhead ÷ 15 pets = $32 per pet, plus $10 materials cost). She is willing to provide her services free of charge, but she realizes that she cannot afford to subsidize the practice further by personally paying for the costs of materials and overhead in the months of low activity. She decides to discuss the matter with her accountant to find a way to cut costs even more. Her accountant tells her that her problem is cost *measurement* rather than cost *cutting*.

Required

Assume that you are Dr. Sterling's accountant. Write a memo describing a pricing strategy that resolves the apparent problem of high costs during months of low volume. Recommend in your memo the price to charge per pet treated during the month of December.

ATC 2-5 **Ethical Dilemma** *Profitability versus social conscience (effects of cost behavior)*

Advances in biological technology have enabled two research companies, Bio Labs, Inc., and Scientific Associates, to develop an insect-resistant corn seed. Neither company is financially strong enough to develop the distribution channels necessary to bring the product to world markets. World Agra Distributors, Inc., has negotiated contracts with both companies for the exclusive right to market their seed. Bio Labs signed an agreement to receive an annual royalty of $1,000,000. In contrast, Scientific Associates chose an agreement that provides for a royalty of $0.50 per pound of seed sold. Both agreements have a 10-year term. During 2011, World Agra sold approximately 1,600,000 pounds of the Bio Labs, Inc., seed and 2,400,000 pounds of the Scientific Associates seed. Both types of seed were sold for $1.25 per pound. By the end of 2011, it was apparent that the seed developed by Scientific Associates was superior. Although insect infestation was virtually nonexistent for both types of seed, the seed developed by Scientific Associates produced corn that was sweeter and had consistently higher yields.

World Agra Distributors' chief financial officer, Roger Weatherstone, recently retired. To the astonishment of the annual planning committee, Mr. Weatherstone's replacement, Ray Borrough, adamantly recommended that the marketing department develop a major advertising campaign to promote the seed developed by Bio Labs, Inc. The planning committee reluctantly approved the recommendation. A $100,000 ad campaign was launched; the ads emphasized the ability of the Bio Labs seed to avoid insect infestation. The campaign was silent with respect to taste or crop yield. It did not mention the seed developed by Scientific Associates. World Agra's sales staff was instructed to push the Bio Labs seed and to sell the Scientific Associates seed only on customer demand. Although total sales remained relatively constant during 2012, sales of the Scientific Associates seed fell to approximately 1,300,000 pounds while sales of the Bio Labs, Inc., seed rose to 2,700,000 pounds.

Required

a. Determine the amount of increase or decrease in profitability experienced by World Agra in 2012 as a result of promoting Bio Labs seed. Support your answer with appropriate commentary.

b. Did World Agra's customers in particular and society in general benefit or suffer from the decision to promote the Bio Labs seed?

c. Review the standards of ethical conduct in Exhibit 1.15 of Chapter 1 and comment on whether Mr. Borrough's recommendation violated any of the standards in the code of ethical conduct.

d. Comment on your belief regarding the adequacy of the Standards of Ethical Conduct for Managerial Accountants to direct the conduct of management accountants.

e. Are the actions of Ray Borrough in violation of the provisions of Sarbanes-Oxley that were described in Chapter 1? Explain your answer.

ATC 2-6 **Spreadsheet Assignment** *Using Excel*

Charlie Stork rented a truck for his business on two previous occasions. Since he will soon be renting a truck again, he would like to analyze his bills and determine how the rental fee is calculated. His two bills for truck rental show that on September 1, he drove 1,000 miles and the bill was $1,500, and on December 5, he drove 600 miles and the bill was $1,380.

Required

Construct a spreadsheet to calculate the variable and fixed costs of this mixed cost that will allow Mr. Stork to predict his cost if he drives the truck 700 miles. The cells that show as numbers should all be formulas except C5, C6, E5, E6, and C18. Constructing the spreadsheet in this manner will allow you to change numbers in these five cells to recalculate variable cost, fixed cost, or predicted total cost.

	ch02-working.xls							
	A	B	C	D	E	F	G	H
1	Chapter 2 - Working with Excel					Name:		
2								
3			Rental		Miles			
4			Cost		Driven			
5		High	$ 1,500		1,000			
6		Low	1,380		600			
7		Difference	$ 120		400			
8								
9		Variable cost per mile =			Change in Total Cost/Change in Miles			
10		Variable cost per mile =			$ 0.30 per mile			
11								
12		Fixed cost =	Total Cost - Variable Cost					
13		Fixed cost =	$ 1,200					
14								
15								
16		Predicted Cost =	$ 1,200 +	$ 0.30 per mile x Predicted Mileage				
17								
18		If predicted mileage is:	700					
19								
20		Predicted Cost =	$ 1,410					
21								

Spreadsheet Tip

1. To format cells to show dollar signs, commas, or both, choose Format, then Cells, then click on the tab titled Numbers, and choose Accounting.

ATC 2-7   Spreadsheet Assignment   *Mastering Excel*

Siwa Company makes and sells a decorative ceramic statue. Each statue costs $50 to manufacture and sells for $75. Siwa spends $3 to ship the statue to customers and pays salespersons a $2 commission for each statue sold. The remaining annual expenses of operation are administrative salaries, $70,000; advertising, $20,000; and rent, $30,000. Siwa plans to sell 9,000 statues in the coming year.

	A	B	C	D	E	F	G	H	I	J	K
1		Chapter 2 - Mastering Excel							Name:		
2											
3											
4		**Contribution Margin Format Income Statement**									
5											
6		Sales Revenue		(9,000 x $75)							$675,000
7		Variable Expenses									
8			Cost of Goods Sold	(9,000 x $50)			$450,000				
9			Sales Commissions	(9,000 x $ 2)			18,000				
10			Shipping Expenses	(9,000 x $ 3)			27,000			495,000	
11		Contribution Margin									$180,000
12		Fixed Expenses									
13			Administrative Salaries				$ 70,000				
14			Advertising				20,000				
15			Rent				30,000			120,000	
16		Net Income									$ 60,000
17											
18											
19		Operating Leverage									3.00
20											

Required

Construct a spreadsheet that shows a contribution margin format income statement and that calculates operating leverage. Place formulas in the spreadsheet to allow changes to any of the preceding information to be automatically reflected in the income statement and operating leverage.

COMPREHENSIVE PROBLEM

Use the same transaction data for Magnificent Modems, Inc., as was used in Chapter 1 (see page 52).

Required

a. Based on these data, identify each cost incurred by the company as (1) fixed versus variable relative to the number of units produced and sold; and (2) product versus selling, general, and administrative (S,G,&A). The solution for the first item is shown as an example.

Cost Item	Fixed	Variable	Product	S,G,&A
Depreciation on manufacturing equipment	X		X	
Direct materials				
Direct labor				
Production supplies				
Rent on manufacturing facility				
Sales commissions				
Depreciation on administrative equipment				
Administrative costs (rent and salaries)				

b. Replace the question marks in the following table to indicate the product cost per unit assuming levels of production of 5,000, 6,000, 7,000, and 8,000.

Cost of goods sold	$455,000	?	?	?
Divided by number of units	5,000	6,000	7,000	8,000
Cost per unit	$ 91	?	?	?

CHAPTER 3

Analysis of Cost, Volume, and Pricing to Increase Profitability

LEARNING OBJECTIVES

After you have mastered the material in this chapter, you will be able to:

1 Use the equation method to determine the break-even point.

2 Use the contribution margin per unit method to determine the break-even point.

3 Use the contribution margin ratio method to determine the break-even point.

4 Determine the sales volume required to attain a desired profit.

5 Set selling prices by using cost-plus, prestige, and target costing.

6 Explain cost-volume-profit relationships.

7 Draw and interpret a cost-volume-profit graph.

8 Calculate and interpret the margin of safety.

9 Conduct sensitivity analysis for cost-volume-profit relationships.

10 Perform multiproduct cost-volume-profit analysis.

CHAPTER OPENING

The president of Bright Day Distributors recently completed a managerial accounting course. He was particularly struck by the operating leverage concept. His instructor had demonstrated how a small percentage increase in sales volume could produce a significantly higher percentage increase in profitability. Unfortunately, the discussion had been limited to the effects of changes in sales volume. In practice, changes in sales volume are often related to changes in sales price. For example, reducing selling prices often leads to increases in sales volume. Sales volume may also change in response to cost changes such as increasing the advertising budget. Furthermore, significant changes in sales volume could redefine the relevant range, changing the fixed and variable costs. Bright Day's president realized that understanding operating leverage was only one piece of understanding how to manage a business. He also needed to understand how changes in prices, costs, and volume affect profitability. Bright Day's president is interested in **cost-volume-profit (CVP) analysis.**

The Curious Accountant

At a meeting in November 2009, InterContinental Hotels Group (IHG) reminded its franchisees that they had until February 1, 2010, to complete renovations of their properties and install new corporate logos. If they did not comply by the deadline, they would no longer be allowed to call themselves Holiday Inns. IHC itself owns only 17 hotels, but it is the global franchisor of 4,400 hotels. These hotels operate under several brand names including Holiday Inn, Holiday Inn Express, and Crown Plaza Hotels, but most of its franchisees operate under the Holiday Inn name. At the time of the meeting, 300 of the 2,700 Holiday Inns in North America had not even started the process of renovation and were likely to lose their franchise rights.

In February, 2009, American Express began offering some of its cardholders a $300 gift card if they would pay off their account balances and close their accounts. Remember that this is the same company that spends millions each year trying to attract new customers.

Why would a company like IHG that earns most of its revenues, and profits, from franchise fees collected from hotels it does not even own threaten to force 300 of them to take down their Holiday Inn signs? Would this not reduce IHG's revenues without significantly reducing its costs? At a time when the economy was slow and hotel occupancy was down, why would IHC take such action? Why would American Express pay some of its customers to leave? (Answers on page 115.)

DETERMINING THE BREAK-EVEN POINT

Bright Day Distributors sells nonprescription health food supplements including vitamins, herbs, and natural hormones in the northwestern United States. Bright Day recently obtained the rights to distribute the new herb mixture Delatine. Recent scientific research found that Delatine delayed aging in laboratory animals. The researchers hypothesized that the substance would have a similar effect on humans. Their theory could not be confirmed because of the relatively long human life span. The news media reported the research findings; as stories turned up on television and radio news, talk shows, and in magazines, demand for Delatine increased.

Bright Day plans to sell the Delatine at a price of $36 per bottle. Delatine costs $24 per bottle. Bright Day's management team suspects that enthusiasm for Delatine will abate quickly as the news media shift to other subjects. To attract customers immediately, the product managers consider television advertising. The marketing manager suggests running a campaign of several hundred cable channel ads at an estimated cost of $60,000.

Bright Day's first concern is whether it can sell enough units to cover its costs. The president made this position clear when he said, "We don't want to lose money on this product. We have to sell at least enough units to break-even." In accounting terms, the **break-even point** is where profit (income) equals zero. So how many bottles of Delatine must be sold to produce a profit of zero? The break-even point is commonly computed using either the *equation method,* the *contribution margin per unit method,* or the *contribution margin ratio method.* All three of these approaches produce the same result. They are merely different ways to arrive at the same conclusion.

Equation Method

The **equation method** begins by expressing the income statement as follows:

$$\text{Sales} - \text{Variable costs} - \text{Fixed costs} = \text{Profit (Net income)}$$

As previously stated, profit at the break-even point is zero. Therefore, the break-even point for Delatine is computed as follows:

$$\text{Sales} - \text{Variable costs} - \text{Fixed costs} = \text{Profit}$$
$$\$36N - \$24N - \$60,000 = \$0$$
$$\$12N = \$60,000$$
$$N = \$60,000 \div \$12$$
$$N = 5,000 \text{ Units}$$

Where:

N = Number of units
$36 = Sales price per unit
$24 = Variable cost per unit
$60,000 = Fixed costs

✓ CHECK YOURSELF 3.1

B-Shoc is an independent musician who is considering whether to independently produce and sell a CD. B-Shoc estimates fixed costs of $5,400 and variable costs of $2.00 per unit. The expected selling price is $8.00 per CD. Use the equation method to determine B-Shoc's break-even point.

Answer

$$\text{Sales} - \text{Variable costs} - \text{Fixed costs} = \text{Profit}$$

$$\$8N - \$2N - \$5,400 = \$0$$

$$\$6N = \$5,400$$

$$N = \$5,400 \div \$6$$

$$N = 900 \text{ Units (CDs)}$$

Where:

N = Number of units
$8 = Sales price per unit
$2 = Variable cost per unit
$5,400 = Fixed costs

Contribution Margin per Unit Method

Recall that the *total contribution margin* is the amount of sales minus total variable cost. The **contribution margin per unit** is the sales price per unit minus the variable cost per unit. Therefore, the contribution margin per unit for Delatine is:

LO 2

Use the contribution margin per unit method to determine the break-even point.

Sales price per unit	$36
Less: Variable cost per unit	(24)
Contribution margin per unit	$12

For every bottle of Delatine it sells, Bright Day earns a $12 contribution margin. In other words, every time Bright Day sells a bottle of Delatine, it receives enough money to pay $24 to cover the variable cost of the bottle of Delatine and still has $12 left to go toward paying the fixed cost. Bright Day will reach the break-even point when it sells enough bottles of Delatine to cover its fixed costs. Therefore the break-even point can be determined as follows:

$$\text{Break-even point in units} = \frac{\text{Fixed costs}}{\text{Contribution margin per unit}}$$

$$\text{Break-even point in units} = \frac{\$60,000}{\$12}$$

$$\text{Break-even point in units} = 5,000 \text{ Units}$$

This result is the same as that determined under the equation method. Indeed, the contribution margin per unit method formula is an abbreviated version of the income statement formula used in the equation method. In other words both methods are simply different derivations of the same formula. The proof is provided in the footnote below.[1]

[1]The formula for the *contribution margin per unit method* is (where N is the number of units at the break-even point):

N = Fixed costs ÷ Contribution margin per unit

The income statement formula for the *equation method* produces the same result as shown below (where N is the number of units at the break-even point):

Sales − Variable costs − Fixed costs = Profit
Sales price per unit (N) − Variable cost per unit (N) − Fixed costs = Profit
Contribution margin per unit (N) − Fixed costs = Profit
Contribution margin per unit (N) − Fixed costs = 0
Contribution margin per unit (N) = Fixed costs
N = Fixed costs ÷ Contribution margin per unit

Both the *equation method* and the *contribution margin per unit method* yield the amount of break-even sales measured *in units.* To determine the amount of break-even sales measured *in dollars,* multiply the number of units times the sales price per unit. For Delatine the break-even point measured in dollars is $180,000 (5,000 units × $36 per unit). The following income statement confirms this result:

Sales revenue (5,000 units × $36)	$180,000
Total variable expenses (5,000 units × $24)	(120,000)
Total contribution margin (5,000 units × $12)	60,000
Fixed expenses	(60,000)
Net income	$ 0

Contribution Margin Ratio Method

Use the contribution margin ratio method to determine the break-even point.

The equation method and the contribution margin per unit method produce a break-even point measured *in units.* The break-even point expressed *in dollars* can be determined using the contribution margin ratio method. We begin by determining the **contribution margin ratio,** which is defined as follows.

$$\text{Contribution margin ratio} = \text{Contribution margin} \div \text{Sales}$$

The ratio can be computed using the total amount of the contribution margin and sales or by using per unit amounts. Either approach will yield the same result, as shown here.
Using total dollar values:

$$\text{Contribution margin ratio} = \text{Contribution margin in dollars} \div \text{Sales in dollars}$$

$$\text{Contribution margin ratio} = \$60,000 \div \$180,000 = .3333333$$

Using per unit values:

$$\text{Contribution margin ratio} = \text{Contribution margin per unit} \div \text{Sales price per unit}$$

$$\text{Contribution margin ratio} = \$12 \div \$36 = .3333333$$

Using the *contribution margin ratio method* the break-even point in dollars is computed by dividing the fixed cost by the contribution margin ratio. The computations for Bright Day follow.

$$\text{Break-even point in dollars} = \frac{\text{Fixed costs}}{\text{Contribution margin ratio}}$$

$$\text{Break-even point in dollars} = \frac{\$60,000}{.333333}$$

$$\text{Break-even point in dollars} = \$180,000 \text{ Sales revenue}$$

The break-even volume measured in units can be determined by dividing the total sales revenue by the sales price per unit as follows:

$$\text{Break-even point} = \$180,000 \text{ Sales revenue} \div \$36 = 5,000 \text{ Units}$$

The *contribution margin ratio method* yields the same results as the *contribution margin per unit method* and the *equation method.* The results are the same because all three methods are merely different derivations of the income statement formula.

DETERMINING THE SALES VOLUME NECESSARY TO REACH A DESIRED PROFIT

Bright Day's president decides the ad campaign should produce a $40,000 profit. He asks the accountant to determine the sales volume that is required to achieve this level of profitability. Using the *equation method,* the sales volume in units required to attain the desired profit is computed as follows:

Determine the sales volume required to attain a desired profit.

$$\text{Sales} - \text{Variable costs} - \text{Fixed costs} = \text{Profit}$$

$$\$36N - \$24N - \$60,000 = \$40,000$$

$$\$12N = \$60,000 + \$40,000$$

$$N = \$100,000 \div \$12$$

$$N = 8,333 \text{ Units}$$

Where:

N = Number of units

$36 = Sales price per unit

$24 = Variable cost per unit

$60,000 = Fixed costs

$40,000 = Desired profit

The accountant used the *contribution margin per unit method* to confirm these computations as follows:

$$\text{Sales volume in units} = \frac{\text{Fixed costs} + \text{Desired profit}}{\text{Contribution margin per unit}}$$

$$= \frac{\$60,000 + \$40,000}{\$12} = 8,333.33 \text{ Units}$$

The required volume in sales dollars is this number of units multiplied by the sales price per unit (8,333.33 units × $36 = $300,000). The following income statement confirms this result; all amounts are rounded to the nearest whole dollar.

Sales revenue (8,333.33 units × $36)	$300,000
Total variable expenses (8,333.33 units × $24)	(200,000)
Total contribution margin (8,333.33 units × $12)	100,000
Fixed expenses	(60,000)
Net income	$ 40,000

In practice, the company will not sell partial bottles of Delatine. The accountant rounds 8,333.33 bottles to whole units. For planning and decision making, managers frequently make decisions using approximate data. Accuracy is desirable, but it is not as important as relevance. Do not be concerned when computations do not produce whole numbers. Rounding and approximation are common characteristics of managerial accounting data.

✓ CHECK YOURSELF 3.2

VolTech Company manufactures small engines that it sells for $130 each. Variable costs are $70 per unit. Fixed costs are expected to be $100,000. The management team has established a target profit of $188,000. Use the contribution margin per unit method to determine how many engines VolTech must sell to attain the target profit. Use the contribution margin ratio method to determine the amount of sales volume in dollars required to attain the desired profit.

Answer

Contribution margin per unit approach:

$$\text{Sales volume in units} = \frac{\text{Fixed costs} + \text{Desired profit}}{\text{Contribution margin per unit}} = \frac{\$100,000 + \$188,000}{\$130 - \$70} = 4,800 \text{ Units}$$

Contribution margin ratio approach:

$$\text{Sales volume in \$} = \frac{\text{Fixed costs} + \text{Desired profit}}{\text{Contribution margin ratio}} = \frac{\$100,000 + \$188,000}{(\$60 \div \$130)} = \$624,000$$

Proof that the two approaches produce the same result:

$$\text{Sales price} \times \text{No. units} = \text{Sales in dollars}$$

$$\$130 \times 4,800 \text{ Units} = \$624,000$$

ASSESSING THE PRICING STRATEGY

LO 5

Set selling prices by using cost-plus, prestige, and target costing.

After reviewing the accountant's computations, the president asked the marketing manager, "What are our chances of reaching a sales volume of 8,334 units?" The manager replied, "Slim to none." She observed that no Bright Day product has ever sold more than 4,000 bottles when initially offered. Further, she feels the $36 price is too high. She asked who set the $36 price and how it was established.

The accountant explained that the price was established using a **cost-plus pricing** strategy. The normal policy is to price products at variable cost plus 50 percent of the variable cost. In this case the variable cost was $24, resulting in a price of $36 [$24 + ($24 × .5)] The accountant knew the price was high but expected Delatine to sell anyway. Indeed, he supported his position by referencing a strategy known as **prestige pricing.** Many people will pay a premium to be the first to use a new product. Similarly, people will pay more for a product with a prestigious brand name. The accountant noted that the widespread news coverage coupled with Bright Day's brand identity makes Delatine a prime product for prestige pricing.

The marketing manager recognized the accountant's arguments, but contended that news coverage will fade rapidly, competitors will enter the market, and therefore, Delatine cannot support a $36 price for an extended period of time. As an alternative, she suggested they use a strategy known as target costing. **Target costing** begins by determining the market price at which a product will sell. This becomes the target price. The focus then shifts to developing the product at a cost that will enable the company to be profitable while selling the product at the target price.

Market research indicates that Delatine could sustain long-term sales at a price of $28 per bottle. At this price, the new contribution margin becomes a mere $4 ($28 Sales price − $24 Variable cost per unit). Lowering the contribution margin per unit will dramatically increase the sales volume necessary to attain the desired profit. Using the *equation method*, the sales volume in units required to attain the desired profit when the sales price per unit is reduced to $28 is as follows:

$$\text{Sales} - \text{Variable costs} - \text{Fixed costs} = \text{Profit}$$

$$\$28N - \$24N - \$60,000 = \$40,000$$

$$\$4N = \$60,000 + \$40,000$$

$$N = \$100,000 \div \$4$$

$$N = 25,000 \text{ Units}$$

Where:

N = Number of units

$28 = Sales price per unit

$24 = Variable cost per unit

$60,000 = Fixed costs

$40,000 = Desired profit

The accountant used the *contribution margin per unit method* to confirm these computations as follows:

$$\text{Sales volume in units} = \frac{\text{Fixed costs} + \text{Desired profit}}{\text{Contribution margin per unit}}$$

$$= \frac{\$60,000 + \$40,000}{\$4} = 25,000 \text{ Units}$$

The required sales volume *in dollars* is $700,000 (25,000 units × $28 per bottle). The following income statement confirms these results.

Sales revenue (25,000 units × $28)	$700,000
Total variable expenses (25,000 units × $24)	(600,000)
Total contribution margin (25,000 units × $4)	100,000
Fixed expenses	(60,000)
Net income	$ 40,000

The marketing manager recognized that it would be impossible to sell 25,000 bottles of Delatine. She noted that this is where target costing enters the picture. Delatine must be made at a cost that will enable the company to earn the desired profit of $40,000 while selling at a price of $28 per bottle. Clearly, the cost structure must change, and the marketing manager has some suggestions for making the necessary changes.

ASSESSING THE EFFECTS OF CHANGES IN VARIABLE COSTS

The previously discussed $24 cost is for a bottle of 100 capsules, each containing 90 milligrams (mg) of pure Delatine. The manufacturer is willing to provide Delatine to Bright Day in two alternative package sizes: (1) a bottle costing $12 that contains 100 capsules of 30 mg strength pure Delatine and (2) a bottle costing $3 that contains 100 capsules containing 5 mg of Delatine mixed with a vitamin C compound. The 5 mg dosage is the minimum required to permit a package label to indicate the product contains Delatine. The marketing manager observes that either option would enable Bright Day to sell Delatine at a price customers would be willing to pay.

LO 6

Explain cost-volume-profit relationships.

The president vehemently rejected the second option, calling it a blatant attempt to deceive customers by suggesting they were buying Delatine when in fact they were getting vitamin C. *He considered the idea unethical and dangerous.* He vowed that he would not be seen on the six o'clock news trying to defend a fast buck scheme while his company's reputation went up in smoke. After calming down, he agreed that the first option had merit. The appropriate dosage for Delatine was uncertain; customers who wanted 90 mg per day could take three capsules instead of one. He asked the accountant, "What's the effect on the bottom line?"

The variable cost changes from $24 to $12 per bottle. The contribution margin per unit increases from $4 per bottle ($28 sales price − $24 variable cost per bottle) to $16 per bottle ($28 sales price − $12 variable cost per bottle). The significant increase in contribution margin per unit dramatically decreases the sales volume necessary to attain the target profit.

FOCUS ON INTERNATIONAL ISSUES

COST-VOLUME-PROFIT ANALYSIS AT A GERMAN CHEMICAL COMPANY

The greater the percentage of a company's total costs that are fixed, the more sensitive the company's earnings are to changes in revenue or volume. Operating leverage, the relationship between the changes in revenue and changes in earnings, introduced earlier, applies to companies throughout the world, large or small.

Large chemical manufacturers have significant fixed costs. It takes a lot of buildings and equipment to produce chemicals. BASF claims to be the largest chemical company in the world. It has its headquarters in Ludwigshafen, Germany. From 2004 through 2006 BASF's revenues increased 40.2 percent, but its earnings increased 60.4 percent. In other words, its earnings grew one and one-half times faster than its revenues.

Studying BASF offers insight into a true global enterprise. Though headquartered in Germany, it has manufacturing facilities at 150 locations throughout the world. Only 21 percent of its 2006 revenue came from sales within Germany, which was 1 percent less than the revenue it earned in the United States. Although its financial statements are presented in euros and prepared in accordance with international financial accounting standards, its stock is traded on the New York Stock Exchange as well as on the Frankfurt Stock Exchange.

Using the *equation method,* the sales volume in units required to attain the desired profit when the variable cost per unit is reduced to $12 per bottle is as follows:

$$\text{Sales} - \text{Variable costs} - \text{Fixed costs} = \text{Profit}$$

$$\$28N - \$12N - \$60{,}000 = \$40{,}000$$

$$\$16N = \$60{,}000 + \$40{,}000$$

$$N = \$100{,}000 \div \$16$$

$$N = 6{,}250 \text{ Units}$$

Where:

N = Number of units

$28 = Sales price per unit

$12 = Variable cost per unit

$60,000 = Fixed costs

$40,000 = Desired profit

The accountant used the *contribution margin per unit method* to confirm these computations as follows:

$$\text{Sales volume in units} = \frac{\text{Fixed costs} + \text{Desired profit}}{\text{Contribution margin per unit}}$$

$$= \frac{\$60{,}000 + \$40{,}000}{\$16} = 6{,}250 \text{ Units}$$

The required sales volume in sales dollars is $175,000 (6,250 units × $28 per bottle). The following income statement confirms these amounts.

Sales revenue (6,250 units × $28)	$175,000
Total variable expenses (6,250 units × $12)	(75,000)
Total contribution margin (6,250 units × $16)	100,000
Fixed expenses	(60,000)
Net income	$ 40,000

Although the drop in required sales from 25,000 units to 6,250 was significant, the marketing manager was still uneasy about the company's ability to sell 6,250 bottles of Delatine. She observed again that no other Bright Day product had produced sales of that magnitude. The accountant suggested reducing projected fixed costs by advertising on radio rather than television. While gathering cost data for the potential television ad campaign, the accountant had consulted radio ad executives who had assured him radio ads could equal the TV audience exposure at about half the cost. Even though the TV ads would likely be more effective, he argued that since radio advertising costs would be half those of TV, the desired profit could be attained at a significantly lower volume of sales. The company president was impressed with the possibilities. He asked the accountant to determine the required sales volume if advertising costs were $30,000 instead of $60,000.

Answers to The Curious Accountant

InterContinental Hotel Group (IHG) obviously believed that the revenue it lost from dropping some hotels that did not meet its new image standards would be more than offset by the fees it received from new franchisees. If the Holiday Inn brand was perceived as a low-quality lodging choice because of a few unattractive properties, new franchisees may not be eager to sign on. Also, existing hotels can charge higher prices if the brand is perceived as more upscale. Since IHG gets a piece of these higher fees, it was willing to eliminate some units in order to, it hopes, improve overall profitability. It would be more difficult for IHG to initiate a marketing campaign based on the quality of Holiday Inns if several of its franchisees were perceived poorly.

American Express (AMEX) was trying to get rid of a small percentage of customers who had relatively large account balances, but who were not using their cards very often. AMEX could receive at least two benefits if these customers left. First, the company could avoid the higher-than-average default risk associated with them. Second, AMEX could avoid the costs of servicing the accounts of these infrequent card users. These costs occur even though the customers do not generate much revenue for the company.

IHC and American Express made their decisions by focusing on multiple factors, not just revenues and not just cost. Their decisions were based on an analysis of the interactions of costs, revenues, and the volume of revenues that would be generated as cost and pricing strategies were altered. Traditionally accountants refer to the topics covered in this chapter as cost-volume-profit analysis, but more accurately it could be called *price*-cost-volume-profit analysis.

Sources: "Hotels Risk Losing Holiday Inn Brand," *The Wall Street Journal,* November 13, 2009, p. B-3, and "AmEx Encourages Cardholders to Leave," *The Wall Street Journal,* February 24, 2009, p. D-2.

ASSESSING THE EFFECTS OF CHANGES IN FIXED COSTS

LO 6

Explain cost-volume-profit relationships.

Changing the fixed costs from $60,000 to $30,000 will dramatically reduce the sales level required to earn the target profit. Using the *equation method* the sales volume in units required to attain the desired profit when fixed costs are reduced to $30,000 is as follows.

$$\text{Sales} - \text{Variable costs} - \text{Fixed costs} = \text{Profit}$$

$$\$28N - \$12N - \$30,000 = \$40,000$$

$$\$16N = \$30,000 + \$40,000$$

$$N = \$70,000 \div \$16$$

$$N = 4,375 \text{ Units}$$

Where:

N = Number of units

$28 = Sales price per unit

$12 = Variable cost per unit

$30,000 = Fixed costs

$40,000 = Desired profit

The accountant used the *contribution margin per unit method* to confirm these computations as follows.

$$\text{Sales volume in units} = \frac{\text{Fixed costs} + \text{Desired profit}}{\text{Contribution margin per unit}}$$

$$= \frac{\$30,000 + \$40,000}{\$16} = 4,375 \text{ units}$$

The required sales volume in sales dollars is $122,500 (4,375 units × $28). The following income statement confirms these amounts.

Sales revenue (4,375 units × $28)	$122,500
Total variable expenses (4,375 units × $12)	(52,500)
Total contribution margin (4,375 units × $16)	70,000
Fixed expenses	(30,000)
Net income	$ 40,000

The marketing manager supported using radio instead of television ads. Obviously, she could not guarantee any specific sales volume, but she felt confident that sales projections within a range of 4,000 to 5,000 units were reasonable.

The Effect of Cost Structure on the Break-Even Point

Reducing fixed cost from $60,000 to $30,000 also significantly reduces the break-even point. This conclusion is confirmed by computing the break-even point before and after the reduction of the fixed cost as follows:

$$\text{Break-even point} = \text{Fixed costs} \div \text{Contribution margin per unit}$$

$$\text{Break-even point before fixed cost reduction} = \$60,000 \div \$16 = 3,750 \text{ units}$$

$$\text{Break-even point after fixed cost reduction} = \$30,000 \div \$16 = 1,875 \text{ units}$$

The lower break-even point is consistent with the conclusion reached in Chapter 2 regarding operating leverage. Recall that higher risk exists for companies with high fixed cost structures while variable cost structures limit risk. It follows that companies with high fixed cost structures will have higher break-even points than companies with low fixed cost structures. A high break-even point suggests that a company must attain a high sales volume or face operating losses. Indeed, failure to attain the required sales volume will result in leveraged losses. In other words, operating leverage will cause any change in sales revenue to have a disproportionately larger impact on net income.

USING THE COST-VOLUME-PROFIT GRAPH

To visually analyze the revised projections, Bright Day's accountant prepared a cost-volume-profit (CVP) graph that pictured CVP relationships over a range of sales activity from zero to 6,000 units. The accountant followed the steps below to produce the CVP graph (sometimes called a *break-even chart*) shown in Exhibit 3.1. The graph is drawn under the following assumptions.

Draw and interpret a cost-volume-profit graph.

- The contribution margin is $16 (sales price $28 − variable cost $12 per bottle).
- The fixed cost is $30,000.
- The desired profit is $40,000.

Procedures for Drawing the CVP Graph

1. *Draw and label the axes:* The horizontal axis represents activity (expressed in units) and the vertical axis represents dollars.
2. *Draw the fixed-cost line:* Total fixed costs are constant for all levels of activity. Draw a horizontal line representing the amount of fixed costs across the graph at $30,000, the fixed-cost level.
3. *Draw the total cost line:* The total cost line representing the combination of fixed and variable costs is a diagonal line that rises as it moves from left to right. To draw the line, plot one point of the total cost line at the intersection of the fixed-cost line and the vertical axis. In this case, plot the first point at the zero level of activity and $30,000 (fixed cost). Next, select an arbitrary activity level. In this case we assume

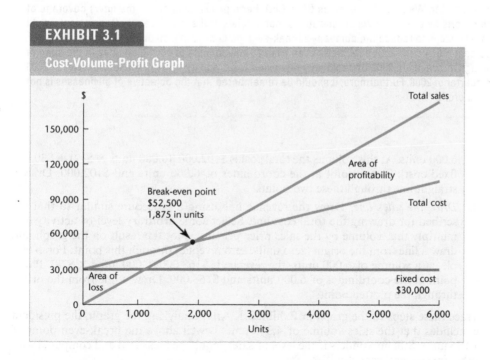

EXHIBIT 3.1

Cost-Volume-Profit Graph

REALITY BYTES

The relationship among the costs to produce goods, the volume of goods produced, the price charged for those goods, and the profit earned is relevant to all industries, but perhaps no industry demonstrates the effects of these relationships more dramatically than automobile manufacturing. First, the automobile industry is characterized by having a lot of fixed production-costs for things such as buildings, equipment, research, and development, but also financing costs associated with borrowed funds, such as the interest expense bonds. Second, the industry is globally competitive, and companies in the United States are often at a cost disadvantage. Some of this cost disadvantage comes from obvious sources, such as having to pay higher wages than do companies in countries such as South Korea. Finally, for many customers, price and quality are more important than brand loyalty.

Over the past decades, domestic auto makers, and in particular General Motors (GM), have used different strategies to try to deal with the issues mentioned above. Early on it had a dominant market share. As long as it produced more cars than its competitors, its fixed cost per car was lower, resulting in better profits. In the 1980s, however, foreign manufactures began increasing their market share and decreasing GM's. As its relative levels of production fell, its fixed cost per unit increased. In response, GM and others tried to regain market share by lowering prices, largely through rebates. Unfortunately this did not work, so the lower prices, combined with the higher relative fixed costs, seriously eroded profits.

These problems reached a crisis in 2008 and 2009 when GM and Chrysler sought financial help from the government and entered expedited bankruptcy proceedings.

What did GM and Chrysler hope to achieve? Primarily they needed to lower their costs, especially their fixed costs. As a result of bankruptcy proceedings, they were able to greatly reduce interest and principal payments on their outstanding bonds (fixed costs), reduce the number of brands (fixed costs), shut down some plants (fixed costs), reduce health care costs to retirees (fixed costs), and reduce the number of dealers. While reducing the number of dealers did reduce some cost to the companies, it also reduced price competition among the dealers, which had the potential of allowing the companies to charge more for their cars. All of these changes, it was hoped, would allow the companies to return to profitability.

However, before a company can be profitable, it must break even. At one time GM's break-even point was estimated at around 16 million vehicles per year. GM's CEO until 2000, Rick Wagoner, had implemented changes that reduced the company's break-even point to 12 million units. On March 29, 2009, as a condition of receiving government support, the administration of President Barack Obama asked Mr. Wagoner to resign as GM's CEO. Perhaps lost by many in the news coverage of Mr. Wagoner's resignation were reports by several news organizations that officials at the U.S. Treasury Department would ask the new leadership at GM to take steps to reduce the company's break-even point to 10 million units.

It would be a major achievement if GM can reduce its break even from 16 million units to 10 million units in the span of a few years. This may not be enough, however. In 2008 GM sold only 8.8 million units, and its sales in the first quarter of 2009 were even lower than the same quarter of 2008. Furthermore, it should be remembered that the objective of businesses is not simply to break even, but to make a profit.

6,000 units. At this volume, the total cost is $102,000 [(6,000 units × $12) + $30,000 fixed cost]. Plot a point at the coordinates of 6,000 units and $102,000. Draw a straight line through these two points.

4. *Draw the sales line:* Draw the revenue line using a procedure similar to that described for drawing the total cost line. Select some arbitrary level of activity and multiply that volume by the sales price per unit. Plot the result on the graph and draw a line from the origin (zero units, zero revenue) through this point. For example, at a volume of 6,000 units, the revenue is $168,000 (6,000 units × $28). Plot a point at the coordinates of 6,000 units and $168,000. Draw a line from the origin through the plotted point.

Trace these steps to the graph in Exhibit 3.1. After analyzing the graph, the president concludes that the sales volume of 4,375 units is well above the break-even point of 1,875 units. Still he wonders if the level of safety could be measured and compared with other investment opportunities.

CALCULATING THE MARGIN OF SAFETY

The final meeting of Bright Day's management team focused on the reliability of the data used to construct the CVP chart. The accountant called attention to the sales volume figures in the area of profitability. Recall that Bright Day must sell 4,375 bottles of Delatine to earn the desired profit. In dollars, budgeted sales are $122,500 (4,375 bottles × $28 per bottle). The accountant highlighted the large gap between these budgeted sales and break-even sales. The amount of this gap, called the *margin of safety,* can be measured in units or in sales dollars as shown here.

	In Units	In Dollars
Budgeted sales	4,375	$122,500
Break-even sales	(1,875)	(52,500)
Margin of safety	2,500	$ 70,000

The **margin of safety** measures the cushion between budgeted sales and the break-even point. It quantifies the amount by which actual sales can fall short of expectations before the company will begin to incur losses.

To help compare diverse products or companies of different sizes, the margin of safety can be expressed as a percentage. Divide the margin of safety by the budgeted sales volume[2] as shown here.

$$\text{Margin of safety} = \frac{\text{Budgeted sales} - \text{Break-even sales}}{\text{Budgeted sales}}$$

$$\text{Margin of safety} = \frac{\$122,500 - \$52,500}{\$122,500} = 57.14\%$$

This analysis suggests actual sales would have to fall short of expected sales by more than 57 percent before Bright Day would experience a loss on Delatine. The large margin of safety suggests the proposed radio advertising program to market bottles of 30mg Delatine capsules has minimal risk. As a result, the project team recommends that Delatine be added to the company's line of products. The steps Bright Day's project team experienced to arrive at this decision are summarized in Exhibit 3.2.

✓ CHECK YOURSELF 3.3

Suppose that Bright Day is considering the possibility of selling a protein supplement that will cost Bright Day $5 per bottle. Bright Day believes that it can sell 4,000 bottles of the supplement for $25 per bottle. Fixed costs associated with selling the supplement are expected to be $42,000. Does the supplement have a wider margin of safety than Delatine?

Answer   Calculate the break-even point for the protein supplement.

$$\text{Break-even volume in units} = \frac{\text{Fixed costs}}{\text{Contribution margin per unit}} = \frac{\$42,000}{\$25 - \$5} = 2,100 \text{ Units}$$

Calculate the margin of safety. Note that the margin of safety expressed as a percentage can be calculated using the number of units or sales dollars. Using either units or dollars yields the same percentage.

$$\text{Margin of safety} = \frac{\text{Budgeted sales} - \text{Break-even sales}}{\text{Budgeted sales}} = \frac{4,000 - 2,100}{4,000} = 47.5\%$$

The margin of safety for Delatine (57.14 percent) exceeds that for the protein supplement (47.5 percent). This suggests that Bright Day is less likely to incur losses selling Delatine than selling the supplement.

[2]The margin of safety percentage can be based on actual as well as budgeted sales. For example, an analyst could compare the margins of safety of two companies under current operating conditions by substituting actual sales for budgeted sales in the computation, as follows: [(Actual sales − Break-even sales) ÷ Actual sales].

EXHIBIT 3.2

Recap of Delatine Decision Process

Management considers a new product named Delatine. Delatine has a projected sales price of $36 and variable cost of $24 per bottle. Fixed cost is projected to be $60,000. The break-even point is 5,000 units [$60,000 ÷ ($36 − $24) = 5,000].

Management desires to earn a $40,000 profit on Delatine. The sales volume required to earn the desired profit is 8,334 units [($60,000 + $40,000) ÷ ($36 − $24) = 8,334].

The marketing manager advocates a target pricing approach that lowers the proposed selling price to $28 per bottle. The sales volume required to earn a $40,000 profit increases to 25,000 units [($60,000 + $40,000) ÷ ($28 − $24) = 25,000].

Target costing is employed to reengineer the product, thereby reducing variable cost to $12 per bottle. The sales volume required to earn a $40,000 profit decreases to 6,250 units [($60,000 + $40,000) ÷ ($28 − $12) = 6,250].

Target costing is applied further to reduce fixed cost to $30,000. The sales volume required to earn a $40,000 profit decreases to 4,375 units [($30,000 + $40,000) ÷ ($28 − $12) = 4,375]. The new break-even point is 1,875 units [$30,000 ÷ ($28 − $12) = 1,875].

In view of a 57.14% margin of safety [(4,375 − 1,875) ÷ 4,375 = .5714], management decides to add Delatine to its product line.

PERFORMING SENSITIVITY ANALYSIS USING SPREADSHEET SOFTWARE

While useful, the margin of safety offers only a one dimensional measure of risk—change in sales volume. Profitability is affected by multidimensional forces. Fixed or variable costs, as well as sales volume, could differ from expectations. Exhibit 3.3 uses data pertaining to Bright Day's proposed project for marketing Delatine to illustrate an Excel spreadsheet showing the sensitivity of profits to simultaneous changes in fixed cost, variable cost, and sales volume. Recall the accountant estimated the radio ad campaign would cost $30,000. The spreadsheet projects profitability if advertising costs are as low as $20,000 or as high as $40,000. The effects of potential simultaneous changes in variable cost and sales volume are similarly projected.

Conduct sensitivity analysis for cost-volume-profit relationships.

The range of scenarios illustrated in the spreadsheet represents only a few of the many alternatives management can analyze with a few quick keystrokes. The spreadsheet program recalculates profitability figures instantly when one of the variables changes. If the president asks what would happen if Bright Day sold 10,000 units, the accountant merely substitutes the new number for one of the existing sales volume figures, and revised profitability numbers are instantly available. By changing the variables, management can get a real feel for the sensitivity of profits to changes in cost and volume. Investigating a multitude of what-if possibilities involving simultaneous changes in fixed cost, variable cost, and volume is called **sensitivity analysis.**

After reviewing the spreadsheet analysis, Bright Day's management team is convinced it should undertake radio advertising for Delatine. Only under the most dire circumstances (if actual sales are significantly below expectations while costs are well above expectations) will the company incur a loss.

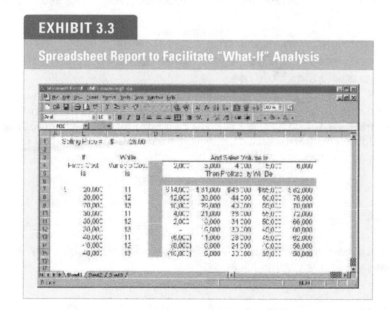

EXHIBIT 3.3

Spreadsheet Report to Facilitate "What-If" Analysis

ASSESSING THE EFFECT OF SIMULTANEOUS CHANGES IN CVP VARIABLES

When spreadsheet software is not available, the effects of simultaneous changes in CVP variables can be examined using the equation method. To illustrate several possible scenarios, assume Bright Day has developed the budgeted income statement in Exhibit 3.4.

EXHIBIT 3.4

Budgeted Income Statement

Sales revenue (4,375 units × $28 sale price)	$122,500
Total variable expenses (4,375 units × $12 cost per bottle)	(52,500)
Total contribution margin (4,375 units × $16)	70,000
Fixed expenses	(30,000)
Net income	$ 40,000

A Decrease in Sales Price Accompanied by an Increase in Sales Volume

The marketing manager believes reducing the sales price per bottle to $25 will increase sales volume by 625 units. The expected sales volume would become 5,000 (4,375 + 625). Variable cost per unit is expected to remain at $12. Should Bright Day reduce the price? Compare the projected profit without these changes ($40,000) with the projected profit if the sales price is $25 and volume increases to 5,000 units.

$$\text{Sales} - \text{Variable costs} - \text{Fixed costs} = \text{Profit}$$
$$(\$25 \times 5{,}000 \text{ units}) - (\$12 \times 5{,}000) - \$30{,}000 = \text{Profit}$$
$$\$35{,}000 = \text{Profit}$$

Since budgeted income falls from $40,000 to $35,000, Bright Day should not reduce the sales price.

An Increase in Fixed Cost Accompanied by an Increase in Sales Volume

Return to the budgeted income statement in Exhibit 3.4. If the company buys an additional $12,000 of advertising, management believes sales can increase to 6,000 units. The sales price remains at $28 and variable cost per unit at $12. Should Bright Day incur the additional advertising cost, increasing fixed costs to $42,000 and sales volume to 6,000 units? The expected profit would be:

$$\text{Sales} - \text{Variable costs} - \text{Fixed costs} = \text{Profit}$$
$$(\$28 \times 6{,}000 \text{ units}) - (\$12 \times 6{,}000) - \$42{,}000 = \text{Profit}$$
$$\$54{,}000 = \text{Profit}$$

Since budgeted income increases from $40,000 to $54,000, Bright Day should seek to increase sales through additional advertising.

A Simultaneous Reduction in Sales Price, Fixed Costs, Variable Costs, and Sales Volume

Return again to the budgeted income statement in Exhibit 3.4. Suppose Bright Day negotiates a $4 reduction in the cost of a bottle of Delatine. The management team considers passing some of the savings on to customers by reducing the sales price to $25 per bottle. Furthermore, the team believes it could reduce advertising costs by $8,000 and still achieve sales of 4,200 units. Should Bright Day adopt this plan to reduce prices and advertising costs?

The contribution margin would increase to $17 per bottle ($25 revised selling price − $8 revised variable cost per bottle) and fixed cost would fall to $22,000 ($30,000 − $8,000). Based on a sales volume of 4,200 units, the expected profit is:

$$\text{Sales} - \text{Variable costs} - \text{Fixed costs} = \text{Profit}$$

$$(\$25 \times 4{,}200 \text{ units}) - (\$8 \times 4{,}200) - \$22{,}000 = \text{Profit}$$

$$\$49{,}400 = \text{Profit}$$

Because budgeted income increases from $40,000 to $49,400, Bright Day should proceed with the revised operating strategy.

Many other possible scenarios could be considered. The contribution approach can be used to analyze independent or simultaneous changes in the CVP variables.

MULTIPRODUCT COST-VOLUME-PROFIT ANALYSIS

To this point we have simplified our discussion of CVP by assuming a company sells only one product. In the real world, most companies sell many products. Each product has an independent impact on the profitability of the company. Calculating the break-even point requires an analyst to consider the simultaneous impact of the contribution margins of all products. This impact can be easily measured by computing the weighted average contribution margin.

LO 10

Perform multiproduct cost-volume-profit analysis.

To illustrate we assume that Bright Day's management team is examining its annual Vitamin C Sales Days event. The sales event focuses on two products. One product is labeled Synthetic C; the other is called Organic C. The sales price, variable cost, and contribution margin for each bottle of each product is shown here.

	Synthetic C	Organic C
Sales price	$7	$9
Variable cost	5	6
Contribution margin	$2	$3

Due to its lower cost, Synthetic C has consistently outsold the Organic C. Indeed, Synthetic C historically accounts for approximately 80 percent of the total sales; with Organic C making up the remaining 20 percent. The fixed costs for the annual sales event are expected to be $2,112. These fixed costs are largely composed of advertising and training expenses. Based on this information the management team begins its examination by determining the break-even point.

Determining the Break-Even Point

The first step in determining the break-even point is to compute the *weighted average contribution margin per unit.* The weighted average depends on each product's proportionate share of the total sales. In accounting terms, the relative proportions in which a company's products are sold is called the **sales mix.** The expected sales mix for the annual sales event is 80 percent for Synthetic C and 20 percent for Organic C. In other words, the two products in the event have an 80/20 sales mix. Base on this sales mix, the weighted average contribution margin per bottle is computed as follows.

	Contribution Margin	Times Proportionate Share	Weighted Average
Synthetic C	$2	× .8	$1.60
Organic C	3	× .2	.60
Weighted average contribution margin			$2.20

Using the per unit contribution margin approach, the break-even point in total units can be determined by dividing the fixed cost by the weighted average contribution margin as follows.

Break-even point = Fixed costs ÷ Weighted average contribution margin per unit

Break-even point = $2,112 ÷ $2.20 = 960 Total units

The 960 units represent the total number of bottles of both products combined. To determine the number of bottles of each product, multiply the total number of bottles times the proportionate share of the sales mix as follows.

Break-even point = Total units × Proportionate share of sales mix

Break-even point for Synthetic C = 960 bottles × .8 share of sales mix = 768 Bottles

Break-even point for Organic C = 960 bottles × .2 share of sales mix = 192 Bottles

The following income statement confirms that these sales volume figures constitute the break-even point.

Sales of Synthetic C (768 bottles × $7)	$5,376
Sales of Organic C (192 bottles × $9)	1,728
Total sales	7,104
Variable cost of Synthetic C (768 bottles × $5)	(3,840)
Variable cost of Organic C (192 bottles × $6)	(1,152)
Contribution margin	2,112
Fixed cost	(2,112)
Net income	$ 0

Determining the Sales Volume Necessary to Reach a Desired Profit

Suppose Bright Day's president wants to know the number of bottles of each product that must be sold to earn a profit of $264 from the sales event. This information can be easily determined by adding the amount of the desired profit to the amount of fixed cost and then dividing the total by the weighted average contribution margin per unit. The computations are as follows.

$$\text{Sales volume in units} = \frac{\text{Fixed cost} + \text{Desired profit}}{\text{Weighted average contribution margin per unit}}$$

$$= \frac{\$2,112 + \$264}{\$2.20} = 1,080 \text{ Total units}$$

The 1,080 units represent the total number of bottles of both products combined. To determine the number of bottles of each product, multiply the total number of bottles times the proportionate share of the sales mix as follows.

Break-even point = Total units × Proportionate share of sales mix

Break-even point for Synthetic C = 1,080 bottles × .8 share of sales mix = 864 Bottles

Break-even point for Organic C = 1,080 bottles × .2 share of sales mix = 216 Bottles

The following income statement confirms that these sales volume figures constitute the sales volumes necessary to earn a desired profit of $264.

Sales of Synthetic C (864 bottles × $7)	$6,048
Sales of Organic C (216 bottles × $9)	1,944
Total sales	7,992
Variable cost of Synthetic C (864 bottles × $5)	(4,320)
Variable cost of Organic C (216 bottles × $6)	(1,296)
Contribution margin	2,376
Fixed cost	(2,112)
Net income	$ 264

Managing the Sales Mix

Bright Day's president asks the management team to consider possibilities for increasing profitability. The team first considers the possibility of increasing the total number of bottles of vitamins sold. The marketing manager is pessimistic about this possibility. She notes that there are only so many people buying vitamin C. Trying to convince the same number of customers to purchase more bottles of the vitamin is not likely. The accountant notes that it is not necessary to sell more bottles of vitamins. Indeed, he argues that profitability can be increased even if sales volume remains flat. His solution is to change the sales mix.

Since Organic C has a higher contribution margin, shifting customers from Synthetic C to Organic C will increase profitability. The accountant demonstrates his point by computing the level of profitability assuming the sales mix shifts from an 80/20 split to a 60/40 mix. The income statement for a total sales volume of 1,080 bottles under a 60/40 sales mix is developed as follows.

The 1,080 units represent the total number of bottles of both products combined. To determine the number of bottles of each product using the 60/40 sales mix, multiply the total number of bottles times the proportionate share of the sales mix as follows.

Break-even point = Total units × Proportionate share of sales mix

Break-even point for Synthetic C = 1,080 bottles × .6 share of sales mix = 648 Bottles

Break-even point for Organic C = 1,080 bottles × .4 share of sales mix = 432 Bottles

The following income statement confirms that revised sales mix produces a higher net income. Indeed, in this case net income increases from $264 to $480 given the same total sales volume of 1,080 total bottles of vitamin C.

Sales of Synthetic C (648 bottles × $7)	$4,536
Sales of Organic C (432 bottles × $9)	3,888
Total sales	8,424
Variable cost of Synthetic C (648 bottles × $5)	(3,240)
Variable cost of Organic C (432 bottles × $6)	(2,592)
Contribution margin	2,592
Fixed cost	(2,112)
Net income	$ 480

The president is very impressed with this potential increase in profitability. His immediate response is to ask, how do we change the sales mix? A number of possibilities are examined, including slanting the advertising to emphasize Organic C and training the sales staff to promote the product. After careful consideration the team implements the most promising ideas. Ultimately, the team would compare the expected income statement with actual results to evaluate and fine tune the strategy. Variance analysis and performance evaluation are important subjects that will be covered in coming chapters.

It is important to note that the sales mix affects all aspects of CVP analysis. For example, the new break-even point for a sales mix of 60/40 is computed as discussed here. The first step is to compute the weighted average contribution margin per unit as follows.

	Contribution Margin	Times Proportionate Share	Weighted Average
Synthetic C	$2	× .6	$1.20
Organic C	3	× .4	1.20
Weighted average contribution margin			$2.40

Using the per unit contribution margin approach, the break-even point in total units can be determined by dividing the fixed cost by the weighted average contribution margin as follows:

Break-even point = Fixed costs ÷ Weighted average contribution margin per unit

Break-even point = $2,112 ÷ $2.40 = 880 Total units

Note that the break-even point is 80 units less (960 units − 880 units) than when the sales mix was 80/20. This demonstrates that shifting the sales mix not only increases net income but also reduces the break-even point. The 880 units represent the total number of bottles of both products combined that must be sold under an 60/40 sales mix for the company to break even. To determine the number of bottles of each product, multiply the total number of bottles times the proportionate share of the sales mix as follows:

Break-even point = Total units × Proportionate share of sales mix

Break-even point for Synthetic C = 880 bottles × .6 share of sales mix = 528 Bottles

Break-even point for Organic C = 880 bottles × .4 share of sales mix = 352 Bottles

The following income statement confirms that these sales volume figures constitute the break-even point.

Sales of Synthetic C (528 bottles × $7)	$3,696
Sales of Organic C (352 bottles × $9)	3,168
Total sales	6,864
Variable cost of Synthetic C (528 bottles × $5)	(2,640)
Variable cost of Organic C (352 bottles × $6)	(2,112)
Contribution margin	2,112
Fixed cost	(2,112)
Net income	$ 0

The contribution margin per unit formula can be used to determine the number of units required to attain a target profit. Simply add the desired profit to the fixed costs and then divide by the weighted average contribution margin per unit. The resulting formula is:

$$\text{Sales volume in units} = \frac{\text{Fixed costs} + \text{Desired profit}}{\text{Weighted average contribution margin per unit}}$$

COST-VOLUME-PROFIT LIMITATIONS

CVP is limited by a number of underlying assumptions. These assumptions include:

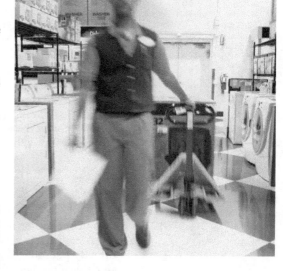

1. The selling price is constant. It does not increase or decrease regardless of changes in sales volume.
2. Costs are linear.
   a. The variable cost per unit is constant and moves in direct proportion with changes in sales volume.
   b. Total fixed costs do not change with changes in sales volume.
   c. Efficiency and productivity are constant.
3. The sales mix in multiproduct companies is constant.
4. Inventory levels in manufacturing companies are constant.
5. All CVP variables are within the relevant range.

Violating these assumptions will produce inaccuracies in CVP analysis. Unfortunately some violations are unavoidable in practice. For example, some companies may offer a discounted sales price for large orders, thereby violating the first assumption. Similarly, managers may desire to analyze operations at levels of sales volume that are outside the relevant range. Fortunately, many violations are insignificant. Further, accountants can make appropriate adjustments if serious violations are unavoidable. The widespread use of CVP in the real world suggests that the benefits of the analysis exceed the minor inaccuracies that inevitably occur. Even so, accountants must remain vigilant to avoid inaccuracies in the advice they render.

A Look Back

Profitability is affected by changes in sales price, costs, and the volume of activity. The relationship among these variables is examined using *cost-volume-profit (CVP) analysis*. The *contribution margin,* determined by subtracting variable costs from the sales price, is a useful variable in CVP analysis. The *contribution margin per unit* is the amount each unit sold provides to cover fixed costs. Once fixed costs have been covered, each additional unit sold increases net income by the amount of the per-unit contribution margin.

The *break-even point* (the point where total revenue equals total cost) can be determined by the equation method, the contribution margin method, or the contribution margin ratio method. All three methods produce the same result because all three methods are derivations of the income statement formula:

$$\text{Sales} - \text{Variable costs} - \text{Fixed costs} = \text{Profit}$$

Beyond determining the break-even point, all three methods can also be used to assess the effects in other CVP relationships.

Many methods are available to determine the prices at which products should sell. In *cost-plus pricing,* the sales price per unit is determined by adding a percentage markup to the cost per unit. In contrast, *target costing* begins with an estimated market price customers would be willing to pay for the product and then develops the product at a cost that will enable the company to earn its desired profit.

A *break-even graph* can depict cost-volume-profit relationships for a product over a range of sales activity. The horizontal axis represents volume of activity and the vertical axis represents dollars. Lines for fixed costs, total costs, and sales are drawn based on the sales price per unit, variable cost per unit, and fixed costs. The graph can be used to determine the break-even point in units and sales dollars.

The *margin of safety* is the number of units or the amount of sales dollars by which actual sales can fall below expected sales before a loss is incurred. The margin of safety can also be expressed as a percentage to permit comparing different size companies. The margin of safety can be computed as a percentage by dividing the difference between budgeted sales and break-even sales by the amount of budgeted sales.

Spreadsheet software as well as the contribution margin approach can be used to conduct sensitivity analysis of cost-volume-profit relationships. *Sensitivity analysis* predicts the effect on profitability of different scenarios of fixed costs, variable costs, and sales volumes. The effects of simultaneous changes in all three variables can be assessed.

Cost-volume-profit analysis is built upon certain simplifying assumptions. The analysis assumes true linearity among the CVP variables and a constant level of inventory. Although these assumptions are not literally valid in actual practice, CVP analysis nevertheless provides managers with helpful insights for decision making.

>> A Look Forward

The next chapter introduces a new cost classification scheme. Specifically, you will learn how to classify costs as being either direct or indirect costs. Direct costs are directly traceable to cost objects. Cost objects are items for which management needs to determine their cost. For example, a manager may need to determine the cost of making a product, providing a service, or operating a department. In these cases the cost object is the product, the service or the department. Indirect costs are those costs that cannot be directly traced to a cost object. The chapter will discuss the techniques such as cost tracing and cost allocation which are used to assign indirect costs to various objects.

A step-by-step audio-narrated series of slides is provided on the text website at www.mhhe.com/edmonds2011.

SELF-STUDY REVIEW PROBLEM

Sharp Company makes and sells pencil sharpeners. The variable cost of each sharpener is $20. The sharpeners are sold for $30 each. Fixed operating expenses amount to $40,000.

Required

a. Determine the break-even point in units and sales dollars.
b. Determine the sales volume in units and dollars that is required to attain a profit of $12,000. Verify your answer by preparing an income statement using the contribution margin format.
c. Determine the margin of safety between sales required to attain a profit of $12,000 and break-even sales.
d. Prepare a break-even graph using the cost and price assumptions outlined above.

Solution to Requirement a

Formula for Computing Break-even Point in Units
Sales − Variable costs − Fixed costs = Profit
Sales price per unit (N) − Variable cost per unit (N) − Fixed costs = Profit
Contribution margin per unit (N) − Fixed costs = Profit
N = (Fixed costs + Profit) ÷ Contribution profit per unit
N = ($40,000 + 0) ÷ ($30 − $20) = 4,000 Units

Break-even Point in Sales Dollars

Sales price	$ 30
× Number of units	4,000
Sales volume in dollars	$120,000

Solution to Requirement b

Formula for Computing Unit Sales Required to Attain Desired Profit

Sales − Variable costs − Fixed costs = Profit
Sales price per unit (N) − Variable cost per unit (N) − Fixed costs = Profit
Contribution margin per unit (N) − Fixed costs = Profit
N = (Fixed costs + Profit) ÷ Contribution profit per unit
N = ($40,000 + 12,000) ÷ ($30 − $20) = 5,200 Units

Sales Dollars Required to Attain Desired Profit

Sales price	$ 30
× Number of units	5,200
Sales volume in dollars	$156,000

Income Statement

Sales volume in units (a)	5,200
Sales revenue (a × $30)	$156,000
Variable costs (a × $20)	(104,000)
Contribution margin	52,000
Fixed costs	(40,000)
Net income	$ 12,000

Solution to Requirement c

Margin of Safety Computations	Units	Dollars
Budgeted sales	5,200	$156,000
Break-even sales	(4,000)	(120,000)
Margin of safety	1,200	$ 36,000

Percentage Computation

$$\frac{\text{Margin of safety in \$}}{\text{Budgeted sales}} = \frac{\$36,000}{\$156,000} = 23.08\%$$

Solution to Requirement d

KEY TERMS

Break-even point 108
Contribution margin per
  unit 109
Contribution margin ratio 110
Cost-plus pricing 112

Cost-volume-profit (CVP)
  analysis 107
Equation method 108
Margin of safety 119
Prestige pricing 112

Sales mix 123
Sensitivity analysis 121
Target costing 112

QUESTIONS

1. What does the term *break-even point* mean? Name the two ways it can be measured.

2. How does a contribution margin income statement differ from the income statement used in financial reporting?

3. In what three ways can the contribution margin be useful in cost-volume-profit analysis?

4. If Company A has a projected margin of safety of 22 percent while Company B has a margin of safety of 52 percent, which company is at greater risk when actual sales are less than budgeted?

5. What variables affect profitability? Name two methods for determining profitability when simultaneous changes occur in these variables.

6. When would the customer be willing to pay a premium price for a product or service? What pricing strategy would be appropriate under these circumstances?

7. What are three alternative approaches to determine the break-even point? What do the results of these approaches show?

8. What is the equation method for determining the break-even point? Explain how the results of this method differ from those of the contribution margin approach.

9. If a company is trying to find the break-even point for multiple products that sell simultaneously, what consideration must be taken into account?

10. What assumptions are inherent in cost-volume-profit analysis? Since these assumptions are usually not wholly valid, why do managers still use the analysis in decision making?

11. Mary Hartwell and Jane Jamail, college roommates, are considering the joint purchase of a computer that they can share to prepare class assignments. Ms. Hartwell wants a particular model that costs $2,000; Ms. Jamail prefers a more economical model that costs $1,500. In fact, Ms. Jamail is adamant about her position, refusing to contribute more than $750 toward the purchase. If Ms. Hartwell is also adamant about her position, should she accept Ms. Jamail's $750 offer and apply that amount toward the purchase of the more expensive computer?

12. How would the algebraic formula used to compute the break-even point under the equation method be changed to solve for a desired target profit?

13. Setting the sales price is easy: Enter cost information and desired profit data into

one of the cost-volume-profit formulas, and the appropriate sales price can be computed mathematically. Do you agree with this line of reasoning? Explain.

14. What is the relationship between cost-volume-profit analysis and the relevant range?

MULTIPLE-CHOICE QUESTIONS

Multiple-choice questions are provided on the text website at www.mhhe.com/edmonds2011.

EXERCISES—SERIES A

All applicable Exercises in Series A are available with McGraw-Hill's _Connect Accounting_.

Exercise 3-1A   _Equation method_   LO 1

Adair Corporation produces products that it sells for $12 each. Variable costs per unit are $5, and annual fixed costs are $140,000. Adair desires to earn a profit of $21,000.

Required

a. Use the equation method to determine the break-even point in units and dollars.

b. Determine the sales volume in units and dollars required to earn the desired profit.

Exercise 3-2A   _Per-unit contribution margin approach_   LO 2

Connor Corporation sells products for $25 each that have variable costs of $13 per unit. Connor's annual fixed cost is $264,000.

Required

Use the per-unit contribution margin approach to determine the break-even point in units and dollars.

Exercise 3-3A   _Contribution margin ratio_   LO 3

Garcia Company incurs annual fixed costs of $60,000. Variable costs for Garcia's product are $22.75 per unit, and the sales price is $35.00 per unit. Garcia desires to earn an annual profit of $45,000.

Required

Use the contribution margin ratio approach to determine the sales volume in dollars and units required to earn the desired profit.

Exercise 3-4A   _Cost structure, risk, and the break-even point_   LO 1, 4, 6

Kennedy Company produces a product that sells for $37 per unit and has a variable cost of $22 per unit. Kennedy incurs annual fixed costs of $75,000.

Required

a. Determine the sales volume in units and dollars required to break even.

b. Calculate the break-even point assuming fixed costs increase to $120,000.

c. Explain how a fixed cost structure affects risk and the break-even point.

Exercise 3-5A   _Target costing_   LO 5

Mote Enterprises produces a product with fixed costs of $36,000 and variable cost of $2.50 per unit. The company desires to earn a $20,000 profit and believes it can sell 10,000 units of the product.

Required

a. Based on this information, determine the target sales price.

b. Assume a competitor is currently selling a similar product for $6.80 per unit. Explain how Mote can use target costing to maintain its desired profitability.

LO 6

Exercise 3-6A   *Determining variable cost from incomplete cost data*

Laya Corporation produced 200,000 watches that it sold for $16 each during 2012. The company determined that fixed manufacturing cost per unit was $7 per watch. The company reported an $800,000 gross margin on its 2012 financial statements.

Required

Determine the variable cost per unit, the total variable, and the total contribution margin.

LO 2, 4

Exercise 3-7A   *Contribution margin per unit approach for break-even and desired profit*

Information concerning a product produced by Salter Company appears here:

Sales price per unit	$175
Variable cost per unit	$75
Total annual fixed manufacturing and operating costs	$600,000

Required

Determine the following:

a. Contribution margin per unit.
b. Number of units that Salter must sell to break even.
c. Sales level in units that Salter must reach to earn a profit of $200,000.

LO 6

Exercise 3-8A   *Changing sales price*

Pettigrew Company produces a product that has a variable cost of $13 per unit; the product sells for $28 per unit. The company's annual fixed costs total $375,000; it had net income of $75,000 in the previous year. In an effort to increase the company's market share, management is considering lowering the selling price to $25 per unit.

Required

If Pettigrew desires to maintain net income of $75,000, how many additional units must it sell to justify the price decline?

LO 4, 6

Exercise 3-9A   *Simultaneous change in sales price and desired profit*

Use the cost data presented in Exercise 3-8A but assume that in addition to increasing its market share by lowering its selling price to $25, Pettigrew desires to increase its net income by $36,000.

Required

Determine the number of units the company must sell to earn the desired income.

LO 1, 7

Exercise 3-10A   *Components of break-even graph*

Required

Match the numbers shown in the graph with the following items.

a. Fixed cost line
b. Total cost line
c. Break-even point

d. Area of profit
e. Revenue line
f. Area of loss

Exercise 3-11A *Evaluating simultaneous changes in fixed and variable costs*   LO 6

Naylor Company currently produces and sells 6,400 units annually of a product that has a variable cost of $18 per unit and annual fixed costs of $161,400. The company currently earns a $69,000 annual profit. Assume that Naylor has the opportunity to invest in new labor-saving production equipment that will enable the company to reduce variable costs to $16 per unit. The investment would cause fixed costs to increase by $9,000 because of additional depreciation cost.

Required

a. Use the equation method to determine the sales price per unit under existing conditions (current equipment is used).
b. Prepare a contribution margin income statement, assuming that Naylor invests in the new production equipment. Recommend whether Naylor should invest in the new equipment.

Exercise 3-12A *Margin of safety*   LO 8

Jensen Company makes a product that sells for $38 per unit. The company pays $16 per unit for the variable costs of the product and incurs annual fixed costs of $176,000. Jensen expects to sell 21,000 units of product.

Required

Determine Jensen's margin of safety expressed as a percentage.

Exercise 3-13A *Cost-volume-profit relationship*   LO 1, 2, 4, 6

Feskin Corporation is a manufacturing company that makes small electric motors it sells for $36 per unit. The variable costs of production are $22 per motor, and annual fixed costs of production are $196,000.

Required

a. How many units of product must Feskin make and sell to break even?
b. How many units of product must Feskin make and sell to earn a $56,000 profit?
c. The marketing manager believes that sales would increase dramatically if the price were reduced to $34 per unit. How many units of product must Feskin make and sell to earn a $56,000 profit, if the sales price is set at $34 per unit?

Exercise 3-14A *Complexities of CVP Analysis in Multinational Companies*   LO 6

Pinero Barrels, Inc. (PBI), manufactures oak barrels for the wine industry at its facility in the United States. One of the raw materials used for some of its barrels is French oak lumber. The company fabricates the oak lumber into the appropriate-sized staves and assembles these staves, along with other components, into barrels. In January 2009, the company signed a contract to buy oak lumber from a French supplier for the coming two years. The contract calls for PBI to pay the supplier in euros (€), although all other costs that PBI incurs are paid for in dollars. A summary of the production cost for one barrel, based on the expected production level, follows:

Variable costs:	
French oak	$100*
All other variable costs	150
Fixed costs:	50

*Based on the exchange rate at the time the contract with the French supplier was signed. The cost of lumber in euros was €77.50 as of January 2009.

The exchange rate between the dollar and the euro was $1.33 = €1.00 in January 2009 when the contract was signed. By September 2009, the exchange rate had changed to $1.48 = €1.00.

Required

a. CVP analysis is based on several assumptions. Explain which of these assumptions would be violated as a result of PBI having to pay for one of its raw materials in euros while its other costs and revenues are priced in dollars.

b. What effect, if any, would the change in the exchange rate have on PBI's variable cost per unit for September versus January 2009?

c. What effect, if any, would the change in the exchange rate have on PBI's contribution margin per unit for September versus January 2009?

d. What effect, if any, would the change in the exchange rate have on PBI's fixed cost per unit for September versus January 2009?

LO 5

Exercise 3-15A   *Target costing*

The marketing manager of Ross Corporation has determined that a market exists for a telephone with a sales price of $19 per unit. The production manager estimates the annual fixed costs of producing between 40,000 and 80,000 telephones would be $344,000.

Required

Assume that Ross desires to earn a $116,000 profit from the phone sales. How much can Ross afford to spend on variable cost per unit if production and sales equal 46,000 phones?

LO 10

Exercise 3-16A   *Multiple product break-even analysis*

Eaton Company manufactures two products. The budgeted per-unit contribution margin for each product follows:

	Super	Supreme
Sales price	$100	$125
Variable cost per unit	(65)	(74)
Contribution margin per unit	$ 35	$ 51

Eaton expects to incur annual fixed costs of $145,160. The relative sales mix of the products is 80 percent for Super and 20 percent for Supreme.

Required

a. Determine the total number of products (units of Super and Supreme combined) Eaton must sell to break even.

b. How many units each of Super and Supreme must Eaton sell to break even?

PROBLEMS—SERIES A

All applicable Problems in Series A are available with McGraw-Hill's *Connect Accounting*.

LO 1, 2, 3

e*X*cel

Problem 3-17A   *Determining the break-even point and preparing a contribution margin income statement*

Inman Manufacturing Company makes a product that it sells for $60 per unit. The company incurs variable manufacturing costs of $24 per unit. Variable selling expenses are $12 per unit, annual fixed manufacturing costs are $189,000, and fixed selling and administrative costs are $141,000 per year.

Required

Determine the break-even point in units and dollars using each of the following approaches:

a. Equation method.

b. Contribution margin per unit.

c. Contribution margin ratio.
d. Confirm your results by preparing a contribution margin income statement for the break-even sales volume.

Problem 3-18A   *Determining the break-even point and preparing a break-even graph*

LO 1, 2, 3, 7

Whitaker Company is considering the production of a new product. The expected variable cost is $48.75 per unit. Annual fixed costs are expected to be $650,000. The anticipated sales price is $65 each.

CHECK FIGURE
a. $2,600,000

Required

Determine the break-even point in units and dollars using each of the following:

a. Equation method.
b. Contribution margin per unit approach.
c. Contribution margin ratio approach.
d. Prepare a break-even graph to illustrate the cost-volume-profit relationships.

Problem 3-19A   *Effect of converting variable to fixed costs*

LO 2, 4, 6

Yule Manufacturing Company reported the following data regarding a product it manufactures and sells. The sales price is $42.

CHECK FIGURE
b. 19,000 units

Variable costs	
Manufacturing	$18 per unit
Selling	6 per unit
Fixed costs	
Manufacturing	$150,000 per year
Selling and administrative	66,000 per year

Required

a. Use the per-unit contribution margin approach to determine the break-even point in units and dollars.
b. Use the per-unit contribution margin approach to determine the level of sales in units and dollars required to obtain a profit of $126,000.
c. Suppose that variable selling costs could be eliminated by employing a salaried sales force. If the company could sell 20,000 units, how much could it pay in salaries for salespeople and still have a profit of $126,000? (*Hint:* Use the equation method.)

Problem 3-20A   *Analyzing change in sales price using the contribution margin ratio*

LO 3, 6

Hugh Company reported the following data regarding the product it sells:

CHECK FIGURE
c. 9,000 units

Sales price	$40
Contribution margin ratio	15%
Fixed costs	$144,000

Required

Use the contribution margin ratio approach and consider each requirement separately.

a. What is the break-even point in dollars? In units?
b. To obtain a profit of $36,000, what must the sales be in dollars? In units?
c. If the sales price increases to $50 and variable costs do not change, what is the new break-even point in dollars? In units?

LO 1, 6

CHECK FIGURE

a. 8,000 units

Problem 3-21A   *Analyzing sales price and fixed cost using the equation method*

Tainan Company is considering adding a new product. The cost accountant has provided the following data.

Expected variable cost of manufacturing	$47 per unit
Expected annual fixed manufacturing costs	$78,000

The administrative vice president has provided the following estimates.

Expected sales commission	$3 per unit
Expected annual fixed administrative costs	$42,000

The manager has decided that any new product must at least break even in the first year.

Required

Use the equation method and consider each requirement separately.

a. If the sales price is set at $65, how many units must Tainan sell to break even?
b. Tainan estimates that sales will probably be 10,000 units. What sales price per unit will allow the company to break even?
c. Tainan has decided to advertise the product heavily and has set the sales price at $66. If sales are 9,000 units, how much can the company spend on advertising and still break even?

LO 8

CHECK FIGURES

b. NI:
  Skin Cream $60,000
  Bath Oil $60,000
  Color Gel $40,000

Problem 3-22A   *Margin of safety and operating leverage*

Santiago Company is considering the addition of a new product to its cosmetics line. The company has three distinctly different options: a skin cream, a bath oil, or a hair coloring gel. Relevant information and budgeted annual income statements for each of the products follow.

	Skin Cream	Bath Oil	Color Gel
Relevant Information			
Budgeted sales in units (a)	50,000	90,000	30,000
Expected sales price (b)	$7.00	$4.00	$13.00
Variable costs per unit (c)	$4.00	$1.50	$9.00
Income statements			
Sales revenue (a × b)	$350,000	$360,000	$390,000
Variable costs (a × c)	(200,000)	(135,000)	(270,000)
Contribution margin	150,000	225,000	120,000
Fixed costs	(120,000)	(210,000)	(104,000)
Net income	$ 30,000	$ 15,000	$ 16,000

Required

a. Determine the margin of safety as a percentage for each product.
b. Prepare revised income statements for each product, assuming a 20 percent increase in the budgeted sales volume.
c. For each product, determine the percentage change in net income that results from the 20 percent increase in sales. Which product has the highest operating leverage?
d. Assuming that management is pessimistic and risk averse, which product should the company add to its cosmetic line? Explain your answer.
e. Assuming that management is optimistic and risk aggressive, which product should the company add to its cosmetics line? Explain your answer.

LO 2, 4, 6, 7, 8

Problem 3-23A   *Comprehensive CVP analysis*

Borysko Company makes and sells products with variable costs of $47 each. Borysko incurs annual fixed costs of $22,400. The current sales price is $63.

Required

The following requirements are interdependent. For example, the $4,800 desired profit introduced in Requirement *c* also applies to subsequent requirements. Likewise, the $55 sales price introduced in Requirement *d* applies to the subsequent requirements.

a. Determine the contribution margin per unit.

b. Determine the break-even point in units and in dollars. Confirm your answer by preparing an income statement using the contribution margin format.

c. Suppose that Borysko desires to earn a $4,800 profit. Determine the sales volume in units and dollars required to earn the desired profit. Confirm your answer by preparing an income statement using the contribution margin format.

d. If the sales price drops to $55 per unit, what level of sales is required to earn the desired profit? Express your answer in units and dollars. Confirm your answer by preparing an income statement using the contribution margin format.

e. If fixed costs drop to $16,800, what level of sales is required to earn the desired profit? Express your answer in units and dollars. Confirm your answer by preparing an income statement using the contribution margin format.

f. If variable cost drops to $39 per unit, what level of sales is required to earn the desired profit? Express your answer in units and dollars. Confirm your answer by preparing an income statement using the contribution margin format.

g. Assume that Borysko concludes that it can sell 1,350 units of product for $55 each. Recall that variable costs are $39 each and fixed costs are $16,800. Compute the margin of safety in units and dollars and as a percentage.

h. Draw a break-even graph using the cost and price assumptions described in Requirement *g.*

Problem 3-24A *Assessing simultaneous changes in CVP relationships*

LO 6, 7, 8, 9

Braun Corporation sells hammocks; variable costs are $75 each, and the hammocks are sold for $125 each. Braun incurs $240,000 of fixed operating expenses annually.

Required

a. Determine the sales volume in units and dollars required to attain a $60,000 profit. Verify your answer by preparing an income statement using the contribution margin format.

b. Braun is considering implementing a quality improvement program. The program will require a $10 increase in the variable cost per unit. To inform its customers of the quality improvements, the company plans to spend an additional $10,000 for advertising. Assuming that the improvement program will increase sales to a level that is 4,000 units above the amount computed in Requirement *a,* should Braun proceed with plans to improve product quality? Support your answer by preparing a budgeted income statement.

c. Determine the new break-even point in units and sales dollars as well as the margin of safety percentage, assuming that the quality improvement program is implemented.

d. Prepare a break-even graph using the cost and price assumptions outlined in Requirement *c.*

Problem 3-25A *Determining the break-even point and margin of safety for a company with multiple products*

LO 10

eXcel

Tottori Company produces two products. Budgeted annual income statements for the two products are provided here:

	Power			Lite			Total	
	Budgeted Number	Per Unit	Budgeted Amount	Budgeted Number	Per Unit	Budgeted Amount	Budgeted Number	Budgeted Amount
Sales	160	@ $500 =	$80,000	640	@ $450 =	$288,000	800	$368,000
Variable cost	160	@ 320 =	(51,200)	640	@ 330 =	(211,200)	800	(262,400)
Contribution margin	160	@ 180 =	28,800	640	@ 120 =	76,800	800	105,600
Fixed cost			(12,000)			(54,000)		(66,000)
Net income			$16,800			$ 22,800		$ 39,600

Required

a. Based on budgeted sales, determine the relative sales mix between the two products.
b. Determine the weighted-average contribution margin per unit.
c. Calculate the break-even point in total number of units.
d. Determine the number of units of each product Tottori must sell to break even.
e. Verify the break-even point by preparing an income statement for each product as well as an income statement for the combined products.
f. Determine the margin of safety based on the combined sales of the two products.

EXERCISES—SERIES B

LO 1

Exercise 3-1B *Equation method*

Jade Corporation manufactures products that it sells for $57 each. Variable costs are $32 per unit, and annual fixed costs are $750,000. Jade desires to earn a profit of $200,000.

Required

a. Use the equation method to determine the break-even point in units and dollars.
b. Determine the sales volume in units and dollars required to earn the desired profit.

LO 2

Exercise 3-2B *Per-unit contribution margin approach*

Kemeth Corporation manufactures products that have variable costs of $43 per unit. Its fixed cost amounts to $84,000. It sells the products for $78 each.

Required

Use the per-unit contribution margin approach to determine the break-even point in units and dollars.

LO 3

Exercise 3-3B *Contribution margin ratio*

Lambert Company incurs annual fixed costs of $960,000. Variable costs for Lambert's product are $36 per-unit, and the sales price is $60 per unit. Lambert desires to earn a profit of $240,000.

Required

Use the contribution margin ratio approach to determine the sales volume in dollars and units required to earn the desired profit.

LO 4, 6

Exercise 3-4B *Cost structure, risk, and the break-even point*

Wava Company manufactures a product that sells for $125 per unit. It incurs fixed costs of $198,000. Variable cost for its product is $81 per unit.

Required

a. Determine the sales volume in units and dollars required to earn the desired profit.
b. Calculate the break-even point assuming fixed costs increase to $308,000.
c. Explain how a fixed cost structure affects risk and the break-even point.

LO 5

Exercise 3-5B *Prestige pricing*

Weng Company is considering the production and sale of a new product with fixed costs of $35,000 and variable cost of $4 per unit. Based on its normal profit margins, Weng desires to earn a $40,000 profit and believes it can sell 5,000 units of the product.

Required

a. Based on this information determine the target sales price.
b. Explain how prestige pricing could be used to increase profitability.

Exercise 3-6B   *Determining variable cost from incomplete data*   **LO 6**

Sohail Corporation produced 80,000 tires and sold them for $100 each during 2011. The company determined that fixed manufacturing cost per unit was $25 per tire. The company reported gross profit of $1,440,000 on its 2011 financial statements.

Required

Determine the variable cost per unit, the total variable cost, and the total contribution margin.

Exercise 3-7B   *Contribution margin per unit approach for break-even and*   **LO 2, 4**
                     desired profit

Information concerning a product produced by Agar Company appears here:

Sales price per unit	$420
Variable cost per unit	$270
Total fixed manufacturing and operating costs	$750,000

Required

Determine the following:

a. Contribution margin per unit.
b. Number of units Agar must sell to break even.
c. Sales level in units that Agar must reach in order to earn a profit of $150,000.

Exercise 3-8B   *Changing sales price*   **LO 6**

Mendez Company manufactures a product that has a variable cost of $30 per unit. The company's fixed costs total $750,000. Mendez had net income of $90,000 in the previous year. Its product sells for $50 per unit. In an effort to increase the company's market share, management is considering lowering the product's selling price to $46 per unit.

Required

If Mendez desires to maintain net income of $90,000, how many additional units must it sell in order to justify the price decline?

Exercise 3-9B   *Simultaneous change in sales price and desired profit*   **LO 4, 6**

Use the cost data presented in Exercise 3-8B but assume that in addition to increasing its market share by lowering its selling price to $46, Mendez desires to increase its net income by $42,000.

Required

Determine the number of units that Mendez must sell to earn the desired income.

Exercise 3-10B   *Components of break-even graph*   **LO 1, 7**

Jimmy, a 10-year-old boy, wants to sell lemonade on a hot summer day. He hopes to make enough money to buy a new iPod. Sam, his elder brother, tries to help him compute his prospect of doing so. The following is the relevant information:

Variable costs	
Lemonade	$0.30 per cup
Paper cups	$0.10 per cup
Fixed costs	
Table and chair	$36.00
Price	$1.00 per cup

The following graph depicts the dollar amount of cost or revenue on the vertical axis and the number of lemonade cups sold on the horizontal axis.

Required

a. Draw a line that depicts the total cost.
b. Draw a line that depicts the total revenue.
c. Identify the break-even point.
d. Identify the area representing profit.
e. Identify the area representing loss.

LO 6

Exercise 3-11B   *Evaluating simultaneous changes in fixed and variable costs*

Kasmira Company currently produces and sells 10,000 units of a telephone per year that has a variable cost of $13 per unit and a fixed cost of $380,000. The company currently earns a $120,000 annual profit. Assume that Kasmira has the opportunity to invest in a new machine that will enable the company to reduce variable costs to $10 per unit. The investment would cause fixed costs to increase by $15,000.

Required

a. Use the equation method to determine the sales price per unit under existing conditions (current machine is used).
b. Prepare a contribution margin income statement assuming Kasmira invests in the new technology. Recommend whether Kasmira should invest in the new technology.

LO 8

Exercise 3-12B   *Margin of safety*

Conway Company manufactures scanners that sell for $250 each. The company pays $130 per unit for the variable costs of the product and incurs fixed costs of $3,600,000. Conway expects to sell 54,000 scanners.

Required

Determine Conway's margin of safety expressed as a percentage.

LO 1, 2, 4, 6

Exercise 3-13B   *Cost-volume-profit relationship*

Dalton Corporation manufactures faucets. The variable costs of production are $27 per faucet. Fixed costs of production are $600,000. Dalton sells the faucets for a price of $52 per unit.

Required

a. How many faucets must Dalton make and sell to break even?
b. How many faucets must Dalton make and sell to earn a $180,000 profit?
c. The marketing manager believes that sales would increase dramatically if the price were reduced to $47 per unit. How many faucets must Dalton make and sell to earn a $180,000 profit, assuming the sales price is set at $47 per unit?

LO 6

Exercise 3-14B   *Complexities of CVP analysis in multinational companies*

Castillo Wood Products (CWP) manufactures disposable chopsticks for the restaurant industry at its highly automated production facility in China. The main raw material used to produce the chopsticks is wood that is purchased in bulk from suppliers in the United States. In September

2007, the company signed a contract to buy wood from a U.S. supplier for the coming two years. The contract calls for CWP to pay the supplier in dollars, although all other costs CWP incurs are paid for in Chinese Renminbi (¥). A summary of the production costs for a box of 1,000 sets of chopsticks, based on the expected production level, follows:

Variable costs:	
Wood	¥6,000*
All other variable costs	600
Fixed costs:	5,400

*Based on the exchange rate at the time the contract with the U.S. supplier was signed. The cost of wood in dollars was $50 as of January 2007.

The exchange rate between the yen and the dollar was ¥100 = $13.24 in September 2007 when the contract was signed. By September 2009, the exchange rate had changed to ¥100 = $14.65. (Exchange rates are rounded to the nearest cent.)

Required

a. CVP analysis is based on several assumptions. Explain which of these assumptions would be violated as a result of CWP having to pay for one of its raw materials in dollars while its other costs and revenues are priced in yen.

b. What effect, if any, would the change in the exchange rate have on CWP's variable cost per unit for September 2007 versus September 2009?

c. What effect, if any, would the change in the exchange rate have on CWP's contribution margin per unit for September 2007 versus September 2009?

d. What effect, if any, would the change in the exchange rate have on CWP's fixed cost per unit for September 2007 versus September 2009?

Exercise 3-15B *Target costing*

LO 5

After substantial marketing research, Ewing Corporation management believes that it can make and sell a new battery with a prolonged life for laptop computers. Management expects the market demand for its new battery to be 12,000 units per year if the battery is priced at $90 per unit. A team of engineers and accountants determines that the fixed costs of producing 8,000 units to 16,000 units is $480,000.

Required

Assume that Ewing desires to earn a $240,000 profit from the battery sales. How much can it afford to spend on the variable cost per unit if production and sales equal 12,000 batteries?

Exercise 3-16B *Multiple product break-even analysis*

LO 10

Harvey Company makes two products. The budgeted per-unit contribution margin for each product follows:

	Deluxe	Luxury
Sales price	$48	$75
Variable cost per unit	33	40
Contribution margin per unit	$15	$35

Harvey expects to incur fixed costs of $115,000. The relative sales mix of the products is 60 percent for Deluxe and 40 percent for Luxury.

Required

a. Determine the total number of products (units of Deluxe and Luxury combined) Harvey must sell to break even.

b. How many units each of Deluxe and Luxury must Harvey sell to break even?

PROBLEMS—SERIES B

LO 1, 2, 3

Problem 3-17B   *Determining the break-even point and preparing a contribution margin income statement*

Nickolas Company manufactures radio and cassette players and sells them for $100 each. According to the company's records, the variable costs, including direct labor and direct materials, are $50. Factory depreciation and other fixed manufacturing costs are $192,000 per year. Nickolas pays its salespeople a commission of $18 per unit. Annual fixed selling and administrative costs are $128,000.

Required

Determine the break-even point in units and dollars, using each of the following:

a. Equation method.
b. Contribution margin per unit approach.
c. Contribution margin ratio approach.
d. Confirm your results by preparing a contribution margin income statement for the break-even point sales volume.

LO 1, 2, 3, 7

Problem 3-18B   *Determining the break-even point and preparing a break-even graph*

Executive officers of Vaclar Company are assessing the profitability of a potential new product. They expect that the variable cost of making the product will be $54 per unit and fixed manufacturing cost will be $720,000. The executive officers plan to sell the product for $72 per unit.

Required

Determine the break-even point in units and dollars using each of the following approaches:

a. Contribution margin per unit.
b. Equation method.
c. Contribution margin ratio.
d. Prepare a break-even graph to illustrate the cost-volume-profit relationships.

LO 2, 3, 4, 6

Problem 3-19B   *Effect of converting variable to fixed costs*

Souta Company manufactures and sells its own brand of digital cameras. It sells each camera for $32. The company's accountant prepared the following data:

Manufacturing costs	
Variable	$15 per unit
Fixed	$150,000 per year
Selling and administrative expenses	
Variable	$9 per unit
Fixed	$50,000 per year

Required

a. Use the per-unit contribution margin approach to determine the break-even point in units and dollars.
b. Use the per-unit contribution margin approach to determine the level of sales in units and dollars required to obtain a $60,000 profit.
c. Suppose that variable selling and administrative costs could be eliminated by employing a salaried sales force. If the company could sell 32,000 units, how much could it pay in salaries for the salespeople and still have a profit of $60,000? (*Hint:* Use the equation method.)

Problem 3-20B *Analyzing change in sales price using the contribution margin ratio*   LO 3, 6

Kaito Company reported the following data regarding the one product it sells:

Sales price	$16
Contribution margin ratio	20%
Fixed costs	$360,000 per year

Required

Use the contribution margin ratio approach and consider each requirement separately.

a. What is the break-even point in dollars? In units?

b. To obtain a $80,000 profit, what must the sales be in dollars? In units?

c. If the sales price increases to $20 and variable costs do not change, what is the new break-even point in units? In dollars?

Problem 3-21B *Analyzing sales price and fixed cost using the equation method*   LO 1, 6

Salazar Company is analyzing whether its new product will be profitable. The following data are provided for analysis:

Expected variable cost of manufacturing	$30 per unit
Expected fixed manufacturing costs	$48,000 per year
Expected sales commission	$6 per unit
Expected fixed administrative costs	$12,000 per year

The company has decided that any new product must at least break even in the first year.

Required

Use the equation method and consider each requirement separately.

a. If the sales price is set at $48, how many units must Salazar sell to break even?

b. Salazar estimates that sales will probably be 6,000 units. What sales price per unit will allow the company to break even?

c. Salazar has decided to advertise the product heavily and has set the sales price at $54. If sales are 9,000 units, how much can the company spend on advertising and still break even?

Problem 3-22B *Margin of safety and operating leverage*   LO 8

Meier Company has three distinctly different options available as it considers adding a new product to its automotive division: engine oil, coolant, or windshield washer. Relevant information and budgeted annual income statements for each product follow:

Relevant Information			
	Engine Oil	Coolant	Windshield Washer
Budgeted sales in units (a)	20,000	30,000	125,000
Expected sales price (b)	$2.40	$2.85	$1.15
Variable costs per unit (c)	$1.00	$1.25	$0.35
Income Statements			
Sales revenue (a × b)	$48,000	$85,500	$143,750
Variable costs (a × c)	(20,000)	(37,500)	(43,750)
Contribution margin	28,000	48,000	100,000
Fixed costs	(21,000)	(32,000)	(50,000)
Net income	$ 7,000	$16,000	$ 50,000

Required

a. Determine the margin of safety as a percentage for each product.

b. Prepare revised income statements for each product, assuming 20 percent growth in the budgeted sales volume.

c. For each product, determine the percentage change in net income that results from the 20 percent increase in sales. Which product has the highest operating leverage?

d. Assuming that management is pessimistic and risk averse, which product should the company add? Explain your answer.

e. Assuming that management is optimistic and risk aggressive, which product should the company add? Explain your answer.

LO 2, 4, 6, 7, 8   **Problem 3-23B**   *Comprehensive CVP analysis*

Dunlop Company makes a product that it sells for $200. Dunlop incurs annual fixed costs of $250,000 and variable costs of $160 per unit.

Required

The following requirements are interdependent. For example, the $50,000 desired profit introduced in Requirement *c* also applies to subsequent requirements. Likewise, the $180 sales price introduced in Requirement *d* applies to the subsequent requirements.

a. Determine the contribution margin per unit.

b. Determine the break-even point in units and in dollars. Confirm your answer by preparing an income statement using the contribution margin format.

c. Suppose that Dunlop desires to earn a $50,000 profit. Determine the sales volume in units and dollars required to earn the desired profit. Confirm your answer by preparing an income statement using the contribution margin format.

d. If the sales price drops to $180 per unit, what level of sales is required to earn the desired profit? Express your answer in units and dollars. Confirm your answer by preparing an income statement using the contribution margin format.

e. If fixed costs drop to $200,000, what level of sales is required to earn the desired profit? Express your answer in units and dollars. Confirm your answer by preparing an income statement using the contribution margin format.

f. If variable costs drop to $130 per unit, what level of sales is required to earn the desired profit? Express your answer in units and dollars. Confirm your answer by preparing an income statement using the contribution margin format.

g. Assume that Dunlop concludes that it can sell 5,000 units of product for $180 each. Recall that variable costs are $130 each and fixed costs are $200,000. Compute the margin of safety in units and dollars and as a percentage.

h. Draw a break-even graph using the cost and price assumptions described in Requirement *g.*

LO 6, 7, 8, 9   **Problem 3-24B**   *Assessing simultaneous changes in CVP relationships*

Haas Company sells tennis racquets; variable costs for each are $45, and each is sold for $135. Haas incurs $540,000 of fixed operating expenses annually.

Required

a. Determine the sales volume in units and dollars required to attain a $270,000 profit. Verify your answer by preparing an income statement using the contribution margin format.

b. Haas is considering establishing a quality improvement program that will require a $15 increase in the variable cost per unit. To inform its customers of the quality improvements, the company plans to spend an additional $150,000 for advertising. Assuming that the improvement program will increase sales to a level that is 5,000 units above the amount computed in Requirement *a*, should Haas proceed with plans to improve product quality? Support your answer by preparing a budgeted income statement.

c. Determine the new break-even point and the margin of safety percentage, assuming Haas adopts the quality improvement program.

d. Prepare a break-even graph using the cost and price assumptions outlined in Requirement *c.*

Problem 3-25B *Determining the break-even point and margin of safety for a company with multiple products*   **LO 10**

Executive officers of Pena Company have prepared the annual budgets for its two products, Washer and Dryer, as follows.

	Washer			Dryer			Total	
	Budgeted Quantity	Per Unit	Budgeted Amount	Budgeted Quantity	Per Unit	Budgeted Amount	Budgeted Quantity	Budgeted Amount
Sales	400	@ $540 =	$216,000	1,200	@ $300 =	$360,000	1,600	$576,000
Variable cost	400	@ 300 =	(120,000)	1,200	@ 180 =	(216,000)	1,600	(336,000)
Contribution margin	400	@ 240 =	96,000	1,200	@ 120 =	144,000	1,600	240,000
Fixed costs			(34,000)			(44,000)		(78,000)
Net income			$ 62,000			$100,000		$162,000

Required

a. Based on the number of units budgeted to be sold, determine the relative sales mix between the two products.

b. Determine the weighted-average contribution margin per unit.

c. Calculate the break-even point in total number of units.

d. Determine the number of units of each product Pena must sell to break even.

e. Verify the break-even point by preparing an income statement for each product as well as an income statement for the combined products.

f. Determine the margin of safety based on the combined sales of the two products.

ANALYZE, THINK, COMMUNICATE

ATC 3-1   Business Applications   *Cost-volume-profit behavior at Apple Inc.*

In July 2009, Apple Inc. announced that its revenues for the third quarter of its 2009 fiscal year rose 11.7 percent, causing its earnings to increase by 14.6 percent compared with the third quarter of 2008. Sales for this period were $8.34 billion.

In July 2007, the company had announced that a 24 percent increase in revenue had produced a 73 percent increase in earnings, compared to the same quarter of the previous year. Sales for the second quarter of 2007 were $5.41 billion.

Required

a. What concept explains how Apple's net income could rise by 14.6 percent when its revenue rose only 11.7 percent?

b. Does the concept identified in Requirement *a* result from fixed costs or variable costs?

c. Notice that in the third quarter of 2007, Apple's percentage increase in earnings was over three times the percentage increase in revenue (73 ÷ 24 = 3.04). In the third quarter of 2009, however, Apple's percentage increase in earnings was only about 1.25 times its increase in revenue (14.6 ÷ 11.7 = 1.25). Explain why the ratio of increase in earnings to increase in revenue was lower in 2009 than in 2007. Assume Apple's general pricing policies and cost structure did not change.

ATC 3-2   Group Assignment   *Effect of changes in fixed and variable cost on profitability*

In a month when it sold 200 units of product, Queen Manufacturing Company (QMC) produced the following internal income statement:

Revenue	$8,000
Variable costs	(4,800)
Contribution margin	3,200
Fixed costs	(2,400)
Net income	$ 800

QMC has the opportunity to alter its operations in one of the following ways:

1. Increasing fixed advertising costs by $1,600, thereby increasing sales by 120 units.
2. Lowering commissions paid to the sales staff by $8 per unit, thereby reducing sales by 10 units.
3. Decreasing fixed inventory holding cost by $800, thereby decreasing sales by 20 units.

Required

a. The instructor will divide the class into groups and then organize the groups into two sections. For a large class (12 or more groups), four sections may be necessary. At least three groups in each section are needed. Having more groups in one section than another section is acceptable because offsetting advantages and disadvantages exist. Having more groups is advantageous because more people will work on the task but is disadvantageous because having more people complicates communication.

Group Task

The sections are to compete with each other to see which section can identify the most profitable alternative in the shortest period of time. No instruction is provided regarding how the sections are to proceed with the task. In other words, each section is required to organize itself with respect to how to accomplish the task of selecting the best alternative. A total quality management (TQM) constraint is imposed that requires zero defects. A section that turns in a wrong answer is disqualified. Once an answer has been submitted to the instructor, it cannot be changed. Sections continue to turn in answers until all sections have submitted a response. The first section to submit the correct answer wins the competition.

b. If any section submits a wrong answer, the instructor or a spokesperson from the winning group should explain how the right answer was determined.

c. Discuss the dynamics of group interaction. How was the work organized? How was leadership established?

ATC 3-3   Research Assignment   *Using real world data from Southwest Airlines*

Use the 2008 Form 10-K for Southwest Airlines to complete the requirements below. To obtain the Form 10-K you can use either the EDGAR system following the instructions in Appendix A, or it can be found under "Investor Relations" which is under the "About Southwest" link on the company's corporate website, www.southwest.com. The company includes its Form 10-K as a part of its 2008 Annual Report. Be sure to read carefully the "Item 6. Selected Financial Data" section of the document.

Required

a. "Item 6. Selected Financial Data," list data for several measures of activity. List the items from this table that might be used by Southwest as an activity base for CVP analysis.

b. Of the activity bases that you identified for Requirement *a*, which do you think would work best for performing CVP at Southwest? Explain the rationale for your choice.

c. Use the "Operating expense" and the "Revenue passenger miles" data from Item 6, to compute the variable cost and fixed cost components of operating expense using the high-low method presented in Chapter 2. *Warning:* the results you get will not seem reasonable, but perform the calculations and report your results.

d. Try to explain the peculiar results you obtained for Requirement *c.* This will require careful thought, and you may wish to review the *Cost-Volume-Profit Limitations* section of this chapter.

e. "Item 6." reports that in 2008 Southwest's "Load factor" was 71.2%. If this load factor could have been increased by 10% to 78.3%, do you think the company's net earnings would have increased by less than 10%, 10%, or more than 10%? Explain.

ATC 3-4 Writing Assignment *Operating leverage, margin of safety, and cost behavior*

In the early years of the 21st century the housing market in the United States was booming. Housing prices were increasing rapidly, new houses were being constructed at a record pace, and companies doing business in the construction and home improvement industry were enjoying rising profits. In 2006 the real estate market had slowed considerably, and the slump continued through 2007.

Home Depot was one major company in the building supplies industry that was adversely affected by the slowdown in the housing market. On August 14, 2007, it announced that its revenues for the first half of the year were 3 percent lower than revenues were for the first six months of 2006. Of even greater concern was the fact that its earnings for the first half of 2007 were 21 percent lower than for the same period in the prior year.

Required

Write a memorandum that explains how a 3 percent decline in sales could cause a 21 percent decline in profits. Your memo should address the following:

a. An identification of the accounting concept involved.

b. A discussion of how various major types of costs incurred by Home Depot were likely affected by the decline in its sales.

c. The effect of the decline in sales on Home Depot's margin of safety.

ATC 3-5 Ethical Dilemma *Opportunity to manipulate earnings*

Sherwin-Williams and PPG Industries are both companies that produce wall coverings, such as paint, among other products. Although they uses similar assets to conduct their businesses, the estimated lives they use to depreciate those assets vary, as shown in the following table:

Asset Category	Estimated Useful Lives	
	PPG Industries	Sherwin-Williams
Buildings	20–40 years	5–40 years
Machinery and equipment	5–25	5–20
Other	3–20	3–10

Managers have significant flexibility in setting the estimated useful lives of depreciable assets, and as the table shows, PPG Industries uses longer estimated lives for its assets than does Sherwin-Williams.

Required

a. How does using a longer estimated life for a depreciable asset potentially affect its earnings?

b. Would using a longer estimated life for a depreciable asset be more likely to affect a company's fixed or variable costs?

c. In the past, some companies, not PPG, have been accused of deliberately overestimating the useful lives of their companies' depreciable assets. Speculate as to what would cause them to do this.

d. Review the standards of ethical conduct shown in Exhibit 1.15 of Chapter 1 and comment on which, if any, of the ethical standards are violated by deliberately overestimating the useful lives of depreciable assets.

e. Comment on the provisions of the Sarbanes-Oxley Act that are designed to prevent a company's executives from deliberately overestimating the useful lives of depreciable assets.

ATC 3-6 Spreadsheet Assignment *Using Excel*

Bishop Company has provided the estimated data that appear in rows 4 to 8 of the following spreadsheet:

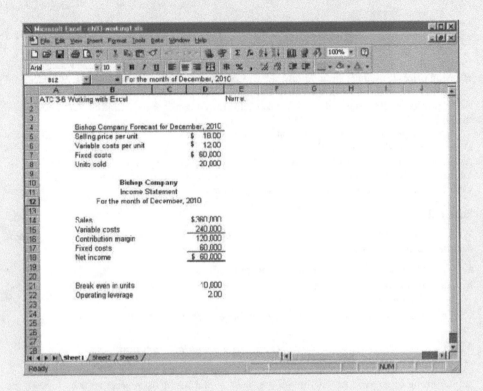

Required

Construct a spreadsheet as follows that would allow you to determine net income, break-even in units, and operating leverage for the estimates at the top of the spreadsheet, and to see the effects of changes to the estimates. Set up this spreadsheet so that any change in the estimates will automatically be reflected in the calculation of net income, break-even, and operating leverage.

Spreadsheet Tip

To center a heading across several columns, such as the Income Statement title, highlight the area to be centered (Columns B, C, and D), choose Format, then choose Cells, and click on the tab titled Alignment. Near the bottom of the alignment window, place a check mark in the box titled Merge cells. The shortcut method to merge cells is to click on the icon near the middle of the top icons that contains an *a* in a box.

ATC 3-7   Spreadsheet Assignment   *Mastering Excel*

Required

Build the spreadsheet pictured in Exhibit 3.3. Be sure to use formulas that will automatically calculate profitability if fixed cost, variable cost, or sales volume is changed.

Spreadsheet Tip

1. The shading in column D and in row 6 can be inserted by first highlighting a section to be shaded, choosing Format from the main menu, then Cells, and then clicking on the tab titled Patterns, and then choosing a color for the shading. The shortcut method to accomplish the shading is to click on the fill color icon (it looks like a tipped bucket and is in the upper right area of the screen).

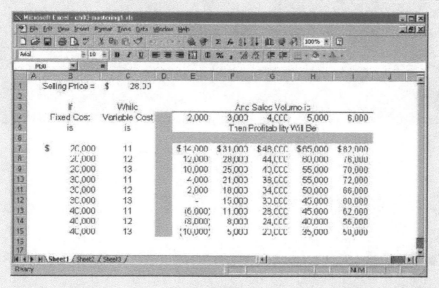

2. Similar to basic math rules, the order of calculation within a formula is multiplication and division before addition and subtraction. Therefore, if you wish to subtract variable cost from selling price and multiply the difference by units sold, the formula must be = (28 − C8)*E5.

3. The quickest way to get the correct formulas in the area of E8 to I16 is to place the proper formula in cell E8 and then copy this formula to the entire block of E8:I16. However, the formulas must use the $ around the cell addresses to lock either the row or the column, or both. For example, the formula = 2*B8 can be copied to any other cell and the cell reference will remain B8 because the $ symbol locks the row and column. Likewise, $B8 indicates that only the column is locked, and B$8 indicates that only the row is locked.

COMPREHENSIVE PROBLEM

Use the same transaction data for Magnificant Modems, Inc., as was used in Chapter 1. (See page 52.)

Required

a. Use the following partially completed form to prepare an income statement using the contribution margin format.

Sales revenue	$600,000
Variable costs:	
Contribution margin	225,000
Fixed costs	
Net income	$31,050

b. Determine the break-even point in units and in dollars.

c. Assume that next year's sales are budgeted to be the same as the current year's sales. Determine the margin of safety expressed as a percentage.

CHAPTER 4

Cost Accumulation, Tracing, and Allocation

LEARNING OBJECTIVES

After you have mastered the material in this chapter, you will be able to:

1 Identify cost objects and cost drivers.

2 Distinguish direct costs from indirect costs.

3 Allocate indirect costs to cost objects.

4 Select appropriate cost drivers for allocating indirect costs.

5 Allocate costs to solve timing problems.

6 Explain the benefits and detriments of allocating pooled costs.

7 Allocate joint product costs.

8 Recognize the effects of cost allocation on employee motivation.

9 Allocate service department costs to operating departments (Appendix).

CHAPTER OPENING

What does it cost? This is one of the questions most frequently asked by business managers. Managers must have reliable cost estimates to price products, evaluate performance, control operations, and prepare financial statements. As this discussion implies, managers need to know the cost of many different things. The things we are trying to determine the cost of are commonly called **cost objects.** For example, if we are trying to determine the cost of operating a department, that department is the cost object. Cost objects may be products, processes, departments, services, activities, and so on. This chapter explains techniques managerial accountants use to determine the cost of a variety of cost objects.

The Curious Accountant

A former patient of a California hospital complained about being charged $7 for a single aspirin tablet. After all, an entire bottle of 100 aspirins can be purchased at the local pharmacy store for around $2.

Can you think of any reasons, other than shameless profiteering, that a hospital would need to charge $7 for an aspirin? Remember that the hospital is not just selling the aspirin; it is also delivering it to the patient. (Answer on page 159.)

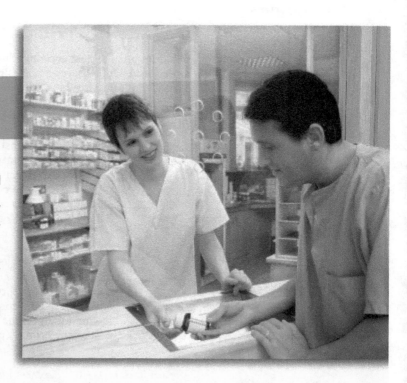

DETERMINE THE COST OF COST OBJECTS

Identify cost objects and cost drivers.

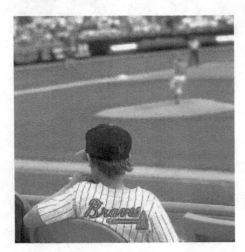

Accountants use **cost accumulation** to determine the cost of a particular object. Suppose the Atlanta Braves advertising manager wants to promote a Tuesday night ball game by offering free baseball caps to all children who attend. What would be the promotion cost? The team's accountant must *accumulate* many individual costs and add them together. For simplicity consider only three cost components: (1) the cost of the caps, (2) the cost of advertising the promotion, and (3) the cost of an employee to work on the promotion.

Cost accumulation begins with identifying the cost objects. The primary cost object is the cost of the promotion. Three secondary cost objects are (1) the cost of caps, (2) the cost of advertising, and (3) the cost of labor. The costs of the secondary cost objects are combined to determine the cost of the primary cost object.

Determining the costs of the secondary cost objects requires identifying what *drives* those costs. A **cost driver** has a *cause-and-effect* relationship with a cost object. For example, the *number of caps* (cost driver) has an effect on the *cost of caps* (cost object). The *number of advertisements* is a cost driver for the *advertising cost* (cost object); the *number of labor hours* worked is a cost driver for the *labor cost* (cost object). Using the following assumptions about unit costs and cost drivers, the accumulated cost of the primary cost object (cost of the cap promotion) is:

Cost Object	Cost Per Unit	×	Cost Driver	=	Total Cost of Object
Cost of caps	$2.50	×	4,000 Caps	=	$10,000
Cost of advertising	$100.00	×	50 Advertisements	=	5,000
Cost of labor	$8.00	×	100 Hours	=	800
Cost of cap promotion					$15,800

The Atlanta Braves should run the promotion if management expects it to produce additional revenues exceeding $15,800.

Estimated versus Actual Cost

The accumulated cost of the promotion—$15,800—is an *estimate.* Management cannot know *actual* costs and revenues until after running the promotion. While actual information is more accurate, it is not relevant for deciding whether to run the promotion because the decision must be made before the actual cost is known. Managers must accept a degree of inaccuracy in exchange for the relevance of timely information. Many business decisions are based on estimated rather than actual costs.

Managers use cost estimates to set prices, bid on contracts, evaluate proposals, distribute resources, plan production, and set goals. Certain circumstances, however, require actual cost data. For example, published financial reports and managerial performance evaluations use actual cost data. Managers frequently accumulate both estimated and actual cost data for the same cost object. For example, companies use cost estimates to establish goals and use actual costs to evaluate management performance in meeting those goals. The following discussion provides a number of business examples that use estimated data, actual data, or a combination of both.

ASSIGNMENT OF COSTS TO OBJECTS IN A RETAIL BUSINESS

Exhibit 4.1 displays the January income statement for In Style, Inc. (ISI), a retail clothing store. ISI subdivides its operations into women's, men's, and children's departments. To encourage the departmental managers to maximize sales, ISI began

paying the manager of each department a bonus based on a percentage of departmental sales revenue.

Although the bonus incentive increased sales revenue, it also provoked negative consequences. The departmental managers began to argue over floor space; each manager wanted more space to display merchandise. The managers reduced prices; they increased sales commissions. In the drive to maximize sales, the managers ignored the need to control costs. To improve the situation, the store manager decided to base future bonuses on each department's contribution to profitability rather than its sales revenue.

IDENTIFYING DIRECT AND INDIRECT COSTS

The new bonus strategy requires determining the cost of operating each department. Each department is a separate *cost object*. Assigning costs to the departments (cost objects) requires **cost tracing** and **cost allocation.** *Direct costs* can be easily traced to a cost object. *Indirect costs* cannot be easily traced to a cost object. Whether or not a cost is easily traceable requires *cost/benefit analysis*.

LO 2

Distinguish direct costs from indirect costs.

Some of ISI's costs can be easily traced to the cost objects (specific departments). The cost of goods sold is an example of an easily traced cost. Price tags on merchandise can be coded so cash register scanners capture the departmental code for each sale. The cost of goods sold is not only easily traceable but also very useful information. Companies need cost of goods sold information for financial reporting (income statement and balance sheet) and for management decisions (determining inventory reorder points, pricing strategies, and cost control). Because the cost of tracing *cost of goods sold* is small relative to the benefits obtained, cost of goods sold is a *direct cost.*

In contrast, the cost of supplies (shopping bags, sales slips, pens, staples, price tags) used by each department is much more difficult to trace. How could the number of staples used to seal shopping bags be traced to any particular department? The sales staff could count the number of staples used, but doing so would be silly for the benefits obtained. Although tracing the cost of supplies to each department may be possible, it is not worth the effort of doing so. The cost of supplies is therefore an *indirect cost*. Indirect costs are also called **overhead costs.**

Direct and indirect costs can be described as follows:

EXHIBIT 4.1

Income Statement

IN STYLE, INC.
Income Statement
For the Month Ended January 31

Sales	$360,000
Cost of goods sold	(216,000)
Gross margin	144,000
Sales commissions	(18,000)
Dept. managers' salaries	(12,000)
Store manager's salary	(9,360)
Depreciation	(16,000)
Rental fee for store	(18,400)
Utilities	(2,300)
Advertising	(7,200)
Supplies	(900)
Net income	$ 59,840

> **Direct costs** can be traced to cost objects in a *cost-effective* manner.
> **Indirect costs** cannot be traced to objects in a *cost-effective* manner.

By analyzing the accounting records, ISI's accountant classified the costs from the income statement in Exhibit 4.1 as direct or indirect, as shown in Exhibit 4.2. The next paragraph explains the classifications.

All figures represent January costs. Items 1 though 4 are direct costs, traceable to the cost objects in a cost-effective manner. Cost of goods sold is traced to departments at the point of sale using cash register scanners. Sales commissions are based on a percentage of departmental sales and are therefore easy to trace to the departments. Departmental managers' salaries are also easily traceable to the departments. Equipment, furniture, and fixtures are tagged with department codes that permit tracing depreciation charges directly to specific departments. Items 5 through 8 are incurred on behalf of the company as a whole and are therefore not directly traceable to a specific department.

EXHIBIT 4.2

Income Statement Classification of Costs

Cost Item	Direct Costs			Indirect Costs
	Women's	Men's	Children's	
1. Cost of goods sold—$216,000	$120,000	$58,000	$38,000	
2. Sales commissions—$18,000	9,500	5,500	3,000	
3. Dept. managers' salaries—$12,000	5,000	4,200	2,800	
4. Depreciation—$16,000	7,000	5,000	4,000	
5. Store manager's salary				$ 9,360
6. Rental fee for store				18,400
7. Utilities				2,300
8. Advertising				7,200
9. Supplies				900
Totals	$141,500	$72,700	$47,800	$38,160

Although Item 9 could be traced to specific departments, the cost of doing so would exceed the benefits. The cost of supplies is therefore also classified as indirect.

Cost Classifications—Independent and Context Sensitive

Whether a cost is direct or indirect is independent of whether it is fixed or variable. In the ISI example, both cost of goods sold and the cost of supplies vary relative to sales volume (both are variable costs), but cost of goods sold is direct and the cost of supplies is indirect. Furthermore, the cost of rent and the cost of depreciation are both fixed relative to sales volume, but the cost of rent is indirect and the cost of depreciation is direct. In fact, the very same cost can be classified as direct or indirect, depending on the cost object. The store manager's salary is not directly traceable to a specific department, but it is traceable to a particular store. As these examples demonstrate, cost classification depends on the context in which the costs occur.

ALLOCATING INDIRECT COSTS TO OBJECTS

LO 3

Allocate indirect costs to cost objects.

Common costs support multiple cost objects, but cannot be directly traced to any specific object. In the case of In Style, Inc., the cost of renting the store (common cost) supports the women's, men's, and children's departments (cost objects). The departmental managers may shirk responsibility for the rental cost by claiming that others higher up the chain of command are responsible. Responsibility can be motivated at the departmental level by assigning (*allocating*) a portion of the total rental cost to each department.

To accomplish appropriate motivation, authority must accompany responsibility. In other words, the departmental managers should be held responsible for a portion of rental cost only if they are able to exercise some degree of control over that cost. For example, if managers are assigned a certain amount of the rental cost for each square foot of space they use, they should have the authority to establish the size of the space used by their departments. **Controllable costs** are costs that can be influenced by a manager's decisions and actions. The controllability concept is discussed in more detail in Chapter 9.

Cost **allocation** involves dividing a total cost into parts and assigning the parts to designated cost objects. How should ISI allocate the $38,160 of indirect costs to each of the three departments? First, identify a cost driver for each cost to be allocated. For example, there is a cause-and-effect relationship between store size and rent cost;

REALITY BYTES

How does Southwest Airlines know the cost of flying a passenger from Houston, Texas, to Los Angeles, California? The fact is that Southwest does not know the actual cost of flying particular passengers anywhere. There are many indirect costs associated with flying passengers. Some of these include the cost of planes, fuel, pilots, office buildings, and ground personnel. Indeed, besides insignificant food and beverage costs, there are few costs that could be traced directly to customers. Southwest and other airlines are forced to use allocation and averaging to determine the estimated cost of providing transportation services to customers. Estimated rather than actual cost is used for decision-making purposes.

Consider that in its 2008 annual report Southwest reported the average operating expenses of flying one passenger one mile (called a *passenger mile*) were 10.2¢. However, this number was based on 103.3 billion "available passenger miles." In 2008 Southwest operated at 71.2 percent of capacity, not 100 percent, so it was only able to charge passengers for 73.5 billion passenger miles. Thus, its average operating expenses were closer to 14.4¢ for each mile for which they were able to charge. Had they operated at a higher capacity, their average costs would have been lower.

---

the larger the building, the higher the rent cost. This relationship suggests that the more floor space a department occupies, the more rent cost that department should bear. To illustrate, assume ISI's store capacity is 23,000 square feet and the women's, men's, and children's departments occupy 12,000, 7,000, and 4,000 square feet, respectively. ISI can achieve a rational allocation of the rent cost using the following two-step process.[1]

Step 1. Compute the *allocation rate* by dividing the *total cost to be allocated* ($18,400 rental fee) by the *cost driver* (23,000 square feet of store space). *The cost driver is also called the* **allocation base.** This computation produces the **allocation rate,** as follows:

Total cost to be allocated ÷ Cost driver (allocation base) = Allocation rate

$18,400 rental fee ÷ 23,000 square feet = $0.80 per square foot

Step 2. Multiply the *allocation rate* by the *weight of the cost driver* (weight of the base) to determine the allocation *per cost object*, as follows:

Cost Object	Allocation Rate	×	Number of Square Feet	=	Allocation per Cost Object
Women's department	$0.80	×	12,000	=	$ 9,600
Men's department	0.80	×	7,000	=	5,600
Children's department	0.80	×	4,000	=	3,200
Total			23,000		$18,400

[1]Other mathematical approaches achieve the same result. This text consistently uses the two-step method described here. Specifically, the text determines allocations by (1) computing a *rate* and (2) multiplying the *rate* by the *weight of the base* (cost driver).

It is also plausible to presume utilities cost is related to the amount of floor space a department occupies. Larger departments will consume more heating, lighting, air conditioning, and so on than smaller departments. Floor space is a reasonable cost driver for utility cost. Based on square footage, ISI can allocate utility cost to each department as follows:

Step 1. Compute the allocation rate by dividing the total cost to be allocated ($2,300 utility cost) by the cost driver (23,000 square feet of store space):

Total cost to be allocated ÷ Cost driver = Allocation rate

$2,300 utility cost ÷ 23,000 square feet = $0.10 per square foot

Step 2. Multiply the *allocation rate* by the *weight of the cost driver* to determine the allocation *per cost object:*

Cost Object	Allocation Rate	×	Number of Square Feet	=	Allocation per Cost Object
Women's department	$0.10	×	12,000	=	$1,200
Men's department	0.10	×	7,000	=	700
Children's department	0.10	×	4,000	=	400
Total			23,000		$2,300

✓ CHECK YOURSELF 4.1

HealthCare, Inc., wants to estimate the cost of operating the three departments (Dermatology, Gynecology, and Pediatrics) that serve patients in its Health Center. Each department performed the following number of patient treatments during the most recent year of operation: Dermatology, 2,600; Gynecology, 3,500; and Pediatrics, 6,200. The annual salary of the Health Center's program administrator is $172,200. How much of the salary cost should HealthCare allocate to the Pediatrics Department?

Answer

Step 1 Compute the *allocation rate.*

Total cost to be allocated ÷ Cost driver (patient treatments) = Allocation rate

$172,200 salary cost ÷ (2,600 + 3,500 + 6,200) = $14 per patient treatment

Step 2 Multiply the *allocation rate* by the *weight of the cost driver* (weight of the base) to determine the allocation per *cost object.*

Cost Object	Allocation Rate	×	No. of Treatments	=	Allocation per Cost Object
Pediatrics department	$14	×	6,200	=	$86,800

SELECTING A COST DRIVER

Companies can frequently identify more than one cost driver for a particular indirect cost. For example, ISI's shopping bag cost is related to both the *number of sales transactions* and the *volume of sales dollars*. As either of these potential cost drivers increases, shopping bag usage also increases. The most useful cost driver is the one with the strongest cause-and-effect relationship.

Consider shopping bag usage for T-shirts sold in the children's department versus T-shirts sold in the men's department. Assume ISI studied T-shirt sales during the first week of June and found the following:

Department	Children's	Men's
Number of sales transactions	120	92
Volume of sales dollars	$1,440	$1,612

Given that every sales transaction uses a shopping bag, the children's department uses far more shopping bags than the men's department even though it has a lower volume of sales dollars. A reasonable explanation for this circumstance is that children's T-shirts sell for less than men's T-shirts. The number of sales transactions is the better cost driver because it has a stronger cause-and-effect relationship with shopping bag usage than does the volume of sales dollars. Should ISI therefore use the number of sales transactions to allocate supply cost to the departments? Not necessarily.

The *availability of information* also influences cost driver selection. While the number of sales transactions is the more accurate cost driver, ISI could not use this allocation base unless it maintains records of the number of sales transactions per department. If the store tracks the volume of sales dollars but not the number of transactions, it must use dollar volume even if the number of transactions is the better cost driver. For ISI, sales volume in dollars appears to be the best *available* cost driver for allocating supply cost.

Assuming that sales volume for the women's, men's, and children's departments was $190,000, $110,000, and $60,000, respectively, ISI can allocate the supplies cost as follows:

Step 1. Compute the allocation rate by dividing the total cost to be allocated ($900 supplies cost) by the cost driver ($360,000 total sales volume):

Total cost to be allocated ÷ Cost driver = Allocation rate

$900 supplies cost ÷ $360,000 sales volume = $0.0025 per sales dollar

Step 2. Multiply the allocation rate by the weight of the cost driver to determine the allocation per cost object:

Cost Object	Allocation Rate	×	Sales Volume	=	Allocation per Cost Object
Women's department	$0.0025	×	$190,000	=	$475
Men's department	0.0025	×	110,000	=	275
Children's department	0.0025	×	60,000	=	150
Total			$360,000		$900

ISI believes sales volume is also the appropriate allocation base for advertising cost. The sales generated in each department were likely influenced by the general advertising campaign. ISI can allocate advertising cost as follows:

Step 1. Compute the allocation rate by dividing the total cost to be allocated ($7,200 advertising cost) by the cost driver ($360,000 total sales volume):

Total cost to be allocated ÷ Cost driver = Allocation rate

$7,200 advertising cost ÷ $360,000 sales volume = $0.02 per sales dollar

Step 2. Multiply the allocation rate by the weight of the cost driver to determine the allocation per cost object:

Cost Object	Allocation Rate	×	Sales Volume	=	Allocation per Cost Object
Women's department	$0.02	×	$190,000	=	$3,800
Men's department	0.02	×	110,000	=	2,200
Children's department	0.02	×	60,000	=	1,200
Total			$360,000		$7,200

There is no strong cause-and-effect relationship between the store manager's salary and the departments. ISI pays the store manager the same salary regardless of sales level, square footage of store space, number of labor hours, or any other identifiable variable. Because no plausible cost driver exists, ISI must allocate the store manager's salary arbitrarily. Here the manager's salary is simply divided equally among the departments as follows:

Step 1. Compute the allocation rate by dividing the total cost to be allocated ($9,360 manager's monthly salary) by the allocation base (number of departments):

Total cost to be allocated   ÷   Cost driver   =   Allocation rate

$9,360 store manager's salary ÷ 3 departments = $3,120 per department

Step 2. Multiply the allocation rate by the weight of the cost driver to determine the allocation per cost object:

Cost Object	Allocation Rate	×	Number of Departments	=	Allocation per Cost Object
Women's department	$3,120	×	1	=	$3,120
Men's department	3,120	×	1	=	3,120
Children's department	3,120	×	1	=	3,120
Total			3		$9,360

As the allocation of the store manager's salary demonstrates, many allocations are arbitrary or based on a weak relationship between the allocated cost and the allocation base (cost driver). Managers must use care when making decisions using allocated costs.

Behavioral Implications

Using the indirect cost allocations just discussed, Exhibit 4.4 shows the profit each department generated in January. ISI paid the three departmental managers bonuses based on each department's contribution to profitability. The store manager noticed an immediate change in the behavior of the departmental managers. For example, the manager of the women's department offered to give up 1,000 square feet of floor space because she believed reducing the selection of available products would not reduce sales significantly. Customers would simply buy different brands. Although sales would not decline dramatically, rent and utility cost allocations to the women's department would decline, increasing the profitability of the department.

Answers to The Curious Accountant

When we compare the cost that a hospital charges for an aspirin to the price we pay for an aspirin, we are probably not considering the full cost that we incur to purchase aspirin. If someone asks you what you pay for an aspirin, you would probably take the price of a bottle, say $2, and divide it by the number of pills in the bottle, say 100. This would suggest their cost is $0.02 each. Now, consider what it cost to buy the aspirins when all costs are considered. First, there is your time to drive to the store; what do you get paid per hour? Then, there is the cost of operating your automobile. You get the idea; in reality, the cost of an aspirin, from a business perspective, is much more than just the cost of the pills themselves.

Exhibit 4.3 shows the income statement of Hospital Corporation of America (HCA) for three recent years. HCA claims to be " . . . one of the leading health care services companies in the United States." In 2008 it operated 271 facilities in 20 states and England. As you can see, while it generated over $28 billion in revenue, it also incurred a lot of expenses. Look at its first two expense categories. Although it incurred $4.6 billion in supplies expenses, it incurred almost two and a half times this amount in compensation expense. In other words, it cost a lot more to have someone deliver the aspirin to your bed than the aspirin itself costs.

In 2008 HCA earned $673 million from its $28.4 billion in revenues. This is a return on sales percentage of 2.4 percent ($.673 ÷ $28.4). Therefore, on a $7 aspirin, HCA would earn 17 cents of profit, which is still not a bad profit for selling one aspirin. As a comparison, in 2008, Walgreens return on sales was 3.7 percent.

EXHIBIT 4.3

HCA, INC.
Consolidated Income Statements
for the Years Ended December 31, 2008, 2007, and 2006
(Dollars in millions, except per share amounts)

	2008	2007	2006
Revenues	$28,374	$26,858	$25,477
Salaries and benefits	11,440	10,714	10,409
Supplies	4,620	4,395	4,322
Other operating expenses	4,554	4,241	4,056
Provision for doubtful accounts	3,409	3,130	2,660
Gains on investments		(8)	(243)
Equity in earnings of affiliates	(223)	(206)	(197)
Depreciation and amortization	1,416	1,426	1,391
Interest expense	2,021	2,215	955
Gains on sales of facilities	(97)	(471)	(205)
Transaction costs			442
Impairment of long-lived assets	64	24	24
Total expenses	27,204	25,460	23,614
Income before minority interests and income taxes	1,170	1,398	1,863
Minority interests in earnings of consolidated entities	229	208	201
Income before income taxes	941	1,190	1,662
Provision for income taxes	268	316	626
Net income	$ 673	$ 874	$ 1,036

EXHIBIT 4.4

Profit Analysis by Department

	Department			
	Women's	Men's	Children's	Total
Sales	$190,000	$110,000	$60,000	$360,000
Cost of goods sold	(120,000)	(58,000)	(38,000)	(216,000)
Sales commissions	(9,500)	(5,500)	(3,000)	(18,000)
Dept. managers' salary	(5,000)	(4,200)	(2,800)	(12,000)
Depreciation	(7,000)	(5,000)	(4,000)	(16,000)
Store manager's salary	(3,120)	(3,120)	(3,120)	(9,360)
Rental fee for store	(9,600)	(5,600)	(3,200)	(18,400)
Utilities	(1,200)	(700)	(400)	(2,300)
Advertising	(3,800)	(2,200)	(1,200)	(7,200)
Supplies	(475)	(275)	(150)	(900)
Departmental profit	$ 30,305	$ 25,405	$ 4,130	$ 59,840

In contrast, the manager of the children's department wanted the extra space. He believed the children's department was losing sales because it did not have enough floor space to display a competitive variety of merchandise. Customers came to the store to shop at the women's department, but they did not come specifically for children's wear. With additional space, the children's department could carry items that would draw customers to the store specifically to buy children's clothing. He believed the extra space would increase sales enough to cover the additional rent and utility cost allocations.

The store manager was pleased with the emphasis on profitability that resulted from tracing and assigning costs to specific departments.

EFFECTS OF COST BEHAVIOR ON SELECTING THE MOST APPROPRIATE COST DRIVER

Select appropriate cost drivers for allocating indirect costs.

As previously mentioned, indirect costs may exhibit variable or fixed cost behavior patterns. Failing to consider the effects of cost behavior when allocating indirect costs can lead to significant distortions in product cost measurement. We examine the critical relationships between cost behavior and cost allocation in the next section of the text.

Using Volume Measures to Allocate Variable Overhead Costs

A *causal relationship* exists between variable overhead product costs (indirect materials, indirect labor, inspection costs, utilities, etc.) and the volume of production. For example, the cost of indirect materials such as glue, staples, screws, nails, and varnish will increase or decrease in proportion to the number of desks a furniture manufacturing company makes. *Volume measures are good cost drivers* for allocating variable overhead costs.

Volume can be expressed by such measures as the number of units produced, the number of labor hours worked, or the amount of *direct* materials used in production. Given the variety of possible volume measures, how does management identify the most appropriate cost driver (allocation base) for assigning particular overhead costs? Consider the case of Filmier Furniture Company.

Using Units as the Cost Driver

During the most recent year, Filmier Furniture Company produced 4,000 chairs and 1,000 desks. It incurred $60,000 of *indirect materials* cost during the period. How much of this cost should Filmier allocate to chairs versus desks? Using number of units as the cost driver produces the following allocation:

Step 1. Compute the allocation rate.

Total cost to be allocated ÷ Cost driver = Allocation rate

$60,000 indirect materials cost ÷ 5,000 units = $12 per unit

Step 2. Multiply the allocation rate by the weight of the cost driver to determine the allocation per cost object.

Product	Allocation Rate	×	Number of Units Produced	=	Allocated Cost
Desks	$12	×	1,000	=	$12,000
Chairs	12	×	4,000	=	48,000
Total			5,000	=	$60,000

Using Direct Labor Hours as the Cost Driver

Using the number of units as the cost driver assigns an *equal amount* ($12) of indirect materials cost to each piece of furniture. However, if Filmier uses more indirect materials to make a desk than to make a chair, assigning the same amount of indirect materials cost to each is inaccurate. Assume Filmier incurs the following direct costs to make chairs and desks:

	Desks	Chairs	Total
Direct labor hours	3,500 hrs.	2,500 hrs.	6,000 hrs.
Direct materials cost	$1,000,000	$500,000	$1,500,000

Both direct labor hours and direct materials cost are volume measures that indicate Filmier uses more indirect materials to make a desk than a chair. It makes sense that the amount of direct labor used is related to the amount of indirect materials used. Because production workers use materials to make furniture, it is plausible to assume that the more hours they work, the more materials they use. Using this reasoning, Filmier could assign the indirect materials cost to the chairs and desks as follows:

Step 1. Compute the allocation rate.

Total cost to be allocated ÷ Cost driver = Allocation rate

$60,000 indirect materials cost ÷ 6,000 hours = $10 per hour

Step 2. Multiply the allocation rate by the weight of the cost driver.

Product	Allocation Rate	×	Number of Labor Hours	=	Allocated Cost
Desks	$10.00	×	3,500	=	$35,000
Chairs	10.00	×	2,500	=	25,000
Total			6,000	=	$60,000

Basing the allocation on labor hours rather than number of units assigns a significantly larger portion of the indirect materials cost to desks ($35,000 versus $12,000). Is this allocation more accurate? Suppose the desks, but not the chairs, require elaborate, labor-intensive carvings. A significant portion of the labor is then not related to consuming indirect materials (glue, staples, screws, nails, and varnish). It would therefore be inappropriate to allocate the indirect materials cost based on direct labor hours.

Using Direct Material Dollars as the Cost Driver

If labor hours is an inappropriate allocation base, Filmier can consider direct material usage, measured in material dollars, as the allocation base. It is likely that the more lumber (direct material) Filmier uses, the more glue, nails, and so forth (indirect materials) it uses. It is reasonable to presume direct materials usage drives indirect materials usage. Using direct materials dollars as the cost driver for indirect materials produces the following allocation:

Step 1.   Compute the allocation rate.

$$\text{Total cost to be allocated} \div \text{Cost driver} = \text{Allocation rate}$$

$$\begin{array}{c} \$60{,}000 \text{ indirect} \\ \text{materials cost} \end{array} \div \begin{array}{c} \$1{,}500{,}000 \text{ direct} \\ \text{material dollars} \end{array} = \begin{array}{c} \$0.04 \text{ per direct} \\ \text{material dollar} \end{array}$$

Step 2.   Multiply the allocation rate by the weight of the cost driver.

Product	Allocation Rate	×	Number of Direct Material Dollars	=	Allocated Cost
Desks	$0.04	×	$1,000,000	=	$40,000
Chairs	0.04	×	500,000	=	20,000
Total			$1,500,000	=	$60,000

Selecting the Best Cost Driver

Which of the three volume-based cost drivers (units, labor hours, or direct material dollars) results in the most accurate allocation of the overhead cost? Management must use judgment to decide. In this case, direct material dollars appears to have the most convincing relationship to indirect materials usage. If the cost Filmier was allocating were fringe benefits, however, direct labor hours would be a more appropriate cost driver. If the cost Filmier was allocating were machine maintenance cost, a different volume-based cost driver, machine hours, would be an appropriate base. The most accurate allocations of indirect costs may actually require using multiple cost drivers.

✓ CHECK YOURSELF 4.2

Boston Boat Company builds custom sailboats for customers. During the current accounting period, the company built five different-sized boats that ranged in cost from $35,000 to $185,000. The company's manufacturing overhead cost for the period was $118,000. Would you recommend using the number of units (boats) or direct labor hours as the base for allocating the overhead cost to the five boats? Why?

Answer   Using the number of units as the allocation base would assign the same amount of overhead cost to each boat. Since larger boats require more overhead cost (supplies, utilities, equipment, etc.) than smaller boats, there is no logical link between the number of boats and the amount of overhead cost required to build a particular boat. In contrast, there is a logical link between direct labor hours used and overhead cost incurred. The more labor used, the more supplies, utilities, equipment, and so on used. Since larger boats require more direct labor than smaller boats, using direct labor hours as the allocation base would allocate more overhead cost to larger boats and less overhead cost to smaller boats, producing a logical overhead allocation. Therefore, Boston should use direct labor hours as the allocation base.

Allocating Fixed Overhead Costs

Fixed costs present a different cost allocation problem. By definition, the volume of production does not drive fixed costs. Suppose Lednicky Bottling Company rents its manufacturing facility for $28,000 per year. The rental cost is fixed regardless of how much product Lednicky bottles. However, Lednicky may still use a volume-based cost driver as the allocation base. The object of allocating fixed costs to products is to distribute a *rational share* of the overhead cost to each product. Selecting an allocation base that spreads total overhead cost equally over total production often produces a rational distribution. For example, assume Lednicky produced 2,000,000 bottles of apple juice during 2011. If it sold 1,800,000 bottles of the juice during 2011, how much of the $28,000 of rental cost should Lednicky allocate to ending inventory and how much to cost of goods sold? A rational allocation follows:

Step 1.   Compute the allocation rate.

Total cost to be allocated ÷ Allocation base (cost driver) =   Allocation rate

$28,000 rental cost   ÷   2,000,000 units   = $0.014 per bottle of juice

Because the base (number of units) used to allocate the cost does not drive the cost, it is sometimes called an *allocation base* instead of a *cost driver*. However, many managers use the term cost driver in conjunction with fixed cost even though that usage is technically inaccurate. The terms allocation base and cost driver are frequently used interchangeably.

Step 2.   Multiply the allocation rate by the weight of the cost driver.

Financial Statement Item	Allocation Rate	×	Number of Bottles	=	Allocated Cost
Inventory	$0.014	×	200,000	=	$ 2,800
Cost of goods sold	0.014	×	1,800,000	=	25,200

Using number of units as the allocation base assigns equal amounts of the rental cost to each unit of product. Equal allocation is appropriate so long as the units are homogeneous. If the units are not identical, however, Lednicky may need to choose a different allocation base to rationally distribute the rental cost. For example, if some of the bottles are significantly larger than others, Lednicky may find using some physical measure, like liters of direct material used, to be a more appropriate allocation base. Whether an indirect cost is fixed or variable, selecting the most appropriate allocation base requires sound reasoning and judgment.

ALLOCATING COSTS TO SOLVE TIMING PROBLEMS

LO 5

Allocate costs to solve timing problems.

Under certain circumstances products may be made before or after the costs associated with making them have been incurred. Suppose, for example, premiums for an annual insurance policy are paid in March. The insurance cost benefits the products made in the months before and after March as well as those produced in March. Allocation can be used to spread the insurance cost over products made during the entire accounting period rather than charging the total cost only to products made in March.

Monthly fluctuations in production volume complicate fixed cost allocations. To illustrate, assume Grave Manufacturing pays its production supervisor a monthly salary of $3,000. Furthermore, assume Grave makes 800 units of product in January and 1,875 in February. How much salary cost should Grave assign to the products made in January and February, respectively? The allocation seems simple. Just divide the $3,000 monthly salary cost by the number of units of product made each month as follows:

January $3,000 ÷   800 units = $3.75 cost per unit

February $3,000 ÷ 1,875 units = $1.60 cost per unit

If Grave Manufacturing based a cost-plus pricing decision on these results, it would price products made in January significantly higher than products made in February. It is likely such price fluctuations would puzzle and drive away customers. Grave needs an allocation base that will spread the annual salary cost evenly over annual production. A timing problem exists, however, because Grave must allocate the salary cost before the end of the year. In order to price its products, Grave needs to know the allocated amount before the actual cost information is available. Grave can manage the timing problem by using estimated rather than actual costs.

Grave Manufacturing can *estimate* the annual cost of the supervisor's salary (indirect labor) as $36,000 ($3,000 × 12 months). The *actual* cost of indirect labor may differ because the supervisor might receive a pay raise or be replaced with a person who earns less. Based on current information, however, $36,000 is a reasonable estimate of the annual indirect labor cost. Grave must also estimate total annual production volume. Suppose Grave produced 18,000 units last year and expects no significant change in the current year. It can allocate indirect labor cost for January and February as follows:

Step 1.   Compute the allocation rate.

Total cost to be allocated ÷ Allocation base = Allocation rate
(cost driver)

$36,000   ÷ 18,000 units   = $2.00 per unit

Step 2.   Multiply the rate by the weight of the base (number of units per month) to determine how much of the salary cost to allocate to each month's production.

Month	Allocation Rate	×	Number of Units Produced	=	Allocation per Month
January	$2.00	×	800	=	$1,600
February	2.00	×	1,875	=	3,750

Grave Manufacturing will add these indirect cost allocations to other product costs to determine the total estimated product cost to use in cost-plus pricing or other managerial decisions.

Because the overhead allocation rate is determined *before* actual cost and volume data are available, it is called the **predetermined overhead rate.** Companies use predetermined overhead rates for product costing estimates and pricing decisions during a year, but they must use actual costs in published year-end financial statements. If necessary, companies adjust their accounting records at year-end when they have used estimated data on an interim basis. The procedures for making such adjustments are discussed in a later chapter.

AGGREGATING AND DISAGGREGATING INDIVIDUAL COSTS INTO COST POOLS

Allocating *individually* every single indirect cost a company incurs would be tedious and not particularly useful relative to the benefit obtained. Instead, companies frequently accumulate many individual costs into a single **cost pool.** The total of the pooled cost is then allocated to the cost objects. For example, a company may accumulate costs for gas, water, electricity, and telephone service into a single utilities cost pool. It would then allocate the total cost in the utilities cost pool to the cost objects rather than individually allocating each of the four types of utility costs.

How far should pooling costs go? Why not pool utility costs with indirect labor costs? If the forces driving the utility costs are different from the forces driving the labor costs, pooling the costs will likely reduce the reliability of any associated cost allocations. To promote accuracy, pooling should be limited to costs with common cost drivers.

Costs that have been pooled for one purpose may require disaggregation for a different purpose. Suppose all overhead costs are pooled for the purpose of determining the cost of making a product. Further, suppose that making the product requires two processes that are performed in different departments. A cutting department makes heavy use of machinery to cut raw materials into product parts. An assembly department uses human labor to assemble the parts into a finished product. Now suppose the objective changes from determining the cost of making the product to determining the cost of operating each department. Under these circumstances, it may be necessary to disaggregate the total overhead cost into smaller pools such as a utility cost pool, an indirect labor cost pool, and so on so that different drivers can be used to allocate these costs to the two departments.

ALLOCATING JOINT COSTS

Joint costs are common costs incurred in the process of making two or more **joint products.** The cost of raw milk is a joint cost of producing the joint products cream, whole milk, 2 percent milk, and skim milk. Joint costs include not only materials costs but also the labor and overhead costs of converting the materials into separate products. The point in the production process at which products become separate and identifiable is the **split-off point.** For financial reporting of inventory and cost of goods sold, companies must allocate the joint costs to the separate joint products. Some joint products require additional processing after the split-off point. Any additional materials, labor, or overhead costs incurred after the split-off point are assigned to the specific products to which they relate.

To illustrate, assume Westar Chemical Company produces from common raw materials the joint products Compound AK and Compound AL. Compound AL requires further processing before Westar can sell it. The diagram in Exhibit 4.5 illustrates the joint product costs.

EXHIBIT 4.5

Allocation of Joint Cost

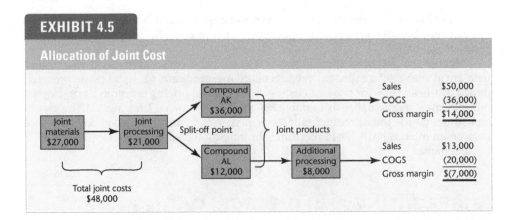

The joint costs of producing a batch of the two compounds are $48,000, representing $27,000 of materials cost and $21,000 of processing cost. A batch results in 3,000 gallons of Compound AK and 1,000 gallons of Compound AL. Westar allocates joint costs to the products based on the number of gallons produced, as follows:

Step 1.   Compute the allocation rate.

$$\text{Total cost to be allocated} \div \text{Allocation base} = \text{Allocation rate}$$

$$\$48,000 \text{ joint costs} \div 4,000 \text{ gallons} = \$12 \text{ per gallon}$$

Step 2.   Multiply the allocation rate by the weight of the base.

Joint Product	Allocation Rate	×	Number of Gallons Produced	=	Allocated Cost
Compound AK	$12	×	3,000	=	$36,000
Compound AL	12	×	1,000	=	12,000

Westar sells 3,000 gallons of Compound AK for $50,000, and 1,000 gallons of Compound AL for $13,000. Exhibit 4.5 shows the gross margins for each product using the joint cost allocations computed above.

Relative Sales Value as the Allocation Base

Because Compound AL shows a $7,000 loss, a manager might mistakenly conclude that Westar should stop making and selling this product. If Westar stops making Compound AL, the total joint cost ($48,000) would be assigned to Compound AK and total gross margin would decline as shown below.

	With Compound AL		Without Compound AL
Sales	$63,000	($50,000 + $13,000)	$50,000
Cost of goods sold	(56,000)	($36,000 + $20,000)	(48,000)
Gross margin	$ 7,000		$ 2,000

To avoid the appearance that a product such as Compound AL is producing losses, many companies allocate joint cost to products based on the relative sales value of each product at the split-off point. Westar Chemical would allocate all of the joint costs to Compound AK because Compound AL has no market value at the split-off point. The resulting gross margins follow.

	Compound AK	Compound AL
Sales	$50,000	$13,000
Cost of goods sold	(48,000)	(8,000)
Gross margin	$ 2,000	$ 5,000

Westar's total profit on the joint products is $7,000 whether it allocates the joint costs using gallons or relative market value. However, using market value as the allocation base produces a positive gross margin for both products, reducing the likelihood that a manager will mistakenly eliminate a product that is contributing to profitability.

✓ CHECK YOURSELF 4.3

What are some logical split-off points for a meat processing company engaged in butchering beef?

Answer   The first logical split-off point occurs when processing separates the hide (used to produce leather) from the carcass. Other split-off points occur as further processing produces different cuts of meat (T-bone and New York strip steaks, various roasts, chops, ground chuck, etc.).

COST ALLOCATION: THE HUMAN FACTOR

Cost allocations significantly affect individuals. They may influence managers' performance evaluations and compensation. They may dictate the amount of resources various departments, divisions, and other organizational subunits receive. Control over resources usually offers managers prestige and influence over organization operations. The following scenario illustrates the emotional impact and perceptions of fairness of cost allocation decisions.

Recognize the effects of cost allocation on employee motivation.

Using Cost Allocations in a Budgeting Decision

Sharon Southport, dean of the School of Business at a major state university, is in dire need of a budgeting plan. Because of cuts in state funding, the money available to the School of Business for copying costs next year will be reduced substantially. Dean Southport supervises four departments: management, marketing, finance, and accounting. The Dean knows the individual department chairpersons will be unhappy and frustrated with the deep cuts they face.

Using Cost Drivers to Make Allocations

To address the allocation of copying resources, Dean Southport decided to meet with the department chairs. She explained that the total budgeted for copying costs will be $36,000. Based on past usage, department allocations would be as follows: $12,000 for management, $10,000 for accounting, $8,000 for finance, and $6,000 for marketing.

Dr. Bill Thompson, the management department chair, immediately protested that his department could not operate on a $12,000 budget for copy costs. Management has more faculty members than any other department. Dr. Thompson argued that copy costs are directly related to the number of faculty members, so copy funds should be allocated based on the number of faculty members. Dr. Thompson suggested that number of faculty members rather than past usage should be used as the allocation base.

Since the School of Business has 72 faculty members (29 in management, 16 in accounting, 12 in finance, and 15 in marketing), the allocation should be as follows:

Step 1. Compute the allocation rate.

Total cost to be allocated ÷ Cost driver = Allocation rate

$36,000 ÷ 72 = $500 per faculty member

Step 2. Multiply the rate by the weight of the driver (the number of faculty per department) to determine the allocation per object (department).

Department	Allocation Rate	×	Number of Faculty	=	Allocation per Department	Allocation Based on Past Usage
Management	$500	×	29		$14,500	$12,000
Accounting	500	×	16		8,000	10,000
Finance	500	×	12		6,000	8,000
Marketing	500	×	15		7,500	6,000
Total					$36,000	$36,000

Seeing these figures, Dr. Bob Smethers, chair of the accounting department, questioned the accuracy of using the number of faculty members as the cost driver. Dr. Smethers suggested the number of *students* rather than the number of *faculty members* drives the cost of copying. He argued that most copying results from duplicating syllabi, exams, and handouts. The accounting department teaches mass sections of introductory accounting that have extremely high student/teacher ratios. Because his department teaches more students, it spends more on copying costs even though it has fewer faculty members. Dr. Smethers recomputed the copy cost allocation as follows:

Step 1. Compute the allocation rate based on number of students. University records indicate that the School of Business taught 1,200 students during the most recent academic year. The allocation rate (copy cost per student) follows.

Total cost to be allocated ÷ Cost driver = Allocation rate

$36,000 ÷ 1,200 = $30 per student

Step 2. Multiply the rate by the weight of the driver (number of students taught by each department) to determine the allocation per object (department).

Department	Allocation Rate	×	Number of Students	=	Allocation per Department	Allocation Based on Past Usage
Management	$30	×	330		$ 9,900	$12,000
Accounting	30	×	360		10,800	10,000
Finance	30	×	290		8,700	8,000
Marketing	30	×	220		6,600	6,000
Total					$36,000	$36,000

Choosing the Best Cost Driver

Dr. Thompson objected vigorously to using the number of students as the cost driver. He continued to argue that the size of the faculty is a more appropriate allocation base. The chair of the finance department sided with Dr. Smethers, the chair of the marketing department kept quiet, and the dean had to settle the dispute.

Dean Southport recognized that the views of the chairpersons were influenced by self-interest. The allocation base affects the amount of resources available to each department. Furthermore, the dean recognized that the size of the faculty does drive some of the copying costs. For example, the cost of copying manuscripts that faculty submit for publication relates to faculty size. The more articles faculty submit, the higher the copying cost. Nevertheless, the dean decided the number of students has the most significant impact on copying costs. She also wanted to encourage faculty members to minimize the impact of funding cuts on student services. Dean Southport therefore decided to allocate copying costs based on the number of students taught by each department. Dr. Thompson stormed angrily out of the meeting. The dean developed a budget by assigning the available funds to each department using the number of students as the allocation base.

Controlling Emotions

Dr. Thompson's behavior may relieve his frustration but it doesn't indicate clear thinking. Dean Southport recognized that Dr. Thompson's contention that copy costs were related to faculty size had some merit. Had Dr. Thompson offered a compromise rather than an emotional outburst, he might have increased his department's share of the funds. Perhaps a portion of the allocation could have been based on the number of faculty members with the balance allocated based on the number of students. Had Dr. Thompson controlled his anger, the others might have agreed to compromise. Technical expertise in computing numbers is of little use without the interpersonal skills to persuade others. Accountants may provide numerical measurements, but they should never forget the impact of their reports on the people in the organization.

A Look Back

Managers need to know the costs of products, processes, departments, activities, and so on. The target for which accountants attempt to determine cost is a *cost object*. Knowing the cost of specific objects enables management to control costs, evaluate performance, and price products. *Direct costs* can be cost-effectively traced to a cost object. *Indirect costs* cannot be easily traced to designated cost objects.

The same cost can be direct or indirect, depending on the cost object to which it is traced. For example, the salary of a Burger King restaurant manager can be directly traced to a particular store but cannot be traced to particular food items made and sold in the store. Classifying a cost as direct or indirect is independent of whether the cost behaves as fixed or variable; it is also independent of whether the cost is relevant to a given decision. A direct cost could be either fixed or variable or either relevant or irrelevant, depending on the context and the designated cost object.

Indirect costs are assigned to cost objects using *cost allocation*. Allocation divides an indirect cost into parts and distributes the parts among the relevant cost objects. Companies frequently allocate costs to cost objects in proportion to the *cost drivers* that cause the cost to be incurred. The first step in allocating an indirect cost is to determine the allocation rate by dividing the total cost to be allocated by the chosen cost driver. The next step is to multiply the allocation rate by the amount of the cost driver for a particular object. The result is the amount of indirect cost to assign to the cost object.

A particular indirect cost may be related to more than one driver. The best cost driver is the one that most accurately reflects the amount of the resource used by the cost object. Objects that consume the most resources should be allocated a proportionately greater share of the costs. If no suitable cost driver exists, companies may use arbitrary allocations such as dividing a total cost equally among cost objects.

Cost allocations have behavioral implications. Using inappropriate cost drivers can distort allocations and lead managers to make choices that are detrimental to the company's profitability.

The joint costs incurred in the process of making two or more products are allocated among the products at the *split-off point,* the point at which products become separate and identifiable. The allocation base can be the products' relative sales values or some quantity measure of the amount of each product made. If one of the joint products requires additional processing costs to bring it to market, only these additional processing costs are relevant to a decision about whether to undertake further processing. The allocated joint costs are not relevant because they will be incurred whether or not the joint product is processed after the split-off point. By-products share common costs with other products but have an insignificant market value relative to their joint products.

>> A Look Forward

The failure to accurately allocate indirect costs to cost objects can result in misinformation that impairs decision making. The next chapter explains how increased use of automation in production has caused distortion in allocations determined using traditional approaches. The chapter introduces the allocation of indirect costs using more recently developed activity-based costing and explains how activity-based management can improve efficiency and productivity. Finally, the chapter introduces total quality management, a strategy that seeks to minimize the costs of conforming to a designated standard of quality.

APPENDIX

Allocating Service Center Costs

LO 9

Allocate service department costs to operating departments.

Most organizations establish departments responsible for accomplishing specific tasks. Departments that are assigned tasks leading to the accomplishment of the primary objectives of the organization are called **operating departments.** Those that provide support to operating departments are called **service departments.** For example, the department of accounting at a university is classified as an operating department because its faculty perform the university's primary functions of teaching, research, and service. In contrast, the maintenance department is classified as a service department because its employees provide janitorial services that support primary university functions. Professors are more likely to be motivated to perform university functions when facilities are clean, but the university's primary purpose is not to clean buildings. Similarly, the lending department in a bank is an operating department and the personnel department is a service department. The bank is in the business of making loans. Hiring employees is a secondary function that assists the lending activity.

The costs to produce a product (or a service) include both operating and service department costs. Therefore, service department costs must somehow be allocated to the products produced (or services provided). Service department costs are frequently distributed to products through a two-stage allocation process. First-stage allocations involve the distribution of costs from service center cost pools to operating department cost pools. In the second stage, costs in the operating cost pools are allocated to products. Three different approaches can be used to allocate costs in the first stage of the two-stage costing process: the *direct method,* the *step method,* and the *reciprocal method.*

Direct Method

The **direct method** is the simplest allocation approach. It allocates service department costs directly to operating department cost pools. To illustrate, assume that Candler & Associates is a law firm that desires to determine the cost of handling each case. The firm has two operating departments, one that represents clients in civil suits and the other that defends clients in criminal cases. The two operating departments are supported by two service departments, personnel and secretarial support. Candler uses a two-stage allocation system to allocate the service centers' costs to the firm's legal cases. In the first stage, the costs to operate each service department are accumulated in separate cost pools. For example, the costs to operate the personnel department are $80,000 in salary, $18,000 in office rental, $12,000 in depreciation, $3,000 in supplies, and $4,000 in miscellaneous costs. These costs are added together in a single services department cost pool amounting to $117,000. Similarly, the costs incurred by the secretarial department are accumulated in a cost pool. We assume that this cost pool contains $156,800 of accumulated costs. The amounts in these cost pools are then allocated to the operating departments' cost pools. The appropriate allocations are described in the following paragraphs.

Assume that Candler's accountant decides that the number of attorneys working in the two operating departments constitutes a rational cost driver for the allocation of the personnel department cost pool and that the number of request forms submitted to the secretarial department constitutes a rational cost driver for the allocation of costs accumulated in the secretarial department cost pool. The total number of attorneys working in the two operating departments is 18, 11 in the civil department and 7 in the criminal department. The secretarial department received 980 work request forms with 380 from the civil department and 600 from the criminal department. Using these cost drivers as the allocation bases, the accountant made the following first-stage allocations.

Determination of Allocation Rates

$$\text{Allocation rate for personnel department cost pool} = \frac{\$117,000}{18} = \$6,500 \text{ per attorney}$$

$$\text{Allocation rate for secretarial department cost pool} = \frac{\$156,800}{980} = \$160 \text{ per request form}$$

EXHIBIT 4.6

First-Stage Allocations for Candler & Associates—Direct Method

Allocated Service Department Overhead	Allocation Rate	×	Weight of Base	=	Civil Department	Criminal Department	Total Service Department Cost Pool
Personnel	$6,500	×	11 attorneys	=	$ 71,500		
	6,500	×	7 attorneys	=		$ 45,500	
Total cost of personnel department							$117,000
Secretarial	160	×	380 requests	=	60,800		
	160	×	600 requests	=		96,000	
Total cost of secretarial department							156,800
Total of cost pools after allocation					132,300	141,500	$273,800
Other operating department overhead costs					785,100	464,788	
Total of operating department overhead cost pools					$917,400	$606,288	

The accountant then multiplied these rates by the weight of the base to determine the amount of each service cost pool to allocate to each operating department cost pool. The appropriate computations are shown in Exhibit 4.6.

As indicated, the allocated service department costs are pooled with other operating department overhead costs to form the operating department cost pools. In the second stage of the costing process, the costs in the operating department cost pools are allocated to the firm's products (cases). To illustrate second-stage allocations, assume that Candler allocates the operating department overhead cost pools on the basis of billable hours. Furthermore, assume that the civil department expects to bill 30,580 hours to its clients and the criminal department expects to bill 25,262 hours. Based on this information, the following predetermined overhead rates are used to allocate operating department cost pools to particular cases.

$$\text{Predetermined overhead rate for the civil department} = \frac{\$917,400}{30,580} = \$30 \text{ per billable hour}$$

$$\text{Predetermined overhead rate for the criminal department} = \frac{\$606,288}{25,262} = \$24 \text{ per billable hour}$$

These rates are used to calculate the amount of operating department cost pools to include in the determination of the cost to litigate specific cases. For example, a case in the civil department that required 300 billable hours of legal service is allocated $9,000 (300 hours × $30 predetermined overhead rate) of overhead cost. Assuming that the direct costs to litigate the case amounted to $25,000, the total cost of this particular case is $34,000 ($25,000 direct cost + $9,000 allocated overhead). This accumulated cost figure could be used as a guide to determine the charge to the client or the profitability of the case.

Step Method

The direct method of allocating service center costs fails to consider the fact that service departments render assistance to other service departments. A service that is performed by one service department for the benefit of another service department is called an **interdepartmental service.** To illustrate this, we return to the case of Candler & Associates. Suppose that Candler's personnel department works with the employees in the secretarial department as well as the attorneys in the civil and criminal operating departments. Under these circumstances, Candler needs a cost approach that recognizes the

EXHIBIT 4.7

Comparison of Direct and Step Allocation Methods

interdepartmental service activity. One such approach is known as the **step method.** The primary difference between the direct method and the step method is depicted graphically in Exhibit 4.7. Focus your attention on the first stage of the allocation process. Notice that the step method includes one additional allocation, specifically from the personnel department cost pool to the secretarial department cost pool. The direct method ignores this interdepartmental service cost allocation. Indeed, the direct method derives its name from the fact that it allocates costs only from service cost pools to operating cost pools.

The fact that the direct method ignores the effect of interdepartmental services may cause distortions in the measurement of cost objects. The primary purpose of the step method is to avoid such distortions, thereby improving the accuracy of product costing. To illustrate this point, consider Candler & Associates. First, note that the interdepartmental portion of the personnel department cost is, in fact, a cost of providing secretarial services. In other words, the personnel service costs could be reduced if the personnel department did not provide service to the secretarial staff. Accordingly, the cost of providing personnel support to the secretarial staff should be included in the secretarial cost pool. Under the direct method, however, the interdepartmental service cost is allocated between the civil and criminal operating departments. This is not a problem in and of itself because the cost of secretarial service is also allocated between the civil and criminal operating departments. Unfortunately, the base used to allocate personnel costs to the operating departments (i.e., number of attorneys) distributes more cost to the civil department than to the criminal department. This is unfortunate because the criminal department uses more secretarial service than the civil department does. In other words, more secretarial cost (i.e., interdepartmental personnel cost) is being allocated to the civil department although the criminal department uses more secretarial services. This means that ultimately the cost to litigate civil cases will be overstated and the cost to litigate criminal cases will be understated.

The step method corrects this distortion by distributing the interdepartmental personnel department cost to the secretarial department cost pool before it is allocated to the operating departments. Because the secretarial cost pool is allocated on the basis of requests for secretarial service, more of the interdepartmental cost will be allocated to the criminal operating deparment. To validate this result, assume that the personnel department cost pool is allocated to the secretarial department cost pool and the two operating department cost pools on the basis of the number of employees in each department. In addition to the 18 attorneys in the firm, assume that two employees work in the secretarial department. Accordingly, the allocation rate for the personnel cost pool is calculated as follows.

$$\text{Allocation rate for personnel department cost pool} = \frac{\$117,000}{20} = \$5,850 \text{ per employee}$$

Based on this rate, the first step in the allocation process distributes the personnel department cost pool as indicated here.

Personnel Cost Pool Allocated to	Allocation Rate		Weight of Base		Allocated Cost
Secretarial	$5,850	×	2 employees	=	$ 11,700
Civil	5,850	×	11 employees	=	64,350
Criminal	5,850	×	7 employees	=	40,950
Total			20 employees		$117,000

The result of the distribution of personnel department costs is shown as the Step 1 allocation in Exhibit 4.8. The $11,700 interdepartmental personnel department cost allocated to the secretarial department cost pool is added to the $156,800 existing balance in that cost pool (See Exhibit 4.8). The result is the accumulation of secretarial cost of $168,500. The second step in the costing process allocates this cost pool to the operating departments. Recall that the secretarial cost pool is allocated on the basis of number of work request forms submitted. Furthermore, recall that 980 request forms were submitted to the secretarial department (380 from the civil department and 600 from the criminal department). Accordingly, the allocation rate for the secretarial department cost pool is computed as follows.

$$\text{Allocation rate for secretarial department cost pool} = \frac{\$168,500}{980} = \$171.93878 \text{ per request form}$$

Based on this rate, the second step in the allocation process distributes the secretarial cost pool as indicated here.

Secretarial Cost Pool Allocated to	Allocation Rate		Weight of Base		Allocated Cost
Civil	$171.93878	×	380 requests	=	$ 65,337
Criminal	171.93878	×	600 requests	=	103,163
Total			980 requests		$168,500

The result of this allocation is shown as the Step 2 allocation in Exhibit 4.8. Notice that the final cost pools for the operating departments reflect the expected shift in the cost distribution between the two departments. Specifically, the cost pool in the criminal department is higher and the cost pool in the civil department is lower than the comparable cost pool amounts computed under the direct method (see Exhibit 4.6 for the appropriate comparison). This distribution of cost is consistent with the fact that more of the interdepartmental service cost should be assigned to the criminal

EXHIBIT 4.8				
First-Stage Allocations for Candler & Associates—Step Method				
	Personnel Cost Pool	Secretarial Cost Pool	Civil Department	Criminal Department
Cost to be allocated	$117,000	$156,800		
Step 1 allocation	(117,000) =	11,700 +	$ 64,350 +	$ 40,950
Step 2 allocation		(168,500) =	65,337 +	103,163
Total in cost pool after allocation	$ 0	$ 0	129,687	144,113
Other operating department overhead costs			785,100	464,788
Total of operating department overhead cost pool			$914,787	$608,901

department because it uses more secretarial services than does the civil department. Accordingly, the step method of allocation more accurately reflects the manner in which the two operating departments consume resources.

The preceding illustration considered a simple two-stage allocation process with only two service departments and two operating departments. In large organizations, the costing process may be significantly more complex. Interdepartmental cost allocations may involve several service departments. For example, a personnel department may provide service to a secretarial department that provides service to an engineering department that provides service to the accounting department that provides service to several operating departments. In addition, general overhead costs may be allocated to both service and operating departments before costs are allocated from service to operating departments. For example, general utility costs may be pooled together and allocated to service and operating departments on the basis of square footage of floor space. These allocated utility costs are then redistributed to other service departments and to operating departments in a sequence of step-down allocations. The step-down process usually begins with the cost pool that represents resources used by the largest number of departments. This constitutes the first step in the costing process. The second step proceeds with allocations from the cost pool that represents resources used by the second largest number of departments and so on, until all overhead costs have been allocated to the operating departments. Accordingly, the first stage of a two-stage costing process may include many allocations (steps) before all costs have been distributed to the operating departments. Regardless of how many allocations are included in the first stage, the second stage begins when costs are allocated from the operating departments to the organization's products.

Reciprocal Method

Note that the step method is limited to one-way interdepartmental relationships. In practice, many departments have two-way working relationships. For example, the personnel department may provide services to the secretarial department and receive services from it. Two-way associations in which departments provide and receive services from one another are called **reciprocal relationships.** Allocations that recognize reciprocal relationships require complex mathematical manipulation involving the use of simultaneous linear equations. The resultant cost distributions are difficult to interpret. Furthermore, the results attained with the **reciprocal method** are not significantly different from those attained through the step method. As a result, the reciprocal method is rarely used in practice.

A step-by-step audio-narrated series of slides is provided on the text website at www.mhhe.com/edmonds2011.

SELF-STUDY REVIEW PROBLEM

New budget constraints have pressured Body Perfect Gym to control costs. The owner of the gym, Mr. Ripple, has notified division managers that their job performance evaluations will be highly influenced by their ability to minimize costs. The gym has three divisions: weight lifting, aerobics, and spinning. The owner has formulated a report showing how much it cost to operate each of the three divisions last year. In preparing the report, Mr. Ripple identified several indirect costs that must be allocated among the divisions. These indirect costs are $4,200 of laundry expense, $48,000 of supplies, $350,000 of office rent, $50,000 of janitorial services, and $120,000 for administrative salaries. To provide a reasonably accurate cost allocation, Mr. Ripple has identified several potential cost drivers. These drivers and their association with each division follow.

Cost Driver	Weight Lifting	Aerobics	Spinning	Total
Number of participants	26	16	14	56
Number of instructors	10	8	6	24
Square feet of gym space	12,000	6,000	7,000	25,000
Number of staff	2	2	1	5

Required

a. Identify the appropriate cost objects.

b. Identify the most appropriate cost driver for each indirect cost, and compute the allocation rate for assigning each indirect cost to the cost objects.

c. Determine the amount of supplies expense that should be allocated to each of the three divisions.

d. The spinning manager wants to use the number of staff rather than the number of instructors as the allocation base for the supplies expense. Explain why the spinning manager would take this position.

e. Identify two cost drivers other than your choice for Requirement *b* that could be used to allocate the cost of the administrative salaries to the three divisions.

Solution to Requirement a

The objective is to determine the cost of operating each division. Therefore, the cost objects are the three divisions (weight lifting, aerobics, and spinning).

Solution to Requirement b

The costs, appropriate cost drivers, and allocation rates for assigning the costs to the departments follow:

Cost	Base	Computation	Allocation Rate
Laundry expense	Number of participants	$ 4,200 ÷ 56	$75 per participant
Supplies	Number of instructors	48,000 ÷ 24	$2,000 per instructor
Office rent	Square feet	350,000 ÷ 25,000	$14 per square foot
Janitorial service	Square feet	50,000 ÷ 25,000	$2 per square foot
Administrative salaries	Number of divisions	120,000 ÷ 3	$40,000 per division

There are other logical cost drivers. For example, the cost of supplies could be allocated based on the number of staff. It is also logical to use a combination of cost drivers. For example, the allocation for the cost of supplies could be based on the combined number of instructors and staff. For this problem, we assumed that Mr. Ripple chose the number of instructors as the base for allocating supplies expense.

Solution to Requirement c

Department	Cost to Be Allocated	Allocation Rate	×	Weight of Base	=	Amount Allocated
Weight lifting	Supplies	$2,000	×	10	=	$20,000
Aerobics	Supplies	2,000	×	8	=	16,000
Spinning	Supplies	2,000	×	6	=	12,000
Total						$48,000

Solution to Requirement d

If the number of staff were used as the allocation base, the allocation rate for supplies would be as follows:

$$\$48,000 \div 5 \text{ staff} = \$9,600 \text{ per staff member}$$

Using this rate, the total cost of supplies would be allocated among the three divisions as follows:

Department	Cost to Be Allocated	Allocation Rate	×	Weight of Base	=	Amount Allocated
Weight lifting	Supplies	$9,600	×	2	=	$19,200
Aerobics	Supplies	9,600	×	2	=	19,200
Spinning	Supplies	9,600	×	1	=	9,600
Total						$48,000

By using the number of staff as the allocation base instead of the number of instructors, the amount of overhead cost allocated to the spinning division falls from $12,000 to $9,600. Since managers are evaluated based on minimizing costs, it is clearly in the spinning manager's self-interest to use the number of staff as the allocation base.

Solution to Requirement e

Among other possibilities, bases for allocating the administrative salaries include the number of participants, the number of lessons, or the number of instructors.

KEY TERMS

allocation 153
allocation base 155
allocation rate 155
common costs 154
controllable costs 154
cost accumulation 152
cost allocation 153
cost driver 152
cost objects 150

cost pools 165
cost tracing 153
direct cost 153
direct method 171
indirect cost 153
interdepartmental service 172
joint costs 165
joint products 165
operating departments 170

overhead costs 153
predetermined
    overhead rate 165
reciprocal method 175
reciprocal relationships 175
service departments 170
split-off point 165
step method 173

QUESTIONS

1. What is a cost object? Identify four different cost objects in which an accountant would be interested.

2. Why is cost accumulation imprecise?

3. If the cost object is a manufactured product, what are the three major cost categories to accumulate?

4. What is a direct cost? What criteria are used to determine whether a cost is a direct cost?

5. Why are the terms *direct cost* and *indirect cost* independent of the terms *fixed cost* and *variable cost*? Give an example to illustrate.

6. Give an example of why the statement, "All direct costs are avoidable," is incorrect.

7. What are the important factors in determining the appropriate cost driver to use in allocating a cost?

8. How is an allocation rate determined? How is an allocation made?

9. In a manufacturing environment, which costs are direct and which are indirect in product costing?

10. Why are some manufacturing costs not directly traceable to products?

11. What is the objective of allocating indirect manufacturing overhead costs to the product?

12. On January 31, the managers of Integra, Inc., seek to determine the cost of producing their product during January for product pricing and control purposes. The company can easily determine the costs of direct materials and direct labor used in January production, but many fixed indirect costs are not affected by the level of production activity and have not yet been incurred. The managers can reasonably estimate the overhead costs for the year based on the fixed indirect costs incurred in past periods. Assume the managers decide to allocate an equal amount of these estimated costs to the products produced each month. Explain why this practice may not provide a reasonable estimate of product costs in January.

13. Respond to the following statement: "The allocation base chosen is unimportant. What is important in product costing is that overhead costs be assigned to production in a specific period by an allocation process."

14. Larry Kwang insists that the costs of his school's fund-raising project should be determined after the project is complete. He argues that only after the project is complete can its costs be determined accurately and that it is a waste of time to try to estimate future costs. Georgia Sundum counters that waiting until the project is complete will not provide timely information for planning expenditures. How would you arbitrate this discussion? Explain the trade-offs between accuracy and timeliness.

15. What are the three methods used for allocating service center costs? How do the methods differ? (Appendix)

MULTIPLE-CHOICE QUESTIONS

Multiple-choice questions are provided on the text website at www.mhhe.com/edmonds2011.

EXERCISES—SERIES A

All applicable Exercises in Series A are available with McGraw-Hill's _Connect Accounting_.

LO 3

Exercise 4-1A   _Allocating costs between divisions_

Sims Services Company (SSC) has 50 employees, 38 of whom are assigned to Division A and 12 to Division B. SSC incurred $296,000 of fringe benefits cost during 2011.

Required

Determine the amount of the fringe benefits cost to be allocated to Division A and to Division B.

LO 2

Exercise 4-2A   _Direct versus indirect costs_

Jeelani Construction Company is composed of two divisions: (1) Home Construction and (2) Commercial Construction. The Home Construction Division is in the process of building 12 houses and the Commercial Construction Division is working on three projects. Cost items of the company follow:

Company president's salary

Depreciation on crane used in commercial construction

Depreciation on home office building

Salary of corporate office manager

Wages of workers assigned to a specific construction project

Supplies used by the Commercial Construction Division

Labor on a particular house

Salary of the supervisor of commercial construction projects

Supplies, such as glue and nails, used by the Home Construction Division

Cost of building permits

Materials used in commercial construction project

Depreciation on home building equipment (small tools such as hammers or saws)

Required

a. Identify each cost as being a direct or indirect cost assuming the cost objects are the individual products (houses or projects).

b. Identify each cost as being a direct or indirect cost, assuming the cost objects are the two divisions.

c. Identify each cost as being a direct or indirect cost assuming the cost object is Jeelani Construction Company as a whole.

Exercise 4-3A *Allocating overhead cost among products*   LO 3, 4

Dew Hats Corporation manufactures three different models of hats: Vogue, Beauty, and Glamour. Dew expects to incur $576,000 of overhead cost during the next fiscal year. Other budget information follows.

	Vogue	Beauty	Glamour	Total
Direct labor hours	2,000	4,000	6,000	12,000
Machine hours	1,200	1,400	1,400	4,000

Required

a. Use direct labor hours as the cost driver to compute the allocation rate and the budgeted overhead cost for each product.

b. Use machine hours as the cost driver to compute the allocation rate and the budgeted overhead cost for each product.

c. Describe a set of circumstances where it would be more appropriate to use direct labor hours as the allocation base.

d. Describe a set of circumstances where it would be more appropriate to use machine hours as the allocation base.

Exercise 4-4A *Allocating overhead costs among products*   LO 3, 4

Nevin Company makes three products in its factory: plastic cups, plastic tablecloths, and plastic bottles. The expected overhead costs for the next fiscal year include the following.

Factory manager's salary	$260,000
Factory utility cost	121,000
Factory supplies	56,000
Total overhead costs	$437,000

Nevin uses machine hours as the cost driver to allocate overhead costs. Budgeted machine hours for the products are as follows:

Cups	420 Hours
Tablecloths	740
Bottles	1,140
Total machine hours	2,300

Required

a. Allocate the budgeted overhead costs to the products.

b. Provide a possible explanation as to why Nevin chose machine hours, instead of labor hours, as the allocation base.

LO 3, 4

Exercise 4-5A *Allocating costs among products*

Deka Construction Company expects to build three new homes during a specific accounting period. The estimated direct materials and labor costs are as follows.

Expected Costs	Home 1	Home 2	Home 3
Direct labor	$60,000	$ 90,000	$170,000
Direct materials	90,000	130,000	180,000

Assume Deka needs to allocate two major overhead costs ($40,000 of employee fringe benefits and $20,000 of indirect materials costs) among the three jobs.

Required

Choose an appropriate cost driver for each of the overhead costs and determine the total cost of each house.

LO 3, 5

Exercise 4-6A *Allocating to smooth cost over varying levels of production*

Production workers for Nabors Manufacturing Company provided 280 hours of labor in January and 500 hours in February. Nabors expects to use 4,000 hours of labor during the year. The rental fee for the manufacturing facility is $8,000 per month.

Required

Explain why allocation is needed. Based on this information, how much of the rental cost should be allocated to the products made in January and to those made in February?

LO 3, 5

Exercise 4-7A *Allocating to solve a timing problem*

Production workers for Bianco Manufacturing Company provided 3,600 hours of labor in January and 1,900 hours in February. The company, whose operation is labor intensive, expects to use 32,000 hours of labor during the year. Bianco paid a $96,000 annual premium on July 1 of the prior year for an insurance policy that covers the manufacturing facility for the following 12 months.

Required

Explain why allocation is needed. Based on this information, how much of the insurance cost should be allocated to the products made in January and to those made in February?

LO 3, 5

Exercise 4-8A *Allocating to solve a timing problem*

Stevens Air is a large airline company that pays a customer relations representative $4,000 per month. The representative, who processed 1,000 customer complaints in January and 1,300 complaints in February, is expected to process 24,000 customer complaints during 2012.

Required

a. Determine the total cost of processing customer complaints in January and in February.
b. Explain why allocating the cost of the customer relations representative would or would not be relevant to decision making.

LO 3, 5

Exercise 4-9A *Allocating overhead cost to accomplish smoothing*

Woods Corporation expects to incur indirect overhead costs of $60,000 per month and direct manufacturing costs of $11 per unit. The expected production activity for the first four months of 2012 is as follows.

	January	February	March	April
Estimated production in units	4,000	7,000	3,000	6,000

Required

a. Calculate a predetermined overhead rate based on the number of units of product expected to be made during the first four months of the year.
b. Allocate overhead costs to each month using the overhead rate computed in Requirement *a*.
c. Calculate the total cost per unit for each month using the overhead allocated in Requirement *b*.

Exercise 4-10A   *Pooling overhead cost*   LO 3, 5, 6

Jasti Manufacturing Company produced 1,000 units of inventory in January 2011. It expects to produce an additional 8,400 units during the remaining 11 months of the year. In other words, total production for 2011 is estimated to be 9,600 units. Direct materials and direct labor costs are $64 and $52 per unit, respectively. Jasti Company expects to incur the following manufacturing overhead costs during the 2011 accounting period.

Production supplies	$ 4,800
Supervisor salary	192,000
Depreciation on equipment	144,000
Utilities	36,000
Rental fee on manufacturing facilities	96,000

Required

a. Combine the individual overhead costs into a cost pool and calculate a predetermined overhead rate assuming the cost driver is number of units.

b. Determine the cost of the 1,200 units of product made in January.

c. Is the cost computed in Requirement *a* actual or estimated? Could Jasti improve accuracy by waiting until December to determine the cost of products? Identify two reasons that a manager would want to know the cost of products in January. Discuss the relationship between accuracy and relevance as it pertains to this problem.

Exercise 4-11A   *How the allocation of fixed cost affects a pricing decision*   LO 3, 5

Mallett Manufacturing Co. expects to make 30,000 chairs during the 2011 accounting period. The company made 3,200 chairs in January. Materials and labor costs for January were $16,000 and $24,000, respectively. Mallett produced 2,500 chairs in February. Material and labor costs for February were $8,000 and $12,000, respectively. The company paid the $240,000 annual rental fee on its manufacturing facility on January 1, 2011.

Required

Assuming that Mallett desires to sell its chairs for cost plus 40 percent of cost, what price should be charged for the chairs produced in January and February?

Exercise 4-12A   *Allocating joint product cost*   LO 3, 7

Turley Chemical Company makes three products, B7, K6, and X9, which are joint products from the same materials. In a standard batch of 300,000 pounds of raw materials, the company generates 70,000 pounds of B7, 150,000 pounds of K6, and 80,000 pounds of X9. A standard batch costs $2,400,000 to produce. The sales prices per pound are $6, $10, and $16 for B7, K6, and X9, respectively.

Required

a. Allocate the joint product cost among the three final products using weight as the allocation base.

b. Allocate the joint product cost among the three final products using market value as the allocation base.

Exercise 4-13A   *Human factor*   LO 8

Dearman Clinics provides medical care in three departments: internal medicine (IM), pediatrics (PD), and obstetrics gynecology (OB). The estimated costs to run each department follow:

	IM	PD	OB
Physicians	$400,000	$300,000	$200,000
Nurses	80,000	120,000	160,000

Dearman expects to incur $450,000 of indirect (overhead) costs in the next fiscal year.

Required

a. Name four allocation bases that could be used to assign the overhead cost to each department.

b. Assume the manager of each department is permitted to recommend how the overhead cost should be allocated to the departments. Which of the allocation bases named in Requirement *a* is the manager of OB most likely to recommend? Explain why. What argument may the manager of OB use to justify his choice of the allocation base?

c. Which of the allocation bases would result in the fairest allocation of the overhead cost from the perspective of the company president?

d. Explain how classifying overhead costs into separate pools could improve the fairness of the allocation of the overhead costs.

Appendix

LO 3, 9

Exercise 4-14A   *Allocating a service center cost to operating departments*

Fowler Corporation's computer services department assists two operating departments in using the company's information system effectively. The annual cost of computer services is $360,000. The production department employs 22 employees, and the sales department employs 18 employees. Fowler uses the number of employees as the cost driver for allocating the cost of computer services to operating departments.

Required

Allocate the cost of computer services to operating departments.

LO 3, 9

Exercise 4-15A   *Allocating costs of service centers to operating departments—step method*

Hardy Health Care Center, Inc., has three clinics servicing the Seattle metropolitan area. The company's legal services department supports the clinics. Moreover, its computer services department supports all of the clinics and the legal services department. The annual cost of operating the legal services department is $217,000. The annual cost of operating the computer services department is $450,000. The company uses the number of patients served as the cost driver for allocating the cost of legal services and the number of computer workstations as the cost driver for allocating the cost of computer services. Other relevant information follows:

	Number of Patients	Number of Workstations
Hoover clinic	6,000	15
Eastwood clinic	4,200	16
Gardendale clinic	5,800	12
Legal services		7
Computer services		10

Required

a. Allocate the cost of computer services to all of the clinics and the legal services department.

b. After allocating the cost of computer services, allocate the cost of legal services to the three clinics.

c. Compute the total allocated cost of service centers for each clinic.

LO 3, 9

Exercise 4-16A   *Allocating costs of service centers to operating departments—direct method*

Jooste Trust Corporation has two service departments: actuary and economic analysis. Jooste also has three operating departments: annuity, fund management, and employee benefit services. The annual costs of operating the service departments are $440,000 for actuary and $720,000 for economic analysis. Jooste uses the direct method to allocate service center costs to operating departments. Other relevant data follow:

	Operating Costs*	Revenue
Annuity	$500,000	$ 840,000
Fund management	900,000	1,260,000
Employee benefit services	600,000	1,100,000

*The operating costs are measured before allocating service center costs.

Required

a. Use operating costs as the cost driver for allocating service center costs to operating departments.

b. Use revenue as the cost driver for allocating service center costs to operating departments.

PROBLEMS—SERIES A

All applicable Problems in Series A are available with McGraw-Hill's
Connect Accounting.

Problem 4-17A *Cost accumulation and allocation*

Singh Manufacturing Company makes two different products, M and N. The company's two departments are named after the products; for example, Product M is made in Department M. Singh's accountant has identified the following annual costs associated with these two products.

LO 1, 2, 3, 4, 5

CHECK FIGURE
(c) N: $531.65

Financial data	
Salary of vice president of production division	$180,000
Salary of supervisor Department M	76,000
Salary of supervisor Department N	56,000
Direct materials cost Department M	300,000
Direct materials cost Department N	420,000
Direct labor cost Department M	240,000
Direct labor cost Department N	680,000
Direct utilities cost Department M	120,000
Direct utilities cost Department N	24,000
General factorywide utilities	36,000
Production supplies	36,000
Fringe benefits	138,000
Depreciation	720,000
Nonfinancial data	
Machine hours Department M	5,000
Machine hours Department N	1,000

Required

a. Identify the costs that are (1) direct costs of Department M, (2) direct costs of Department N, and (3) indirect costs.

b. Select the appropriate cost drivers for the indirect costs and allocate these costs to Departments M and N.

c. Determine the total estimated cost of the products made in Departments M and N. Assume that Singh produced 2,000 units of Product M and 4,000 units of Product N during the year. If Singh prices its products at cost plus 40 percent of cost, what price per unit must it charge for Product M and for Product N?

LO 1, 3, 4

Problem 4-18A   *Selecting an appropriate cost driver (What is the base?)*

The Vest School of Vocational Technology has organized the school training programs into three departments. Each department provides training in a different area as follows: nursing assistant, dental hygiene, and office technology. The school's owner, Wilma Vest, wants to know how much it costs to operate each of the three departments. To accumulate the total cost for each department, the accountant has identified several indirect costs that must be allocated to each. These costs are $10,080 of phone expense, $2,016 of office supplies, $720,000 of office rent, $144,000 of janitorial services, and $150,000 of salary paid to the dean of students. To provide a reasonably accurate allocation of costs, the accountant has identified several possible cost drivers. These drivers and their association with each department follow.

Cost Driver	Department 1	Department 2	Department 3
Number of telephones	28	32	52
Number of faculty members	20	16	12
Square footage of office space	28,800	16,800	12,000
Number of secretaries	2	2	2

Required

a. Identify the appropriate cost objects.

b. Identify the appropriate cost driver for each indirect cost and compute the allocation rate for assigning each indirect cost to the cost objects.

c. Determine the amount of telephone expense that should be allocated to each of the three departments.

d. Determine the amount of supplies expense that should be allocated to Department 3.

e. Determine the amount of office rent that should be allocated to Department 2.

f. Determine the amount of janitorial services cost that should be allocated to Department 1.

g. Identify two cost drivers not listed here that could be used to allocate the cost of the dean's salary to the three departments.

LO 1, 2

CHECK FIGURE
b. To NY: $802

Problem 4-19A   *Cost allocation in a service industry*

Kirby Airlines is a small airline that occasionally carries overload shipments for the overnight delivery company Never-Fail, Inc. Never-Fail is a multimillion-dollar company started by Jack Never immediately after he failed to finish his first accounting course. The company's motto is "We Never-Fail to Deliver Your Package on Time." When Never-Fail has more freight than it can deliver, it pays Kirby to carry the excess. Kirby contracts with independent pilots to fly its planes on a per-trip basis. Kirby recently purchased an airplane that cost the company $5,500,000. The plane has an estimated useful life of 25,000,000 miles and a zero salvage value. During the first week in January, Kirby flew two trips. The first trip was a round trip flight from Chicago to San Francisco, for which Kirby paid $350 for the pilot and $300 for fuel. The second flight was a round trip from Chicago to New York. For this trip, it paid $300 for the pilot and $150 for fuel. The round trip between Chicago and San Francisco is approximately 4,400 miles and the round trip between Chicago and New York is 1,600 miles.

Required

a. Identify the direct and indirect costs that Kirby incurs for each trip.

b. Determine the total cost of each trip.

c. In addition to depreciation, identify three other indirect costs that may need to be allocated to determine the cost of each trip.

LO 1, 3, 4

CHECK FIGURE
d. Feb.: $7,200

Problem 4-20A   *Cost allocation in a manufacturing company*

Hunt Manufacturing Company makes tents that it sells directly to camping enthusiasts through a mail-order marketing program. The company pays a quality control expert $72,000 per year to inspect completed tents before they are shipped to customers. Assume that the company completed 1,600 tents in January and 1,200 tents in February. For the entire year, the company expects to produce 12,000 tents.

Required

a. Explain how changes in the cost driver (number of tents inspected) affect the total amount of fixed inspection cost.

b. Explain how changes in the cost driver (number of tents inspected) affect the amount of fixed inspection cost per unit.

c. If the cost objective is to determine the cost per tent, is the expert's salary a direct or an indirect cost?

d. How much of the expert's salary should be allocated to tents produced in January and February?

Problem 4-21A *Fairness and cost pool allocations*

LO 1, 4, 6, 8

Daniel Manufacturing Company uses two departments to make its products. Department I is a cutting department that is machine intensive and uses very few employees. Machines cut and form parts and then place the finished parts on a conveyor belt that carries them to Department II where they are assembled into finished goods. The assembly department is labor intensive and requires many workers to assemble parts into finished goods. The company's manufacturing facility incurs two significant overhead costs: employee fringe benefits and utility costs. The annual costs of fringe benefits are $252,000 and utility costs are $180,000. The typical consumption patterns for the two departments are as follows.

	Department I	Department II	Total
Machine hours used	16,000	4,000	20,000
Direct labor hours used	5,000	13,000	18,000

The supervisor of each department receives a bonus based on how well the department controls costs. The company's current policy requires using a single allocation base (machine hours or labor hours) to allocate the total overhead cost of $432,000.

Required

a. Assume that you are the supervisor of Department I. Choose the allocation base that would minimize your department's share of the total overhead cost. Calculate the amount of overhead that would be allocated to both departments using the base that you selected.

b. Assume that you are the supervisor of Department II. Choose the allocation base that would minimize your department's share of the total overhead cost. Calculate the amount of overhead that would be allocated to both departments using the base that you selected.

c. Assume that you are the plant manager and have the authority to change the company's overhead allocation policy. Formulate an overhead allocation policy that would be fair to the supervisors of both Department I and Department II. Compute the overhead allocations for each department using your policy.

d. Explain why it is necessary to disaggregate the overhead cost pool in order to accomplish fairness.

Problem 4-22A *Allocation to accomplish smoothing*

LO 1, 3, 5
CHECK FIGURES
a. $4
c. March: $42

O'Hara Corporation estimated its overhead costs would be $24,000 per month except for January when it pays the $72,000 annual insurance premium on the manufacturing facility. Accordingly, the January overhead costs were expected to be $96,000 ($72,000 + $24,000). The company expected to use 7,000 direct labor hours per month except during July, August, and September when the company expected 9,000 hours of direct labor each month to build inventories for high demand that normally occurs during the Christmas season. The company's actual direct labor hours were the same as the estimated hours. The company made 3,500 units of product in each month except July, August, and September in which it produced 4,500 units each month. Direct labor costs were $24 per unit, and direct materials costs were $10 per unit.

Required

a. Calculate a predetermined overhead rate based on direct labor hours.

b. Determine the total allocated overhead cost for January, March, and August.

c. Determine the cost per unit of product for January, March, and August.
d. Determine the selling price for the product, assuming that the company desires to earn a gross margin of $20 per unit.

LO 1, 3, 5

CHECK FIGURES
a. Cost/unit for
   EZRecords: $200
b. Cost/unit for
   ProOffice: $220

Problem 4-23A   *Allocating indirect costs between products*

Erin Tarver is considering expanding her business. She plans to hire a salesperson to cover trade shows. Because of compensation, travel expenses, and booth rental, fixed costs for a trade show are expected to be $12,000. The booth will be open 30 hours during the trade show. Ms. Tarver also plans to add a new product line, ProOffice, which will cost $180 per package. She will continue to sell the existing product, EZRecords, which costs $100 per package. Ms. Tarver believes that the salesperson will spend approximately 20 hours selling EZRecords and 10 hours marketing ProOffice.

Required

a. Determine the estimated total cost and cost per unit of each product, assuming that the salesperson is able to sell 80 units of EZRecords and 50 units of ProOffice.
b. Determine the estimated total cost and cost per unit of each product, assuming that the salesperson is able to sell 200 units of EZRecords and 100 units of ProOffice.
c. Explain why the cost per unit figures calculated in Requirement *a* are different from the amounts calculated in Requirement *b*. Also explain how the differences in estimated cost per unit will affect pricing decisions.

LO 1, 6

Problem 4-24A   *Cost Pools*

Richter Department Stores, Inc. has three departments: women's, men's, and children's. The following are the indirect costs related to its operations:

Medical insurance
Salaries of secretaries
Water bill
Vacation pay
Sewer bill
Staples
Natural gas bill
Pens
Ink cartridges
Payroll taxes
Paper rolls for cash registers

Required

a. Organize the costs in the following three pools: indirect materials, indirect labor, and indirect utilities, assuming that each department is a cost object.
b. Identify an appropriate cost driver for each pool.
c. Explain why accountants use cost pools.

LO 3, 7

CHECK FIGURES
a. GM for drumsticks: $(980)
b. Total cost of breasts: $7,087.50

Problem 4-25A   *Allocating joint product cost*

Koch Chicken Corporation processes and packages chicken for grocery stores. It purchases chickens from farmers and processes them into two different products: chicken drumsticks and chicken steak. From a standard batch of 12,000 pounds of raw chicken that costs $7,000, the company produces two parts: 2,800 pounds of drumsticks and 4,200 pounds of breast for a processing cost of $2,450. The chicken breast is further processed into 3,200 pounds of steak for a processing cost of $2,000. The market price of drumsticks per pound is $1.00 and the market price per pound of chicken steak is $3.40. If Koch decided to sell chicken breast instead of chicken steak, the price per pound would be $2.00.

Required

a. Allocate the joint cost to the joint products, drumsticks and breasts, using weight as the allocation base. Calculate the net income for each product. Since the drumsticks are producing a net loss, should that product line be eliminated?

b. Reallocate the joint cost to the joint products, drumsticks and breasts, using relative market values as the allocation base. Calculate the net income for each product. Compare the total net income (drumsticks + breasts) computed in Requirement *b* with that computed in Requirement *a* above. Explain why the total amount is the same. Comment on which allocation base (weight or market value) is more appropriate.

c. Should Koch further process chicken breasts into chicken steak?

Appendix

Problem 4-26A   *Allocating service center costs—step method and direct method*

Romero Information Services, Inc., has two service departments: human resources and billing. Romero's operating departments, organized according to the special industry each department serves, are health care, retail, and legal services. The billing department supports only the three operating departments, but the human resources department supports all operating departments and the billing department. Other relevant information follows.

LO 3, 9

CHECK FIGURES
a. Allocated cost from
   Billing to Retail: $558,000
b. Allocated cost from
   HR to LS: $240,000

	Human Resources	Billing	Health Care	Retail	Legal Services
Number of employees	20	50	190	140	120
Annual cost*	$900,000	$1,710,000	$6,000,000	$4,800,000	$2,800,000
Annual revenue	—	—	$9,000,000	$6,200,000	$4,800,000

*This is the operating cost before allocating service department costs.

Required

a. Allocate service department costs to operating departments, assuming that Romero adopts the step method. The company uses the number of employees as the base for allocating human resources department costs and department annual revenue as the base for allocating the billing department costs.

b. Allocate service department costs to operating departments, assuming that Romero adopts the direct method. The company uses the number of employees as the base for allocating the human resources department costs and department annual revenue as the base for allocating the billing department costs.

c. Compute the total allocated cost of service centers for each operating department using each allocation method.

EXERCISES—SERIES B

Exercise 4-1B   *Allocating costs between divisions*

LO 1, 3

Smith and Warren, LLP, has three departments: auditing, tax, and information systems. The departments occupy 2,500 square feet, 1,500 square feet, and 1,000 square feet of office space, respectively. The firm pays $6,000 per month to rent its offices.

Required

How much monthly rent cost should Smith and Warren allocate to each department?

Exercise 4-2B   *Direct versus indirect costs*

LO 2

Kenta and Associates, LLP, is an accounting firm that provides two major types of professional services: (1) tax services as provided by the tax department and (2) auditing services as provided by the audit department. Each department has numerous clients. Engagement with each individual client is a separate service (i.e., product) and each department has several engagements in each period. Cost items of the firm follow:

Secretarial labor supporting both departments

Professional labor for an audit engagement

Depreciation of computers used in the audit department

Salary of the partner in charge of the tax department
Travel expenditures for an audit engagement
Salary of the partner in charge of the audit department
Salary of the managing partner of the firm
Cost of office supplies such as paper, pencils, erasers, etc.
Depreciation of computers used in the tax department
License fees of the firm
Professional labor for a tax engagement

Required

a. Identify each cost as being a direct or indirect cost assuming the cost objects are the individual engagements (audit engagements or tax engagements).

b. Identify each cost as being a direct or indirect cost assuming the cost objects are the two departments.

c. Identify each cost as being a direct or indirect cost assuming the cost object is Kenta and Associates, LLP, as a whole.

LO 3, 5

Exercise 4-3B   *Allocating overhead costs among products*

Diat Company manufactures three different sizes of automobile sunscreens: large, medium, and small. Diat expects to incur $480,000 of overhead costs during the next fiscal year. Other budget information for the coming year follows:

	Large	Medium	Small	Total
Direct labor hours	2,500	5,000	4,500	12,000
Machine hours	700	1,300	1,000	3,000

Required

a. Use direct labor hours as the cost driver to compute the allocation rate and the budgeted overhead cost for each product.

b. Use machine hours as the cost driver to compute the allocation rate and the budgeted overhead cost for each product.

c. Describe a set of circumstances where it would be more appropriate to use direct labor hours as the allocation base.

d. Describe a set of circumstances where it would be more appropriate to use machine hours as the allocation base.

LO 3, 4

Exercise 4-4B   *Allocating overhead costs among products*

Yunan Company makes three models of jump drives in its factory: J512, J1G, and J4G. The expected overhead costs for the next fiscal year are as follows:

Payroll for factory managers	$100,000
Factory maintenance costs	45,000
Factory insurance	23,000
Total overhead costs	$168,000

Yunan uses labor hours as the cost driver to allocate overhead cost. Budgeted labor hours for the products are as follows:

J512	1,000 hours
J1G	650
J4G	450
Total labor hours	2,100

Required

a. Allocate the budgeted overhead costs to the products.

b. Provide a possible explanation as to why Yunan chose labor hours, instead of machine hours, as the allocation base.

Exercise 4-5B   *Allocating costs among products*

LO 3, 4

Blotski Company makes household plastic bags in three different sizes: Snack, Sandwich, and Storage. The estimated direct materials and direct labor costs are as follows.

Expected Costs	Snack	Sandwich	Storage
Direct materials	$112,000	$188,000	$300,000
Direct labor	60,000	116,000	224,000

Blotski allocates two major overhead costs among the three products: $36,000 of indirect labor cost for workers who move various materials and products to different stations in the factory and $28,000 of employee pension costs.

Required

Determine the total cost of each product.

Exercise 4-6B   *Allocating indirect cost over varying levels of production*

LO 3, 5

Denver Company's annual factory depreciation is $108,000. Denver estimated it would operate the factory a total of 2,400 hours this year. The factory operated 200 hours in November and 150 hours in December.

Required

Why would Denver need to allocate factory depreciation cost? How much depreciation cost should Denver allocate to products made in November and those made in December?

Exercise 4-7B   *Allocating indirect cost over varying levels of production*

LO 3, 5

On January 1, Glaze Corporation paid the annual royalty of $720,000 for rights to use patented technology to make batteries for laptop computers. Glaze plans to use the patented technology to produce five different models of batteries. Glaze uses machine hours as a common cost driver and plans to operate its machines 48,000 hours in the coming year. The company used 3,000 machine hours in June and 3,600 hours in July.

Required

Why would Glaze need to allocate the annual royalty payment rather than simply assign it in total to January production? How much of the royalty cost should Glaze allocate to products made in June and those made in July?

Exercise 4-8B   *Allocating a fixed cost*

LO 3, 5

Last year, Sean Tapper bought an automobile for $24,000 to use in his taxi business. He expected to drive the vehicle for 140,000 miles before disposing of it for $3,000. Sean drove 3,200 miles this week and 2,800 miles last week.

Required

a. Determine the total cost of vehicle depreciation this week and last week.

b. Explain why allocating the vehicle cost would or would not be relevant to decision making.

Exercise 4-9B   *Allocating overhead cost to accomplish smoothing*

LO 3, 5

In 2012, Pingtung Corporation incurred direct manufacturing costs of $35 per unit and manufacturing overhead costs of $175,000. The production activity for the four quarters of 2012 follows:

	1st Quarter	2nd Quarter	3rd Quarter	4th Quarter
Number of units produced	3,300	2,700	4,500	2,000

Required

a. Calculate a predetermined overhead rate based on the number of units produced during the year.

b. Allocate overhead costs to each quarter using the overhead rate computed in Requirement *a*.

c. Using the overhead allocation determined in Requirement *b*, calculate the total cost per unit for each quarter.

LO 3, 5, 6

Exercise 4-10B   *Pooling overhead cost*

Rosen Manufacturing Company produced 500 units of inventory in January 2011. The company expects to produce an additional 5,500 units of inventory during the remaining 11 months of the year, for total estimated production of 6,000 units in 2011. Direct materials and direct labor costs are $70 and $82 per unit, respectively. Rosen expects to incur the following manufacturing overhead costs during the 2011 accounting period:

Indirect materials	$ 6,800
Depreciation on equipment	24,000
Utilities cost	10,200
Salaries of plant manager and staff	96,800
Rental fee on manufacturing facilities	19,000

Required

a. Combine the individual overhead costs into a cost pool and calculate a predetermined overhead rate assuming the cost driver is number of units.

b. Determine the estimated cost of the 500 units of product made in January.

c. Is the cost computed in Requirement *a* actual or estimated? Could Rosen improve accuracy by waiting until December to determine the cost of products? Identify two reasons that a manager would want to know the cost of products in January. Discuss the relationship between accuracy and relevance as it pertains to this problem.

LO 3, 5

Exercise 4-11B   *How fixed cost allocation affects a pricing decision*

Neumann Manufacturing Company expects to make 30,000 travel sewing kits during 2012. In January, the company made 1,800 kits. Materials and labor costs for January were $7,200 and $9,000, respectively. In February, Neumann produced 2,200 kits. Material and labor costs for February were $8,800 and $11,000, respectively. The company paid $69,000 for annual factory insurance on January 10, 2012. Ignore other manufacturing overhead costs.

Required

Assuming that Neumann desires to sell its sewing kits for cost plus 20 percent of cost, what price should it charge for the kits produced in January and February?

LO 3, 6

Exercise 4-12B   *Allocating joint product cost*

Pannier Food Corporation makes two products from soybeans: cooking oil and cattle feed. From a standard batch of 100,000 pounds of soybeans, Pannier produces 20,000 pounds of cooking oil and 80,000 pounds of cattle feed. Producing a standard batch costs $10,000. The sales prices per pound are $1.00 for cooking oil and $0.75 for cattle feed.

Required

a. Allocate the joint product cost to the two products using weight as the allocation base.

b. Allocate the joint product cost to the two products using market value as the allocation base.

LO 8

Exercise 4-13B   *Human factor*

Duddley Company builds custom sailboats. Duddley currently has three boats under construction. The estimated costs to complete each boat are shown below.

	Boat 1	Boat 2	Boat 3
Direct materials	$25,000	$32,000	$12,000
Direct labor	22,000	20,000	14,000

Duddley expects to incur $48,000 of indirect (overhead) costs in the process of making the boats.

Required

a. Based on the information provided, name four allocation bases that could be used to assign the overhead costs to each boat.

b. Assume that the production manager of each boat is permitted to recommend how the overhead costs should be allocated to the boats. Which of the allocation bases named in Requirement *a* is the manager of Boat 2 most likely to recommend? Explain why. What argument may the manager of Boat 2 use to justify his choice of the allocation base?

c. Which of the allocation bases would result in the fairer allocation of the overhead costs from the perspective of the company president?

d. Explain how classifying overhead costs into separate pools could improve the fairness of the allocation of the overhead costs.

Appendix

Exercise 4-14B   *Allocating a service center cost to operating departments*   LO 3, 9

The administrative department of Andrews Consulting, LLC, provides office administration and professional support to its two operating departments. Annual administrative costs are $540,000. In 2010, the hours chargeable to clients generated by the information services department and the financial planning department were 24,000 and 36,000, respectively. Andrews uses chargeable hours as the cost driver for allocating administrative costs to operating departments.

Required

Allocate the administrative costs to the two operating departments.

Exercise 4-15B   *Allocating service centers' costs to operating departments—*   LO 3, 9
                       step method

Shepard Consulting, LLP, has three operating departments: tax, estate planning, and small business. The company's internal accounting and maintenance departments support the operating departments. Moreover, the maintenance department also supports the internal accounting department. Other relevant information follows:

	Annual Cost*	Square Feet	Operating Revenue
Tax	$5,000,000	8,000	$8,000,000
Estate planning	2,000,000	2,000	3,500,000
Small business	3,000,000	4,000	6,500,000
Internal accounting	690,000	1,000	0
Maintenance	450,000	1,000	0

*The annual cost figures do not include costs allocated from service departments.

Shepard allocates its maintenance cost based on the square footage of each department's office space. The firm allocates the internal accounting cost based on each department's operating revenue.

Required

a. Allocate the maintenance cost to the operating and internal accounting departments.

b. After allocating the maintenance cost, allocate the internal accounting cost to the three operating departments.

c. Compute the total allocated cost of the service departments for each operating department.

Exercise 4-16B   *Allocating service centers' costs to operating departments—*   LO 3, 9
                       direct method

Quebec Corporation, a book publisher, has two service departments: editing and typesetting. Quebec also has three operating departments: children's fiction, youth fiction, and adult fiction. The annual costs of operating the editing department are $240,000 and of operating the typesetting department are $210,000. Quebec uses the direct method to allocate service center costs to operating departments. Other relevant data follow.

	Number of Pages	Number of Hours
Children	15,000	5,000
Youth	10,000	8,000
Adult	5,000	7,000

Required

a. Allocate the service center costs to the operating departments using the number of pages as the cost driver.

b. Allocate the service center costs to the operating departments using the number of hours as the cost driver.

PROBLEMS—SERIES B

LO 1, 2, 3, 4, 5

Problem 4-17B   *Cost accumulation and allocation*

Otto Tools Company has two production departments in its manufacturing facilities. Home tools specializes in hand tools for individual home users, and professional tools makes sophisticated tools for professional maintenance workers. Otto's accountant has identified the following annual costs associated with these two products:

Financial data	
Salary of vice president of production	$150,000
Salary of manager, home tools	54,000
Salary of manager, professional tools	43,500
Direct materials cost, home tools	300,000
Direct materials cost, professional tools	375,000
Direct labor cost, home tools	336,000
Direct labor cost, professional tools	414,000
Direct utilities cost, home tools	75,000
Direct utilities cost, professional tools	30,000
General factorywide utilities	31,500
Production supplies	40,500
Fringe benefits	150,000
Depreciation	360,000
Nonfinancial data	
Machine hours, home tools	4,000
Machine hours, professional tools	2,000

Required

a. Identify the costs that are the (1) direct costs of home tools, (2) direct costs of professional tools, and (3) indirect costs.

b. Select the appropriate cost drivers and allocate the indirect costs to home tools and to professional tools.

c. Assume that each department makes only a single product. Home tools produces its Deluxe Drill for home use, and professional tools produces the Professional Drill. The company made 30,000 units of Deluxe Drill and 20,000 units of Professional Drill during the year. Determine the total estimated cost of the products made in each department. If Otto prices its products at cost plus 30 percent of cost, what price per unit must it charge for the Deluxe Drill and the Professional Drill?

Problem 4-18B *Selecting an appropriate cost driver (What is the base?)* LO 1, 3, 4

Letterman Research Institute has three departments: biology, chemistry, and physics. The institute's controller wants to estimate the cost of operating each department. He has identified several indirect costs that must be allocated to each department including $11,200 of phone expense, $2,400 of office supplies, $1,120,000 of office rent, $150,000 of janitorial services, and $150,000 of salary paid to the director. To provide a reasonably accurate allocation of costs, the controller identified several possible cost drivers. These drivers and their association with each department follow.

Cost Driver	Biology	Chemistry	Physics
Number of telephones	10	14	16
Number of researchers	8	10	12
Square footage of office space	8,000	8,000	12,000
Number of secretaries	1	1	1

Required

a. Identify the appropriate cost objects.

b. Identify the appropriate cost driver for each indirect cost, and compute the allocation rate for assigning each indirect cost to the cost objects.

c. Determine the amount of telephone expense that should be allocated to each of the three departments.

d. Determine the amount of supplies expense that should be allocated to the physics department.

e. Determine the amount of office rent cost that should be allocated to the chemistry department.

f. Determine the amount of janitorial services cost that should be allocated to the biology department.

g. Identify two cost drivers not listed here that could be used to allocate the cost of the director's salary to the three departments.

Problem 4-19B *Cost allocation in a service industry* LO 1, 2

Cook, Newton, and Associates provides legal services for its local community. In addition to its regular attorneys, the firm hires some part-time attorneys to handle small cases. Two secretaries assist all part-time attorneys exclusively. In 2010, the firm paid $48,000 for the two secretaries who worked a total of 4,000 hours. Moreover, the firm paid Jean Sutton $60 per hour and Eric Veasy $50 per hour for their part-time legal services.

In August 2010, Ms. Sutton completed a case that took her 60 hours. Mr. Veasy finished a case on which he worked 30 hours. The firm also paid a private investigator to uncover relevant facts. The investigation fees cost $1,000 for Ms. Sutton's case and $750 for Mr. Veasy's case. Ms. Sutton used 30 hours of secretarial assistance, and Mr. Veasy used 40 hours.

Required

a. Identify the direct and indirect costs incurred in each case completed in August 2010.

b. Determine the total cost of each case.

c. In addition to secretaries' salaries, identify three other indirect costs that may need to be allocated to determine the cost of the cases.

Problem 4-20B *Cost allocation in a manufacturing company* LO 1, 3, 4

Solid Door Corporation makes a particular type of door. The labor cost is $90 per door and the material cost is $160 per door. Solid rents a factory building for $60,000 a month. Solid plans to produce 24,000 doors annually. In March and April, it made 2,000 and 3,000 doors, respectively.

Required

a. Explain how changes in the cost driver (number of doors made) affect the total amount of fixed rental cost.

b. Explain how changes in the cost driver (number of doors made) affect the fixed rental cost per unit.

c. If the cost objective is to determine the cost per door, is the factory rent a direct or an indirect cost?

d. How much of the factory rent should be allocated to doors produced in March and April?

LO 1, 4, 6, 8

Problem 4-21B   *Fairness and cost pool allocations*

Pettway Furniture Company has two production departments. The parts department uses automated machinery to make parts; as a result, it uses very few employees. The assembly department is labor intensive because workers manually assemble parts into finished furniture. Employee fringe benefits and utility costs are the two major overhead costs of the company's production division. The fringe benefits and utility costs for the year are $300,000 and $144,000, respectively. The typical consumption patterns for the two departments follow.

	Parts	Assembly	Total
Machine hours used	26,000	$ 4,000	30,000
Direct labor hours used	3,500	20,500	24,000

The supervisor of each department receives a bonus based on how well the department controls costs. The company's current policy requires using a single activity base (machine hours or labor hours) to allocate the total overhead cost of $444,000.

Required

a. Assume that you are the parts department supervisor. Choose the allocation base that would minimize your department's share of the total overhead cost. Calculate the amount of overhead to allocate to both departments using the base that you selected.

b. Assume that you are the assembly department supervisor. Choose the allocation base that would minimize your department's share of the total overhead cost. Calculate the amount of overhead to allocate to both departments using the base that you selected.

c. Assume that you are the plant manager and that you have the authority to change the company's overhead allocation policy. Formulate an overhead allocation policy that would be fair to the supervisors of both the parts and assembly departments. Compute the overhead allocation for each department using your policy.

d. Explain why it is necessary to disaggregate the overhead cost pool in order to accomplish fairness.

LO 1, 3, 5

Problem 4-22B   *Allocation to accomplish smoothing*

Lagatta Corporation's overhead costs are usually $24,000 per month. However, the company pays $54,000 of real estate tax on the factory facility in March. Thus, the overhead costs for March increase to $78,000. The company normally uses 5,000 direct labor hours per month except for August, September, and October, in which the company requires 9,000 hours of direct labor per month to build inventories for high demand in the Christmas season. Last year, the company's actual direct labor hours were the same as usual. The company made 5,000 units of product in each month except August, September, and October in which it produced 9,000 units per month. Direct labor costs were $8 per unit; direct materials costs were $7 per unit.

Required

a. Calculate a predetermined overhead rate based on direct labor hours.

b. Determine the total allocated overhead cost for the months of March, August, and December.

c. Determine the cost per unit of product for the months of March, August, and December.

d. Determine the selling price for the product, assuming that the company desires to earn a gross margin of $7 per unit.

Problem 4-23B   *Allocating indirect cost between products*

LO 1, 3, 5

McCombs Corporation has hired a marketing representative to sell the company's two products: Marvelous and Wonderful. The representative's total salary and fringe benefits are $10,000 monthly. The product cost is $90 per unit for Marvelous and $144 per unit for Wonderful. McCombs expects the representative to spend 48 hours per month marketing Marvelous and 112 hours promoting Wonderful.

Required

a. Determine the estimated total cost and cost per unit, assuming that the representative is able to sell 100 units of Marvelous and 70 units of Wonderful in a month. Allocate indirect cost on the basis of labor hours.

b. Determine the estimated total cost and cost per unit, assuming that the representative is able to sell 250 units of Marvelous and 140 units of Wonderful. Allocate indirect cost on the basis of labor hours.

c. Explain why the cost per unit figures calculated in Requirement *a* differ from the amounts calculated in Requirement *b.* Also explain how the differences in estimated cost per unit will affect pricing decisions.

Problem 4-24B   *Cost Pools*

LO 1, 6

Esquire Furniture Company incurred the following costs in the process of making tables and chairs.

Glue	Paint
Supervisor salaries	Water bill
Gas bill	Vacation pay
Payroll taxes	Sewer bill
Cost of nails	Staples
Medical insurance	Electric bill

Required

a. Organize the costs in the following three pools: indirect materials, indirect labor, and indirect utilities.

b. Identify an appropriate cost driver for each pool.

c. Explain why accountants use cost pools.

Problem 4-25B   *Allocating joint product cost*

LO 3, 9

Mountain Tea Co. makes two products: a high-grade tea branded Wulong and a low-grade tea branded San Tea for the Asian market. Mountain purchases tea leaves from tea firms in mountainous villages of Taiwan and processes the tea leaves into a high-quality product. The tea leaves are dried and baked in the manufacturing process. Mountain pays farmers $600 for 900 kilograms of tea leaves. For 900 kilograms of green leaves, the company can produce 100 kilograms of Wulong and 200 kilograms of tea fragments including dried leave stems and broken dried leaves. The cost of this process is $300 per batch. The tea fragments are packaged into San Tea. The market price for San Tea is $2.00 per kilogram. The market price is $20 per kilogram for Wulong. Mountain has an option of taking an additional process to refine the 100 kilograms of Wulong into 30 kilograms of Donding, a prestigious brand. The market price of Donding is $100 per kilogram. The cost of the additional process is $250 per batch.

Required

a. Allocate the joint cost to the joint products, Wulong and San Tea, using weight as the allocation base. Calculate the net income for each product. Since the San Tea is sold at a loss, should that product line be eliminated?

b. Allocate the joint cost to the joint products, Wulong and San Tea, using relative market value as the allocation base. Calculate the net income for each product. Compare the total net income (Wulong + San Tea) computed in Requirement *b* with that computed in Requirement *a* above. Explain why the total amount is the same. Comment on which allocation base (weight or relative market value) is more appropriate.

c. Should Mountain Tea further process Wulong into Donding?

Appendix

LO 3, 9

Problem 4-26B   *Allocating service center costs—step method and direct method*

Dunne Corporation has three production departments: forming, assembly, and packaging. The maintenance department supports only the production departments; the computer services department supports all departments including maintenance. Other relevant information follows.

	Forming	Assembly	Packaging	Maintenance	Computer Services
Machine hours	6,000	2,500	1,500	400	0
Number of computers	14	20	11	15	8
Annual cost*	$450,000	$800,000	$250,000	$100,000	$90,000

*This is the annual operating cost before allocating service department costs.

Required

a. Allocate service department costs to operating departments, assuming that Dunne adopts the step method. The company uses the number of computers as the base for allocating the computer services costs and machine hours as the base for allocating the maintenance costs.

b. Use machine hours as the base for allocating maintenance department costs and the number of computers as the base for allocating computer services cost. Allocate service department costs to operating departments, assuming that Dunne adopts the direct method.

c. Compute the total allocated cost of service centers for each operating department using each allocation method.

ANALYZE, THINK, COMMUNICATE

ATC 4-1   Business Applications Case   *Allocating fixed costs at Porsche*

During its fiscal year ending on July 31, 2008, the Dr. Ing. h. c. F. Porsche AG, commonly known as "Porsche," manufactured 105,162 vehicles. During that same year, Porsche recorded depreciation on property, plant and equipment of €281,813,000. (Porsche's financial information is reported in euros, and € is the symbol for the euro.) For the purposes of this problem, assume that all of the depreciation is related to manufacturing activities.

Required

a. Indicate whether the depreciation charge is a:

   (1) Product cost, or a general, selling and administrative costs.

   (2) Fixed or variable cost relative to the volume of production.

   (3) Direct or indirect if the cost object is the cost of vehicles made in the 2008 fiscal year.

b. Assume that Porsche incurred depreciation of €23,500,000 during each month of the 2008 fiscal year, but that it produced 10,000 vehicles during February and 7,000 vehicles during March. Based on monthly costs and production levels, what was the average amount of depreciation cost per vehicle produced during each of these two months, assuming each vehicle was charged the same amount of depreciation?

c. If Porsche had expected to produce 108,000 vehicles during 2008, and had estimated its annual depreciation costs to be €285,000,000, what would have been its predetermined overhead charge per vehicle for depreciation? Explain the advantage of using this amount to determine the cost of manufacturing a car in February and March versus the amounts you computed in Requirement *b*.

d. If Porsche's management had estimated the profit per vehicle based on its budgeted production of 108,000 units, would you expect its actual profit per vehicle to be higher or lower than expected? Explain.

ATC 4-2   Group Assignment   *Selection of the cost driver*

Vulcan College School of Business is divided into three departments: accounting, marketing, and management. Relevant information for each of the departments follows.

Cost Driver	Accounting	Marketing	Management
Number of students	1,400	800	400
Number of classes per semester	64	36	28
Number of professors	20	24	10

Vulcan is a private school that expects each department to generate a profit. It rewards departments for profitability by assigning 20 percent of each department's profits back to that department. Departments have free rein as to how to use these funds. Some departments have used them to supply professors with computer technology. Others have expanded their travel budgets. The practice has been highly successful in motivating the faculty to control costs. The revenues and direct costs for the year 2011 follow:

	Accounting	Marketing	Management
Revenue	$29,600,000	$16,600,000	$8,300,000
Direct costs	24,600,000	13,800,000	6,600,000

Vulcan allocates to the School of Business $4,492,800 of indirect overhead costs such as administrative salaries and the costs of operating the registrar's office and the bookstore.

Required

a. Divide the class into groups and organize the groups into three sections. Assign each section a department. For example, groups in Section 1 should represent the Accounting Department Groups in Sections 2 and 3 should represent the Marketing Department and Management Department, respectively. Assume that the dean of the school is planning to assign an equal amount of the college overhead to each department. Have the students in each group prepare a response to the dean's plan. Each group should select a spokesperson who is prepared to answer the following questions.

   (1) Is your group in favor of or opposed to the allocation plan suggested by the dean?

   (2) Does the plan suggested by the dean provide a fair allocation? Why?

   The instructor should lead a discussion designed to assess the appropriateness of the dean's proposed allocation plan.

b. Have each group select the cost driver (allocation base) that best serves the self-interest of the department it represents.

c. Consensus on Requirement *c* should be achieved before completing Requirement *d*. Each group should determine the amount of the indirect cost to be allocated to each department using the cost driver that best serves the self-interest of the department it represents. Have a spokesperson from each section go to the board and show the income statement that would result for each department.

d. Discuss the development of a cost driver(s) that would promote fairness rather than self-interest in allocating the indirect costs.

ATC 4-3   Research Assignment   *Using real world data from Pepsi Bottling Group*

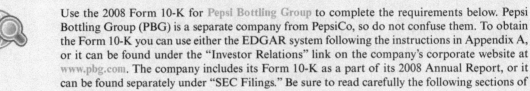

Use the 2008 Form 10-K for Pepsi Bottling Group to complete the requirements below. Pepsi Bottling Group (PBG) is a separate company from PepsiCo, so do not confuse them. To obtain the Form 10-K you can use either the EDGAR system following the instructions in Appendix A, or it can be found under the "Investor Relations" link on the company's corporate website at www.pbg.com. The company includes its Form 10-K as a part of its 2008 Annual Report, or it can be found separately under "SEC Filings." Be sure to read carefully the following sections of the document:

> Under "Item 1. Business," read subsections titled "Introduction," "Principal Products," "Raw Materials and Other Supplies," and "Seasonality."
>
> In the footnotes section of the report, under "Note 2—Summary of Significant Accounting Policies," read the subsections titled "Advertising and Marketing Costs" and "Shipping and Handling Costs"
>
> "Note 4—Balance Sheet Details," in the footnotes section of the report.

Required

a. Does PBG consider *shipping and handling costs* and *advertising and marketing costs* to be direct or indirect cost in relation to the manufacturing of its products? Explain.

b. Assume that when PBG ships orders of bottled drinks each shipment includes several different products such as Pepsi, Lipton tea, and Starbucks Frappuccino. If PBG wanted to allocate the shipping costs among the various products, what would be an appropriate cost driver? Explain the rationale for your choice.

c. Assume that PBG incurs some advertising costs that cannot be directly traced to a single product such as Pepsi or Diet Pepsi. If PBG wanted to allocate the advertising costs among the various products being advertised jointly, what would be an appropriate way of making this allocation? Explain the rationale for your choice.

d. As *Note 4* indicates, PBG computes depreciation expense on three separate classes of assets. For which of these classes of assets could its depreciation expense be directly traced to the production of soft drinks? Which class would least likely be traceable to the production of soft drinks? Explain.

e. Based on PBG's discussion of the seasonality of its business, should the depreciation of production equipment recorded in a given month be based on the volume of drinks produced that month, or should the depreciation be one-twelfth of the estimated annual depreciation PBG expects to incur? Explain your answer.

ATC 4-4   Writing Assignment   *Selection of the appropriate cost driver*

Bullions Enterprises, Inc. (BEI), makes gold, silver, and bronze medals used to recognize outstanding athletic performance in regional and national sporting events. The per-unit direct costs of producing the medals follow.

	Gold	Silver	Bronze
Direct materials	$300	$130	$ 35
Labor	120	120	120

During 2012, BEI made 1,200 units of each type of medal for a total of 3,600 (1,200 × 3) medals. All medals are created through the same production process, and they are packaged and shipped in identical containers. Indirect overhead costs amounted to $324,000. BEI currently uses the number of units as the cost driver for the allocation of overhead cost. As a result, BEI allocated $90 ($324,000 ÷ 3,600 units) of overhead cost to each medal produced.

Required

The president of the company has questioned the wisdom of assigning the same amount of over-head to each type of medal. He believes that overhead should be assigned on the basis of the cost to produce the medals. In other words, more overhead should be charged to expensive gold medals, less to silver, and even less to bronze. Assume that you are BEI's chief financial officer. Write a memo responding to the president's suggestion.

ATC 4-5 Ethical Dilemma *Allocation to achieve fairness*

The American Acupuncture Association offers continuing professional education courses for its members at its annual meeting. Instructors are paid a fee for each student attending their courses but are charged a fee for overhead costs that is deducted from their compensation. Overhead costs include fees paid to rent instructional equipment such as overhead projectors, provide supplies to participants, and offer refreshments during coffee breaks. The number of courses offered is used as the allocation base for determining the overhead charge. For example, if overhead costs amount to $5,000 and 25 courses are offered, each course is allo-cated an overhead charge of $200 ($5,000 ÷ 25 courses). Heidi McCarl, who taught one of the courses, received the following statement with her check in payment for her instructional services.

Instructional fees (20 students × $50 per student)	$1,000
Less: Overhead charge	(200)
Less: Charge for sign language assistant	(240)
Amount due instructor	$ 560

Although Ms. McCarl was well aware that one of her students was deaf and required a sign language assistant, she was surprised to find that she was required to absorb the cost of this service.

Required

a. Given that the Americans with Disabilities Act stipulates that the deaf student cannot be charged for the cost of providing sign language, who should be required to pay the cost of sign language services?

b. Explain how allocation can be used to promote fairness in distributing service costs to the disabled. Describe two ways to treat the $240 cost of providing sign language services that improve fairness.

ATC 4-6 Spreadsheet Assignment *Using Excel*

Brook Health Care Center, Inc., has three clinics servicing the Birmingham metropolitan area. The company's legal services department supports the clinics. Moreover, its computer services department supports all of the clinics and the legal services department. The company uses the number of computer workstations as the cost driver for allocating the cost of computer services and the number of patients as the cost driver for allocating the cost of legal services. The annual cost of the Department of Legal Services was $340,000, and the annual cost of the Department of Computer Services was $250,000. Other relevant informa-tion follows.

	Number of Patients	Number of Workstations
Hoover Clinic	3,100	17
Eastwood Clinic	2,300	13
Gardendale Clinic	2,800	6
Legal Services	0	14

Required

a. Construct a spreadsheet like the following one to allocate the service costs using the step method.

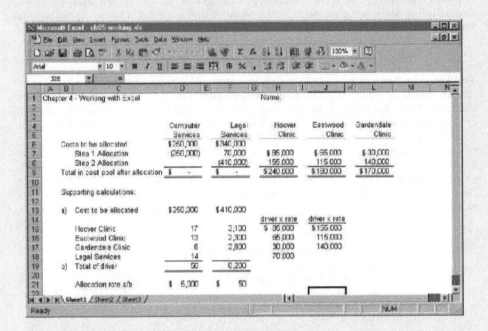

Spreadsheet Tips

1. The headings in rows 4 and 5 are right aligned. To right align text, choose Format, then Cells, and then click on the tab titled Alignment, and set the horizontal alignment to Right. The shortcut method to right align text is to click on the right align icon in the middle of the second tool bar.

2. The supporting calculation section must be completed simultaneously with the allocation table. However, most of the supporting calculations can be completed first. The exception is that the value in cell F13 refers to the sum of cells F6 and F7.

ATC 4-7   Spreadsheet Assignment   *Mastering Excel*

Phillips Paints manufactures three types of paint in a joint process: rubberized paint, rust-proofing paint, and aluminum paint. In a standard batch of 500,000 gallons of raw material, the outputs are 240,000 gallons of rubberized paint, 80,000 gallons of rust-proofing paint, and 180,000 gallons of aluminum paint. The production cost of a batch is $2,700,000. The sales prices per gallon are $15, $18, and $20 for rubberized, rust-proofing, and aluminum paint, respectively.

Required

a. Construct a spreadsheet to allocate joint costs to the three products using the number of gallons as the allocation base.

b. Include formulas in your spreadsheet to calculate the gross margin for each paint.

COMPREHENSIVE PROBLEM

Magnificent Modems has excess production capacity and is considering the possibility of making and selling paging equipment. The following estimates are based on a production and sales volume of 1,000 pagers.

Unit-level manufacturing costs are expected to be $20. Sales commissions will be established at $1 per unit. The current facility-level costs, including depreciation on manufacturing equipment ($60,000), rent on the manufacturing facility ($50,000), depreciation on the administrative equipment ($12,000), and other fixed administrative expenses ($71,950), will not be affected by the production of the pagers. The chief accountant has decided to allocate the facility-level costs to the existing product (modems) and to the new product (pagers) on the basis of the number of units of product made (i.e., 5,000 modems and 1,000 pagers).

Required

a. Determine the per-unit cost of making and selling 1,000 pagers.

b. Assuming the pagers could be sold at a price of $34 each, should Magnificent make the pagers?

c. Comment on the validity of using the number of units as an allocation base.

CHAPTER 5

Cost Management in an Automated Business Environment

ABC, ABM, and TQM

LEARNING OBJECTIVES

After you have mastered the material in this chapter you will be able to:

1 Explain how activity-based costing improves accuracy in determining the cost of products and services.

2 Identify cost centers and cost drivers in an activity-based costing system.

3 Use activity-based costing to calculate costs of products and services.

4 Identify the components of quality costs.

5 Prepare and interpret quality cost reports.

CHAPTER OPENING

Worldwide growth in capitalism has fostered an increasingly competitive global business environment. Companies have responded by using technology to increase productivity. Management accountants have worked with engineers to more accurately measure and control costs. They have eliminated many nonvalue-added activities and have employed quality control procedures that reduce costs and enhance customer satisfaction. These innovative business practices have enabled companies to eliminate unprofitable products and to promote products that maximize profitability. This chapter focuses on newer and emerging business practices employed by world-class companies.

The Curious Accountant

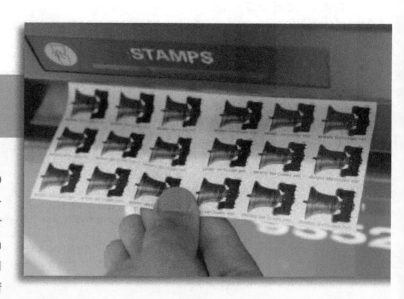

A vendor incurs a cost when it allows customers to pay using a credit or debit card. Credit card companies, such as American Express, charge the vendor either a fixed fee or a percentage of the transaction amount. For example, when the United States Postal Service (USPS) allows a customer to pay for $100 of stamps using a credit card, the USPS receives less than $100 from the credit card company, perhaps $97. The actual discount rate the credit card company charges depends on its agreement with the individual vendor. Large customers such as the USPS usually get better rates than smaller customers. Considering that total revenues at the USPS were $74.9 billion in 2008 and that $38.2 billion of these were from first-class mail, the costs of allowing customers to use debit and credit cards to pay for postage can be high.

Most companies that accept credit cards as payment do so believing that customers will spend more money using "plastic" than if forced to pay cash. Also, a company's competitors may be accepting credit cards, leaving the company little choice. However, the USPS has a virtual monopoly on many types of mail services in the United States, so why is it willing to allow customers to pay with credit cards? Why not make everyone pay with cash or checks?

Now consider this: Another large government agency, the Internal Revenue Service (IRS) will not accept debit or credit card payments unless the taxpayer pays the credit card fee. If the USPS does not require a surcharge for credit card users, why does the IRS? (Answers on page 215.)

DEVELOPMENT OF A SINGLE COMPANYWIDE COST DRIVER

Explain how activity-based costing improves accuracy in determining the cost of products and services.

When accountants first developed cost systems, manufacturing processes were labor intensive. Indirect manufacturing costs were relatively minor and highly correlated with labor use; products that used large amounts of labor consumed large amounts of overhead. This link made the number of labor hours a suitable cost driver for allocating overhead costs.

To illustrate, suppose during an eight-hour day Friedman Company production employees worked on two jobs, Job 1 for two hours and Job 2 for six hours. Friedman consumed utilities of $120 during the day. How much of the $120 should the company assign to each job? Friedman cannot trace the utility cost directly to a specific job, but the job that required more labor likely consumed more of the utility cost. The longer employees work the more heat, lights, and water they use. Allocating the utility cost to the two jobs based on *direct labor hours* produces rational results. Friedman could allocate the utility cost at $15 per hour ($120 ÷ 8 hours). It could assign Job 1 $30 of the utility cost ($15 per hour × 2 hours), and Job 2 the remaining $90 ($15 × 6 hours).

In addition to utilities, direct labor drives many other indirect costs. Consider the depreciation cost of tools employees use while working on production jobs. The more time employees work, the more they use the tools. Direct labor hours could be an effective cost driver (allocation base) for allocating tool depreciation costs. The same logic applies to supervisory salaries, production supplies, factory rent expense, and other overhead costs. Many companies applied this reasoning to justify using direct labor hours as the *sole base* for establishing a **companywide allocation rate.** These companies then allocated all overhead costs to their products or other cost objects using the single labor-based, companywide overhead rate. Even though using one base to allocate all overhead costs inaccurately measured some cost objects, in the labor intensive environment that spawned companywide allocation rates, overhead costs were relatively small compared to the costs of labor and materials. Allocation inaccuracies were relatively insignificant in amount.

Automation has changed the nature of manufacturing processes. The number of direct labor hours is no longer an effective allocation base in many modern manufacturing companies. Machines have replaced most human workers. Because they operate technically complex equipment, the remaining workers are highly skilled and not easily replaced. Companies resist laying off these trained workers when production declines. Neither do companies add employees when production increases. Adjusting production volume merely requires turning additional machines on or off. In such circumstances, direct labor is not related to production volume. Direct labor is therefore not an effective base for allocating overhead costs. Former labor-intensive companies that adopt automation usually must develop more sophisticated ways to allocate overhead costs.

When companies replace people with machines, overhead costs such as machinery depreciation and power usage become greater in proportion to total manufacturing costs. In highly automated companies, overhead costs may be greater than direct labor and direct materials costs combined. Although misallocating minor overhead amounts does little harm, misallocating major costs destroys the usefulness of accounting information and leads to poor decisions. Managers must consider how automation affects overhead cost allocation.

Effects of Automation on Selecting a Cost Driver

In an automated manufacturing environment, robots and sophisticated machinery, rather than human labor, transform raw materials into finished goods. To illustrate the effect of these changes on selecting a cost driver, return to the previous Friedman Company example. Suppose Friedman automates the production process for Job 2, replacing most labor with four hours of machine processing and reducing the number of direct labor hours required from six to one. Assume the new machinery acquired increases utility consumption and depreciation charges, raising daily overhead costs from $120 to $420. Because Job 1 requires two hours of direct labor and Job 2 now requires one hour of direct labor, Friedman's companywide allocation rate increases to $140 per direct labor hour ($420 ÷ 3 hours). The company would allocate $280 ($140 × 2 hours) of the total overhead cost to Job 1 and $140 ($140 × 1 hour) to Job 2. The pre- and postautomation allocations are compared here.

Product	Preautomation Cost Distribution	Postautomation Cost Distribution
Job 1	$ 30	$280
Job 2	90	140
Total	$120	$420

Using direct labor hours as the cost driver after automating production of Job 2 distorts the overhead cost allocation. Although Friedman did not change the production process for Job 1 at all, Job 1 received a $250 ($280 − $30) increase in its share of allocated overhead cost. This increase should have been assigned to Job 2 because automating production of Job 2 caused overhead costs to increase. The decrease in direct labor hours for Job 2 causes the distortion. Prior to automation, Job 2 used six of eight total direct labor hours and was therefore allocated 75 percent (6 ÷ 8) of the overhead cost. After automation, Job 2 consumed only one of three total direct labor hours, reducing its overhead allocation to only 33 percent of the total. These changes in the allocation base, coupled with the increase in total overhead cost, caused the postautomation overhead cost allocation for Job 1 to be significantly overstated and for Job 2 to be significantly understated.

One way to solve the misallocation problem is to find a more suitable volume-based cost driver. For example, Friedman could allocate utility costs using machine hours instead of direct labor hours. This text illustrated using different **volume-based cost drivers** (such as material dollars and direct labor hours) in Chapter 4. Unfortunately, automated production processes often generate costs which have no cause-and-effect relationship with volume-based cost drivers. Many companies have therefore adopted **activity-based cost drivers** to improve the accuracy of indirect cost allocations. To illustrate, consider the case of Carver Soup Company.

Activity-Based Cost Drivers

Carver Soup Company (CSC) produces batches of vegetable and tomato soup. Each time CSC switches production from vegetable soup to tomato soup or vice versa, it incurs certain costs. For example, production workers must clean the mixing, blending, and cooking equipment. They must change settings on the equipment to the specifications for the particular soup to be processed. CSC must test each batch for quality to ensure the recipe has been correctly followed. Because these costs are incurred for each new batch, they are called **start-up,** or **setup, costs.** CSC plans to make 180 batches of each type of soup during the coming year. The following table summarizes expected production information:

	Vegetable	Tomato	Total
Number of cans	954,000	234,000	1,188,000
Number of setups	180	180	360

CSC expects each setup will cost $264, for total expected setup costs of $95,040 ($264 × 360 setups). Using number of cans as the cost driver (volume-based driver) produces an allocation rate of $0.08 per can ($95,040 ÷ 1,188,000 cans). Multiplying the allocation rate by the weight of the base (number of cans) produces the following setup cost allocation:

Product	Allocation Rate	×	Number of Cans Produced	=	Allocated Setup Cost
Vegetable	$0.08	×	954,000	=	$76,320
Tomato	0.08	×	234,000	=	18,720

As expected, the volume-based (number of cans) allocation rate assigns more cost to the high-volume vegetable soup product. However, assigning more setup cost to the vegetable soup makes little sense. Since both products require the *same number* of setups, the setup cost should be distributed equally between them. The volume-based cost driver *overcosts* the high-volume product (vegetable soup) and *undercosts* the low-volume product (tomato soup).

Setup costs are driven by the number of times CSC employees perform the setup activities. The more setups employees undertake, the greater the total setup cost. An *activity-based cost driver* (number of setups) provides a more accurate allocation base for setup costs. Using the allocation rate of $264 ($95,040 ÷ 360 setups) per setup assigns the same amount of setup cost to each product, as follows:

Product	Allocation Rate	×	Number of Setups	=	Allocated Setup Cost
Vegetable	$264	×	180	=	$47,520
Tomato	264	×	180	=	47,520

Activity-Based Cost Drivers Enhance Relevance

The *activity-based cost driver* produces a better allocation because it distributes the *relevant* costs to the appropriate products. If CSC were to stop producing tomato soup, it could *avoid* spending $47,520 for 180 setups (assuming CSC could eliminate labor, supplies, and other resources used in the setup process). *Avoidable costs are relevant* to decision making. The inaccurate volume-based product cost data could mislead a manager into making a poor decision. Suppose a company specializing in setup activities offered to provide CSC 180 tomato soup setups for $40,000. A manager relying on the volume-based allocated cost of $18,720 would reject the $40,000 offer to outsource as too costly. In fact, CSC should accept the offer because it could avoid $47,520 of cost if the outside company performs the setup activity. In a highly automated environment in which companies produce many different products at varying volume levels, it is little wonder that many companies have turned to activity-based costing to improve the accuracy of cost allocations and the effectiveness of decisions.

✓ **CHECK YOURSELF 5.1**

Professional Training Services, Inc. (PTSI), offers professional exam review courses for both the certified public accountant (CPA) and the certified management accountant (CMA) exams. Many more students take the CPA review courses than the CMA review courses. PTSI uses the same size and number of classrooms to teach both courses; its CMA courses simply have more empty seats. PTSI is trying to determine the cost of offering the two courses. The company's accountant has decided to allocate classroom rental cost based on the number of students enrolled in the courses. Explain why this allocation base will likely result in an inappropriate assignment of cost to the two cost objects. Identify a more appropriate allocation base.

Answer   Using the number of students as the allocation base will assign more of the rental cost to the CPA review courses because those courses have higher enrollments. This allocation is inappropriate because the number of classrooms, not the number of students, drives the amount of rental cost. Since both courses require the same number of classrooms, the rental cost should be allocated equally between them. Several allocation bases would produce an equal allocation, such as the number of classrooms, the number of courses, or a 50/50 percentage split.

ACTIVITY-BASED COSTING

A company that allocates indirect costs using **activity-based costing (ABC)** follows a two-stage process. In the first stage, costs are assigned to pools based on the activities that cause the costs to be incurred. In the second stage, the costs in the activity cost pools are allocated to products using a variety of cost drivers. The first step in developing an ABC system is to identify essential activities and the costs of performing those activities.

LO 2

Identify cost centers and cost drivers in an activity-based costing system.

A business undertakes **activities** to accomplish its mission. Typical activities include acquiring raw materials, transforming raw materials into finished products, and delivering products to customers. These broadly defined activities can be divided into subcategories. For example, the activity of acquiring raw materials involves separate subcategory activities such as identifying suppliers, obtaining price quotations, evaluating materials specifications, completing purchase orders, and receiving purchased materials. Each of these subcategories can be subdivided into yet more detailed activities. For instance, identifying suppliers may include such activities as reviewing advertisements, searching Internet sites, and obtaining recommendations from business associates. Further subdivisions are possible. Companies perform thousands of activities.

Identifying Activity Centers

Maintaining separate cost records for thousands of activities is expensive. To reduce record-keeping costs, companies group related activities into hubs called **activity centers.** The overhead costs of these related activities are combined into a cost pool for each activity center. Because the activities assigned to each center are related, a business can obtain rational cost allocations using a common cost driver for an entire cost pool. Determining the optimal number of activity centers requires *cost/benefit analysis.* Companies will incur the higher record-keeping costs for additional activity centers only to the extent that the additional accuracy improves decision making.

Comparing ABC with Traditional Cost Allocation

How do ABC systems differ from traditional allocation systems? Traditional allocation systems pool costs by departments, then allocate departmental cost pools to cost objects using volume-based cost drivers. In contrast, ABC systems pool costs

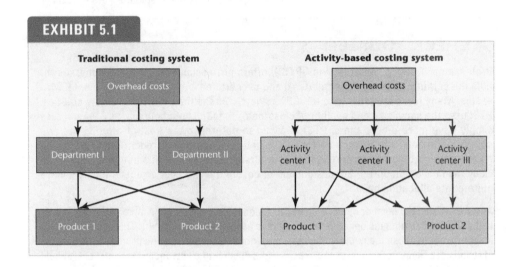

EXHIBIT 5.1

by activity centers, then allocate activity center cost pools to cost objects using a variety of volume- and activity-based cost drivers. ABC systems use many more activity centers than the number of departments in a traditional allocation system. As a result, ABC improves cost tracing by using more cause-and-effect relationships in assigning indirect costs to numerous activity centers. Exhibit 5.1 illustrates the primary differences between a traditional two-stage allocation system and an ABC system.

Types of Production Activities

Many companies organize activities into four hierarchical categories to improve cost tracing. These categories are (1) unit-level activities, (2) batch-level activities, (3) product-level activities, and (4) facility-level activities.[1] The overhead costs in each category are pooled and allocated to products based on how the products benefit from the activities. *The primary objective is to trace the cost of performing activities to the products that are causing the activities to be performed.* To illustrate, consider the overhead costs incurred by Unterman Shirt Company.

Unterman has two product lines, dress shirts and casual shirts. The company expects to incur overhead costs of $5,730,000 in the course of producing 680,000 dress shirts and 120,000 casual shirts during 2011. Currently, Unterman assigns an equal amount of overhead to each shirt, simply dividing the total expected overhead cost by the total expected production ($5,730,000 ÷ 800,000 units = $7.16 per shirt, rounded). Each type of shirt requires approximately the same amount of direct materials, $8.20 per shirt, and the same amount of direct labor, $6.80 per shirt. The total cost per shirt is $22.16 ($7.16 + $8.20 + $6.80). Unterman sells shirts for $31 each, yielding a gross margin of $8.84 per shirt ($31 − $22.16).

Bob Unterman, president and owner of the company, believes the direct materials and direct labor costs are reasonable, but the overhead costs must not be the same for both product lines. Mr. Unterman hired a consultant, Rebecca Lynch, to trace the overhead costs. Ms. Lynch decided to use an *activity-based cost* system. She identified the activities necessary to make shirts and classified them into the following four activity cost centers.

Unit-Level Activity Center

Unit-level activities occur each time a unit of product is made. For example, for every shirt made, Unterman incurs inspection costs, machine-related utility costs, and costs

---

[1]The types of costs in each category will be in Chapter 6.

for production supplies. Total unit-level cost increases with every shirt made and decreases with reductions in production volume. Some costs behave so much like unit-level costs that they may be accounted for as unit-level even though they are not strictly unit-level. For example, suppose Unterman employees lubricate production machinery after every eight hours of continuous operation. Although Unterman does not incur lubrication cost for each shirt produced, the cost behavior pattern is so closely tied to production levels that it may be accounted for as a unit-level cost.

Ms. Lynch identified the following unit-level overhead costs: (1) $300,000 for machine-related utilities, (2) $50,000 for machine maintenance, (3) $450,000 for indirect labor and indirect materials, (4) $200,000 for inspection and quality control, and (5) $296,000 for miscellaneous unit-level costs. She assigned these costs into a single *unit-level activity center* overhead cost pool of $1,296,000. This assignment illustrates the first stage of the two-stage ABC allocation system. Of the total $5,730,000 overhead cost, Ms. Lynch has allocated $1,296,000 to one of the four activity centers. The remaining overhead cost is allocated among the three other activity centers.

The second-stage cost assignment involves allocating the $1,296,000 unit-level cost pool between the two product lines. Because unit-level costs are incurred each time a shirt is produced, they should be allocated using a base correlated to production levels. Ms. Lynch chose direct labor hours as the allocation base. Past performance indicates the dress shirts will require 272,000 direct labor hours and the casual shirts will require 48,000 direct labor hours. Based on this information, Ms. Lynch allocated the unit-level overhead costs and computed the cost per unit as shown in Exhibit 5.2.

EXHIBIT 5.2

Allocation of Unit-Level Overhead Costs

	Product Lines		
	Dress Shirts	Casual Shirts	Total
Number of direct labor hours (a)	272,000	48,000	320,000
Cost per labor hour ($1,296,000 ÷ 320,000 hours) (b)	$4.05	$4.05	NA
Total allocated overhead cost (c = a × b)	$1,101,600	$194,400	$1,296,000
Number of shirts (d)	680,000	120,000	800,000
Cost per shirt (c ÷ d)	$1.62	$1.62	NA

The unit-level costs exhibit a variable cost behavior pattern. Total cost varies in direct proportion to the number of units produced. Cost per unit is constant. Because production volume does not affect the unit-level overhead cost, the pricing of shirts should not be affected by the fact that the company makes more dress shirts than casual shirts.

Batch-Level Activity Center

Batch-level activities relate to producing groups of products. Batch-level costs are fixed regardless of the number of units produced in a single batch. For example, the costs of setting up machinery to cut fabric for a certain size shirt remain unchanged regardless of the number of shirts cut at that particular machine setting. Similarly, the cost of a first-item batch test is the same whether 200 or 2,000 shirts are made in the batch. Materials handling costs are also commonly classified as batch-level because materials are usually transferred from one department to another in batches. For example, all of the size small casual shirts are cut in the sizing department, then the entire batch of cut fabric is transferred in one operation to the sewing department. The cost of materials handling is the same regardless of whether the batch load is large or small.

Because total batch costs depend on the number of batches produced, more batch costs should be allocated to products that require more batches. Ms. Lynch identified $690,000 of total batch-level overhead costs and assigned this amount to a batch-level cost pool.

For the second-stage allocation, Ms. Lynch determined that the casual-shirt line requires considerably more setups than the dress-shirt line because the casual shirts are subject to frequent style changes. Because customers buy limited amounts of items with short shelf lives, Unterman must produce casual shirts in small batches. Ms. Lynch decided more of the batch-level costs should be allocated to the casual-shirt line than to the dress-shirt line. She chose number of setups as the most rational allocation base. Since casual shirts require 1,280 setups and dress shirts require 1,020 setups, Ms. Lynch allocated the batch-level costs as shown in Exhibit 5.3.

EXHIBIT 5.3

Allocation of Batch-Level Overhead Costs

	Product Lines		
	Dress Shirts	Casual Shirts	Total
Number of setups performed (a)	1,020	1,280	2,300
Cost per setup ($690,000 ÷ 2,300 setups) (b)	$300	$300	NA
Total allocated overhead cost (c = a × b)	$306,000	$384,000	$690,000
Number of shirts (d)	680,000	120,000	800,000
Cost per shirt (c ÷ d)	$0.45	$3.20	NA

ABC demonstrates that the per shirt batch-level cost for casual shirts ($3.20 per shirt) is considerably more than for dress shirts ($0.45). One reason is that the casual-shirt line incurs more batch-level costs ($384,000 versus $306,000). The other is that Unterman produces far fewer casual shirts than dress shirts (120,000 units versus 680,000). Because batch-level costs are fixed relative to the number of units in a particular batch, the cost per unit is greater the smaller the batch. For example, if setup costs are $300, the setup cost per unit for a batch of 100 units is $3 ($300 ÷ 100 units). For a batch of only 10 units, however, the setup cost per unit is $30 ($300 ÷ 10 units). When batch-level costs are significant, companies should pursue high-volume products. Low-volume products are more expensive to make because the fixed costs must be spread over fewer units. To the extent that cost affects pricing, Unterman should charge more for casual shirts than dress shirts.

Product-Level Activity Center

Product-level activities support specific products or product lines. Examples include raw materials inventory holding costs; engineering development costs; and legal fees for patents, copyrights, trademarks, and brand names. Unterman Shirt Company positions itself as a fashion leader. It incurs extensive design costs to ensure that it remains a trendsetter. The company also incurs engineering costs to continually improve the quality of materials used in its shirts and legal fees to protect its brand names. After reviewing Unterman's operations, Ms. Lynch concluded she could trace $1,800,000 of the total overhead cost to the product-level activity center.

The second-stage allocation requires dividing these activities between the dress-shirt line and the casual-shirt line. Interviews with fashion design staff disclosed that they spend more time on casual shirts because of the frequent style changes. Similarly, the engineers spend more of their time developing new fabric, buttons, and zippers for casual shirts. The materials used in dress shirts are fairly stable. Although engineers spend some time improving the quality of dress-shirt materials, they devote far more

EXHIBIT 5.4

Allocation of Product-Level Overhead Costs

	Product Lines		
	Dress Shirts	Casual Shirts	Total
Percent of product-level activity utilization (a)	30%	70%	100%
Total allocated overhead cost (b = a × $1,800,000)	$540,000	$1,260,000	$1,800,000
Total units produced (c)	680,000	120,000	800,000
Cost per unit (b ÷ c)	$0.79*	$10.50	NA

*Rounded to the nearest whole cent.

time to the more unusual materials used in the casual shirts. Similarly, the legal department spends more time developing and protecting patents, trademarks, and brand names for the casual-shirt line. Ms. Lynch concluded that 70 percent of the product-level cost pool applied to casual shirts and 30 percent to dress shirts. She allocated product-level costs to the two product lines as shown in Exhibit 5.4.

Product-level costs are frequently distributed unevenly among different product lines. Unterman Shirt Company incurs substantially more costs to sustain its casual-shirt line than its dress-shirt line. Using a single companywide overhead rate in such circumstances distorts cost measurements. Distorted product cost measurements can lead to negative consequences such as irrational pricing policies and rewards for inappropriate decisions. Activity-based costing reduces measurement distortions by more accurately tracing costs to the products that cause their incurrence.

Facility-Level Activity Center

Facility-level activities benefit the production process as a whole and are not related to any specific product, batch, or unit of production. For example, insuring the manufacturing facility against fire losses does not benefit any particular product or product line. Facility-level costs include depreciation on the manufacturing plant, security, landscaping, plant maintenance, general utilities, and property taxes. For Unterman Shirt Company, Ms. Lynch identified $1,944,000 of facility-level overhead costs. Because no cause-and-effect relationship exists between these facility-level manufacturing costs and the two product lines, she must allocate these costs arbitrarily. Basing the arbitrary allocation on the total number of units produced, Ms. Lynch allocated 85 percent (680,000 ÷ 800,000) of the facility-level cost pool to the dress-shirt line and 15 percent (120,000 ÷ 800,000) to the casual-shirt line as shown in Exhibit 5.5.

EXHIBIT 5.5

Allocation of Facility-Level Overhead Costs

	Product Lines		
	Dress Shirts	Casual Shirts	Total
Percent of total units (a)	85%	15%	100%
Total allocated overhead cost (b = a × $1,944,000)	$1,652,400	$291,600	$1,944,000
Total units produced (c)	680,000	120,000	800,000
Cost per unit (b ÷ c)	$2.43	$2.43	NA

Classification of Activities Not Limited to Four Categories

The number of activity centers a business uses depends on cost/benefit analysis. The four categories illustrated for Unterman Shirt Company represent a useful starting point. Any of the four categories could be further subdivided into more detailed activity centers. Unterman could establish an activity cost center for unit-level labor-related activities and a different activity center for unit-level machine-related activities. Identifying all potential activity centers in a real-world company can be daunting. Paulette Bennett describes the process used in the Material Control Department at Compumotor, Inc., as follows:

> Recognizing that ordinarily the two biggest problems with an ABC project are knowing where to start and how deep to go, we began by analyzing the activities that take place in our procurement process. As the old saying goes, to find the biggest alligators you usually have to wade into the weeds; therefore, we started by writing down all the procurement activities. Creating a real world picture of costs by activity was our aim. But had we used our initial list we would have designed a spreadsheet so large that no human could ever have emerged alive at the other end.[2]

Ms. Bennett's abbreviated list still included 83 separate activities. The list represented the activity centers for only one department of a very large company. Although the Unterman example used only four categories, the real-world equivalent is far more complex.

✓ CHECK YOURSELF 5.2

Under what circumstances would the number of units produced be an inappropriate allocation base for batch-level costs?

Answer Using the number of units produced as the allocation base would allocate more of the batch-level costs to high-volume products and less of the costs to low-volume products. Since batch-level costs are normally related to the number of batches rather than the number of units made in each batch, allocation of batch-level costs based on units produced would result in poor product cost estimates; the costing system would overcost high-volume products and undercost low-volume products. It would be appropriate to use the number of units produced only when each batch consists of the same number of product units. Even under these circumstances, the number of units merely serves as a proxy for the number of batches. It would still be more appropriate to use the number of batches to allocate batch-level costs.

Context-Sensitive Classification of Activities

Particular activities could fall into any of the four hierarchical categories. For example, inspecting each individual item produced is a unit-level activity. Inspecting the first item of each batch to ensure the setup was correct is a batch-level activity. Inspecting a specific product line is a product-level activity. Finally, inspecting the factory building is a facility-level activity. To properly classify activities, you must learn to analyze the context within which they occur.

Selecting Cost Drivers

Activity-based costing uses both *volume-based* cost drivers and *activity-based* cost drivers. Volume-based drivers are appropriate for indirect costs that increase or decrease relative to the volume of activity. Using cost drivers such as units, direct labor hours, or

---

[2]Paulette Bennett, "ABM and the Procurement Cost Model," *Management Accounting*, March 1996, pp. 28–32.

machine hours is appropriate for unit-level activities. The flaw in traditional costing systems is that they use a volume-based measure (usually direct labor hours) to allocate all indirect costs. In contrast, the more sophisticated ABC approach uses activity drivers such as number of setups or percentage of utilization for overhead costs that are not influenced by volume. ABC improves the accuracy of allocations by using a combination of volume- and activity-based cost drivers.

USING ABC INFORMATION TO TRACE COSTS TO PRODUCT LINES

Exhibit 5.6 summarizes the ABC allocations Ms. Lynch prepared. Mr. Unterman was shocked to learn that overhead costs for casual shirts are virtually three times those for dress shirts. Exhibit 5.7 compares the per-unit gross margins for the two product lines using the traditional cost system and using the ABC system. Recall that direct materials and direct labor costs for dress and casual shirts are $8.20 and $6.80, respectively. The difference in the margins is attributable to the overhead allocation. Using a traditional companywide overhead rate allocates an equal amount of overhead to each shirt ($5,730,000 ÷ 800,000 units = $7.16 per shirt). In contrast, the ABC approach assigns $5.29 to each dress shirt and $17.75 to each casual shirt. Total overhead cost is $5,730,000 under both approaches. It is the *allocation* of rather than the *amount* of the overhead cost that differs. ABC shows that making a casual

LO 3

Use activity-based costing to calculate costs of products and services.

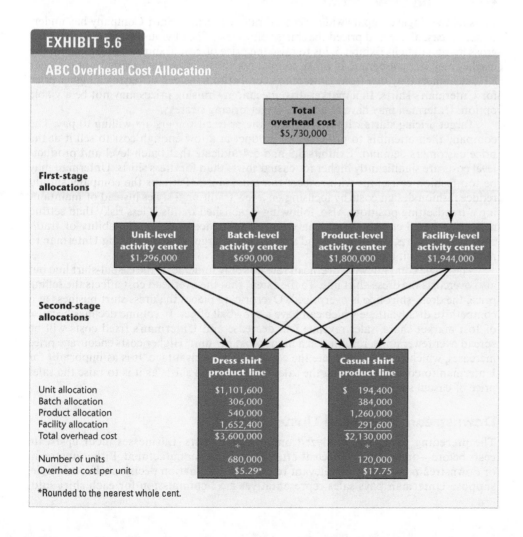

EXHIBIT 5.6

ABC Overhead Cost Allocation

Total overhead cost **$5,730,000**

First-stage allocations

| Unit-level activity center $1,296,000 | Batch-level activity center $690,000 | Product-level activity center $1,800,000 | Facility-level activity center $1,944,000 |

Second-stage allocations

	Dress shirt product line	Casual shirt product line
Unit allocation	$1,101,600	$ 194,400
Batch allocation	306,000	384,000
Product allocation	540,000	1,260,000
Facility allocation	1,652,400	291,600
Total overhead cost	$3,600,000	$2,130,000
	÷	÷
Number of units	680,000	120,000
Overhead cost per unit	$5.29*	$17.75

*Rounded to the nearest whole cent.

EXHIBIT 5.7

Gross Margins Using Traditional Versus ABC Costing

	Gross Margins Traditional System		Gross Margins ABC Costing	
	Dress Shirts	Casual Shirts	Dress Shirts	Casual Shirts
Sales price	$31.00	$31.00	$31.00	$31.00
Cost of goods sold				
Materials cost	(8.20)	(8.20)	(8.20)	(8.20)
Labor cost	(6.80)	(6.80)	(6.80)	(6.80)
Overhead	(7.16)	(7.16)	(5.29)	(17.75)
Gross margin	$ 8.84	$ 8.84	$10.71	$ (1.75)

---

shirt costs more than making a dress shirt. After reviewing the data in Exhibit 5.7, Mr. Unterman realized the company was incurring losses on the casual-shirt line. What options does he have?

Under- and Overcosting

In using the single companywide overhead rate, Unterman Shirt Company has undercosted its casual line and priced the shirts below cost. The obvious response to the ABC gross margin data in Exhibit 5.7 is to raise the price of casual shirts. Unfortunately, the market may not cooperate. If other companies are selling casual shirts at prices near $31, customers may buy from Unterman's competitors instead of paying a higher price for Unterman's shirts. In a market-driven economy, raising prices may not be a viable option. Unterman may have to adopt a target-pricing strategy.

Target pricing starts with determining the price customers are willing to pay. The company then attempts to produce the product at a low enough cost to sell it at the price customers demand. Exhibits 5.3 and 5.4 indicate that batch-level and product-level costs are significantly higher for casual shirts than for dress shirts. Unterman may be too fashion conscious with respect to casual shirts. Perhaps the company should reduce fashion design costs by focusing on a few traditional styles instead of maintaining a trendsetting position. Also, following established trends is less risky than setting new ones. Retail customers may have more confidence in the marketability of traditional casual shirts, which could lead them to place larger orders, enabling Unterman to reduce its per-unit batch costs.

The single companywide overhead rate not only undercosts the casual-shirt line but also overcosts the dress-shirt line. To the extent that the overhead cost affects the selling price, the dress-shirt line is overpriced. Overpricing places the dress shirt business at a competitive disadvantage which can have a snowball effect. If volume declines because of lost market share, sales revenue will decrease and Unterman's fixed costs will be spread over fewer units, resulting in a higher cost per unit. Higher costs encourage price increases, which further aggravate the competitive disadvantage. It is as important for Unterman to consider reducing the sales price of dress shirts as it is to raise the sales price of casual shirts.

Downstream Costs and Upstream Costs

The preceding paragraph analyzed only product costs. Businesses incur **upstream costs** before—and **downstream costs** after—goods are manufactured. Either upstream or downstream costs may be relevant to product elimination decisions. For example, suppose Unterman pays sales representatives a $2 commission for each shirt sold.

Answers to The Curious Accountant

The USPS commissioned Coopers & Lybrand (C&L) (now Pricewaterhouse-Coopers), a large accounting firm, to conduct activity-based costing (ABC) studies of its key revenue collection processes. C&L developed an ABC model for USPS's existing cash and check revenue collection and a similar ABC model for debit and credit card activities. The ABC model identified costs associated with unit, batch, and product activities. *Unit-level activity* was defined as the acceptance and processing of a payment by item. *Batch-level activities* involved the closeout at the end of the day, consolidation, and supervisory review. *Product-level activities* included maintenance for bank accounts and deposit reconciliation for the cash and checks model and terminal maintenance and training for the credit and debit card system. A comparison of the cost of the two activity models revealed that a significant cost savings could be achieved in the long term by implementing a debit and credit card system. Some examples of expected cost savings included a decrease in the per-unit transaction cost due to the fact that credit card customers tend to spend more per transaction than do cash customers. In addition, the cost of activities associated with the collection of bad debts falls to virtually zero when debit or credit cards are used and the cost of cash management activities declines. Funds are collected earlier (no check collection float occurs), thereby reducing the need for financing and the resultant interest cost.

Payments received by the IRS are very different from those received by the USPS. The USPS experiences billions of payment transactions each year, many of which are for relatively small amounts; for example, a customer may pay to send one package priority mail for $5.70. The IRS receives fewer payments than the USPS, but most of these payments are for significantly larger amounts. Also, while the USPS has over 36,000 post offices processing payments, the IRS has less than a dozen payment processing centers. In ABC costing terms, the IRS has fewer unit-level activities and batch-level activities associated with processing payments than does the USPS, so the financial analysis used by the USPS is not relevant to the IRS. There is another very good reason the IRS does not accept credit card payments unless the taxpayer pays a surcharge; Congress passed a law stipulating this condition.

Source: Terrel L. Carter, Ali M. Sedghat, and Thomas D. Williams, "How ABC Changed the Post Office," *Management Accounting*, February 1998, pp. 28–36; and the USPS 2008 Annual Report.

Although sales commissions are selling, not product, costs, they are relevant to deciding whether to eliminate the casual-shirt line. Unterman can avoid the commission expense if it sells no casual shirts. Including the sales commission increases the total avoidable cost to $32.32 ($30.32 product costs + $2.00 sales commissions) which is more than the $31 sales price. Unterman would therefore be more profitable if it abandoned the casual-shirt line. Management must also consider upstream costs such as those for research and development. To continue in business, companies must sell products at prices that exceed the *total* cost to develop, make, and sell them.

Employee Attitudes and the Availability of Data

Activity-based costing can lead management to implement cost-cutting measures, including product and product line eliminations, that can result in the loss of jobs. Employees are therefore sometimes uncooperative with management efforts to adopt an ABC system. Companies must help employees recognize that ABC and other **strategic cost management** techniques frequently result in redirecting workers rather than displacing them. Ultimately, jobs depend on the employer's competitive health. The implementation of an ABC system is more likely to succeed when both managers and rank-and-file employees are convinced their own well-being is tied to the company's well-being.

Even when employees cooperate, implementing an ABC system can be difficult. Frequently, the accounting system is not collecting some of the needed data. For example, suppose a manager wants to allocate inspection costs based on the number of hours job inspections take. Inspectors may not record the time spent on individual jobs. Basing the allocation on inspection hours requires inspectors to begin keeping more detailed time records. The accuracy of the allocation then depends on how conscientiously inspectors complete their time reports. Obtaining employee support and accurate data are two of the more challenging obstacles to successfully implementing ABC.

TOTAL QUALITY MANAGEMENT

Quality is key to a company's ability to obtain and retain customers. What does *quality* mean? It does not always mean the best. A spoon made of silver is of higher quality than a spoon made of plastic, but customers are perfectly willing to use plastic spoons at fast-food restaurants. **Quality** represents the degree to which products or services *conform* to design specifications. The costs companies incur to ensure quality conformance can be classified into four categories: prevention, appraisal, internal failure, and external failure.

Companies incur **prevention costs** to avoid nonconforming products. They incur **appraisal costs** to identify nonconforming products produced in spite of prevention cost expenditures. **Failure costs** result from correcting defects in nonconforming products produced. **Internal failure costs** pertain to correcting defects before goods reach customers; **external failure costs** result from delivering defective goods to customers.

Because prevention and appraisal costs are a function of managerial discretion, they are often called **voluntary costs.** Management chooses how much to spend on these voluntary costs. In contrast, management does not directly control failure costs. The cost of dissatisfied customers may not be measurable, much less controllable. Even though failure costs may not be directly controllable, they are related to voluntary costs. When management spends additional funds on prevention and appraisal controls, failure costs tend to decline. As the level of control increases, quality conformance increases, reducing failure costs. When control activities are reduced, quality conformance decreases and failure cost increases. *Voluntary costs and failure costs move in opposite directions.*

Minimizing Total Quality Cost

Total quality control cost is the sum of voluntary costs plus failure costs. Because voluntary costs and failure costs are negatively correlated, the minimum amount of *total* quality cost is located at the point on a graph where the marginal voluntary expenditures equal the marginal savings on failure cost as shown in Exhibit 5.8.

EXHIBIT 5.8

Relationships Among Components of Quality Cost

Cost per Unit

Total quality cost

Voluntary cost (prevention and appraisal)

Failure cost (internal and external)

0   100

Percent of Products without Defects

Exhibit 5.8 indicates that the minimum total quality cost per unit occurs at quality level of less than 100 percent. At very low levels of quality assurance, significant failure costs outweigh any cost savings available by avoiding voluntary costs. In contrast, extremely high levels of quality assurance result in voluntary cost expenditures that are not offset by failure cost savings. Although the goal of zero defects is appealing, it is not a cost-effective strategy. Realistic managers seek to minimize total quality cost rather than to eliminate all defects.

✓ CHECK YOURSELF 5.3

Is it wiser to spend money on preventing defects or on correcting failures?

Answer   The answer depends on where a company's product falls on the "total quality cost" line (see Exhibit 5.8). If the product falls left of the cost minimization point, spending more on preventing defects would produce proportionately greater failure cost savings. In other words, a company would spend less in total by reducing failure costs through increasing prevention costs. Under these circumstances, it would be wise to incur prevention costs. On the other hand, if the product falls right of the cost minimization point line, the company would spend more to prevent additional defects than it would save by reducing failure costs. Under these circumstances, it makes more sense to pay the failure costs than attempt to avoid them by incurring prevention costs.

FOCUS ON INTERNATIONAL ISSUES

GLOBAL CONSEQUENCES OF EXTERNAL FAILURE COSTS

In late September 2009, Toyota Motor Company announced that it would be conducting a recall related to problems with floor mats in several models of Toyota and Lexus model cars and trucks. In some cases the floor mats had moved, preventing the vehicle's accelerator from moving properly. As an immediate solution, Toyota asked drivers of the affected vehicles to remove the driver's side floor mat, but the company said it would replace the accelerator pedals in the vehicles to prevent the floor mats from causing them to get stuck. The company estimated that 3.8 million vehicles had been sold with the mats under suspicion. A few months later, in February 2010, the company announced further recalls for additional vehicles with faulty accelerator pedals and braking systems.

These are examples of an *external failure cost* since the product made it into costumers' hands before the defect was found. Toyota did not immediately say how much this product failure was estimated to cost the company, but some analysts projected the costs of these recalls, along with lost sales, to be $1.5 to $2.0 billion. First, there is the cost of notifying all affected customers of the potential risk and advising them of what to do. This includes the obvious costs of printing and mailing, but also the costs of lawyers and public-relations consultants. Then there is the replacement cost of the new accelerator pedals. Since some individuals had already been injured and killed in cars that were alleged to have the defects, there will certainly be the costs of lawsuits and settlements. Finally, there is the cost of the potential damage to the company's reputation. Product recalls are nothing unusual in the automobile industry; cars are complex products with thousands of parts. However, Toyota, and particularly its Lexus brand, have reputations for being among the highest quality vehicles. A company can lose its reputation for quality a lot more quickly that it can be developed.

It may cost a little more to make sure your products are made correctly in the first place, but in the long run it is often cheaper than paying the external failure costs.

Prepare and interpret quality
cost reports.

Quality Cost Reports

Managing quality costs to achieve the highest level of customer satisfaction is known as **total quality management (TQM).** Accountants support TQM by preparing a **quality cost report,** which typically lists the company's quality costs and analyzes horizontally each item as a percentage of the total cost. Data are normally displayed for two or more accounting periods to disclose the effects of changes over time. Exhibit 5.9 shows a quality cost report for Unterman Shirt Company. The company's accountant prepared the report to assess the effects of a quality control campaign the company recently initiated. Review Exhibit 5.9. What is Unterman's quality control strategy? Is it succeeding?

Exhibit 5.9 indicates Unterman is seeking to control quality costs by focusing on appraisal activities. The total expenditures for prevention activities remained unchanged, but expenditures for appraisal activities increased significantly. The results of this strategy are apparent in the failure cost data. Internal failure costs increased significantly while external failure costs decreased dramatically. The strategy succeeded in lowering total quality costs. The report suggests, however, that more improvement is possible. Notice that 86.13 percent (appraisal 19.63 percent + internal failure 39.01 percent + external failure 27.49 percent) of total quality costs is spent on finding and correcting mistakes. The adage "an ounce of prevention is worth a pound of cure," applied to Unterman, implies spending more on prevention could perhaps eliminate many of the appraisal and failure costs.

EXHIBIT 5.9

Quality Cost Report for Unterman Shirt Company

	2013		2012	
	Amount	Percentage*	Amount	Percentage*
Prevention costs				
Product design	$ 50,000	6.54%	$ 52,000	6.60%
Preventive equipment (depreciation)	7,000	0.92	7,000	0.89
Training costs	27,000	3.53	25,000	3.17
Promotion and awards	22,000	2.88	22,000	2.79
Total prevention	106,000	13.87	106,000	13.45
Appraisal costs				
Inventory inspection	75,000	9.82	25,000	3.17
Reliability testing	43,000	5.63	15,000	1.90
Testing equipment (depreciation)	20,000	2.62	12,000	1.52
Supplies	12,000	1.57	8,000	1.02
Total appraisal	150,000	19.63	60,000	7.61
Internal failure costs				
Scrap	90,000	11.78	40,000	5.08
Repair and rework	140,000	18.32	110,000	13.96
Downtime	38,000	4.97	20,000	2.54
Reinspection	30,000	3.93	12,000	1.52
Total internal failure	298,000	39.01	182,000	23.10
External failure costs				
Warranty repairs and replacement	120,000	15.71	260,000	32.99
Freight	20,000	2.62	50,000	6.35
Customer relations	40,000	5.24	60,000	7.61
Restocking and packaging	30,000	3.93	70,000	8.88
Total external failure	210,000	27.49	440,000	55.84
Grand total	$764,000	100.00%	$788,000	100.00%

*Percentages do not add exactly because of rounding.

REALITY BYTES

Improving the quality of a product can increase its costs. Are the benefits of the higher quality worth the higher costs? In other words, are companies that spend money to improve the quality of their products rewarded with higher profit margins? This is a difficult question to answer empirically because, among other things, there is not always a definitive, objective measure of the quality of competing products or services.

Nevertheless, we can make some general comparisons based on objective data available for automobile manufactures. Every year JD Power and Associates releases reports on various aspects of quality among auto manufacturers, including the *Vehicle Dependability Study (VDS)*. This study surveys owners who have had their cars for three years, asking what problems they have experienced related to their vehicles' dependability. According to the company, "the study finds that the frequency and severity of component replacement has a potentially strong impact on customer loyalty intentions."

On March 19, JD Power released its 2009 VDS, which looked at the reliability of 2006 model cars. Although Buick came in first as an overall brand-name winner, other GM brands, including Saab, Hummer, Pontiac, and Saturn, came in well below average. Toyota and Lexus, a division of Toyota, were close to Buick at the top of the dependability rankings. Toyota and Lexus are usually near the top of JD Power's VDS as well as its Initial Quality Study, which is based on a survey of owners of new cars. Ford and its Lincoln, Mercury, and Jaguar divisions were also ranked as being above average in the 2009 VDS.

What about these companies' comparative profitability? The table below shows return on assets ratios for the 2008 and 2007 fiscal years of Toyota, Ford, and GM. Although 2008 was not a good year for car manufacturers in general, due to the economic recession, the data show that, generally, car companies with better quality had better financial results. It would certainly be an oversimplification to attribute all of Toyota's financial success to its higher quality evaluations. However, many experts in the automotive business believe Toyota's reputation for building high-quality vehicles has been a significant contributor to its success.

	Return on Assets Ratios	
	2008	2007
Toyota	(1.4)%	5.3%
Ford	(5.9)	(1.0)
GM	(33.9)	(26.0)
Source: jdpower.com		

These data are for years prior to Toyota's recalls for faulty accelerator and braking systems that occurred in late 2009 and early 2010. These widespread recalls had an immediate, negative, effect on the company's sales, and a positive effect on Ford's sales. It is a lot easier to lose customers due to quality problems than it was to attract them in the first place.

A Look Back

Many traditional cost systems used direct labor hours as the sole base for allocating overhead costs. Labor hours served as an effective *companywide allocation base* because labor was highly correlated with overhead cost incurrence. It made sense to assign more overhead to cost objects that required more labor. Because direct labor was related to production volume, it was frequently called a *volume-based cost driver*. Other volume-based cost drivers included machine hours, number of units, and labor dollars. Companywide, volume-based cost drivers were never perfect measures of overhead consumption. However, misallocation was not a serious problem because overhead costs were relatively small. If a manager misallocated an insignificant cost, it did not matter.

Automation has changed the nature of the manufacturing process. This change may cause significant distortions in the allocation of overhead costs when the allocation base is a companywide, volume-based cost driver. There are two primary reasons for distortions. First, in an automated environment, the same amount of labor (e.g., flipping a switch) may produce a large or a small volume of products. Under these circumstances, labor use is not related to the incurrence of overhead and is not a rational allocation base. Second, the distortions may be significant because overhead costs are much higher relative to the cost of labor and materials. For example, when robots replace people in the production process, depreciation becomes a larger portion of total product cost and labor becomes a smaller portion of the total.

To improve the accuracy of allocations, managerial accountants began to study the wide array of activities required to make a product. Such activities may include acquiring raw materials, materials handling and storage activities, product design activities, legal activities, and traditional production labor activities. Various measures of these activities can be used as bases for numerous overhead allocations related to determining product cost. Using activity measures to allocate overhead costs has become known as *activity-based costing (ABC)*. In an ABC system, costs are allocated in a two-stage process. First, activities are organized into *activity centers* and the related costs of performing these activities are combined into *cost pools*. Second, the pooled costs are allocated to designated cost objects using activity-based cost drivers. Implementing ABC is most likely to succeed when employees understand that it will positively affect their fate and that of the company. Without employee cooperation, collecting data necessary for the system's success may be difficult.

Many ABC systems begin by organizing activities into one of four categories. Total *unit-level activity cost* increases each time a unit of product is made and decreases when production volume declines. Unit-level activity costs can be allocated with a base correlated to the level of production (volume-based cost drivers). *Batch-level activities* are related to producing groups of products. Their costs are fixed regardless of the number of units in a batch. Batch-level costs are assigned so that the products requiring the most batches are assigned the most batch costs. *Product-level activities* support a specific product or product line. Product-level costs are frequently assigned to products based on the product's percentage use of product-level activities. *Facility-level activities* are performed for the benefit of the production process as a whole. The allocation of these costs is often arbitrary.

Accurate allocations prevent the distortions of overcosted or undercosted products. Over-costing can cause a product line to be overpriced. Overpriced products may cause a company to lose market share, and the decline in sales revenue will cause profits to fall. When products are underpriced, revenue is less than it could be, and profitability suffers.

Product costs are frequently distinguished from upstream and downstream costs. *Upstream costs* result from activities that occur *before* goods are manufactured. Examples include research and development, product design, and legal work. *Downstream costs* result from activities that occur *after* goods are manufactured. Examples of downstream costs include selling and administrative expenses. Upstream and downstream costs affect pricing decisions and product elimination decisions.

 A Look Forward

The next chapter introduces the concept of cost relevance. Applying the concepts you have learned to real-world business problems can be challenging. Frequently, so much data is available that it is difficult to distinguish important from useless information. The next chapter will help you learn to identify information that is relevant in a variety of short-term decision-making scenarios including special offers, outsourcing, segment elimination, and asset replacement.

A step-by-step audio-narrated series of slides is provided on the text website at www.mhhe.com/edmonds2011.

SELF-STUDY REVIEW PROBLEM

Adventure Luggage Company makes two types of airline carry-on bags. One bag type designed to meet mass-market needs is constructed of durable polyester. The other bag type aimed at the high-end luxury market is made of genuine leather. Sales of the polyester bag have declined recently because of stiff price competition. Indeed, Adventure would have to sell this bag at less than production cost to match the competition. Adventure's president suspects that something is wrong with how the company estimates the bag's cost. He has asked the company's accountant to investigate that possibility. The accountant gathered the following information relevant to estimating the cost of the company's two bag types.

Both bags require the same amount of direct labor. The leather bags have significantly higher materials costs, and they require more inspections and rework because of higher quality standards. Since the leather bags are produced in smaller batches of different colors, they require significantly more setups. Finally, the leather bags generate more legal costs due to patents and more promotion costs because Adventure advertises them more aggressively. Specific cost and activity data follow.

	Polyester Bags	Leather Bags
Per unit direct materials cost	$30	$90
Per unit direct labor cost	2 hours @ $14 per hour	2 hours @ $14 per hour
Annual sales volume	7,000 units	3,000 units

Total annual overhead costs are $872,000. Adventure currently allocates overhead costs using a traditional costing system based on direct labor hours.

To reassess the overhead allocation policy and the resulting product cost estimates, the accountant subdivided the overhead into four categories and gathered information about these cost categories and the activities that caused the company to incur the costs. These data follow.

Category	Estimated Cost	Cost Driver	Amount of Cost Driver Polyester	Leather	Total
Unit level	$480,000	Number of machine hours	20,000	60,000	80,000
Batch level	190,000	Number of machine setups	1,500	3,500	5,000
Product level	152,000	Number of inspections	200	600	800
Facility level	50,000	Equal percentage	50%	50%	100%
Total	$872,000				

Required

a. Determine the total cost and cost per unit for each product line, assuming that Adventure allocates overhead costs to each product line using direct labor hours as a companywide allocation base. Also determine the combined cost of the two product lines.

b. Determine the total cost and cost per unit for each product line, assuming that Adventure allocates overhead costs using an ABC system. Determine the combined cost of the two product lines.

c. Explain why the total combined cost computed in Requirements *a* and *b* is the same. Given that the combined cost is the same using either system, why is an ABC system with many different allocation rates better than a traditional system with a single companywide overhead rate?

Solution to Requirement a
Predetermined Overhead Rate

Polyester		Leather		
2 hr. × 7,000 units	+	2 hr. × 3,000 units		
14,000 direct labor hours		6,000 direct labor hours	=	20,000 hours

Allocation rate = $872,000 ÷ 20,000 hours = $43.60 per direct labor hour

Allocated Overhead Costs

Type of Bag	Allocation Rate	×	Number of Hours	=	Allocated Cost
Polyester	$43.60	×	14,000	=	$610,400
Leather	43.60	×	6,000	=	261,600
Total			20,000		$872,000

Total Cost of Each Product Line and Combined Cost

Type of Bag	Direct Materials*	+	Direct Labor†	+	Allocated Overhead	=	Total
Polyester	$210,000	+	$196,000	+	$610,400	=	$1,016,400
Leather	270,000	+	84,000	+	261,600	=	615,600
Total	$480,000	+	$280,000	+	$872,000	=	$1,632,000

*Direct materials
Polyester $30 × 7,000 units = $210,000
Leather $90 × 3,000 units = $270,000
†Direct labor
Polyester $14 × 14,000 hours = $196,000
Leather $14 × 6,000 hours = $84,000

Cost per Unit Computations Using Traditional Cost System

Type of Bag	Total Cost	÷	Units	=	Cost per Unit
Polyester	$1,016,400	÷	7,000	=	$145.20
Leather	615,600	÷	3,000	=	205.20
Total	$1,632,000				

Solution to Requirement b
Overhead Cost Allocation Using ABC

	Unit	Batch	Product	Facility	Total
Cost pool	$480,000	$190,000	$152,000	$50,000	$872,000
÷ Cost drivers	Number of machine hours	Number of setups	Number of inspections	Equally	
	80,000	5,000	800	50%	
= Rate	$6 per machine hour	$38 per setup	$190 per inspection	$25,000	

Overhead Allocation for Polyester Bags

	Unit	Batch	Product	Facility	Total
Weight	20,000	1,500	200	1	
× Rate	$ 6	$ 38	$ 190	$25,000	
Allocation	$120,000	$57,000	$38,000	$25,000	$240,000

Overhead Allocation for Leather Bags

	Unit	Batch	Product	Facility	Total
Weight	60,000	3,500	600	1	
× Rate	$ 6	$ 38	$ 190	$25,000	
Allocation	$360,000	$133,000	$114,000	$25,000	$632,000

Total Cost of Each Product Line and Combined Cost

Type of Bag	Direct Materials	+	Direct Labor	+	Allocated Overhead	=	Total
Polyester	$210,000	+	$196,000	+	$240,000	=	$ 646,000
Leather	270,000	+	84,000	+	632,000	=	986,000
Total	$480,000	+	$280,000	+	$872,000	=	$1,632,000

Cost per Unit Computations Under ABC System

Type of Bag	Total Cost	÷	Units	=	Cost per Unit
Polyester	$ 646,000	÷	7,000	=	$ 92.29
Leather	986,000	÷	3,000	=	328.67
Total	$1,632,000				

Solution to Requirement c

The allocation method (ABC versus traditional costing) does not affect the total amount of cost to be allocated. Therefore, the total cost is the same using either method. However, the allocation method (ABC versus traditional costing) does affect the cost assigned to each product line. Since the ABC system more accurately traces costs to the products that cause the costs to be incurred, it provides a more accurate estimate of the true cost of making the products. The difference in the cost per unit using ABC versus traditional costing is significant. For example, the cost of the polyester bag was determined to be $145.20 using the traditional allocation method and $92.29 using ABC. This difference could have led Adventure to overprice the polyester bag, thereby causing the decline in sales volume. To the extent that ABC is more accurate, using it will improve pricing and other strategic decisions that significantly affect profitability.

KEY TERMS

Activities 207
Activity-based cost drivers 205
Activity-based costing (ABC) 207
Activity centers 207
Appraisal costs 216
Batch-level activities 209
Companywide allocation rate 204

Downstream costs 214
External failure costs 216
Facility-level activities 211
Failure costs 216
Internal failure costs 216
Prevention costs 216
Product-level activities 210
Quality 216
Quality cost report 218

Start-up (setup) costs 205
Strategic cost management 216
Target pricing 214
Total quality management (TQM) 218
Unit-level activities 208
Upstream costs 214
Volume-based cost drivers 205
Voluntary costs 216

QUESTIONS

1. Why did traditional costing systems base allocations on a single companywide cost driver?

2. Why are labor hours ineffective as a companywide allocation base in many industries today?

3. What is the difference between volume-based cost drivers and activity-based cost drivers?

4. Why do activity-based cost drivers provide more accurate allocations of overhead in an automated manufacturing environment?

5. When would it be appropriate to use volume-based cost drivers in an activity-based costing system?

6. Martinez Manufacturing makes two products, one of which is produced at a significantly higher volume than the other. The low-volume product consumes more of the company's engineering resources because it is technologically complex. Even so, the company's cost accountant chose to allocate engineering department costs based on the number of units produced. How could selecting this allocation base affect a decision about outsourcing engineering services for the low-volume product?

7. Briefly describe the activity-based costing allocation process.

8. Tom Rehr made the following comment: "Facility-level costs should not be allocated to products because they are irrelevant for decision-making purposes." Do you agree or disagree with this statement? Justify your response.

9. To facilitate cost tracing, a company's activities can be subdivided into four hierarchical categories. What are these four categories? Describe them and give at least two examples of each category.

10. Beth Nelson, who owns and runs a small sporting goods store, buys most of her merchandise directly from manufacturers. Ms. Nelson was shocked at the $7.50 charge for a container of three ping-pong balls. She found it hard to believe that it could have cost more than $1.00 to make the balls. When she complained to Jim Wilson, the marketing manager of the manufacturing company, he tried to explain that the cost also included companywide overhead costs. How could companywide overhead affect the cost of ping-pong balls?

11. If each patient in a hospital is considered a cost object, what are examples of unit-, batch-, product- and facility-level costs that would be allocated to this object using an activity-based costing system?

12. Milken Manufacturing has three product lines. The company's new accountant, Marvin LaSance, is responsible for allocating facility-level costs to these product lines. Mr. LaSance is finding the allocation assignment a daunting task. He knows there have been disagreements among the product managers over the allocation of facility costs, and he fears being asked to defend his method of allocation. Why would the allocation of facility-level costs be subject to disagreements?

13. Why would machine hours be an inappropriate allocation base for batch-level costs?

14. Alisa Kamuf's company has reported losses from operations for several years. Industry standards indicate that prices are normally set at 30 percent above manufacturing cost, which Ms. Kamuf has done. Assuming that her other costs are in line with industry norms, how could she continue to lose money while her competitors earn a profit?

15. Issacs Corporation produces two lines of pocket knives. The Arrowsmith product line involves very complex engineering designs; the Starscore product line involves relatively simple designs. Since its introduction, the low-volume Arrowsmith products have gained market share at the expense of the high-volume Starscore products. This pattern of sales has been accompanied by an overall decline in company profits. Why may the existing cost system be inadequate?

16. What is the relationship between activity-based management and just-in-time inventory?

MULTIPLE-CHOICE QUESTIONS

Multiple-choice questions are provided on the text website at www.mhhe.com/edmonds2011.

EXERCISES—SERIES A

All applicable Exercises in Series A are available with McGraw-Hill's *Connect Accounting*.

LO 3

Exercise 5-1A *Classifying the costs of unit-, batch-, product-, or facility-level activities*

Humphrey Manufacturing is developing an activity-based costing system to improve overhead cost allocation. One of the first steps in developing the system is to classify the costs of performing production activities into activity cost pools.

Required

Using your knowledge of the four categories of activities, classify the cost of each activity in the following list into unit-, batch-, product-, or facility-level cost pools.

Cost Activity	Cost Pool
a. Engineering product design	
b. Supplies	
c. Wages of maintenance staff	
d. Labeling and packaging	
e. Plant security	
f. Ordering materials for a specific type of product	
g. Wages of workers moving units of work between work stations	
h. Factorywide electricity	
i. Salary of a manager in charge of a product line	
j. Sales commissions	

Exercise 5-2A *Identifying appropriate cost drivers*   LO 2

Required

Provide at least one example of an appropriate cost driver (allocation base) for each of the following activities.

a. Maintenance is performed on manufacturing equipment.
b. Sales commissions are paid.
c. Direct labor is used to change machine configurations.
d. Production equipment is set up for new production runs.
e. Engineering drawings are produced for design changes.
f. Purchase orders are issued.
g. Products are labeled, packaged, and shipped.
h. Machinists are trained on new computer-controlled machinery.
i. Lighting is used for production facilities.
j. Materials are unloaded and stored for production.

Exercise 5-3A *Classifying costs and identifying the appropriate cost driver*   LO 2, 3

Fairfield Manufacturing incurred the following costs during 2011 to produce its high-quality precision instruments. The company used an activity-based costing system and identified the following activities.

1. Inspection of each batch produced.
2. Salaries of receiving clerks.
3. Setup for each batch produced.
4. Insurance on production facilities.
5. Depreciation on manufacturing equipment.
6. Materials handling.
7. Inventory storage.

Required

a. Classify each activity as a unit-level, batch-level, product-level, or facility-level activity.
b. Identify an appropriate cost driver (allocation base) for each activity.

Exercise 5-4A *Context-sensitive nature of activity classification*   LO 3

Required

Describe a set of circumstances in which the cost of painting could be classified as a unit-level, a batch-level, a product-level, or a facility-level cost.

LO 3

Exercise 5-5A   *Context-sensitive nature of activity classification*

Wayne Company makes two types of circuit boards. One is a high-caliber board designed to accomplish the most demanding tasks; the other is a low-caliber board designed to provide limited service at an affordable price. During its most recent accounting period, Wayne incurred $170,000 of inspection cost. When Wayne recently established an activity-based costing system, its activities were classified into four categories. Categories and appropriate cost drivers follow.

	Direct Labor Hours	Number of Batches	Number of Inspectors	Number of Square Feet
High caliber	3,000	20	3	30,000
Low caliber	14,000	20	2	70,000
Total	17,000	40	5	100,000

Required

Allocate the inspection cost between the two products assuming that it is driven by (a) unit-level activities, (b) batch-level activities, (c) product-level activities, or (d) facility-level activities. Note that each allocation represents a separate alternative. In other words, the $170,000 of inspection cost will be allocated four times, once for each cost driver.

LO 2, 3

Exercise 5-6A   *Computing overhead rates based on different cost drivers*

Roebuck Industries produces two electronic decoders, P and Q. Decoder P is more sophisticated and requires more programming and testing than does Decoder Q. Because of these product differences, the company wants to use activity-based costing to allocate overhead costs. It has identified four activity pools. Relevant information follows.

Activity Pools	Cost Pool Total	Cost Driver
Repair and maintenance on assembly machine	$ 50,000	Number of units produced
Programming cost	84,000	Number of programming hours
Software inspections	6,000	Number of inspections
Product testing	8,000	Number of tests
Total overhead cost	$148,000	

Expected activity for each product follows.

	Number of Units	Number of Programming Hours	Number of Inspections	Number of Tests
Decoder P	20,000	2,000	190	1,400
Decoder Q	30,000	1,500	60	1,100
Total	50,000	3,500	250	2,500

Required

a. Compute the overhead rate for each activity pool.
b. Determine the overhead cost allocated to each product.

LO 1, 3

Exercise 5-7A   *Comparing an ABC system with a traditional costing system*

Use the information in Exercise 5-6A to complete the following requirements. Assume that before shifting to activity-based costing, Roebuck Industries allocated all overhead costs based on direct labor hours. Direct labor data pertaining to the two decoders follow.

	Direct Labor Hours
Decoder P	15,000
Decoder Q	22,000
Total	37,000

Required

a. Compute the amount of overhead cost allocated to each type of decoder when using direct labor hours as the allocation base.

b. Determine the cost per unit for overhead when using direct labor hours as the allocation base and when using ABC.

c. Explain why the per unit overhead cost is lower for the high-volume product when using ABC.

Exercise 5-8A   *Allocating costs with different cost drivers*   LO 1, 3

Wykle Company produces commercial gardening equipment. Since production is highly automated, the company allocates its overhead costs to product lines using activity-based costing. The costs and cost drivers associated with the four overhead activity cost pools follow.

	Activities			
	Unit Level	Batch Level	Product Level	Facility Level
Cost	$50,000	$20,000	$10,000	$120,000
Cost driver	2,000 labor hrs.	40 setups	Percentage of use	12,000 units

Production of 800 sets of cutting shears, one of the company's 20 products, took 200 labor hours and 6 setups and consumed 15 percent of the product-sustaining activities.

Required

a. Had the company used labor hours as a companywide allocation base, how much overhead would it have allocated to the cutting shears?

b. How much overhead is allocated to the cutting shears using activity-based costing?

c. Compute the overhead cost per unit for cutting shears using first activity-based costing and then using direct labor hours for allocation if 800 units are produced. If direct product costs are $100 and the product is priced at 30 percent above cost (rounded to the nearest whole dollar), for what price would the product sell under each allocation system?

d. Assuming that activity-based costing provides a more accurate estimate of cost, indicate whether the cutting shears would be over- or underpriced if direct labor hours are used as an allocation base. Explain how over- or undercosting can affect Wykle's profitability.

e. Comment on the validity of using the allocated facility-level cost in the pricing decision. Should other costs be considered in a cost-plus pricing decision? If so, which ones? What costs would you include if you were trying to decide whether to accept a special order?

Exercise 5-9A   *Allocating costs with different cost drivers*   LO 2, 3

Swartz Publishing identified the following overhead activities, their respective costs, and their cost drivers to produce the three types of textbooks the company publishes.

Activity (Cost)	Cost Driver	Type of Textbook		
		Deluxe	Moderate	Economy
Machine maintenance ($240,000)	Number of machine hours	250	750	1,000
Setups ($420,000)	Number of setups	30	15	5
Packing ($108,000)	Number of cartons	10	30	50
Photo development ($336,000)	Number of pictures	4,000	2,000	1,000

Deluxe textbooks are made with the finest-quality paper, six-color printing, and many photographs. Moderate texts are made with three colors and a few photographs spread throughout each chapter. Economy books are printed in black and white and include pictures only in chapter openings.

Required

a. Swartz currently allocates all overhead costs based on machine hours. The company produced the following number of books during the prior year.

Deluxe	Moderate	Economy
50,000	150,000	200,000

Determine the overhead cost per book for each book type.

b. Determine the overhead cost per book, assuming that the volume-based allocation system described in Requirement *a* is replaced with an activity-based costing system.

c. Explain why the per-unit overhead costs determined in Requirements *a* and *b* differ.

LO 3

Exercise 5-10A   *Computing product cost with given activity allocation rates*

Gamble Manufacturing produces two modems, one for laptop computers and the other for desktop computers. The production process is automated, and the company has found activity-based costing useful in assigning overhead costs to its products. The company has identified five major activities involved in producing the modems.

Activity	Allocation Base	Allocation Rate
Materials receiving & handling	Cost of material	2% of material cost
Production setup	Number of setups	$100.00 per setup
Assembly	Number of parts	$5.00 per part
Quality inspection	Inspection time	$1.50 per minute
Packing and shipping	Number of orders	$10.00 per order

Activity measures for the two kinds of modems follow.

	Labor Cost	Material Cost	Number of Setups	Number of Parts	Inspection Time	Number of Orders
Laptops	$1,260	$6,000	30	42	7,200 min.	65
Desktops	1,150	7,500	12	24	5,100 min.	20

Required

a. Compute the cost per unit of laptop and desktop modems, assuming that Gamble made 300 units of each type of modem.

b. Explain why laptop modems cost more to make even though they have less material cost and are smaller than desktop modems.

LO 3

Exercise 5-11A   *Allocating facility-level costs and a product elimination decision*

Jacob Boards produces two kinds of skateboards. Selected unit data for the two boards for the last quarter follow.

	Basco Boards	Shimano Boards
Production costs		
Direct materials	$27	$36
Direct labor	$39	$51
Allocated overhead	$15	$18
Total units produced and sold	4,000	8,000
Total sales revenue	$336,000	$888,000

Jacob allocates production overhead using activity-based costing. It allocates delivery expense and sales commissions, which amount to $54,000 per quarter, to the two products equally.

Required

a. Compute the net profit for each product.
b. Assuming that the overhead allocation for Basco boards includes $12,000 of facility-level costs, would you advise Jacob to eliminate these boards? (*Hint:* Consider the method used to allocate the delivery and selling expense.)

Exercise 5-12A   *Quality cost components and relationships*   **LO 4**

Required

The preceding graph depicts the relationships among the components of total quality cost.

a. Label the lines identified as A, B, and C.
b. Explain the relationships depicted in the graph.

PROBLEMS—SERIES A

All applicable Problems in Series A are available with McGraw-Hill's *Connect Accounting.*

Problem 5-13A   *Comparing an ABC system with a traditional costing system*   **LO 1, 3**

Peck Electronics produces video games in three market categories, commercial, home, and miniature. Peck has traditionally allocated overhead costs to the three products using the company-wide allocation base of direct labor hours. The company recently implemented an ABC system when it installed computer-controlled assembly stations that rendered the traditional costing system ineffective. In implementing the ABC system, the company identified the following activity cost pools and cost drivers.

Category	Total Pooled Cost	Types of Costs	Cost Driver
Unit	$720,000	Indirect labor wages, supplies, depreciation, machine maintenance	Machine hours
Batch	388,800	Materials handling, inventory storage, labor for setups, packaging, labeling and shipping, scheduling	Number of production orders
Product	211,200	Research and development	Time spent by research department
Facility	600,000	Rent, utilities, maintenance, admin. salaries, security	Square footage

Additional data for each of the product lines follow.

	Commercial	Home	Miniature	Total
Direct materials cost	$36.00/unit	$24.00/unit	$30.00/unit	—
Direct labor cost	$14.40/hour	$14.40/hour	$18.00/hour	—
Number of labor hours	6,000	12,000	2,000	20,000
Number of machine hours	10,000	45,000	25,000	80,000
Number of production orders	200	2,000	800	3,000
Research and development time	10%	20%	70%	100%
Number of units	15,000	45,000	14,000	74,000
Square footage	20,000	50,000	30,000	100,000

Required

a. Determine the total cost and cost per unit for each product line, assuming that overhead costs are allocated to each product line using direct labor hours as a companywide allocation base. Also determine the combined cost of all three product lines.

b. Determine the total cost and cost per unit for each product line, assuming that an ABC system is used to allocate overhead costs. Determine the combined cost of all three product lines.

c. Explain why the combined total cost computed in Requirements a and b is the same amount. Given that the combined cost is the same using either allocation method, why is an ABC system with many different allocation rates more accurate than a traditional system with a single companywide overhead rate?

Problem 5-14A   Effect of automation on overhead allocation

Hewitt Rug Company makes two types of rugs, seasonal and all-purpose. Both types of rugs are hand-made, but the seasonal rugs require significantly more labor because of their decorative designs. The annual number of rugs made and the labor hours required to make each type of rug follow.

	Seasonal	All-Purpose	Totals
Number of rugs	1,200	2,800	4,000
Number of direct labor hours	120,000	168,000	288,000

Required

a. Assume that annual overhead costs total $72,000. Select the appropriate cost driver and determine the amount of overhead to allocate to each type of rug.

b. Hewitt automates the seasonal rug line resulting in a dramatic decline in labor usage, to make 1,200 rugs in only 12,000 hours. Hewitt continues to make the all-purpose rugs the same way as before. The number of rugs made and the labor hours required to make them after automation follow.

	Seasonal	All-Purpose	Totals
Number of rugs	1,200	2,800	4,000
Number of direct labor hours	12,000	168,000	180,000

Overhead costs are expected to increase to $90,000 as a result of the automation. Allocate the increased overhead cost to the two types of rugs using direct labor hours as the allocation base and comment on the appropriateness of the allocation.

Problem 5-15A   Using activity-based costing to improve allocation accuracy

This problem is an extension of Problem 5-14A, which must be completed first.

Hewitt's accounting staff has disaggregated the $90,000 of overhead costs into the following items.

(1) Inspection costs	$ 32,000
(2) Setup costs	21,600
(3) Engineering costs	32,000
(4) Legal costs related to products	12,000
(5) Materials movement cost per batch	4,800
(6) Salaries of production supervisors	80,000
(7) Fringe benefit costs	16,000
(8) Utilities costs	8,000
(9) Plant manager's salary	48,000
(10) Depreciation on production equipment	72,000
(11) Depreciation on building	16,000
(12) Miscellaneous costs	10,000
(13) Indirect materials costs	5,600
(14) Production employee incentive costs	2,000
Total	$360,000

Required

a. Each of Hewitt's rug lines operates as a department. The all-purpose department occupies 6,000 square feet of floor space, and the seasonal department occupies 12,000 square feet of space. Comment on the validity of allocating the overhead costs by square footage.

b. Assume that the following additional information is available.

   (1) Rugs are individually inspected.

   (2) Hewitt incurs setup costs each time a new style of seasonal rug is produced. The seasonal rugs were altered nine times during the year. The manual equipment for all-purpose rugs is reset twice each year to ensure accurate weaving. The setup for the technical equipment used to weave seasonal rugs requires more highly skilled workers, but the all-purpose rugs require more manual equipment, thereby resulting in a *per setup* charge that is roughly equal for both types of rugs. Hewitt undertook 22 setups during the year, 18 of which applied to seasonal rugs and 4 that applied to all-purpose rugs.

   (3) Ninety percent of the product-level costs can be traced to producing seasonal rugs.

   (4) Six supervisors oversee the production of all-purpose rugs. Because seasonal rugs are made in an automated department, only two production supervisors are needed.

   (5) Each rug requires an equal amount of indirect materials.

   (6) Costs associated with production activities are assigned to six activity cost pools: (1) labor-related activities, (2) unit-level activities, (3) batch-level activities, (4) product-level supervisory activities, (5) other product-level activities, and (6) facility-level activities.

   Organize the $360,000 of overhead costs into activity center cost pools and allocate the costs to the two types of rugs.

c. Assuming that 90 seasonal and 240 all-purpose rugs were made in January, determine the overhead costs that would be assigned to each of the two rug types for the month of January.

Problem 5-16A *Using activity-based costing to improve allocation accuracy*

LO 1, 3

Soloman Academy, is a profit-oriented education business. Soloman provides remedial training for high school students who have fallen behind in their classroom studies. It charges its students $500 per course. During the previous year, Soloman provided instruction for 1,000 students. The income statement for the company follows.

CHECK FIGURES
a. Cost per student:
   Computer-Assisted: $327
   Classroom: $237

Revenue	$ 400,000
Cost of instructors	(170,000)
Overhead costs	(85,000)
Net income	$ 145,000

The company president, Susan Doubleday, indicated in a discussion with the accountant, Merrill Archer, that she was extremely pleased with the growth in the area of computer-assisted instruction. She observed that this department served 200 students using only two part-time instructors. In contrast, the classroom-based instructional department required 32 instructors to teach 800 students. Ms. Doubleday noted that the per-student cost of instruction was dramatically lower for the computer-assisted department. She based her conclusion on the following information.

Soloman pays its part-time instructors an average of $5,000 per year. The total cost of instruction and the cost per student are computed as follows.

Type of Instruction	Computer-Assisted	Classroom
Number of instructors (a)	2	32
Number of students (b)	200	800
Total cost (c = a × $5,000)	$10,000	$160,000
Cost per student (c ÷ b)	$50	$200

Assuming that overhead costs were distributed equally across the student population, Ms. Doubleday concluded that the cost of instructors was the critical variable in the company's capacity to generate profits. Based on her analysis, her strategic plan called for heavily increased use of computer-assisted instruction.

Mr. Archer was not so sure that computer-assisted instruction should be stressed. After attending a seminar on activity-based costing (ABC), he believed that the allocation of overhead cost could be more closely traced to the different types of learning activities. To facilitate an activity-based analysis, he developed the following information about the costs associated with computer-assisted versus classroom instructional activities. He identified $48,000 of overhead costs that were directly traceable to computer-assisted activities, including the costs of computer hardware, software, and technical assistance. He believed the remaining $37,000 of overhead costs should be allocated to the two instructional activities based on the number of students enrolled in each program.

Required

a. Based on the preceding information, determine the total cost and the cost per student to provide courses through computer-assisted instruction versus classroom instruction.

b. Comment on the validity of stressing growth in the area of computer-assisted instruction.

LO 1

Problem 5-17A   *Key activity-based costing concepts*

Friar Paint Company makes paint in many different colors; it charges the same price for all of its paint regardless of the color. Recently, Friar's chief competitor cut the price of its white paint, which normally outsells any other color by a margin of 4 to 1. Friar's marketing manager requested permission to match the competitor's price. When Phillip Keaton, Friar's president, discussed the matter with Candice Smalley, the chief accountant, he was told that the competitor's price was below Friar's cost. Mr. Keaton responded, "If that's the case, then there is something wrong with our accounting system. I know the competition wouldn't sell below cost. Prepare a report showing me how you determine our paint cost and get back to me as soon as possible."

The next day, Ms. Smalley returned to Mr. Keaton's office and began by saying, "Determining the cost per gallon is a pretty simple computation. It includes $1.10 of labor, $3.10 of materials, and $4.00 of overhead for a total cost of $8.20 per gallon. The problem is that the competition is selling the stuff for $7.99 per gallon. They've got to be losing money."

Mr. Keaton then asked Ms. Smalley how she determined the overhead cost. She replied, "We take total overhead cost and divide it by total labor hours and then assign it to the products based on the direct labor hours required to make the paint." Mr. Keaton then asked what kinds of costs are included in the total overhead cost. Ms. Smalley said, "It includes the depreciation on the building and equipment, the cost of utilities, supervisory salaries, and interest. Just how detailed do you want me to go with this list?"

Mr. Keaton responded, "Keep going, I'll tell you when I've heard enough."

Ms. Smalley continued, "There is the cost of setups. Every time a color is changed, the machines have to be cleaned, the color release valves reset, a trial batch prepared, and color quality tested. Sometimes mistakes occur and the machines must be reset. In addition, purchasing and handling the color ingredients must be accounted for as well as adjustments in the packaging department to change the paint cans and to mark the boxes to show the color change. Then . . ."

Mr. Keaton interrupted, "I think I've heard enough. We sell so much white paint that we run it through a separate production process. White paint is produced continuously. There are no shutdowns and setups. White uses no color ingredients. So why are these costs being assigned to our white paint production?"

Ms. Smalley replied, "Well, sir, these costs are just a part of the big total that is allocated to all of the paint, no matter what color it happens to be."

Mr. Keaton looked disgusted and said, "As I told you yesterday, Ms. Smalley, something is wrong with our accounting system!"

Required

a. Explain what the terms *overcost* and *undercost* mean. Is Friar's white paint over- or under-costed?

b. Explain what the term *companywide overhead rate* means. Is Friar using a companywide overhead rate?

c. Explain how Friar could improve the accuracy of its overhead cost allocations.

Problem 5-18A   *Pricing decisions made with ABC system cost data*

LO 3

Morello Sporting Goods Corporation makes two types of racquets, tennis and badminton. The company uses the same facility to make both products even though the processes are quite different. The company has recently converted its cost accounting system to activity-based costing. The following are the cost data that June Searight, the cost accountant, prepared for the third quarter of 2011 (during which Morello made 70,000 tennis racquets and 30,000 badminton racquets).

CHECK FIGURES
a. Cost per unit:
 Tennis Racquet: $64.71
 Badminton Racquet: $65.67

Direct Cost	Tennis Racquet (TR)	Badminton Racquet (BR)
Direct materials	$18 per unit	$14 per unit
Direct labor	32 per unit	26 per unit

Category	Estimated Cost	Cost Driver	Amount of Cost Driver
Unit level	$ 750,000	Number of inspection hours	TR: 15,000 hours; BR: 10,000 hours
Batch level	250,000	Number of setups	TR: 80 setups; BR: 45 setups
Product level	150,000	Number of TV commercials	TR: 4; BR: 1
Facility level	650,000	Number of machine hours	TR: 30,000 hours; BR: 35,000 hours
Total	$1,800,000		

Inspectors are paid according to the number of actual hours worked, which is determined by the number of racquets inspected. Engineers who set up equipment for both products are paid monthly salaries. TV commercial fees are paid at the beginning of the quarter. Facility-level cost includes depreciation of all production equipment.

Required

a. Compute the cost per unit for each product.

b. If management wants to price badminton racquets 30 percent above cost, what price should the company set?

c. The market price of tennis racquets has declined substantially because of new competitors entering the market. Management asks you to determine the minimum cost of producing tennis racquets in the short term. Provide that information.

Problem 5-19A   *Target pricing and target costing with ABC*

LO 3

Heisler Cameras, Inc., manufactures two models of cameras. Model ZM has a zoom lens; Model DS has a fixed lens. Heisler uses an activity-based costing system. The following are the relevant cost data for the previous month.

Direct Cost per Unit	Model ZM	Model DS
Direct materials	$20	$10
Direct labor	28	12

Category	Estimated Cost	Cost Driver	Use of Cost Driver
Unit level	$ 27,000	Number of units	ZM: 2,400 units; DS: 9,600 units
Batch level	50,000	Number of setups	ZM: 25 setups; DS: 25 setups
Product level	90,000	Number of TV commercials	ZM: 15; DS: 10
Facility level	300,000	Number of machine hours	ZM: 500 hours; DS: 1,000 hours
Total	$467,000		

Heisler's facility has the capacity to operate 4,500 machine hours per month.

Required

a. Compute the cost per unit for each product.

b. The current market price for products comparable to Model ZM is $135 and for DS is $47. If Heisler sold all of its products at the market prices, what was its profit or loss for the previous month?

c. A market expert believes that Heisler can sell as many cameras as it can produce by pricing Model ZM at $130 and Model DS at $45. Heisler would like to use those estimates as its target prices and have a profit margin of 20 percent of target prices. What is the target cost for each product?

d. Is there any way for the company to reach its target costs?

Problem 5-20A *Cost management with an ABC system*

Fazel Chairs, Inc., makes two types of chairs. Model Diamond is a high-end product designed for professional offices. Model Gold is an economical product designed for family use. Irene Fazel, the president, is worried about cut-throat price competition in the chairs market. Her company suffered a loss last quarter, an unprecedented event in its history. The company's accountant prepared the following cost data for Ms. Fazel.

Direct Cost per Unit	Model Diamond (D)	Model Gold (G)
Direct materials	$20 per unit	$10 per unit
Direct labor	$18/hour × 2 hours production time	$18/hour × 1 hour production time

Category	Estimated Cost	Cost Driver	Use of Cost Driver
Unit level	$ 300,000	Number of units	D: 15,000 units; G: 35,000 units
Batch level	750,000	Number of setups	D: 104 setups; G: 146 setups
Product level	450,000	Number of TV commercials	D: 5; G: 10
Facility level	500,000	Number of machine hours	D: 1,500 hours; G: 3,500 hours
Total	$2,000,000		

The market price for office chairs comparable to Model Diamond is $118 and to Model Gold is $73.

Required

a. Compute the cost per unit for both products.

b. Judson Regland, the chief engineer, told Ms. Fazel that the company is currently making 150 units of Model Diamond per batch and 245 units of Model Gold per batch. He suggests doubling the batch sizes to cut the number of setups in half, thereby reducing the setup cost by 50 percent. Compute the cost per unit for each product if Ms. Fazel adopts his suggestion.

c. Is there any side effect if Ms. Fazel increases the production batch size by 100 percent?

Problem 5-21A *Assessing a quality control strategy*   LO 4, 5

The following quality cost report came from the records of Nelson Company.

	2011 Amount	2011 Percentage	2010 Amount	2010 Percentage
Prevention costs				
Engineering and design	$136,000	13.74%	$ 58,000	3.86%
Training and education	34,000	3.43	12,000	0.80
Depreciation on prevention equipment	58,000	5.86	30,000	1.99
Incentives and awards	88,000	8.89	40,000	2.66
Total prevention	316,000	31.92%	140,000	9.31%
Appraisal costs				
Inventory inspection	50,000	5.05	50,000	3.32
Reliability testing	32,000	3.23	30,000	1.99
Testing equipment (depreciation)	22,000	2.22	24,000	1.60
Supplies	14,000	1.41	16,000	1.06
Total appraisal	118,000	11.92%	120,000	7.98%
Internal failure costs				
Scrap	48,000	4.85	80,000	5.32
Repair and rework	98,000	9.90	220,000	14.63
Downtime	24,000	2.42	40,000	2.66
Reinspection	8,000	0.81	24,000	1.60
Total internal failure	178,000	17.98%	364,000	24.20%
External failure cost				
Warranty repairs and replacement	220,000	22.22	520,000	34.57
Freight	48,000	4.85	100,000	6.65
Customer relations	56,000	5.66	120,000	7.98
Restocking and packaging	54,000	5.45	140,000	9.31
Total external failure	378,000	38.18%	880,000	58.51%
Grand total	$990,000	100.00%	$1,504,000	100.00%

Required

a. Explain the strategy that Nelson Company initiated to control its quality costs.
b. Indicate whether the strategy was successful or unsuccessful in reducing quality costs.
c. Explain how the strategy likely affected customer satisfaction.

EXERCISES—SERIES B

Exercise 5-1B *Classifying the costs of unit-, batch-, product-, or facility-level activities*   LO 3

Tucker Manufacturing is developing an activity-based costing system to improve overhead cost allocation. One of the first steps in developing the system is to classify the costs of performing production activities into activity cost pools.

Required

Using the four-tier cost hierarchy described in the chapter, classify each of the following costs into unit-level, batch-level, product-level, or facility-level cost pools.

Cost Activity	Cost Pool
a. Wages of assembly line workers	
b. Product design costs	
c. Materials requisition costs for a particular work order	
d. Security guard wages	
e. Lubricant for machines	
f. Parts used to make a particular product	
g. Machine setup cost	
h. Salary of the plant manager's secretary	
i. Factory depreciation	
j. Advertising costs for a particular product	

LO 2

Exercise 5-2B   *Identifying appropriate cost drivers*

Required

Provide at least one example of an appropriate cost driver (allocation base) for each of the following activities.

a. Workers count completed goods before moving them to a warehouse.
b. A logistics manager runs a computer program to determine the materials release schedule.
c. Janitors clean the factory floor after workers have left.
d. Mechanics apply lubricant to machines.
e. Engineers design a product production layout.
f. Engineers set up machines to produce a product.
g. The production supervisor completes the paperwork initiating a work order.
h. The production manager prepares materials requisition forms.
i. Workers move materials from the warehouse to the factory floor.
j. Assembly line machines are operated.

LO 2, 3

Exercise 5-3B   *Classifying costs and identifying the appropriate cost driver*

Astro Corporation, a furniture manufacturer, uses an activity-based costing system. It has identified the following selected activities:

1. Incurring property taxes on factory buildings.
2. Incurring paint cost for furniture produced.
3. Setting up machines for a particular batch of production.
4. Inspecting wood prior to using it in production.
5. Packaging completed furniture in boxes for shipment.
6. Inspecting completed furniture for quality control.
7. Purchasing TV time to advertise a particular product.

Required

a. Classify each activity as a unit-level, batch-level, product-level, or facility-level activity.
b. Identify an appropriate cost driver (allocation base) for each of the activities.

LO 3

Exercise 5-4B   *Understanding the context-sensitive nature of classifying activities*

Required

Describe a set of circumstances in which labor cost could be classified as a unit-level, a batch-level, a product-level, or a facility-level cost.

LO 3

Exercise 5-5B   *Understanding the context-sensitive nature of classifying activities*

Mauldin Company makes two types of cell phones. Handy is a thin, pocket-size cell phone that is easy to carry around. Action is a palm-size phone convenient to hold while the user is talking.

During its most recent accounting period, Mauldin incurred $150,000 of quality-control costs. Recently Mauldin established an activity-based costing system, which involved classifying its activities into four categories. The categories and appropriate cost drivers follow.

	Direct Labor Hours	Number of Batches	Number of Engineers	Number of Square Feet
Handy	26,000	38	10	37,000
Action	24,000	22	5	83,000
Totals	50,000	60	15	120,000

Mauldin uses direct labors hours to allocate unit-level activities, number of batches to allocate batch-level activities, number of engineers to allocate product-level activities, and number of square feet to allocate facility-level activities.

Required

Allocate the quality-control cost between the two products, assuming that it is driven by (a) unit-level activities, (b) batch-level activities, (c) product-level activities, and (d) facility-level activities. Note that each allocation represents a separate allocation. In other words, the $300,000 of quality-control costs will be allocated four times, once for each cost driver.

Exercise 5-6B   *Computing overhead rates based on different costing drivers*   LO 2, 3

Chase Industries produces two surge protectors: VC620 with six outlets and PH630 with eight outlets and two telephone line connections. Because of these product differences, the company plans to use activity-based costing to allocate overhead costs. The company has identified four activity pools. Relevant information follows.

Activity Pools	Cost Pool Total	Cost Driver
Machine setup	$120,000	Number of setups
Machine operation	300,000	Number of machine hours
Quality control	48,000	Number of inspections
Packaging	32,000	Number of units
Total overhead cost	$500,000	

Expected activity for each product follows.

	Number of Setups	Number of Machine Hours	Number of Inspections	Number of Units
VC620	48	1,400	78	25,000
PH630	72	2,600	172	15,000
Total	120	4,000	250	40,000

Required

a. Compute the overhead rate for each activity pool.
b. Determine the overhead cost allocated to each product.

Exercise 5-7B   *Comparing an ABC system with a traditional cost system*   LO 1, 3

Use the information in Exercise 5-6B to complete the following requirements. Assume that before shifting to activity-based costing, Chase Industries allocated all overhead costs based on direct labor hours. Direct labor data pertaining to the two surge protectors follow.

	Direct Labor Hours
VC620	16,000
PH630	9,000
Total	25,000

Required

a. Compute the amount of overhead cost allocated to each type of surge protector when using direct labor hours as the allocation base.

b. Determine the cost per unit for overhead when using direct labor hours as the allocation base and when using ABC.

c. Explain why the per unit overhead cost is lower for the higher-volume product when using ABC.

LO 1, 2, 3

Exercise 5-8B   *Allocating costs with different cost drivers*

Rigsby Sporting Goods, Inc., produces indoor treadmills. The company allocates its overhead costs using activity-based costing. The costs and cost drivers associated with the four overhead activity cost pools follow.

Activities	Unit Level	Batch Level	Product Level	Facility Level
Cost	$500,000	$250,000	$150,000	$450,000
Cost driver	12,500 labor hours	50 setups	Percentage of use	15,000 units

Producing 5,000 units of PFT200, one of the company's five products, took 4,000 labor hours, 25 setups, and consumed 30 percent of the product-sustaining activities.

Required

a. Had the company used labor hours as a companywide allocation base, how much overhead would it have allocated to the 5,000 units of PFT200?

b. How much overhead is allocated to the 5,000 PFT200 units using activity-based costing?

c. Compute the overhead cost per unit for PFT200 using activity-based costing and direct labor hours if 5,000 units are produced. If direct product costs are $120 and PFT200 is priced at 20 percent above cost (rounded to the nearest whole dollar), compute the product's selling price under each allocation system.

d. Assuming that activity-based costing provides a more accurate estimate of cost, indicate whether PFT200 would be over- or underpriced if Rigsby uses direct labor hours as the allocation base. Explain how over- or undercosting can affect Rigsby's profitability.

e. Comment on the validity of using the allocated facility-level costs in the pricing decision. Should other costs be considered in a cost-plus pricing decision? If so, which ones? What costs would you include if you were trying to decide whether to accept a special order?

LO 2, 3

Exercise 5-9B   *Allocating costs with different cost drivers*

Talton Shoes Corporation produces three brands of shoes, Brisk, Pro, and Runner. Relevant information about Talton overhead activities, their respective costs, and their cost drivers follows.

Overhead Costs	Cost Driver	Brisk	Pro	Runner
Fringe benefits ($360,000)	Labor hours	10,000	20,000	20,000
Setups ($200,000)	Number of setups	15	25	10
Packing costs ($40,000)	Number of cartons	200	300	300
Quality control ($300,000)	Number of tests	120	200	80

Required

a. Talton currently allocates all overhead costs based on labor hours. The company produced the following numbers of pairs of shoes during the prior year.

Brisk	Pro	Runner
10,000	15,000	20,000

Determine the overhead cost per pair of shoes for each brand.

b. Determine the overhead cost per pair of shoes for each brand, assuming that the volume-based allocation system described in Requirement *a* is replaced with an activity-based costing system.

c. Explain why the per pair overhead costs determined in Requirements *a* and *b* differ.

Exercise 5-10B *Computing product cost with given activity allocation rates*

LO 3

Using automated production processes, Stegall Videos produces two kinds of digital camcorders: N100 for the novice and D200 for the hobbyist. The company has found activity-based costing useful in assigning overhead costs to its products. It has identified the following five major activities involved in producing the camcorders.

Activity	Allocation Base	Allocation Rate
Materials receiving and handling	Cost of materials	3% of materials cost
Production setup	Number of setups	$800 per setup
Assembly	Number of parts	$10 per part
Quality inspection	Inspection time	$25 per minute
Packing and shipping	Number of orders	$80 per order

Activity measures for the two kinds of camcorders follow.

	Labor Cost*	Materials Cost*	Number of Setups	Number of Parts	Inspection Time	Number of Orders
N100	$225,000	$125,000	10	10,000	800 min.	25
D200	150,000	150,000	25	10,000	4,800 min.	50

*Both are direct costs.

Required

a. Compute the cost per unit of N100 and D200, assuming that Stegall made 1,000 units of N100 and 500 units of D200.

b. Explain why the D200 camcorders cost more to make although their direct costs are less than those for the N100 camcorders.

Exercise 5-11B *Allocating facility-level costs and a product elimination decision*

LO 3

Adgar Corporation produces two types of juice that it packages in cases of 24 cans per case. Selected per case data for the two products for the last month follow.

	Orange Juice	Tomato Juice
Production costs		
Direct material	$2.25	$1.50
Direct labor	$1.50	$2.25
Allocated overhead	$2.25	$3.00
Total cases produced and sold	25,000	15,000
Total sales revenue	$210,000	$127,500

Adgar allocates production overhead using activity-based costing but allocates monthly packaging expense, which amounted to $60,000 last month, to the two products equally.

Required

a. Compute the net profit for each product.
b. Assuming that the overhead allocation for the tomato juice includes $30,000 of facility-level costs, would you advise Adgar to eliminate this product? (*Hint:* Consider the method used to allocate the monthly packaging expense.)

LO 4

Exercise 5-12B   *Applying concepts of quality cost management*

Lucas Weldon, the president of Easeley Industries, Inc., was beaming when he was reviewing the company's quality cost report. After he had implemented a quality-control program for three years, the company's defect rate had declined from 20 percent to 3 percent. Mr. Weldon patted Kenyata Terry, the production manager, on her back and said: "You have done a great job! I plan to reward you for your hard work. However, I want the defects to disappear completely before I promote you to the position of executive vice president. So, zero-defect is going to be your personal goal for the coming year." Ms. Terry responded wearily, "I'm not sure that's really a good idea."

Required

Write a memorandum to the president explaining that zero defect is not a practical policy.

PROBLEMS—SERIES B

LO 1, 3

Problem 5-13B   *Comparing an ABC system with a traditional costing system*

Since its inception, Ray Laboratory, has produced a single product, Product S109. With the advent of automation, the company added the technological capability to begin producing a second product, Product N227. Because of the success of Product N227, manufacturing has been shifting toward its production. Sales of Product N227 are now 50 percent of the total annual sales of 20,000 units, and the company is optimistic about the new product's future sales growth. One reason the company is excited about the sales potential of its new product is that the new product's gross profit margin is higher than that of Product S109. Management is thrilled with the new product's initial success but concerned about the company's declining profits since the product's introduction. Suspecting a problem with the company's costing system, management hires you to investigate.

In reviewing the company's records, product specifications, and manufacturing processes, you discover the following information.

1. The company is in an extremely competitive industry in which markups are low and accurate estimates of cost are critical to success.
2. Product N227 has complex parts that require more labor, machine time, setups, and inspections than Product S109.
3. Budgeted costs for direct materials and labor follow.

Direct Cost per Unit	Product S109	Product N227
Direct materials	$25	$25
Direct labor	$10/hour × 2 hours production time	$10/hour × 2.8 hours production time

4. The company presently allocates overhead costs to its products based on direct labor hours. After carefully studying the company's overhead, you identify four different categories of overhead costs. Using your knowledge of this company and similar companies in the same industry, you estimate the total costs for each of these categories and identify the most appropriate cost driver for measuring each product's overhead consumption. Detailed information for each cost category follows.

Category	Estimated Cost	Cost Driver	Use of Cost Driver
Unit level	$ 540,000	Number of machine hours	S109: 20,000 hours; N227: 60,000 hours
Batch level	228,000	Number of machine setups	S109: 1,500; N227: 3,500
Product level	180,000	Number of inspections	S109: 200; N227: 600
Facility level	60,000	Equal percentage for products	S109: 50%; N227: 50%
Total	$1,008,000		

Required

a. Determine the predetermined overhead rate the company is using.

b. Compute the amount of overhead the company assigns to each product using this rate.

c. Determine the cost per unit and total cost of each product when overhead is assigned based on direct labor hours.

d. To remain competitive, the company prices its products at only 20 percent above cost. Compute the price for each product with this markup.

e. Compute the overhead rate for each category of activity.

f. Determine the amount of overhead cost, both in total and per unit, that would be assigned to each product if the company switched to activity-based costing.

g. Assuming that prices are adjusted to reflect activity-based costs, determine the revised price for each product.

h. Based on your results for Requirements *f* and *g*, explain why Product N227 costs more to make than previously apparent and why sales prices therefore need to be adjusted.

Problem 5-14B   *Using activity-based costing to improve allocation accuracy*

LO 1, 3

Kelvin's Commemoratives makes and sells two types of decorative plates. One plate displays a hand-painted image of Princess Diana; the other plate displays a machine-pressed image of Marilyn Monroe. The Diana plates require 25,000 hours of direct labor to make; the Monroe plates require only 5,000 hours of direct labor. Overhead costs are composed of (1) $210,000 machine-related activity costs including indirect labor, utilities, and depreciation and (2) $150,000 labor-related activity costs including overtime pay, fringe benefits, and payroll taxes.

Required

a. Assuming that Kelvin's uses direct labor hours as the allocation base, determine the amount of the total $240,000 overhead cost that would be allocated to each type of plate.

b. Explain why using direct labor hours may distort the allocation of overhead cost to the two products.

c. Explain how activity-based costing could improve the accuracy of the overhead cost allocation.

Problem 5-15B   *Using activity-based costing to improve allocation accuracy*

LO 1, 3

This problem is an extension of Problem 5-14B, which must be completed first.
Assume the same data as in Problem 5-14B with the following additional information. The hours of machine time for processing plates are 1,000 for Diana plates and 2,500 for Monroe plates.

Required

a. Establish two activity centers, one for machine-related activities and the second for labor-related activities. Assign the total overhead costs to the two activity centers.

b. Allocate the machine-related overhead costs to each product based on machine hours.

c. Allocate the labor-related overhead costs to each product based on direct labor hours.

d. Draw a diagram that compares the one-stage allocation method used in Problem 5-14B with the two-stage activity-based costing approach used in this problem.

LO 1, 3

Problem 5-16B   *Using activity-based costing to improve business decisions*

Wattson CPA and Associates is a local accounting firm specializing in bookkeeping and tax services. The firm has four certified public accountants who supervise 20 clerks. The clerks handle basic bookkeeping jobs and prepare tax return drafts. The CPAs review and approve the bookkeeping jobs and tax returns. Each CPA receives a fixed salary of $7,500 per month; the clerks earn an hourly rate of $18. Because the clerks are paid by the hour and their work hours can be directly traced to individual jobs, their wages are considered direct costs. The CPAs' salaries are not traced to individual jobs and are therefore treated as indirect costs. The firm allocates overhead based on direct labor hours. The following is Wattson's income statement for the previous month.

	Bookkeeping	Tax	Total
Revenues	$70,000	$70,000	$140,000
Direct expenses	(22,500)*	(22,500)*	(45,000)
Indirect supervisory expenses	(15,000)	(15,000)	(30,000)
Net income	$32,500	$32,500	$ 65,000

*1,250 clerical hours were used in each category during the previous month.

Loretta Wattson, CPA and chief executive officer, is not sure that the two operations are equally profitable as the income statement indicates. First, she believes that most of the CPAs' time was spent instructing clerks in tax return preparation. The bookkeeping jobs appear to be routine, and most of the clerks can handle them with little supervision. After attending a recent professional development seminar on activity-based costing (ABC), Ms. Wattson believes that the allocation of indirect costs can be more closely traced to different types of services. To facilitate an activity-based analysis, she asked the CPAs to document their work hours on individual jobs for the last week. The results indicate that, on average, 25 percent of the CPAs' hours was spent supervising bookkeeping activities and the remaining 75 percent was spent supervising tax activities.

Required

a. Based on the preceding information, reconstruct the income statement for bookkeeping services, tax services, and the total, assuming that Wattson revises its allocation of indirect supervisory costs based on ABC.

b. Comment on the results and recommend a new business strategy.

LO 1

Problem 5-17B   *Key activity-based costing concepts*

Yoder Boot and Shoe Company makes hand-sewn boots and shoes. Yoder uses a companywide overhead rate based on direct labor hours to allocate indirect manufacturing costs to its products. Making a pair of boots normally requires 2.4 hours of direct labor, and making a pair of shoes requires 1.8 hours. The company's shoe division, facing increased competition from international companies that have access to cheap labor, has responded by automating its shoe production. The reengineering process was expensive, requiring the purchase of manufacturing equipment and the restructuring of the plant layout. In addition, utility and maintenance costs increased significantly for operating the new equipment. Even so, labor costs decreased significantly. Now making a pair of shoes requires only 18 minutes of direct labor. As predicted, the labor savings more than offset the increase in overhead cost, thereby reducing the total cost to make a pair of shoes. The company experienced an unexpected side effect, however; according to the company's accounting records, the cost to make a pair of boots increased although the manufacturing process in the boot division was not affected by the reengineering of the shoe division. In other words, the cost of boots increased although Yoder did not change anything about the way it makes them.

Required

a. Explain why the accounting records reflected an increase in the cost to make a pair of boots.
b. Explain how the companywide overhead rate could result in the underpricing of shoes.
c. Explain how activity-based costing could improve the accuracy of overhead cost allocations.

Problem 5-18B   *Pricing decisions made with ABC system cost data*   LO 3

Pittman Furniture Corporation makes two types of dining tables, Elegance for formal dining and Comfort for casual dining, at its single factory. With the economy beginning to experience a recession, Justin Pittman, the president, is concerned about whether the company can stay in business as market prices fall. At Mr. Pittman's request, Yamini Sing, the controller, prepared cost data for analysis.

Inspectors are paid according to the number of actual hours worked, determined by the number of tables inspected. Engineers, who set up equipment for both products, are paid monthly salaries. TV commercial fees are paid at the beginning of the quarter.

Direct Cost	Elegance (E)	Comfort (C)
Direct materials	$50 per unit	$30 per unit
Direct labor	$36 per hour × 1.5 hours production time	$36 per hour × 1 hour production time

Category	Estimated Cost	Cost Driver	Use of Cost Driver
Product inspection	$120,000	Number of units	E: 2,500 units; C: 7,500 units
Machine setups	75,000	Number of setups	E: 23 setups; C: 27 setups
Product advertising	210,000	Number of TV commercials	E: 5; C: 9
Facility depreciation	405,000	Number of machine hours	E: 5,000 hours; C: 5,000 hours
Total	$810,000		

Required

a. Compute the cost per unit for each product.
b. If management wants to make 30 percent of cost as a profit margin for Elegance, what price should the company set?
c. The market price of tables in the Comfort class has declined because of the recession. Management asks you to determine the minimum cost of producing Comfort tables in the short term. Provide that information.

Problem 5-19B   *Target pricing and target costing with ABC*   LO 3

Ricardo Corporation manufactures two models of watches. Model Wonder displays cartoon characters and has simple features designed for kids. Model Marvel has sophisticated features such as dual time zones and an attached calculator. Ricardo's product design team has worked with a cost accountant to prepare a budget for the two products for the next fiscal year as follows.

Direct Cost	Wonder (W)	Marvel (M)
Direct materials	$10 per unit	$20 per unit
Direct labor	$40/hour × 0.3 hour production time	$40/hour × 0.7 hour production time

Category	Estimated Cost	Cost Driver	Use of Cost Driver
Materials handling	$366,000	Number of parts	W: 700,000; M: 520,000
Machine setups	180,000	Number of setups	W: 50; M: 40
Product testing	28,000	Number of units tested	W: 1,000; M: 400
Facility depreciation	360,000	Number of machine hours	W: 3,200; M: 4,000
Total	$934,000		

Wonder watches have 35 parts, and Marvel watches have 65 parts. The budget calls for producing 20,000 units of Wonder and 8,000 units of Marvel. Ricardo tests 5 percent of its products for quality assurance. It sells all its products at market prices.

Required

a. Compute the cost per unit for each product.

b. The current market price for products comparable to Wonder is $43 and for products comparable to Marvel is $115. What will Ricardo's profit or loss for the next year be?

c. Ricardo likes to have a 25 percent profit margin based on the current market price for each product. What is the target cost for each product? What is the total target profit?

d. The president of Ricardo has asked the design team to refine the production design to bring down the product cost. After a series of redesigns, the team recommends a new process that requires purchasing a new machine that costs $400,000 and has five years of useful life and no salvage value. With the new process and the new machine, Ricardo can decrease the number of machine setups to four for each product and cut the cost of materials handling in half. The machine hours used will be 4,500 for Wonder and 6,500 for Marvel. Does this new process enable Ricardo to achieve its target costs?

LO 3

Problem 5-20B *Cost management with an ABC system*

Hayne Corporation manufactures two different coffee makers, Professional for commercial use and Home for family use. Dwight Hayne, the president, recently received complaints from some members of the board of directors about the company's failure to reach the expected profit of $200,000 per month. Mr. Hayne is, therefore, under great pressure to improve the company's bottom line. Under his direction, Alicia Meek, the controller, prepared the following monthly cost data for Mr. Hayne.

Direct Cost	Professional (P)	Home (H)
Direct materials	$25 per unit	$9 per unit
Direct labor	$16 per hour × 0.8 hour production time	$16 per hour × 0.3 hour production time

Category	Estimated Cost	Cost Driver	Use of Cost Driver
Product inspection	$ 60,000	Number of units	P: 15,000 units; H: 45,000 units
Machine setups	15,000	Number of setups	P: 30 setups; H: 45 setups
Product promotion	200,000	Number of TV commercials	P: 10; H: 10
Facility depreciation	295,000	Number of machine hours	P: 7,160 hours; H: 4,640 hours
Total	$570,000		

The market price for coffee makers comparable to Professional is $65 and to Home is $22. The company's administrative expenses amount to $125,000.

Required

a. Compute the cost per unit for both products.

b. Determine the company's profit or loss.

c. Charlie Chen, the marketing manager, recommends that the company implement a focused marketing strategy. He argues that advertisements in trade journals would be more effective for the commercial market than on TV. In addition, the cost of journal ads would be only $21,000. He also proposes sending discount coupons to targeted households to reach a broad market base. The coupons program would cost $72,000. Compute the new cost of each product, assuming that Mr. Hayne replaces TV advertising with Mr. Chen's suggestions.

d. Determine the company's profit or loss using the information in Requirement *c.*

Problem 5-21B *Assessing a quality control strategy*

LO 4, 5

Carl Wallace, the president of Ritch Plastic Company, is a famous cost cutter in the plastics industry. Two years ago, he accepted an offer from Ritch's board of directors to help the company cut costs quickly. In fact, Mr. Wallace's compensation package included a year-end bonus tied to the percentage of cost decrease over the preceding year. On February 12, 2012, Mr. Wallace received comparative financial information for the two preceding years. He was especially interested in the results of his cost-cutting measures on quality control. The quality report shown below was extracted from the company's financial information.

Required

a. Explain the strategy that Mr. Wallace initiated to control Ritch's costs.

b. Indicate whether the strategy was successful or unsuccessful in reducing quality costs.

c. Explain how the strategy will likely affect the company's business in the long term.

	2011		2010	
	Amount	Percentage	Amount	Percentage
Prevention costs				
Engineering and design	$ 65,000	6.57%	$ 69,000	7.39%
Training and education	26,000	2.63	76,000	8.14
Depreciation on prevention equipment	15,000	1.51	15,000	1.60
Incentives and awards	20,000	2.02	20,000	2.14
Total prevention	126,000	12.73%	180,000	19.27%
Appraisal costs				
Product and materials inspection	33,000	3.33	73,000	7.82
Reliability testing	27,000	2.73	67,000	7.17
Testing equipment (depreciation)	38,000	3.83	38,000	4.07
Supplies	10,000	1.01	16,000	1.71
Total appraisal	108,000	10.90%	194,000	20.77%
Internal failure costs				
Scrap	52,000	5.25	120,000	12.85
Repair and rework	46,000	4.65	150,000	16.06
Downtime	64,000	6.46	40,000	4.28
Reinspection	8,000	0.81	24,000	2.57
Total internal failure	170,000	17.17%	334,000	35.76%
External failure cost				
Warranty repairs and replacement	347,000	35.05	125,000	13.38
Freight	75,000	7.58	31,000	3.32
Customer relations	45,000	4.55	28,000	3.00
Restocking and packaging	119,000	12.02	42,000	4.50
Total external failure	586,000	59.20%	226,000	24.20%
Grand total	$990,000	100.00%	$934,000	100.00%

ANALYZE, THINK, COMMUNICATE

ATC 5-1 Business Applications Case *Using ABC to improve product pricing*

Drilling Innovations, Inc., produces specialized cutting heads used by companies that drill for oil and natural gas. The company has recently implemented an ABC system for three of its products and is interested in evaluating its effectiveness before converting to an ABC system for all products. To perform this evaluation, the company compiled data for the three products using both the traditional system and the new ABC system. The traditional system used a single driver (machine hours). The ABC system uses a variety of cost drivers related to the activities used to produce the cutting heads. The three products involved in the trial run of the ABC system were GS-157, HS-241, and OS-367. The following data relate to these products; unit data have been rounded to the nearest penny.

Product	Selling Price per Unit	Units Produced	Total Costs Allocated: Traditional Costing	Cost per Unit: Traditional Costing	Total Cost Allocated: ABC	Costs per Unit: ABC
GS-157	$19.30	120,000	$1,600,000	$13.33	$1,500,000	$12.50
HS-241	17.50	90,000	1,100,000	12.22	1,050,000	11.67
OS-367	15.10	40,000	400,000	10.00	550,000	13.75
Totals			$3,100,000		$3,100,000	

Required

a. Determine the gross profit margin for each product produced based on the ABC data [(Selling price − ABC cost per unit) × Units produced].

b. Determine the gross profit margin for each product produced based on the traditional costing data [(Selling price − Traditional cost per unit) × Units produced].

c. Provide an explanation as to why the cost of OS-367 may have increased under the ABC system while the cost of GS-157 decreased.

d. Suggest what action management might take with respect to the discoveries resulting from the ABC versus traditional costing analysis. Assume that Drilling Innovations expects to produce a gross profit margin on each product of at least 30 percent of the selling price.

ATC 5-2 Group Assignment *Using ABC in a service business*

A dialysis clinic provides two types of treatment for its patients. Hemodialysis (HD), an in-house treatment, requires that patients visit the clinic three times each week for dialysis treatments. Peritoneal dialysis (PD) permits patients to self-administer their treatments at home on a daily basis. On average, the clinic serves 102 HD patients and 62 PD patients. A recent development caused clinic administrators to develop a keen interest in cost measurement for the two separate services. Managed care plans such as HMOs began to pay treatment providers a fixed payment per insured participant regardless of the level of services provided by the clinic. With fixed fee revenues, the clinic was forced to control costs to ensure profitability. As a result, knowing the cost to provide HD versus PD services was critically important for the clinic. It needed accurate cost measurements to answer the following questions. Were both services profitable, or was one service carrying the burden of the other service? Should advertising be directed toward acquiring HD or PD patients? Should the clinic eliminate HMO service?

Management suspected the existing cost allocation system was inaccurate in measuring the true cost of providing the respective services; it had been developed in response to Medicare reporting requirements. It allocated costs between HD and PD based on the ratio of cost to charges (RCC). In other words, RCC allocates indirect costs in proportion to revenues. To illustrate, consider the allocation of $883,280 of indirect nursing services costs, which are allocated to the two treatment groups in relation to the revenue generated by each group.

Given that the clinic generated total revenue of $3,006,775, an allocation rate of 0.2937633 per revenue dollar was established ($883,280 ÷ $3,006,775). This rate was multiplied by the proportionate share of revenue generated by each service category to produce the following allocation.

Type of Service	Service Revenue	×	Allocation Rate	=	Allocated Cost
HD	$1,860,287	×	0.2937633	=	$546,484
PD	1,146,488	×	0.2937633	=	336,796
Total	$3,006,775	×	0.2937633	=	$883,280

To better assess the cost of providing each type of service, the clinic initiated an activity-based costing (ABC) system. The ABC approach divided the nursing service cost into four separate cost pools. A separate cost driver (allocation base) was identified for each cost pool. The cost pools and their respective cost drivers follow.

	Total	HD	PD
Nursing services cost pool categories			
RNs	$239,120	?	?
LPNs	404,064	?	?
Nursing administration and support staff	115,168	?	?
Dialysis machine operations (tech. salaries)	124,928	?	?
Total	$883,280	?	?

	Total	HD	PD
Activity cost drivers (corresponding to cost pools)			
Number of RNs	7	5	2
Number of LPNs	19	15	4
Number of treatments (nursing administration)	34,967	14,343	20,624
Number of dialyzer treatments (machine operations)	14,343	14,343	0

Data Source: T. D. West and D. A. West, "Applying ABC to Healthcare," *Management Accounting,* February 1999, pp. 22–33.

Required

a. Organize the class into four sections and divide the sections into groups of four or five students each. Assign Task 1 to the first section of groups, Task 2 to the second section, Task 3 to the third section, and Task 4 to the fourth section.

Group Tasks

(1) Allocate the RN cost pool between the HD and PD service centers.

(2) Allocate the LPN cost pool between the HD and PD service centers.

(3) Allocate the nursing administration and support staff cost pool between the HD and PD service centers.

(4) Allocate the dialysis machine operations cost pool between the HD and PD service centers.

b. Have the class determine the total cost to allocate to the two service centers in the following manner. Select a representative from each section and have the selected person go to the board. Each representative should supply the allocated cost for the cost pool assigned by her respective section. The instructor should total the amounts and compare the ABC cost allocations with those developed through the traditional RCC system.

c. The instructor should lead the class in a discussion that addresses the following questions.

    (1) Assuming that the ABC system provides a more accurate measure of cost, which service center (HD or PD) is overcosted by the traditional allocation system and which is undercosted?

    (2) What is the potential impact on pricing and profitability for both service centers?

    (3) How could management respond to the conditions described in the problem?

ATC 5-3   Research Assignment   *Evaluating external failure costs with real world data*

The federal government maintains a website devoted to providing information about product recalls. To complete this assignment you will need to obtain information from this site as follows:

Go to recalls.gov

Click on the Consumer Products tab at the top of the screen

Click on CPSC Recalls—Home

Use the "Find Recalls by" month and year options to look up information about the following recalls that occurred in November 2009:

- Maclaren USA Recalls to Repair Strollers Following Fingertip Amputations, and

- Infant Entrapment and Suffocation Prompts Stork Craft to Recall . . .

Required

For each of these two recalls:

a. Explain why the product was recalled.

b. Who was most responsible for the problem that resulted in the recall?

c. Who will be negatively affected by the faulty product?

d. What are the external failure costs related to the faulty product? Describe the nature of these costs; you will not be able to identify dollar amounts.

e. At what point in the pre-sale process could steps have been taken to prevent the faulty product from being produced and/or sold?

ATC 5-4   Writing Assignment   *Assessing a strategy to control quality cost*

Lucy Sawyer, who owns and operates Sawyer Toy Company, is a perfectionist. She believes literally in the "zero-defects" approach to quality control. Her favorite saying is, "You can't spend too much on quality." Even so, in 2010 her company experienced an embarrassing breach of quality that required the national recall of a defective product. She vowed never to repeat the experience and instructed her staff to spend whatever it takes to ensure that products are delivered free of defects in 2011. She was somewhat disappointed with the 2011 year-end quality cost report shown here.

	2010	2011
Prevention costs	$120,000	$ 80,000
Appraisal costs	240,000	430,000
Internal failure costs	140,000	560,000
External failure cost	320,000	210,000
Total	$820,000	$1,280,000

Although external failure costs had declined, they remained much higher than expected. The increased inspections had identified defects that were corrected, thereby avoiding another recall; however, the external failure costs were still too high. Ms. Sawyer responded by saying, "We will have to double our efforts." She authorized hiring additional inspectors and instructed her production supervisors to become more vigilant in identifying and correcting errors.

Required

Assume that you are the chief financial officer (CFO) of Sawyer Toy Company. Ms. Sawyer has asked you to review the company's approach to quality control. Prepare a memo to her that evaluates the existing approach, and recommend changes in expenditure patterns that can improve profitability as well as increase the effectiveness of the quality control system.

ATC 5-5   Ethical Dilemma   *Conflicts between controlling cost and providing social responsibility to patients*

This case examines potential ethical issues faced by the dialysis clinic described in ATC 5-2. It is, however, an independent case that students may study in conjunction with or separately from ATC 5-2. The dialysis clinic provides two types of treatment for its patients. Hemodialysis (HD), an in-house treatment, requires patients to visit the clinic three times each week. Peritoneal dialysis (PD) permits patients to self-administer their treatments at home on a daily basis. The clinic serves a number of HMO patients under a contract that limits collections from the HMO insurer to a fixed amount per patient. As a result, the clinic's profitability is directly related to its ability to control costs. To illustrate, assume that the clinic is paid a fixed annual fee of $15,000 per HMO patient served. Also assume that the current cost to provide health care averages $14,000 a year per patient, resulting in an average profitability of $1,000 per patient ($15,000 − $14,000). Because the revenue base is fixed, the only way the clinic can increase profitability is to lower its average cost of providing services. If the clinic fails to control costs and the average cost of patient care increases, profitability will decline. A recent ABC study suggests that the cost to provide HD service exceeds the amount of revenue generated from providing that service. The clinic is profitable because PD services generate enough profit to more than make up for losses on HD services.

Required

Respond to each potential scenario described here. Each scenario is independent of the others.

a. Suppose that as a result of the ABC analysis, the chief accountant, a certified management accountant (CMA), recommends that the clinic discontinue treating HD patients referred by the HMO provider. Based on this assumption, answer the following questions.

  (1) Assume that the clinic is located in a small town. If it discontinues treating the HD patients, they will be forced to drive 50 miles to the nearest alternative treatment center. Does the clinic have a moral obligation to society to continue to provide HD service although it is not profitable to do so?

  (2) The accountant's recommendation places profitability above the needs of HD patients. Does this recommendation violate any of the standards of ethical conduct described in Chapter 1, Exhibit 1.15?

b. Assume that the clinic continues to treat HD patients referred by HMOs. However, to compensate for the loss incurred on these patients, the clinic raises prices charged to non-HMO patients. Is it fair to require non-HMO patients to subsidize services provided to the HMO patients?

c. Suppose that the clinic administrators respond to the ABC data by cutting costs. The clinic overbooks HMO patients to ensure that downtime is avoided when cancellations occur. It reduces the RN nursing staff and assigns some of the technical work to less-qualified assistants. Ultimately, an overworked, underqualified nurse's aide makes a mistake, and a patient dies. Who is at fault—the HMO, the accountant who conducted the ABC analysis, or the clinic administrators who responded to the ABC information?

ATC 5-6   Spreadsheet Assignment   *Using Excel*

Tameron Corporation produces video games in three market categories: commercial, home line, and miniature handheld. Tameron has traditionally allocated overhead costs to the three product categories using the companywide base of direct labor hours. The company recently switched to an ABC system when it installed computer-controlled assembly stations that rendered the traditional costing system ineffective. In implementing the ABC system, the company identified the cost pools and drivers shown in the following spreadsheet. The activity in each of the three product lines appears in rows 3 to 9. The pooled costs are shown in cells E11 to E15.

Required

Construct a spreadsheet like the following one to compute the total cost and cost per unit for each product line. Cells K4 to K9, G12 to I15, E19 to E28, G19 to G28, I19 to I28, and K26 should all be formulas.

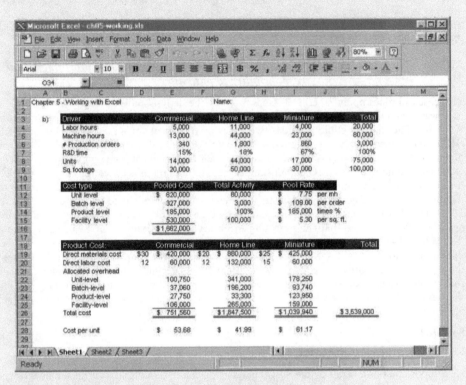

ATC 5-7   Spreadsheet Assignment   *Mastering Excel*

Beasley Company makes three types of exercise machines. Data have been accumulated for four possible overhead drivers. Data for these four possible drivers are shown in rows 3 to 7 of the following spreadsheet.

Required

Construct a spreadsheet that will allocate overhead and calculate unit cost for each of these alternative drivers. A screen capture of the spreadsheet and data follows.

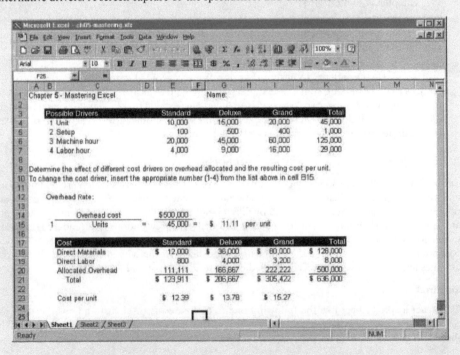

Spreadsheet Tips

1. This spreadsheet uses a function called *vertical lookup.* This function can pull the appropriate values from a table. The form of this function is =VLOOKUP (value, table, column#). In this example, the table is in cells B4 to K7. Three examples of the use of VLOOKUP follow.

2. Cell C15 is =VLOOKUP (B15, B4:K7, 2). This function operates by using the one (1) in cell B15 to look up a value in the table. Notice that the table is defined as B4:K7 and that the function is looking up the value in the second column, which is Units.

3. Cell E15 is =VLOOKUP (B15, B4:K7, 10). In this case, the function is looking up the value in the tenth column, which is 45,000. Be sure to count empty columns.

4. Cell E20 is =VLOOKUP (B15, B4:K7, 4)*G15. In this case, the function is looking up the value in the fourth column, which is $10,000. Be sure to count empty columns.

5. Cells I15, G20, and I20 also use the VLOOKUP function.

6. After completing the spreadsheet, you can change the value in cell B15 (1-4) to see the effect of choosing a different driver for overhead.

COMPREHENSIVE PROBLEM

To this point we have assumed the Magnificent Modems produced only one type of modem. Suppose instead we assume the company produces several different kinds of modems. The production process differs for each type of product. Some require more setup time than others, they are produced in different batch sizes, and they require different amounts of indirect labor (supervision). Packaging and delivery to customers also differs for each type of modem. Even so, Magnificent Modems uses a single allocation base (number of units) to allocate overhead costs.

Required

Write a brief memo that explains how Magnificent Modems could benefit from an ABC costing system.

CHAPTER 6

Relevant Information for Special Decisions

LEARNING OBJECTIVES

After you have mastered the material in this chapter, you will be able to:

1 Identify the characteristics of relevant information.

2 Distinguish between unit-level, batch-level, product-level, and facility-level costs and understand how these costs affect decision making.

3 Make appropriate special order decisions.

4 Make appropriate outsourcing decisions.

5 Make appropriate segment elimination decisions.

6 Make appropriate asset replacement decisions.

7 Explain the conflict between short-term and long-term profitability (Appendix).

8 Make decisions about allocating scarce resources (Appendix).

CHAPTER OPENING

Mary Daniels paid $25,000 to purchase a car that was used in her rental business. After one year the car had a book value of $21,000. Ms. Daniels needs cash and is considering selling the car. After advertising the vehicle for sale, the best offer she received was $19,000. Ms. Daniels really needed the money, but ultimately decided not to sell because she did not want to incur a $2,000 loss ($21,000 market value − $19,000 book value). Did Ms. Daniels make the right decision?

Whether Ms. Daniels will be better off selling the car or keeping it is unknown. However, it is certain that she based her decision on irrelevant data. Ms. Daniels incurred a loss when the market value of the car dropped. She cannot avoid a loss that already exists. Past mistakes should not affect current decisions. The current value of the car is $19,000. Ms. Daniels's decision is whether to take the money or keep the car. The book value of the car is not relevant. This chapter explains how to isolate and focus on the variables that are relevant in the decision-making process.

The Curious Accountant

In July 2009, the authors compared the prices of 10 of the top selling prescription drugs at two large on-line pharmacies, one in the United States and one in Canada. The analysis showed the Canadian prices for these 10 popular prescription drugs, such as Lipitor and Zocor, were only 51 percent of prices charged in the United States.

Major pharmaceutical companies have earnings before tax that average around 25 percent of sales, indicating that their costs average around 75 percent of the prices they charge. In other words, it costs approximately $75 to generate $100 of revenue. Given that drugs are sold in Canada for 51 percent of the U.S. sales price, a drug that is sold in the U.S. for $100 would be sold in Canada for only $51.

How can drugs be sold in Canada for less ($51) than cost ($75)? (Answer on page 259.)

Identify the characteristics of relevant information.

RELEVANT INFORMATION

How can you avoid irrelevant information when making decisions? Two primary characteristics distinguish relevant from useless information. Specifically, **relevant information** (1) differs among the alternatives and (2) is future oriented.

The first characteristic recognizes that relevant information differs for one or more of the alternatives being considered. Suppose the car Ms. Daniels is considering selling is due for a state required safety inspection. Further assume that the inspection must be completed before the car can be sold or driven. Since the inspection fee must be paid regardless of whether Ms. Daniels keeps or sells the car, it does not differ among the alternatives and therefore is not relevant to her decision. In contrast, assume the car is due for an oil change that can be delayed until after the car is sold. Since Ms. Daniels can avoid the cost of the oil change if she sells the car but must pay for the oil change if she keeps the car, the cost of the oil change differs between the alternatives and is relevant to her decision.

The second characteristic of relevant information is that it impacts the future. "Don't cry over spilt milk." "It's water over the dam." These aphorisms remind people they cannot change the past. With regard to business decisions, the principle means you cannot avoid a cost that has already been incurred. In the Daniels example, the historical cost ($25,000) of the car is not relevant to a decision regarding whether to sell the car today. The current market value of $19,000 is relevant to the decision regarding whether to sell the car today.

It is interesting to note that the two characteristics are merely different views of the same concept because historical information does not differ between the alternatives. In other words, we could say that historical costs are not relevant because they do not differ between alternatives associated with current decisions.

Sunk Cost

Historical costs are frequently called *sunk costs*. Since **sunk costs** have been incurred in past transactions, they cannot be changed and are not relevant for making current decisions. The $25,000 original cost of the car in the Daniels example is a sunk cost.

Why even bother to collect historical information if it is not relevant? Historical information may be useful in predicting the future. A company that earned $5 million last year is more likely to earn $5 million this year than a company that earned $5,000 last year. The predictive capacity is relevant because it provides insight into the future.

Opportunity Costs

An **opportunity cost** is the sacrifice that is incurred in order to obtain an alternative opportunity. For example, in the above case, Ms. Daniels must give up the opportunity to obtain $19,000 in order to keep the car. So, the opportunity cost of owning the car is $19,000. Since this cost differs between the alternatives of owning the car versus selling it and since it affects the present or future, it is relevant to the decision regarding whether to keep or sell the car.

The best offer that Ms. Daniels received for the car was $19,000. Suppose Ms. Daniels also received the less favorable offer of $18,000. Does this mean that the opportunity cost of keeping the car is $37,000 ($18,000 + $19,000)? No. Opportunity costs are not cumulative. Ms. Daniels really has only one opportunity. If she accepts the $19,000 offer, she must reject the $18,000 offer or vice versa. Accountants normally measure opportunity cost as the highest value of the available alternatives. In this case, the opportunity cost of keeping the car is $19,000.

✓ CHECK YOURSELF 6.1

Aqua, Inc., makes statues for use in fountains. On January 1, 2011, the company paid $13,500 for a mold to make a particular type of statue. The mold had an expected useful life of four years and a salvage value of $1,500. On January 1, 2013, the mold had a market value of $3,000 and a salvage value of $1,200. The expected useful life did not change. What is the relevant cost of using the mold during 2013?

Answer The relevant cost of using the mold in 2013 is the opportunity cost [(market value − salvage value) ÷ remaining useful life], in this case, ($3,000 − $1,200) ÷ 2 = $900. The book value of the asset and associated depreciation is based on a sunk cost that cannot be avoided because it has already been incurred and therefore is not relevant to current decisions. In contrast, Aqua could avoid the opportunity cost (market value) by selling the mold.

Relevance Is an Independent Concept

The concept of relevance is independent from the concept of cost behavior. In a given circumstance, **relevant costs** could be either fixed or variable. Consider the following illustration. Executives of Better Bakery Products are debating whether to add a new product, either cakes or pies, to the company's line. Projected costs for the two options follow.

Cost of Cakes		Cost of Pies	
Materials (per unit)	$ 1.50	Materials (per unit)	$ 2.00
Direct labor (per unit)	1.00	Direct labor (per unit)	1.00
Supervisor's salary*	25,000.00	Supervisor's salary*	25,000.00
Franchise fee†	50,000.00	Advertising‡	40,000.00

*It will be necessary to hire a new production supervisor at a cost of $25,000 per year.

†Cakes will be distributed under a nationally advertised label. Better Bakery pays an annual franchise fee for the right to use the product label. Because of the established brand name, Better Bakery will not be required to advertise the product.

‡Better Bakery will market the pies under its own name and will advertise the product in the local market in which the product sells.

Which costs are relevant? Fifty cents per unit of the materials can be avoided by choosing cakes instead of pies. A portion of the materials cost is therefore relevant. Labor costs will be one dollar per unit whether Better Bakery makes cakes or pies.

REALITY BYTES

Determining what price to charge for their company's goods or services is one of the most difficult decisions that business managers make. Charge too much and customers will go elsewhere. Charge less than customers are willing to pay and lose the opportunity to earn profits. This problem is especially difficult when managers are deciding if they should reduce (mark down) the price of aging inventory—for example, flowers that are beginning to wilt, fruit that is beginning to overripen, or clothing that is going out of season.

At first managers may be reluctant to mark down the inventory below its cost because this would cause the company to take a loss on the aging inventory. However, the concept of sunk cost applies here. Since the existing inventory has already been paid for, its cost is sunk. Since the cost is sunk it is not relevant to the decision. Does this mean the merchandise should be sold for any price? Not necessarily. The concept of opportunity cost must also be considered.

If the goods are marked down too far, too quickly, they may be sold for less than is possible. The lost potential revenue is an opportunity cost. To minimize the opportunity cost, the amount of a markdown must be the smallest amount necessary to sell the merchandise. The decision is further complicated by qualitative considerations. If a business develops a reputation for repeated markdowns, customers may hesitate to buy goods, thinking that the price will fall further if they only wait a while. The result is a dilemma as to when and how much to mark down aging inventories.

How do managers address this dilemma? Part of the answer has been the use of technology. For years airlines have used computerized mathematical models to help them decide how many seats on a particular flight should be sold at a discount. More recently, retailers began using this same type of modeling software. Such software allows retailers to take fewer markdowns at more appropriate times, thereby resulting in higher overall gross profit margins.

Labor cost is therefore not relevant. Although both materials and direct labor are variable costs, one is relevant but the other is not.

Since Better Bakery must hire a supervisor under either alternative, the supervisor's salary is not relevant. The franchise fee can be avoided if Better Bakery makes pies and advertising costs can be avoided if it makes cakes. All three of these costs are fixed, but only two are relevant. Finally, all the costs (whether fixed or variable) could be avoided if Better Bakery rejects both products. Whether a cost is fixed or variable has no bearing on its relevance.

Relevance Is Context Sensitive

A particular cost that is relevant in one context may be irrelevant in another. Consider a store that carries men's, women's, and children's clothing. The store manager's salary could not be avoided by eliminating the children's department, but it could be avoided if the entire store were closed. The salary is not relevant to deciding whether to eliminate the children's department but is relevant with respect to deciding to close the store. In one context, the salary is not relevant. In the other context, it is relevant.

Relationship between Relevance and Accuracy

Information need not be exact to be relevant. You may decide to delay purchasing a laptop computer you want if you know its price is going to drop even if you don't know exactly how much the price decrease will be. You know part of the cost can be avoided by waiting; you are just not sure of the amount.

The most useful information is both relevant and precise. Totally inaccurate information is useless. Likewise, irrelevant information is useless regardless of its accuracy.

Quantitative versus Qualitative Characteristics of Decision Making

Relevant information can have both **quantitative** and **qualitative characteristics.** The previous examples focused on quantitative data. Now consider qualitative issues. Suppose you are deciding which of two laptop computers to purchase. Computer A costs $300 more than Computer B. Both computers satisfy your technical requirements; however, Computer A has a more attractive appearance. From a quantitative standpoint, you would select Computer B because you could avoid $300 of cost. However, if the laptop will be used in circumstances where clients need to be impressed, appearance—a qualitative characteristic—may be more important than minimizing cost. You might purchase Computer A even though quantitative factors favor Computer B. Both qualitative and quantitative data are relevant to decision making.

As with quantitative data, qualitative features must *differ* between the alternatives to be relevant. If the two computers were identical in appearance, attractiveness would not be relevant to making the decision.

Differential Revenue and Avoidable Cost

Since relevant revenue *differs* among the alternatives, it is sometimes called **differential revenue.** To illustrate, assume Pecks Department Stores sells men's, women's, and children's clothing and is considering eliminating the children's line. The revenue generated by the children's department is differential (relevant) revenue because Pecks' total revenue would be different if the children's department were eliminated.

Why would Pecks consider eliminating the children's department and thereby lose the differential (relevant) revenue? Pecks may be able to save more by eliminating the cost of operating the department than it loses in differential revenue. Some but not all of the costs associated with operating the children's department can be saved. For example, if Pecks Department Stores eliminates the children's department, the company can eliminate the cost of the department manager's salary but cannot get rid of the salary of the company president. The costs that stay the same are not relevant. The costs that can be *avoided* by closing the department are relevant. Indeed, relevant costs are frequently called *avoidable costs.*

Avoidable costs are the costs managers can eliminate by making specific choices. In the Pecks example, the cost of the department manager's salary is an avoidable (relevant) cost. The cost of the president's salary is not avoidable and is not relevant to the elimination decision.

RELATIONSHIP OF COST AVOIDANCE TO A COST HIERARCHY

Classifying costs into one of four hierarchical levels helps identify avoidable costs.[1]

1. *Unit-level costs.* Costs incurred each time a company generates one unit of product are **unit-level costs.**[2] Examples include the cost of direct materials, direct labor, inspections, packaging, shipping, and handling. Incremental (additional) unit-level costs increase *with each additional unit of product generated. Unit-level costs can be avoided by eliminating the production of a single unit of product.*

2. *Batch-level costs.* Many products are generated in batches rather than individual units. For example, a heating and air conditioning technician may service a batch of air conditioners in an apartment complex. Some of the job costs apply only to individual units, and other costs relate to the entire batch. For instance, the labor to service each air conditioner is a unit-level cost, but the cost of driving to the site is a **batch-level cost.**

   Classifying costs as unit- versus batch-level frequently depends on the context rather than the type of cost. For example, shipping and handling costs to send 200 computers to a university are batch-level costs. In contrast, the shipping and handling cost to deliver a single computer to each of a number of individual customers is a unit-level cost. Eliminating a batch of work avoids both batch-level and unit-level costs. Similarly, adding a batch of work increases batch-level and unit-level costs. Increasing the number of units in a particular batch increases unit-level but not batch-level costs. Decreasing the number of units in a batch reduces unit-level costs but not batch-level costs.

3. *Product-level costs.* Costs incurred to support specific products or services are called **product-level costs.** Product-level costs include quality inspection costs, engineering design costs, the costs of obtaining and defending patents, the costs of regulatory compliance, and inventory holding costs such as interest, insurance, maintenance, and storage. *Product-level costs can be avoided by discontinuing a product line.* For example, suppose the Snapper Company makes the engines used in its lawn mowers. Buying engines from an outside supplier instead of making them would allow Snapper to avoid the product-level costs such as legal fees for patents, manufacturing supervisory costs of producing the engines, and the maintenance and inventory costs of holding engine parts.

4. *Facility-level costs.* **Facility-level costs** are incurred to support the entire company. They are not related to any specific product, batch, or unit of product. Because these costs maintain the facility as a whole, they are frequently called *facility-sustaining costs.* Facility-level costs include building rent or depreciation, personnel administration and training, property and real estate taxes, insurance, maintenance, administrative salaries, general selling costs, landscaping, utilities,

---

[1]R. Cooper and R. S. Kaplan, *The Design of Cost Management Systems* (Englewood Cliffs, NJ: Prentice-Hall, 1991). Our classifications are broader than those typically presented. They encompass service and merchandising companies as well as manufacturing businesses. The original cost hierarchy was developed as a platform for activity-based costing, a topic introduced in the previous chapter. These classifications are equally useful as a tool for identifying avoidable costs.

[2]Recall that we use the term *product* in a generic sense to represent producing goods or services.

and security. Total facility-level costs cannot be avoided unless the entire company is dissolved. However, eliminating a business segment (such as a division, department, or office) may enable a company to avoid some facility-level costs. For example, if a bank eliminates one of its branches, it can avoid the costs of renting, maintaining, and insuring that particular branch building. In general, *segment-level* facility costs can be avoided when a segment is eliminated. In contrast, *corporate-level* facility costs cannot be avoided unless the corporation is eliminated.

Precise distinctions between the various categories are often difficult to draw. One company may incur sales staff salaries as a facility-level cost while another company may pay sales commissions traceable to product lines or even specific units of a product line. Cost classifications cannot be memorized. Classifying specific cost items into the appropriate categories requires thoughtful judgment.

RELEVANT INFORMATION AND SPECIAL DECISIONS

LO 3

Make appropriate special order decisions.

Five types of special decisions are frequently encountered in business practice: (1) special order, (2) outsourcing, (3) segment elimination, (4) asset replacement, and (5) scarce resource allocation. The following sections discuss using relevant information in making the first four types of special decisions. The Appendix to this chapter discusses scarce resource decisions.

Special Order Decisions

Occasionally, a company receives an offer to sell its goods at a price significantly below its normal selling price. The company must make a **special order decision** to accept or reject the offer.

EXHIBIT 6.1

Budgeted Cost for Expected Production of 2,000 Printers

Unit-level costs		
Materials costs (2,000 units × $90)	$180,000	
Labor costs (2,000 units × $82.50)	165,000	
Overhead (2,000 units × $7.50)	15,000	
Total unit-level costs (2,000 × $180)		$360,000
Batch-level costs		
Assembly setup (10 batches × $1,700)	17,000	
Materials handling (10 batches × $500)	5,000	
Total batch-level costs (10 batches × $2,200)		22,000
Product-level costs		
Engineering design	14,000	
Production manager salary	63,300	
Total product-level costs		77,300
Facility-level costs		
Segment-level costs:		
Division manager's salary	85,000	
Administrative costs	12,700	
Allocated—corporate-level costs:		
Company president's salary	43,200	
Building rental	27,300	
General expenses	31,000	
Total facility-level costs		199,200
Total expected cost		$658,500
Cost per unit: $658,500 ÷ 2,000 = $329.25		

Quantitative Analysis

Assume Premier Office Products manufactures printers. Premier expects to make and sell 2,000 printers in 10 batches of 200 units per batch during the coming year. Expected production costs are summarized in Exhibit 6.1.

Adding its normal markup to the total cost per unit, Premier set the selling price at $360 per printer.

Suppose Premier receives a *special order* from a new customer for 200 printers. If Premier accepts the order, its expected sales would increase from 2,000 units to 2,200 units. But the special order customer is willing to pay only $250 per printer. This price is well below not only Premier's normal selling price of $360 but also the company's expected per unit cost of $329.25. Should Premier accept or reject the special order? At first glance, it seems Premier should reject the special order because the customer's offer is below the expected cost per unit. Analyzing relevant costs and revenue leads, however, to a different conclusion.

The quantitative analysis follows in three steps.

Step 1.   **Determine the amount of the relevant (differential) revenue Premier will earn by accepting the special order.** Premier's alternatives are (1) to accept or (2) to reject the special order. If Premier accepts the special order, additional revenue will be $50,000 ($250 × 200 units). If Premier rejects the special order, additional revenue will be zero. Since the amount of revenue differs between the alternatives, the $50,000 is relevant.

Step 2. **Determine the amount of the relevant (differential) cost Premier will incur by accepting the special order.** Examine the costs in Exhibit 6.1. If Premier accepts the special order, it will incur additional unit-level costs (materials, labor, and overhead). It will also incur the cost of one additional 200-unit batch. The unit- and batch-level costs are relevant because Premier could avoid them by rejecting the special order. The other costs in Exhibit 6.1 are not relevant because Premier will incur them whether it accepts or rejects the special order.

Step 3. **Accept the special order if the relevant revenue exceeds the relevant (avoidable) cost. Reject the order if relevant cost exceeds relevant revenue.** Exhibit 6.2 summarizes the relevant figures. Since the relevant revenue exceeds the relevant cost, Premier should accept the special order because profitability will increase by $11,800.

EXHIBIT 6.2

Relevant Information for Special Order of 200 Printers

Differential revenue ($250 × 200 units)	$50,000
Avoidable unit-level costs ($180 × 200 units)	(36,000)
Avoidable batch-level costs ($2,200 × 1 batch)	(2,200)
Contribution to income	$11,800

Opportunity Costs

Premier can consider the special order because it has enough excess productive capacity to make the additional units. Suppose Premier has the opportunity to lease its excess capacity (currently unused building and equipment) for $15,000. If Premier uses the excess capacity to make the additional printers, it must forgo the opportunity to lease the excess capacity to a third party. Sacrificing the potential leasing income represents an opportunity cost of accepting the special order. Adding this opportunity cost to the other relevant costs increases the cost of accepting the special order to $53,200 ($38,200 unit-level and batch-level costs + $15,000 opportunity cost). The avoidable costs would then exceed the differential revenue, resulting in a projected loss of $3,200 ($50,000 differential revenue − $53,200 avoidable costs). Under these circumstances Premier would be better off rejecting the special order and leasing the excess capacity.

Relevance and the Decision Context

Assume Premier does not have the opportunity to lease its excess capacity. Recall the original analysis indicated the company could earn an $11,800 contribution to profit by accepting a special order to sell 200 printers at $250 per unit (see Exhibit 6.2). Because Premier can earn a contribution to profit by selling printers for $250 each, can the company reduce its normal selling price (price charged to existing customers) to $250? The answer is no, as illustrated in Exhibit 6.3.

EXHIBIT 6.3		
Projections Based on 2,200 Printers at a Sales Price of $250 per Unit		
Revenue ($250 × 2,200 units)		$ 550,000
Unit-level supplies and inspection ($180 × 2,200 units)	$396,000	
Batch-level costs ($2,200 × 11 batches)	24,200	
Product-level costs	77,300	
Facility-level costs	199,200	
Total cost		(696,700)
Projected loss		$(146,700)

If a company is to be profitable, it must ultimately generate revenue in excess of total costs. Although the facility-level and product-level costs are not relevant to the special order decision, they are relevant to the operation of the business as a whole.

Qualitative Characteristics

Should a company ever reject a special order if the relevant revenues exceed the relevant costs? Qualitative characteristics may be even more important than quantitative ones. If Premier's regular customers learn the company sold printers to another buyer at $250 per unit, they may demand reduced prices on future purchases. Exhibit 6.3 shows Premier cannot reduce the price for all customers. Special order customers should therefore come from outside Premier's normal sales territory. In addition, special order customers should be advised that the special price does not apply to repeat business. Cutting off a special order customer who has been permitted to establish a continuing relationship is likely to lead to ill-feelings and harsh words. A business's reputation can depend on how management handles such relationships. Finally, at full capacity, Premier should reject any special orders at reduced prices because filling those orders reduces its ability to satisfy customers who pay full price.

Outsourcing Decisions

Make appropriate outsourcing decisions.

Companies can sometimes purchase products they need for less than it would cost to make them. This circumstance explains why automobile manufacturers purchase rather than make many of the parts in their cars or why a caterer might buy gourmet desserts from a specialty company. Buying goods and services from other companies rather than producing them internally is commonly called **outsourcing.**

Quantitative Analysis

Assume Premier Office Products is considering whether to outsource production of the printers it currently makes. A supplier has offered to sell an unlimited supply of printers to Premier for $240 each. The estimated cost of making the printers is $329.25 per unit (see Exhibit 6.1). The data suggest that Premier could save money by outsourcing. Analyzing relevant costs proves this presumption wrong.

A two-step quantitative analysis for the outsourcing decision follows:

Step 1. **Determine the production costs Premier can avoid if it outsources printer production.** A review of Exhibit 6.1 discloses the costs Premier could avoid by outsourcing. If Premier purchases the printers, it can avoid the unit-level costs (materials, labor, overhead), and the batch-level costs (assembly setup, and materials handling). It can also avoid the product-level costs (engineering design costs and production manager salary). Deciding to outsource will not, however, affect the facility-level costs. Because Premier will incur them whether or not it outsources printer production, the facility-level costs are not relevant to the outsourcing decision. Exhibit 6.4 shows the avoidable (relevant) costs of outsourcing.

Step 2. **Compare the avoidable (relevant) production costs with the cost of buying the product and select the lower-cost option.** Because the relevant production cost is less than the purchase price of the printers ($229.65 per unit versus $240.00), the quantitative analysis suggests that Premier should continue to make the printers. Profitability would decline by $20,700 [$459,300 − ($240 × 2,000)] if printer production were outsourced.

Opportunity Costs

Suppose Premier's accountant determines that the space Premier currently uses to manufacture printers could be leased to a third party for $40,000 per year. By using the space to manufacture printers, Premier is *forgoing the opportunity* to earn $40,000. Because this *opportunity cost* can be avoided by purchasing the printers, it is relevant to the outsourcing decision. After adding the opportunity cost to the other relevant costs, the total relevant cost increases to $499,300 ($459,300 + $40,000) and the relevant cost per

EXHIBIT 6.4

Relevant Cost for Expected Production for Outsourcing 2,000 Printers

Unit-level costs ($180 × 2,000 units)	$360,000
Batch-level costs ($2,200 × 10 batches)	22,000
Product-level costs	77,300
Total relevant cost	$459,300
Cost per unit: $459,300 ÷ 2,000 = $229.65	

unit becomes $249.65 ($499,300 ÷ 2,000). Since Premier can purchase printers for $240, it should outsource printer production. It would be better off buying the printers and leasing the manufacturing space.

Evaluating the Effect of Growth on the Level of Production

The decision to outsource would change if expected production increased from 2,000 to 3,000 units. Because some of the avoidable costs are fixed relative to the level of production, cost per unit decreases as volume increases. For example, the product-level costs (engineering design, production manager's salary, and opportunity cost) are fixed relative to the level of production. Exhibit 6.5 shows the relevant cost per unit if Premier expects to produce 3,000 printers.

At 3,000 units of production, the relevant cost of making printers is less than the cost of outsourcing ($230.10 versus $240.00). If management believes the company is likely to experience growth in the near future, it should reject

EXHIBIT 6.5

Relevant Cost for Expected Production for Outsourcing 3,000 Printers

Unit-level costs ($180 × 3,000 units)	$540,000
Batch-level costs ($2,200 × 15 batches)	33,000
Product-level costs	77,300
Opportunity cost	40,000
Total relevant cost	$690,300
Cost per unit: $690,300 ÷ 3,000 units = $230.10	

FOCUS ON INTERNATIONAL ISSUES

ARE YOU SURE YOUR GERMAN CAR WAS MADE IN GERMANY?

In recent years there has been much discussion about American companies outsourcing work to other workers in other countries. However, some activities that are seldom outsourced by American companies are routinely outsourced by companies in other countries. In fact, sometimes the "foreign country" who provides the outsourcing is the United States.

   Consider an example from the automotive industry. While American automobile companies may use parts that were manufactured in another country, the final assembly of cars they sell in the United States is usually performed in their own plants in the United States or Canada. Japanese auto companies also tend to perform the final assembly of their cars in their own plants, which may be located in another country. In contrast, European car makers are more willing to outsource the final assembly, as well as engineering and parts production, to independent companies. For example, most, if not all BMW X3s are not assembled at a BMW plant, but by the employees of Magna Steyr in Graz, Austria. This company, by the way, is a subsidiary of Magna International, which is a Canadian company. And that Porsche Boxster or Cayman you are hoping to receive as a graduation gift—it almost certainly will be built by Valmet Automotive in Finland. In fact, Valmet assembled 22,356 of the 105,162 vehicles that Porsche produced in 2008.

Source: Companies' annual reports.

the outsourcing option. Managers must consider potential growth when making outsourcing decisions.

Qualitative Features

A company that uses **vertical integration** controls the full range of activities from acquiring raw materials to distributing goods and services. Outsourcing reduces the level of vertical integration, passing some of a company's control over its products to outside suppliers. The reliability of the supplier is critical to an outsourcing decision. An unscrupulous supplier may lure an unsuspecting manufacturer into an outsourcing decision using **low-ball pricing.** Once the manufacturer is dependent on the supplier, the supplier raises prices. If a price sounds too good to be true, it probably is too good to be true. Other potential problems include product quality and delivery commitments. If the printers do not work properly or are not delivered on time, Premier's customers will be dissatisfied with Premier, not the supplier. Outsourcing requires that Premier depend on the supplier to deliver quality products at designated prices according to a specified schedule. Any supplier failures will become Premier's failures.

   To protect themselves from unscrupulous or incompetent suppliers, many companies establish a select list of reliable **certified suppliers.** These companies seek to become the preferred customers of the suppliers by offering incentives such as guaranteed volume purchases with prompt payments. These incentives motivate the suppliers to ship high-quality products on a timely basis. The purchasing companies recognize that prices ultimately depend on the suppliers' ability to control costs, so the buyers and suppliers work together to minimize costs. For example, buyers may share confidential information about their production plans with suppliers if such information would enable the suppliers to more effectively control costs.

   Companies must approach outsourcing decisions cautiously even when relationships with reliable suppliers are ensured. Outsourcing has both internal and external effects. It usually displaces employees. If the supplier experiences difficulties, reestablishing internal production capacity is expensive once a trained workforce has been released. Loyalty and trust are difficult to build but easy to destroy. In fact, companies must consider not only the employees who will be discharged but also the morale of those who remain. Cost reductions achieved through outsourcing are of little benefit if they are acquired at the expense of low morale and reduced productivity.

In spite of the potential pitfalls outsourcing entails, the vast majority of U.S. businesses engage in some form of it. Such widespread acceptance suggests that most companies believe the benefits achieved through outsourcing exceed the potential shortcomings.

✓ CHECK YOURSELF 6.2

Addison Manufacturing Company pays a production supervisor a salary of $48,000 per year. The supervisor manages the production of sprinkler heads that are used in water irrigation systems. Should the production supervisor's salary be considered a relevant cost to a special order decision? Should the production supervisor's salary be considered a relevant cost to an outsourcing decision?

Answer   The production supervisor's salary is not a relevant cost to a special order decision because Addison would pay the salary regardless of whether it accepts or rejects a special order. Since the cost does not differ for the alternatives, it is not relevant. In contrast, the supervisor's salary would be relevant to an outsourcing decision. Addison could dismiss the supervisor if it purchased the sprinkler heads instead of making them. Since the salary could be avoided by purchasing heads instead of making them, the salary is relevant to an outsourcing decision.

Segment Elimination Decisions

Businesses frequently organize their operations into subcomponents called **segments.** Segment data are used to make comparisons among different products, departments, or divisions. For example, in addition to the companywide income statement provided for external users, JCPenney may prepare separate income statements for each retail store for internal users. Executives can then evaluate managerial performance by comparing profitability measures among stores. *Segment reports* can be prepared for products, services, departments, branches, centers, offices, or divisions. These reports normally show segment revenues and costs. The primary objective of segment analysis is to determine whether relevant revenues exceed relevant costs.

LO 5

Make appropriate segment elimination decisions.

Quantitative Analysis

Assume Premier Office Products makes copy equipment and computers as well as printers. Each product line is made in a separate division of the company. Division (segment) operating results for the most recent year are shown in Exhibit 6.6. Initial review of the results suggests the copier division should be eliminated because it is operating at a loss. However, analyzing the relevant revenues and expenses leads to a different conclusion.

A three-step quantitative analysis for the segment elimination decision follows:

Step 1.   Determine the amount of relevant (differential) revenue that pertains to eliminating the copier division. The alternatives are (1) to eliminate or (2) to continue to operate the copier division. If Premier eliminates the copier line it will lose the $550,000 of revenue the copier division currently produces. If the division continues to operate, Premier will earn the revenue. Since the revenue differs between the alternatives, it is relevant.

Step 2.   Determine the amount of cost Premier can avoid if it eliminates the copier division. If it eliminates copiers, Premier can avoid the unit-level, batch-level,

EXHIBIT 6.6

Projected Revenues and Costs by Segment

	Copiers	Computers	Printers	Total
Projected revenue	$550,000	$850,000	$720,000	$2,120,000
Projected costs				
Unit-level costs				
Materials costs	(120,000)	(178,000)	(180,000)	(478,000)
Labor costs	(160,000)	(202,000)	(165,000)	(527,000)
Overhead	(30,800)	(20,000)	(15,000)	(65,800)
Batch-level costs				
Assembly setup	(15,000)	(26,000)	(17,000)	(58,000)
Materials handling	(6,000)	(8,000)	(5,000)	(19,000)
Product-level costs				
Engineering design	(10,000)	(12,000)	(14,000)	(36,000)
Production manager salary	(52,000)	(55,800)	(63,300)	(171,100)
Facility-level costs				
Segment level				
Division manager salary	(82,000)	(92,000)	(85,000)	(259,000)
Administrative costs	(12,200)	(13,200)	(12,700)	(38,100)
Allocated—corporate-level				
Company president salary	(34,000)	(46,000)	(43,200)	(123,200)
Building rental	(19,250)	(29,750)	(27,300)	(76,300)
General facility expenses	(31,000)	(31,000)	(31,000)	(93,000)
Projected income (loss)	$(22,250)	$136,250	$ 61,500	$ 175,500

product-level, and segment-level facility-sustaining costs. The relevant revenue and the avoidable costs are shown in Exhibit 6.7.

Premier will incur the corporate-level facility-sustaining costs whether it eliminates the copier segment or continues to operate it. Since these costs do not differ between the alternatives, they are not relevant to the elimination decision.

Step 3. **If the relevant revenue is less than the avoidable cost, eliminate the segment (division). If not, continue to operate it.** Because operating the segment is contributing $62,000 per year to company profitability (see Exhibit 6.7), Premier should not eliminate the copiers division. Exhibit 6.8 shows Premier's estimated revenues and costs if the computers and printers divisions were operated without the copiers division. Projected company profit declines by $62,000 ($175,500 − $113,500) without the copiers segment, confirming that eliminating it would be detrimental to Premier's profitability.

EXHIBIT 6.7

Relevant Revenue and Cost Data for Copier Segment

Projected revenue	$550,000
Projected costs	
Unit-level costs	
Materials costs	(120,000)
Labor costs	(160,000)
Overhead	(30,800)
Batch-level costs	
Assembly setup	(15,000)
Materials handling	(6,000)
Product-level costs	
Engineering design	(10,000)
Production manager salary	(52,000)
Facility-level costs	
Segment level	
Division manager salary	(82,000)
Administrative costs	(12,200)
Projected income (loss)	$ 62,000

Qualitative Considerations in Decisions to Eliminate Segments

As with other special decisions, management should consider qualitative factors when determining whether to eliminate segments. Employee lives will be disrupted; some employees may be reassigned elsewhere in the company, but others will be discharged. As with outsourcing decisions, reestablishing internal production capacity is difficult once a trained workforce has been released. Furthermore, employees in other segments, suppliers, customers, and investors may believe that the elimination of a segment implies the company as a whole is experiencing financial difficulty. These individuals may lose confidence in the company and seek business contacts with other companies they perceive to be more stable.

EXHIBIT 6.8

Projected Revenues and Costs without Copier Division

	Computers	Printers	Total
Projected revenue	$850,000	$720,000	$1,570,000
Projected costs			
Unit-level costs			
Materials costs	(178,000)	(180,000)	(358,000)
Labor costs	(202,000)	(165,000)	(367,000)
Overhead	(20,000)	(15,000)	(35,000)
Batch-level costs			
Assembly setup	(26,000)	(17,000)	(43,000)
Materials handling	(8,000)	(5,000)	(13,000)
Product-level costs			
Engineering design	(12,000)	(14,000)	(26,000)
Production manager salary	(55,800)	(63,300)	(119,100)
Facility-level costs			
Segment level			
Division manager salary	(92,000)	(85,000)	(177,000)
Administrative costs	(13,200)	(12,700)	(25,900)
Allocated—corporate-level*			
Company president salary	(63,000)	(60,200)	(123,200)
Building rental	(39,375)	(36,925)	(76,300)
General facility expenses	(46,500)	(46,500)	(93,000)
Projected income (loss)	$ 94,125	$ 19,375	$ 113,500

*The corporate-level facility costs that were previously *allocated* to the copier division have been reassigned on the basis of one-half to the computer division and one-half to the printer division.

Management must also consider the fact that sales of different product lines are frequently interdependent. Some customers prefer one-stop shopping; they want to buy all their office equipment from one supplier. If Premier no longer sells copiers, customers may stop buying its computers and printers. Eliminating one segment may reduce sales of other segments.

What will happen to the space Premier used to make the copiers? Suppose Premier decides to make telephone systems in the space it previously used for copiers. The contribution to profit of the telephone business would be an *opportunity cost* of operating the copier segment. As demonstrated in previous examples, adding the opportunity cost to the avoidable costs of operating the copier segment could change the decision.

As with outsourcing, volume changes can affect elimination decisions. Because many costs of operating a segment are fixed, the cost per unit decreases as production increases. Growth can transform a segment that is currently producing real losses into a segment that produces real profits. Managers must consider growth potential when making elimination decisions.

✓ CHECK YOURSELF 6.3

Capital Corporation is considering eliminating one of its operating segments. Capital employed a real estate broker to determine the marketability of the building that houses the segment. The broker obtained three bids for the building: $250,000, $262,000, and $264,000. The book value of the building is $275,000. Based on this information alone, what is the relevant cost of the building?

Answer The book value of the building is a sunk cost that is not relevant. There are three bids for the building, but only one is relevant because Capital could sell the building only once. The relevant cost of the building is the highest opportunity cost, which in this case is $264,000.

Distinguish between unit-level,
batch-level, product-level, and
facility-level costs and understand
how these costs affect decision
making.

Summary of Relationships between Avoidable Costs and the Hierarchy of Business Activity

A relationship exists between the cost hierarchy and the different types of special decisions just discussed. A special order involves making additional units of an existing product. Deciding to accept a special order affects unit-level and possibly batch-level costs. In contrast, outsourcing a product stops the production of that product. Outsourcing can avoid many product-level as well as unit- and batch-level costs. Finally, if a company eliminates an entire business segment, it can avoid some of the facility-level costs. The more complex the decision level, the more opportunities there are to avoid costs. Moving to a higher category does not mean, however, that all costs at the higher level of activity are avoidable. For example, all product-level costs may not be avoidable if a company chooses to outsource a product. The company may still incur inventory holding costs or advertising costs whether it makes or buys the product. Understanding the relationship between decision type and level of cost hierarchy helps when identifying avoidable costs. The relationships are summarized in Exhibit 6.9. For each type of decision, look for avoidable costs in the categories marked with an X. Remember also that sunk costs cannot be avoided.

EXHIBIT 6.9

Relationship between Decision Type and Level of Cost Hierarchy

Decision Type	Unit level	Batch level	Product level	Facility level
Special order	X	X		
Outsourcing	X	X	X	
Elimination	X	X	X	X

Equipment Replacement Decisions

Equipment may become technologically obsolete long before it fails physically. Managers should base **equipment replacement decisions** on profitability analysis rather than physical deterioration. Assume Premier Office Products is considering replacing an existing machine with a new one. The following table summarizes pertinent information about the two machines:

Old Machine		New Machine	
Original cost	$ 90,000	Cost of the new machine	$29,000
Accumulated depreciation	(33,000)	Salvage value (in 5 years)	4,000
Book value	$ 57,000	Operating expenses	
		($4,500 × 5 years)	22,500
Market value (now)	$ 14,000		
Salvage value (in 5 years)	2,000		
Annual depreciation expense	11,000		
Operating expenses			
($9,000 × 5 years)	45,000		

Quantitative Analysis

First determine what relevant costs Premier will incur if it keeps the *old machine*.

1. The *original cost* ($90,000), *current book value* ($57,000), *accumulated depreciation* ($33,000), and *annual depreciation expense* ($11,000) are different measures of a cost that was incurred in a prior period. They represent irrelevant sunk costs.

2. The $14,000 market value represents the current sacrifice Premier must make if it keeps using the existing machine. In other words, if Premier does not keep the

machine, it can sell it for $14,000. In economic terms, *forgoing the opportunity to sell the machine costs as much as buying it.* The *opportunity cost* is therefore relevant to the replacement decision.

3. The salvage value of the old machine reduces the opportunity cost. Premier can sell the old machine now for $14,000 or use it for five more years and then sell it for $2,000. The opportunity cost of using the old machine for five more years is therefore $12,000 ($14,000 − $2,000).

4. Because the $45,000 ($9,000 × 5) of operating expenses will be incurred if the old machine is used but can be avoided if it is replaced, the operating expenses are relevant costs.

Next, determine what relevant costs will be incurred if Premier purchases and uses the *new machine.*

1. The cost of the new machine represents a future economic sacrifice Premier must incur if it buys the new machine. It is a relevant cost.

2. The salvage value reduces the cost of purchasing the new machine. Part ($4,000) of the $29,000 cost of the new machine will be recovered at the end of five years. The relevant cost of purchasing the new machine is $25,000 ($29,000 − $4,000).

3. The $22,500 ($4,500 × 5) of operating expenses will be incurred if the new machine is purchased; it can be avoided if the new machine is not purchased. The operating expenses are relevant costs.

The relevant costs for the two machines are summarized here:

Old Machine		New Machine	
Opportunity cost	$14,000	Cost of the new machine	$29,000
Salvage value	(2,000)	Salvage value	(4,000)
Operating expenses	45,000	Operating expenses	22,500
Total	$57,000	Total	$47,500

The analysis suggests that Premier should acquire the new machine because buying it produces the lower relevant cost. The $57,000 cost of using the old machine can be *avoided* by incurring the $47,500 cost of acquiring and using the new machine. Over the five-year period, Premier would save $9,500 ($57,000 − $47,500) by purchasing the new machine. One caution: this analysis ignores income tax effects and the time value of money, which are explained later. The discussion in this chapter focuses on identifying and using relevant costs in decision making.

A Look Back

Decision making requires managers to choose from alternative courses of action. Successful decision making depends on a manager's ability to identify *relevant information.* Information that is relevant for decision making differs among the alternatives and is future oriented. Relevant revenues are sometimes called *differential revenues* because they differ among the alternatives. Relevant costs are sometimes called *avoidable costs* because they can be eliminated or avoided by choosing a specific course of action.

Costs that do not differ among the alternatives are not avoidable and therefore not relevant. *Sunk costs* are not relevant in decision making because they have been incurred in past transactions and therefore cannot be avoided. *Opportunity costs* are relevant because they represent potential benefits that may or may not be realized, depending on the decision maker's choice. In other words, future benefits that differ among the alternatives are relevant. Opportunity costs are not recorded in the financial accounting records.

Cost behavior (fixed or variable) is independent from the concept of relevance. Furthermore, a cost that is relevant in one decision context may be irrelevant in another context. Decision making depends on qualitative as well as quantitative information. *Quantitative information refers to information that can be measured using numbers. Qualitative information* is nonquantitative information such as personal preferences or opportunities.

Classifying costs into one of four hierarchical levels facilitates identifying relevant costs. *Unit-level costs* such as materials and labor are incurred each time a single unit of product is made. These costs can be avoided by eliminating the production of a single unit of product. *Batch-level costs* are associated with producing a group of products. Examples include setup costs and inspection costs related to a batch (group) of work rather than a single unit. Eliminating a batch would avoid both batch-level costs and unit-level costs. *Product-level costs* are incurred to support specific products or services (design and regulatory compliance costs). Product-level costs can be avoided by discontinuing a product line. *Facility-level costs,* like the president's salary, are incurred on behalf of the whole company or a segment of the company. In segment elimination decisions, the facility-level costs related to a particular segment being considered for elimination are relevant and avoidable. Those applying to the company as a whole are not avoidable.

Four types of special decisions that are frequently encountered in business are (1) *special orders,* (2) *outsourcing,* (3) *elimination decisions,* and (4) *asset replacement.* The relevant costs in a special order decision are the unit-level and batch-level costs that will be incurred if the special order is accepted. If the differential revenues from the special order exceed the relevant costs, the order should be accepted. Outsourcing decisions determine whether goods and services should be purchased from other companies. The relevant costs are the unit-level, batch-level, and product-level costs that could be avoided if the company outsources the product or service. If these costs are more than the cost to buy and the qualitative characteristics are satisfactory, the company should outsource. Segment-related unit-level, batch-level, product-level, and facility-level costs that can be avoided when a segment is eliminated are relevant. If the segment's avoidable costs exceed its differential revenues, it should be eliminated, assuming favorable qualitative factors. Asset replacement decisions compare the relevant costs of existing equipment with the relevant costs of new equipment to determine whether replacing the old equipment would be profitable.

>> A Look Forward

The next chapter introduces planning and cost control, including how to prepare budgets and projected (pro forma) financial statements. In addition to quantitative aspects, it illustrates the effects of the budgeting process on human behavior.

APPENDIX

Short-Term versus Long-Term Goals

Explain the conflict between short-term and long-term profitability.

To examine conflicts between short-term versus long-term goals, we return to the equipment replacement decision made by the management team of Premier Office Products (see page 266 for details). Suppose that the final equipment replacement decision is made by a departmental supervisor who is under significant pressure to maximize profitability. She is told that if profitability declines, she will lose her job. Under these circumstances, the supervisor may choose to keep the old machine even though it is to the company's advantage to purchase the new one. This occurs because the beneficial impact of the new machine is realized in the second through fifth years. Indeed, replacing the equipment will result in more expense/loss recognition in the first year. To illustrate, study the following information.

Year	First	Second	Third	Fourth	Fifth	Totals
Keep old machine						
Depreciation expense*	$11,000	$11,000	$11,000	$11,000	$11,000	$ 55,000
Operating expense	9,000	9,000	9,000	9,000	9,000	45,000
Total	$20,000	$20,000	$20,000	$20,000	$20,000	$100,000
Replace old machine						
Loss on disposal†	$43,000	$ 0	$ 0	$ 0	$ 0	$ 43,000
Depreciation expense‡	5,000	5,000	5,000	5,000	5,000	25,000
Operating expense	4,500	4,500	4,500	4,500	4,500	22,500
Total	$52,500	$ 9,500	$ 9,500	$ 9,500	$ 9,500	$ 90,500

*($57,000 book value − $2,000 salvage) ÷ 5 years = $11,000

†($57,000 book value − $14,000 market value) = $43,000

‡($29,000 cost − $4,000 salvage) ÷ 5 years = $5,000

This analysis verifies that total cost at the end of the five-year period is $9,500 less if the equipment is replaced ($100,000 − $90,500). Notice, however, that total costs at the end of the first year are higher by $32,500 ($52,500 − $20,000) if the old machine is replaced. A decision maker under significant pressure to report higher profitability may be willing to sacrifice tomorrow's profits to look better today. By emphasizing short-term profitability, she may secure a promotion before the long-term effects of her decision become apparent. Even if she stays in the same position, her boss may be replaced by someone not so demanding in terms of reported profitability. The department supervisor's intent is to survive the moment and let the future take care of itself. Misguided reward systems can be as detrimental as threats of punishment. For example, a manager may choose short-term profitability to obtain a bonus that is based on reported profitability. It is the responsibility of upper-level management to establish policies and procedures that motivate subordinates to perform in ways that maximize the company's long-term profitability.

Decisions Regarding the Allocation of Scarce Resources

Suppose that Premier Office Products makes two types of computers: a high-end network server and an inexpensive personal computer. The relevant sales and variable cost data for each unit follow.

LO 8

Make decisions about allocating scarce resources.

Network Server		Personal Computer	
Sales price	$4,000	Sales price	$1,500
Less: Variable cost	(3,760)	Less: Variable cost	(1,370)
Contribution margin	$ 240	Contribution margin	$ 130

In many circumstances, variable costs act as proxies for *avoidable costs.* For example, by definition, unit-level costs increase and decrease in direct proportion with the number of units of product made and sold. As previously indicated, unit-level costs are avoidable with respect to many special decision scenarios. To the extent that variable costs are proxies for avoidable costs, the contribution margin can be used as a measure of profitability. Other things being equal, higher contribution margins translate into more profitable products. If Premier could sell 1,000 computers, the company would certainly prefer that they be network servers. The contribution to profitability on those machines is almost double the contribution margin on the personal computer.

Even though the contribution margin is higher for network servers, selling personal computers may be more profitable. Why? If Premier can sell considerably more of the personal computers, the volume of activity will make up for the lower margin. In other words, selling three personal computers produces more total margin (3 × $130 = $390) than selling one network server (1 × $240). Many factors could limit the sales of one or both of the products. Factors that limit a business's ability to satisfy the demand for its product are called **constraints.** Suppose that warehouse space is limited (i.e., the warehouse is a scarce resource that constrains sales). Accordingly, Premier cannot warehouse all of the computers that it needs to satisfy its customer orders. If a network server requires considerably more warehouse space than a personal computer, stocking and selling personal computers may be more profitable than stocking and selling network servers. To illustrate, assume that it requires 5 square feet of warehouse space for a network server and 2 square feet for a personal computer. If only 2,100 square feet of warehouse space are available, which computer should Premier stock and sell?

In this case, the warehouse space is considered a scarce resource. The computer that produces the highest contribution margin per unit of scarce resource (i.e., per square foot) is the more profitable product. The per unit computations for each product are shown here.

	Network Server	Personal Computer
Contribution margin per unit (a)	$240	$130
Divide by warehouse space needed to store one unit (b)	÷5	÷2
Contribution margin per square foot of warehouse space (a ÷ b)	$ 48	$ 65

The data suggest that Premier should focus on the personal computer. Even though the personal computer produces a lower contribution margin per product, its contribution margin per scarce resource is higher. The effect on total profitability is shown as follows.

	Network Server	Personal Computer
Amount of available warehouse space in square feet (a)	2,100	2,100
Divided by warehouse space needed to store one unit (b)	÷ 5	÷ 2
Warehouse capacity in number of units (a ÷ b) = (c)	420	1,050
Times contribution margin per unit (d)	× $ 240	× $ 130
Total profit potential (c × d)	$100,800	$136,500

Although the quantitative data suggest that Premier will maximize profitability by limiting its inventory to personal computers, qualitative considerations may force the company to maintain a reasonable sales mix between the two products. For example, a business that buys several personal computers may also need a network server. A customer who cannot obtain both products from Premier may choose to buy nothing at all. Instead, the customer will find a supplier who will satisfy all of his needs. In other words, Premier may still need to stock some servers to offer a competitive product line.

The chairman of the board of directors asked Premier's president why company sales had remained level while the company's chief competitor had experienced significant increases. The president replied, "You cannot sell what you do not have. Our warehouse is too small. We stop production when we fill up the warehouse. The products sell out rapidly, and then we have to wait around for the next batch of computers to be made. When we are out of stock, our customers turn to the competition. We are constrained by the size of the warehouse." In business terms, the warehouse is a **bottleneck.** Its size is limiting the company's ability to produce and sell its products.

Many businesses use a management practice known as the **theory of constraints (TOC)** to increase profitability by managing bottlenecks or constrained resources. TOC's primary objective is to identify the bottlenecks restricting the operations of the business and then to open those bottlenecks through a practice known as **relaxing the constraints.** The effect of applying TOC to the Premier case is apparent via contribution margin analysis. According to the preceding computations, a new server and a new personal computer produce a contribution margin of $48 and $65 per square foot of storage space, respectively. So long as additional warehouse space can be purchased for less than these amounts, Premier can increase its profitability by acquiring the space.

A step-by-step audio-narrated series of slides is provided on the text website at www.mhhe.com/edmonds2011.

SELF-STUDY REVIEW PROBLEM

Flying High, Inc. (FHI), is a division of The Master Toy Company. FHI makes remote-controlled airplanes. During 2011, FHI incurred the following costs in the process of making 5,000 planes:

Unit-level materials costs (5,000 units × $80)	$ 400,000
Unit-level labor costs (5,000 units × $90)	450,000
Unit-level overhead costs (5,000 × $70)	350,000
Depreciation cost on manufacturing equipment*	50,000
Other manufacturing overhead†	140,000
Inventory holding costs	240,000
Allocated portion of The Master Toy Company's facility-level costs	600,000
Total costs	$2,230,000

*The manufacturing equipment, which originally cost $250,000, has a book value of $200,000, a remaining useful life of four years, and a zero salvage value. If the equipment is not used in the production process, it can be leased for $30,000 per year.

†Includes supervisors' salaries and rent for the manufacturing building.

Required

a. FHI uses a cost-plus pricing strategy. FHI sets its price at product cost plus $100. Determine the price that FHI should charge for its remote-controlled airplanes.

b. Assume that a potential customer that operates a chain of high-end toy stores has approached FHI. A buyer for this chain has offered to purchase 1,000 planes from FHI at a price of $275 each. Ignoring qualitative considerations, should FHI accept or reject the order?

c. FHI has the opportunity to purchase the planes from Arland Manufacturing Company for $325 each. Arland maintains adequate inventories so that it can supply its customers with planes on demand. Should FHI accept the opportunity to outsource the making of its planes?

d. When completing this requirement use the sales price computed in Requirement *a*. Use the contribution margin format to prepare an income statement based on historical cost data. Prepare a second income statement that reflects the relevant cost data that Master Toy should consider in a segment elimination decision. Based on a comparison of these two statements, indicate whether Master Toy should eliminate the FHI division.

e. FHI is considering replacing the equipment it currently uses to manufacture its planes. It could purchase replacement equipment for $480,000 that has an expected useful life of four years and a salvage value of $40,000. The new equipment would increase productivity substantially, reducing unit-level labor costs by 20 percent. Assume that FHI would maintain its production and sales at 5,000 planes per year. Prepare a schedule that shows the relevant costs of operating the old equipment versus the costs of operating the new equipment. Should FHI replace the equipment?

Solution to Requirement a

Product Cost for Remote-Controlled Airplanes	
Unit-level materials costs (5,000 units × $80)	$ 400,000
Unit-level labor costs (5,000 units × $90)	450,000
Unit-level overhead costs (5,000 units × $70)	350,000
Depreciation cost on manufacturing equipment	50,000
Other manufacturing overhead	140,000
Total product cost	$1,390,000

The cost per unit is $278 ($1,390,000 ÷ 5,000 units). The sales price per unit is $378 ($278 + $100). Depreciation expense is included because cost-plus pricing is usually based on historical cost rather than relevant cost. To be profitable in the long run, a company must ultimately recover the amount it paid for the equipment (the historical cost of the equipment).

Solution to Requirement b

The incremental (relevant) cost of making 1,000 additional airplanes follows. The depreciation expense is not relevant because it represents a sunk cost. The other manufacturing overhead costs are not relevant because they will be incurred regardless of whether FHI makes the additional planes.

Per Unit Relevant Product Cost for Airplanes	
Unit-level materials costs	$ 80
Unit-level labor costs	90
Unit-level overhead costs	70
Total relevant product cost	$240

Since the relevant (incremental) cost of making the planes is less than the incremental revenue, FHI should accept the special order. Accepting the order will increase profits by $35,000 [($275 incremental revenue − $240 incremental cost) × 1,000 units].

Solution to Requirement c

Distinguish this decision from the special order opportunity discussed in Requirement *b*. That special order (Requirement *b*) decision hinged on the cost of making additional units with the existing production process. In contrast, a make-or-buy decision compares current production with the possibility of making zero units (closing down the entire manufacturing process). If the manufacturing process were shut down, FHI could avoid the unit-level costs, the cost of the lost opportunity to lease the equipment, the other manufacturing overhead costs, and the inventory holding costs. Since the planes can be purchased on demand, there is no need to maintain any inventory. The allocated portion of the facility-level costs is not relevant because it would be incurred regardless of whether FHI manufactured the planes. The relevant cost of making the planes follows.

Relevant Manufacturing Cost for Airplanes	
Unit-level materials costs (5,000 units × $80)	$ 400,000
Unit-level labor costs (5,000 units × $90)	450,000
Unit-level overhead costs (5,000 units × $70)	350,000
Opportunity cost of leasing the equipment	30,000
Other manufacturing overhead costs	140,000
Inventory holding cost	240,000
Total product cost	$1,610,000

The relevant cost per unit is $322 ($1,610,000 ÷ 5,000 units). Since the relevant cost of making the planes ($322) is less than the cost of purchasing them ($325), FHI should continue to make the planes.

Solution to Requirement d

Income Statements

	Historical Cost Data	Relevant Cost Data
Revenue (5,000 units × $378)	$1,890,000	$1,890,000
Less variable costs:		
Unit-level materials costs (5,000 units × $80)	(400,000)	(400,000)
Unit-level labor costs (5,000 units × $90)	(450,000)	(450,000)
Unit-level overhead costs (5,000 units × $70)	(350,000)	(350,000)
Contribution margin	690,000	690,000
Depreciation cost on manufacturing equipment	(50,000)	
Opportunity cost of leasing manufacturing equipment		(30,000)
Other manufacturing overhead costs	(140,000)	(140,000)
Inventory holding costs	(240,000)	(240,000)
Allocated facility-level administrative costs	(600,000)	
Net loss	$ (340,000)	
Contribution to Master Toy's profitability		$ 280,000

Master Toy should not eliminate the segment (FHI). Although it appears to be incurring a loss, the allocated facility-level administrative costs are not relevant because Master Toy would incur these costs regardless of whether it eliminated FHI. Also, the depreciation cost on the manufacturing equipment is not relevant because it is a sunk cost. However, since the company could lease the equipment if the segment were eliminated, the $30,000 potential rental fee represents a relevant opportunity cost. The relevant revenue and cost data show that FHI is contributing $280,000 to the profitability of The Master Toy Company.

Solution to Requirement e

The relevant costs of using the old equipment versus the new equipment are the costs that differ for the two alternatives. In this case relevant costs include the purchase price of the new equipment, the opportunity cost of the old equipment, and the labor costs. These items are summarized in the following table. The data show the total cost over the four-year useful life of the replacement equipment.

Relevant Cost Comparison

	Old Equipment	New Equipment
Opportunity to lease the old equipment ($30,000 × 4 years)	$ 120,000	
Cost of new equipment ($480,000 − $40,000)		$ 440,000
Unit-level labor costs (5,000 units × $90 × 4 years)	1,800,000	
Unit-level labor costs (5,000 units × $90 × 4 years × .80)		1,440,000
Total relevant costs	$1,920,000	$1,880,000

Since the relevant cost of operating the new equipment is less than the cost of operating the old equipment, FHI should replace the equipment.

KEY TERMS

Avoidable costs 257
Batch-level costs 257
Bottleneck 270
Certified suppliers 262
Constraints 270
Differential revenue 256
Equipment replacement
    decisions 266

Facility-level costs 257
Low-ball pricing 262
Opportunity cost 254
Outsourcing 260
Product-level costs 257
Qualitative characteristics 256
Quantitative characteristics 256
Relaxing the constraints 271

Relevant costs 254
Relevant information 254
Segment 263
Special order decisions 258
Sunk costs 254
Theory of constraints (TOC) 271
Unit-level costs 257
Vertical integration 262

QUESTIONS

1. Identify the primary qualities of revenues and costs that are relevant for decision making.

2. Are variable costs always relevant? Explain.

3. Identify the four hierarchical levels used to classify costs. When can each of these levels of costs be avoided?

4. Describe the relationship between relevance and accuracy.

5. "It all comes down to the bottom line. The numbers never lie." Do you agree with this conclusion? Explain your position.

6. Carmon Company invested $300,000 in the equity securities of Mann Corporation. The current market value of Carmon's investment in Mann is $250,000. Carmon currently needs funds for operating purposes. Although interest rates are high, Carmon's president has decided to borrow the needed funds instead of selling the investment in Mann. He explains that his company cannot afford to take a $50,000 loss on the Mann stock. Evaluate the president's decision based on this information.

7. What is an opportunity cost? How does it differ from a sunk cost?

8. A local bank advertises that it offers a free noninterest-bearing checking account if the depositor maintains a $500 minimum balance in the account. Is the checking account truly free?

9. A manager is faced with deciding whether to replace machine A or machine B. The original cost of machine A was $20,000 and that of machine B was $30,000. Because the two cost figures differ, they are relevant to the manager's decision. Do you agree? Explain your position.

10. Are all fixed costs unavoidable?

11. Identify two qualitative considerations that could be associated with special order decisions.

12. Which of the following would not be relevant to a make-or-buy decision?

  (a) Allocated portion of depreciation expense on existing facilities.

  (b) Variable cost of labor used to produce products currently purchased from suppliers.

  (c) Warehousing costs for inventory of completed products (inventory levels will be constant regardless of whether products are purchased or produced).

  (d) Cost of materials used to produce the items currently purchased from suppliers.

  (e) Property taxes on the factory building.

13. What two factors should be considered in deciding how to allocate shelf space in a retail establishment?

14. What level(s) of costs is(are) relevant in special order decisions?

15. Why would a company consider outsourcing products or services?

16. Chris Sutter, the production manager of Satellite Computers, insists that the floppy drives used in the company's upper-end computers be outsourced since they can be purchased from a supplier at a lower cost per unit than the company is presently incurring to produce the drives. Jane Meyers, his assistant, insists that if sales growth continues at the current levels, the company will be able to produce the drives in the near future at a lower cost because of the company's predominately fixed cost structure. Does Ms. Meyers have a legitimate argument? Explain.

17. Identify some qualitative factors that should be considered in addition to quantitative costs in deciding whether to outsource.

18. The managers of Wilcox, Inc., are suggesting that the company president eliminate one of the company's segments that is operating at a loss. Why may this be a hasty decision?

19. Why would a supervisor choose to continue using a more costly old machine instead of replacing it with a less costly new machine?

20. Identify some of the constraints that limit a business's ability to satisfy the demand for its products or services.

MULTIPLE-CHOICE QUESTIONS

Multiple-choice questions are provided on the text website at www.mhhe.com/edmonds2011.

EXERCISES—SERIES A

All applicable Exercises in Series A are available with McGraw-Hill's *Connect Accounting.*

Exercise 6-1A *Distinction between relevance and cost behavior* LO 1

Leah Friend is trying to decide which of two different kinds of candy to sell in her retail candy store. One type is a name brand candy that will practically sell itself. The other candy is cheaper to purchase but does not carry an identifiable brand name. Ms. Friend believes that she will have to incur significant advertising costs to sell this candy. Several cost items for the two types of candy are as follows:

Brandless Candy		Name Brand Candy	
Cost per box	$ 6.00	Cost per box	$ 7.00
Sales commissions per box	1.00	Sales commissions per box	1.00
Rent of display space	1,500.00	Rent of display space	1,500.00
Advertising	3,000.00	Advertising	2,000.00

Required

Identify each cost as being relevant or irrelevant to Ms. Friend's decision and indicate whether it is fixed or variable relative to the number of boxes sold.

Exercise 6-2A *Distinction between relevance and cost behavior* LO 1

Stanley Company makes and sells a single product. Stanley incurred the following costs in its most recent fiscal year.

Cost Items Appearing on the Income Statement	
Materials cost ($10 per unit)	Sales commissions (2% of sales)
Company president's salary	Salaries of administrative personnel
Depreciation on manufacturing equipment	Shipping and handling ($0.50 per unit)
Customer billing costs (1% of sales)	Depreciation on office furniture
Rental cost of manufacturing facility	Manufacturing supplies ($0.25 per unit)
Advertising costs ($200,000 per year)	Production supervisor's salary
Labor cost ($8 per unit)	

Stanley could purchase the products that it currently makes. If it purchased the items, the company would continue to sell them using its own logo, advertising program, and sales staff.

Required

Identify each cost as relevant or irrelevant to the outsourcing decision and indicate whether the cost is fixed or variable relative to the number of products manufactured and sold.

Exercise 6-3A *Distinction between avoidable costs and cost behavior* LO 1

Medallion Company makes fine jewelry that it sells to department stores throughout the United States. Medallion is trying to decide which of two bracelets to manufacture. Cost data pertaining to the two choices follow.

	Bracelet A	Bracelet B
Cost of materials per unit	$ 25	$ 32
Cost of labor per unit	32	32
Advertising cost per year	8,000	6,000
Annual depreciation on existing equip.	5,000	4,000

Required

a. Identify the fixed costs and determine the amount of fixed cost for each product.
b. Identify the variable costs and determine the amount of variable cost per unit for each product.
c. Identify the avoidable costs and determine the amount of avoidable cost for each product.

LO 2

Exercise 6-4A   *Cost hierarchy*

Costs can be classified into one of four categories including unit-level, batch-level, product-level, or facility-level costs.

Required

Classify each of the items listed below into one of the four categories listed above. The first item has been categorized as an example.

Cost Description	Cost Classification
Salary of company president	Facility-level cost
Research and development cost	
Factory lawn care cost	
Cost of patent	
Startup cost to change color of a product	
Cost of resetting sewing machines to change shirt size	
Real estate tax for the factory	
Direct labor	

LO 2, 3

Exercise 6-5A   *Special order decision*

Norman Concrete Company pours concrete slabs for single-family dwellings. Wayne Construction Company, which operates outside Norman's normal sales territory, asks Norman to pour 40 slabs for Wayne's new development of homes. Norman has the capacity to build 300 slabs and is presently working on 250 of them. Wayne is willing to pay only $2,500 per slab. Norman estimates the cost of a typical job to include unit-level materials, $1,000; unit-level labor, $600; and an allocated portion of facility-level overhead, $700.

Required

Should Norman accept or reject the special order to pour 40 slabs for $2,500 each? Support your answer with appropriate computations.

LO 2, 3

Exercise 6-6A   *Special order decision*

Issa Company manufactures a personal computer designed for use in schools and markets it under its own label. Issa has the capacity to produce 25,000 units a year but is currently producing and selling only 15,000 units a year. The computer's normal selling price is $1,600 per unit with no volume discounts. The unit-level costs of the computer's production are $600 for direct materials, $300 for direct labor, and $120 for indirect unit-level manufacturing costs. The total product- and facility-level costs incurred by Issa during the year are expected to be $2,100,000 and $800,000, respectively. Assume that Issa receives a special order to produce and sell 3,000 computers at $1,200 each.

Required

Should Issa accept or reject the special order? Support your answer with appropriate computations.

Exercise 6-7A *Identifying qualitative factors for a special order decision* LO 3

Required

Describe the qualitative factors that Issa should consider before accepting the special order described in Exercise 6-6A.

Exercise 6-8A *Using the contribution margin approach for a special order decision* LO 3

Shenyang Company, which produces and sells a small digital clock, bases its pricing strategy on a 35 percent markup on total cost. Based on annual production costs for 10,000 units of product, computations for the sales price per clock follow.

Unit-level costs	$150,000
Fixed costs	50,000
Total cost (a)	200,000
Markup (a × 0.35)	70,000
Total sales (b)	$270,000
Sales price per unit (b ÷ 10,000)	$ 27

Required

a. Shenyang has excess capacity and receives a special order for 4,000 clocks for $17 each. Calculate the contribution margin per unit; based on it, should Shenyang accept the special order?

b. Support your answer by preparing a contribution margin income statement for the special order.

Exercise 6-9A *Outsourcing decision* LO 4

Roaming Bicycle Manufacturing Company currently produces the handlebars used in manufacturing its bicycles, which are high-quality racing bikes with limited sales. Roaming produces and sells only 6,000 bikes each year. Due to the low volume of activity, Roaming is unable to obtain the economies of scale that larger producers achieve. For example, Roaming could buy the handlebars for $35 each; they cost $32 each to make. The following is a detailed breakdown of current production costs.

Item	Unit Cost	Total
Unit-level costs		
Materials	$18	$108,000
Labor	12	72,000
Overhead	3	18,000
Allocated facility-level costs	5	30,000
Total	$38	$228,000

After seeing these figures, Roaming's president remarked that it would be foolish for the company to continue to produce the handlebars at $38 each when it can buy them for $35 each.

Required

Do you agree with the president's conclusion? Support your answer with appropriate computations.

Exercise 6-10A *Establishing price for an outsourcing decision* LO 4

Lunn Company makes and sells lawn mowers for which it currently makes the engines. It has an opportunity to purchase the engines from a reliable manufacturer. The annual costs of making the engines are shown here.

Cost of materials (15,000 Units × $24)	$360,000
Labor (15,000 Units × $26)	390,000
Depreciation on manufacturing equipment*	42,000
Salary of supervisor of engine production	85,000
Rental cost of equipment used to make engines	23,000
Allocated portion of corporate-level facility-sustaining costs	80,000
Total cost to make 15,000 engines	$980,000

*The equipment has a book value of $90,000 but its market value is zero.

Required

a. Determine the maximum price per unit that Lunn would be willing to pay for the engines.

b. Would the price computed in Requirement *a* change if production increased to 18,750 units? Support your answer with appropriate computations.

LO 4

Exercise 6-11A *Outsourcing decision with qualitative factors*

Nadir Corporation which makes and sells 79,400 radios annually, currently purchases the radio speakers it uses for $12 each. Each radio uses one speaker. The company has idle capacity and is considering the possibility of making the speakers that it needs. Nadir estimates that the cost of materials and labor needed to make speakers would be a total of $10 for each speaker. In addition, the costs of supervisory salaries, rent, and other manufacturing costs would be $168,000. Allocated facility-level costs would be $99,600.

Required

a. Determine the change in net income Nadir would experience if it decides to make the speakers.

b. Discuss the qualitative factors that Nadir should consider.

LO 2, 4

Exercise 6-12A *Outsourcing decision affected by opportunity costs*

Pace Electronics currently produces the shipping containers it uses to deliver the electronics products it sells. The monthly cost of producing 9,000 containers follows.

Unit-level materials	$ 6,000
Unit-level labor	6,600
Unit-level overhead	4,200
Product-level costs*	10,800
Allocated facility-level costs	26,400

*One-third of these costs can be avoided by purchasing the containers.

Ace Container Company has offered to sell comparable containers to Pace for $2.70 each.

Required

a. Should Pace continue to make the containers? Support your answer with appropriate computations.

b. Pace could lease the space it currently uses in the manufacturing process. If leasing would produce $10,800 per month, would your answer to Requirement *a* be different? Explain.

LO 6

Exercise 6-13A *Opportunity cost*

Lynch Freight Company owns a truck that cost $30,000. Currently, the truck's book value is $18,000, and its expected remaining useful life is four years. Lynch has the opportunity to purchase for $26,000 a replacement truck that is extremely fuel efficient. Fuel cost for the old truck is expected to be $5,000 per year more than fuel cost for the new truck. The old truck is paid for but, in spite of being in good condition, can be sold for only $12,000.

Required

Should Lynch replace the old truck with the new fuel-efficient model, or should it continue to use the old truck until it wears out? Explain.

Exercise 6-14A *Opportunity costs*

Steve Denmark owns his own taxi, for which he bought an $18,000 permit to operate two years ago. Mr. Denmark earns $36,000 a year operating as an independent but has the opportunity to sell the taxi and permit for $73,000 and take a position as dispatcher for Sartino Taxi Co. The dispatcher position pays $31,000 a year for a 40-hour week. Driving his own taxi, Mr. Denmark works approximately 55 hours per week. If he sells his business, he will invest the $73,000 and can earn a 10 percent return.

Required

a. Determine the opportunity cost of owning and operating the independent business.
b. Based solely on financial considerations, should Mr. Denmark sell the taxi and accept the position as dispatcher?
c. Discuss the qualitative as well as quantitative factors that Mr. Denmark should consider.

Exercise 6-15A *Segment elimination decision*

Chamberline Company operates three segments. Income statements for the segments imply that profitability could be improved if Segment A were eliminated.

CHAMBERLINE COMPANY			
Income Statements for the Year 2011			
Segment	A	B	C
Sales	$162,000	$235,000	$245,000
Cost of goods sold	(121,000)	(92,000)	(95,000)
Sales commissions	(15,000)	(22,000)	(22,000)
Contribution margin	26,000	121,000	128,000
General fixed oper. exp. (allocation of president's salary)	(44,000)	(52,000)	(44,000)
Advertising expense (specific to individual divisions)	(3,000)	(10,000)	0
Net income	$(21,000)	$ 59,000	$ 84,000

Required

a. Explain the effect on profitability if Segment A is eliminated.
b. Prepare comparative income statements for the company as a whole under two alternatives: (1) the retention of Segment A and (2) the elimination of Segment A.

Exercise 6-16A *Segment elimination decision*

Baich Transport Company divides its operations into four divisions. A recent income statement for Koslov Division follows.

BAICH TRANSPORT COMPANY	
Koslov Division	
Income Statement for the Year 2012	
Revenue	$ 500,000
Salaries for drivers	(350,000)
Fuel expenses	(50,000)
Insurance	(70,000)
Division-level facility-sustaining costs	(40,000)
Companywide facility-sustaining costs	(130,000)
Net loss	$(140,000)

Required

a. Should Koslov Division be eliminated? Support your answer by explaining how the division's elimination would affect the net income of the company as a whole. By how much would companywide income increase or decrease?

b. Assume that Koslov Division is able to increase its revenue to $540,000 by raising its prices. Would this change the decision you made in Requirement *a*? Determine the amount of the increase or decrease that would occur in companywide net income if the segment were eliminated if revenue were $540,000.

c. What is the minimum amount of revenue required to justify continuing the operation of Koslov Division?

LO 5

Exercise 6-17A   *Identifying avoidable cost of a segment*

Safar Corporation is considering the elimination of one of its segments. The segment incurs the following fixed costs. If the segment is eliminated, the building it uses will be sold.

Advertising expense	$ 80,000
Supervisory salaries	160,000
Allocation of companywide facility-level costs	49,000
Original cost of building	110,000
Book value of building	50,000
Market value of building	80,000
Maintenance costs on equipment	70,000
Real estate taxes on building	6,000

Required

Based on this information, determine the amount of avoidable cost associated with the segment.

LO 6

Exercise 6-18A   *Asset replacement decision*

A machine purchased three years ago for $300,000 has a current book value using straight-line depreciation of $175,000; its operating expenses are $30,000 per year. A replacement machine would cost $240,000, have a useful life of nine years, and would require $13,000 per year in operating expenses. It has an expected salvage value of $57,000 after nine years. The current disposal value of the old machine is $70,000; if it is kept 9 more years, its residual value would be $10,000.

Required

Based on this information, should the old machine be replaced? Support your answer.

LO 6

Exercise 6-19A   *Asset replacement decision*

Rainger Company is considering replacement of some of its manufacturing equipment. Information regarding the existing equipment and the potential replacement equipment follows.

Existing Equipment		Replacement Equipment	
Cost	$120,000	Cost	$105,000
Operating expenses*	120,000	Operating expenses*	95,000
Salvage value	30,000	Salvage value	20,000
Market value	60,000	Useful life	8 years
Book value	33,000		
Remaining useful life	8 years		

*The amounts shown for operating expenses are the cumulative total of all such expected expenses to be incurred over the useful life of the equipment.

Required

Based on this information, recommend whether to replace the equipment. Support your recommendation with appropriate computations.

LO 6

Exercise 6-20A   *Asset replacement decision*

Hardin Company paid $90,000 to purchase a machine on January 1, 2009. During 2011, a technological breakthrough resulted in the development of a new machine that costs $120,000. The old machine costs $45,000 per year to operate, but the new machine could be operated for only

$15,000 per year. The new machine, which will be available for delivery on January 1, 2012, has an expected useful life of four years. The old machine is more durable and is expected to have a remaining useful life of four years. The current market value of the old machine is $30,000. The expected salvage value of both machines is zero.

Required

Based on this information, recommend whether to replace the machine. Support your recommendation with appropriate computations.

Exercise 6-21A   *Annual versus cumulative data for replacement decision*   **LO 6, 7**

Because of rapidly advancing technology, Andersen Publications Corporation is considering replacing its existing typesetting machine with leased equipment. The old machine, purchased two years ago, has an expected useful life of six years and is in good condition. Apparently, it will continue to perform as expected for the remaining four years of its expected useful life. A four-year lease for equipment with comparable productivity can be obtained for $14,000 per year. The following data apply to the old machine:

Original cost	$160,000
Accumulated depreciation	55,000
Current market value	74,000
Estimated salvage value	10,000

Required

a. Determine the annual opportunity cost of using the old machine. Based on your computations, recommend whether to replace it.
b. Determine the total cost of the lease over the four-year contract. Based on your computations, recommend whether to replace the old machine.

Appendix

Exercise 6-22A   *Scarce resource decision*   **LO 8**

Joyful Novelties has the capacity to produce either 30,000 corncob pipes or 14,000 cornhusk dolls per year. The pipes cost $4 each to produce and sell for $7 each. The dolls sell for $11 each and cost $5 to produce.

Required

Assuming that Joyful Novelties can sell all it produces of either product, should it produce the corncob pipes or the cornhusk dolls? Show computations to support your answer.

PROBLEMS—SERIES A

All applicable Problems in Series A are available with McGraw-Hill's *Connect Accounting*.

connect
ACCOUNTING

Problem 6-23A   *Context-sensitive relevance*   **LO 1**

Required

Respond to each requirement independently.

a. Describe two decision-making contexts, one in which unit-level materials costs are avoidable, and the other in which they are unavoidable.
b. Describe two decision-making contexts, one in which batch-level setup costs are avoidable, and the other in which they are unavoidable.
c. Describe two decision-making contexts, one in which advertising costs are avoidable, and the other in which they are unavoidable.

d. Describe two decision-making contexts, one in which rent paid for a building is avoidable, and the other in which it is unavoidable.

e. Describe two decision-making contexts, one in which depreciation on manufacturing equipment is avoidable, and the other in which it is unavoidable.

LO 1

CHECK FIGURES

a. Contribution to profit for
   Job A: $264,250

b. Contribution to profit: $(3,220)

Problem 6-24A   *Context-sensitive relevance*

Chapman Construction Company is a building contractor specializing in small commercial buildings. The company has the opportunity to accept one of two jobs; it cannot accept both because they must be performed at the same time and Chapman does not have the necessary labor force for both jobs. Indeed, it will be necessary to hire a new supervisor if either job is accepted. Furthermore, additional insurance will be required if either job is accepted. The revenue and costs associated with each job follow.

Cost Category	Job A	Job B
Contract price	$800,000	$700,000
Unit-level materials	243,700	223,450
Unit-level labor	249,150	305,000
Unit-level overhead	18,000	12,600
Supervisor's salary	116,670	116,670
Rental equipment costs	24,900	27,300
Depreciation on tools (zero market value)	19,900	19,900
Allocated portion of companywide facility-sustaining costs	10,400	8,600
Insurance cost for job	18,200	18,200

Required

a. Assume that Chapman has decided to accept one of the two jobs. Identify the information relevant to selecting one job versus the other. Recommend which job to accept and support your answer with appropriate computations.

b. Assume that Job A is no longer available. Chapman's choice is to accept or reject Job B alone. Identify the information relevant to this decision. Recommend whether to accept or reject Job B. Support your answer with appropriate computations.

LO 2, 3

CHECK FIGURE

a. Relevant cost per unit: $57

Problem 6-25A   *Effect of order quantity on special order decision*

Ellis Quilting Company makes blankets that it markets through a variety of department stores. It makes the blankets in batches of 1,000 units. Ellis made 20,000 blankets during the prior accounting period. The cost of producing the blankets is summarized here.

Materials cost ($25 per unit × 20,000)	$ 500,000
Labor cost ($22 per unit × 20,000)	440,000
Manufacturing supplies ($2 × 20,000)	40,000
Batch-level costs (20 batches at $4,000 per batch)	80,000
Product-level costs	160,000
Facility-level costs	290,000
Total costs	$1,510,000

Cost per unit = $1,510,000 ÷ 20,000 = $75.50

Required

a. Kent Motels has offered to buy a batch of 500 blankets for $56 each. Ellis normal selling price is $90 per unit. Based on the preceding quantitative data, should Ellis accept the special order? Support your answer with appropriate computations.

b. Would your answer to Requirement *a* change if Kent offered to buy a batch of 1,000 blankets for $56 per unit? Support your answer with appropriate computations.

c. Describe the qualitative factors that Ellis Quilting Company should consider before accepting a special order to sell blankets to Kent Motels.

Problem 6-26A   *Effects of the level of production on an outsourcing decision*

LO 2, 4

Seymour Chemical Company makes a variety of cosmetic products, one of which is a skin cream designed to reduce the signs of aging. Seymour produces a relatively small amount (15,000 units) of the cream and is considering the purchase of the product from an outside supplier for $4.50 each. If Seymour purchases from the outside supplier, it would continue to sell and distribute the cream under its own brand name. Seymour's accountant constructed the following profitability analysis.

Revenue (15,000 units × $10)	$150,000
Unit-level materials costs (15,000 units × $1.40)	(21,000)
Unit-level labor costs (15,000 units × $0.50)	(7,500)
Unit-level overhead costs (15,000 × $0.10)	(1,500)
Unit-level selling expenses (15,000 × $0.20)	(3,000)
Contribution margin	117,000
Skin cream production supervisor's salary	(44,000)
Allocated portion of facility-level costs	(11,300)
Product-level advertising cost	(34,000)
Contribution to companywide income	$ 27,700

CHECK FIGURE
a. Total relevant cost: $74,000

Required

a. Identify the cost items relevant to the make-or-outsource decision.

b. Should Seymour continue to make the product or buy it from the supplier? Support your answer by determining the change in net income if Seymour buys the cream instead of making it.

c. Suppose that Seymour is able to increase sales by 10,000 units (sales will increase to 25,000 units). At this level of production, should Seymour make or buy the cream? Support your answer by explaining how the increase in production affects the cost per unit.

d. Discuss the qualitative factors that Seymour should consider before deciding to outsource the skin cream. How can Seymour minimize the risk of establishing a relationship with an unreliable supplier?

Problem 6-27A   *Outsourcing decision affected by equipment replacement*

LO 2, 4, 6

Jenkins Bike Company (JBC) makes the frames used to build its bicycles. During 2011, JBC made 20,000 frames; the costs incurred follow.

CHECK FIGURES
a. Avoidable cost per unit: $123.60
b. Avoidable cost per unit with new equipment: $30.90

Unit-level materials costs (20,000 units × $45)	$ 900,000
Unit-level labor costs (20,000 units × $51)	1,020,000
Unit-level overhead costs (20,000 × $9)	180,000
Depreciation on manufacturing equipment	90,000
Bike frame production supervisor's salary	70,000
Inventory holding costs	290,000
Allocated portion of facility-level costs	500,000
Total costs	$3,050,000

JBC has an opportunity to purchase frames for $110 each.

Additional Information

1. The manufacturing equipment, which originally cost $550,000, has a book value of $450,000, a remaining useful life of four years, and a zero salvage value. If the equipment is not used to produce bicycle frames, it can be leased for $70,000 per year.

2. JBC has the opportunity to purchase for $910,000 new manufacturing equipment that will have an expected useful life of four years and a salvage value of $70,000. This equipment will increase productivity substantially, reducing unit-level labor costs by 60 percent. Assume that JBC will continue to produce and sell 20,000 frames per year in the future.

3. If JBC outsources the frames, the company can eliminate 80 percent of the inventory holding costs.

Required

a. Determine the avoidable cost per unit of making the bike frames, assuming that JBC is considering the alternatives of making the product using the existing equipment or outsourcing the product to the independent contractor. Based on the quantitative data, should JBC outsource the bike frames? Support your answer with appropriate computations.

b. Assuming that JBC is considering whether to replace the old equipment with the new equipment, determine the avoidable cost per unit to produce the bike frames using the new equipment and the avoidable cost per unit to produce the bike frames using the old equipment. Calculate the impact on profitability if the bike frames were made using the old equipment versus the new equipment.

c. Assuming that JBC is considering whether to either purchase the new equipment or outsource the bike frame, calculate the impact on profitability between the two alternatives.

d. Discuss the qualitative factors that JBC should consider before making a decision to outsource the bike frame. How can JBC minimize the risk of establishing a relationship with an unreliable supplier?

LO 5

CHECK FIGURE
a. Contribution to profit: $14,225

Problem 6-28A   *Eliminating a segment*

Brandt Boot Co. sells men's, women's, and children's boots. For each type of boot sold, it operates a separate department that has its own manager. The manager of the men's department has a sales staff of nine employees, the manager of the women's department has six employees, and the manager of the children's department has three employees. All departments are housed in a single store. In recent years, the children's department has operated at a net loss and is expected to continue to do so. Last year's income statements follow.

	Men's Department	Women's Department	Children's Department
Sales	$ 600,000	$ 420,000	$160,000
Cost of goods sold	(265,500)	(176,400)	(96,875)
Gross margin	334,500	243,600	63,125
Department manager's salary	(52,000)	(41,000)	(21,000)
Sales commissions	(106,200)	(75,600)	(27,900)
Rent on store lease	(21,000)	(21,000)	(21,000)
Store utilities	(4,000)	(4,000)	(4,000)
Net income (loss)	$ 151,300	$ 102,000	$ (10,775)

Required

a. Determine whether to eliminate the children's department.

b. Confirm the conclusion you reached in Requirement *a* by preparing income statements for the company as a whole with and without the children's department.

c. Eliminating the children's department would increase space available to display men's and women's boots. Suppose management estimates that a wider selection of adult boots would increase the store's net earnings by $32,000. Would this information affect the decision that you made in Requirement *a*? Explain your answer.

LO 5

CHECK FIGURE
a. Contribution to profit: $(32,500)

Problem 6-29A   *Effect of activity level and opportunity cost on segment elimination decision*

Levert Manufacturing Co. produces and sells specialized equipment used in the petroleum industry. The company is organized into three separate operating branches: Division A, which manufactures and sells heavy equipment; Division B, which manufactures and sells hand tools; and Division C, which makes and sells electric motors. Each division is housed in a separate manufacturing facility. Company headquarters is located in a separate building. In recent years, Division B has been operating at a net loss and is expected to continue to do so. Income statements for the three divisions for 2010 follow.

	Division A	Division B	Division C
Sales	$ 3,000,000	$ 900,000	$ 3,800,000
Less: Cost of goods sold			
Unit-level manufacturing costs	(1,800,000)	(600,000)	(2,280,000)
Rent on manufacturing facility	(410,000)	(225,000)	(300,000)
Gross margin	790,000	75,000	1,220,000
Less: Operating expenses			
Unit-level selling and admin. expenses	(187,500)	(42,500)	(237,500)
Division-level fixed selling and			
admin. expenses	(250,000)	(65,000)	(310,000)
Headquarters facility-level costs	(150,000)	(150,000)	(150,000)
Net income (loss)	$ 202,500	$(182,500)	$ 522,500

Required

a. Based on the preceding information, recommend whether to eliminate Division B. Support your answer by preparing companywide income statements before and after eliminating Division B.

b. During 2010, Division B produced and sold 20,000 units of hand tools. Would your recommendation in response to Requirement *a* change if sales and production increase to 30,000 units in 2011? Support your answer by comparing differential revenue and avoidable cost for Division B, assuming that it sells 30,000 units.

c. Suppose that Levert could sublease Division B's manufacturing facility for $475,000. Would you operate the division at a production and sales volume of 30,000 units, or would you close it? Support your answer with appropriate computations.

Problem 6-30A   *Comprehensive problem including special order, outsourcing, and segment elimination decisions*

Huffman Corporation makes and sells state-of-the-art electronics products. One of its segments produces The Math Machine, an inexpensive calculator. The company's chief accountant recently prepared the following income statement showing annual revenues and expenses associated with the segment's operating activities. The relevant range for the production and sale of the calculators is between 30,000 and 60,000 units per year.

LO 3, 4, 5

CHECK FIGURE
a. CM: $3,750

Revenue (40,000 units × $8)	$320,000
Unit-level variable costs	
Materials cost (40,000 × $2)	(80,000)
Labor cost (40,000 × $1)	(40,000)
Manufacturing overhead (40,000 × $0.50)	(20,000)
Shipping and handling (40,000 × $0.25)	(10,000)
Sales commissions (40,000 × $1)	(40,000)
Contribution margin	130,000
Fixed expenses	
Advertising costs	(20,000)
Salary of production supervisor	(60,000)
Allocated companywide facility-level expenses	(80,000)
Net loss	$ (30,000)

Required (Consider each of the requirements independently.)

a. A large discount store has approached the owner of Huffman about buying 5,000 calculators. It would replace The Math Machine's label with its own logo to avoid affecting Huffman's existing customers. Because the offer was made directly to the owner, no sales commissions on the transaction would be involved, but the discount store is willing to pay only $4.50 per calculator. Based on quantitative factors alone, should Huffman accept the special order? Support your answer with appropriate computations. Specifically, by what amount would the special order increase or decrease profitability?

b. Huffman has an opportunity to buy the 40,000 calculators it currently makes from a reliable competing manufacturer for $4.90 each. The product meets Huffman's quality standards. Huffman could continue to use its own logo, advertising program, and sales force to distribute the products. Should Huffman buy the calculators or continue to make them? Support your answer with appropriate computations. Specifically, how much more or less would it cost to buy the calculators than to make them? Would your answer change if the volume of sales were increased to 60,000 units?

c. Because the calculator division is currently operating at a loss, should it be eliminated from the company's operations? Support your answer with appropriate computations. Specifically, by what amount would the segment's elimination increase or decrease profitability?

Appendix

Problem 6-31A   *Allocating scarce resources*

The following information applies to the products of Kaito Company.

	Product A	Product B
Selling price per unit	$13	$12
Variable cost per unit	11	9

Required

Identify the product that should be produced or sold under each of the following constraints. Consider each constraint separately.

a. One unit of Product A requires 2 hours of labor to produce, and one unit of Product B requires 4 hours of labor to produce. Due to labor constraints, demand is higher than the company's capacity to make both products.

b. The products are sold to the public in retail stores. The company has limited floor space and cannot stock as many products as it would like. Display space is available for only one of the two products. Expected sales of Product A are 10,000 units and of Product B are 8,000 units.

c. The maximum number of machine hours available is 40,000. Product A uses 2 machine hours, and Product B uses 5 machine hours. The company can sell all the products it produces.

Problem 6-32A   *Conflict between short-term and long-term performance*

Julio Sanchez manages the cutting department of Guzman Timber Company. He purchased a tree-cutting machine on January 1, 2011, for $400,000. The machine had an estimated useful life of five years and zero salvage value, and the cost to operate it is $90,000 per year. Technological developments resulted in the development of a more advanced machine available for purchase on January 1, 2012, that would allow a 25 percent reduction in operating costs. The new machine would cost $240,000 and have a four-year useful life and zero salvage value. The current market value of the old machine on January 1, 2012, is $200,000, and its book value is $320,000 on that date. Straight-line depreciation is used for both machines. The company expects to generate $224,000 of revenue per year from the use of either machine.

Required

a. Recommend whether to replace the old machine on January 1, 2012. Support your answer with appropriate computations.

b. Prepare income statements for four years (2012 through 2015) assuming that the old machine is retained.

c. Prepare income statements for four years (2012 through 2015) assuming that the old machine is replaced.

d. Discuss the potential ethical conflicts that could result from the timing of the loss and expense recognition reported in the two income statements.

EXERCISES—SERIES B

Exercise 6-1B *Distinction between relevance and cost behavior*

LO 1

Joe Awad is planning to rent a small shop for a new business. He can sell either sandwiches or donuts. The following costs pertain to the two products.

Sandwiches		Donuts	
Cost per sandwich	$ 2.00	Cost per dozen donuts	$ 1.75
Sales commissions per sandwich	0.05	Sales commissions per dozen donuts	0.07
Monthly shop rental cost	1,000.00	Monthly shop rental cost	1,000.00
Monthly advertising cost	500.00	Monthly advertising cost	300.00

Required

Identify each cost as relevant or irrelevant to Mr. Awad's product decision and indicate whether the cost is fixed or variable relative to the number of units sold.

Exercise 6-2B *Distinction between relevance and cost behavior*

LO 1

Gromyko Company makes and sells a toy plane. Gromyko incurred the following costs in its most recent fiscal year:

> **Cost Items Reported on Income Statement**
>
> Sales commissions (1% of sales)
> Sales manager's salary
> Shipping and handling costs ($0.75 per unit)
> Cost of renting the administrative building
> Utility costs for the manufacturing plant ($0.25 per unit produced)
> Manufacturing plant manager's salary
> Materials costs ($4 per unit produced)
> Real estate taxes on the manufacturing plant
> Depreciation on manufacturing equipment
> Packaging cost ($1 per unit produced)
> Wages of the plant security guard
> Costs of TV commercials
> Labor costs ($3 per unit)

Gromyko could purchase the toy planes from a supplier. If it did, the company would continue to sell them using its own logo, advertising program, and sales staff.

Required

Identify each cost as relevant or irrelevant to the outsourcing decision and indicate whether the cost is fixed or variable relative to the number of toy planes manufactured and sold.

Exercise 6-3B *Distinction between avoidable costs and cost behavior*

LO 1

Preston Phones, Inc., makes telephones that it sells to department stores throughout the United States. Preston is trying to decide which of two telephone models to manufacture. The company could produce either telephone with its existing machinery. Cost data pertaining to the two choices follow:

	Model 90	Model 30
Materials cost per unit	$ 57	$ 57
Labor cost per unit	46	27
Product design cost	12,000	$7,000
Depreciation on existing manufacturing machinery	3,000	3,000

Required

a. Identify the fixed costs and determine the amount of fixed cost for each model.
b. Identify the variable costs and determine the amount of variable cost for each model.
c. Identify the avoidable costs.

LO 2

Exercise 6-4B   *Cost hierarchy*

Costs can be classified into one of four categories including unit-level, batch-level, product-level, or facility-level costs.

Required

Classify each of the items listed below into one of the four categories listed above. The first item has been categorized as an example.

Cost Description	Cost Classification
Wages of factory janitors	Facility-level cost
Machine setup cost for different production jobs	
Direct materials	
Salary of the manager in charge of making a product	
Tires used to assemble a car	
Payroll cost for assembly-line workers	
Electricity bill of the factory	
Product design	

LO 2, 3

Exercise 6-5B   *Special order decision*

Ragan Textile Company manufactures high-quality bed sheets and sells them in sets to a well-known retail company for $54 a set. Ragan has sufficient capacity to produce 150,000 sets of sheets annually; the retail company currently purchases 90,000 sets each year. Ragan's unit-level cost is $30 per set and its fixed cost is $810,000 per year. A motel chain has offered to purchase 15,000 sheet sets from Ragan for $40 per set. If Ragan accepts the order, the contract will prohibit the motel chain from reselling the bed sheets.

Required

Should Ragan accept or reject the special order? Support your answer with appropriate computations.

LO 2, 3

Exercise 6-6B   *Special order decision*

Mansour Automotive Company manufactures an engine designed for motorcycles and markets the product using its own brand name. Although Mansour has the capacity to produce 40,000 engines annually, it currently produces and sells only 30,000 units per year. The engine normally sells for $500 per unit, with no quantity discounts. The unit-level costs to produce the engine are $200 for direct materials, $150 for direct labor, and $30 for indirect manufacturing costs. Mansour expects total annual product- and facility-level costs to be $540,000 and $750,000, respectively. Assume Mansour receives a special order from a new customer seeking to buy 1,000 engines for $370 each.

Required

Should Mansour accept or reject the special order? Support your answer with appropriate computations.

LO 3

Exercise 6-7B   *Identifying qualitative factors for a special order decision*

Required

Describe the qualitative factors that Mansour should consider before making the decision described in Exercise 6-6B.

LO 3

Exercise 6-8B   *Using the contribution margin approach for a special order decision*

Winchester Company produces and sells a food processor that it prices at a 25 percent markup on total cost. Based on data pertaining to producing and selling 50,000 food processors, Winchester computes the sales price per food processor as follows:

Unit-level costs	$ 900,000
Fixed costs	640,000
Total cost (a)	$1,540,000
Markup (a × .25)	385,000
Total sales revenue (b)	$1,925,000
Sales price per unit (b ÷ 50,000)	$38.50

Required

a. Winchester receives a special order for 7,000 food processors for $20 each. Winchester has excess capacity. Calculate the contribution margin per unit for the special order. Based on the contribution margin per unit, should Winchester accept the special order?

b. Support your answer by preparing a contribution margin income statement for the special order.

Exercise 6-9B   *Making an outsourcing decision*   LO 4

Upton Boats Company currently produces a battery used in manufacturing its boats. The company annually manufactures and sells 5,000 units of a particular model of fishing boat. Because of the low volume of activity, Upton is unable to obtain the economies of scale that larger producers achieve. For example, the costs associated with producing the batteries it uses are almost 30 percent more than the cost of purchasing comparable batteries. Upton could buy batteries for $86 each; it costs $110 each to make them. A detailed breakdown of current production costs for the batteries follows:

Item	Unit Cost	Total
Unit-level costs:		
Materials	$ 40	$200,000
Labor	25	125,000
Overhead	5	25,000
Allocated facility-level costs	40	200,000
Total	$110	$550,000

Based on these figures, Upton's president asserted that it would be foolish for the company to continue to produce the batteries at $100 each when it can buy them for $86 each.

Required

Do you agree with the president's conclusion? Support your answer with appropriate computations.

Exercise 6-10B   *Establishing a price for an outsourcing decision*   LO 4

Romero Corporation makes and sells skateboards. Romero currently makes the 60,000 wheels used annually in its skateboards but has an opportunity to purchase the wheels from a reliable manufacturer. The costs of making the wheels follow.

Annual Costs Associated with Manufacturing Skateboard Wheels	
Materials (60,000 units × $5)	$300,000
Labor (60,000 units × $3)	180,000
Depreciation on manufacturing equipment*	24,000
Salary of wheel production supervisor	65,000
Rental cost of equipment used to make wheels	55,000
Allocated portion of corporate-level facility-sustaining costs	33,000
Total cost to make 60,000 wheels	$657,000

*The equipment has a book value of $74,000 but its market value is zero.

Required

a. Determine the maximum price per unit that Romero would be willing to pay for the wheels.

b. Would the price computed in Requirement *a* change if production were increased to 80,000 units? Support your answer with appropriate computations.

LO 4

Exercise 6-11B   *Making an outsourcing decision with qualitative factors considered*

Keating Computers currently purchases for $16 each keyboard it uses in the 50,000 computers it makes and sells annually. Each computer uses one keyboard. The company has idle capacity and is considering whether to make the keyboards that it needs. Keating estimates that materials and labor costs for making keyboards would be $10 each. In addition, supervisory salaries, rent, and other manufacturing costs would be $400,000. Allocated facility-level costs would amount to $70,000.

Required

a. Determine the change in net income that Keating would experience if it decides to make the keyboards.

b. Discuss the qualitative factors that Keating should consider.

LO 2, 4

Exercise 6-12B   *Outsourcing decision affected by opportunity costs*

Oakey Doors Company currently produces the doorknobs for the doors it makes and sells. The monthly cost of producing 5,000 doorknobs is as follows:

Unit-level materials	$4,000
Unit-level labor	7,500
Unit-level overhead	1,000
Product-level costs*	8,000
Allocated facility-level costs	5,000

*Twenty percent of these costs can be avoided if the doorknobs are purchased.

Venice Company has offered to sell comparable doorknobs to Oakey for $3.80 each.

Required

a. Should Oakey continue to make the doorknobs? Support you answer with appropriate computations.

b. For $6,000 per month, Oakey could lease the manufacturing space to another company. Would this potential cash inflow affect your response to Requirement *a*? Explain.

LO 6

Exercise 6-13B   *Asset replacement decision*

Porter Fishing Tours, Inc., owns a boat that originally cost $120,000. Currently, the boat's net book value is $36,000, and its expected remaining useful life is four years. Porter has an opportunity to purchase for $80,000 a replacement boat that is extremely fuel efficient. Fuel costs for the old boat are expected to be $15,000 per year more than fuel costs would be for the replacement boat. Porter could sell the old boat, which is fully paid for and in good condition, for only $32,000.

Required

Should Porter replace the old boat with the new fuel-efficient model, or should it continue to use the old one until it wears out? Explain.

LO 1

Exercise 6-14B   *Opportunity costs*

Two years ago, Victor Baldwin bought a truck for $22,000 to offer delivery services. Victor earns $32,000 a year operating as an independent trucker. He has an opportunity to sell his truck for $15,000 and take a position as an instructor in a truck driving school. The instructor position pays $25,000 a year for working 40 hours per week. Driving his truck, Victor works approximately 60 hours per week. If Victor sells his truck, he will invest the proceeds of the sale in bonds that pay a 12 percent return.

Required

a. Determine the opportunity cost of owning and operating the independent delivery business.
b. Based solely on financial considerations, should Victor sell his truck and accept the instructor position?
c. Discuss the qualitative as well as quantitative characteristics that Victor should consider.

Exercise 6-15B *Segment elimination decision*

LO 5

Evan Company operates three segments. Income statements for the segments imply that Evan could improve profitability if Segment X is eliminated.

THE EVAN COMPANY			
Income Statement			
For the Year 2011			
Segment	X	Y	Z
Sales	$ 87,000	$210,000	$200,000
Cost of goods sold	(67,000)	(82,000)	(85,000)
Sales commissions	(14,000)	(22,000)	(20,000)
Contribution margin	6,000	106,000	95,000
General fixed oper. exp. (allocation of president's salary)	(20,000)	(20,000)	(20,000)
Advertising expense (specific to individual segments)	(3,000)	(18,000)	0
Net income	$(17,000)	$ 68,000	$ 75,000

Required

a. Explain the effect on Evan's profitability if Segment X is eliminated.
b. Prepare comparative income statements for the company as a whole under the two alternatives: (1) Segment X is retained or (2) Segment X is eliminated.

Exercise 6-16B *Segment elimination decision*

LO 5

Jevon Company divides its operations into six divisions. A recent income statement for the Heath Division follows:

Income Statement	
Revenue	$ 700,000
Salaries for employees	(325,000)
Operating expenses	(250,000)
Insurance	(45,000)
Division-level facility-sustaining costs	(90,000)
Companywide facility-sustaining costs	(74,000)
Net loss	$ (84,000)

Required

a. Should Jevon eliminate the Heath Division? Support your answer by explaining how the division's elimination would affect the net income of the company as a whole. By how much would companywide income increase or decrease?
b. Assume that the Heath Division could increase its revenue to $760,000 by raising prices. Would this change the decision you made in response to Requirement *a*? Assuming Jevon's revenue becomes $760,000, determine the amount of the increase or decrease that would occur in companywide net income if the segment were eliminated.
c. What is the minimum amount of revenue the Heath Division must generate to justify its continued operation?

Exercise 6-17B *Identifying avoidable cost of a segment*

LO 5

Norton Corporation is considering the elimination of one of its segments. The following fixed costs pertain to the segment. If the segment is eliminated, the building it uses will be sold.

Annual advertising expense	$240,000
Market value of the building	36,000
Annual depreciation on the building	18,000
Annual maintenance costs on equipment	26,000
Annual real estate taxes on the building	8,000
Annual supervisory salaries	72,000
Annual allocation of companywide facility-level costs	30,000
Original cost of the building	75,000
Current book value of the building	54,000

Required

Based on this information, determine the amount of avoidable cost associated with the segment.

LO 6

Exercise 6-18B   *Asset replacement decision*

Quigley Electronics purchased a manufacturing plant four years ago for $7,000,000. The plant costs $1,800,000 per year to operate. Its current book value using straight-line depreciation is $5,000,000. Quigley could purchase a replacement plant for $14,000,000 that would have a useful life of 10 years. Because of new technology, the replacement plant would require only $500,000 per year in operating expenses. It would have an expected salvage value of $3,000,000 after 10 years. The current disposal value of the old plant is $1,200,000, and if Quigley keeps it 10 more years, its residual value would be $300,000.

Required

Based on this information, should Quigley replace the old plant? Support your answer with appropriate computations.

LO 6

Exercise 6-19B   *Asset replacement decision*

Fenwick Company is considering whether to replace some of its manufacturing equipment. Information pertaining to the existing equipment and the potential replacement equipment follows:

Existing Equipment		Replacement Equipment	
Cost	$45,000	Cost	$42,000
Operating expenses*	48,000	Operating expenses*	8,000
Salvage value	8,000	Salvage value	10,000
Market value	16,000	Useful life	10 years
Book value	21,000		
Remaining useful life	10 years		

*The amounts shown for operating expenses are the cumulative total of all such expenses expected to be incurred over the useful life of the equipment.

Required

Based on this information, recommend whether to replace the equipment. Support your recommendation with appropriate computations.

LO 6

Exercise 6-20B   *Asset replacement decision*

Gilchrist Company, a Texas-based corporation, paid $57,000 to purchase an air conditioner on January 1, 2000. During 2010, surging energy costs prompted management to consider replacing the air conditioner with a more energy-efficient model. The new air conditioner would cost $80,000. Electricity for the existing air conditioner costs the company $30,000 per year; the new model would cost only $20,000 per year. The new model, which has an expected useful life of 10 years, would be installed on January 1, 2011. Because the old air conditioner is more durable, Gilchrist estimates it still has a remaining useful life of 10 years even though it has been used. The current market value of the old air conditioner is $27,000. The expected salvage value of both air conditioners is zero.

Required

Based on this information, recommend whether to replace the equipment. Support your recommendation with appropriate computations.

Exercise 6-21B   *Annual versus cumulative data for replacement decision*   LO 6, 7

Because their three adult children have all at last left home, Paul and Cindy Bender recently moved to a smaller house. Paul owns a riding lawnmower he bought three years ago to take care of the former house's huge yard; it should last another five years. With the new house's smaller yard, Paul thinks he could hire someone to cut his grass for $400 per year. He wonders if this option is financially sound. Relevant information follows.

Riding Lawn Mower	Amount
Original cost	$2,400
Accumulated depreciation	900
Current market value	1,300
Estimated salvage value	0

Required

a. What is the annual opportunity cost of using the riding mower? Based on your computations, recommend whether Paul should sell it and hire a lawn service.
b. Determine the total cost of hiring a lawn service for the next five years. Based on your computations, recommend whether Paul should sell the mower and hire a lawn service.

Appendix

Exercise 6-22B   *Scarce resource decision*   LO 8

Quantum Technologies has the capacity to annually produce either 50,000 desktop computers or 28,000 laptop computers. Relevant data for each product follow:

	Desktop	Laptop
Sales price	$1,000	$1,800
Variable costs	400	650

Required

Assuming that Quantum can sell all it produces of either product, should the company produce the desktop computers or the laptop computers? Provide computations to support your answer.

PROBLEMS—SERIES B

Problem 6-23B   *Context-sensitive relevance*   LO 1

Required

Respond to each requirement independently.

a. Describe two decision-making contexts, one in which unit-level labor costs are avoidable, and the other in which they are unavoidable.
b. Describe two decision-making contexts, one in which batch-level shipping costs are avoidable, and the other in which they are unavoidable.
c. Describe two decision-making contexts, one in which administrative costs are avoidable, and the other in which they are unavoidable.
d. Describe two decision-making contexts, one in which the insurance premium paid on a building is avoidable, and the other in which it is unavoidable.
e. Describe two decision-making contexts, one in which amortization of a product patent is avoidable, and the other in which it is unavoidable.

LO 1

Problem 6-24B   *Context-sensitive relevance*

Inman Machines Company is evaluating two customer orders from which it can accept only one because of capacity limitations. The data associated with each order follow.

Cost Category	Order A	Order B
Contract price	$900,000	$770,000
Unit-level materials	350,000	286,000
Unit-level labor	324,000	264,800
Unit-level overhead	106,000	98,000
Supervisor's salary	80,000	80,000
Rental equipment costs	20,000	24,000
Depreciation on tools (zero market value)	28,000	28,000
Allocated portion of companywide facility-sustaining costs	8,000	7,200
Insurance coverage	54,000	54,000

Required

a. Assume that Inman has decided to accept one of the two orders. Identify the information relevant to selecting one order versus the other. Recommend which job to accept, and support your answer with appropriate computations.

b. The customer presenting Order A has withdrawn it because of its financial hardship. Under this circumstance, Inman's choice is to accept or reject Order B alone. Identify the information relevant to this decision. Recommend whether to accept or reject Order B. Support your answer with appropriate computations.

LO 2, 3

Problem 6-25B   *Effect of order quantity on special order decision*

Lang Company made 100,000 electric drills in batches of 1,000 units each during the prior accounting period. Normally, Lang markets its products through a variety of hardware stores. The following is the summarized cost to produce electric drills.

Materials cost ($8.00 per unit × 100,000)	$ 800,000
Labor cost ($4.00 per unit × 100,000)	400,000
Manufacturing supplies ($0.50 × 100,000)	50,000
Batch-level costs (100 batches at $2,000 per batch)	200,000
Product-level costs	150,000
Facility-level costs	180,000
Total costs	$1,780,000
Cost per unit = $1,780,000 ÷ 100,000 = $17.80	

Required

a. Bypassing Lang's regular distribution channel, Chekhol's Home Maintenance Company, has offered to buy a batch of 500 electric drills for $15.50 each directly from Lang. Lang's normal selling price is $23 per unit. Based on the preceding quantitative data, should Lang accept the special order? Support your answer with appropriate computations.

b. Would your answer to Requirement *a* change if Chekhol's offered to buy a batch of 1,000 electric drills for $14.90 each? Support your answer with appropriate computations.

c. Describe the qualitative factors that Lang should consider before accepting a special order to sell electric drills to Chekhol's.

LO 2, 4

Problem 6-26B   *Effects of the level of production on an outsourcing decision*

One of Yamamoto Company's major products is a fuel additive designed to improve fuel efficiency and keep engines clean. Yamamoto, a petrochemical firm, makes and sells 200,000 units of the fuel additive per year. Its management is evaluating the possibility of having an outside supplier manufacture the product for Yamamoto for $2 each. Yamamoto would continue to sell and distribute the fuel additive under its own brand name for either alternative. Yamamoto's accountant constructed the following profitability analysis:

Revenue (100,000 units × $3.50)	$350,000
Unit-level materials costs (100,000 units × $0.80)	(80,000)
Unit-level labor costs (100,000 units × $0.12)	(12,000)
Unit-level overhead costs (100,000 × $0.38)	(38,000)
Unit-level selling expenses (100,000 × $0.20)	(20,000)
Contribution margin	200,000
Fuel additive production supervisor's salary	(80,000)
Allocated portion of facility-level costs	(25,000)
Product-level advertising cost	(40,000)
Contribution to companywide income	$ 55,000

Required

a. Identify the cost items relevant to the make-or-outsource decision.

b. Should Yamamoto continue to make the fuel additive or buy it from the supplier? Support your answer by determining the change in net income if Yamamoto buys the fuel additive instead of making it.

c. Suppose that Yamamoto is able to increase sales by 60,000 units (sales will increase to 160,000 units). At this level of sales, should Yamamoto make or buy the fuel additive? Support your answer by explaining how the increase in production affects the cost per unit.

d. Discuss the qualitative factors that Yamamoto should consider before deciding to outsource the fuel additive. How can Yamamoto minimize the risk of establishing a relationship with an unreliable supplier?

Problem 6-27B   *Outsourcing decision affected by equipment replacement*   LO 2, 5, 6

During 2011, Vance Toy Company made 10,000 units of Model K, the costs of which follow.

Unit-level materials costs (10,000 units × $10)	$100,000
Unit-level labor costs (10,000 units × $40)	400,000
Unit-level overhead costs (10,000 × $4)	40,000
Depreciation on manufacturing equipment	60,000
Model K production supervisor's salary	60,000
Inventory holding costs	120,000
Allocated portion of facility-level costs	80,000
Total costs	$860,000

An independent contractor has offered to make the same product for Vance for $50 each.

Additional Information:

1. The manufacturing equipment originally cost $420,000 and has a book value of $240,000, a remaining useful life of four years, and a zero salvage value. If the equipment is not used to produce Model K in the production process, it can be leased for $40,000 per year.

2. Vance has the opportunity to purchase for $240,000 new manufacturing equipment that will have an expected useful life of four years and a salvage value of $80,000. This equipment will increase productivity substantially, thereby reducing unit-level labor costs by 20 percent.

3. If Vance discontinues the production of Model K, the company can eliminate 50 percent of its inventory holding cost.

Required

a. Determine the avoidable cost per unit to produce Model K assuming that Vance is considering the alternatives between making the product using the existing equipment and outsourcing the product to the independent contractor. Based on the quantitative data, should Vance outsource Model K? Support your answer with appropriate computations.

b. Assuming that Vance is considering whether to replace the old equipment with the new equipment, determine the avoidable cost per unit to produce Model K using the new equipment and the avoidable cost per unit to produce Model K using the old equipment. Calculate the impact on profitability if Model K were made using the old equipment versus the new equipment.

c. Assuming that Vance is considering either to purchase the new equipment or to outsource Model K, calculate the impact on profitability between the two alternatives.

d. Discuss the qualitative factors that Vance should consider before making a decision to outsource Model K. How can Vance minimize the risk of establishing a relationship with an unreliable supplier?

LO 5

Problem 6-28B   *Eliminating a segment*

Dexier's Grocery Store has three departments, meat, canned food, and produce, each of which has its own manager. All departments are housed in a single store. Recently, the produce department has been suffering a net loss and is expected to continue doing so. Last year's income statements follow.

	Meat Department	Canned Food Department	Produce Department
Sales	$650,000	$590,000	$425,000
Cost of goods sold	(270,000)	(330,000)	(245,000)
Gross margin	380,000	260,000	180,000
Departmental manager's salary	(42,000)	(30,000)	(35,000)
Rent on store lease	(80,000)	(80,000)	(80,000)
Store utilities	(20,000)	(20,000)	(20,000)
Other general expenses	(98,000)	(98,000)	(98,000)
Net income (loss)	$140,000	$ 32,000	$(53,000)

Required

a. Determine whether to eliminate the produce department.

b. Confirm the conclusion you reached in Requirement *a* by preparing a before and an after income statement, assuming that the produce department is eliminated.

c. Eliminating the produce department would allow the meat department to expand. It could add seafood to its products. Suppose that management estimates that offering seafood would increase the store's net earnings by $160,000. Would this information affect the decision that you made in Requirement *a*? Explain your answer.

LO 2, 5

Problem 6-29B   *Effect of activity level and opportunity cost on segment elimination decision*

Aquilar Company has three separate operating branches: Division X, which manufactures utensils; Division Y, which makes plates; and Division Z, which makes cooking pots. Each division operates its own facility. The company's administrative offices are located in a separate building. In recent years, Division Z has experienced a net loss and is expected to continue to do so. Income statements for 2011 follow.

	Division X	Division Y	Division Z
Sales	$1,800,000	$1,400,000	$1,500,000
Less: Cost of goods sold			
Unit-level manufacturing costs	(1,100,000)	(580,000)	(400,000)
Rent on manufacturing facility	(240,000)	(220,000)	(360,000)
Gross margin	460,000	600,000	240,000
Less: Operating expenses			
Unit-level selling and admin. expenses	(60,000)	(45,000)	(90,000)
Division-level fixed selling and admin. expenses	(140,000)	(125,000)	(180,000)
Administrative facility-level costs	(80,000)	(80,000)	(80,000)
Net income (loss)	$ 180,000	$ 350,000	$ (110,000)

Required

a. Based on the preceding information, recommend whether to eliminate Division Z. Support your answer by preparing companywide income statements before and after eliminating Division Z.

b. During 2011, Division Z produced and sold 30,000 units of product. Would your recommendation in Requirement *a* change if sales and production increase to 45,000 units in 2012? Support your answer by comparing differential revenue and avoidable cost for Division Z, assuming that 45,000 units are sold.

c. Suppose that Aquilar could sublease Division Z's manufacturing facility for $740,000. Would you operate the division at a production and sales volume of 45,000 units, or would you close it? Support your answer with appropriate computations.

Problem 6-30B   *Comprehensive problem including special order, outsourcing, and segment elimination decisions*   **LO 2, 3, 4, 5**

Emerson Company's electronics division produces an MP3 player. The vice president in charge of the division is evaluating the income statement showing annual revenues and expenses associated with the division's operating activities. The relevant range for the production and sale of the radio/cassette player is between 50,000 and 150,000 units per year.

Income Statement	
Revenue (60,000 units × $30)	$1,800,000
Unit-level variable costs	
Materials cost (60,000 × $15)	(900,000)
Labor cost (60,000 × $8)	(480,000)
Manufacturing overhead (60,000 × $1.50)	(90,000)
Shipping and handling (60,000 × $0.50)	(30,000)
Sales commissions (60,000 × $2)	(120,000)
Contribution margin	180,000
Fixed expenses	
Advertising costs related to the division	(30,000)
Salary of production supervisor	(126,000)
Allocated companywide facility-level expenses	(120,000)
Net loss	$ (96,000)

Required (Consider each of the requirements independently.)

a. An international trading firm has approached top management about buying 30,000 MP3 players for $26.50 each. It would sell the product in a foreign country, so that Emerson's existing customers would not be affected. Because the offer was made directly to top management, no sales commissions on the transaction would be involved. Based on quantitative features alone, should Emerson accept the special order? Support your answer with appropriate computations. Specifically, by what amount would profitability increase or decrease if the special order is accepted?

b. Emerson has an opportunity to buy the 60,000 MP3 players it currently makes from a foreign manufacturer for $26 each. The manufacturer has a good reputation for reliability and quality, and Emerson could continue to use its own logo, advertising program, and sales force to distribute the products. Should Emerson buy the MP3 players or continue to make them? Support your answer with appropriate computations. Specifically, how much more or less would it cost to buy the MP3 players than to make them? Would your answer change if the volume of sales were increased to 140,000 units?

c. Because the electronics division is currently operating at a loss, should it be eliminated from the company's operations? Support your answer with appropriate computations. Specifically, by what amount would the segment's elimination increase or decrease profitability?

Appendix

LO 8

Problem 6-31B *Allocating scarce resources*

Minter Company makes two products, M and N. Product information follows.

	Product M	Product N
Selling price per unit	$69	$84
Variable cost per unit	45	54

Required

Identify the product that should be produced or sold under each of the following constraints. Consider each constraint separately.

a. One unit of Product M requires 3 hours of labor to produce, and one unit of Product N requires 5 hours of labor to produce. Due to labor constraints, demand is higher than the company's capacity to make both products.

b. The products are sold to the public in retail stores. The company has limited floor space and cannot stock as many products as it would like. Display space is available for only one of the two products. Expected sales of Product M are 8,000 units, and expected sales of Product N are 7,000 units.

c. The maximum number of machine hours available is 24,000. Product M uses 4 machine hours, and Product N uses 6 machine hours. The company can sell all the products it produces.

LO 7

Problem 6-32B *Conflict between short-term and long-term performance*

Traywick Construction Components, Inc., purchased a machine on January 1, 2009, for $240,000. The chief engineer estimated the machine's useful life to be six years and its salvage value to be zero. The operating cost of this machine is $120,000 per year. By January 1, 2011, a new machine that requires 30 percent less operating cost than the existing machine has become available for $180,000; it would have a four-year useful life with zero salvage. The current market value of the old machine on January 1, 2011, is $100,000, and its book value is $160,000 on that date. Straight-line depreciation is used for both machines. The company expects to generate $320,000 of revenue per year from the use of either machine.

Required

a. Recommend whether to replace the old machine on January 1, 2011. Support your answer with appropriate computations.

b. Prepare income statements for four years (2011 through 2014) assuming that the old machine is retained.

c. Prepare income statements for four years (2011 through 2014) assuming that the old machine is replaced.

d. Discuss the potential ethical conflicts that could result from the timing of the loss and expense recognition reported in the two income statements.

ANALYZE, THINK, COMMUNICATE

ACT 6-1 Business Application Case *Analyzing inventory reductions at Supervalu*

On January 12, 2010, Supervalu, Inc., announced it was planning to reduce the number of different items it carries in its inventory by as much as 25 percent. Supervalu is one of the largest grocery store companies in the United States. It operates more than 2,400 stores under 14 different brand names, including Albertsons, Farm Fresh, Jewel-Osco, and Save-A-Lot. The company also has a segment that provides third-party supply-chain services.

The planned reduction in inventory items was going to be accomplished more by reducing the number of different package sizes than by reducing entire product brands. The new approach was also intended to allow the company to get better prices from its vendors and to put more emphasis on its own store brands.

Required

a. Identify some costs savings Supervalu might realize by reducing the number of items it carries in inventory by 25 percent. Be as specific as possible and use your imagination.

b. Consider the additional information presented below, which is hypothetical. All dollar amounts are in thousands; unit amounts are not. Assume that Supervalu decides to eliminate one product line, Sugar-Bits, for one of its segments that currently produces three products. As a result, the following are expected to occur:

(1) The number of units sold for the segment is expected to drop by only 40,000 because of the elimination of Sugar-Bits, since most customers are expected to purchase a Fiber-Treats or Carbo-Crunch product instead. The shift of sales from Sugar-Bits to Fiber-Treats and Carbo-Crunch is expected to be evenly split. In other words, the sales of Fiber-Treats and Carbo-Crunch will each increase by 100,000 units.

(2) Rent is paid for the entire production facility, and the space used by Sugar-Bits cannot be sublet.

(3) Utilities costs are expected to be reduced by $24,000.

(4) The supervisors for Sugar-Bits were all terminated. No new supervisor will be hired for Fiber-Treats or Carbo-Crunch.

(5) The equipment being used to produce Sugar-Bits is also used to produce the other two products. The company believes that as a result of eliminating Sugar-Bits it can eliminate equipment that has a remaining useful life of five years, and a projected salvage value of $20,000. Its current market value is $35,000.

(6) Facility-level costs will continue to be allocated between the product lines based on the number of units produced.

Product-line Earnings Statements
(Dollar amounts are in thousands)

Annual Costs of Operating Each Product Line	Fiber-Treats	Carbo-Crunch	Sugar-Bits	Total
Sales in units	480,000	480,000	240,000	1,200,000
Sales in dollars	$480,000	$480,000	$240,000	$1,200,000
Unit-level costs:				
Cost of production	48,000	48,000	26,400	122,400
Sales commissions	6,000	6,000	2,400	14,400
Shipping and handling	10,800	9,600	4,800	25,200
Miscellaneous	3,600	2,400	2,400	8,400
Total unit-level costs	68,400	66,000	36,000	170,400
Product-level costs:				
Supervisors salaries	4,800	3,600	1,200	9,600
Facility-level costs:				
Rent	48,000	48,000	24,000	120,000
Utilities	60,000	60,000	30,000	150,000
Depreciation on equipment	192,000	192,000	96,000	480,000
Allocated company-wide expenses	12,000	12,000	6,000	30,000
Total facility-level costs	312,000	312,000	156,000	780,000
Total product cost	385,200	381,600	193,200	960,000
Profit on products	$94,800	$98,400	$46,800	$240,000

Prepare revised product-line earnings statements based on the elimination of Sugar-Bits. It will be necessary to calculate some per-unit data to accomplish this.

ACT 6-2 Group Assignment *Relevance and cost behavior*

Maccoa Soft, a division of Zayer Software Company, produces and distributes an automated payroll software system. A contribution margin format income statement for Maccoa Soft for the past year follows.

Revenue (12,000 units × $1,200)	$14,400,000
Unit-level variable costs	
Product materials cost (12,000 × $60)	(720,000)
Installation labor cost (12,000 × $200)	(2,400,000)
Manufacturing overhead (12,000 × $2)	(24,000)
Shipping and handling (12,000 × $25)	(300,000)
Sales commissions (12,000 × $300)	(3,600,000)
Nonmanufacturing miscellaneous costs (12,000 × $5)	(60,000)
Contribution margin (12,000 × $608)	7,296,000
Fixed costs	
Research and development	(2,700,000)
Legal fees to ensure product protection	(780,000)
Advertising costs	(1,200,000)
Rental cost of manufacturing facility	(600,000)
Depreciation on production equipment (zero market value)	(300,000)
Other manufacturing costs (salaries, utilities, etc.)	(744,000)
Division-level facility sustaining costs	(1,730,000)
Allocated companywide facility-level costs	(1,650,000)
Net loss	$ (2,408,000)

a. Divide the class into groups and then organize the groups into three sections. Assign Task 1 to the first section, Task 2 to the second section, and Task 3 to the third section. Each task should be considered independently of the others.

Group Tasks

(1) Assume that Maccoa has excess capacity. The sales staff has identified a large franchise company with 200 outlets that is interested in Maccoa's software system but is willing to pay only $800 for each system. Ignoring qualitative considerations, should Maccoa accept the special order?

(2) Maccoa has the opportunity to purchase a comparable payroll system from a competing vendor for $600 per system. Ignoring qualitative considerations, should Maccoa outsource producing the software? Maccoa would continue to sell and install the software if the manufacturing activities were outsourced.

(3) Given that Maccoa is generating a loss, should Zayer eliminate it? Would your answer change if Maccoa could increase sales by 1,000 units?

b. Have a representative from each section explain its respective conclusions. Discuss the following:

(1) Representatives from Section 1 should respond to the following: The analysis related to the special order (Task 1) suggests that all variable costs are always relevant. Is this conclusion valid? Explain your answer.

(2) Representatives from Section 2 should respond to the following: With respect to the outsourcing decision, identify a relevant fixed cost and a nonrelevant fixed cost. Discuss the criteria for determining whether a cost is or is not relevant.

(3) Representatives from Section 3 should respond to the following: Why did the segment elimination decision change when the volume of production and sales increased?

ATC 6-3 Research Assignment *Using real world data from Pfizer*

On September 20, 2008, *The Wall Street Journal* (WSJ) reported that Pfizer was going to discontinue efforts to develop drugs related to the treatment of heart disease, obesity, and bone health. Pfizer wanted to focus its resources on areas it thought would be more profitable (p. B-1). On January 17, 2009, the WSJ reported that Pfizer planned to lay off as many as 2,400 salespersons, which would be one-third of its sales force. As a part of its efforts to reduce costs, Pfizer had reduced its workforce by 35,000 employees from January 2007 to January 2009 (p. B-5). On July 7, 2009, the WSJ reported that Pfizer, along with other pharmaceutical companies, was increasing its efforts to sell patented durgs (versus generic drugs) to customers in poorer nations. To accomplish this they were offering these customers lower prices. For example, Pfizer sells drugs in Venezuela for 30 percent less than it sells the same drugs in the United States (p. A-1).

Required

a. By stopping the development of drugs related to the treatment of heart disease, obesity, and bone health Pfizer hoped to reduce the amount spend on research and development. Relative to the level of sales, should R&D costs be considered:
- Fixed costs or variable costs
- Marginal costs or not

b. Were the R&D costs that Pfizer had spent in past years to develop drugs related to heart disease relevant to its decision to discontinue their future development? If they were not relevant costs, what kind of cost were they?

c. Explain how Pfizer can afford to sell drugs in Venezuela for 30 percent lower prices than it sells them for in the United States.

d. Obtain Pfizer's annual report for 2008. Pfizer's annual reports can be found at its website: www.pfizer.com. Calculate its operating costs as a percentage of revenue for 2006, 2007, and 2008. (The easiest way to do this is to calculate its "income from continuing operations" as a percentage of revenue, and subtract that amount from 1.0.) Does it appear that Pfizer is accomplishing its goal of reducing its cost? Show supporting computations.

ATC 6-4   Writing Assignment   *Relevant versus full cost*

State law permits the State Department of Revenue to collect taxes for municipal governments that operate within the state's jurisdiction and allows private companies to collect taxes for municipalities. To promote fairness and to ensure the financial well-being of the state, the law dictates that the Department of Revenue must charge municipalities a fee for collection services that is above the cost of providing such services but does not define the term *cost*. Until recently, Department of Revenue officials have included a proportionate share of all departmental costs such as depreciation on buildings and equipment, supervisory salaries, and other facility-level overhead costs when determining the cost of providing collection services, a measurement approach known as *full costing*. The full costing approach has led to a pricing structure that places the Department of Revenue at a competitive disadvantage relative to private collection companies. Indeed, highly efficient private companies have been able to consistently underbid the Revenue Department for municipal customers. As a result, it has lost 30 percent of its municipal collection business over the last two years. The inability to be price competitive led the revenue commissioner to hire a consulting firm to evaluate the current practice of determining the cost to provide collection services.

The consulting firm concluded that the cost to provide collection services should be limited to the relevant costs associated with providing those services, defined as the difference between the costs that would be incurred if the services were provided and the costs that would be incurred if the services were not provided. According to this definition, the costs of depreciation, supervisory salaries, and other facility-level overhead costs are not included because they are the same regardless of whether the Department of Revenue provides collection services to municipalities. The Revenue Department adopted the relevant cost approach and immediately reduced the price it charges municipalities to collect their taxes and rapidly recovered the collection business it had lost. Indeed, several of the private collection companies were forced into bankruptcy. The private companies joined together and filed suit against the Revenue Department, charging that the new definition of cost violates the intent of the law.

Required

a. Assume that you are an accountant hired as a consultant for the private companies. Write a brief memo explaining why it is inappropriate to limit the definition of the costs of providing collection services to relevant costs.

b. Assume that you are an accountant hired as a consultant for the Department of Revenue. Write a brief memo explaining why it is appropriate to limit the definition of the costs of providing collection services to relevant costs.

c. Speculate on how the matter will be resolved.

ATC 6-5   Ethical Dilemma   *Asset replacement clouded by self-interest*

John Dillworth is in charge of buying property used as building sites for branch offices of the National Bank of Commerce. Mr. Dillworth recently paid $110,000 for a site located in a growing section of the city. Shortly after purchasing this lot, Mr. Dillworth had the opportunity to purchase a more desirable lot at a significantly lower price. The traffic count at the new site is virtually twice that of the old site, but the price of the lot is only $80,000. It was immediately apparent that he had overpaid for the previous purchase. The current market value of the purchased property is only $75,000. Mr. Dillworth believes that it would be in the bank's best interest to buy the new lot, but he does not want to report a loss to his boss, Kelly Fullerton. He knows that Ms. Fullerton will severely reprimand him, even though she has made her share of mistakes. In fact, he is aware of a significant bad loan that Ms. Fullerton recently approved. When confronted with the bad debt by the senior vice president in charge of commercial lending, Ms. Fullerton blamed the decision on one of her former subordinates, Ira Sacks. Ms. Fullerton implied that Mr. Sacks had been dismissed for reckless lending decisions when, in fact, he had been an excellent loan officer with an uncanny ability to assess the creditworthiness of his customers. Indeed, Mr. Sacks had voluntarily resigned to accept a better position.

Required

a. Determine the amount of the loss that would be recognized on the sale of the existing branch site.

b. Identify the type of cost represented by the $110,000 original purchase price of the land. Also identify the type of cost represented by its current market value of $75,000. Indicate which cost is relevant to a decision as to whether the original site should be replaced with the new site.

c. Is Mr. Dillworth's conclusion that the old site should be replaced supported by quantitative analysis? If not, what facts do justify his conclusion?

d. Assuming that Mr. Dillworth is a certified management accountant (CMA), do you believe the failure to replace the land violates any of the standards of ethical conduct in Exhibit 1.15 in Chapter 1? If so, which standards would be violated?

e. Discuss the ethical dilemma that Mr. Dillworth faces within the context of the fraud triangle that was discussed in Chapter 1.

f. Would Mr. Dillworth be subject to criminal penalties under the Sarbanes-Oxley Act? Explain your answer.

ATC 6-6   Spreadsheet Assignment   *Using Excel*

Dorina Company makes cases of canned dog food in batches of 1,000 cases and sells each case for $15. The plant capacity is 50,000 cases; the company currently makes 40,000 cases. DoggieMart has offered to buy 1,500 cases for $12 per case. Because product-level and facility-level costs are unaffected by a special order, they are omitted.

Required

a. Prepare a spreadsheet like the following one to calculate the contribution to income if the special order is accepted. Construct formulas so that the number of cases or the price could be changed and the new contribution would be automatically calculated.

b. Try different order sizes (such as 2,000) or different prices to see the effect on contribution to profit.

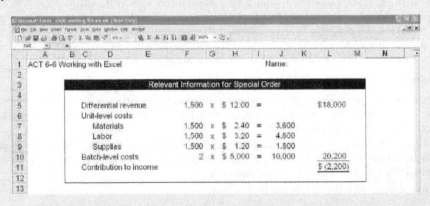

Spreadsheet Tips

1. The numbers in cells F7 to F9 should be formulas that refer to F5. This allows the number of cases to be changed in cell F5 with the other cells changing automatically.

2. The formula in cell F10 uses a function named ROUNDUP to calculate the even number of batches. The formula should be = ROUNDUP(F5/1000,0) where the zero refers to rounding up to the nearest whole number.

ATC 6-7   Spreadsheet Assignment   *Mastering Excel*

Refer to Problem 6-31A.

Required

a. Prepare a spreadsheet to solve Requirements *a*, *b*, and *c* in Problem 6-31A.

b. While constructing formulas for Requirement *a* of Problem 6-31A, include a formula to calculate contribution margin per labor hour.

c. While constructing formulas for Requirement *b* of Problem 6-31A, include formulas to calculate total contribution margin for each product.

d. While constructing formulas for Requirement *c* of Problem 6-31A, include formulas to calculate contribution margin per machine hour and total contribution margin for each product.

COMPREHENSIVE PROBLEM

Use the same transaction data for Magnificent Modems, Inc., as was used in Chapter 1. (See page 52.)

Required

a. One of Magnificent Modems' sales representatives receives a special offer to sell 1,000 modems at a price of $72 each. Should the offer be accepted?

b. Magnificent Modems has the opportunity to purchase the modems that it currently makes. The modems can be purchased at a price of $76 each. Assuming the manufacturing equipment has a zero market value, should Magnificent buy the modems?

c. Assume that Magnificent Modems expects production and sales to grow to 10,000. At this volume of production, should Magnificent buy the modems?

CHAPTER 7

Planning for Profit and Cost Control

LEARNING OBJECTIVES

After you have mastered the material in this chapter you will be able to:

1 Describe the budgeting process and the benefits it provides.

2 Explain the relationship between budgeting and human behavior.

3 Prepare a sales budget and related schedule of cash receipts.

4 Prepare an inventory purchases budget and related schedule of cash payments.

5 Prepare a selling and administrative expense budget and related schedule of cash payments.

6 Prepare a cash budget.

7 Prepare a pro forma income statement, balance sheet, and statement of cash flows.

CHAPTER OPENING

Planning is crucial to operating a profitable business. Expressing business plans in financial terms is commonly called **budgeting.** The budgeting process involves coordinating the financial plans of all areas of the business. For example, the production department cannot prepare a manufacturing plan until it knows how many units of product to produce. The number of units to produce depends on the marketing department's sales projection. The marketing department cannot project sales volume until it knows what products the company will sell. Product information comes from the research and development department. The point should be clear: a company's master budget results from combining numerous specific plans prepared by different departments.

Master budget preparation is normally supervised by a committee. The budget committee is responsible for settling disputes among various departments over budget matters. The committee also monitors reports on how various segments are progressing toward achieving their budget goals. The budgeting committee is not an accounting committee. It is a high-level committee that normally includes the company president, vice presidents of marketing, purchasing, production, and finance, and the controller.

The Curious Accountant

People in television commercials often say they shop at a particular store because, "my family is on a budget." The truth is, most families do not have a formal budget. What these people mean is that they need to be sure their spending does not exceed their available cash.

When a family expects to spend more money in a given year than it will earn, it must plan on borrowing funds needed to make up the difference. However, even if a family's income for a year will exceed its spending, it may still need to borrow money because the timing of its cash inflows may not match the timing of its cash outflows. Whether a budget is being prepared for a family or a business, those preparing the budget must understand the specific issues facing that entity if potential financial problems are to be anticipated. There is no such thing as a "one size fits all" budget.

The United States Olympic Committee (USOC), like all large organizations, devotes considerable effort to budget planning.

Think about the Olympic Games, and how the USOC generates revenues and incurs expenditures. Can you identify any unusual circumstances facing the USOC that complicate its budgeting efforts? (Answer on page 319.)

Describe the budgeting process and the benefits it provides.

THE PLANNING PROCESS

Planning normally addresses short, intermediate, and long-range time horizons. Short-term plans are more specific than long-term plans. Consider, for example, your decision to attend college. Long-term planning requires considering general questions such as:

- Do I want to go to college?
- How do I expect to benefit from the experience?
- Do I want a broad knowledge base, or am I seeking to learn specific job skills?
- In what field do I want to concentrate my studies?

Many students go to college before answering these questions. They discover the disadvantages of poor planning the hard way. While their friends are graduating, they are starting over in a new major.

Intermediate-range planning usually covers three to five years. In this stage, you consider which college to attend, how to support yourself while in school, and whether to live on or off campus.

Short-term planning focuses on the coming year. In this phase you plan specific courses to take, decide which instructors to choose, schedule part-time work, and join a study group. Short-term plans are specific and detailed. Their preparation may seem tedious, but careful planning generally leads to efficient resource use and high levels of productivity.

THREE LEVELS OF PLANNING FOR BUSINESS ACTIVITY

Businesses describe the three levels of planning as *strategic planning, capital budgeting,* and *operations budgeting.* **Strategic planning** involves making long-term decisions such as defining the scope of the business, determining which products to develop or discontinue, and identifying the most profitable market niche. Upper-level management is responsible for these decisions. Strategic plans are descriptive rather than quantitative. Objectives such as "to have the largest share of the market" or "to be the best-quality producer" result from strategic planning. Although strategic planning is an integral component of managing a business, an in-depth discussion of it is beyond the scope of this text.

Capital budgeting focuses on intermediate range planning. It involves such decisions as whether to buy or lease equipment, whether to stimulate sales, or whether to increase the company's asset base. Capital budgeting is discussed in detail in a later chapter.

Operations budgeting concentrates on short-term plans. A key component of operations budgeting is the *master budget,* which describes short-term objectives in specific amounts of sales targets, production goals, and financing plans. The master budget describes how management intends to achieve its objectives and directs the company's short-term activities.

The master budget normally covers one year. It is frequently divided into quarterly projections and often subdivides quarterly data by month. Effective managers cannot wait until year-end to know whether operations conform to budget targets. Monthly data provide feedback to permit making necessary corrections promptly.

Many companies use **perpetual,** or **continuous, budgeting** covering a 12-month reporting period. As the current month draws to a close, an additional month is added at the end of the budget period, resulting in a continuous 12-month budget. A perpetual budget offers the advantage of keeping management constantly focused on thinking ahead to the next 12 months. The more traditional annual approach to budgeting invites a frenzied stop-and-go mentality, with managers preparing the budget in a year-end rush that is soon forgotten. Changing conditions may not be discussed until the next year-end budget is due. A perpetual budget overcomes these disadvantages.

ADVANTAGES OF BUDGETING

Budgeting is costly and time-consuming. The sacrifices, however, are more than offset by the benefits. Budgeting promotes planning and coordination; it enhances performance measurement and corrective action.

Planning

Almost everyone makes plans. Each morning, most people think about what they will do during the day. Thinking ahead is planning. Most business managers think ahead about how they will direct operations. Unfortunately, planning is frequently as informal as making a few mental notes. Informal planning cannot be effectively communicated. The business manager might know what her objectives are, but neither her superiors nor her subordinates know. Because it serves as a communication tool, budgeting can solve these problems. The budget formalizes and documents managerial plans, clearly communicating objectives to both superiors and subordinates.

Coordination

Sometimes a choice benefits one department at the expense of another. For example, a purchasing agent may order large quantities of raw materials to obtain discounts from suppliers. But excessive quantities of materials pose a storage problem for the inventory supervisor who must manage warehouse costs. The budgeting process forces coordination among departments to promote decisions in the best interests of the company as a whole.

Performance Measurement

Budgets are specific, quantitative representations of management's objectives. Comparing actual results to budget expectations provides a way to evaluate performance. For example, if a company budgets sales of $10 million, it can judge the performance of the sales department against that level. If actual sales exceed $10 million, the company should reward the sales department; if actual sales fall below $10 million, the company should seek an explanation for the shortfall from the sales manager.

Corrective Action

Budgeting provides advance notice of potential shortages, bottlenecks, or other weaknesses in operating plans. For example, a cash budget alerts management to when the company can expect cash shortages during the coming year. The company can make borrowing arrangements well before it needs the money. Without knowing ahead of time, management might be unable to secure necessary financing on short notice, or it may have to pay excessively high interest rates to obtain funds. Budgeting advises managers of potential problems in time for them to carefully devise effective solutions.

BUDGETING AND HUMAN BEHAVIOR

Effective budgeting requires genuine sensitivity on the part of upper management to the effect on employees of budget expectations. People are often uncomfortable with budgets. Budgets are constraining. They limit individual freedom in favor of an established plan. Many people find evaluation based on budget expectations stressful. Most students experience a similar fear about testing. Like examinations, budgets represent

LO 2

Explain the relationship between budgeting and human behavior.

standards by which performance is evaluated. Employees worry about whether their performance will meet expectations.

The attitudes of high-level managers significantly impact budget effectiveness. Subordinates are keenly aware of management's expectations. If upper-level managers degrade, make fun of, or ignore the budget, subordinates will follow suit. If management uses budgets to humiliate, embarrass, or punish subordinates, employees will resent the treatment and the budgeting process. Upper-level managers must demonstrate that they view the budget as a sincere effort to express realistic goals employees are expected to meet. An honest, open, respectful atmosphere is essential to budgeting success.

Participative budgeting has frequently proved successful in creating a healthy atmosphere. This technique invites participation in the budget process by personnel at all levels of the organization, not just upper-level managers. Information flows from the bottom up as well as from the top down during budget preparation. Because they are directly responsible for meeting budget goals, subordinates can offer more realistic targets. Including them in budget preparation fosters development of a team effort. Participation fosters more cooperation and motivation, and less fear. With participative budgeting, subordinates cannot complain that the budget is management's plan. The budget is instead a self-imposed constraint. Employees can hold no one responsible but themselves if they fail to accomplish the budget objectives they established.

Upper management participates in the process to ensure that employee-generated objectives are consistent with company objectives. Furthermore, if subordinates were granted complete freedom to establish budget standards, they might be tempted to adopt lax standards to ensure they will meet them. Both managers and subordinates must cooperate if the participatory process is to produce an effective budget. If developed carefully, budgets can motivate employees to achieve superior performance. Normal human fears must be overcome, and management must create an honest budget atmosphere.

THE MASTER BUDGET

The **master budget** is a group of detailed budgets and schedules representing the company's operating and financial plans for a future accounting period. The master budget usually includes (1) *operating budgets,* (2) *capital budgets,* and (3) *pro forma financial statements.* The budgeting process normally begins with preparing the **operating budgets,** which focus on detailed operating activities. This chapter illustrates operating budgets for Hampton Hams, a retail sales company that uses (1) a sales budget, (2) an inventory purchases budget, (3) a selling and administrative (S&A) expense budget, and (4) a cash budget.

The sales budget includes a schedule of cash receipts from customers. The inventory purchases and S&A expense budgets include schedules of cash payments for inventory and expenses. Preparing the master budget begins with the sales forecast. Based on the sales forecast, the detailed budgets for inventory purchases and operating expenses are developed. The schedules of cash receipts and cash payments provide the foundation for preparing the cash budget.

The **capital budget** describes the company's intermediate-range plans for investments in facilities, equipment, new products, store outlets, and lines of business. The capital budget affects several operating budgets. For example, equipment acquisitions result in additional depreciation expense on the S&A expense budget. The cash flow effects of capital investments influence the cash budget.

The operating budgets are used to prepare *pro forma statements.* **Pro forma financial statements** are based on projected (budgeted) rather than historical information. Hampton Hams prepares a pro forma income statement, balance sheet, and statement of cash flows.

Exhibit 7.1 shows how information flows in a master budget.

EXHIBIT 7.1

Information Flows in the Master Budget

Cash receipts and payments schedules
- Cash receipts
- Cash payments for inventory
- Cash payments for S & A expenses

Operating budgets | Starting point
- Sales budget
- Inventory purchases budget
- S & A expense budget
- Cash budget

Pro forma financial statements
- Income statement
- Balance sheet
- Statement of cash flows

HAMPTON HAMS BUDGETING ILLUSTRATION

Hampton Hams (HH), a major corporation, sells cured hams nationwide through retail outlets in shopping malls. By focusing on a single product and standardized operations, the company controls costs stringently. As a result, it offers high-quality hams at competitive prices.

HAMPTON HAMS

Hampton Hams has experienced phenomenal growth during the past five years. It opened two new stores in Indianapolis, Indiana, last month and plans to open a third new store in October. Hampton Hams finances new stores by borrowing on a line of credit arranged with National Bank. National's loan officer has requested monthly budgets for each of the first three months of the new store's operations. The accounting department is preparing the new store's master budget for October, November, and December. The first step is developing a sales budget.

Sales Budget

Preparing the master budget begins with the sales forecast. The accuracy of the sales forecast is critical because all the other budgets are derived from the sales budget. Normally, the marketing department coordinates the development of the sales forecast. Sales estimates frequently flow from the bottom up to the higher management levels. Sales personnel prepare sales projections for their products and territories and pass them up the line where they are combined with the estimates of other sales personnel to develop regional and national estimates. Using various information sources, upper-level sales managers adjust the estimates generated by sales personnel. Adjustment information comes from industry periodicals and trade journals, economic analysis, marketing surveys, historical sales figures, and changes in competition. Companies assimilate this data using sophisticated computer programs, statistical techniques, and quantitative methods, or, simply, professional judgment. Regardless of the technique, the senior vice president of sales ultimately develops a sales forecast for which she is held responsible.

LO 3

Prepare a sales budget and related schedule of cash receipts.

To develop the sales forecast for HH's new store, the sales manager studied the sales history of existing stores operating in similar locations. He then adjusted for start-up conditions. October is an opportune time to open a new store because customers will learn the store's location before the holiday season. The sales manager expects significant sales growth in November and December as customers choose the company's hams as the centerpiece for many Thanksgiving and winter holiday dinner tables.

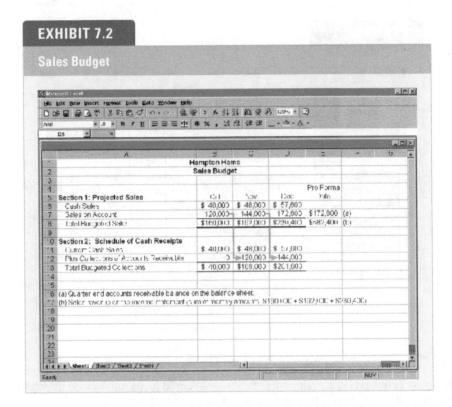

EXHIBIT 7.2

Sales Budget

The new store's sales are expected to be $160,000 in October ($40,000 in cash and $120,000 on account). Sales are expected to increase 20 percent per month during November and December. Based on these estimates, the sales manager prepared the sales budget in Exhibit 7.2.

Projected Sales

The sales budget has two sections. Section 1 shows the projected sales for each month. The November sales forecast reflects a 20 percent increase over October sales. For example, November *cash sales* are calculated as $48,000 [$40,000 + ($40,000 × 0.20)] and December *cash sales* as $57,600 [$48,000 + ($48,000 × 0.20)]. *Sales on account* are similarly computed.

Schedule of Cash Receipts

Section 2 is a schedule of the cash receipts for the projected sales. This schedule is used later to prepare the cash budget. The accountant has assumed in this schedule that Hampton Hams will collect accounts receivable from credit sales *in full* in the month following the sale. In practice, collections may be spread over several months, and some receivables may become bad debts that are never collected. Regardless of additional complexities, the objective is to estimate the amount and timing of expected cash receipts.

In the HH case, *total cash receipts* are determined by adding the current month's *cash sales* to the cash collected from the previous month's *credit sales* (accounts receivable balance). Cash receipts for each month are determined as follows:

- October receipts are projected to be $40,000. Because the store opens in October, no accounts receivable from September exist to be collected in October. Cash receipts for October equal the amount of October's cash sales.

- November receipts are projected to be $168,000 ($48,000 November cash sales + $120,000 cash collected from October sales on account).

- December receipts are projected to be $201,600 ($57,600 December cash sales + $144,000 cash collected from November sales on account).

FOCUS ON INTERNATIONAL ISSUES

CASH FLOW PLANNING IN BORDEAUX

The year 2005 was considered a great year for wine in the Bordeaux region of France, and the winemakers could look forward to selling their wines for high prices, but there was one catch; these wines would not be released to consumers until late in 2008. The winemakers had incurred most of their costs in 2005 when the vines were being tended and the grapes were being processed into wine. In many industries this would mean the companies would have to finance their inventory for almost four years—not an insignificant cost. The company must finance the inventory by either borrowing the money, which results in out-of-pocket interest expense, or using its own funds. The second option generates an opportunity cost resulting from the interest revenue that could have been earned if these funds were not being used to finance the inventory.

To address this potential cash flow problem, many of the winemakers in Bordeaux offer some of their wines for sale as "futures." That means the wines are purchased and paid for while they are still aging in barrels in France. Selling wine as futures reduces the time inventory must be financed from four years to only one to two years. Of course there are other types of costs in such deals. For one, the wines must be offered at lower prices than they are expected to sell for upon release. The winemakers have obviously decided this cost is less than the cost of financing inventory through borrowed money, or they would not do it.

Companies in other industries use similar techniques to speed up cash flow, such as factoring of accounts receivable. A major reason entities prepare cash budgets is to be sure they will have enough cash on hand to pay bills as they come due. If the budget indicates a temporary cash flow deficit, action must be taken to avoid the problem, and new budgets must be prepared based on these options. Budgeting is not a static process.

Pro Forma Financial Statement Data

The Pro Forma Data column in the sales budget displays two figures HH will report on the quarter-end (December 31) budgeted financial statements. Since HH expects to collect December credit sales in January, the *accounts receivable balance* will be $172,800 on the December 31, pro forma balance sheet (shown later in Exhibit 7.7).

The $582,400 of *sales revenue* in the Pro Forma Data column will be reported on the budgeted income statement for the quarter (shown later in Exhibit 7.6). The sales revenue represents the sum of October, November, and December sales ($160,000 + $192,000 + $230,400 = $582,400).

Inventory Purchases Budget

The inventory purchases budget shows the amount of inventory HH must purchase each month to satisfy the demand projected in the sales budget. The *total inventory needed* each month equals the amount of inventory HH plans to sell that month plus the amount of inventory HH wants on hand at month-end. To the extent that total inventory needed exceeds the inventory on hand at the beginning of the month, HH will need to purchase additional inventory. The amount of inventory to purchase is computed as follows:

Prepare an inventory purchases budget and related schedule of cash payments.

Cost of budgeted sales	XXX
Plus: Desired ending inventory	XXX
Total inventory needed	XXX
Less: Beginning inventory	(XXX)
Required purchases	XXX

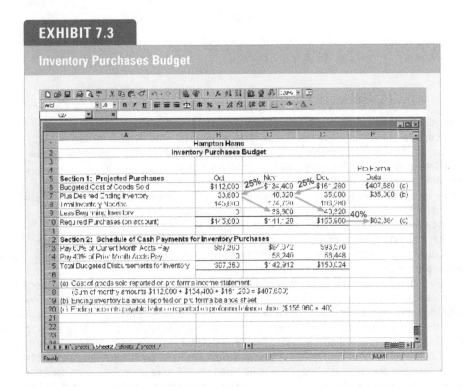

EXHIBIT 7.3

Inventory Purchases Budget

It is HH's policy to maintain an ending inventory equal to 25 percent of the next month's *projected cost of goods sold.* HH's cost of goods sold normally equals 70 percent of *sales.* Using this information and the sales budget, the accounting department prepared the inventory purchases budget shown in Exhibit 7.3.

Section 1 of the inventory purchases budget shows required purchases for each month. HH determined *budgeted cost of goods sold* for October by multiplying October *budgeted sales* by 70 percent ($160,000 × 0.70 = $112,000). Budgeted cost of goods sold for November and December were similarly computed. The October *desired ending inventory* was computed by multiplying November *budgeted cost of goods sold* by 25 percent ($134,400 × 0.25 = $33,600). Desired ending inventory for November is $40,320 ($161,280 × .25). Desired ending inventory for December is based on January projected cost of goods sold (not shown in the exhibit). HH expects ham sales to decline after the winter holidays. Because January projected cost of goods sold is only $140,000, the December desired ending inventory falls to $35,000 ($140,000 × .25).

Schedule of Cash Payments for Inventory Purchases

Section 2 is the schedule of cash payments for inventory purchases. HH makes all inventory purchases on account. The supplier requires that HH pay for 60 percent of inventory purchases in the month goods are purchased. HH pays the remaining 40 percent the month after purchase.

Cash payments are projected as follows (amounts are rounded to the nearest whole dollar):

■ October cash payments for inventory are $87,360. Because the new store opens in October, no accounts payable balance from September remains to be paid in October. Cash payments for October equal 60 percent of October inventory purchases.

■ November cash payments for inventory are $142,912 (40 percent of October purchases + 60 percent of November purchases).

■ December cash payments for inventory are $150,024 (40 percent of November purchases + 60 percent of December purchases).

Pro Forma Financial Statement Data

The Pro Forma Data column in the inventory purchases budget displays three figures HH will report on the quarter-end budgeted financial statements. The $407,680 *cost of goods sold* reported on the pro forma income statement (shown later in Exhibit 7.6) is the sum of the monthly cost of goods sold amounts ($112,000 + $134,400 + $161,280 = $407,680).

The $35,000 *ending inventory* as of December 31 is reported on the pro forma balance sheet (shown later in Exhibit 7.7). December 31 is the last day of both the month of December and the three-month quarter represented by October, November, and December.

The $62,384 of *accounts payable* reported on the pro forma balance sheet (shown later in Exhibit 7.7) represents the 40 percent of December inventory purchases HH will pay for in January ($155,960 × .40).

✓ CHECK YOURSELF 7.1

Main Street Sales Company purchased $80,000 of inventory during June. Purchases are expected to increase by 2 percent per month in each of the next three months. Main Street makes all purchases on account. It normally pays cash to settle 70 percent of its accounts payable during the month of purchase and settles the remaining 30 percent in the month following purchase. Based on this information, determine the accounts payable balance Main Street would report on its July 31 balance sheet.

Answer   Purchases for the month of July are expected to be $81,600 ($80,000 × 1.02). Main Street will pay 70 percent of the resulting accounts payable in cash during July. The remaining 30 percent represents the expected balance in accounts payable as of July 31. Therefore, the balance would be $24,480 ($81,600 × 0.3).

Selling and Administrative Expense Budget

Section 1 of Exhibit 7.4 shows the selling and administrative (S&A) expense budget for Hampton Hams' new store. Most of the projected expenses are self-explanatory; depreciation and interest, however, merit comment. The depreciation expense is based on projections in the *capital expenditures budget*. Although not presented in this chapter, the capital budget calls for the cash purchase of $130,000 of store fixtures. The fixtures were purchased on October 1. The supplier allows a 30-day inspection period. As a result, payment for the fixtures was made at the end of October. The fixtures are expected to have a useful life of 10 years and a $10,000 salvage value. Using the straight-line method, HH estimates annual depreciation expense at $12,000 ([$130,000 − $10,000] ÷ 10). Monthly depreciation expense is $1,000 ($12,000 annual charge ÷ 12 months).

Interest expense is missing from the S&A expense budget. HH cannot estimate interest expense until it completes its borrowing projections. Expected borrowing (financing activities) and related interest expense are shown in the **cash budget.**

Schedule of Cash Payments for Selling and Administrative Expenses

Section 2 of the S&A expense budget shows the schedule of cash payments. There are several differences between the S&A expenses recognized on the pro forma income statement and the cash payments for S&A expenses. First, Hampton Hams' pays sales commissions and utilities expense the month following their incurrence. Since the store opens in October there are no payments due from September. Cash payments for sales commissions and utilities in October are zero. In November, HH will pay the October expenses for these items and in December it will pay the November sales commissions and utilities expenses. Depreciation expense does not affect the cash payments schedule.

LO 5

Prepare a selling and administrative expense budget and related schedule of cash payments.

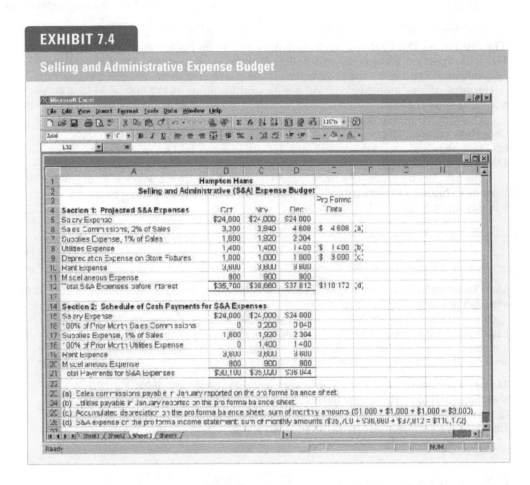

EXHIBIT 7.4

Selling and Administrative Expense Budget

The cash outflow for the store fixtures occurs when the assets are purchased, not when they are depreciated. The cost of the investment in store fixtures is in the cash budget, not in the cash outflow for S&A expenses.

Pro Forma Financial Statement Data

The Pro Forma Data column of the S&A expense budget displays four figures HH will report on the quarter-end budgeted financial statements. The first and second figures are the sales commissions payable ($4,608) and utilities payable ($1,400) on the pro forma balance sheet in Exhibit 7.7. Because December sales commissions and utilities expense are not paid until January, these amounts represent liabilities as of December 31. The third figure in the column ($3,000) is the amount of accumulated depreciation on the pro forma balance sheet in Exhibit 7.7. Since depreciation accumulates, the $3,000 balance is the sum of the monthly depreciation amounts ($1,000 + $1,000 + $1,000 = $3,000). The final figure in the Pro Forma Data column ($110,172) is the total S&A expenses reported on the pro forma income statement in Exhibit 7.6. The total S&A expense is the sum of the monthly amounts ($35,700 + $36,660 + 37,812 = $110,172).

Cash Budget

Little is more important to business success than effective cash management. If a company experiences cash shortages, it will be unable to pay its debts and may be forced into bankruptcy. If excess cash accumulates, a business loses the opportunity to earn investment income or reduce interest costs by repaying debt. Preparing a **cash budget** alerts management to anticipated cash shortages or excess cash balances. Management

LO 6

Prepare a cash budget.

EXHIBIT 7.5

Cash Budget

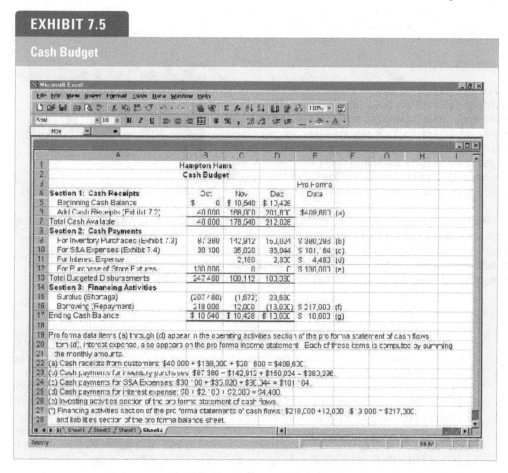

can plan financing activities, making advance arrangements to cover anticipated shortages by borrowing and planning to repay past borrowings and make appropriate investments when excess cash is expected.

The cash budget is divided into three major sections: (1) a cash receipts section, (2) a cash payments section, and (3) a financing section. Much of the data needed to prepare the cash budget are included in the cash receipts and payments schedules previously discussed; however, further refinements to project financing needs and interest costs are sometimes necessary. The completed cash budget is shown in Exhibit 7.5.

Cash Receipts Section

The total cash available (Exhibit 7.5, row 7) is determined by adding the beginning cash balance to the cash receipts from customers. There is no beginning cash balance in October because the new store is opening that month. The November beginning cash balance is the October ending cash balance. The December beginning cash balance is the November ending cash balance. Cash receipts from customers comes from the *schedule of cash receipts* in the sales budget (Exhibit 7.2, section 2, row 13).

Cash Payments Section

Cash payments include expected cash outflows for inventory purchases, S&A expenses, interest expense, and investments. The cash payments for inventory purchases comes from the *schedule of cash payments for inventory purchases* (Exhibit 7.3, section 2, row 15). The cash payments for S&A expenses comes from the *schedule of cash payments for S&A expenses* (Exhibit 7.4, section 2, row 21).

REALITY BYTES

BUDGETING IN GOVERNMENTAL ENTITIES

This chapter has presented several reasons organizations should prepare budgets, but for governmental entities, budgets are not simply good planning tools—law requires them. If a manager at a commercial enterprise does not accomplish the budget objectives established for his or her part of the business, the manager may receive a poor performance evaluation. At worst, they may be fired. If managers of governmental agencies spend more than their budgets allow, they may have broken the law. In some cases the manager could be required to personally repay the amount by which

the budget was exceeded. Since governmental budgets are enacted by the relevant elected bodies, to violate the budget is to break the law.

   Because budgets are so important for governments and are not to be exceeded, government accounting practices require that budgeted amounts be formally entered into the bookkeeping system. As you learned in your first course of accounting, companies do not make formal accounting entries when they order goods; they only make an entry when the goods are received. Governmental accounting systems are different. Each time goods or services are ordered by a government, an "encumbrance" is recorded against the budgeted amount so that agencies do not commit to spend more money than their budgets allow.

HH borrows or repays principal and pays interest on the last day of each month. The cash payments for interest are determined by multiplying the loan balance for the month by the monthly interest rate. Since there is no outstanding debt during October, there is no interest payment at the end of October. HH expects outstanding debt of $218,000 during the month of November. The bank charges interest at the rate of 12 percent per year, or 1 percent per month. The November interest expense and cash payment for interest is $2,180 ($218,000 × .01). The outstanding loan balance during December is $230,000. The December interest expense and cash payment for interest is $2,300 ($230,000 × .01). Determining the amount to borrow or repay at the end of each month is discussed in more detail in the next section of the text.

   Finally, the cash payment for the store fixtures comes from the *capital expenditures budget* (not shown in this chapter).

Financing Section

HH has a line of credit under which it can borrow or repay principal in increments of $1,000 at the end of each month as needed. HH desires to maintain an ending cash balance of at least $10,000 each month. With the $207,460 projected cash shortage in row 15 of the cash budget ($40,000 cash balance in row 7 less $247,460 budgeted cash payments in row 13), HH must borrow $218,000 on October 31 to maintain an ending cash balance of at least $10,000. This $218,000 balance is outstanding during November. On November 30, HH must borrow an additional $12,000 to cover the November projected cash shortage of $1,572 plus the $10,000 desired ending cash balance. HH projects a surplus of $23,660 for the month of December. This surplus will allow HH to repay $13,000 of debt and still maintain the desired $10,000 cash balance.

Pro Forma Financial Statement Data

Figures in the Pro Forma Data column of the cash budget (Exhibit 7.5) are alphabetically referenced. The cash receipts from customers, item (a), and the cash payment items (b), (c), and (d) are reported in the operating activities section of the pro forma statement of cash flows (Exhibit 7.8). The interest expense, item (d), is also reported on the pro forma income statement (Exhibit 7.6). The figures are determined by summing the monthly amounts. The $130,000 purchase of store fixtures, item (e), is reported in the investing activities section of the pro forma statement of cash flows. The $217,000 net borrowings, item (f), is reported in the financing activities section of the pro forma statement of cash flows (Exhibit 7.8) and also as a liability on the pro forma balance sheet (Exhibit 7.7). The $10,660 ending cash balance, item (g), is reported as the ending balance on the pro forma statement of cash flows and as an asset on the pro forma balance sheet.

✓ CHECK YOURSELF 7.2

Astor Company expects to incur the following operating expenses during September: Salary Expense, $25,000; Utility Expense, $1,200; Depreciation Expense, $5,400; and Selling Expense, $14,000. In general, it pays operating expenses in cash in the month in which it incurs them. Based on this information alone, determine the total amount of cash outflow Astor would report in the Operating Activities section of the pro forma statement of cash flows.

Answer　Depreciation is not included in cash outflows because companies do not pay cash when they recognize depreciation expense. The total cash outflow is $40,200 ($25,000 + $1,200 + $14,000).

Pro Forma Income Statement

Exhibit 7.6 shows the budgeted income statement for Hampton Hams' new store. The figures for this statement come from Exhibits 7.2, 7.3, 7.4, and 7.5. The budgeted income statement provides an advance estimate of the new store's expected profitability. If expected profitability is unsatisfactory, management could decide to abandon the project or modify planned activity. Perhaps HH could lease less costly store space, pay employees a lower rate, or reduce the number of employees hired. The pricing strategy could also be examined for possible changes.

Budgets are usually prepared using spreadsheets or computerized mathematical models that allow managers to easily undertake "what-if" analysis. What if the growth rate differs from expectations? What if interest rates increase or decrease? Exhibits 7.2 through 7.5 in this chapter were prepared using Microsoft Excel. When variables such as growth rate, collection assumptions, or interest rates are changed, the spreadsheet software instantly recalculates the budgets. Although managers remain responsible for data analysis and decision making, computer technology offers powerful tools to assist in those tasks.

LO 7

Prepare a pro forma income statement, balance sheet, and statement of cash flows.

EXHIBIT 7.6

HAMPTON HAMS
Pro Forma Income Statement
For the Quarter Ending December 31

		Data Source
Sales revenue	$ 582,400	Exhibit 7.2
Cost of goods sold	(407,680)	Exhibit 7.3
Gross margin	174,720	
Selling and administrative expenses	(110,172)	Exhibit 7.4
Operating income	64,548	
Interest expense	(4,480)	Exhibit 7.5
Net income	$ 60,068	

Pro Forma Balance Sheet

Most of the figures on the pro forma balance sheet in Exhibit 7.7 have been explained. The new store has no contributed capital because its operations will be financed through debt and retained earnings. The amount of retained earnings equals the amount of net income because no earnings from prior periods exist and no distributions are planned.

EXHIBIT 7.7

HAMPTON HAMS
Pro Forma Balance Sheet
As of the Quarter Ending December 31

			Data Source
Assets			
Cash		$ 10,660	Exhibit 7.5
Accounts receivable		172,800	Exhibit 7.2
Inventory		35,000	Exhibit 7.3
Store fixtures	$130,000		Exhibit 7.4 Discussion
Accumulated depreciation	(3,000)		Exhibit 7.4 Discussion
Book value of store fixtures		127,000	
Total assets		$345,460	
Liabilities			
Accounts payable		$ 62,384	Exhibit 7.3
Sales commissions payable		4,608	Exhibit 7.4
Utilities payable		1,400	Exhibit 7.4
Line of credit borrowings		217,000	Exhibit 7.5
Equity			
Retained earnings		60,068	
Total liabilities and equity		$345,460	

Pro Forma Statement of Cash Flows

Exhibit 7.8 shows the pro forma statement of cash flows. All information for this statement comes from the cash budget in Exhibit 7.5.

EXHIBIT 7.8

HAMPTON HAMS
Pro Forma Statement of Cash Flows
For the Quarter Ending December 31

Cash flow from operating activities		
Cash receipts from customers	$409,600	
Cash payments for inventory	(380,296)	
Cash payments for S&A expenses	(101,164)	
Cash payments for interest expense	(4,480)	
Net cash flow for operating activities		$ (76,340)
Cash flow from investing activities		
Cash outflow to purchase fixtures		(130,000)
Cash flow from financing activities		
Inflow from borrowing on line of credit		217,000
Net change in cash		10,660
Plus beginning cash balance		0
Ending cash balance		$ 10,660

Answers to The Curious Accountant

Budget preparation at the USOC is complicated by the fact that the timing of its revenues does not match the timing of its expenditures. The USOC spends a lot of money helping to train athletes for the United States Olympic team. Training takes place year-round, every year, for many athletes. The USOC's training facilities in Colorado must also be maintained continuously.

Conversely, much of the USOC's revenues are earned in big batches, received every two years. This money comes from fees the USOC receives for the rights to broadcast the Olympic games on television in the United States. Most companies have a one-year budget cycle during which they attempt to anticipate the coming year's revenues and expenses. This model would not work well for the USOC. For example, in 2008, a year of summer Olympics, the USOC reported revenues of $201.7 million and a deficit of $30.6 million. In 2007, a year with no Olympic games, the USOC reported revenues of $146.1 million and a deficit of $35.0 million. In 2006, a year of winter games, the USOC had revenues of $239.7 million and a surplus of $74.9 million.

Every business, like every family, faces its own set of circumstances. Those individuals responsible for preparing an entity's budget must have a thorough understanding of the environment in which the entity operates. This is the reason the budget process must be participatory if it is to be successful. No one person, or small group, can anticipate all the issues that will face a large organization in the coming budget period; they need input from employees at all levels.

Source: Form 990s filed by the USOC with the IRS.

✓ CHECK YOURSELF 7.3

How do pro forma financial statements differ from the financial statements presented in a company's annual report to stockholders?

Answer Pro forma financial statements are based on estimates and projections about business events that a company expects to occur in the future. The financial statements presented in a company's annual report to stockholders are based on historical events that occurred prior to the preparation of the statements.

A Look Back

The planning of financial matters is called *budgeting*. The degree of detail in a company's budget depends on the budget period. Generally, the shorter the time period, the more specific the plans. *Strategic planning* involves long-term plans, such as the overall objectives of the business. Examples of strategic planning include which products to manufacture and sell and which market niches to pursue. Strategic plans are stated in broad, descriptive terms. Capital budgeting deals with intermediate investment planning. *Operations budgeting* focuses on short-term plans and is used to create the master budget.

A budgeting committee is responsible for consolidating numerous departmental budgets into a master budget for the whole company. The *master budget* has detailed objectives stated in specific amounts; it describes how management intends to achieve its objectives. The master budget usually covers one year. Budgeting supports planning, coordination, performance measurement, and corrective action.

Employees may be uncomfortable with budgets, which can be constraining. Budgets set standards by which performance is evaluated. To establish an effective budget system, management should recognize the effect on human behavior of budgeting. Upper-level management must set a positive atmosphere by taking budgets seriously and avoiding using them to humiliate subordinates. One way to create the proper atmosphere is to encourage subordinates' participation in the budgeting process; *participative budgeting* can lead to goals that are more realistic about what can be accomplished and to establish a team effort in trying to reach those goals.

The primary components of the master budget are the *operating budgets,* the *capital budgets,* and the *pro forma financial statements.* The budgeting process begins with preparing the operating budgets, which consist of detailed schedules and budgets prepared by various company departments. The first operating budget to be prepared is the sales budget. The detailed operating budgets for inventory purchases and S&A expenses are based on the projected sales from the sales budget. The information in the schedules of cash receipts (prepared in conjunction with the sales budget) and cash payments (prepared in conjunction with the inventory purchases and S&A expense budgets) is used in preparing the cash budget. The cash budget subtracts cash payments from cash receipts; the resulting cash surplus or shortage determines the company's financing activities.

The capital budget describes the company's long-term plans regarding investments in facilities, equipment, new products, or other lines of business. The information from the capital budget is used as input to several of the operating budgets.

The pro forma financial statements are prepared from information in the operating budgets. The operating budgets for sales, inventory purchases, and S&A expenses contain information that is used to prepare the income statement and balance sheet. The cash budget includes the amount of interest expense reported on the income statement, the ending cash balance, the capital acquisitions reported on the balance sheet, and most of the information included in the statement of cash flows.

>> A Look Forward

Once a company has completed its budget, it has defined its plans. Then the plans must be followed. The next chapter investigates the techniques used to evaluate performance. You will learn to compare actual results to budgets, to calculate variances, and to identify the parties who are normally accountable for deviations from expectations. Finally, you will learn about the human impact management must consider in taking corrective action when employees fail to accomplish budget goals.

A step-by-step audio-narrated series of slides is provided on the text website at www.mhhe.com/edmonds2011.

SELF-STUDY REVIEW PROBLEM

The Getaway Gift Company operates a chain of small gift shops that are located in prime vacation towns. Getaway is considering opening a new store on January 1, 2012. Getaway's president recently attended a business seminar that explained how formal budgets could be useful in judging the new store's likelihood of succeeding. Assume you are the company's accountant. The president has asked you to explain the budgeting process and to provide sample reports that show the new store's operating expectations for the first three months (January, February, and March). Respond to the following specific requirements:

Required

a. List the operating budgets and schedules included in a master budget.

b. Explain the difference between pro forma financial statements and the financial statements presented in a company's annual reports to shareholders.

c. Prepare a sample sales budget and a schedule of expected cash receipts using the following assumptions. Getaway estimates January sales will be $400,000 of which $100,000 will be cash and $300,000 will be credit. The ratio of cash sales to sales on account is expected to remain constant over the three-month period. The company expects sales to increase 10 percent per month. The company expects to collect 100 percent of the accounts receivable generated by credit sales in the month following the sale. Use this information to determine the amount of accounts receivable that Getaway would report on the March 31 pro forma balance sheet and the amount of sales it would report on the first quarter pro forma income statement.

d. Prepare a sample inventory purchases budget using the following assumptions. Cost of goods sold is 60 percent of sales. The company desires to maintain a minimum ending inventory equal to 25 percent of the following month's cost of goods sold. Getaway makes all inventory purchases on account. The company pays 70 percent of accounts payable in the month of purchase. It pays the remaining 30 percent in the following month. Prepare a schedule of expected cash payments for inventory purchases. Use this information to determine the amount of cost of goods sold Getaway would report on the first quarter pro forma income statement and the amounts of ending inventory and accounts payable it would report on the March 31 pro forma balance sheet.

Solution to Requirement a

A master budget would include (1) a sales budget and schedule of cash receipts, (2) an inventory purchases budget and schedule of cash payments for inventory, (3) a general, selling, and administrative expenses budget and a schedule of cash payments related to these expenses, and (4) a cash budget.

Solution to Requirement b

Pro forma statements result from the operating budgets listed in the response to Requirement *a*. Pro forma statements describe the results of expected future events. In contrast, the financial statements presented in a company's annual report reflect the results of events that have actually occurred in the past.

Solution to Requirement c

General Information				
Sales growth rate 10%				**Pro Forma Statement Data**
Sales Budget	January	February	March	
Sales				
Cash sales	$100,000	$110,000	$121,000	
Sales on account	300,000	330,000	363,000	$ 363,000*
Total sales	$400,000	$440,000	$484,000	$1,324,000†
Schedule of Cash Receipts				
Current cash sales	$100,000	$110,000	$121,000	
Plus 100% of previous month's credit sales	0	300,000	330,000	
Total budgeted collections	$100,000	$410,000	$451,000	

*Ending accounts receivable balance reported on March 31 pro forma balance sheet.

†Sales revenue reported on first quarter pro forma income statement (sum of monthly sales).

Solution to Requirement d

General Information				
Cost of goods sold percentage 60%				**Pro Forma**
Desired ending inventory percentage of CGS 25%				**Statement Data**
Inventory Purchases Budget	**January**	**February**	**March**	
Budgeted cost of goods sold	$240,000	$264,000	$290,400	$794,400*
Plus: Desired ending inventory	66,000	72,600	79,860	79,860†
Inventory needed	306,000	336,600	370,260	
Less: Beginning inventory	0	(66,000)	(72,600)	
Required purchases	$306,000	$270,600	$297,660	89,298‡
Schedule of Cash Payments for Inventory Purchases				
70% of current purchases	$214,200	$189,420	$208,362	
30% of prior month's purchases	0	91,800	81,180	
Total budgeted payments for inventory	$214,200	$281,220	$289,542	

*Cost of goods sold reported on first quarter pro forma income statement (sum of monthly amounts).
†Ending inventory balance reported on March 31 pro forma balance sheet.
‡Ending accounts payable balance reported on pro forma balance sheet ($297,660 × 0.3).

KEY TERMS

Budgeting 304	**Operating budgets** 306	**Pro forma financial**
Capital budget 308	**Operations budgeting** 306	**statements** 308
Capital budgeting 306	**Participative budgeting** 308	**Strategic planning** 306
Cash budget 313	**Perpetual (continuous)**	
Master budget 308	**budgeting** 306	

QUESTIONS

1. Budgets are useful only for small companies that can estimate sales with accuracy. Do you agree with this statement?

2. Why does preparing the master budget require a committee?

3. What are the three levels of planning? Explain each briefly.

4. What is the primary factor that distinguishes the three different levels of planning from each other?

5. What is the advantage of using a perpetual budget instead of the traditional annual budget?

6. What are the advantages of budgeting?

7. How may budgets be used as a measure of performance?

8. Ken Shilov, manager of the marketing department, tells you that "budgeting simply does not work." He says that he made budgets for his employees and when he reprimanded them for failing to accomplish budget goals, he got unfounded excuses. Suggest how Mr. Shilov could encourage employee cooperation.

9. What is a master budget?

10. What is the normal starting point in developing the master budget?

11. How does the level of inventory affect the production budget? Why is it important to manage the level of inventory?

12. What are the components of the cash budget? Describe each.

13. The primary reason for preparing a cash budget is to determine the amount of cash to include on the budgeted balance sheet. Do you agree or disagree with this statement? Explain.

14. What information does the pro forma income statement provide? How does its preparation depend on the operating budgets?

15. How does the pro forma statement of cash flows differ from the cash budget?

MULTIPLE-CHOICE QUESTIONS

Multiple-choice questions are provided on the text website at www.mhhe.com/edmonds2011.

EXERCISES—SERIES A

All applicable Exercises in Series A are available with McGraw-Hill's *Connect Accounting*.

Exercise 7-1A *Budget responsibility* **LO 1, 2**

Sonya Huffman, the accountant, is a perfectionist. No one can do the job as well as she can. Indeed, she has found budget information provided by the various departments to be worthless. She must change everything they give her. She has to admit that her estimates have not always been accurate, but she shudders to think of what would happen if she used the information supplied by the marketing and operating departments. No one seems to care about accuracy. Indeed, some of the marketing staff have even become insulting. When Ms. Huffman confronted one of the salesmen with the fact that he was behind in meeting his budgeted sales forecast, he responded by saying, "They're your numbers. Why don't you go out and make the sales? It's a heck of a lot easier to sit there in your office and make up numbers than it is to get out and get the real work done." Ms. Huffman reported the incident, but, of course, nothing was done about it.

Required

Write a short report suggesting how the budgeting process could be improved.

Exercise 7-2A *Preparing a sales budget* **LO 3, 7**

Welch Company, which expects to start operations on January 1, 2011, will sell digital cameras in shopping malls. Welch has budgeted sales as indicated in the following table. The company expects a 10 percent increase in sales per month for February and March. The ratio of cash sales to sales on account will remain stable from January through March.

Sales	January	February	March
Cash sales	$ 40,000	?	?
Sales on account	100,000	?	?
Total budgeted sales	$140,000	?	?

Required

a. Complete the sales budget by filling in the missing amounts.
b. Determine the amount of sales revenue Welch will report on its first quarter pro forma income statement.

Exercise 7-3A *Preparing a schedule of cash receipts* **LO 3, 7**

The budget director of Ginger's Florist has prepared the following sales budget. The company had $300,000 in accounts receivable on July 1. Ginger's Florist normally collects 100 percent of accounts receivable in the month following the month of sale.

	July	August	September
Sales Budget			
Cash sales	$ 70,000	$ 75,000	$ 80,000
Sales on account	90,000	108,000	129,600
Total budgeted sales	$160,000	$183,000	$209,600
Schedule of Cash Receipts			
Current cash sales	?	?	?
Plus: Collections from accounts receivable	?	?	?
Total budgeted collections	$370,000	$165,000	$188,000

Required

a. Complete the schedule of cash receipts by filling in the missing amounts.

b. Determine the amount of accounts receivable the company will report on its third quarter pro forma balance sheet.

LO 3

Exercise 7-4A *Preparing sales budgets with different assumptions*

Applebaum Corporation, which has three divisions, is preparing its sales budget. Each division expects a different growth rate because economic conditions vary in different regions of the country. The growth expectations per quarter are 4 percent for East Division, 2 percent for West Division, and 6 percent for South Division.

Division	First Quarter	Second Quarter	Third Quarter	Fourth Quarter
East Division	$100,000	?	?	?
West Division	300,000	?	?	?
South Division	200,000	?	?	?

Required

a. Complete the sales budget by filling in the missing amounts. (Round figures to the nearest dollar.)

b. Determine the amount of sales revenue that the company will report on its quarterly pro forma income statements.

LO 3

Exercise 7-5A *Determining cash receipts from accounts receivable*

Janice's Dress Delivery operates a mail-order business that sells clothes designed for frequent travelers. It had sales of $560,000 in December. Because Janice's Dress Delivery is in the mail-order business, all sales are made on account. The company expects a 30 percent drop in sales for January. The balance in the Accounts Receivable account on December 31 was $96,400 and is budgeted to be $73,600 as of January 31. Janice's Dress Delivery normally collects accounts receivable in the month following the month of sale.

Required

a. Determine the amount of cash Janice's Dress Delivery expects to collect from accounts receivable during January.

b. Is it reasonable to assume that sales will decline in January for this type of business? Why or why not?

LO 3

Exercise 7-6A *Using judgment in making a sales forecast*

Contrell Company operates a candy store located in a large shopping mall.

Required

Write a brief memo describing the sales pattern that you would expect Contrell to experience during the year. In which months will sales likely be high? In which months will sales likely be low? Explain why.

LO 4

Exercise 7-7A *Preparing an inventory purchases budget*

Naftel Company sells lamps and other lighting fixtures. The purchasing department manager prepared the following inventory purchases budget. Naftel's policy is to maintain an ending inventory balance equal to 10 percent of the following month's cost of goods sold. April's budgeted cost of goods sold is $75,000.

	January	February	March
Budgeted cost of goods sold	$50,000	$54,000	$60,000
Plus: Desired ending inventory	5,400	?	?
Inventory needed	55,400	?	?
Less: Beginning inventory	5,000	?	?
Required purchases (on account)	$50,400	?	?

Required

a. Complete the inventory purchases budget by filling in the missing amounts.

b. Determine the amount of cost of goods sold the company will report on its first quarter pro forma income statement.

c. Determine the amount of ending inventory the company will report on its pro forma balance sheet at the end of the first quarter.

Exercise 7-8A   *Preparing a schedule of cash payments for inventory purchases*   LO 4

Sciara Books buys books and magazines directly from publishers and distributes them to grocery stores. The wholesaler expects to purchase the following inventory.

	April	May	June
Required purchases (on account)	$100,000	$120,000	$132,000

Sciara Books' accountant prepared the following schedule of cash payments for inventory purchases. Sciara Books' suppliers require that 90 percent of purchases on account be paid in the month of purchase; the remaining 10 percent are paid in the month following the month of purchase.

Schedule of Cash Payments for Inventory Purchases

	April	May	June
Payment for current accounts payable	$90,000	?	?
Payment for previous accounts payable	8,000	?	?
Total budgeted payments for inventory	$98,000	?	?

Required

a. Complete the schedule of cash payments for inventory purchases by filling in the missing amounts.

b. Determine the amount of accounts payable the company will report on its pro forma balance sheet at the end of the second quarter.

Exercise 7-9A   *Determining the amount of expected inventory purchases and cash payments*   LO 4

Tobert Company, which sells electric razors, had $300,000 of cost of goods sold during the month of June. The company projects a 5 percent increase in cost of goods sold during July. The inventory balance as of June 30 is $28,000, and the desired ending inventory balance for July is $29,000. Tobert pays cash to settle 70 percent of its purchases on account during the month of purchase and pays the remaining 30 percent in the month following the purchase. The accounts payable balance as of June 30 was $35,000.

Required

a. Determine the amount of purchases budgeted for July.

b. Determine the amount of cash payments budgeted for inventory purchases in July.

Exercise 7-10A   *Preparing a schedule of cash payments for selling and administrative expenses*   LO 5

The budget director for Metro Cleaning Services prepared the following list of expected selling and administrative expenses. All expenses requiring cash payments are paid for in the month incurred except salary expense and insurance. Salary is paid in the month following the month in which it is incurred. The insurance premium for six months is paid on October 1. October is the first month of operations; accordingly, there are no beginning account balances.

	October	November	December
Budgeted S&A Expenses			
Equipment lease expense	$ 6,000	$ 6,000	$ 6,000
Salary expense	6,100	6,600	7,000
Cleaning supplies	2,800	2,730	3,066
Insurance expense	1,200	1,200	1,200
Depreciation on computer	1,800	1,800	1,800
Rent	1,700	1,700	1,700
Miscellaneous expenses	700	700	700
Total operating expenses	$20,300	$20,730	$21,466
Schedule of Cash Payments for S&A Expenses			
Equipment lease expense	?	?	?
Prior month's salary expense, 100%	?	?	?
Cleaning supplies	?	?	?
Insurance premium	?	?	?
Depreciation on computer	?	?	?
Rent	?	?	?
Miscellaneous expenses	?	?	?
Total disbursements for operating expenses	$18,400	$17,230	$18,066

Required

a. Complete the schedule of cash payments for S&A expenses by filling in the missing amounts.

b. Determine the amount of salaries payable the company will report on its pro forma balance sheet at the end of the fourth quarter.

c. Determine the amount of prepaid insurance the company will report on its pro forma balance sheet at the end of the fourth quarter.

LO 4

Exercise 7-11A *Preparing inventory purchases budgets with different assumptions*

Executive officers of Dominick Company are wrestling with their budget for the next year. The following are two different sales estimates provided by two difference sources.

Source of Estimate	First Quarter	Second Quarter	Third Quarter	Fourth Quarter
Sales manager	$380,000	$310,000	$280,000	$480,000
Marketing consultant	520,000	460,000	410,000	650,000

Dominick's past experience indicates that cost of goods sold is about 60 percent of sales revenue. The company tries to maintain 10 percent of the next quarter's expected cost of goods sold as the current quarter's ending inventory. This year's ending inventory is $29,000. Next year's ending inventory is budgeted to be $30,000.

Required

a. Prepare an inventory purchases budget using the sales manager's estimate.

b. Prepare an inventory purchases budget using the marketing consultant's estimate.

LO 5, 7

Exercise 7-12A *Determining the amount of cash payments and pro forma statement data for selling and administrative expenses*

January budgeted selling and administrative expenses for the retail shoe store that Kathy Sibley plans to open on January 1, 2011, are as follows: sales commissions, $25,000; rent, $16,000; utilities, $5,000; depreciation, $4,000; and miscellaneous, $2,000. Utilities are paid in the month after incurrence. Other expenses are expected to be paid in cash in the month in which they are incurred.

Required

a. Determine the amount of budgeted cash payments for January selling and administrative expenses.

b. Determine the amount of utilities payable the store will report on the January 31st pro forma balance sheet.

c. Determine the amount of depreciation expense the store will report on the income statement for the year 2011, assuming that monthly depreciation remains the same for the entire year.

Exercise 7-13A   *Preparing a cash budget*   LO 6, 7

The accountant for Teresa's Dress Shop prepared the following cash budget. Teresa's desires to maintain a cash cushion of $14,000 at the end of each month. Funds are assumed to be borrowed and repaid on the last day of each month. Interest is charged at the rate of 2 percent per month.

Cash Budget	July	August	September
Section 1: Cash receipts			
Beginning cash balance	$ 42,500	$?	$?
Add cash receipts	180,000	200,000	240,600
Total cash available (a)	222,500	?	?
Section 2: Cash payments			
For inventory purchases	165,526	140,230	174,152
For S&A expenses	54,500	60,560	61,432
For interest expense	0	?	?
Total budgeted disbursements (b)	220,026	?	?
Section 3: Financing activities			
Surplus (shortage)	2,474	?	?
Borrowing (repayments) (c)	11,526	?	?
Ending cash balance (a − b + c)	$ 14,000	$ 14,000	$ 14,000

Required

a. Complete the cash budget by filling in the missing amounts. Round all computations to the nearest whole dollar.

b. Determine the amount of net cash flows from operating activities Teresa's will report on the third quarter pro forma statement of cash flows.

c. Determine the amount of net cash flows from financing activities Teresa's will report on the third quarter pro forma statement of cash flows.

Exercise 7-14A   *Determining amount to borrow and pro forma statement balances*   LO 6, 7

Athena Sudsberry owns a small restaurant in New York City. Ms. Sudsberry provided her accountant with the following summary information regarding expectations for the month of June. The balance in accounts receivable as of May 31 is $60,000. Budgeted cash and credit sales for June are $150,000 and $600,000, respectively. Credit sales are made through Visa and MasterCard and are collected rapidly. Eighty percent of credit sales is collected in the month of sale, and the remainder is collected in the following month. Ms. Sudsberry's suppliers do not extend credit. Consequently, she pays suppliers on the last day of the month. Cash payments for June are expected to be $700,000. Ms. Sudsberry has a line of credit that enables the restaurant to borrow funds on demand; however, they must be borrowed on the last day of the month. Interest is paid in cash also on the last day of the month. Ms. Sudsberry desires to maintain a $30,000 cash balance before the interest payment. Her annual interest rate is 9 percent.

Required

a. Compute the amount of funds Ms. Sudsberry needs to borrow for June.

b. Determine the amount of interest expense the restaurant will report on the June pro forma income statement.

c. What amount will the restaurant report as interest expense on the July pro forma income statement?

LO 7

Exercise 7-15A   *Preparing pro forma income statements with different assumptions*

Norman Jelen, the controller of Wing Corporation, is trying to prepare a sales budget for the coming year. The income statements for the last four quarters follow.

	First Quarter	Second Quarter	Third Quarter	Fourth Quarter	Total
Sales revenue	$170,000	$200,000	$210,000	$260,000	$840,000
Cost of goods sold	102,000	120,000	126,000	156,000	504,000
Gross profit	68,000	80,000	84,000	104,000	336,000
Selling & admin. expenses	17,000	20,000	21,000	26,000	84,000
Net income	$ 51,000	$ 60,000	$ 63,000	$ 78,000	$252,000

Historically, cost of goods sold is about 60 percent of sales revenue. Selling and administrative expenses are about 10 percent of sales revenue.

Sam Wing, the chief executive officer, told Mr. Jelen that he expected sales next year to be 10 percent for each respective quarter above last year's level. However, Glenda Sullivan, the vice president of sales, told Mr. Jelen that she believed sales growth would be only 5 percent.

Required

a. Prepare a pro forma income statement including quarterly budgets for the coming year using Mr. Wing's estimate.

b. Prepare a pro forma income statement including quarterly budgets for the coming year using Ms. Sullivan's estimate.

c. Explain why two executive officers in the same company could have different estimates of future growth.

PROBLEMS—SERIES A

connect
[ACCOUNTING]

All applicable Problems in Series A are available with McGraw-Hill's *Connect Accounting.*

LO 3

Problem 7-16A   *Preparing a sales budget and schedule of cash receipts*

McCarty Pointers Corporation expects to begin operations on January 1, 2012; it will operate as a specialty sales company that sells laser pointers over the Internet. McCarty expects sales in January 2012 to total $200,000 and to increase 10 percent per month in February and March. All sales are on account. McCarty expects to collect 70 percent of accounts receivable in the month of sale, 20 percent in the month following the sale, and 10 percent in the second month following the sale.

Required

a. Prepare a sales budget for the first quarter of 2012.

b. Determine the amount of sales revenue McCarty will report on the first 2012 quarterly pro forma income statement.

c. Prepare a cash receipts schedule for the first quarter of 2012.

d. Determine the amount of accounts receivable as of March 31, 2012.

LO 4, 7

Problem 7-17A   *Preparing an inventory purchases budget and schedule of cash payments*

Spratt, Inc., sells fireworks. The company's marketing director developed the following cost of goods sold budget for April, May, June, and July.

	April	May	June	July
Budgeted cost of goods sold	$60,000	$70,000	$80,000	$86,000

Spratt had a beginning inventory balance of $3,600 on April 1 and a beginning balance in accounts payable of $14,800. The company desires to maintain an ending inventory balance equal to 10 percent of the next period's cost of goods sold. Spratt makes all purchases on account. The company pays 60 percent of accounts payable in the month of purchase and the remaining 40 percent in the month following purchase.

Required

a. Prepare an inventory purchases budget for April, May, and June.

b. Determine the amount of ending inventory Spratt will report on the end-of-quarter pro forma balance sheet.

c. Prepare a schedule of cash payments for inventory for April, May, and June.

d. Determine the balance in accounts payable Spratt will report on the end-of-quarter pro forma balance sheet.

Problem 7-18A   *Preparing pro forma income statements with different assumptions*

LO 7

Top executive officers of Zottoli Company, a merchandising firm, are preparing the next year's budget. The controller has provided everyone with the current year's projected income statement.

CHECK FIGURE
a. 12.75%

	Current Year
Sales revenue	$2,000,000
Cost of goods sold	1,400,000
Gross profit	600,000
Selling & admin. expenses	260,000
Net income	$ 340,000

Cost of goods sold is usually 70 percent of sales revenue, and selling and administrative expenses are usually 10 percent of sales plus a fixed cost of $60,000. The president has announced that the company's goal is to increase net income by 15 percent.

Required

The following items are independent of each other.

a. What percentage increase in sales would enable the company to reach its goal? Support your answer with a pro forma income statement.

b. The market may become stagnant next year, and the company does not expect an increase in sales revenue. The production manager believes that an improved production procedure can cut cost of goods sold by 2 percent. What else can the company do to reach its goal? Prepare a pro forma income statement illustrating your proposal.

c. The company decides to escalate its advertising campaign to boost consumer recognition, which will increase selling and administrative expenses to $340,000. With the increased advertising, the company expects sales revenue to increase by 15 percent. Assume that cost of goods sold remains a constant proportion of sales. Can the company reach its goal?

Problem 7-19A   *Preparing a schedule of cash payments for selling and administrative expenses*

LO 5, 6

Prestia is a retail company specializing in men's hats. Its budget director prepared the list of expected operating expenses that follows. All items are paid when incurred except sales commissions and utilities, which are paid in the month following their incurrence. July is the first month of operations, so there are no beginning account balances.

CHECK FIGURE
a. Sept: $28,510

	July	August	September
Salary expense	$18,000	$18,000	$18,000
Sales commissions (4 percent of sales)	1,700	1,700	1,700
Supplies expense	360	390	420
Utilities	1,100	1,100	1,100
Depreciation on store equipment	3,000	3,000	3,000
Rent	6,600	6,600	6,600
Miscellaneous	690	690	690
Total S&A expenses before interest	$31,450	$31,480	$31,510

Required

a. Prepare a schedule of cash payments for selling and administrative expenses.

b. Determine the amount of utilities payable as of September 30.

c. Determine the amount of sales commissions payable as of September 30.

LO 6

CHECK FIGURE
Feb. cash surplus before
financing activities: $7,010

Problem 7-20A   *Preparing a cash budget*

Kinnion Medical Clinic has budgeted the following cash flows.

	January	February	March
Cash receipts	$100,000	$106,000	$126,000
Cash payments			
For inventory purchases	90,000	72,000	85,000
For S&A expenses	31,000	32,000	27,000

Kinnion Medical had a cash balance of $8,000 on January 1. The company desires to maintain a cash cushion of $5,000. Funds are assumed to be borrowed, in increments of $1,000, and repaid on the last day of each month; the interest rate is 1 percent per month. Repayments may be made in any amount available. Kinnion pays its vendors on the last day of the month also. The company had a monthly $40,000 beginning balance in its line of credit liability account from this year's quarterly results.

Required

Prepare a cash budget. (Round all computations to the nearest whole dollar.)

LO 3, 4, 5

CHECK FIGURES
c. 1st QTR purchases for
peaches: $141,120
2nd QTR purchases for
oranges: $312,840

Problem 7-21A   *Preparing budgets with multiple products*

Hammond Fruits Corporation wholesales peaches and oranges. Lashanda King is working with the company's accountant to prepare next year's budget. Ms. King estimates that sales will increase 5 percent for peaches and 10 percent for oranges. The current year's sales revenue data follow.

	First Quarter	Second Quarter	Third Quarter	Fourth Quarter	Total
Peaches	$220,000	$240,000	$300,000	$240,000	$1,000,000
Oranges	400,000	450,000	570,000	380,000	1,800,000
Total	$620,000	$690,000	$870,000	$620,000	$2,800,000

Based on the company's past experience, cost of goods sold is usually 60 percent of sales revenue. Company policy is to keep 10 percent of the next period's estimated cost of goods sold as the current period's ending inventory. (*Hint:* Use the cost of goods sold for the first quarter to determine the beginning inventory for the first quarter.)

Required

a. Prepare the company's sales budget for the next year for each quarter by individual product.

b. If the selling and administrative expenses are estimated to be $700,000, prepare the company's budgeted annual income statement.

c. Ms. King estimates next year's ending inventory will be $34,000 for peaches and $56,000 for oranges. Prepare the company's inventory purchases budgets for the next year showing quarterly figures by product.

LO 3, 4, 5

excel

Problem 7-22A   *Preparing a master budget for retail company with no beginning account balances*

Patel Company is a retail company that specializes in selling outdoor camping equipment. The company is considering opening a new store on October 1, 2012. The company president formed a planning committee to prepare a master budget for the first three months of operation. As budget coordinator, you have been assigned the following tasks.

Required

a. October sales are estimated to be $120,000 of which 40 percent will be cash and 60 percent will be credit. The company expects sales to increase at the rate of 25 percent per month. Prepare a sales budget.

b. The company expects to collect 100 percent of the accounts receivable generated by credit sales in the month following the sale. Prepare a schedule of cash receipts.

c. The cost of goods sold is 60 percent of sales. The company desires to maintain a minimum ending inventory equal to 10 percent of the next month's cost of goods sold. However, ending inventory of December is expected to be $12,000. Assume that all purchases are made on account. Prepare an inventory purchases budget.

d. The company pays 70 percent of accounts payable in the month of purchase and the remaining 30 percent in the following month. Prepare a cash payments budget for inventory purchases.

e. Budgeted selling and administrative expenses per month follow.

Salary expense (fixed)	$18,000
Sales commissions	5 percent of Sales
Supplies expense	2 percent of Sales
Utilities (fixed)	$1,400
Depreciation on store fixtures (fixed)*	$4,000
Rent (fixed)	$4,800
Miscellaneous (fixed)	$1,200

*The capital expenditures budget indicates that Patel will spend $164,000 on October 1 for store fixtures, which are expected to have a $20,000 salvage value and a three-year (36-month) useful life.

Use this information to prepare a selling and administrative expenses budget.

f. Utilities and sales commissions are paid the month after they are incurred; all other expenses are paid in the month in which they are incurred. Prepare a cash payments budget for selling and administrative expenses.

g. Patel borrows funds, in increments of $1,000, and repays them on the last day of the month. Repayments may be made in any amount available. The company also pays its vendors on the last day of the month. It pays interest of 1 percent per month in cash on the last day of the month. To be prudent, the company desires to maintain a $12,000 cash cushion. Prepare a cash budget.

h. Prepare a pro forma income statement for the quarter.

i. Prepare a pro forma balance sheet at the end of the quarter.

j. Prepare a pro forma statement of cash flows for the quarter.

Problem 7-23A *Behavioral impact of budgeting*

LO 2

Shahid Corporation has three divisions, each operating as a responsibility center. To provide an incentive for divisional executive officers, the company gives divisional management a bonus equal to 15 percent of the excess of actual net income over budgeted net income. The following is Chaudhry Division's current year's performance.

	Current Year
Sales revenue	$4,000,000
Cost of goods sold	2,500,000
Gross profit	1,500,000
Selling & admin. expenses	900,000
Net income	$ 600,000

The president has just received next year's budget proposal from the vice president in charge of Chaudhry Division. The proposal budgets a 5 percent increase in sales revenue with an extensive explanation about stiff market competition. The president is puzzled. Chaudhry has enjoyed revenue growth of around 10 percent for each of the past five years. The president had consistently approved the division's budget proposals based on 5 percent growth in the past. This time, the president wants to show that he is not a fool. "I will impose a 15 percent revenue increase to teach them a lesson!" the president says to himself smugly.

Assume that cost of goods sold and selling and administrative expenses remain stable in proportion to sales.

Required

a. Prepare the budgeted income statement based on Chaudhry Division's proposal of a 5 percent increase.

b. If growth is actually 10 percent as usual, how much bonus would Chaudhry Division's executive officers receive if the president had approved the division's proposal?

c. Prepare the budgeted income statement based on the 15 percent increase the president imposed.

d. If the actual results turn out to be a 10 percent increase as usual, how much bonus would Chaudhry Division's executive officers receive since the president imposed a 15 percent increase?

e. Propose a better budgeting procedure for Shahid.

EXERCISES—SERIES B

LO 1, 2

Exercise 7-1B *Budget responsibility*

Bennia Judson, the controller of Mullins Industries, is very popular. He is easygoing and does not offend anybody. To develop the company's most recent budget, Mr. Judson first asked all department managers to prepare their own budgets. He then added together the totals from the department budgets to produce the company budget. When Lonnie Morgan, Mullins' president, reviewed the company budget, she sighed and asked, "Is our company a charitable organization?"

Required

Write a brief memo describing deficiencies in the budgeting process and suggesting improvements.

LO 3, 7

Exercise 7-2B *Preparing a sales budget*

Gardner Restaurant is opening for business in a new shopping center. Ed Rozell, the owner, is preparing a sales budget for the next three months. After consulting friends in the same business, Mr. Rozell estimated July revenues as shown in the following table. He expects revenues to increase 5 percent per month in August and September.

	July	August	September
Food sales	$40,000	?	?
Beverage and liquor sales	24,000	?	?
Total budgeted revenues	$64,000	?	?

Required

a. Complete the sales budget by filling in the missing amounts.

b. Determine the total amount of revenue Gardner Restaurant will report on its quarterly pro forma income statement.

LO 3, 7

Exercise 7-3B *Preparing a schedule of cash receipts*

Brown Imports, Inc., sells goods imported from the Far East. Using the second quarter's sales budget, Mark Yao is trying to complete the schedule of cash receipts for the quarter. The company had accounts receivable of $310,000 on April 1. Brown Imports normally collects 100 percent of accounts receivable in the month following the month of sale.

Sales	April	May	June
Sales Budget			
Cash sales	$120,000	$140,000	$150,000
Sales on account	480,000	568,000	500,000
Total budgeted sales	$600,000	$708,000	$650,000
Schedule of Cash Receipts			
Current cash sales	?	?	?
Plus: Collections from accounts receivable	?	?	?
Total budgeted collections	$410,000	$604,000	$704,000

Required

a. Help Mr. Yao complete the schedule of cash receipts by filling in the missing amounts.

b. Determine the amount of accounts receivable the company will report on the quarterly pro forma balance sheet.

Exercise 7-4B   *Preparing sales budgets with different assumptions*   LO 3

Lagrave International Company has three subsidiaries, Moore Trading Company, Pickrell Medical Supplies Company, and Rice Shipping Company. Because the subsidiaries operate in different industries, Lagrave's corporate budget for the coming year must reflect the different growth potentials of the individual industries. The growth expectations per quarter for the subsidiaries are 4 percent for Moore, 1 percent for Pickrell, and 3 percent for Rice.

Subsidiary	Current Quarter Sales	First Quarter	Second Quarter	Third Quarter	Fourth Quarter
Moore	$160,000	?	?	?	?
Pickrell	200,000	?	?	?	?
Rice	320,000	?	?	?	?

Required

a. Complete the sales budget by filling in the missing amounts. (Round the figures to the nearest dollar.)

b. Determine the amount of sales revenue Lagrave will report on the quarterly pro forma income statements.

Exercise 7-5B   *Determining cash receipts from accounts receivable*   LO 3

Hancock Corporation is about to start a business as an agricultural products distributor. Because its customers will all be retailers, Hancock will sell its products solely on account. The company expects to collect 50 percent of accounts receivable in the month of sale and the remaining 50 percent in the following month. Hancock expects sales revenues of $300,000 in July, the first month of operation, and $280,000 in August.

Required

a. Determine the amount of cash Hancock expects to collect in July.

b. Determine the amount of cash Hancock expects to collect in August.

Exercise 7-6B   *Using judgment in making a sales forecast*   LO 3

Starr Greetings Corporation sells greeting cards for various occasions.

Required

Write a brief memo describing the sales pattern that you would expect Starr Greetings to experience during the year. In which months will sales likely be high? Explain why.

LO 4

Exercise 7-7B *Preparing an inventory purchases budget*

Young Drugstores, Inc., sells prescription drugs, over-the-counter drugs, and some groceries. The purchasing manager prepared the following inventory purchases budget. For this year, Young expects an ending inventory balance equal to 16 percent of the following month's cost of goods sold. April's budgeted cost of goods sold amounts to $63,000.

Inventory Purchases Budget	January	February	March
Budgeted cost of goods sold	$80,000	$56,000	$60,000
Plus: Desired ending inventory	8,960	?	?
Inventory needed	88,960	?	?
Less: Beginning inventory	12,000	?	?
Required purchases (on account)	$76,960	?	?

Required

a. Complete the inventory purchases budget by filling in the missing amounts.

b. Determine the amount of cost of goods sold the company will report on the first quarter pro forma income statement.

c. Determine the amount of ending inventory the company will report on the first quarter pro forma balance sheet.

LO 4

Exercise 7-8B *Preparing a schedule of cash payments for inventory purchases*

Waldrop Grocery buys and sells groceries in a community far from any major city. Cedric Waldrop, the owner, budgeted the store's purchases as follows:

	October	November	December
Required purchases (on account)	$40,000	$30,000	$36,000

Waldrop's suppliers require that 70 percent of accounts payable be paid in the month of purchase. The remaining 30 percent is paid in the month following the month of purchase.

Schedule of Cash Payments for Inventory Purchases			
	October	November	December
Payment for current accounts payable	$28,000	?	?
Payment for previous accounts payable	9,000	?	?
Total budgeted payments for inventory	$37,000	?	?

Required

a. Complete the schedule of cash payments for inventory purchases by filling in the missing amounts.

b. Determine the amount of accounts payable Waldrop will report on the store's quarterly pro forma balance sheet.

LO 4

Exercise 7-9B *Determining the amount of inventory purchases and cash payments*

Bellaire Oil Corporation, which distributes gasoline products to independent gasoline stations, had $320,000 of cost of goods sold in January. The company expects a 2.5 percent increase in cost of goods sold during February. The ending inventory balance for January is $25,000, and the desired ending inventory for February is $30,000. Bellaire pays cash to settle 60 percent of its purchases on account during the month of purchase and pays the remaining 40 percent in the month following the purchase. The accounts payable balance as of January 31 was $30,000.

Required

a. Determine the amount of purchases budgeted for February.

b. Determine the amount of cash payments budgeted for inventory purchases in February.

Exercise 7-10B *Preparing a schedule of cash payments for selling and administrative expenses*

LO 5

The controller for Robinson Laundry Services prepared the following list of expected selling and administrative expenses. All expenses requiring cash payments except salary expense and insurance are paid for in the month incurred. Salary is paid in the month following its incursion. The annual insurance premium is paid in advance on January 1. January is the first month of operations. Accordingly, there are no beginning account balances.

	January	February	March
Budgeted Selling and Administrative Expenses			
Equipment depreciation	$ 5,000	$ 5,000	$ 5,000
Salary expense	3,400	3,200	3,600
Cleaning supplies	1,000	940	1,100
Insurance expense	600	600	600
Equipment maintenance expense	500	500	500
Leases expense	1,600	1,600	1,600
Miscellaneous expenses	400	400	400
Total S&A expenses	$12,500	$12,240	$12,800
Schedule of Cash Payments for Selling and Administrative Expenses			
Equipment depreciation	?	?	?
Prior month's salary expense, 100%	?	?	?
Cleaning supplies	?	?	?
Insurance premium	?	?	?
Equipment maintenance expense	?	?	?
Leases expense	?	?	?
Miscellaneous expenses	?	?	?
Total payments for S&A expenses	$10,700	$ 6,840	$ 6,800

Required

a. Complete the schedule of cash payments for selling and administrative expenses by filling in the missing amounts.

b. Determine the amount of salaries payable the company will report on its quarterly pro forma balance sheet.

c. Determine the amount of prepaid insurance the company will report on its quarterly pro forma balance sheet.

Exercise 7-11B *Preparing inventory purchases budgets with different assumptions*

LO 4

Rachel Khan has been at odds with her brother and business partner, David, since childhood. The sibling rivalry is not all bad, however; their garden shop, Khan Gardens and Gifts, has been very successful. When the partners met to prepare the coming year's budget, their forecasts were different, naturally. Their sales revenue estimates follow.

Source of Estimate	First Quarter	Second Quarter	Third Quarter	Fourth Quarter
Rachel	$360,000	$400,000	$300,000	$420,000
David	300,000	320,000	340,000	480,000

Past experience indicates that cost of goods sold is about 60 percent of sales revenue. The company tries to maintain 15 percent of the next quarter's expected cost of goods sold as the current quarter's ending inventory. The ending inventory this year is $25,000. Next year's ending inventory is budgeted to be $35,000.

Required

a. Prepare an inventory purchases budget using Rachel's estimate.
b. Prepare an inventory purchases budget using David's estimate.

LO 5, 7 **Exercise 7-12B** *Determining the amount of cash payments for selling and administrative expenses*

Jensi Berger, managing partner of Berger Business Consulting, is preparing a budget for January 2013, the first month of business operations. Jensi estimates the following monthly selling and administrative expenses: office lease, $4,000; utilities, $1,900; office supplies, $2,400; depreciation, $12,000; referral fees, $5,000; and miscellaneous, $1,000. Referral fees will be paid in the month following the month they are incurred. Other expenses will be paid in the month in which they are incurred.

Required

a. Determine the amount of budgeted cash payments for January selling and administrative expenses.
b. Determine the amount of referral fees payable the firm will report on the January 31st pro forma balance sheet.
c. Determine the amount of office lease expense the company will report on its 2013 pro forma income statement, assuming that the monthly lease expense remains the same throughout the whole year.

LO 6, 7 **Exercise 7-13B** *Preparing a cash budget*

Antonio Kinnard, the accounting manager of Sparks Antique Company, is preparing his company's cash budget for the next quarter. Sparks desires to maintain a cash cushion of $4,000 at the end of each month. As cash flows fluctuate, the company either borrows or repays funds at the end of a month. It pays interest on borrowed funds at the rate of 1 percent per month.

Cash Budget	July	August	September
Section 1: Cash Receipts			
Beginning cash balance	$ 16,000	$?	$?
Add cash receipts	180,000	192,000	208,000
Total cash available (a)	196,000	?	?
Section 2: Cash Payments			
For inventory purchases	158,000	153,000	171,000
For S&A expenses	37,000	36,000	39,000
For interest expense	0	?	?
Total budgeted disbursements (b)	195,000	?	?
Section 3: Financing Activities			
Surplus (shortage)	1,000	?	?
Borrowing (repayments) (c)	3,000	?	?
Ending Cash Balance (a − b + c)	$ 4,000	$ 4,000	$ 4,000

Required

a. Complete the cash budget by filling in the missing amounts. Round all computations to the nearest whole dollar.
b. Determine the amount of net cash flows from operating activities Sparks will report on its quarterly pro forma statement of cash flows.
c. Determine the amount of net cash flows from financing activities Sparks will report on its quarterly pro forma statement of cash flows.

Exercise 7-14B *Determining amount to borrow and pro forma statement balances*   LO 6, 7

Kerry Norton, the president of Donnelly Corporation, has been working with his controller to manage the company's cash position. The controller provided Kerry the following data.

Balance of accounts receivable, June 30	$ 50,000
Balance of line of credit, June 30	0
Budgeted cash sales for July	70,000
Budgeted credit sales for July	320,000
Budgeted cash payments for July	380,000

The company typically collects 75 percent of credit sales in the month of sale and the remainder in the month following the sale. Norton's line of credit enables the company to borrow funds readily, with the stipulation that any borrowing must take place on the last day of the month. The company pays its vendors on the last day of the month also. Mr. Norton likes to maintain a $15,000 cash balance before any interest payments. The annual interest rate is 12 percent.

Required

a. Compute the amount of funds Mr. Norton needs to borrow on July 31.

b. Determine the amount of interest expense the company will report on the July pro forma income statement.

c. Determine the amount of interest expense the company will report on the August pro forma income statement.

Exercise 7-15B *Preparing pro forma income statements with different assumptions*   LO 2, 7

Revell Corporation's budget planning meeting is like a zoo. Millard McFerrin, the credit manager, is naturally conservative and Dorothy Dester, the marketing manager, is the opposite. They have argued back and forth about the effect of various factors that influence the sales growth rate, such as credit policies and market potential. Based on the following current year data provided by Elaine Gann, the controller, Millard expects Revell's revenues to grow 5 percent each quarter above last year's level; Dorothy insists the growth rate will be 8 percent per quarter.

Current Year	First Quarter	Second Quarter	Third Quarter	Fourth Quarter	Total
Sales revenue	$240,000	$200,000	$216,000	$314,000	$970,000
Cost of goods sold	122,000	101,000	106,000	156,000	485,000
Gross margin	118,000	99,000	110,000	158,000	485,000
Selling & admin. expenses	32,000	26,000	26,400	40,600	125,000
Net income	$ 86,000	$ 73,000	$ 83,600	$117,400	$360,000

Historically, cost of goods sold is projected at 50 percent of sales revenue. Selling and administrative expenses are expected to be 12.5 percent of sales revenue.

Required

a. Prepare a pro forma income statement for the coming year using the credit manager's growth estimate.

b. Prepare a pro forma income statement for the coming year using the marketing manager's growth estimate.

c. Explain why two executives in the same company could have different estimates of future growth.

PROBLEMS—SERIES B

LO 3

Problem 7-16B   *Preparing a sales budget and schedule of cash receipts*

Cobb Corporation sells mail-order computers. In December 2011, it has generated $450,000 of sales revenue; the company expects a 20 percent increase in sales in January and 10 percent in February. All sales are on account. Cobb normally collects 80 percent of accounts receivable in the month of sale and 20 percent in the next month.

Required

a. Prepare a sales budget for January and February 2012.
b. Determine the amount of sales revenue Cobb would report on the bimonthly pro forma income statement for January and February 2012.
c. Prepare a cash receipts schedule for January and February 2012.
d. Determine the amount of accounts receivable as of February 28, 2012.

LO 4, 7

Problem 7-17B   *Preparing an inventory purchases budget and schedule of cash payments*

Drennan Company's purchasing manager, Neil Grey, is preparing a purchases budget for the next quarter. At his request, Robert Chan, the manager of the sales department, forwarded him the following preliminary sales budget.

	October	November	December	January
Budgeted sales	$600,000	$750,000	$900,000	$800,000

For budgeting purposes, Drennan estimates that cost of goods sold is 75 percent of sales. The company desires to maintain an ending inventory balance equal to 20 percent of the next period's cost of goods sold. The September ending inventory is $90,000. Drennan makes all purchases on account and pays 70 percent of accounts payable in the month of purchase and the remaining 30 percent in the following month. The balance of accounts payable at the end of September is $90,000.

Required

a. Prepare an inventory purchases budget for October, November, and December.
b. Determine the amount of ending inventory Drennan will report on the end-of-quarter pro forma balance sheet.
c. Prepare a schedule of cash payments for inventory for October, November, and December.
d. Determine the balance in accounts payable Drennan will report on the end-of-quarter pro forma balance sheet.

LO 7

Problem 7-18B   *Preparing pro forma income statements with different assumptions*

Drexel Morris, a successful entrepreneur, is reviewing the results of his first year in business. His accountant delivered the following income statement just five minutes ago.

	Current Year
Sales revenue	$500,000
Cost of goods sold	350,000
Gross profit	150,000
Selling & admin. expenses	90,000
Net income	$ 60,000

Mr. Morris would like net income to increase 20 percent in the next year. This first year, selling and administrative expenses were 10 percent of sales revenue plus $40,000 of fixed expenses.

Required

The following questions are independent of each other.

a. Mr. Morris expects that cost of goods sold and variable selling and administrative expenses will remain stable in proportion to sales next year. The fixed selling and administrative expenses will increase to $68,000. What percentage increase in sales would enable the company to reach Mr. Morris's goal? Prepare a pro forma income statement to illustrate.

b. Market competition may become serious next year, and Mr. Morris does not expect an increase in sales revenue. However, he has developed a good relationship with his supplier, who is willing to give him a volume discount that will decrease cost of goods sold by 3 percent. What else can the company do to reach Mr. Morris's goal? Prepare a pro forma income statement illustrating your proposal.

c. If the company escalates its advertising campaign to boost consumer recognition, the selling and administrative expenses will increase to $150,000. With the increased advertising, the company expects sales revenue to increase by 25 percent. Assume that cost of goods sold remains constant in proportion to sales. Can the company reach Mr. Morris's goal?

Problem 7-19B *Preparing a schedule of cash payments for selling and administrative expenses*   **LO 5**

Redney's Travel Services has prepared its selling and administrative expenses budget for the next quarter. It pays all expenses when they are incurred except sales commissions, advertising expense, and telephone expense. These three items are paid in the month following the one in which they are incurred. January is the first month of operations, so there are no beginning account balances.

	January	February	March
Salary expense	$ 9,000	$ 9,000	$ 9,000
Sales commissions	600	640	800
Advertising expense	500	500	600
Telephone expense	1,000	1,080	1,100
Depreciation on store equipment	4,000	4,000	4,000
Rent	10,000	10,000	10,000
Miscellaneous	800	800	800
Total S&A expenses before interest	$25,900	$26,020	$26,300

Required

a. Prepare a schedule of cash payments for selling and administrative expenses.
b. Determine the amount of telephone expense payable as of March 31.
c. Determine the amount of sales commissions payable as of February 28.

Problem 7-20B *Preparing a cash budget*   **LO 6**

Pope Company has budgeted the following cash flows:

	April	May	June
Cash receipts	$320,000	$470,000	$624,000
Cash payments			
For inventory purchases	410,000	420,000	464,000
For S&A expenses	80,000	106,000	132,000

Pope had a $36,000 cash balance on April 1. The company desires a $60,000 cash cushion before paying interest. Funds are assumed to be borrowed, in increments of $1,000, and repaid on the last day of each month; the interest rate is 1.50 percent per month. Pope also pays its vendors on the last day of the month.

Required

Prepare a cash budget.

LO 3, 4, 5

Problem 7-21B *Preparing budgets with multiple products*

Lowden Enterprises, Inc., has two products, palm-size computers and programmable calculators. Pamela Mason, the chief executive officer, is working with her staff to prepare next year's budget. Ms. Mason estimates that sales will increase at an annual rate of 10 percent for palm-size computers and 4 percent for programmable calculators. The current year sales revenue data follow.

	First Quarter	Second Quarter	Third Quarter	Fourth Quarter	Total
Palm-size computers	$500,000	$550,000	$620,000	$730,000	$2,400,000
Programmable calculators	250,000	275,000	290,000	325,000	1,140,000
Total	$750,000	$825,000	$910,000	$1,055,000	$3,540,000

Based on the company's past experience, cost of goods sold is usually 75 percent of sales revenue. Company policy is to keep 10 percent of the next period's estimated cost of goods sold as the current period ending inventory.

Required

a. Prepare the company's sales budget for the next year for each quarter by individual products.

b. If the selling and administrative expenses are estimated to be $500,000, prepare the company's budgeted annual income statement for the next year.

c. Ms. Mason estimates the current year's ending inventory will be $78,000 for computers and $32,000 for calculators and the ending inventory next year will be $88,000 for computers and $42,000 for calculators. Prepare the company's inventory purchases budget for the next year showing quarterly figures by product.

LO 3, 4, 5

Problem 7-22B *Preparing a master budget for a retail company with no beginning account balances*

McGriff Gifts Corporation begins business today, December 31, 2010. Janet Novak, the president, is trying to prepare the company's master budget for the first three months (January, February, and March) of 2011. Since you are her good friend and an accounting student, Ms. Novak asks you to prepare the budget based on the following specifications.

Required

a. January sales are estimated to be $250,000 of which 30 percent will be cash and 70 percent will be credit. The company expects sales to increase at the rate of 10 percent per month. Prepare a sales budget.

b. The company expects to collect 100 percent of the accounts receivable generated by credit sales in the month following the sale. Prepare a schedule of cash receipts.

c. The cost of goods sold is 50 percent of sales. The company desires to maintain a minimum ending inventory equal to 20 percent of the next month's cost of goods sold. The ending inventory of March is expected to be $33,000. Assume that all purchases are made on account. Prepare an inventory purchases budget.

d. The company pays 60 percent of accounts payable in the month of purchase and the remaining 40 percent in the following month. Prepare a cash payments budget for inventory purchases.

e. Budgeted selling and administrative expenses per month follow.

Salary expense (fixed)	$25,000
Sales commissions	8 percent of Sales
Supplies expense	4 percent of Sales
Utilities (fixed)	$1,800
Depreciation on store fixtures (fixed)*	$5,000
Rent (fixed)	$7,200
Miscellaneous (fixed)	$2,000

*The capital expenditures budget indicates that McGriff will spend $350,000 on January 1 for store fixtures. The fixtures are expected to have a $50,000 salvage value and a five-year (60-month) useful life.

Use this information to prepare a selling and administrative expenses budget.

f. Utilities and sales commissions are paid the month after they are incurred; all other expenses are paid in the month in which they are incurred. Prepare a cash payments budget for selling and administrative expenses.

g. The company borrows funds, in increments of $1,000, and repays them in any amount available on the last day of the month. It pays interest of 1.5 percent per month in cash on the last day of the month. For safety, the company desires to maintain a $50,000 cash cushion. The company pays its vendors on the last day of the month. Prepare a cash budget.

h. Prepare a pro forma income statement for the quarter.

i. Prepare a pro forma balance sheet at the end of the quarter.

j. Prepare a pro forma statement of cash flows for the quarter.

Problem 7-23B   *Behavioral impact of budgeting*   LO 2, 7

Geraldin Rollin, the director of Diaz Corporation's Mail-Order Division, is preparing the division's budget proposal for next year. The company's president will review the proposal for approval. Ms. Rollin estimates the current year final operating results will be as follows.

	Current Year
Sales revenue	$8,000,000
Cost of goods sold	4,800,000
Gross profit	3,200,000
Selling & admin. expenses	1,280,000
Net income	$1,920,000

Ms. Rollin believes that the cost of goods sold as well as selling and administrative expenses will continue to be stable in proportion to sales revenue.

Diaz has an incentive policy to reward division managers whose performance exceeds their budget. Division directors receive a 10 percent bonus based on the excess of actual net income over the division's budget. For the last two years, Ms. Rollin has proposed a 4 percent rate of increase, which proved accurate. However, her honesty and accuracy in forecasting caused her to receive no year-end bonus at all. She is pondering whether she should do something differently this time. If she continues to be honest, she should propose an 8 percent growth rate because of robust market demand. Alternatively, she can propose a 4 percent growth rate as usual and thereby expect to receive some bonus at year-end.

Required

a. Prepare a pro forma income statement, assuming a 4 percent estimated increase.

b. Prepare a pro forma income statement, assuming an 8 percent increase.

c. Assume the president eventually approves the division's proposal with the 4 percent growth rate. If growth actually is 8 percent, how much bonus would Ms. Rollin receive?

d. Propose a better budgeting procedure for Diaz Corporation.

ANALYZE, THINK, COMMUNICATE

ATC 7-1   Business Applications Case   *Preparing and using pro forma statements*

Nancy Pinedo and Justin Johnson recently graduated from the same university. After graduation they decided not to seek jobs at established organizations but, rather, to start their own small business hoping they could have more flexibility in their personal lives for a few years. Nancy's family has operated Mexican restaurants and taco-trucks for the past two generations, and Nancy noticed there were no taco-truck services in the town where their university was located. To reduce the amount they would need for an initial investment, they decided to start a business operating a taco-cart rather than a taco-truck, from which they would cook and serve traditional Mexican styled street food.

They bought a used taco-cart for $15,000. This cost, along with the cost for supplies to get started, a business license, and street vendor license brought their initial expenditures to $20,000.

Five-thousand dollars came from personal savings they had accumulated by working part time during college, and they borrowed $15,000 from Nancy's parents. They agreed to pay interest on the outstanding loan balance each month based on an annual rate of 6 percent. They will repay the principal over the next few years as cash becomes available. They were able to rent space in a parking lot near the campus they had attended, believing that the students would welcome their food as an alternative to the typical fast food that was currently available.

After two months in business, September and October, they had average monthly revenues of $20,000 and out of pocket costs of $16,000 for rent, ingredients, paper supplies, and so on, but not interest. Justin thinks they should repay some of the money they borrowed, but Nancy thinks they should prepare a set of forecasted financial statements for their first year in business before deciding whether or not to repay any principal on the loan. She remembers a bit about budgeting from a survey of accounting course she took and thinks the results from their first two months in business can be extended over the next 10 months to prepare the budget they need. They estimate the cart will last at least five years, after which they expect to sell it for $5,000 and move on to something else in their lives. Nancy agrees to prepare a forecasted (pro forma) income statement, balance sheet, and statement of cash flows for their first year in business, which includes the two months already passed.

Required

a. Prepare the annual pro forma financial statements that you would expect Nancy to prepare based on her comments about her expectations for the business. Assume no principal will be repaid on the loan.

b. Review the statements you prepared for the first requirement and prepare a list of reasons why actual results for Justin and Nancy's business probably will not match their budgeted statements.

ATC 7-2   Group Assignment   *Master budget and pro forma statements*

The following trial balance was drawn from the records of Havel Company as of October 1, 2011.

Cash	$ 16,000	
Accounts receivable	60,000	
Inventory	40,000	
Store equipment	200,000	
Accumulated depreciation		$ 76,800
Accounts payable		72,000
Line of credit loan		100,000
Common stock		50,000
Retained earnings		17,200
Totals	$316,000	$316,000

Required

a. Divide the class into groups, each with 4 or 5 students. Organize the groups into three sections. Assign Task 1 to the first section, Task 2 to the second section, and Task 3 to the third section.

Group Tasks

(1) Based on the following information, prepare a sales budget and a schedule of cash receipts for October, November, and December. Sales for October are expected to be $180,000, consisting of $40,000 in cash and $140,000 on credit. The company expects sales to increase at the rate of 10 percent per month. All accounts receivable are collected in the month following the sale.

(2) Based on the following information, prepare a purchases budget and a schedule of cash payments for inventory purchases for October, November, and December. The inventory balance as of October 1 was $40,000. Cost of goods sold for October is expected to be $72,000. Cost of goods sold is expected to increase by 10 percent per month. The company expects to maintain a minimum ending inventory equal to 20 percent of the current month cost of goods sold. Seventy-five percent of accounts payable is paid in the month that the purchase occurs; the remaining 25 percent is paid in the following month.

(3) Based on the following selling and administrative expenses budgeted for October, prepare a selling and administrative expenses budget for October, November, and December.

Sales commissions (10% increase per month)	$7,200
Supplies expense (10% increase per month)	1,800
Utilities (fixed)	2,200
Depreciation on store equipment (fixed)	1,600
Salary expense (fixed)	34,000
Rent (fixed)	6,000
Miscellaneous (fixed)	1,000

Cash payments for sales commissions and utilities are made in the month following the one in which the expense is incurred. Supplies and other operating expenses are paid in cash in the month in which they are incurred.

b. Select a representative from each section. Have the representatives supply the missing information in the following pro forma income statement and balance sheet for the fourth quarter of 2011. The statements are prepared as of December 31, 2011.

Income Statement	
Sales revenue	$?
Cost of goods sold	?
Gross margin	357,480
Operating expenses	?
Operating income	193,290
Interest expense	(2,530)
Net income	$190,760

Balance Sheet		
Assets		
Cash		$ 9,760
Accounts receivable		?
Inventory		?
Store equipment	$200,000	
Accumulated depreciation store equipment	?	
Book value of equipment		118,400
Total assets		$314,984
Liabilities		
Accounts payable		?
Utilities payable		?
Sales commissions payable		?
Line of credit		23,936
Equity		
Common stock		50,000
Retained earnings		?
Total liabilities and equity		$314,984

c. Indicate whether Havel will need to borrow money during October.

ATC 7-3   Research Assignment   *Analyzing budget data for the United States government*

The annual budget of the United States is very complex, but this case requires that you analyze only a small portion of the historical tables that are presented as a part of each year's budget. The fiscal year of the federal government ends on September 30. Obtain the budget documents needed at www.gpoaccess.gov/usbudget by following these steps:

- Under the "Previous Budgets" heading, click on "Browse"
- Under the Barack H. Obama heading, click on "Fiscal Year 2010"

■ There are two options that can be used on the page that appears next:
   • Under the "Budget Documents" heading, you can select the PDF link beside the "Historical Table" subheading.
   • Scroll down to the "Spreadsheets" heading and click on the "Historical Tables" subheading. This option provides the data in an Excel compatible format.

■ Under whichever option you choose above, you will need to review Table 1.1, Table 1.2, and Table 4.2 to complete the requirements below.

Required

a. Table 1.2 shows the budget as a *percentage of gross domestic product* (GDP). Using the data in the third column, "Surplus of Deficit," determine how many years since 1960 the budget has shown a surplus and how many times it has shown a deficit. Ignore the "TQ" data between 1976 and 1977. This was a year that the government changed the ending date of its fiscal year.

b. Based on the data in Table 1.2, identify the three years with the highest deficits as a percentage of GDP. What were the deficit percentages for these years? Which year had the largest surplus and by what percentage?

c. Using your findings for Requirement *b*, regarding the year with the highest deficit as a percentage of GDP, go to Table 1.1 and calculate the deficit for that year as a *percentage of revenues*.

d. The president of the United States from 1993 through 2000 was Bill Clinton, a Democrat. The president from 2001 through 2009 was George Bush, a Republican. These men had significant input into the federal budget for the fiscal years 1994–2001 and 2002–2009, respectively. Table 4.2 shows what percentage of the total federal budget was directed toward each department within the government. Compare the data on Table 4.2 for 1994–2001, the Clinton years, to the data for 2002–2009, the Bush years. Identify the five departments that appear to have changed the most from the Clinton years to the Bush years. Ignore "Allowances" and "Undistributed offsetting receipts." Note, if you wish to approach this assignment more accurately, you can compute the average percentage for each department for the eight years each president served, and compare the two averages. The gpoaccess website includes a spreadsheet version of the historical data tables, allowing for a reasonably easy Excel analysis.

ATC 7-4   Writing Assignment   *Continuous budgeting*

HON Company is the largest maker of mid-priced office furniture in the United States and Canada. Its management has expressed dissatisfaction with its *annual* budget system. Fierce competition requires businesses to be flexible and innovative. Unfortunately, building the effects of innovation into an annual budget is difficult because actions and outcomes often are evolutionary. Innovation unfolds as the year progresses. Consequently, HON's management team reached the conclusion that "when production processes undergo continuous change, standards developed annually for static conditions no longer offer meaningful targets for gauging their success."

Required

Assume that you are HON Company's budget director. Write a memo to the management team explaining how the practice of continuous budgeting could overcome the shortcomings of an annual budget process. (For insight, read the article "Continuous Budgeting at the HON Company," *Management Accounting,* January 1996. This article describes HON's real-world experience with a continuous budget system.)

ATC 7-5   Ethical Dilemma   *Bad budget system or unethical behavior?*

Clarence Cleaver is the budget director for the Harris County School District. Mr. Cleaver recently sent an urgent E-mail message to Sally Simmons, principal of West Harris County High. The message severely reprimanded Ms. Simmons for failing to spend the funds allocated to her to purchase computer equipment. Ms. Simmons responded that her school already has a sufficient supply of computers; indeed, the computer lab is never filled to capacity and usually is less than half filled. Ms. Simmons suggested that she would rather use the funds for teacher training. She argued that the reason the existing computers are not fully utilized is that the teachers lack sufficient computer literacy necessary to make assignments for their students.

Mr. Cleaver responded that it is not Ms. Simmons's job to decide how the money is to be spent; that is the school board's job. It is the principal's job to spend the money as the board directed. He informed Ms. Simmons that if the money is not spent by the fiscal closing date, the school board would likely reduce next year's budget allotment. To avoid a potential budget cut, Mr. Cleaver reallocated Ms. Simmons's computer funds to Jules Carrington, principal of East Harris County High. Mr. Carrington knows how to buy computers regardless of whether they are needed. Mr. Cleaver's final words were, "Don't blame me if parents of West High students complain that East High has more equipment. If anybody comes to me, I'm telling them that you turned down the money."

Required

a. Do Mr. Cleaver's actions violate the standards of ethical conduct shown in Exhibit 1.15 of Chapter 1?

b. Does the Sarbanes-Oxley Act apply to this case? Explain your answer.

c. Explain how participative budgeting could improve the allocation of resources for the Harris County School District.

ATC 7-6 Spreadsheet Assignment *Using Excel*

The accountant for Nelly's Dress Shop prepared the fourth quarter 2011 cash budget that appears on the following spreadsheet. Nelly's has a policy to maintain a minimum cash balance of $14,000 before the interest payment at the end of each month. The shop borrows and repays funds on the first day of the month. The interest rate is 2 percent per month.

Required

a. Construct a spreadsheet to model the cash budget as in the following screen capture. Be sure to use formulas where possible so that any changes to the estimates will be automatically reflected in the spreadsheet.

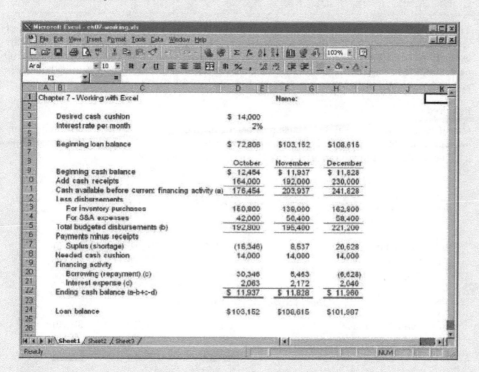

Spreadsheet Tips

(1) Rows 11, 15, 17, 18, 20 to 22, and 24 should be based on formulas.

(2) Cells F6, H6, F9, and H9 should be based on formulas also. For example, cell F6 should be = D24.

ATC 7-7   Spreadsheet Assignment   *Mastering Excel*

Spitzer Company has collected sales forecasts for next year from three people.

Sources of Sales Estimate	First Quarter	Second Quarter	Third Quarter	Fourth Quarter
a. Sales manager	$520,000	$410,000	$370,000	$610,000
b. Marketing consultant	540,000	480,000	400,000	630,000
c. Production manager	460,000	360,000	350,000	580,000

They have estimated that the cost of goods sold is 70 percent of sales. The company tries to maintain 10 percent of next quarter's expected cost of goods sold as the current quarter's ending inventory. The ending inventory of this year is $25,000. For budgeting, the ending inventory of the next year is expected to be $28,000.

Required

a. Construct a spreadsheet that allows the inventory purchases budget to be prepared for each of the preceding estimates.

Spreadsheet Tips

The VLOOKUP function can be used to choose one line of the preceding estimates. See the spreadsheet tips in Chapter 6 for an explanation of VLOOKUP.

COMPREHENSIVE PROBLEM

The management team of Magnificent Modems, Inc. (MMI), wants to investigate the effect of several different growth rates on sales and cash receipts. Cash sales for the month of January are expected to be $10,000. Credit sales for January are expected to be $50,000. MMI collects 100 percent of credit sales in the month following the month of sale. Assume a beginning balance in accounts receivable of $48,000.

Required

Calculate the amount of sales and cash receipts for the months of February and March assuming a growth rate of 1 percent, 2 percent, and 4 percent.
The results at a growth rate of 1 percent are shown as an example.

Sales Budget			
	Jan	Feb	Mar
Cash sales	$10,000	$10,100	$10,201
Sales on account	50,000	50,500	51,005
Total budgeted sales	$60,000	$60,600	$61,206
Schedule of Cash Receipts			
Current cash sales	$10,000	$10,100	$10,201
Plus collections from accts. rec.	48,000	50,000	50,500
Total budgeted collections	$58,000	$60,100	$60,701

Use the following forms, assuming a growth rate of 2 percent.

Sales Budget

	Jan	Feb	Mar
Cash sales	$10,000	_____	_____
Sales on account	50,000	_____	_____
Total budgeted sales	$60,000	_____	_____

Schedule of Cash Receipts

	Jan	Feb	Mar
Current cash sales	$10,000	_____	_____
Plus collections from accts. rec.	48,000	_____	_____
Total budgeted collections	$58,000	_____	_____

Use the following forms, assuming a growth rate of 4 percent.

Sales Budget

	Jan	Feb	Mar
Cash sales	$10,000	_____	_____
Sales on account	50,000	_____	_____
Total budgeted sales	$60,000	_____	_____

Schedule of Cash Receipts

	Jan	Feb	Mar
Current cash sales	$10,000	_____	_____
Plus collections from accts. rec.	48,000	_____	_____
Total budgeted collections	$58,000	_____	_____

CHAPTER 8

Performance Evaluation

LEARNING OBJECTIVES

After you have mastered the material in this chapter you will be able to:

1 Describe flexible and static budgets.

2 Classify variances as being favorable or unfavorable.

3 Compute and interpret sales and variable cost volume variances.

4 Compute and interpret flexible budget variances.

5 Calculate and interpret fixed cost variances.

6 Explain standard cost systems.

7 Calculate and interpret price and usage variances.

CHAPTER OPENING

Suppose you are a carpenter who builds picnic tables. You normally build 200 tables each year (the planned volume of activity), but because of unexpected customer demand, you are asked to build 225 tables (the actual volume of activity). You work hard and build the tables. Should management chastise you for using more materials, labor, or overhead than you normally use? Should management criticize the sales staff for selling more tables than expected? Of course not. Management must evaluate performance based on the actual volume of activity, not the planned volume of activity. To help management plan and evaluate performance, managerial accountants frequently prepare flexible budgets based on different levels of volume. Flexible budgets flex, or change, when the volume of activity changes.

The Curious Accountant

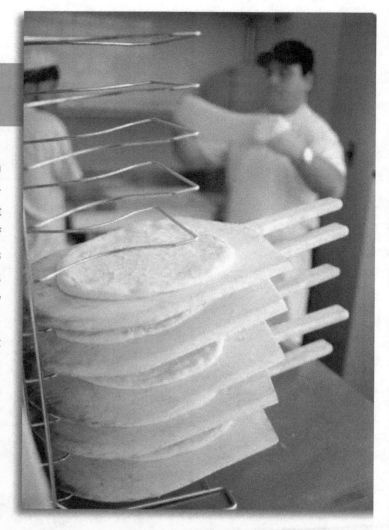

Gourmet Pizzas is located in an affluent section of a major metropolitan area. Its owner worked at a national-chain pizza restaurant while in college. He knew that even though the national pizza chains had a lot of stores, (in 2010 Domino's, Pizza Hut, and Papa John's had approximately 14,000 stores in the United States), more than half of the country's pizzas were sold by other, mostly independently owned, restaurants. Knowing he could not beat the big guys on price, Gourmet Pizzas focuses on quality. Its pizza dough is made from scratch on the premises from organically grown flour, and it offers a wide variety of unusual toppings, such as pancetta.

In order to determine a proper selling price for his pizzas, the owner estimated the cost of making the crusts, among other things. Knowing how much flour, yeast, and so on was needed to make the dough for one pizza and estimating the cost of these ingredients, he determined that the materials for the dough for each pizza should cost him 25 cents. However, after six months in business, he had spent $10,150 on materials for making his dough and had sold 32,750 pizzas. This resulted in an actual price per pizza of 31 cents.

What are two general reasons that may explain why the materials cost for pizza dough was higher than Gourmet Pizzas' owner estimated? (Answer on page 360.)

Sources: Companies' SEC filings and PMQ.com.

PREPARING FLEXIBLE BUDGETS

Describe flexible and static budgets.

A **flexible budget** is an extension of the *master budget* discussed previously. The master budget is based solely on the planned volume of activity. The master budget is frequently called a **static budget** because it remains unchanged even if the actual volume of activity differs from the planned volume. Flexible budgets differ from static budgets in that they show expected revenues and costs at a *variety* of volume levels.

To illustrate the differences between static and flexible budgets, consider Melrose Manufacturing Company, a producer of small, high-quality trophies used in award ceremonies. Melrose plans to make and sell 18,000 trophies during 2011. Management's best estimates of the expected sales price and per unit costs for the trophies are called *standard* prices and costs. The standard price and costs for the 18,000 trophies follow.

Per unit sales price and variable costs	
Expected sales price	$ 80.00
Standard materials cost	12.00
Standard labor cost	16.80
Standard overhead cost	5.60
Standard general, selling, and administrative cost	15.00
Total fixed costs	$291,600

The static budget is highlighted with red shading in Exhibit 8.1. Sales revenue is determined by multiplying the expected sales price per unit times the planned volume of activity ($80 × 18,000 = $1,440,000). Similarly, the variable costs are calculated by multiplying the standard cost per unit times the planned volume of activity. For example, the manufacturing materials cost is $216,000 ($12 × 18,000). The same computational procedures apply to the other variable costs. The variable costs are subtracted from the sales revenue to produce a contribution margin of $550,800. The fixed costs are subtracted from the contribution margin to produce a budgeted net income of $259,200.

EXHIBIT 8.1

Static and Flexible Budgets in Excel Spreadsheet

	Per Unit Standards	Static Budget		Flexible Budgets				
Number of Units		18,000		16,000	17,000	18,000	19,000	20,000
Sales Revenue	$80.00	$1,440,000		$1,280,000	$1,360,000	$1,440,000	$1,520,000	$1,600,000
Variable Manuf. Costs								
Materials	$12.00	216,000		192,000	204,000	216,000	228,000	240,000
Labor	16.80	302,400		268,800	285,600	302,400	319,200	336,000
Overhead	5.60	100,800		89,600	95,200	100,800	106,400	112,000
Variable G,S,&A	15.00	270,000		240,000	255,000	270,000	285,000	300,000
Contribution Margin		550,800		489,600	520,200	550,800	581,400	612,000
Fixed Costs		291,600		291,600	291,600	291,600	291,600	291,600
Net Income		$ 259,200		$ 198,000	$ 228,600	$ 259,200	$ 289,800	$ 320,400

What happens if the number of units sold is different from the planned volume? In other words, *what* happens to net income *if* Melrose sells more or less than 18,000 units? Managers frequently use flexible budgets to examine such *what if* scenarios. Flexible budget income statements for Melrose at sales volumes of 16,000, 17,000, 18,000, 19,000, and 20,000 are highlighted with blue shading in Exhibit 8.1.

The flexible budgets are prepared with the same per-unit standard amounts and fixed cost data used to produce the static budget. The only difference is the expected number of units sold. For example, the sales revenue at 16,000 units is $1,280,000 ($80 × 16,000), at 17,000 units it is $1,360,000 ($80 × 17,000), and so on. The variable materials cost at 16,000 units is $192,000 ($12 × 16,000), at 17,000 units it is $204,000 ($12 × 17,000), and so on. The other variable costs are computed in the same manner. Note that the fixed costs are the same at all levels of activity because, by definition, they are not affected by changes in volume.

Other flexible budgets are possible. Indeed, a flexible budget can be prepared for any number of units sold. You have probably noticed that Exhibit 8.1 was prepared using an Excel spreadsheet. Excel offers the opportunity to prepare an unlimited number of flexible budgets with minimal effort. For example, formulas can be created with cell references so that new budgets can be created simply by changing the number of units entered in a single cell.

Managers use flexible budgets for both planning and performance evaluation. For example, managers may assess whether the company's cash position is adequate by assuming different levels of volume. They may judge if the number of employees, amounts of materials, and equipment and storage facilities are appropriate for a variety of different potential levels of volume. In addition to helping plan, flexible budgets are critical to implementing an effective performance evaluation system.

✓ CHECK YOURSELF 8.1

The static (master) budget of Parcel, Inc., called for a production and sales volume of 25,000 units. At that volume, total budgeted fixed costs were $150,000 and total budgeted variable costs were $200,000. Prepare a flexible budget for an expected volume of 26,000 units.

Answer   Budgeted fixed costs would remain unchanged at $150,000 because changes in the volume of activity do not affect budgeted fixed costs. Budgeted variable costs would increase to $208,000, computed as follows: Calculate the budgeted variable cost per unit ($200,000 ÷ 25,000 units = $8) and then multiply that variable cost per unit by the expected volume ($8 × 26,000 units = $208,000).

DETERMINING VARIANCES FOR PERFORMANCE EVALUATION

One means of evaluating managerial performance is to compare *standard* amounts with *actual* results. The differences between the standard and actual amounts are called **variances;** variances can be either **favorable** or **unfavorable.** When actual sales revenue is greater than expected (planned) revenue, a company has a favorable sales variance because higher sales increase net income. When actual sales are less than expected, an unfavorable sales variance exists. When actual costs are *less* than standard costs, cost variances are favorable because lower costs increase net income. Unfavorable cost variances exist when actual costs are *more* than standard costs. These relationships are summarized below.

LO 2

Classify variances as being favorable or unfavorable.

- ■ When actual sales exceed expected sales, variances are favorable.
- ■ When actual sales are less than expected sales, variances are unfavorable.
- ■ When actual costs exceed standard costs, variances are unfavorable.
- ■ When actual costs are less than standard costs, variances are favorable.

SALES AND VARIABLE COST VOLUME VARIANCES

LO 3

Compute and interpret sales and variable cost volume variances.

The amount of a **sales volume variance** is the difference between the static budget (which is based on planned volume) and a flexible budget based on actual volume. Likewise, the **variable cost volume variances** are determined by calculating the differences between the static and flexible budget amounts. These variances measure management effectiveness in attaining the planned volume of activity. To illustrate, assume Melrose Manufacturing Company actually makes and sells 19,000 trophies during 2011. The planned volume of activity was 18,000 trophies. Exhibit 8.2 shows Melrose's static budget, flexible budget, and volume variances.

EXHIBIT 8.2

Melrose Manufacturing Company's Volume Variances

	Static Budget	Flexible Budget	Volume Variances	
Number of units	18,000	19,000	1,000	Favorable
Sales revenue	$1,440,000	$1,520,000	$80,000	Favorable
Variable manufacturing costs				
Materials	216,000	228,000	12,000	Unfavorable
Labor	302,400	319,200	16,800	Unfavorable
Overhead	100,800	106,400	5,600	Unfavorable
Variable SG&A	270,000	285,000	15,000	Unfavorable
Contribution margin	550,800	581,400	30,600	Favorable
Fixed costs	291,600	291,600	0	
Net income	$ 259,200	$ 289,800	$30,600	Favorable

Interpreting the Sales and Variable Cost Volume Variances

Because the static and flexible budgets are based on the same standard sales price and per-unit variable costs, the variances are solely attributable to the difference between the planned and actual volume of activity. Marketing managers are usually responsible for the volume variances. Because the sales volume drives production levels, production managers have little control over volume. Exceptions occur; for example, if poor production quality control leads to inferior goods that are difficult to sell, the production manager is responsible. The production manager is responsible for production delays that affect product availability, which may restrict sales volume. Under normal circumstances, however, the marketing campaign determines the volume of sales. Upper-level marketing managers develop the promotional program and create the sales plan; they are in the best position to explain why sales goals are or are not met. When marketing managers refer to **making the numbers,** they usually mean reaching the sales volume in the static (master) budget.

In the case of Melrose Manufacturing Company, the marketing manager not only achieved but also exceeded by 1,000 units the planned volume of sales. Exhibit 8.2 shows the activity variances resulting from the extra volume. At the standard price, the additional volume produces a favorable revenue variance of $80,000 (1,000 units × $80 per unit). The increase in volume also produces unfavorable variable cost variances. The net effect of producing and selling the additional 1,000 units is an increase of $30,600 in the contribution margin, a positive result. These preliminary results suggest that the marketing manager is to be commended. The analysis, however, is incomplete. For example, examining market share could reveal whether the manager won customers from competitors or whether the manager simply reaped the benefit of an unexpected industrywide increase in demand. The increase in sales volume could have been attained by reducing the sales price; the success of that strategy will be analyzed further in a later section of this chapter.

Since the variable costs in the flexible budget are higher than the variable costs in the static budget, the variable cost volume variances are *unfavorable*. The unfavorable classification may be misleading because it focuses solely on the cost component of the income statement. While costs are higher than expected, so too may be revenue. Indeed, as shown in Exhibit 8.2, the total of the unfavorable variable cost variances is more than offset by the favorable revenue variance, resulting in a higher contribution margin. Frequently, the assessment of variances requires a holistic perspective.

Fixed Cost Considerations

At this point, it is important to note that the reason the fixed cost variance shown in Exhibit 8.2 is zero is because we are comparing two budgets (static versus flexible). Variances occur only because the budgets are created using different volumes of activity. Since total fixed cost is not affected by the level of activity, there will be no fixed cost variances associated with static versus flexible budgets.

FLEXIBLE BUDGET VARIANCES

For performance evaluation, management compares actual results to a flexible budget based on the *actual* volume of activity. Because the actual results and the flexible budget reflect the same volume of activity, any variances in revenues and variable costs result from differences between standard and actual per unit amounts. To illustrate computing and analyzing flexible budget variances, we assume that Melrose's *actual* per unit amounts during 2011 were those shown in the following table. The 2011 per unit *standard* amounts are repeated here for your convenience.

Compute and interpret flexible budget variances.

	Standard	Actual
Sales price	$80.00	$78.00
Variable materials cost	12.00	11.78
Variable labor cost	16.80	17.25
Variable overhead cost	5.60	5.75

Actual and budgeted fixed costs are shown in Exhibit 8.3.

Exhibit 8.3 shows Melrose's 2011 flexible budget, actual results, and flexible budget variances. The flexible budget is the same one compared to the static budget in Exhibit 8.2.

EXHIBIT 8.3

Flexible Budget Variances for Melrose Manufacturing Company

	Flexible Budget	Actual Results	Flexible Budget Variances	
Number of units	19,000	19,000	0	
Sales revenue	$1,520,000	$1,482,000	$38,000	Unfavorable
Variable manufacturing costs				
Materials	228,000	223,820	4,180	Favorable
Labor	319,200	327,750	8,550	Unfavorable
Overhead	106,400	109,250	2,850	Unfavorable
Variable SG&A	285,000	283,100	1,900	Favorable
Contribution margin	581,400	538,080	43,320	Unfavorable
Fixed costs	291,600	295,000	3,400	Unfavorable
Net income	$ 289,800	$ 243,080	$46,720	Unfavorable

Recall the flexible budget amounts come from multiplying the standard per-unit amounts by the actual volume of production. For example, the sales revenue in the flexible budget comes from multiplying the standard sales price by the actual volume ($80 × 19,000). The variable costs are similarly computed. The *actual results* are calculated by multiplying the actual per-unit sales price and cost figures from the preceding table by the actual volume of activity. For example, the sales revenue in the Actual Results column comes from multiplying the actual sales price by the actual volume ($78 × 19,000 = $1,482,000). The actual cost figures are similarly computed. The differences between the flexible budget figures and the actual results are the **flexible budget variances.**

Calculating the Sales Price Variance

Because both the flexible budget and actual results are based on the actual volume of activity, the flexible budget variance is attributable to sales price, not sales volume. In this case, the actual sales price of $78 per unit is less than the standard price of $80 per unit. Because Melrose sold its product for less than the standard sales price, the **sales price variance** is *unfavorable.* Even though the price variance is unfavorable, however, sales volume was 1,000 units more than expected. It is possible the marketing manager generated the additional volume by reducing the sales price. Whether the combination of lower sales price and higher sales volume is favorable or unfavorable depends on the amount of the unfavorable sales price variance versus the amount of the favorable sales volume variance. The *total* sales variance (price and volume) follows:

Actual sales (19,000 units × $78 per unit)	$1,482,000	
Expected sales (18,000 units × $80 per unit)	1,440,000	
Total sales variance	$ 42,000	Favorable

Alternatively,

Activity variance (sales volume)	$ 80,000	Favorable
Sales price variance	(38,000)	Unfavorable
Total sales variance	$ 42,000	Favorable

This analysis indicates that reducing the sales price had a favorable impact on *total* contribution margin. Use caution when interpreting variances as good or bad; in this instance, the unfavorable sales price variance was more than offset by the favorable sales volume variance. All unfavorable variances are not bad; all favorable variances are not good. Variances signal the need to investigate.

✓ CHECK YOURSELF 8.2

Scott Company's master budget called for a planned sales volume of 30,000 units. Budgeted direct materials cost was $4 per unit. Scott actually produced and sold 32,000 units with an actual materials cost of $131,000. Determine the materials volume variance and identify the organizational unit most likely responsible for this variance. Determine the flexible budget variance and identify the organizational unit most likely responsible for this variance.

Answer The variable cost volume variance is the difference between the expected materials usage at the planned volume of activity and the expected materials usage at the actual volume of activity [($4 × 30,000 units) − ($4 × 32,000) = $8,000]. The variance is unfavorable because expected direct materials cost at actual volume was higher than budgeted direct materials cost at planned volume. The unfavorable variance might not be a bad thing. The variance is due to increased volume, which could be a good thing. The organizational unit most likely responsible for the volume variance is the marketing department.

    The flexible budget variance is the difference between the expected materials cost at the actual volume ($4 × 32,000 units = $128,000) and the actual materials cost of $131,000. The $3,000 ($128,000 − $131,000) variance is unfavorable because it cost more than expected to make the 32,000 units. Either the production department or the purchasing department is most likely responsible for this variance.

The Human Element Associated with Flexible Budget Variances

The flexible budget cost variances offer insight into management efficiency. For example, Melrose Manufacturing Company's favorable materials variance could mean purchasing agents were shrewd in negotiating price concessions, discounts, or delivery terms and therefore reduced the price the company paid for materials. Similarly, production employees may have used materials efficiently, using less than expected. The unfavorable labor variance could mean managers failed to control employee wages or motivate employees to work hard. As with sales variances, cost variances require careful analysis. A favorable variance may, in fact, mask unfavorable conditions. For example, the favorable materials variance might have been caused by paying low prices for inferior goods. Using substandard materials could have required additional labor in the production process, which would explain the unfavorable labor variance. Again, we caution that variances, whether favorable or unfavorable, alert management to investigate further.

FIXED COST VARIANCES

Because fixed costs do not fluctuate with volume, does not mean that the actual costs will be the same as the budgeted costs. Indeed, there are two fixed cost variances commonly investigated by management. One is called a *fixed cost spending variance;* the other is called a *fixed cost volume variance.*

Calculate and interpret fixed cost variances.

Fixed Cost Spending Variance

Companies frequently pay more or less than expected for fixed costs. For example, a supervisor may receive an unplanned raise, causing actual salary cost to be more than the amount budgeted. The difference between the *actual fixed cost* and the *budgeted fixed cost* (amount shown in the static budget) is called a **fixed cost spending variance.** The *fixed cost spending variance* for Melrose is $3,400 (295,000 actual fixed cost − $291,600 budgeted fixed cost). Since actual fixed costs are higher than the budgeted fixed cost, the variance is unfavorable. In other words the company had to pay more than it expected for the fixed costs.

    In the Melrose case, there is no way to know who is responsible for the $3,400 unfavorable fixed cost spending variance because all of the costs have been pooled together. To promote accountability, fixed costs that are controllable by a specific manager must be disaggregated and tagged for individual analysis. For example, the plant manager may control the assistant manager's salary cost. If a fixed cost spending variance is associated with the salary cost, the plant manager is responsible for explaining why the variance occurred. Other managers will be held accountable for the specific fixed costs they control.

Uncontrollable fixed costs should also be reported for management oversight. Even if these costs are not controllable in the short term, management should stay abreast of them because they may be controllable in the long term.

Fixed Cost Volume Variance

Companies frequently need to know the cost of something before the actual cost can be determined. For example, a company may base its selling price on the cost of making and selling a product. Even so, the actual cost of making and selling the product may not be known until after the product has been sold. In order to price the product, the company will be required to use estimated costs rather than actual costs. Likewise it may be necessary to use estimated costs to prepare quarterly financial statements because the actual cost will not be known until after the quarterly statements have been published. To solve such problems, accountants frequently estimate the total annual cost and then apply (allocate) a portion of the estimated annual cost to the products as they are made and sold.

To illustrate, assume that Melrose develops an allocation rate based on its budgeted fixed cost and the planned volume of production as shown below:

$$\text{Budgeted fixed cost} \div \text{Planned volume of activity} = \text{Allocation rate}$$
$$\$291{,}600 \div 18{,}000 \text{ units} = \$16.20 \text{ per unit}$$

As production proceeds, Melrose would apply $16.20 to the appropriate accounts each time an actual unit of product (trophy) is made and sold. Since the allocation rate is determined *before* the actual cost and volume are known, it is frequently called the *predetermined* allocation rate. Since fixed costs are frequently classified as overhead costs this rate is more frequently called the predetermined *overhead* rate. In summary the **predetermined overhead rate** is calculated as follows:

$$\text{Predetermined overhead rate} = \frac{\text{Budgeted fixed cost from the static budget}}{\text{Planned volume of activity}}$$

The total cost determined by multiplying the *predetermined overhead rate* times the *actual volume* of production is called the **applied fixed cost.** Given that Melrose produced and sold 19,000 units of product during 2011, the amount of applied fixed cost is $307,800 ($16.20 × 19,000 units).

The difference between the *applied fixed cost based on actual volume* and the *budgeted fixed cost based on planned volume* is called the **fixed cost volume variance.** In this case Melrose has a fixed cost volume variance of $16,200 ($307,800 budgeted fixed cost − $291,600 applied fixed cost).

To interpret the fixed cost volume variance, consider the effect that volume changes have on the behavior of fixed cost per unit. As volume increases, fixed cost per unit decreases. In this case, the planned volume was 18,000 units and the actual volume was 19,000 units. Since the higher than expected volume decreases the fixed cost per unit, the volume variance is *favorable.* An *unfavorable* fixed cost volume variance occurs when actual volume is less than planned volume, a condition that increases fixed costs per unit.

The fixed cost volume variance is a measure of facility utilization. If the fixed cost volume variance is unfavorable, the facilities are considered to be underutilized. This is just another way of saying that the company suffered an unfavorable variance because it did not utilize its facilities to make and sell the number of units of product it had planned to make and sell. A favorable fixed cost volume variance suggests that a company utilized its facilities to make and sell *more* than the planned volume of activity. In summary, a fixed cost volume variance indicates over- or underutilization of facilities, not over- or underspending.

For your convenience, the two fixed cost overhead variances are summarized as follows:

---

1. Fixed cost spending variance = Actual fixed cost − Budgeted fixed cost

   If actual costs are less than the budgeted costs the variance is favorable.
   If actual costs are greater than the budgeted costs the variance is unfavorable.

2. Fixed cost volume variance = Applied fixed cost based on actual volume − Budgeted fixed cost based on planned volume

   If actual volume is more than the planned volume the variance is favorable.
   If actual volume is less than the planned volume the variance is unfavorable.

Fixed Cost Volume Variance and Product Pricing

Changes in the fixed cost per unit have important implications for decision making. For example, consider the impact on cost-plus pricing decisions. Because the actual volume is unknown until the end of the accounting period, selling prices must be based on planned volume. Recall that at the planned volume of activity, Melrose's predetermined overhead rate is $16.20 ($291,600 ÷ 18,000 units). Compare this figure with the rate based on actual volume which is $15.35 ($291,600 ÷ 19,000 units). Since the price of the product was based on the predetermined overhead rate ($16.20), instead of the rate based on actual volume ($15.35), the product was overpriced. It follows that if actual volume is less than planned volume, products will be underpriced.

Overpricing can be problematic because it encourages competitors to enter the market. Eventually, these competitors will draw customers away from Melrose by offering lower prices. As Melrose loses customers, its actual fixed cost per unit increases, thereby exacerbating the pricing problem. Underpricing (not encountered by Melrose in this example) can also be detrimental. If planned volume is overstated, the predetermined overhead rate will be understated and prices will be set too low. When the higher amount of actual costs is eventually subtracted from revenues, actual profits will be lower than expected. As this discussion demonstrates, over- or understating the planned volume will cause pricing problems. It is critically important to be as accurate as possible when establishing the planned volume.

Responsibility for the Fixed Cost Volume Variance

Normally upper-level marketing managers are held accountable for the fixed cost volume variance because they control the volume of sales, which in turn dictates the volume of production. Even so, other possibilities must be considered. For example, goods may not sell because they are poorly constructed, which may be the fault of design engineers or production managers. Likewise, buyers may be at fault for purchasing undesirable products that are difficult to resell. In this case the purchasing department rather than the marketing department would be responsible for the fixed cost volume variance. Determining the amount of the variance is the easy part of performance evaluation; determining responsibility is usually more difficult.

STANDARD COST SYSTEMS

Standard cost systems help managers plan and also establish benchmarks against which actual performance can be judged. By highlighting differences between standard (expected) and actual performance, standard costing focuses management attention on the areas of greatest need. Because management talent is a valuable and expensive resource, businesses cannot afford to have managers spend large amounts of time on operations that are functioning normally. Instead, managers should concentrate on areas not performing as expected. In other words, management should attend to the exceptions; this management philosophy is known as **management by exception.**

LO 6

Explain standard cost systems.

Standard costing fosters using the management by exception principle. By reviewing performance reports that show differences between actual and standard costs, management can focus its attention on the items that show significant variances. Areas with only minor variances need little or no review.

Establishing Standards

Establishing standards is probably the most difficult part of using a standard cost system. A **standard** represents the amount that a price, cost, or quantity *should be* under certain anticipated circumstances. Consider the complexity of establishing the standard cost to produce a pair of blue jeans. Among other things, managers need to know where they can get the best price for materials, who will pay transportation costs, if cash or volume discounts are available, whether the suppliers with the lowest price can reliably supply the quantities needed on a timely basis, how the material should be cut to conserve time and labor, in what order to sew pieces of material together, the wage rates of the relevant production employees, whether overtime will be needed, and how many pairs of jeans will be produced. Obtaining this information requires the combined experience, judgment, and forecasting ability of all personnel who have responsibility for price and usage decisions. Even when a multitalented group of experienced persons is involved in standard setting, the process involves much trial and error. Revising standards is common even with established systems.

Historical data provide a good starting point for establishing standards. These data must be updated for changes in technology, plant layout, new methods of production, and worker productivity. Frequently, changes of this nature result from initiating a standard cost system. Remember that a *standard* represents what *should be* rather than what *is* or *was*. Engineers often help establish standards, recommending the most efficient way to perform required tasks. The engineers undertake time and motion studies and review material utilization in the process of developing standards. Established practices and policies are frequently changed in response to engineers' reports.

Management must consider behavioral implications when developing standards. Managers, supervisors, purchasing agents, and other affected employees should be consulted for two reasons: (1) their experience and expertise provide invaluable input to standard development and (2) persons who are involved in standard setting are more likely to accept and be motivated to reach the resulting standards. Management should also consider how difficult it should be to achieve standard performance. Difficulty levels can be described as follows: (1) ideal standards, (2) practical standards, and (3) lax standards.

Ideal standards represent flawless performance; they represent what costs should be under the best possible circumstances. They do not allow for normal materials waste and spoilage or ordinary labor inefficiencies caused by machine downtime, cleanups, breaks, or personal needs. Meeting ideal standards is beyond the capabilities of most, if not all, employees. Ideal standards may motivate some individuals to constantly strive for improvement, but unattainable standards discourage most people. When people consistently fail, they become demotivated and stop trying to succeed. In addition, variances associated with ideal standards lose significance. They reflect deviations that are largely beyond employees' control, and they mask true measures of superior or inferior performance, considerably reducing their usefulness.

Practical standards represent reasonable effort; they are attainable for most employees. Practical standards allow for normal levels of inefficiency in materials and labor usage. An average worker performing diligently would be able to achieve standard performance. Practical standards motivate most employees; the feeling of accomplishment attained through earnest effort encourages employees to do their best. Practical standards also produce meaningful variances. Deviations from practical standards usually result from factors employees control. Positive variances normally represent superior performance, and negative variances indicate inferior performance.

Lax standards represent easily attainable goals. Employees can achieve standard performance with minimal effort. Lax standards do not motivate most people; continual success with minimal effort leads to boredom and lackluster performance. In addition, variances lose meaning. Deviations caused by superior or inferior performance are obscured by the built-in slack.

Management must consider employee ability levels when establishing standards. Standards that seasoned workers can attain may represent ideal standards to inexperienced workers. Management should routinely monitor standards and adjust them when it is appropriate to do so.

Selecting Variances to Investigate

Managerial judgment, developed through experience, plays a significant role in deciding which variances to investigate. Managers consider the *materiality* of a variance, the *frequency* with which it occurs, their *capacity to control* the variance, and the *characteristics* of the items behind the variance.

Standard costs are estimates. They cannot perfectly predict actual costs. Most business experience minor variances as part of normal operations. Investigating minor variances is not likely to produce useful information. Many companies therefore establish *materiality* guidelines for selecting variances to analyze. They set dollar or percentage thresholds and ignore variances that fall below these limits, investigating material variances only. A **material variance** is one that could influence management decisions. Material variances should be investigated whether they are favorable or unfavorable. As mentioned earlier, a favorable price variance can result from purchasing substandard materials; the quality of the company's products, however, will suffer from the inferior materials and sales will fall.

How *frequently* a variance occurs impacts materiality. A variance of $20,000 may be immaterial in a single month, but if the same variance occurs repeatedly throughout the year, it can become a material $240,000 variance. Variance reports should highlight frequent as well as large variations.

Capacity to control refers to whether management action can influence the variance. If utility rates cause differences between actual and standard overhead costs, management has little control over the resulting variances. Conversely, if actual labor costs exceed standard costs because a supervisor fails to motivate employees, management can take some action. To maximize their value to the firm, managers should concentrate on controllable variances.

The *characteristics* of the items behind the variance may invite management abuse. For example, managers can reduce actual costs in the short term by delaying expenditures for maintenance, research and development, and advertising. Although cost reductions in these areas may produce favorable variances in the current period, they will have a long-term detrimental impact on profitability. Managers under stress may be tempted to focus on short-term benefits. Variances associated with these critical items should be closely analyzed.

The primary advantage of a standard cost system is efficient use of management talent to control costs. Secondary benefits include the following.

1. Standard cost systems quickly alert management to trouble spots. For example, a standard amount of materials may be issued for a particular job. If requisitions of additional materials require supervisory approval, each time a supervisor must grant such approval, she is immediately aware that excess materials are being used and can act before excessive material usage becomes unmanageable.

2. If established and maintained properly, standard cost systems can boost morale and motivate employees. Reward systems can be linked to accomplishments that exceed the established performance standards. Under such circumstances, employees become extremely conscious of the time and materials they use, minimizing waste and reducing costs.

3. Standard cost systems encourage good planning. The failure to plan well leads to overbuying, excessive inventory, wasted time, and so on. A standard cost system forces managers to plan, resulting in more effective operations with less waste.

Avoiding Gamesmanship

In general, variances should not be used to praise or punish managers. The purpose of identifying variances is to help management improve efficiency and productivity.

If variances are used to assign rewards and blame, managers are likely to respond by withholding or manipulating information. For example, a manager might manipulate the cost standard for a job by deliberately overstating the amount of materials or labor needed to complete it. The manager's performance will later appear positive when the actual cost of materials or labor is less than the inflated standard. This practice is so common it has a name: **budget slack** is the difference between inflated and realistic standards. Sales staff may play a game called *lowballing* in which they deliberately underestimate the amount of expected sales, anticipating a reward when actual sales subsequently exceed the budget.

Answers to The Curious Accountant

As this chapter demonstrates, there are two primary reasons a company spends more or less to produce a product than it estimated it would. First, the company may have paid more or less to purchase the inputs needed to produce the product than it estimated. Second, the company used a greater or lesser quantity of these inputs than expected. In the case of Gourmet Pizzas, it may have had to pay more for flour, yeast, cheese, and so on than the owner estimated. Or, it may have used more of these ingredients than expected. For example, if pizza dough sits around too long before being used, it may have to be thrown out. This waste was not anticipated when computing the cost to make only one pizza. Of course, the higher than expected cost could have been a combination of price and quantity factors.

Gourmet Pizza needs to determine if the difference between its expected costs and actual costs was because the estimates were faulty, or because the production process was inefficient. If the estimates were to blame, the owner would need to revise them so he can charge the proper price to his customers. If the production process is inefficient, he needs to correct it if he is to earn an acceptable level of profit.

Gamesmanship can be reduced if superiors and subordinates participate sincerely in setting mutually agreeable, attainable standards. Once standards are established, the evaluation system that uses them must promote long-term respect among superiors and their subordinates. If standards are used solely for punitive purposes, gamesmanship will rapidly degrade the standard costing system.

PRICE AND USAGE VARIANCES[1]

Under a standard cost system, it is common practice to subdivide the *flexible budget variances* into component parts that more clearly define the cause of these variances. For example, a favorable flexible budget materials cost variance may be the result of paying less than expected for the materials or of using fewer materials than expected, or some combination of *price and usage variances*. To demonstrate, we return to the Melrose Manufacturing Company case that was introduced earlier in the chapter.

LO 7

Calculate and interpret price and usage variances.

We will limit our discussion to the flexible budget variable manufacturing cost variances shown in Exhibit 8.3. Specifically, there are three of these variances including:

1. Flexible budget materials cost variance: $4,180 Favorable.
2. Flexible budget labor cost variance: $8,550 Unfavorable.
3. Flexible budget variable overhead cost variance: $2,850 Unfavorable.

Recall that these variances were calculated by determining the difference between the flexible budget costs (standard cost per unit times the actual volume) and the actual costs (actual cost per unit times the actual volume). The standard and actual per unit costs for Melrose were shown previously and are repeated here for your convenience.

	Standard	Actual
Variable materials cost per unit of product	$12.00	$11.78
Variable labor cost per unit of product	16.80	17.25
Variable overhead cost per unit of product	5.60	5.75

Using the cost per unit data, the flexible budget manufacturing cost variances can be determined algebraically as shown in Exhibit 8.4. We suggest that you compare the variances shown in the two exhibits to confirm that the algebraic approach in Exhibit 8.4 yields the same result as the variances previously computed in Exhibit 8.3.

Note that the difference between the actual and standard cost is expressed as an absolute value. This mathematical notation suggests that the mathematical sign is not useful in interpreting the condition of the variance. To assess the condition of a variance, you must consider the type of variance being analyzed. With respect to cost

EXHIBIT 8.4

Flexible Budget Variances Calculated Algebraically

Variable Mfg. Costs	Actual Cost *Per Unit* of Product	−	Standard Cost *Per Unit* of Product	×	Actual Units	=	Flexible Budget Variance
Materials	$11.78	−	$12.00	×	19,000	=	$4,180 Favorable
Labor	17.25	−	16.80	×	19,000	=	8,550 Unfavorable
Overhead	5.75	−	5.60	×	19,000	=	2,850 Unfavorable

[1]Businesses use various names for price and usage variances. For example, materials price and usage variances are frequently called materials price and quantity variances; labor price and usage variances are frequently called labor rate and efficiency variances. Regardless of the names, the underlying concepts and computations are the same for all variable price and usage variances.

variances, managers seek to attain actual prices that are lower than standard prices. In this case, the actual price of materials is less than the standard price, so the materials variance is favorable. Since the actual prices for labor and overhead are higher than the standard prices, those variances are unfavorable.

For insight into what caused the flexible budget variances, a separate price and usage variance can be computed for each of the total flexible budget variances. We begin with the $4,180 favorable flexible budget materials cost variance. This variance indicates that Melrose spent less than expected on materials to make 19,000 trophies. Why? The price per unit of material may have been less than expected (price variance), or the company may have used less material than expected (usage variance). To determine what caused the total favorable variance, Melrose must separate the cost per unit of product into two parts, price per unit of material and quantity of material used.

Calculating Materials Price and Usage Variances

Melrose's accounting records indicate the materials cost per unit of product (trophy) is as follows:

	Actual Data	Standard Data
Price **per pound** of material	$ 1.90	$ 2.00
Quantity of materials per unit of product	× 6.2 pounds	× 6.0 pounds
Cost **per unit** of product	$11.78	$12.00

Based on this detail, the total quantity of materials is:

	Actual Data	Standard Data
Actual production volume	19,000 units	19,000 units
Quantity of materials per unit of product	× 6.2 pounds	× 6.0 pounds
Total quantity of materials	117,800 pounds	114,000 pounds

Confirm the price and usage components that make up the total flexible budget materials variance, as follows:

Actual Cost		Standard Cost	
Actual quantity used	117,800	Standard quantity	114,000
×	×	×	×
Actual price per pound	$1.90	Standard price per pound	$2.00
	$223,820		$228,000
		Total variance: $4,180 Favorable	

To isolate the price and usage variances, insert a Variance Dividing column between the Actual Cost and Standard Cost columns. The Variance Dividing column combines standard and actual data, showing the *standard cost* multiplied by the *actual quantity* of materials purchased and used.[2] Exhibit 8.5 shows the result.

---

[2]In practice, raw materials are frequently stored in inventory prior to use. Differences may exist between the amount of materials purchased and the amount of materials used. In such cases, the price variance is based on the quantity of materials *purchased*, and the usage variance is based on the quantity of materials *used*. This text makes the simplifying assumption that the amount of materials purchased equals the amount of materials used during the period.

EXHIBIT 8.5

Materials Price and Usage Variances

Actual Cost		Variance Dividing Data		Standard Cost	
Actual quantity used	117,800	Actual quantity used	117,800	Standard quantity	114,000
×	×	×	×	×	×
Actual price per pound	$1.90	Standard price per pound	$2.00	Standard price per pound	$2.00
	$223,820		$235,600		$228,000
		Materials price variance $11,780 Favorable		Materials usage variance $7,600 Unfavorable	
		Total variance: $4,180 Favorable			

Algebraic solution.   The materials price variance (difference between the Actual Cost column and the Variance Dividing column) can be computed algebraically as follows:

$$\text{Price variance} = |\text{Actual price} - \text{Standard price}| \times \text{Actual quantity}$$
$$= |\$1.90 - \$2.00| \times 117,800$$
$$= \$0.10 \times 117,800$$
$$= \$11,780 \text{ Favorable}$$

Since the actual price ($1.90) is less than the standard price ($2.00), the materials price variance is favorable.

The materials usage variance (difference between the Variance Dividing column and the Standard Cost column) also can be determined algebraically, as follows:

$$\text{Usage variance} = |\text{Actual quantity} - \text{Standard quantity}| \times \text{Standard price}$$
$$= |117,800 - 114,000| \times \$2.00$$
$$= 3,800 \times \$2.00$$
$$= \$7,600 \text{ Unfavorable}$$

Responsibility for materials variances.   A purchasing agent is normally responsible for the **materials price variance.** Management establishes the standard materials cost based on a particular grade of material and assumptions about purchasing terms including volume discounts, cash discounts, transportation costs, and supplier services. A diligent purchasing agent places orders that take advantage of positive trading terms. In such circumstances, the company pays less than standard costs, resulting in a favorable price variance. Investigating the favorable price variance could result in identifying purchasing strategies to share with other purchasing agents. Analyzing favorable as well as unfavorable variances can result in efficiencies that benefit the entire production process.

In spite of a purchasing agent's diligence, unfavorable price variances may still occur. Suppliers may raise prices, poor scheduling by the production department may require more costly rush orders, or a truckers' strike may force the company to use a more expensive delivery system. These conditions are beyond a purchasing agent's control. Management must be careful to identify the real causes of unfavorable variances. False accusations and overreactions lead to resentment that will undermine the productive potential of the standard costing system.

The nature of the **materials usage variance** is readily apparent from the quantity data. Because the actual quantity used was more than the standard quantity, the variance is unfavorable. If management seeks to minimize cost, using more materials than expected is unfavorable. The materials usage variance is largely controlled by the production department. Materials waste caused by inexperienced workers, faulty machinery, negligent processing, or poor planning results in unfavorable usage variances.

REALITY BYTES

Most airlines will allow customers to book a flight approximately one year in advance at a price set on the day the reservation is made. Since the airline does not know what it will actual cost to operate a particular flight a year in advance, the price of the ticket will be based on its estimated costs. This can present a problem if costs rise significantly before the flight occurs.

Imagine that on December 14, 2007, Calvin Haines booked a flight from Boston to Seattle for July 19, 2008, and that the ticket price was $309. Between December 2007 and July 2008 many of the airline's costs would not change unexpectedly; for example the airplane has already been purchased and the salaries of the flight crew have already been set. However, in 2008 approximately 30 percent of the cost of operating an airline was for fuel. In December 2007, the spot price of jet fuel was $2.66 per gallon. The spot price of a commodity is the price it would sell for on a given day to someone who had not placed an advance order at a set price. By July 2008 the spot price for jet fuel had risen to $3.97 per gallon. In standard costing terminology, this would result in an unfavorable price variance. Of course, fuel prices can also rapidly change for the better. By February 2009 the price of jet fuel was down to $1.31 per gallon—one-third of its price just seven months earlier.

How can companies avoid some of the problems of having to set the prices they charge before they know what it will cost them to deliver the promised goods or services? Sometimes they cannot, but jet fuel prices can be hedged. That is, a company can commit to purchase fuel at an agreed-upon price at a future data. As of December 2008 Southwest Airlines had already contracted to buy 10 percent of its fuel needs through 2013, and Delta had hedged 26 percent of its needs through 2010.

Hedging has its own risks. When fuel prices drop the airline will still have had to honor its commitments to buy some of its fuel at a price higher than the spot price.

Sources: Federal government data and the companies' annual reports.

Unfavorable variances may also be caused by factors beyond the control of the production department. If the purchasing agent buys substandard materials the inferior materials may lead to more scrap (waste) during production, which would be reflected in unfavorable usage variances.

Calculating Labor Variances

Labor variances are calculated using the same general formulas as those used to compute materials price and usage variances. To illustrate, assume the labor cost per unit of product (trophy) for Melrose Manufacturing is as follows:

	Actual Data	Standard Data
Price *per hour*	$11.50	$12.00
Quantity of labor per unit of product	× 1.5 hours	× 1.4 hours
Cost *per unit* of product	$17.25	$16.80

Based on this detail, the total quantity of labor is:

	Actual Data	Standard Data
Actual production volume	19,000 units	19,000 units
Quantity of labor per unit of product	× 1.5 hours	× 1.4 hours
Total quantity of labor	28,500 hours	26,600 hours

Using this cost and quantity information, the labor price and usage variances are computed in Exhibit 8.6.

EXHIBIT 8.6

Labor Price and Usage Variances

Actual Cost		Variance Dividing Data		Standard Cost	
Actual hours used	28,500	Actual hours used (AHrs)	28,500	Standard hours (SHrs)	26,600
×	×	×	×	×	×
Actual price per labor hour (AP)	$11.50	Standard price per labor hour (SP)	$12.00	Standard price per labor hour	$12.00
	$327,750		$342,000		$319,200

Labor price variance $14,250 Favorable   Labor usage variance $22,800 Unfavorable

Algebraic solution: $|AP - SP| \times AHrs$ Algebraic solution: $|AHrs - SHrs| \times SP$

$|$11.50 - $12.00| \times 28,500 = $14,250$ $|28,500 - 26,600| \times $12.00 = $22,800$

Total variance: $8,550 Unfavorable

Responsibility for labor variances. The **labor price variance** is favorable because the actual rate paid for labor is less than the standard rate. The production supervisor is usually responsible for the labor price variance because price variances normally result from labor assignments rather than underpayment or overpayment of the hourly rate. Because labor costs are usually fixed by contracts, paying more or less than established rates is not likely. However, using semiskilled labor to perform highly skilled tasks or vice versa will produce price variances. Similarly, using unanticipated overtime will cause unfavorable variances. Production department supervisors control which workers are assigned to which tasks and are therefore accountable for the resulting labor price variances.

Labor usage variances measure the productivity of the labor force. Because Melrose used more labor than expected, the labor usage variance is unfavorable. Unsatisfactory labor performance has many causes; low morale or poor supervision are possibilities. Furthermore, machine breakdowns, inferior materials, and poor planning can waste workers' time and reduce productivity. Production department supervisors generally control and are responsible for labor usage variances.

Price and usage variances may be interrelated. Using less-skilled employees who earned less but took longer to do the work could have caused both the favorable labor price variance and the unfavorable labor usage variance. As mentioned earlier, management must exercise diligence in determining causes of variances before concluding who should be held responsible for them.

✓ CHECK YOURSELF 8.3

DogHouse, Inc., expected to build 200 doghouses during July. Each doghouse was expected to require 2 hours of direct labor. Labor cost was expected to be $10 per hour. The company actually built 220 doghouses using an average of 2.1 labor hours per doghouse at an actual labor rate averaging $9.80 per hour. Determine the labor rate and usage variances.

Answer

Labor price variance = |Actual rate − Standard rate| × Actual quantity

Labor price variance = $|$9.80 - $10.00| \times (220 \text{ units} \times 2.1 \text{ hours}) = 92.40 Favorable

Labor usage variance = |Actual quantity − Standard quantity| × Standard rate

Labor usage variance = $|[220 \times 2.1] - [220 \times 2.0]| \times $10 = 220.00 Unfavorable

REALITY BYTES

Does standard costing apply to service companies as well as manufacturers? Absolutely! If you take your car into an auto dealership to be repaired and the service invoice shows that the repair took one hour to perform, you should not assume that was the actual time the repair required. The time for which you were charged was probably based on the standard time a repair of that type should have taken. The mechanic may have gotten this standard time from a reference manual such as the *Chilton Labor Guide* or the *Real-Time Labor Guide,* which are available in either print or CD versions. Some repair jobs can be completed in less time than the guides suggest, and some jobs will take longer. But since customers are charged based on a standard time allowed, two customers having the same repair performed will be charged the same price.

Variable Overhead Variances

Variable overhead variances are based on the same general formulas used to compute the materials and labor price and usage variances. Unique characteristics of variable overhead costs, however, require special attention. First, variable overhead represents many inputs such as supplies, utilities, and indirect labor. The variable overhead cost pool is normally assigned to products based on a predetermined variable overhead allocation rate. Using a single rate to assign a mixture of different costs complicates variance interpretation. Suppose the actual variable overhead rate is higher than the predetermined rate. Did the company pay more than expected for supplies, utilities, maintenance, or some other input variable? The cost of some variable overhead items may have been higher than expected while others were lower than expected. Similarly, a variable overhead usage variance provides no clue about which overhead inputs were over- or underused. Because meaningful interpretation of the results is difficult, many companies do not calculate price and usage variances for variable overhead costs. We therefore limit coverage of this subject to the total flexible budget variances shown in Exhibit 8.3.

Selling, General, and Administrative Cost Variances

Variable selling, general, and administrative (SG&A) costs can have *price and usage* variances. For example, suppose Melrose decides to attach a promotional advertising brochure to each trophy it sells. Melrose may pay more or less than expected for each brochure (a price variance). Melrose also could use more or fewer of the brochures than expected (a usage variance). Businesses frequently compute variances for SG&A costs such as sales commissions, food and entertainment, postage, and supplies. The same algebraic formulas used to compute variances for variable manufacturing costs apply to computing variable SG&A cost variances.

For your convenience the general formulas for determining price and usage variances are shown in Exhibit 8.7.

EXHIBIT 8.7

Algebraic Formulas for Variances

Variable cost variances (materials, labor, and overhead)

a. Price variance

|Actual price − Standard price| × Actual quantity

b. Usage variance

|Actual quantity − Standard quantity| × Standard price

A Look Back

The essential topics of this chapter are the master budget, flexible budgets, and variance analysis. The *master budget* is determined by multiplying the standard sales price and per unit variable costs by the planned volume of activity. The master budget is prepared at the beginning of the accounting period for planning purposes. It is not adjusted to reflect differences between the planned and actual volume of activity. Since this budget remains unchanged regardless of actual volume, it is also called a *static budget. Flexible budgets* differ from static budgets in that they show the estimated amount of revenue and costs expected at different levels of volume. Both static and flexible budgets are based on the same per unit standard amounts and the same fixed costs. The total amounts of revenue and costs in a static budget differ from those in a flexible budget because they are based on different levels of volume. Flexible budgets are used for planning, cost control, and performance evaluation.

The differences between standard (sometimes called *expected* or *estimated*) and actual amounts are called *variances.* Variances are used to evaluate managerial performance and can be either favorable or unfavorable. *Favorable sales variances* occur when actual sales are greater than expected sales. *Unfavorable sales variances* occur when actual sales are less than expected sales. *Favorable cost variances* occur when actual costs are less than expected costs. *Unfavorable cost variances* occur when actual costs are more than expected costs.

Volume variances are caused by the difference between the static and flexible budgets. Since both static and flexible budgets are based on the same standard sales price and costs per unit, the volume variances are attributable solely to differences between the planned and the actual volume of activity. Favorable sales volume variances suggest that the marketing manager has performed well by selling more than was expected. Unfavorable sales volume variances suggest the inverse. Favorable or unfavorable variable cost volume variances are not meaningful for performance evaluation because variable costs are expected to change in proportion to changes in the volume of activity.

Flexible budget variances are computed by taking the difference between the amounts of revenue and variable costs that are expected at the actual volume of activity and the actual amounts of revenue and variable costs incurred at the actual volume of activity. Since the volume of activity is the same for the flexible budget and the actual results, variances are caused by the differences between the standard and actual sales price and per unit costs. Flexible budget variances are used for cost control and performance evaluation.

The total fixed cost variance is composed of the following:

a. Fixed manufacturing overhead cost spending variance

|Actual fixed overhead costs − Budgeted fixed overhead|

b. Fixed manufacturing overhead cost volume variance

|Applied fixed overhead costs − Budgeted fixed overhead costs|

The fixed overhead spending variance occurs because actual costs may be more or less than expected. For example, a production supervisor's salary will remain unchanged regardless of the volume of activity, but the supervisor may receive a raise resulting in higher than expected fixed costs. The fixed overhead volume variance is favorable if the actual volume of production is greater than the expected volume. A higher volume of production results in a lower fixed cost per unit. The volume variance measures how effectively production facilities are being used.

Flexible budget variances can be subdivided into *price and usage variances.* Price and usage variances for materials and labor can be computed with the following formulas. Variable overhead variances are calculated with the same general formulas; interpreting the results is difficult, however, because of the variety of inputs combined in variable overhead.

Price variance = |Actual price − Standard price| × Actual quantity

Usage variance = |Actual quantity − Standard quantity| × Standard price

The purchasing agent is normally accountable for the material price variance. The production department supervisor is usually responsible for the materials usage variance and the labor price and usage variances.

Management must interpret variances with care. For example, a purchasing agent may produce a favorable price variance by buying inferior materials at a low cost. However, an unfavorable labor usage variance may result because employees have difficulty using the substandard materials. The production supervisor is faced with an unfavorable usage variance for which she is not responsible. In addition, the purchasing agent's undesirable choice produced a favorable price variance. Favorable variances do not necessarily reflect good performance and unfavorable variances do not always suggest poor performance. The underlying causes of variances must be investigated before assigning responsibility for them.

 ## A Look Forward

Chapter 9 introduces other techniques for evaluating managerial performance. The concept of decentralization and its relationship to responsibility accounting will be covered. You will learn how to calculate and interpret return on investment and residual income. Finally, you will study approaches used to establish the price of products that are transferred between divisions of the same company.

A step-by-step audio-narrated series of slides is provided on the text website at www.mhhe.com/edmonds2011.

SELF-STUDY REVIEW PROBLEM

Bugout Pesticides, Inc., established the following standard price and costs for a termite control product that it sells to exterminators.

Variable price and cost data (per unit)	Standard	Actual
Sales price	$52.00	$49.00
Materials cost	10.00	10.66
Labor cost	12.00	11.90
Overhead cost	7.00	7.05
General, selling, and administrative (GS&A) cost	8.00	7.92
Expected fixed costs (in total)		
Manufacturing overhead	$150,000	$140,000
General, selling, and administrative	60,000	64,000

The 2010 master budget was established at an expected volume of 25,000 units. Actual production and sales volume for the year was 26,000 units.

Required

a. Prepare the pro forma income statement for Bugout's 2010 master budget.

b. Prepare a flexible budget income statement at the actual volume.

c. Determine the sales and variable cost volume variances and indicate whether they are favorable or unfavorable. Comment on how Bugout would use the variances to evaluate performance.

d. Determine the flexible budget variances and indicate whether they are favorable or unfavorable. Provide another name for the fixed cost flexible budget variances.

e. Identify the two variances Bugout is most likely to analyze further. Explain why you chose these two variances. Who is normally responsible for the variances you chose to investigate?

f. Each unit of product was expected to require 4 pounds of material, which has a standard price of $2.50 per pound. Actual materials usage was 4.1 pounds per unit at an actual price of $2.60 per pound. Determine the materials price and usage variances.

Solution to Requirements a, b, and c

Number of units		25,000	26,000	
	Per Unit Standards	Master Budget	Flexible Budget	Volume Variances
Sales revenue	$52	$1,300,000	$1,352,000	$52,000 F
Variable manufacturing costs				
Materials	10	250,000	260,000	10,000 U
Labor	12	300,000	312,000	12,000 U
Overhead	7	175,000	182,000	7,000 U
Variable SG&A	8	200,000	208,000	8,000 U
Contribution margin		375,000	390,000	15,000 F
Fixed costs				
Manufacturing overhead		150,000	150,000	0
SG&A		60,000	60,000	0
Net income		$ 165,000	$ 180,000	$15,000 F

The sales and variable cost volume variances are useful in determining how changes in sales volume affect revenues and costs. Since the flexible budget is based on standard prices and costs, the variances do not provide insight into differences between standard prices and costs versus actual prices and costs.

Solution to Requirement d

Number of units		26,000	26,000	
	Actual Unit Price/Cost	Flexible Budget*	Actual Results	Flexible Budget Variances
Sales revenue	$49.00	$1,352,000	$1,274,000	$78,000 U
Variable manufacturing costs				
Materials	10.66	260,000	277,160	17,160 U
Labor	11.90	312,000	309,400	2,600 F
Overhead	7.05	182,000	183,300	1,300 U
Variable SG&A	7.92	208,000	205,920	2,080 F
Contribution margin		390,000	298,220	91,780 U
Fixed costs				
Manufacturing overhead		150,000	140,000	10,000 F[†]
SG&A		60,000	64,000	4,000 U[†]
Net income		$ 180,000	$ 94,220	$85,780 U

*The price and cost data for the flexible budget come from the table shown at the beginning of the problem.
[†]The flexible budget variances for the fixed costs are also called *spending variances*.

Solution to Requirement e

The management by exception doctrine focuses attention on the sales price variance and the materials variance. The two variances are material in size and are generally under the control of management. Upper-level marketing managers are responsible for the sales price variance.

These managers are normally responsible for establishing the sales price. In this case, the actual sales price is less than the planned sales price, resulting in an unfavorable flexible budget variance. Mid-level production supervisors and purchasing agents are normally responsible for the materials cost variance. This variance could have been caused by waste or by paying more for materials than the standard price. Further analysis of the materials cost variance follows in Requirement *f*.

Solution to Requirement f

(Actual price − Standard price)	×	Actual quantity		= Price variance
($2.60 − $2.50)	×	(4.1 pounds × 26,000 units)	=	$10,660 U

(Actual quantity − Standard quantity)	× Standard price	= Usage variance
[(4.1 × 26,000) − (4.0 × 26,000)]	× $2.50	= $6,500 U

The total of the price and usage variances [($10,660 + $6,500) = $17,160] equals the total materials flexible budget variance computed in Requirement *d*.

KEY TERMS

Applied fixed cost 356	Labor usage variance 365	Predetermined overhead
Budget slack 360	Lax standard 358	rate 356
Fixed cost spending	Making the numbers 352	Sales price variance 354
variance 356	Management by	Sales volume variance 352
Fixed cost volume variance 350	exception 357	Standard 358
Flexible budget 350	Material variance 359	Static budget 350
Flexible budget variance 354	Materials price variance 363	Variable cost volume
Ideal standard 358	Materials usage variance 363	variance 352
Labor price variance 365	Practical standard 358	Variances 351

QUESTIONS

1. What is the difference between a static budget and a flexible budget? When is each used?

2. When the operating costs for Bill Smith's production department were released, he was sure that he would be getting a raise. His costs were $20,000 less than the planned cost in the master budget. His supervisor informed him that the results look good but that a more in-depth analysis is necessary before raises can be assigned. What other considerations could Mr. Smith's supervisor be interested in before she rates his performance?

3. When are sales and cost variances favorable and unfavorable?

4. Joan Mason, the marketing manager for a large manufacturing company, believes her unfavorable sales volume variance is the responsibility of the production department. What production circumstances that she does not control could have been responsible for her poor performance?

5. When would variable cost volume variances be expected to be unfavorable? How

should unfavorable variable cost volume variances be interpreted?

6. What factors could lead to an increase in sales revenues that would not merit congratulations to the marketing manager?

7. With respect to fixed costs, what are the consequences of the actual volume of activity exceeding the planned volume?

8. How are flexible budget variances determined? What causes these variances?

9. Minnie Divers, the manager of the marketing department for one of the industry's leading retail businesses, has been notified by the accounting department that her department experienced an unfavorable sales volume variance in the preceding period but a favorable sales price variance. Based on these contradictory results, how would you interpret her overall performance as suggested by her variances?

10. What three attributes are necessary for establishing the best standards? What information and considerations should be taken into account when establishing standards?

11. What are the three ranges of difficulty in standard setting? What level of difficulty normally results in superior employee motivation?

12. "So many variances," exclaimed Carl, a production manager with Bonnyville Manufacturing. "How do I determine the variances that need investigation? I can't possibly investigate all of them." Which variances will lead to useful information?

13. What is the primary benefit associated with using a standard cost system?

14. A processing department of Carmine Corporation experienced a high unfavorable materials quantity variance. The plant manager initially commented, "The best way to solve this problem is to fire the supervisor of the processing department." Do you agree? Explain.

15. Sara Anderson says that she is a busy woman with no time to look at favorable variances. Instead, she concentrates solely on the unfavorable ones. She says that favorable variances imply that employees are doing better than expected and need only

quick congratulations. In contrast, unfavorable variances indicate that change is needed to get the substandard performance up to par. Do you agree? Explain.

16. What two factors affect the total materials and labor variances?

17. Who is normally responsible for a materials price variance? Identify two factors that may be beyond this individual's control that could cause an unfavorable price variance.

18. John Jamail says that he doesn't understand why companies have labor price variances because most union contracts or other binding agreements set wage rates that do not normally change in the short term. How could rate variances occur even when binding commitments hold the dollar per hour rate constant?

19. Which individuals are normally held responsible for labor usage variances?

20. What is the primary cause of an unfavorable fixed cost volume variance?

21. What is the primary cause of a favorable fixed cost spending variance?

MULTIPLE-CHOICE QUESTIONS

Multiple-choice questions are provided on the text website at www.mhhe.com/edmonds2011.

EXERCISES—SERIES A

All applicable Exercises in Series A are available with McGraw-Hill's *Connect Accounting*.

Exercise 8-1A *Classifying variances as favorable or unfavorable*

LO 2

Required

Indicate whether each of the following variances is favorable or unfavorable. The first one has been done as an example.

Item to Classify	Standard	Actual	Type of Variance
Labor cost	$10.00 per hour	$9.60 per hour	Favorable
Labor usage	61,000 hours	61,800 hours	
Fixed cost spending	$400,000	$390,000	
Fixed cost per unit (volume)	$3.20 per unit	$3.16 per unit	
Sales volume	40,000 units	42,000 units	
Sales price	$3.60 per unit	$3.63 per unit	
Materials cost	$2.90 per pound	$3.00 per pound	
Materials usage	91,000 pounds	90,000 pounds	

LO 2

Exercise 8-2A *Determining amount and type (favorable vs. unfavorable) of variance*

Required

Compute variances for the following items and indicate whether each variance is favorable (F) or unfavorable (U).

Item	Budget	Actual	Variance	F or U
Sales price	$650	$525		
Sales revenue	$580,000	$600,000		
Cost of goods sold	$385,000	$360,000		
Material purchases at 5,000 pounds	$275,000	$280,000		
Materials usage	$180,000	$178,000		
Production volume	950 units	900 units		
Wages at 4,000 hours	$60,000	$58,700		
Labor usage at $16 per hour	$96,000	$97,000		
Research and development expense	$22,000	$25,000		
Selling and administrative expenses	$49,000	$40,000		

LO 1

Exercise 8-3A *Preparing master and flexible budgets*

Sexton Manufacturing Company established the following standard price and cost data.

Sales price	$8.00 per unit
Variable manufacturing cost	$4 per unit
Fixed manufacturing cost	$3,000 total
Fixed selling and administrative cost	$1,000 total

Sexton planned to produce and sell 2,000 units. Actual production and sales amounted to 2,200 units.

Required

a. Prepare the pro forma income statement in contribution format that would appear in a master budget.

b. Prepare the pro forma income statement in contribution format that would appear in a flexible budget.

LO 3

Exercise 8-4A *Determining sales and variable cost volume variances*

Required

Use the information provided in Exercise 8-3A.

a. Determine the sales and variable cost volume variances.

b. Classify the variances as favorable (F) or unfavorable (U).

c. Comment on the usefulness of the variances with respect to performance evaluation and identify the member of the management team most likely to be responsible for these variances.

d. Determine the amount of fixed cost that will appear in the flexible budget.

e. Determine the fixed cost per unit based on planned activity and the fixed cost per unit based on actual activity. Assuming Sexton uses information in the master budget to price the company's product, comment on how the fixed cost volume variance could affect the company's profitability.

LO 4

Exercise 8-5A *Determining flexible budget variances*

Use the standard price and cost data provided in Exercise 8-3A. Assume that the actual sales price is $7.65 per unit and that the actual variable cost is $4.25 per unit. The actual fixed manufacturing cost is $2,500, and the actual selling and administrative costs are $1,025.

Required

a. Determine the flexible budget variances.

b. Classify the variances as favorable (F) or unfavorable (U).

c. Provide another name for the fixed cost flexible budget variances.

d. Comment on the usefulness of the variances with respect to performance evaluation and identify the member(s) of the management team who is (are) most likely to be responsible for these variances.

Exercise 8-6A   *Using a flexible budget to accommodate market uncertainty*

LO 4

According to its original plan, Darey Consulting Services Company would charge its customers for service at $125 per hour in 2011. The company president expects consulting services provided to customers to reach 45,000 hours at that rate. The marketing manager, however, argues that actual results may range from 40,000 hours to 50,000 hours because of market uncertainty. Darey's standard variable cost is $48 per hour, and its standard fixed cost is $1,500,000.

Required

Develop flexible budgets based on the assumptions of service levels at 40,000 hours, 45,000 hours, and 50,000 hours.

Exercise 8-7A   *Evaluating a decision to increase sales volume by lowering sales price*

LO 3, 4

Ender Educational Services had budgeted its training service charge at $75 per hour. The company planned to provide 30,000 hours of training services during 2012. By lowering the service charge to $60 per hour, the company was able to increase the actual number of hours to 31,500.

Required

a. Determine the sales volume variance, and indicate whether it is favorable (F) or unfavorable (U).

b. Determine the flexible budget variance, and indicate whether it is favorable (F) or unfavorable (U).

c. Did lowering the price of training services increase revenue? Explain.

Exercise 8-8A   *Responsibility for the fixed cost volume variance*

LO 5

Ragan Company expected to sell 400,000 of its pagers during 2011. It set the standard sales price for the pager at $30 each. During June, it became obvious that the company would be unable to attain the expected volume of sales. Ragan's chief competitor, Selma Corporation, had lowered prices and was pulling market share from Ragan. To be competitive, Ragan matched Selma's price, lowering its sales price to $28 per pager. Selma responded by lowering its price even further to $24 per pager. In an emergency meeting of key personnel, Ragan's accountant, Suzy Kennedy, stated, "Our cost structure simply won't support a sales price in the $24 range." The production manager, Larry Jones, said, "I don't understand why I'm here. The only unfavorable variance on my report is a fixed manufacturing overhead cost volume variance and that one is not my fault. We shouldn't be making the product if the marketing department isn't selling it."

Required

a. Describe a scenario in which the production manager is responsible for the fixed cost volume variance.

b. Describe a scenario in which the marketing manager is responsible for the fixed cost volume variance.

c. Explain how a decline in sales volume would affect Ragan's ability to lower its sales price.

Exercise 8-9A   *Responsibility for variable manufacturing cost variance*

LO 4

Goslin Manufacturing Company set its standard variable manufacturing cost at $24 per unit of product. The company planned to make and sell 4,000 units of product during 2012. More specifically, the master budget called for total variable manufacturing cost to be $96,000. Actual production during 2012 was 4,200 units, and actual variable manufacturing costs amounted to

$101,640. The production supervisor was asked to explain the variance between budgeted and actual cost ($101,640 − $96,000 = $5,640). The supervisor responded that she was not responsible for the variance that was caused solely by the increase in sales volume controlled by the marketing department.

Required

Do you agree with the production supervisor? Explain.

LO 7

Exercise 8-10A   *Calculating the materials usage variance*

Laura Pierre is the manager of the Roebuck Bagel Shop. The corporate office had budgeted her store to sell 3,000 ham sandwiches during the week beginning July 17. Each sandwich was expected to contain 7 ounces of ham. During the week of July 17, the store actually sold 3,500 sandwiches and used 25,000 ounces of ham. The standard cost of ham is $0.20 per ounce. The variance report from company headquarters showed an unfavorable materials usage variance of $800. Ms. Pierre thought the variance was too high, but she had no accounting background and did not know how to register a proper objection.

Required

a. Is the variance calculated properly? If not, recalculate it.
b. Provide three independent explanations as to what could have caused the materials usage variance that you determined in Requirement *a*.

LO 7

Exercise 8-11A   *Determining materials price and usage variances*

Gwen's Florals produced a special Mother's Day arrangement that included six roses. The standard and actual costs of the roses used in each arrangement follow.

	Standard	Actual
Average number of roses per arrangement	6.5	7
Price per rose	× $0.36	× $0.32
Cost of roses per arrangement	$2.34	$2.24

Gwen's Florals planned to make 750 arrangements but actually made 790.

Required

a. Determine the total flexible budget materials variance and indicate whether it is favorable (F) or unfavorable (U).
b. Determine the materials price variance and indicate whether it is favorable (F) or unfavorable (U).
c. Determine the materials usage variance and indicate whether it is favorable (F) or unfavorable (U).
d. Confirm the accuracy of Requirements *a*, *b*, and *c* by showing that the sum of the price and usage variances equals the total variance.

LO 7

Exercise 8-12A   *Responsibility for materials usage variance*

Lehman Fruit Basket Company makes baskets of assorted fruit. The standard and actual costs of oranges used in each basket of fruit follow.

	Standard	Actual
Average number of oranges per basket	4.50	6.30
Price per orange	× $0.28	× $0.25
Cost of oranges per basket	$1.26	$1.58

Lehman actually produced 25,000 baskets.

Required

a. Determine the materials price variance and indicate whether it is favorable (F) or unfavorable (U).

b. Determine the materials usage variance and indicate whether it is favorable (F) or unfavorable (U).

c. Explain why the purchasing agent may have been responsible for the usage variance.

Exercise 8-13A *Responsibility for labor price and usage variances* LO 7

Aman Manufacturing Company incurred a favorable labor price variance and an unfavorable labor usage variance.

Required

a. Describe a scenario in which the personnel manager is responsible for the unfavorable usage variance.

b. Describe a scenario in which the production manager is responsible for the unfavorable usage variance.

Exercise 8-14A *Calculating and explaining labor price and usage variances* LO 7

Huber and Sons, a CPA firm, established the following standard labor cost data for completing what the firm referred to as a Class 2 tax return. Huber expected each Class 2 return to require 4.0 hours of labor at a cost of $50 per hour. The firm actually completed 600 returns. Actual labor hours averaged 4.4 hours per return and actual labor cost amounted to $46 per hour.

Required

a. Determine the total labor variance and indicate whether it is favorable (F) or unfavorable (U).

b. Determine the labor price variance and indicate whether it is favorable (F) or unfavorable (U).

c. Determine the labor usage variance and indicate whether it is favorable (F) or unfavorable (U).

d. Explain what could have caused these variances.

Exercise 8-15A *Determining the standard labor price* LO 7

Kerensky Car Wash, Inc., expected to wash 1,000 cars during the month of August. Washing each car was expected to require 0.2 hours of labor. The company actually used 210 hours of labor to wash 940 cars. The labor usage variance was $352 unfavorable.

Required

a. Determine the standard labor price.

b. If the actual labor rate is $14, indicate whether the labor price variance would be favorable (F) or unfavorable (U).

Exercise 8-16A *Calculating the variable overhead variance* LO 5, 6, 7

Pena Company established a predetermined variable overhead cost rate at $9.40 per direct labor hour. The actual variable overhead cost rate was $8.30 per hour. The planned level of labor activity was 73,000 hours of labor. The company actually used 80,000 hours of labor.

Required

a. Determine the total flexible budget variable overhead cost variance.

b. Like many companies, Pena has decided not to separate the total variable overhead cost variance into price and usage components. Explain why Pena made this choice.

Exercise 8-17A *Determining and interpreting fixed cost variances* LO 5, 6, 7

Sloan Company established a predetermined fixed overhead cost rate of $29 per unit of product. The company planned to make 7,000 units of product but actually produced only 6,500 units. Actual fixed overhead costs were $212,000.

Required

a. Determine the fixed cost spending variance and indicate whether it is favorable or unfavorable. Explain what this variance means. Identify the manager(s) who is (are) responsible for the variance.

b. Determine the fixed cost volume variance and indicate whether it is favorable or unfavorable. Explain why this variance is important. Identify the manager(s) who is (are) responsible for the variance.

PROBLEMS—SERIES A

All applicable Problems in Series A are available with McGraw-Hill's *Connect Accounting*.

≡ connect
[ACCOUNTING]

LO 1, 3

CHECK FIGURES
a. NI = $81,000
b. NI at 29,000 units: $72,000

Problem 8-18A   *Determining sales and variable cost volume variances*

Todhunter Publications established the following standard price and costs for a hardcover picture book that the company produces.

Standard price and variable costs	
Sales price	$36.00
Materials cost	9.00
Labor cost	4.50
Overhead cost	6.30
Selling, general, and administrative costs	7.20
Planned fixed costs	
Manufacturing overhead	$135,000
Selling, general, and administrative	54,000

Todhunter planned to make and sell 30,000 copies of the book.

Required

a. Prepare the pro forma income statement that would appear in the master budget.

b. Prepare flexible budget income statements, assuming production volumes of 29,000 and 31,000 units.

c. Determine the sales and variable cost volume variances, assuming volume is actually 31,000 units.

d. Indicate whether the variances are favorable (F) or unfavorable (U).

e. Comment on how Todhunter could use the variances to evaluate performance.

LO 4

CHECK FIGURE
Flexible budget variance
of NI: $20,450 U

Problem 8-19A   *Determining and interpreting flexible budget variances*

Use the standard price and cost data supplied in Problem 8-18A. Assume that Todhunter actually produced and sold 31,000 books. The actual sales price and costs incurred follow.

Actual price and variable costs	
Sales price	$35.00
Materials cost	9.20
Labor cost	4.40
Overhead cost	6.35
Selling, general, and administrative costs	7.00
Actual fixed costs	
Manufacturing overhead	$120,000
Selling, general, and administrative	60,000

Required

a. Determine the flexible budget variances. Provide another name for the fixed cost flexible budget variances.

b. Indicate whether each variance is favorable (F) or unfavorable (U).

c. Identify the management position responsible for each variance. Explain what could have caused the variance.

Problem 8-20A *Flexible budget planning*

Luke Chou, the president of Digitech Computer Services, needs your help. He wonders about the potential effects on the firm's net income if he changes the service rate that the firm charges its customers. The following basic data pertain to fiscal year 2012.

Standard rate and variable costs	
Service rate per hour	$80.00
Labor cost	40.00
Overhead cost	7.20
Selling, general, and administrative cost	4.30
Expected fixed costs	
Facility repair	$525,000.00
Selling, general, and administrative	150,000.00

Required

a. Prepare the pro forma income statement that would appear in the master budget if the firm expects to provide 30,000 hours of services in 2012.

b. A marketing consultant suggests to Mr. Chou that the service rate may affect the number of service hours that the firm can achieve. According to the consultant's analysis, if Digitech charges customers $75 per hour, the firm can achieve 38,000 hours of services. Prepare a flexible budget using the consultant's assumption.

c. The same consultant also suggests that if the firm raises its rate to $85 per hour, the number of service hours will decline to 25,000. Prepare a flexible budget using the new assumption.

d. Evaluate the three possible outcomes you determined in Requirements *a*, *b*, and *c* and recommend a pricing strategy.

Problem 8-21A *Determining materials price and usage variances*

Vacher Fruit Drink Company planned to make 200,000 containers of apple juice. It expected to use two cups of frozen apple concentrate to make each container of juice, thus using 400,000 cups (200,000 containers × 2 cups) of frozen concentrate. The standard price of one cup of apple concentrate is $0.25. Vacher actually paid $110,168.10 to purchase 408,030 cups of concentrate, which was used to make 201,000 containers of apple juice.

Required

a. Are flexible budget materials variances based on the planned volume of activity (200,000 containers) or actual volume of activity (201,000 containers)?

b. Compute the actual price per cup of concentrate.

c. Compute the standard quantity (number of cups of concentrate) required to produce the containers.

d. Compute the materials price variance and indicate whether it is favorable (F) or unfavorable (U).

e. Compute the materials usage variance and indicate whether it is favorable (F) or unfavorable (U).

Problem 8-22A *Determining labor price and usage variances*

Lakesha's Doll Company produces handmade dolls. The standard amount of time spent on each doll is 1.5 hours. The standard cost of labor is $7.72 per hour. The company planned to make 8,000 dolls during the year but actually used 12,500 hours of labor to make 9,000 dolls. The payroll amounted to $98,875.

Required

a. Should labor variances be based on the planned volume of 8,000 dolls or the actual volume of 9,000 dolls?

b. Prepare a table that shows the standard labor price, the actual labor price, the standard labor hours, and the actual labor hours.

c. Compute the labor price variance and indicate whether it is favorable (F) or unfavorable (U).
d. Compute the labor usage variance and indicate whether it is favorable (F) or unfavorable (U).

Problem 8-23A   *Computing fixed cost variances*

In addition to other costs, Fenwick Telephone Company planned to incur $441,000 of fixed manufacturing overhead in making 350,000 telephones. Fenwick actually produced 359,000 telephones, incurring actual overhead costs of $447,000. Fenwick establishes its predetermined overhead rate based on the planned volume of production (expected number of telephones).

Required

a. Calculate the predetermined overhead rate.
b. Determine the fixed cost spending variance and indicate whether it is favorable (F) or unfavorable (U).
c. Determine the fixed cost volume variance and indicate whether it is favorable (F) or unfavorable (U).

LO 5, 7

eXcel

CHECK FIGURES
d. Price variance: $3,864 F
g. Fixed cost volume variance
   $940 F

Problem 8-24A   *Computing materials, labor, and cost variances*

The following data were drawn from the records of Inman Corporation.

Planned volume for year (static budget)	4,000 units
Standard direct materials cost per unit	3.1 lbs. @ $1.50 per pound
Standard direct labor cost per unit	2 hours @ $4.00 per hour
Total expected fixed overhead costs	$18,800
Actual volume for the year (flexible budget)	4,200 units
Actual direct materials cost per unit	2.7 lbs. @ $2.00 per pound
Actual direct labor cost per unit	2.3 hrs. @ $3.60 per hour
Total actual fixed overhead costs	$15,000

Required

a. Prepare a materials variance information table showing the standard price, the actual price, the standard quantity, and the actual quantity.
b. Calculate the materials price and usage variances. Indicate whether the variances are favorable (F) or unfavorable (U).
c. Prepare a labor variance information table showing the standard price, the actual price, the standard hours, and the actual hours.
d. Calculate the labor price and usage variances. Indicate whether the variances are favorable (F) or unfavorable (U).
e. Calculate the predetermined overhead rate, assuming that Inman uses the number of units as the allocation base.
f. Calculate the fixed cost spending variance. Indicate whether the variance is favorable (F) or unfavorable (U).
g. Calculate the fixed cost volume variance. Indicate whether the variance is favorable (F) or unfavorable (U).

LO 5, 7

CHECK FIGURES
b. Usage variance: $2,781 U
d. Price variance: $8,916 U

Problem 8-25A   *Computing materials, labor, and fixed cost variances*

Lennox Manufacturing Company produces a component part of a top secret military communication device. Standard production and cost data for the part, Product X, follow.

Planned production	30,000 units
Per unit direct materials	2 lbs. @ $1.80 per lb.
Per unit direct labor	3 hrs. @ $8.00 per hr.
Total estimated fixed overhead costs	$702,000

Lennox purchased and used 63,345 pounds of material at an average cost of $1.85 per pound. Labor usage amounted to 89,160 hours at an average of $8.10 per hour. Actual production amounted to 30,900 units. Actual fixed overhead costs amounted to $738,000. The company completed and sold all inventory for $1,800,000.

Required

a. Prepare a materials variance information table showing the standard price, the actual price, the standard quantity, and the actual quantity.

b. Calculate the materials price and usage variances. Indicate whether the variances are favorable (F) or unfavorable (U).

c. Prepare a labor variance information table showing the standard price, the actual price, the standard hours, and the actual hours.

d. Calculate the labor price and usage variances. Indicate whether the variances are favorable (F) or unfavorable (U).

e. Calculate the predetermined overhead rate, assuming that Lennox uses the number of units as the allocation base.

f. Calculate the fixed cost spending and volume variances and indicate whether they are favorable (F) or unfavorable (U).

g. Determine the amount of gross margin Lennox would report on the year-end income statement.

Problem 8-26A *Computing variances*

LO 7

Osmond Manufacturing Company produces a single product. The following data apply to the standard cost of materials and labor associated with making the product.

Materials quantity per unit	1 pound
Materials price	$5.00 per pound
Labor quantity per unit	2 hours
Labor price	$9.00 per hour

During the year, the company made 1,800 units of product. At the end of the year, the following variances had been calculated.

Materials usage variance	$400 Favorable
Materials price variance	$352 Unfavorable
Labor usage variance	$1,800 Unfavorable
Labor price variance	$2,850 Favorable

Required

a. Determine the actual amount of materials used.

b. Determine the actual price paid per pound for materials.

c. Determine the actual labor hours used.

d. Determine the actual labor price per hour.

Problem 8-27A *Computing standard cost and analyzing variances*

LO 5, 7

Quilter Company manufactures molded candles that are finished by hand. The company developed the following standards for a new line of drip candles:

Amount of direct materials per candle	1.6 pounds
Price of direct materials per pound	$0.60
Quantity of labor per unit	1 hours
Price of direct labor per hour	$8.00/hour
Total budgeted fixed overhead	$156,000

CHECK FIGURES
e. Usage variance for
   direct materials: $960 U
f. Volume variance: $31,200 U

During 2010, Quilter planned to produce 30,000 drip candles. Production lagged behind expectations, and it actually produced only 24,000 drip candles. At year-end, direct materials purchased and used amounted to 40,000 pounds at a unit price of $0.54 per pound. Direct labor costs were actually $7.50 per hour and 26,400 actual hours were worked to produce the drip candles. Overhead for the year actually amounted to $132,000. Overhead is applied to products using a predetermined overhead rate based on estimated units.

Required

(Round all computations to two decimal places.)

a. Compute the standard cost per candle for direct materials, direct labor, and overhead.
b. Determine the total standard cost for one drip candle.
c. Compute the actual cost per candle for direct materials, direct labor, and overhead.
d. Compute the total actual cost per candle.
e. Compute the price and usage variances for direct materials and direct labor. Identify any variances that Quilter should investigate. Offer possible cause(s) for the variances.
f. Compute the fixed cost spending and volume variances. Explain your findings.
g. Although the individual variances (price, usage, and overhead) were large, the standard cost per unit and the actual cost per unit differed by only a few cents. Explain why.

LO 1, 2, 3, 4

CHECK FIGURE
b. Variance of surplus: $1,134 U

Problem 8-28A *Analyzing not-for-profit entity variances*

The Midwest Management Association held its annual public relations luncheon in April 2012. Based on the previous year's results, the organization allocated $21,360 of its operating budget to cover the cost of the luncheon. To ensure that costs would be appropriately controlled, Michelle Laird, the treasurer, prepared the following budget for the 2012 luncheon.

The budget for the luncheon was based on the following expectations.

1. The meal cost per person was expected to be $11.80. The cost driver for meals was attendance, which was expected to be 1,400 individuals.
2. Postage was based on $0.44 per invitation and 3,000 invitations were expected to be mailed. The cost driver for postage was number of invitations mailed.
3. The facility charge is $1,000 for a room that will accommodate up to 1,600 people; the charge for one to hold more than 1,600 people is $1,500.
4. A fixed amount was designated for printing, decorations, the speaker's gift, and publicity.

MIDWEST MANAGEMENT ASSOCIATION
Public Relations Luncheon Budget
April 2012

Operating funds allocated	$21,360
Expenses	
Variable costs	
Meals (1,400 × $11.80)	16,520
Postage (3,000 × 0.44)	1,320
Fixed costs	
Facility	1,000
Printing	950
Decorations	840
Speaker's gift	130
Publicity	600
Total expenses	21,360
Budget surplus (deficit)	$ 0

Actual results for the luncheon follow.

MIDWEST MANAGEMENT ASSOCIATION
Actual Results for Public Relations Luncheon
April 2012

Operating funds allocated	<u>$21,360</u>
Expenses	
Variable costs	
Meals (1,620 × $12.50)	20,250
Postage (4,000 × 0.44)	1,760
Fixed costs	
Facility	1,500
Printing	950
Decorations	840
Speaker's gift	130
Publicity	<u>600</u>
Total expenses	<u>26,030</u>
Budget deficit	<u>$ (4,670)</u>

Reasons for the differences between the budgeted and actual data follow.

1. The president of the organization, Yvonne Davis, increased the invitation list to include 1,000 former members. As a result, 4,000 invitations were mailed.
2. Attendance was 1,620 individuals. Because of higher-than-expected attendance, the luncheon was moved to a larger room, thereby increasing the facility charge to $1,500.
3. At the last minute, Ms. Laird decided to add a dessert to the menu, which increased the meal cost to $12.50 per person.
4. Printing, decorations, the speaker's gift, and publicity costs were as budgeted.

Required

a. Prepare a flexible budget and compute the sales and variable cost volume variances based on a comparison between the master budget and the flexible budget.

b. Compute flexible budget variances by comparing the flexible budget with the actual results.

c. Ms. Davis was extremely upset with the budget deficit. She immediately called Ms. Laird to complain about the budget variance for the meal cost. She told Ms. Laird that the added dessert caused the meal cost to be $3,730 ($20,250 − $16,520) over budget. She added, "I could expect a couple hundred dollars one way or the other, but several thousand is totally unacceptable. At the next meeting of the budget committee, I want you to explain what happened." Assume that you are Ms. Laird. What would you tell the members of the budget committee?

d. Since this is a not-for-profit organization, why should anyone be concerned with meeting the budget?

EXERCISES—SERIES B

Exercise 8-1B *Classifying variances as favorable or unfavorable*   LO 2

Required

Indicate whether each of the following variances is favorable (F) or unfavorable (U). The first one has been done as an example.

Item to Classify	Standard	Actual	Type of Variance
Sales volume	38,000 units	36,750 units	Unfavorable
Sales price	$6.90 per unit	$6.78 per unit	
Materials cost	$2.10 per pound	$2.30 per pound	
Materials usage	102,400 pounds	103,700 pounds	
Labor cost	$8.25 per hour	$8.80 per hour	
Labor usage	56,980 hours	55,790 hours	
Fixed cost spending	$249,000	$244,000	
Fixed cost per unit (volume)	$2.51 per unit	$3.22 per unit	

LO 2

Exercise 8-2B *Recognizing favorable vs. unfavorable variances*

Compute variances for the following items and indicate whether each variance is favorable (F) or unfavorable (U).

Item	Budget	Actual	Variance	F or U
Sales price	$550	$560		
Sales revenue	$690,000	$720,000		
Cost of goods sold	$520,000	$470,000		
Materials purchases at 10,000 pounds	$330,000	$360,000		
Materials usage	$270,000	$260,000		
Production volume	890 units	900 units		
Wages at 7,600 hours	$91,200	$90,800		
Labor usage	7,600 hours	8,000 hours		
Research and development expense	$81,000	$90,000		
Selling and administrative expenses	$75,000	$71,000		

LO 1

Exercise 8-3B *Preparing master and flexible budgets*

Clyde Manufacturing Company established the following standard price and cost data.

Sales price	$20 per unit
Variable manufacturing cost	$12 per unit
Fixed manufacturing cost	$20,000 total
Fixed selling and administrative cost	$18,000 total

Clyde planned to produce and sell 18,000 units. It actually produced and sold 19,000 units.

Required

a. Prepare the pro forma income statement that would appear in a master budget. Use the contribution margin format.

b. Prepare the pro forma income statement that would appear in a flexible budget. Use the contribution margin format.

LO 3

Exercise 8-4B *Determining sales and variable cost volume variances*

Required

Use the information provided in Exercise 8-3B.

a. Determine the sales and variable cost volume variances.

b. Classify the variances as favorable or unfavorable.

c. Comment on the usefulness of the variances with respect to performance evaluation and identify the member of the management team most likely to be responsible for these variances.

d. Determine the amounts of fixed cost that will appear in the flexible budget.

e. Determine the fixed cost per unit based on planned activity and the fixed cost per unit based on actual activity. Assuming Clyde uses information in the master budget to price its product, explain how the fixed cost volume variance could affect the company's profitability.

Exercise 8-5B *Determining flexible budget variances* LO 4

Use the standard price and cost data provided in Exercise 8-3B. Assume the actual sales price was $19.60 per unit and the actual variable cost was $11.80 per unit. The actual fixed manufacturing cost was $21,000, and the actual selling and administrative expenses were $17,300.

Required

a. Determine the flexible budget variances.
b. Classify the variances as favorable or unfavorable.
c. Provide another name for the fixed cost flexible budget variances.
d. Comment on the usefulness of the variances with respect to performance evaluation and identify the member(s) of the management team that is (are) most likely to be responsible for these variances.

Exercise 8-6B *Using a flexible budget to accommodate market uncertainty* LO 4

Flemming Cable Installation Services, Inc., is planning to open a new regional office. Based on a market survey Flemming commissioned, the company expects services demand for the new office to be between 30,000 and 40,000 hours annually. The firm normally charges customers $50 per hour for its installation services. Flemming expects the new office to have a standard variable cost of $30 per hour and standard fixed cost of $660,000 per year.

Required

a. Develop flexible budgets based on 30,000 hours, 35,000 hours, and 40,000 hours of services.
b. Based on the results for Requirement *a*, comment on the likely success of Flemming's new office.

Exercise 8-7B *Evaluating a decision to increase sales volume by reducing sales price* LO 3, 4

At the beginning of its most recent accounting period, Jackora Company had planned to clean 400 house roofs at an average price of $250 per roof. By reducing the service charge to $225 per roof, the company was able to increase the actual number of roofs cleaned to 450.

Required

a. Determine the sales volume variance and indicate whether it is favorable (F) or unfavorable (U).
b. Determine the flexible budget variance and indicate whether it is favorable (F) or unfavorable (U).
c. Did reducing the price charged for cleaning roofs increase revenue? Explain.

Exercise 8-8B *Responsibility for fixed cost volume and spending variances* LO 5

Dill Manufacturing Company had an excellent year. The company hired a new marketing director in January. The new director's great motivational appeal inspired the sales staff, and, as a result, sales were 20 percent higher than expected. In a recent management meeting, the company president, Joe Ezell, congratulated the marketing director and then criticized Gene Hartley, the company's production manager, because of an unfavorable fixed cost spending variance. Mr. Hartley countered that the favorable fixed cost volume variance more than offset the unfavorable fixed cost spending variance. He argued that Mr. Ezell should evaluate the two variances in total and that he should be rewarded rather than criticized.

Required

Do you agree with Mr. Hartley's defense of the unfavorable fixed cost spending variance? Explain.

Exercise 8-9B *Assessing responsibility for a labor cost variance* LO 4

Orlov Technologies Company's 2011 master budget called for using 60,000 hours of labor to produce 180,000 units of software. The standard labor rate for the company's employees is $38 per direct labor hour. Demand exceeded expectations, resulting in production and sales of 210,000 software units. Actual direct labor costs were $2,646,000. The year-end variance report showed a total unfavorable labor variance of $366,000.

Required

Assume you are the vice president of manufacturing. Should you criticize or praise the production supervisor's performance? Explain.

LO 7

Exercise 8-10B *Calculating the materials usage variance*

Stella Minten manages the Sweet Candy Shop, which was expected to sell 4,000 servings of its trademark candy during July. Each serving was expected to contain 6 ounces of candy. The standard cost of the candy was $0.60 per ounce. The shop actually sold 3,800 servings and actually used 22,100 ounces of candy.

Required

a. Compute the materials usage variance.
b. Explain what could have caused the variance that you computed in Requirement *a*.

LO 7

Exercise 8-11B *Determining materials price and usage variances*

Howe Company makes paint that it sells in 1-gallon containers to retail home improvement stores. During 2012, the company planned to make 190,000 gallons of paint. It actually produced 198,000 gallons. The standard and actual quantity and cost of the color pigment for 1 gallon of paint follow.

	Standard	Actual
Quantity of materials per gallon	12 ounces	13 ounces
Price per ounce	× $0.50	× $0.52
Cost per gallon	$6.00	$6.76

Required

a. Determine the total flexible budget materials variance for pigment. Indicate whether the variance is favorable or unfavorable.
b. Determine the materials price variance and indicate whether the variance is favorable (F) or unfavorable (U).
c. Determine the materials usage variance and indicate whether the variance is favorable (F) or unfavorable (U).
d. Confirm your answers to Requirements *a*, *b*, and *c* by showing that the sum of the price and usage variances equals the total variance.

LO 7

Exercise 8-12B *Responsibility for materials price variance*

Sweer Chill, Inc., makes ice cream that it sells in 5-gallon containers to retail ice cream parlors. During 2011, the company planned to make 100,000 containers of ice cream. It actually produced 97,000 containers. The actual and standard quantity and cost of sugar per container follow.

	Standard	Actual
Quantity of materials per container	2 pounds	2.1 pounds
Price per pound	× $0.75	× $0.80
Cost per container	$1.50	$1.68

Required

a. Determine the materials price variance and indicate whether the variance is favorable (F) or unfavorable (U).
b. Determine the materials usage variance and indicate whether the variance is favorable (F) or unfavorable (U).
c. Explain how the production manager could have been responsible for the price variance.

Exercise 8-13B *Responsibility for labor price and usage variance*

LO 7

Newhouse Manufacturing Company incurred an unfavorable labor price variance.

Required

a. Describe a scenario in which the personnel manager is responsible for the unfavorable price variance.

b. Describe a scenario in which the production manager is responsible for the unfavorable price variance.

Exercise 8-14B *Calculating and explaining labor price and usage variances*

LO 7

Albertson Landscaping Company established the following standard labor cost data to provide complete lawn care service (cutting, edging, trimming, and blowing) for a small lawn. Albertson planned each lawn to require 2 hours of labor at a cost of $30 per hour. The company actually serviced 500 lawns using an average of 1.75 labor hours per lawn. Actual labor costs were $32 per hour.

Required

a. Determine the total labor variance and indicate whether the variance is favorable (F) or unfavorable (U).

b. Determine the labor price variance and indicate whether the variance is favorable (F) or unfavorable (U).

c. Determine the labor usage variance and indicate whether the variance is favorable (F) or unfavorable (U).

d. Explain what could have caused the variances computed in Requirements *b* and *c*.

Exercise 8-15B *Determining standard labor hours*

LO 7

Stylish Hair is a hair salon. It planned to provide 240 hair color treatments during December. Each treatment was planned to require 0.5 hours of labor at the standard labor price of $18 per hour. The salon actually provided 250 treatments. The actual labor price averaged $17.76. The labor price variance was $36 favorable.

Required

a. Determine the actual number of labor hours used per treatment.

b. Indicate whether the labor usage variance would be favorable (F) or unfavorable (U).

Exercise 8-16B *Calculating a variable overhead variance*

LO 5, 7

Hahn Manufacturing Company established a predetermined variable overhead cost rate of $40 per direct labor hour. The actual variable overhead cost rate was $38 per direct labor hour. Hahn planned to use 150,000 hours of direct labor. It actually used 152,000 hours of direct labor.

Required

a. Determine the total flexible budget variable overhead cost variance.

b. Many companies do not subdivide the total variable overhead cost variance into price and usage components. Under what circumstances would it be appropriate to distinguish between the price and usage components of a variable overhead cost variance? What would be required to accomplish this type of analysis?

Exercise 8-17B *Determining and interpreting fixed cost variances*

LO 5, 7

Smitter Manufacturing Company established a predetermined fixed overhead cost rate of $200 per unit of product. The company planned to make 19,000 units of product but actually produced 20,000 units. Actual fixed overhead costs were $4,000,000.

Required

a. Determine the fixed cost spending variance. Indicate whether the variance is favorable (F) or unfavorable (U). Explain what this variance means. Identify the manager(s) who is (are) responsible for the variance.

b. Determine the fixed cost volume variance. Indicate whether the variance is favorable (F) or unfavorable (U). Explain what the designations *favorable* and *unfavorable* mean with respect to the fixed manufacturing overhead cost volume variance.

PROBLEMS—SERIES B

LO 1, 3

Problem 8-18B *Determining sales and variable cost volume variances*

Vlascenko Food Corporation developed the following standard price and costs for a refrigerated TV dinner that the company produces.

Standard price and variable costs	
Sales price	$25.96
Materials cost	9.00
Labor cost	2.60
Overhead cost	0.56
Selling, general, and administrative costs	4.20
Planned fixed costs	
Manufacturing overhead cost	$500,000
Selling, general, and administrative costs	360,000

Vlascenko plans to make and sell 200,000 TV dinners.

Required

a. Prepare the pro forma income statement that would appear in the master budget.

b. Prepare flexible budget income statements, assuming production and sales volumes of 180,000 and 220,000 units.

c. Determine the sales and variable cost volume variances, assuming volume is actually 190,000 units.

d. Indicate whether the variances are favorable (F) or unfavorable (U).

e. Comment on how Vlascenko could use the variances to evaluate performance.

LO 4

Problem 8-19B *Determining and interpreting flexible budget variances*

Use the standard price and cost data supplied in Problem 8-18B. Assume that Vlascenko actually produced and sold 216,000 units. The actual sales price and costs incurred follow.

Actual price and variable costs	
Sales price	$25.80
Materials cost	8.80
Labor cost	2.68
Overhead cost	0.56
Selling, general, and administrative costs	4.40
Actual fixed costs	
Manufacturing overhead	$512,000
Selling, general, and administrative costs	356,000

Required

a. Determine the flexible budget variances. Provide another name for the fixed cost flexible budget variances.

b. Indicate whether each variance is favorable (F) or unfavorable (U).

c. Identify the management position responsible for each variance. Explain what could have caused the variance.

LO 1

Problem 8-20B *Flexible budget planning*

Executive officers of Ortiz Seafood Processing Company are holding a planning session for fiscal year 2012. They have already established the following standard price and costs for their canned seafood product.

Standard price and variable costs	
Price per can	$3.00
Materials cost	1.05
Labor cost	0.64
Overhead cost	0.10
Selling, general, and administrative costs	0.25
Expected fixed costs	
Production facility costs	$215,000
Selling, general, and administrative costs	180,000

Required

a. Prepare the pro forma income statement that would appear in the master budget if the company expects to produce 600,000 cans of seafood in 2012.

b. A marketing consultant suggests to Ortiz's president that the product's price may affect the number of cans the company can sell. According to the consultant's analysis, if the firm sets its price at $2.70, it could sell 810,000 cans of seafood. Prepare a flexible budget based on the consultant's suggestion.

c. The same consultant also suggests that if the company raises its price to $3.25 per can, the volume of sales would decline to 400,000. Prepare a flexible budget based on this suggestion.

d. Evaluate the three possible outcomes developed in Requirements a, b, and c and recommend a pricing strategy.

Problem 8-21B   *Determining materials price and usage variances* LO 7

Tiffany Swimsuit Specialties, Inc., makes fashionable women's swimsuits. Its most popular swimsuit, with the Sarong trade name, uses a standard fabric amount of 6 yards of raw material with a standard price of $5.00 per yard. The company planned to produce 100,000 Sarong swimsuits in 2011. At the end of 2011, the company's cost accountant reported that Tiffany had used 636,000 yards of fabric to make 102,000 swimsuits. Actual cost for the raw material was $3,307,200.

Required

a. Are flexible budget material variances based on the planned volume of 100,000 swimsuits or actual volume of 102,000 swimsuits?

b. Compute the actual price per yard of fabric.

c. Compute the standard quantity (yards of fabric) required to produce the swimsuits.

d. Compute the materials price variance and indicate whether it is favorable (F) or unfavorable (U).

e. Compute the materials usage variance and indicate whether it is favorable (F) or unfavorable (U).

Problem 8-22B   *Determining labor price and usage variances* LO 7

As noted in Problem 8-21B, Tiffany Swimsuit makes swimsuits. In 2011, Tiffany produced its most popular swimsuit, the Sarong, for a standard labor price of $30 per hour. The standard amount of labor was 1.0 hour per swimsuit. The company had planned to produce 100,000 Sarong swimsuits. At the end of 2011, the company's cost accountant reported that Tiffany had used 107,000 hours of labor to make 102,000 swimsuits. The total labor cost was $3,295,600.

Required

a. Should the labor variances be based on the planned volume of 100,000 swimsuits or on the actual volume of 102,000 swimsuits?

b. Prepare a table that shows the standard labor price, the actual labor price, the standard labor hours, and the actual labor hours.

c. Compute the labor price variance and indicate whether it is favorable (F) or unfavorable (U).

d. Compute the labor usage variance and indicate whether it is favorable (F) or unfavorable (U).

LO 5

Problem 8-23B   *Computing fixed cost variances*

Goodwin Sporting Goods Co. manufactures baseballs. According to Goodwin's 2013 budget, the company planned to incur $300,000 of fixed manufacturing overhead costs to make 200,000 baseballs. Goodwin actually produced 187,000 balls, incurring $296,000 of actual fixed manufacturing overhead costs. Goodwin establishes its predetermined overhead rate on the basis of the planned volume of production (expected number of baseballs).

Required

a. Calculate the predetermined overhead rate.

b. Determine the fixed cost spending variance and indicate whether it is favorable (F) or unfavorable (U).

c. Determine the fixed cost volume variance and indicate whether it is favorable (F) or unfavorable (U).

LO 5, 7

Problem 8-24B   *Computing materials, labor, and manufacturing overhead cost variances*

Frank Trawick was a new cost accountant at Skoney Plastics Corporation. He was assigned to analyze the following data that his predecessor left him.

Planned volume for year (static budget)	10,000 units
Standard direct materials cost per unit	2 lbs. @ $1.50 per pound
Standard direct labor cost per unit	0.5 hours @ $10.00 per hour
Total planned fixed overhead costs	$12,000
Actual volume for the year (flexible budget)	10,800 units
Actual direct materials cost per unit	1.9 lbs. @ $1.60 per pound
Actual direct labor cost per unit	0.6 hrs. @ $8.00 per hour
Total actual fixed overhead costs	$12,400

Required

a. Prepare a materials variance information table showing the standard price, the actual price, the standard quantity, and the actual quantity.

b. Calculate the materials price and usage variances and indicate whether they are favorable (F) or unfavorable (U).

c. Prepare a labor variance information table showing the standard price, the actual price, the standard hours, and the actual hours.

d. Calculate the labor price and usage variances and indicate whether they are favorable (F) or unfavorable (U).

e. Calculate the predetermined overhead rate, assuming that Skoney Plastics uses the number of units as the allocation base.

f. Calculate the fixed manufacturing overhead cost spending variance and indicate whether it is favorable (F) or unfavorable (U).

g. Calculate the fixed manufacturing overhead cost volume variance and indicate whether it is favorable (F) or unfavorable (U).

LO 5, 7

Problem 8-25B   *Computing materials, labor, and fixed cost variances*

Keedy Corporation makes mouse pads for computer users. After the first year of operation, Diane Keedy, the president and chief executive officer, was eager to determine the efficiency of the company's operation. In her analysis, she used the following standards provided by her assistant.

Units of planned production	400,000
Per-unit direct materials	1 square foot @ $0.25 per square foot
Per-unit direct labor	0.2 hrs. @ $7.00 per hr.
Total estimated fixed overhead costs	$200,000

Keedy purchased and used 460,000 square feet of material at an average cost of $0.24 per square foot. Labor usage amounted to 79,200 hours at an average of $6.90 per hour. Actual production amounted to 208,000 units. Actual fixed overhead costs amounted to $204,000. The company completed and sold all inventory for $1,414,400.

Required

a. Prepare a materials variance information table showing the standard price, the actual price, the standard quantity, and the actual quantity.

b. Calculate the materials price and usage variances and indicate whether they are favorable (F) or unfavorable (U).

c. Prepare a labor variance information table showing the standard price, the actual price, the standard hours, and the actual hours.

d. Calculate the labor price and usage variances and indicate whether they are favorable (F) or unfavorable (U).

e. Calculate the predetermined overhead rate, assuming that Keedy uses the number of units as the allocation base.

f. Calculate the fixed cost spending and volume variances and indicate whether they are favorable (F) or unfavorable (U).

g. Determine the amount of gross margin Keedy would report on the year-end income statement.

Problem 8-26B   *Computing variances*   LO 7

A fire destroyed most of Salazar Products Corporation's records. Rose Penwell, the company's accountant, is trying to piece together the company's operating results from salvaged documents. She discovered the following data.

Standard materials quantity per unit	2.5 pounds
Standard materials price	$2 per pound
Standard labor quantity per unit	0.6 hour
Standard labor price	$12 per hour
Actual number of products produced	8,000 units
Materials price variance	$792 Favorable
Materials quantity variance	$400 Favorable
Labor price variance	$1,952 Unfavorable
Labor usage variance	$960 Unfavorable

Required

a. Determine the actual amount of materials used.

b. Determine the actual price per pound paid for materials.

c. Determine the actual labor hours used.

d. Determine the actual labor price per hour.

Problem 8-27B   *Computing standard cost and analyzing variances*   LO 5, 7

Scofield Manufacturing Company, which makes aluminum alloy wheels for automobiles, recently introduced a new luxury wheel that fits small sports cars. The company developed the following standards for its new product.

Amount of direct materials per wheel	2 pounds
Price of direct materials per pound	$5.50
Quantity of labor per wheel	2.5 hours
Price of direct labor per hour	$8.00/hour
Total budgeted fixed overhead	$168,000

In its first year of operation, Scofield planned to produce 3,000 sets of wheels (four wheels per set). Because of unexpected demand, it actually produced 3,600 sets of wheels. By year-end direct materials purchased and used amounted to 30,000 pounds of aluminum at a cost of $175,500. Direct labor costs were actually $8.40 per hour. Actual hours worked were 2.2 hours per wheel. Overhead for the year actually amounted to $180,000. Overhead is applied to products using a predetermined overhead rate based on the total estimated number of wheels to be produced.

Required

(Round all computations to two decimal places.)

a. Compute the standard cost per wheel for direct materials, direct labor, and overhead.
b. Determine the total standard cost per wheel.
c. Compute the actual cost per wheel for direct materials, direct labor, and overhead.
d. Compute the actual cost per wheel.
e. Compute the price and usage variances for direct materials and direct labor. Identify any variances that Scofield should investigate. Based on your results, offer a possible explanation for the labor usage variance.
f. Compute the fixed manufacturing overhead cost spending and volume variances. Explain your findings.

LO 1, 2, 3, 4

Problem 8-28B *Analyzing not-for-profit organization variances*

The Marketing Department of Hammell State University planned to hold its annual distinguished visiting lecturer (DVL) presentation in October 2012. The secretary of the department prepared the following budget based on costs that had been incurred in the past for the DVL presentation.

MARKETING DEPARTMENT Distinguished Visiting Lecturer Budget October 2012	
Variable costs	
Refreshments	$ 375
Postage	352
Step costs*	
Printing	500
Facility	250
Fixed costs	
Dinner	200
Speaker's gift	100
Publicity	50
Total costs	$1,827

*Step costs are costs that change abruptly after a defined range of volume (attendance). They do not change proportionately with unit volume increases (i.e., the cost is fixed within a range of activity but changes to a different fixed cost when the volume changes to a new range). For instance, the facility charge is $250 for from 1 to 400 attendees. From 401 to 500 attendees, the next larger room is needed, and the charge is $350. If more than 500 attended, the room size and cost would increase again.

The budget for the presentation was based on the following expectations:

1. Attendance was estimated at 50 faculty from Hammell State and neighboring schools, 125 invited guests from the business community, and 200 students. Refreshments charge per attendee would be $1.00. The cost driver for refreshments is the number of attendees.
2. Postage was based on $0.44 per invitation; 800 invitations were expected to be mailed to faculty and finance business executives. The cost driver for postage is the number of invitations mailed.

3. Printing cost was expected to be $500 for 800 invitations and envelopes. Additional invitations and envelopes could be purchased in batches of 100 units with each batch costing $50.

4. The DVL presentation was scheduled at a downtown convention center. The facility charge was $250 for a room that has a capacity of 400 persons; the charge for one to hold more than 400 people was $350.

5. After the presentation, three Hammell State faculty members planned to take the speaker to dinner. The dinner had been prearranged at a local restaurant for $200 for a three-course dinner.

6. A gift for the speaker was budgeted at $100.

7. Publicity would consist of flyers and posters placed at strategic locations around campus and business offices, articles in the business section of the local newspapers, and announcements made in business classes and school newspapers. Printing for the posters and flyers had been prearranged for $50.

8. The speaker lives in the adjoining state and had agreed to drive to the presentation at his own expense.

The actual results of the presentation follow.

1. Attendance consisted of 450 faculty, business executives, and students.

2. An additional 100 invitations were printed and mailed when the Marketing Department decided that selected alumni should also be invited.

3. Based on RSVP responses, the department rented the next size larger room at a cost of $350 for the presentation.

4. The speaker's gift cost was as budgeted.

5. The department chairperson decided to have a four-course dinner, which cost $230.

6. Because of poor planning, the posters and flyers were not distributed as widely as expected. It was decided at the last minute to hire a temporary assistant to make phone calls to alumni. The actual publicity cost was $75.

Required

a. Prepare a flexible budget and compute sales and variable cost variances based on a comparison between the master budget and the flexible budget. Briefly explain the meaning of the activity variances.

b. Compute flexible budget variances by comparing the flexible budget with the actual results. Briefly explain the meaning of the variable cost flexible budget variances. Discuss the fixed cost variances.

c. Calculate the expected and actual fixed cost per attendee. Discuss the significance of the difference in these amounts.

d. Since the department is a not-for-profit entity, why is it important for it to control the cost of sponsoring the distinguished visiting lecturer presentation?

ANALYZE, THINK, COMMUNICATE

ATC 8-1 Business Applications Case *Static versus flexible budget variances*

Dan Ludwig is the manufacturing production supervisor for Atlantic Lighting Systems. Trying to explain why he did not get the year-end bonus that he had expected, he told his wife, "This is the dumbest place I ever worked. Last year the company set up this budget assuming it would sell 150,000 units. Well, it sold only 140,000. The company lost money and gave me a bonus for not using as much materials and labor as was called for in the budget. This year, the company has the same 150,000 units goal and it sells 160,000. The company's making all kinds of money. You'd think I'd get this big fat bonus. Instead, management tells me I used more materials and labor than was budgeted. They said the company would have made a lot more money if I'd stayed within my budget. I guess I gotta wait for another bad year before I get a bonus. Like I said, this is the dumbest place I ever worked."

Atlantic Lighting Systems's master budget and the actual results for the most recent year of operating activity follow.

	Master Budget	Actual Results	Variances	F or U
Number of units	150,000	160,000	10,000	
Sales revenue	$33,000,000	$35,520,000	$2,520,000	F
Variable manufacturing costs				
Materials	(4,800,000)	(5,300,000)	(500,000)	U
Labor	(4,200,000)	(4,400,000)	(200,000)	U
Overhead	(2,100,000)	(2,290,000)	(190,000)	U
Variable selling, general, and admin. costs	(5,250,000)	(5,450,000)	(200,000)	U
Contribution margin	16,650,000	18,080,000	1,430,000	F
Fixed costs				
Manufacturing overhead	(7,830,000)	(7,751,000)	79,000	F
Sellings, general, and admin. costs	(6,980,000)	(7,015,000)	(35,000)	U
Net income	$ 1,840,000	$ 3,314,000	$1,474,000	F

Required

a. Did Atlantic increase unit sales by cutting prices or by using some other strategy?

b. Is Mr. Ludwig correct in his conclusion that something is wrong with the company's performance evaluation process? If so, what do you suggest be done to improve the system?

c. Prepare a flexible budget and recompute the budget variances.

d. Explain what might have caused the fixed costs to be different from the amount budgeted.

e. Assume that the company's material price variance was favorable and its material usage variance was unfavorable. Explain why Mr. Ludwig may not be responsible for these variances. Now, explain why he may have been responsible for the material usage variance.

f. Assume the labor price variance is unfavorable. Was the labor usage variance favorable or unfavorable?

g. Is the fixed cost volume variance favorable or unfavorable? Explain the effect of this variance on the cost of each unit produced.

ATC 8-2   Group Assignment   *Variable price and usage variances and fixed manufacturing overhead cost variances*

Kemp Tables, Inc. (KTI), makes picnic tables of 2 × 4 planks of treated pine. It sells the tables to large retail discount stores such as Walmart. After reviewing the following data generated by KTI's chief accountant, the company president, Arianne Darwin, expressed concern that the total manufacturing cost was more than $0.5 million above budget ($7,084,800 − $6,520,000 = $564,800).

	Actual Results	Master Budget
Cost of planks per table	$ 44.10	$ 40.00
Cost of labor per table	26.10	25.50
Total variable manufacturing cost per table (a)	$ 70.20	$ 65.50
Total number of tables produced (b)	82,000	80,000
Total variable manufacturing cost (a × b)	$5,756,400	$5,240,000
Total fixed manufacturing cost	1,328,400	1,280,000
Total manufacturing cost	$7,084,800	$6,520,000

Ms. Darwin asked Conrad Pearson, KTI's chief accountant, to explain what caused the increase in cost. Mr. Pearson responded that things were not as bad as they seemed. He noted that part of the cost variance resulted from making and selling more tables than had been expected. Making more tables naturally causes the cost of materials and labor to be higher. He explained that the flexible budget cost variance was less than $0.5 million. Specifically, he provided the following comparison.

	Actual Results	Flexible Budget
Cost of planks per table	$ 44.10	$ 40.00
Cost of labor per table	26.10	25.50
Total variable manufacturing cost per table (a)	$ 70.20	$ 65.50
Total number of tables produced (b)	82,000	82,000
Total variable manufacturing cost (a × b)	$5,756,400	$5,371,000
Total fixed manufacturing cost	1,328,400	1,280,000
Total manufacturing cost	$7,084,800	$6,651,000

Based on this information, he argued that the relevant variance for performance evaluation was only $433,800 ($7,084,800 − $6,651,000). Ms. Darwin responded, "*Only* $433,800! I consider that a very significant number. By the end of the day, I want a full explanation as to what is causing our costs to increase."

Required

a. Divide the class into groups of four or five students and divide the groups into three sections. Assign Task 1 to the first section, Task 2 to the second section, and Task 3 to the third section.

Group Tasks

(1) Based on the following information, determine the total materials cost variance and the price and usage variances. Assuming that the variances are an appropriate indicator of cause, explain what could have caused the variances. Identify the management position responsible.

	Actual Data	Standard Data
Number of planks per table	21	20
Price per plank	× $2.10	× $2.00
Material cost per table	$44.10	$40.00

(2) Based on the following information, determine the total labor cost variance and the price and usage variances. Assuming that the variances are an appropriate indicator of cause, explain what could have caused each variance. Identify the management position responsible.

	Actual Data	Standard Data
Number of hours per table	2.9	3.0
Price per hour	× $9.00	× $8.50
Labor cost per table	$26.10	$25.50

(3) Determine the amount of the fixed cost spending and volume variances. Explain what could have caused these variances. Based on the volume variance, indicate whether the actual fixed cost per unit would be higher or lower than the budgeted fixed cost per unit.

b. Select a spokesperson from each section to report the amount of the variances computed by the group. Reconcile any differences in the variances reported by the sections. Reconcile the individual variances with the total variance. Specifically, show that the total of the materials, labor, and overhead variances equals the total flexible budget variance ($433,800).

c. Discuss how Ms. Darwin should react to the variance information.

ATC 8-3 Research Assignment *Using real world data from Papa John's*

Obtain the 2004, 2005, 2006, 2007, and 2008 income statements for Papa John's International, Inc. The 2006–2008 statements are included in Papa John's 2008 annual report and Form 10-Ks. The 2004 and 2005 statements are in its 2005 annual report.

To obtain the Form 10-Ks you can use either the EDGAR system following the instructions in Appendix A, or they can be found under "Investors" link on the company's corporate website; www.papajohns.com. The company's annual reports are also available on its website.

Required

a. Compute the percentage change for each of the following categories of revenues and expenses for 2004 to 2005, 2005 to 2006, and 2006 to 2007:

> **Domestic revenues:**
>   Company-owned restaurant sales
> **Domestic company-owned restaurant expenses:**
>   Cost of sales
>   Salaries and benefits
>   Advertising and related costs
>   Occupancy costs
>   Other operating expenses

Using an Excel spreadsheet will make this task much easier. Once these averages are obtained, (you should have three averages for each of the six revenue and expense items), calculate an average of the changes for each item. The answer for the "Occupancy coats" item is show as an example:

	Percentage Change
2004–2005	1.7%
2005–2006	3.2
2006–2007	17.0
Average of the changes	7.3%

b. Prepare a budgeted income statement for 2008 and compare the budgeted data to the actual results for 2008. To calculate budgeted amounts, multiply the average change in each revenue and expense item, from Requirement *b*, by the dollar amount of the corresponding revenue or expense from 2007. This will represent the budgeted amount for that item for 2008. Don't forget to use decimal data and not percentage data. Subtract the actual 2008 results from the budgeted results. Finally, divide the actual versus budgeted difference by the budgeted amount to determine a percentage variance from the budget. Calculate total for "Total domestic company-owned restaurant expenses" by adding the appropriate items. The answer for the "Occupancy costs" item is show as an example: (Dollar amounts are in thousands.)

	(1) 2007 Actual	(2) Average 3-year Change	(3) (1 × 2) 2008 Budget	(4) 2008 Actual	(5) (3 − 4) Variance	(5 ÷ 3) Percentage Variance from Budget
Occupancy costs	$31,866	1.073	$34,192	$34,973	$(781)	.028 [2.8%]

ATC 8-4 Writing Assignment *Standard costing—The human factor*

Kemp Corporation makes a protein supplement called Power Punch™. Its principal competitor for Power Punch is the protein supplement Superior Strength™, made by Jim Adams Company (JAC). Mr. Adams, a world-renowned weight-lifting champion, founded JAC. The primary market for both products is athletes. Kemp sells Power Punch to wellness stores, which sell it, other supplements, and health foods to the public. In contrast, Superior Strength is advertised in sports magazines and sold through orders generated by the ads.

Mr. Adams's fame is an essential factor in his company's advertising program. He is a dynamic character whose personality motivates people to strive for superior achievement. His demeanor not only stimulates sales but also provides a strong inspirational force for company employees. He is a kind, understanding individual with high expectations who is fond of saying that "mistakes are just opportunities for improvement." Mr. Adams is a strong believer in total quality management.

Mr. Quayle, president of Kemp Corporation, is a stern disciplinarian who believes in team-work. He takes pride in his company's standard costing system. Managers work as a team to establish standards and then are held accountable for meeting them. Managers who fail to meet expectations are severely chastised, and continued failure leads to dismissal. After several years of rigorous enforcement, managers have fallen in line. Indeed, during the last two years, all managers have met their budget goals.

Even so, costs have risen steadily. These cost increases have been passed on to customers through higher prices. As a result, Power Punch is now priced significantly higher than Superior Strength. In fact, Superior Strength is selling directly to the public at a price that is below the wholesale price that Kemp is charging the wellness stores. The situation has reached a critical juncture. Sales of Power Punch are falling while Superior Strength is experiencing significant growth. Given that industry sales have remained relatively stable, it is obvious that customers are shifting from Power Punch to Superior Strength. Mr. Quayle is perplexed. He wonders how a company with direct marketing expenses can price its products so low.

Required

a. Explain why JAC has been able to gain a pricing advantage over Kemp.

b. Assume that you are a consultant whom Kemp's board of directors has asked to recommend how to halt the decline in sales of Power Punch. Provide appropriate recommendations.

ATC 8-5   Ethical Dilemma   *Budget games*

Melody Lovelady is the most highly rewarded sales representative at Swift Corporation. Her secret to success is always to understate her abilities. Ms. Lovelady is assigned to a territory in which her customer base is increasing at approximately 25 percent per year. Each year she estimates that her budgeted sales will be 10 percent higher than her previous year's sales. With little effort, she is able to double her budgeted sales growth. At Swift's annual sales meeting, she receives an award and a large bonus. Of course, Ms. Lovelady does not disclose her secret to her colleagues. Indeed, she always talks about how hard it is to continue to top her previous performance. She tells herself: "If they are dumb enough to fall for this rubbish, I'll milk it for all it's worth."

Required

a. What is the name commonly given to the budget game Ms. Lovelady is playing?

b. Does Ms. Lovelady's behavior violate any of the standards of ethical conduct shown in Exhibit 1.15 of Chapter 1?

c. Recommend how Ms. Lovelady's budget game could be stopped.

ATC 8-6   Spreadsheet Assignment   *Using Excel*

Irvine Publications established the following standard price and costs for a hardcover picture book that the company produces.

Standard price and variable costs	
Sales price	$ 48.00
Materials cost	12.00
Labor cost	6.00
Overhead cost	8.40
Selling, general, and administrative costs	9.60
Expected fixed costs	
Manufacturing overhead	$180,000
Selling, general, and administrative	72,000

Irvine planned to make and sell 30,000 copies of the book.

Required

Construct a spreadsheet like the one shown in Exhibit 8.1 to illustrate a static budget and a flexible budget for production volumes of 28,000, 29,000, 30,000, 31,000, and 32,000.

ATC 8-7 Spreadsheet Assignment *Mastering Excel*

Wilkin Fruit Drink Company planned to make 400,000 containers of apple juice. It expected to use two cups of frozen apple concentrate to make each container of juice, thus using 800,000 cups (400,000 containers × 2 cups) of frozen concentrate. The standard price of one cup of apple concentrate is $0.25. Actually, Wilkin produced 404,000 containers of apple juice and purchased and used 820,000 cups of concentrate at $0.26 per cup.

Required

a. Construct a spreadsheet template that could be used to calculate price and usage variances. The template should be constructed so that it could be used for any problem in the chapter that refers to price and usage variances by changing the data in the spreadsheet. The screen capture on this page represents a template for price and usage variances.

Spreadsheet Tip

(1) The shaded cells can be changed according to the data in each problem. All other cells are formulas based on the numbers in the shaded cells.

(2) The cells that label the variances as F or U (favorable (F) or unfavorable (U)) are based on a function called IF. The IF function is needed because the variance can be either favorable or unfavorable. The formula must determine whether actual expenditures exceed budgeted expenditures to determine whether the variance is unfavorable or favorable. As an example, the formula in cell D13 is =IF(B11>E11,'U','F'). The formula evaluates the expression B11>E11. If this expression is true (B11 is greater than E11), the text U is inserted in cell D13. The IF function can also be used to place formulas or numbers in a cell based on whether an expression is true or false. For example, the formula =IF(B11>E11,B11−E11,E11−B11) would calculate the amount of the variance as a positive number regardless of which amount is larger.

(3) An easier way to make the variance a positive number regardless of whether it is favorable or unfavorable is to use the absolute value function. The format of the formula in cells C13 and F13 would be =ABS(left number − right number).

(4) The lines around the variances are produced by using the borders in Excel (Format, Cells, Border).

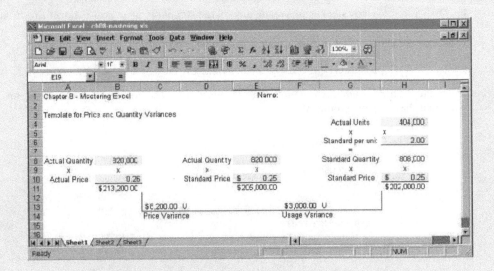

COMPREHENSIVE PROBLEM

The management of Magnificent Modems, Inc. (MMI), is uncertain as to the volume of sales that will exist in 2011. The president of the company asked the chief accountant to prepare flexible budget income statements assuming that sales activity amounts to 3,000 and 6,000 units. The static budget is shown in the form below.

Required

a. Complete the following worksheet to prepare the appropriate flexible budgets.
b. Calculate and show the flexible budget variances for the static budget versus the flexible budget at 6,000 units.
c. Indicate whether each variance is favorable or unfavorable.

Flexible Budget Income Statements				
		Static Budget	Flexible Budget	Flexible Budget
Number of units		5,000	3,000	6,000
	Cost per Unit			
Sales revenue	$120.00	$600,000		
Variable manuf. costs				
Materials	40.00	200,000		
Labor	25.00	125,000		
Overhead	4.00	20,000		
Variable SG&A	6.00	30,000	_____	_____
Contribution margin		225,000		
Fixed costs				
Manufacturing rent		50,000		
Dep. on manu. equip.		60,000		
SG&A expenses		71,950		
Dep. on admin. equip.		12,000		
Net income (loss)		$ 31,050	$(58,950)	$76,050

CHAPTER 10

Planning for
Capital Investments

LEARNING OBJECTIVES

After you have mastered the material in this chapter you will be able to:

1 Explain the time value of money concept and apply it to capital investment decisions.

2 Determine the present value of future cash flows.

3 Determine and interpret the net present value of an investment opportunity.

4 Determine and interpret the internal rate of return of an investment opportunity.

5 Identify cash flows associated with an investment opportunity.

6 Compare capital investment alternatives.

7 Determine the payback period for an investment opportunity.

8 Determine the unadjusted rate of return for an investment opportunity.

9 Conduct a postaudit of a completed investment.

CHAPTER OPENING

The president of EZ Rentals (EZ) is considering expanding the company's rental service business to include LCD projectors that can be used with notebook computers. A marketing study forecasts that renting projectors could generate revenue of $200,000 per year. The possibility of increasing revenue is alluring, but EZ's president has a number of unanswered questions. How much do the projectors cost? What is their expected useful life? Will they have a salvage value? Does EZ have the money to buy them? Does EZ have the technical expertise to support the product? How much will training cost? How long will customer demand last? What if EZ buys the projectors and they become technologically obsolete? How quickly will EZ be able to recover the investment? Are there more profitable ways to invest EZ's funds?

Spending large sums of money that will have long-term effects on company profits makes most managers anxious. What if a cell phone manufacturer spends millions of dollars to build a factory in the United States and its competitors locate their manufacturing facilities in countries that provide cheap labor? The manufacturer's cell phones will be overpriced, but it cannot move overseas because it cannot find a buyer for the factory. What if a pharmaceutical company spends millions of dollars to develop a drug which then fails to receive FDA approval? What if a communications company installs underground cable but satellite transmission steals its market? What if a company buys computer equipment that rapidly becomes technologically obsolete? Although these possibilities may be remote, they can be expensive when they do occur. For example, Wachovia Bank's 1997 annual report discloses a $70 million dollar write-off of computer equipment. This chapter discusses some of the analytical techniques companies use to evaluate major investment opportunities.

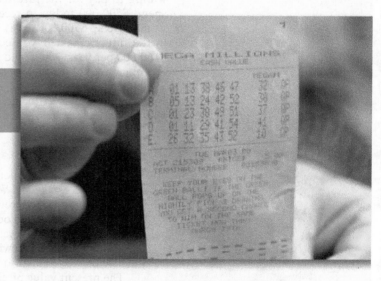

The Curious Accountant

The August 28, 2009, drawing for the Mega millions multi-state lottery produced two winning tickets. The tickets, which were purchased in California and New York, had an advertised value of $338 million. This amount, however, was based on the assumption that the winners would take their prize as 26 equal annual payments of $14,153,384. If the winnings were taken in this manner, the first payment would be made immediately, and the others would be paid annually over the next 25 years. The winner also had the option of taking an immediate, lump-sum payment of $231 million. With two winning tickets, each winner would receive one-half of these amounts.

Assume that you work as a personal financial planner and that one of your clients held one of the winning lottery tickets. If you think you could invest your client's winnings and earn an annual return of 7 percent, would you advise your client to take the lump-sum payment or the annual payments? Why? (The answer is on page 457.)

CAPITAL INVESTMENT DECISIONS

LO I

Explain the time value of money concept and apply it to capital investment decisions.

Purchases of long-term operational assets are **capital investments.** Capital investments differ from stock and bond investments in an important respect. Investments in stocks and bonds can be sold in organized markets such as the New York Stock Exchange. In contrast, investments in capital assets normally can be recovered only by using those assets. Once a company purchases a capital asset, it is committed to that investment for an extended period of time. If the market turns sour, the company is stuck with the consequences. It may also be unable to seize new opportunities because its capital is committed. Business profitability ultimately hinges, to a large extent, on the quality of a few key capital investment decisions.

A capital investment decision is essentially a decision to exchange current cash outflows for the expectation of receiving future cash inflows. For EZ Rentals, purchasing LCD projectors, cash outflows today, provides the opportunity to collect $200,000 per year in rental revenue, cash inflows in the future. Assuming the projectors have useful lives of four years and no salvage value, how much should EZ be willing to pay for the future cash inflows? If you were EZ's president, would you spend $700,000 today to receive $200,000 each year for the next four years? You would give up $700,000 today for the opportunity to receive $800,000 (4 × $200,000) in the future. What if you collect less than $200,000 per year? If revenue is only $160,000 per year, you would lose $60,000 [$700,000 − (4 × $160,000)]. Is $700,000 too much to pay for the opportunity to receive $200,000 per year for four years? If $700,000 is too much, would you spend $600,000? If not, how about $500,000? There is no one right answer to these questions. However, understanding the *time value of money* concept can help you develop a rational response.

Time Value of Money

The **time value of money** concept recognizes that *the present value of a dollar received in the future is less than a dollar.* For example, you may be willing to pay only $0.90 today for a promise to receive $1.00 one year from today. The further into the future the receipt is expected to occur, the smaller is its present value. In other words, one dollar to be received two years from today is worth less than one dollar to be received one year from today. Likewise, one dollar to be received three years from today is less valuable than one dollar to be received two years from today, and so on.

The present value of cash inflows decreases as the time until expected receipt increases for several reasons. First, you could deposit today's dollar in a savings account to earn *interest* that increases its total value. If you wait for your money, you lose the opportunity to earn interest. Second, the expectation of receiving a future dollar carries an element of *risk*. Changed conditions may result in the failure to collect. Finally, *inflation* diminishes the buying power of the dollar. In other words, the longer you must wait to receive a dollar, the less you will be able to buy with it.

When a company invests in capital assets, it sacrifices present dollars in exchange for the opportunity to receive future dollars. Since trading current dollars for future dollars is risky, companies expect compensation before they invest in capital assets. The compensation a company expects is called *return on investment (ROI)*. As discussed in Chapter 9, ROI is expressed as a percentage of the investment. For example, the ROI for a $1,000 investment that earns annual income of $100 is 10 percent ($100 ÷ $1,000 = 10%).

Determining the Minimum Rate of Return

To establish the minimum expected *return on investment* before accepting an investment opportunity, most companies consider their cost of capital. To attract capital, companies must provide benefits to their creditors and owners. Creditors expect interest payments; owners expect dividends and increased stock value. Companies that earn lower returns than their cost of capital eventually go bankrupt; they cannot continually pay out more than they collect. *The* **cost of capital** *represents the* **minimum rate of return** *on investments.* Calculating the cost of capital is a complex exercise which is beyond the scope of this text. It is addressed in finance courses. We discuss how management accountants *use* the cost of capital to evaluate investment opportunities. Companies describe the cost of capital in a variety of ways: the *minimum rate of return,* the *desired rate of return,* the *required rate of return,* the *hurdle rate,* the *cutoff rate,* or the *discount rate.* These terms are used interchangeably throughout this chapter.

✓ CHECK YOURSELF 10.1

Study the following cash inflow streams expected from two different potential investments.

	Year 1	Year 2	Year 3	Total
Alternative 1	$2,000	$3,000	$4,000	$9,000
Alternative 2	4,000	3,000	2,000	9,000

Based on visual observation alone, which alternative has the higher present value? Why?

Answer Alternative 2 has the higher present value. The size of the discount increases as the length of the time period increases. In other words, a dollar received in year 3 has a lower present value than a dollar received in year 1. Since most of the expected cash inflows from Alternative 2 are received earlier than those from Alternative 1, Alternative 2 has a higher present value even though the total expected cash inflows are the same.

CONVERTING FUTURE CASH INFLOWS TO THEIR EQUIVALENT PRESENT VALUES

Given a desired rate of return and the amount of a future cash flow, present value can be determined using algebra. To illustrate, refer to the $200,000 EZ expects to earn the first year it leases LCD projectors.[1] Assuming EZ desires a 12 percent rate of return, what amount of cash would EZ be willing to invest today (present value outflow) to obtain a $200,000 cash inflow at the end of the year (future value)? The answer follows:[2]

LO 2

Determine the present value of future cash flows.

$$\text{Investment} + (0.12 \times \text{Investment}) = \text{Future cash inflow}$$
$$1.12 \text{ Investment} = \$200,000$$
$$\text{Investment} = \$200,000 \div 1.12$$
$$\text{Investment} = \$178,571$$

If EZ invests $178,571 cash on January 1 and earns a 12 percent return on the investment, EZ will have $200,000 on December 31. An investor who is able to earn a 12 percent return on investment is indifferent between having $178,571 now or receiving

---

[1]The following computations assume the $200,000 cash inflow is received on the last day of each year. In actual practice the timing of cash inflows is less precise and present value computations are recognized to be approximate, not exact.

[2]All computations in this chapter are rounded to the nearest whole dollar.

$200,000 one year from now. The two options are equal, as shown in the following mathematical proof:

$$\text{Investment} + (0.12 \times \text{Investment}) = \$200,000$$

$$\$178,571 + (0.12 \times \$178,571) = \$200,000$$

$$\$178,571 + \$21,429 = \$200,000$$

$$\$200,000 = \$200,000$$

Present Value Table for Single-Amount Cash Inflows

The algebra illustrated above is used to convert a one-time future receipt of cash to its present value. One-time receipts of cash are frequently called **single-payment,** or **lump-sum,** cash flows. Because EZ desires a 12 percent rate of return, the present value of the first cash inflow is $178,571. We can also determine the present value of a $200,000 single amount (lump sum) at the end of the second, third, and fourth years. Instead of using cumbersome algebraic computations to convert these future values to their present value equivalents, financial analysts frequently use a table of conversion factors to convert future values to their present value equivalents. The table of conversion factors used to convert future values into present values is commonly called a **present value table.**[3] A typical present value table presents columns with different return rates and rows with different periods of time, like Table 1 in the Appendix located at the end of this chapter.

To illustrate using the present value table, locate the conversion factor in Table 1 at the intersection of the 12% column and the one-period row. The conversion factor is 0.892857. Multiplying this factor by the $200,000 expected cash inflow yields $178,571 ($200,000 × 0.892857). This is the same value determined algebraically in the previous section of this chapter. The conversion factors in the present value tables simplify converting future values to present values.

The conversion factors for the second, third, and fourth periods are 0.797194, 0.711780, and 0.635518, respectively. These factors are in the 12% column at rows 2, 3, and 4, respectively. Locate these factors in Table 1 of the Appendix. Multiplying the conversion factors by the future cash inflow for each period produces their present value equivalents, shown in Exhibit 10.1. Exhibit 10.1 indicates that investing $607,470 today at a 12 percent rate of return is equivalent to receiving $200,000 per year for four years. Because EZ Rentals desires to earn (at least) a 12 percent rate of return, the company should be willing to pay up to $607,470 to purchase the LCD projectors.

Present Value Table for Annuities

The algebra described previously for converting equal lump-sum cash inflows to present value equivalents can be further simplified by adding the present value table factors

EXHIBIT 10.1

Present Value of a $200,000 Cash Inflow to be Received for Four Years

PV	=	FV	×	Present Value Table Factor	=	Present Value Equivalent
Period 1 PV	=	$200,000	×	0.892857	=	$178,571
Period 2 PV	=	200,000	×	0.797194	=	159,439
Period 3 PV	=	200,000	×	0.711780	=	142,356
Period 4 PV	=	200,000	×	0.635518	=	127,104
Total						$607,470

[3]The present value table is based on the formula $[1 \div (1 + r)^n]$ where r equals the rate of return and n equals the number of periods.

together before multiplying them by the cash inflows. The total of the present value table factors in Exhibit 10.1 is 3.037349 (0.892857 + 0.797194 + 0.711780 + 0.635518). Multiplying this **accumulated conversion factor** by the expected annual cash inflow results in the same present value equivalent of $607,470 ($200,000 × 3.037349). As with lump-sum conversion factors, accumulated conversion factors can be calculated and organized in a table with *columns* for different rates of return and *rows* for different periods of time. Table 2 in the Appendix is a present value table of accumulated conversion factors. Locate the conversion factor at the intersection of the 12% column and the fourth time-period row. The factor at this intersection is 3.037349, confirming that the accumulated conversion factors represent the sum of the single-payment conversion factors.

The conversion factors in Table 2 apply to annuities. An **annuity** is a series of cash flows that meets three criteria: (1) equal payment amounts; (2) equal time intervals between payments; and (3) a constant rate of return. For EZ Rentals, the expected cash inflows from renting LCD projectors are all for equivalent amounts ($200,000); the expected intervals between cash inflows are equal lengths of time (one year); and the rate of return for each inflow is constant at 12 percent. The series of expected cash inflows from renting the projectors is therefore an annuity. The present value of an annuity table can be used only if all of these conditions are satisfied.

The present value of an annuity table (Table 2) simplifies converting future cash inflows to their present value equivalents. EZ Rentals can convert the cash inflows as shown in Exhibit 10.1, using four conversion factors, multiplying each conversion factor by the annual cash inflow (four multiplications), and adding the resulting products. In contrast, EZ can recognize that the series of payments is an annuity, which requires multiplying a single conversion factor from Table 2 by the amount of the annuity payment. Regardless of the conversion method, the result is the same (a present value of $607,470). Recall that EZ can also make the conversion using algebra. The table values are derived from algebraic formulas. The present value tables reduce the computations needed to convert future values to present values.

Software Programs that Calculate Present Values

Software programs offer an even more efficient means of converting future values into present value equivalents. These programs are frequently built into handheld financial calculators and computer spreadsheet programs. As an example, we demonstrate the procedures used in a Microsoft Excel spreadsheet.

An Excel spreadsheet offers a variety of financial functions, one of which converts a future value annuity into its present value equivalent. This present value function uses the syntax *PV(rate,nper,pmt)* in which *rate* is the desired rate of return, *nper* is the number of periods, and *pmt* is the amount of the payment (periodic cash inflow). To convert a future value annuity into its present value equivalent, provide the function with the appropriate amounts for the rate, number of periods, and amount of the annuity (cash inflows) into a spreadsheet cell. Press the Enter key and the present value equivalent appears in the spreadsheet cell.

The power of the spreadsheet to perform computations instantly is extremely useful for answering what-if questions. Exhibit 10.2 demonstrates this power by providing spreadsheet conversions for three different scenarios. The first scenario demonstrates the annuity assumptions for EZ Rentals, providing the present value equivalent ($607,470) of a four-year cash inflow of $200,000 per year at a 12 percent rate of interest. The present value is a *negative* number. This format indicates that an initial $607,470 *cash outflow* is required to obtain the four-year series of cash inflows. The present value equivalent in Scenario 2 shows the present value if the annuity assumptions reflect a 14 percent, rather than 12 percent, desired rate of return. The present value equivalent in Scenario 3 shows the present value if the annuity assumptions under Scenario 1 are changed to reflect annual cash inflows of $300,000, rather than $200,000. A wide range of scenarios could be readily considered by changing any or all the variables in the spreadsheet function. In each case, the computer does the calculations, giving the manager more time to analyze the data rather than compute it.

EXHIBIT 10.2

Microsoft Excel Spreadsheet Present Value Function

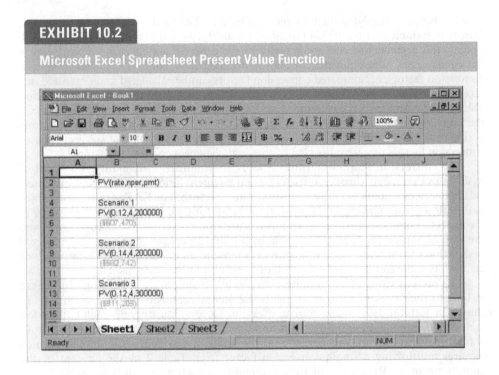

Although software is widely used in business practice, the diversity of interfaces used by different calculators and spreadsheet programs makes it unsuitable for textbook presentations. This text uses the present value tables in the Appendix in the text illustrations and the end-of-chapter exercises and problems. If you use software to solve these problems, your answers will be the same. All these tools—formulas, conversion tables, software—are based on the same mathematical principles and will produce the same results.

Ordinary Annuity Assumption

All the conversion methods described above assume the cash inflows occur at the *end* of each accounting period. This distribution pattern is called an **ordinary annuity.**[4] In practice, cash inflows are likely to be received throughout the period, not just at the end. For example, EZ Rentals is likely to collect cash revenue from renting projectors each month rather than in a single lump-sum receipt at the end of each of the four years. Companies frequently use the ordinary annuity assumption in practice because it simplifies time value of money computations. Because capital investment decisions are necessarily based on uncertain projections about future cash inflows, the lives of investment opportunities, and the appropriate rates of return, achieving pinpoint accuracy is impossible. Sacrificing precision for simplicity by using the ordinary annuity assumption is a reasonable trade-off in the decision-making process.

Reinvestment Assumption

The present value computations in the previous sections show that investing $607,470 today at a 12 percent rate of return is equivalent to receiving four individual $200,000 payments at the end of four successive years. Exhibit 10.3 illustrates that a cash inflow of $200,000 per year is equivalent to earning a 12 percent rate of return on a $607,470 investment.[5]

---

[4]When equal cash inflows occur at the *beginning* of each accounting period, the distribution is called an *annuity due.* Although some business transactions are structured as annuities due, they are less common than ordinary annuities. This text focuses on the ordinary annuity assumption.

[5]Exhibit 10.3 is analogous to an amortization table for a long-term note with equal payments of principal and interest.

EXHIBIT 10.3

Cash Flow Classifications for EZ's Investment in Projectors

Time Period	(a) Investment Balance During the Year	(b) Annual Cash Inflow	(c) Return on Investment (a × 0.12)	(d) Recovered Investment (b − c)	(e) Year-End Investment Balance (a − d)
1	$607,470	$200,000	$ 72,896	$127,104	$480,366
2	480,366	200,000	57,644	142,356	338,010
3	338,010	200,000	40,561	159,439	178,571
4	178,571	200,000	21,429	178,571	0
Totals		$800,000	$192,530	$607,470	

It is customary to assume that the desired rate of return includes the effects of *compounding*.[6] Saying an investment is "earning the desired rate of return," assumes the cash inflows generated by the investment are reinvested at the desired rate of return. In this case, we are assuming that EZ will reinvest the $200,000 annual cash inflows in other investments that will earn a 12 percent return.

TECHNIQUES FOR ANALYZING CAPITAL INVESTMENT PROPOSALS

Managers can choose from among numerous analytical techniques to help them make capital investment decisions. Each technique has advantages and disadvantages. A manager may apply more than one technique to a particular proposal to take advantage of more information. Since most companies have computer capabilities that include a variety of standard capital budgeting programs, applying different techniques to the same proposal normally requires little extra effort. Limiting analysis to only one tool could produce biased results. Obtaining more than one perspective offers substantial benefit.

Net Present Value

By using the present value conversion techniques described earlier, EZ Rentals' management determined it would be willing to invest $607,470 today (present value) to obtain a four-year, $200,000 future value annuity cash inflow. The $607,470 investment is *not* the cost of the LCD projectors; it is the amount EZ is willing to pay for them. The projectors may cost EZ Rentals more or less than their present value. To determine whether EZ should invest in the projectors, management must compare the present value of the future cash inflows ($607,470) to the cost of the projectors (the current cash outflow required to purchase them). Subtracting the cost of the investment from the present value of the future cash inflows determines the **net present value** of the investment opportunity. A positive net present value indicates the investment will yield a rate of return higher than 12 percent. A negative net present value means the return is less than 12 percent.

LO 3

Determine and interpret the net present value of an investment opportunity.

[6]*Compounding* refers to reinvesting investment proceeds so the total amount of invested capital increases, resulting in even higher returns. For example, assume $100 is invested at a 10 percent compounded annual rate of return. At the end of the first year, the investment yields a $10 return ($100 × 0.10). The $10 return plus any recovered investment is reinvested so that the total amount of invested capital at the beginning of the second year is $110. The return for the second year is $11 ($110 × 0.10). All funds are reinvested so that the return for the third year is $12.10 [($110 + $11) × 0.10].

To illustrate, assume EZ can purchase the projectors for $582,742. Assuming the desired rate of return is 12 percent, EZ should buy them. The net present value of the investment opportunity is computed as follows.

Present value of future cash inflows	$607,470
Cost of investment (required cash outflow)	(582,742)
Net present value	$ 24,728

The positive net present value suggests the investment will earn a rate of return in excess of 12 percent (if cash flows are indeed $200,000 each year). Because the projected rate of return is higher than the desired rate of return, this analysis suggests EZ should accept the investment opportunity. Based on the above analysis we are able to establish the following decision rule:

Net present value decision rule: If the net present value is equal to or greater than zero, accept the investment opportunity.

✓ **CHECK YOURSELF 10.2**

To increase productivity, Wald Corporation is considering the purchase of a new machine that costs $50,000. Wald expects using the machine to increase annual net cash inflows by $12,500 for each of the next five years. Wald desires a minimum annual rate of return of 10 percent on the investment. Determine the net present value of the investment opportunity and recommend whether Wald should acquire the machine.

Answer

Present value of future cash flows = Future cash flow × Table 2 factor ($n = 5$, $r = 10\%$)

Present value of future cash flows = $12,500 × 3.790787 = $47,385

Net present value = PV of future cash flows − Cost of machine

Net present value = $47,385 − $50,000 = ($2,615)

The negative net present value indicates the investment will yield a rate of return below the desired rate of return. Wald should not acquire the new machine.

Internal Rate of Return

The net present value method indicates EZ's investment in the projectors will provide a return in excess of the desired rate, but it does not provide the actual rate of return to expect from the investment. If EZ's management team wants to know the rate of return to expect from investing in the projectors, it must use the *internal rate of return method*. The **internal rate of return** is the rate at which the present value of cash inflows equals the cash outflows. It is the rate that will produce a zero net present value. For EZ Rentals, the internal rate of return can be determined as follows. First, compute the *present value table factor* for a $200,000 annuity that would yield a $582,742 present value cash outflow (cost of investment).

Present value table factor × $200,000 = $582,742

Present value table factor = $582,742 ÷ $200,000

Present value table factor = 2.91371

Second, since the expected annual cash inflows represent a four-year annuity, scan Table 2 in the Appendix at period $n = 4$. Try to locate the table factor 2.91371.

The rate listed at the top of the column in which the factor is located is the internal rate of return. Turn to Table 2 and determine the internal rate of return for EZ Rentals before you read further. The above factor is in the 14 percent column. The difference in the table value (2.913712) and the value computed here (2.91371) is not significant. If EZ invests $582,742 in the projectors and they produce a $200,000 annual cash flow for four years, EZ will earn a 14 percent rate of return on the investment.

The *internal rate of return* may be compared with a *desired rate of return* to determine whether to accept or reject a particular investment project. Assuming EZ desires to earn a minimum rate of return of 12 percent, the preceding analysis suggests it should accept the investment opportunity because the internal rate of return (14 percent) is higher than the desired rate of return (12 percent). An internal rate of return below the desired rate suggests management should reject a particular proposal. The desired rate of return is sometimes called the *cutoff rate* or the *hurdle rate*. To be accepted, an investment proposal must provide an internal rate of return higher than the hurdle rate, cutoff rate, or desired rate of return. These terms are merely alternatives for the *cost of capital*. Ultimately, to be accepted, an investment must provide an internal rate of return higher than a company's cost of capital. Based on the above analysis we are able to establish the following decision rule:

Internal rate of return decision rule: If the internal rate of return is equal to or greater than the desired rate of return, accept the investment opportunity.

TECHNIQUES FOR MEASURING INVESTMENT CASH FLOWS

The EZ Rentals example represents a simple capital investment analysis. The investment option involved only one cash outflow and a single annuity inflow. Investment opportunities often involve a greater variety of cash outflows and inflows. The following section of this chapter discusses different types of cash flows encountered in business practice.

LO 5

Identify cash flows associated with an investment opportunity.

Cash Inflows

Cash inflows generated from capital investments come from *four basic sources.* As in the case of EZ Rentals, the most common source of cash inflows is incremental revenue. **Incremental revenue** refers to the *additional* cash inflows from operating activities generated by using additional capital assets. For example, a taxi company expects revenues from taxi fares to increase if it purchases additional taxicabs. Similarly, investing in new apartments should increase rent revenue; opening a new store should result in additional sales revenue.

A second type of cash inflow results from *cost savings.* Decreases in cash outflows have the same beneficial effect as increases in cash inflows. Either way, a firm's cash position improves. For example, purchasing an automated computer system may enable a company to reduce cash outflows for salaries. Similarly, relocating a manufacturing facility closer to its raw materials source can reduce cash outflows for transportation costs.

An investment's *salvage value* provides a third source of cash inflows. Even when one company has finished using an asset, the asset may still be useful to another company. Many assets are sold after a company no longer wishes to use them. The salvage value represents a one-time cash inflow obtained when a company terminates an investment.

Companies can also experience a cash inflow through a *reduction in the amount of* **working capital** needed to support an investment. A certain level of working capital is required to support most business investments. For example, a new retail store outlet requires cash, receivables, and inventory to operate. When an investment is terminated, the decrease in the working capital commitment associated with the investment normally results in a cash inflow.

Cash Outflows

Cash outflows fall into *three primary categories.* One category consists of outflows for the *initial investment.* Managers must be alert to all the cash outflows connected with purchasing a capital asset. The purchase price, transportation costs, installation costs, and training costs are examples of typical cash outflows related to an initial investment.

A second category of cash outflows may result from *increases in operating expenses.* If a company increases output capacity by investing in additional equipment, it may experience higher utility bills, labor costs, and maintenance expenses when it places the equipment into service. These expenditures increase cash outflows.

Third, *increases in working capital* commitments result in cash outflows. Frequently, investments in new assets must be supported by a certain level of working capital. For example, investing in a copy machine requires spending cash to maintain a supply of paper and toner. Managers should treat an increased working capital commitment as a cash outflow in the period the commitment occurs.

Exhibit 10.4 lists the cash inflows and outflows discussed above. The list is not exhaustive but does summarize the most common cash flows businesses experience.

EXHIBIT 10.4

Typical Cash Flows Associated With Capital Investments

Inflows	Outflows
1. Incremental revenue	1. Initial investment
2. Cost savings	2. Incremental expenses
3. Salvage values	3. Working capital commitments
4. Recovery of working capital	

TECHNIQUES FOR COMPARING ALTERNATIVE CAPITAL INVESTMENT OPPORTUNITIES

Compare capital investment alternatives.

The management of Torres Transfer Company is considering two investment opportunities. One alternative, involving the purchase of new equipment for $80,000, would enable Torres to modernize its maintenance facility. The equipment has an expected useful life of five years and a $4,000 salvage value. It would replace existing equipment that had originally cost $45,000. The existing equipment has a current book value of $15,000 and a trade-in value of $5,000. The old equipment is technologically obsolete but can operate for an additional five years. On the day Torres purchases the new equipment, it would also pay the equipment manufacturer $3,000 for training costs to teach employees to operate the new equipment. The modernization has two primary advantages. One, it will improve management of the small parts inventory. The company's accountant believes that by the end of the first year, the carrying value of the small parts inventory could be reduced by $12,000. Second, the modernization is expected to increase efficiency, resulting in a $21,500 reduction in annual operating expenses.

The other investment alternative available to Torres is purchasing a truck. Adding another truck would enable Torres to expand its delivery area and increase revenue. The truck costs $115,000. It has a useful life of five years and a $30,000 salvage value. Operating the truck will require the company to increase its inventory of supplies, its petty cash account, and its accounts receivable and payable balances. These changes would add $5,000 to the company's working capital base immediately upon buying the truck. The working capital cash outflow is expected to be recovered at the end of the truck's useful life. The truck is expected to produce $69,000 per year in additional revenues. The driver's salary and other operating expenses are expected to be $32,000 per year. A major overhaul costing $20,000 is expected to be required at the end of the third year of operation. Assuming Torres desires to earn a rate of return of 14 percent, which of the two investment alternatives should it choose?

Net Present Value

Begin the analysis by calculating the net present value of the two investment alternatives. Exhibit 10.5 shows the computations. Study this exhibit. Each alternative is analyzed using three steps. Step 1 requires identifying all cash inflows; some may be annuities, and others may be lump-sum receipts. In the case of Alternative 1, the cost

EXHIBIT 10.5

Net Present Value Analysis

	Amount	×	Conversion Factor	=	Present Value
Alternative 1: Modernize Maintenance Facility					
Step 1: Cash inflows					
1. Cost savings	$21,500	×	3.433081*	=	$ 73,811
2. Salvage value	4,000	×	0.519369†	=	2,077
3. Working capital recovery	12,000	×	0.877193‡	=	10,526
Total					$ 86,414
Step 2: Cash outflows					
1. Cost of equipment					
($80,000 cost—$5,000 trade-in)	$75,000	×	1.000000§	=	$ 75,000
2. Training costs	3,000	×	1.000000§	=	3,000
Total					$ 78,000
Step 3: Net present value					
Total present value of cash inflows					$ 86,414
Total present value of cash outflows					(78,000)
Net present value					$ 8,414
Alternative 2: Purchase Delivery Truck					
Step 1: Cash inflows					
1. Incremental revenue	$69,000	×	3.433081*	=	$236,883
2. Salvage value	30,000	×	0.519369†	=	15,581
3. Working capital recovery	5,000	×	0.519369†	=	2,597
Total					$255,061
Step 2: Cash outflows					
1. Cost of truck	$115,000	×	1.000000§	=	$115,000
2. Working capital increase	5,000	×	1.000000§	=	5,000
3. Increased operating expense	32,000	×	3.433081§§	=	109,859
4. Major overhaul	20,000	×	0.674972§§	=	13,499
Total					$243,358
Step 3: Net present value					
Total present value of cash inflows					$255,061
Total present value of cash outflows					(243,358)
Net present value					$ 11,703

*Present value of annuity table 2, $n = 5$, $r = 14\%$.   §Present value at beginning of period 1.
†Present value of single payment table 1, $n = 5$, $r = 14\%$.   §§Present value of single payment table 1, $n = 3$, $r = 14\%$.
‡Present value of single payment table 1, $n = 1$, $r = 14\%$.

saving is an annuity, and the inflow from the salvage value is a lump-sum receipt. Once the cash inflows have been identified, the appropriate conversion factors are identified and the cash inflows are converted to their equivalent present values. Step 2 follows the same process to determine the present value of the cash outflows. Step 3 subtracts the present value of the outflows from the present value of the inflows to determine the net present value. The same three-step approach is used to determine the net present value of Alternative 2.

With respect to Alternative 1, the original cost and the book value of the existing equipment are ignored. As indicated in a previous chapter, these measures represent *sunk costs;* they are not relevant to the decision. The concept of relevance applies to long-term capital investment decisions just as it applies to the short-term special decisions that were discussed in Chapter 5. To be relevant to a capital investment decision, costs or revenues must involve different present and future cash flows for each alternative. Since the historical cost of the old equipment does not differ between the alternatives, it is not relevant.

Since the *net present value* of each investment alternative is *positive*, either investment will generate a return in excess of 14 percent. Which investment is the more favorable? The data could mislead a careless manager. Alternative 2 might seem the better choice because it has a greater present value than Alternative 1 ($11,703 vs. $8,414). Net present value, however, is expressed in *absolute dollars*. The net present value of a more costly capital investment can be greater than the net present value of a smaller investment even though the smaller investment earns a higher rate of return.

To compare different size investment alternatives, management can compute a **present value index** by dividing the present value of cash inflows by the present value of cash outflows. *The higher the ratio, the higher the rate of return per dollar invested in the proposed project.* The present value indices for the two alternatives Torres Transfer Company is considering are as follows.

$$\text{Present value index for Alternative 1} = \frac{\text{Present value of cash inflows}}{\text{Present value of cash outflows}} = \frac{\$86,414}{\$78,000} = 1.108$$

$$\text{Present value index for Alternative 2} = \frac{\text{Present value of cash inflows}}{\text{Present value of cash outflows}} = \frac{\$255,061}{\$243,358} = 1.048$$

Management can use the present value indices to rank the investment alternatives. In this case, Alternative 1 yields a higher return than Alternative 2.

Internal Rate of Return

Management can also rank investment alternatives using the internal rate of return for each investment. Generally, *the higher the internal rate of return, the more profitable the investment.* We previously demonstrated how to calculate the internal rate of return for an investment that generates a simple cash inflow annuity. The computations are significantly more complex for investments with uneven cash flows. Recall that the internal rate of return is the rate that produces a zero net present value. Manually computing the rate that produces a zero net present value is a tedious trial-and-error process. You must first estimate the rate of return for a particular investment, then calculate the net present value. If the calculation produces a negative net present value, you try a lower estimated rate of return and recalculate. If this calculation produces a positive net present value, the actual internal rate of return lies between the first and second estimates. Make a third estimate and once again recalculate the net present value, and so on. Eventually you will determine the rate of return that produces a net present value of zero.

Many calculators and spreadsheet programs are designed to make these computations. We illustrate the process with a Microsoft Excel spreadsheet. Excel uses the syntax *IRR (values, guess)* in which *values* refers to cells that specify the cash flows for which you want to calculate the internal rate of return and *guess* is a number you estimate is close to the actual internal rate of return (IRR). The IRRs for the two investment alternatives available to Torres Transfer Company are shown in Exhibit 10.6. Study this exhibit. Excel requires netting cash outflows against cash inflows for each period in which both outflows and inflows are expected. For your convenience, we have labeled the net cash flows in the spreadsheet. Labeling is not necessary to execute the IRR function. The entire function, including values and guess, can be entered into a single cell of the spreadsheet. Persons familiar with spreadsheet programs learn to significantly simplify the input required.

The IRR results in Exhibit 10.6 confirm the ranking determined using the present value index. Alternative 1 (modernize maintenance facility), with an internal rate of return of 18.69 percent, ranks above Alternative 2 (purchase a truck) with an internal rate of return of 17.61 percent, even though Alternative 2 has a higher net present value (see Exhibit 10.5). Alternative 2, however, still may be the better investment option, depending on the amount available to invest. Suppose Torres has $120,000 of available funds to invest. Because Alternative 1 requires an initial investment of only $78,000, $42,000 ($120,000 − $78,000) of capital will not be invested. If Torres has

REALITY BYTES

Developing proficiency with present value mathematics is usually the most difficult aspect of capital budgeting for students taking their first managerial accounting course. In real-world companies, the most difficult aspect of capital budgeting is forecasting cash flows for several years into the future. Consider the following capital budgeting project.

In 1965 representatives from the Georgia Power Company visited Ms. Taylor's fifth grade class to tell her students about the Edwin I. Hatch Nuclear Plant that was going to be built nearby. One of the authors of this text was a student in that class.

In 1966 construction began on the first unit of the plant, and the plant started producing electricity in 1975. The next year, 10 years after hearing the presentation in his fifth grade class, the author worked on construction of the second unit of the plant during the summer before his senior year of college. This second unit began operations in 1978.

In its 2009 annual report, the Southern Company, which is now the major owner of the plant, stated that the Hatch plant is expected to operate until 2038, and that decommissioning of the plant will continue until 2061. The cost to construct both units of the plant was $934 million. The estimated cost to dismantle and decommission the plant is over $1 billion.

It seems safe to assume that the students in Ms. Taylor's fifth grade class were not among the first to hear about the power company's plans for the Hatch plant. Thus, we can reasonably conclude that the life of this capital project will be over 100 years, from around 1960 until 2061.

Try to imagine that you were assigned the task of predicting the cost inflows and outflows for a project that was expected to last 100 years. Clearly, mastering present value mathematics would not be your biggest worry.

EXHIBIT 10.6

Microsoft Excel Spreadsheet Internal Rate of Return Function

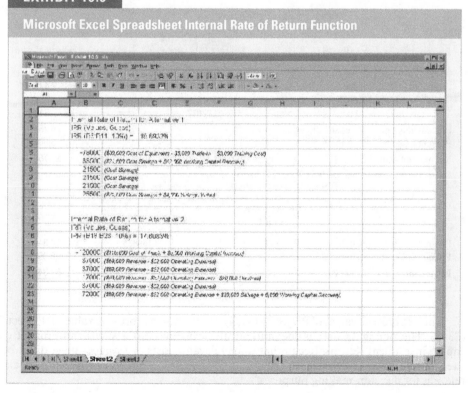

no other investment opportunities for this $42,000, the company would be better off investing the entire $120,000 in Alternative 2 ($115,000 cost of truck + $5,000 working capital increase). Earning 17.61 percent on a $120,000 investment is better than earning 18.69 percent on a $78,000 investment with no return on the remaining $42,000. Management accounting requires exercising judgment when making decisions.

Relevance and the Time Value of Money

Suppose you have the opportunity to invest in one of two capital projects. Both projects require an immediate cash outflow of $6,000 and will produce future cash inflows of $8,000. The only difference between the two projects is the timing of the inflows. The receipt schedule for both projects follows.

Year	Project 1	Project 2
1	$3,500	$2,000
2	3,000	2,000
3	1,000	2,000
4	500	2,000
Total	$8,000	$8,000

Because both projects cost the same and produce the same total cash inflows, they may appear to be equal. Whether you select Project 1 or Project 2, you pay $6,000 and receive $8,000. Because of the time value of money, however, Project 1 is preferable to Project 2. To see why, determine the net present value of both projects, assuming a 10 percent desired rate of return.

Computation of Net Present Value for Project 1 and Project 2

Net Present Value for Project 1

Period	Cash Inflow	×	Conversion Factor Table 1, $r = 10\%$	=	Present Value
1	$3,500	×	0.909091	=	$3,182
2	3,000	×	0.826446	=	2,479
3	1,000	×	0.751315	=	751
4	500	×	0.683013	=	342
Present value of future cash inflows					6,754
Present value of cash outflow					(6,000)
Net present value Project 1					$ 754

Net Present Value for Project 2

	Cash Inflow Annuity	×	Conversion Factor Table 2, $r = 10\%$, $n = 4$		
Present value of cash inflow	$2,000	×	3.169865		$6,340
Present value of cash outflow					(6,000)
Net present value Project 2					$ 340

The net present value of Project 1 ($754) exceeds the net present value of Project 2 ($340). The timing as well as the amount of cash flows has a significant impact on capital investment returns. Recall that to be relevant, costs or revenues must differ between alternatives. Differences in the timing of cash flow payments or receipts are also relevant for decision-making purposes.

Answers to The Curious Accountant

One way to answer your client's question is to determine which option has the highest net present value. The present value of the lump-sum payment option is simple; it is the $115.5 [$231 ÷ 2] million the lottery is prepared to pay them now. The present value of the annuity option must be calculated, and it consists of two parts. The first of the 26 payments of $7,076,692 will be paid immediately, so it is worth $7,076,692 today. The remaining 25 payments will occur at one-year intervals, so their present value is computed as:

$$\$7,076,692 \times 11.653583^* = \$82,468,818$$

Adding $7,076,692 to $82,468,818 yields a present value of $89,545,510, which is a lot less than $115.5 million. This suggests your client should take the lump-sum payment. Of course, the risk of the lottery not making its annual payments is very low. There is a greater risk that a financial planner may not find investments to earn a 7% annual return, so the winner would have to consider his or her tolerance for risk before making a final decision.

In the case of these particular lottery winners, one chose the lump-sum payment and the other chose the annuity.

*This factor is not included in the tables at the end of the chapter, so it is provided here for the purposes of this illustration.

Tax Considerations

The previous examples have ignored the effect of income taxes on capital investment decisions. Taxes affect the amount of cash flows generated by investments. To illustrate, assume Wu Company purchases an asset that costs $240,000. The asset has a four-year useful life, no salvage value, and is depreciated on a straight-line basis. The asset generates cash revenue of $90,000 per year. Assume Wu's income tax rate is 40 percent. What is the net present value of the asset, assuming Wu's management desires to earn a 10 percent rate of return after taxes? The first step in answering this question is to calculate the annual cash flow generated by the asset, as shown in Exhibit 10.7.

EXHIBIT 10.7

Determining Cash Flow from Investment

	Period 1	Period 2	Period 3	Period 4
Cash revenue	$ 90,000	$ 90,000	$ 90,000	$ 90,000
Depreciation expense (noncash)	(60,000)	(60,000)	(60,000)	(60,000)
Income before taxes	30,000	30,000	30,000	30,000
Income tax at 40%	(12,000)	(12,000)	(12,000)	(12,000)
Income after tax	18,000	18,000	18,000	18,000
Depreciation add back	60,000	60,000	60,000	60,000
Annual cash inflow	$ 78,000	$ 78,000	$ 78,000	$ 78,000

Because recognizing depreciation expense does not require a cash payment (cash is paid when assets are purchased, not when depreciation is recognized), depreciation expense must be added back to after-tax income to determine the annual cash inflow. Once the cash flow is determined, the net present value is computed as shown here.

Cash flow annuity	×	Conversion factor Table 2, $r = 10\%$, $n = 4$	=	Present value cash inflows	−	Present value cash outflows	=	Net present value
$78,000	×	3.169865	=	$247,249	−	$240,000	=	$7,249

The depreciation sheltered some of the income from taxation. Income taxes apply to income after deducting depreciation expense. Without depreciation expense, income taxes each year would have been $36,000 ($90,000 × 0.40) instead of $12,000 ($30,000 × 0.40). The $24,000 difference ($36,000 − $12,000) is known as a *depreciation tax shield*. The amount of the depreciation tax shield can also be computed by multiplying the depreciation expense by the tax rate ($60,000 × 0.40 = $24,000).

Because of the time value of money, companies benefit by maximizing the depreciation tax shield early in the life of an asset. For this reason, most companies calculate depreciation expense for tax purposes using the *modified accelerated cost recovery system (MACRS)* permitted by tax law rather than using straight-line depreciation. MACRS recognizes depreciation on an accelerated basis, assigning larger amounts of depreciation in the early years of an asset's useful life. The higher depreciation charges result in lower amounts of taxable income and lower income taxes. In the later years of an asset's useful life, the reverse is true, and lower depreciation charges result in higher taxes. Accelerated depreciation does not allow companies to avoid paying taxes but to delay them. The longer companies can delay paying taxes, the more cash they have available to invest.

TECHNIQUES THAT IGNORE THE TIME VALUE OF MONEY

LO 7

Determine the payback period for an investment opportunity.

Several techniques for evaluating capital investment proposals ignore the time value of money. Although these techniques are less accurate, they are quick and simple. When investments are small or the returns are expected within a short time, these techniques are likely to result in the same decisions that more sophisticated techniques produce.

Payback Method

The **payback method** is simple to apply and easy to understand. It shows how long it will take to recover the initial cash outflow (the cost) of an investment. The formula for computing the payback period, measured in years, is as follows.

$$\text{Payback period} = \text{Net cost of investment} \div \text{Annual net cash inflow}$$

To illustrate, assume Winston Cleaners can purchase a new ironing machine that will press shirts in half the time of the one currently used. The new machine costs $100,000 and will reduce labor cost by $40,000 per year over a four-year useful life. The payback period is computed as follows.

$$\text{Payback period} = \$100,000 \div \$40,000 = 2.5 \text{ years}$$

Interpreting Payback

Generally, investments with shorter payback periods are considered better. Because the payback method measures only investment recovery, not profitability, however, this conclusion can be invalid when considering investment alternatives. To illustrate, assume Winston Cleaners also has the opportunity to purchase a different machine that costs $100,000 and provides an annual labor savings of $40,000. However, the second machine will last for five instead of four years. The payback period is still 2.5 years ($100,000 ÷ $40,000), but the second machine is a better investment because it improves profitability by providing an additional year of cost savings. The payback analysis does not measure this difference between the alternatives.

Unequal Cash Flows

The preceding illustration assumed Winston's labor cost reduction saved the same amount of cash each year for the life of the new machine. The payback method requires adjustment when cash flow benefits are unequal. Suppose a company purchases a machine for $6,000. The machine will be used erratically and is expected to provide incremental revenue over the next five years as follows.

2007	2008	2009	2010	2011
$3,000	$1,000	$2,000	$1,000	$500

Based on this cash inflow pattern, what is the payback period? There are two acceptable solutions. One accumulates the incremental revenue until the sum equals the amount of the original investment.

Year	Annual Amount	Cumulative Total
2007	$3,000	$3,000
2008	1,000	4,000
2009	2,000	6,000

This approach indicates the payback period is three years.

A second solution uses an averaging concept. The average annual cash inflow is determined. This figure is then used in the denominator of the payback equation. Using the preceding data, the payback period is computed as follows.

1. Compute the average annual cash inflow.

$$2007 \ + \ 2008 \ + \ 2009 \ + \ 2010 \ + 2011 = \ \text{Total} \ \div 5 = \text{Average}$$

$$\$3{,}000 + \$1{,}000 + \$2{,}000 + \$1{,}000 + \$500 = \$7{,}500 \div 5 = \ \$1{,}500$$

2. Compute the payback period.

$$\frac{\text{Net cost of}}{\text{investment}} \div \frac{\text{Average annual}}{\text{net cash inflow}} = 6{,}000 \div 1{,}500 = 4 \text{ years}$$

The average method is useful when a company purchases a number of similar assets with differing cash return patterns.

Unadjusted Rate of Return

The **unadjusted rate of return** method is another common evaluation technique. Investment cash flows are not adjusted to reflect the time value of money. The unadjusted rate of return is sometimes called the *simple rate of return*. It is computed as follows.

Determine the unadjusted rate of return for an investment opportunity.

$$\frac{\text{Unadjusted}}{\text{rate of return}} = \frac{\text{Average incremental increase in annual net income}}{\text{Net cost of original investment}}$$

To illustrate computing the unadjusted rate of return, assume The Dining Table, Inc., is considering establishing a new restaurant that will require a $2,000,000 original investment. Management anticipates operating the restaurant for 10 years before significant renovations will be required. The restaurant is expected to provide an average after-tax return of $280,000 per year. The unadjusted rate of return is computed as follows.

$$\text{Unadjusted rate of return} = \$280{,}000 \div \$2{,}000{,}000 = 14\% \text{ per year}$$

The accuracy of the unadjusted rate of return suffers from the failure to recognize the recovery of invested capital. With respect to a depreciable asset, the capital investment is normally recovered through revenue over the life of the asset. To illustrate, assume we purchase a $1,000 asset with a two-year life and a zero salvage value. For simplicity, ignore income taxes. Assume the asset produces $600 of cash revenue per year. The income statement for the first year of operation appears as follows.

Revenue	$ 600
Depreciation expense	(500)
Net income	$ 100

What is the amount of invested capital during the first year? First, a $1,000 cash outflow was used to purchase the asset (the original investment). Next, we collected $600 of cash revenue of which $100 was a *return on investment* (net income) and $500 was a **recovery of investment.** As a result, $1,000 was invested in the asset at the beginning of the year and $500 was invested at the end of the year. Similarly, we will recover an additional $500 of capital during the second year of operation, leaving zero invested capital at the end of the second year. Given that the cash inflows from revenue are collected somewhat evenly over the life of the investment, the amount of invested capital will range from a beginning balance of $1,000 to an ending balance of zero. On average, we will have $500 invested in the asset (the midpoint between $1,000 and zero). The average investment can be determined by dividing the total original investment by 2 ($1,000 ÷ 2 = $500). The unadjusted rate of return based on average invested capital can be calculated as follows.

$$\text{Unadjusted rate of return} \atop \text{(Based on average investment)} = \frac{\text{Average incremental increase in annual net income}}{\text{Net cost of original investment} \div 2}$$

$$= \frac{\$100}{\$1,000 \div 2} = 20\%$$

To avoid distortions caused by the failure to recognize the recovery of invested capital, the unadjusted rate of return should be based on the *average investment* when working with investments in depreciable assets.

✓ CHECK YOURSELF 10.3

EZ Rentals can purchase a van that costs $24,000. The van has an expected useful life of three years and no salvage value. EZ expects rental revenue from the van to be $12,000 per year. Determine the payback period and the unadjusted rate of return.

Answer

Payback = Cost of the investment ÷ Annual cash inflow

Payback = $24,000 ÷ $12,000 = 2 years

Unadjusted rate of return = Net income ÷ Average cost of the investment

Revenue	$12,000	
Depreciation expense	(8,000)	[$24,000 ÷ 3 years]
Net income	$ 4,000	

Unadjusted rate of return = $4,000 ÷ ($24,000 ÷ 2) = 33.33%

REAL-WORLD REPORTING PRACTICES

In a study, researchers found that companies in the forest products industry use discounted cash flow techniques more frequently when the capital project being considered is a long-term timber investment. The use of techniques that ignore the time value of money increased when other shorter-term capital investment projects were being considered. Exhibit 10.8 shows the researchers' findings.

EXHIBIT 10.8

Forestry Industry Investments

Long-term investments in timber

Net present value **38%**

9% Unadjusted rate of return

Internal rate of return **38%**

15% Payback period

Investments in other assets

Net present value **22%**

13% Unadjusted rate of return

Internal rate of return **33%**

32% Payback period

Data Source: J. Bailes, J. Nielsen, and S. Lawton, "How Forest Product Companies Analyze Capital Budgets," *Management Accounting,* October 1998, pp. 24–30.

POSTAUDITS

The analytical techniques for evaluating capital investment proposals depend highly on estimates of future cash flows. Although predictions cannot be perfectly accurate, gross miscalculations can threaten the existence of an organization. For example, optimistic projections of future cash inflows that do not materialize will lead to investments that do not return the cost of capital. Managers must take their projections seriously. A postaudit policy can encourage managers to carefully consider their capital investment decisions. A **postaudit** is conducted at the completion of a capital investment project, using the same analytical technique that was used to justify the original investment. For example, if an internal rate of return was used to justify approving an investment project, the internal rate of return should be computed in the postaudit. In the postaudit computation, *actual* rather than estimated cash flows are used. Postaudits determine whether the expected results were achieved.

Conduct a postaudit of a completed investment.

Postaudits should focus on continuous improvement rather than punishment. Managers who are chastised for failing to achieve expected results might become overly cautious when asked to provide estimates for future projects. Being too conservative can create problems as serious as those caused by being too optimistic. Managers can err two ways with respect to capital investment decisions. First, a manager might accept a project that should have been rejected. This mistake usually stems from excessively optimistic future cash flow projections. Second, a manager might reject a project that should have been accepted. These missed opportunities are usually the result of underestimating future cash flows. A too cautious manager can become unable to locate enough projects to fully invest the firm's funds.

Idle cash earns no return. If projects continue to outperform expectations, managers are probably estimating future cash flows too conservatively. If projects consistently fail to live up to expectations, managers are probably being too optimistic in their projections of future cash flows. Either way, the company suffers. The goal of a postaudit is to provide feedback that will help managers improve the accuracy of future cash flow projections, maximizing the quality of the firm's capital investments.

A Look Back

Capital expenditures have a significant, long-term effect on profitability. They usually involve major cash outflows that are recovered through future cash inflows. The most common cash inflows include incremental revenue, operating cost savings, salvage value, and working capital releases. The most common outflows are the initial investment, increases in operating expenses, and working capital commitments.

Several techniques for analyzing the cash flows associated with capital investments are available. The techniques can be divided into two categories: (1) techniques that use time value of money concepts and (2) techniques that ignore the time value of money. Generally, techniques that ignore the time value of money are less accurate but simpler and easier to understand. These techniques include the *payback method* and the *unadjusted rate of return method*.

The techniques that use time value of money concepts are the *net present value method* and the *internal rate of return method*. These methods offer significant improvements in accuracy but are more difficult to understand. They may involve tedious computations and require using experienced judgment. Computer software and programmed calculators that ease the tedious computational burden are readily available to most managers. Furthermore, the superiority of the techniques justifies learning how to use them. These methods should be used when investment expenditures are larger or when cash flows extend over a prolonged time period.

 A Look Forward

The next chapter moves into unexplored territory. It introduces the concept of inventory cost flow. It discusses how costs move through the inventory accounts Raw Materials, Work in Process, and Finished Goods. It presents techniques for assigning overhead costs to inventory as the inventory is produced. It identifies differences in product costing for service and manufacturing companies. Finally, it contrasts two approaches used to value inventory, variable costing versus full-absorption costing.

APPENDIX

TABLE 1				Present Value of $1							
n	4%	5%	6%	7%	8%	9%	10%	12%	14%	16%	20%
1	0.961538	0.952381	0.943396	0.934579	0.925926	0.917431	0.909091	0.892857	0.877193	0.862069	0.833333
2	0.924556	0.907029	0.889996	0.873439	0.857339	0.841680	0.826446	0.797194	0.769468	0.743163	0.694444
3	0.888996	0.863838	0.839619	0.816298	0.793832	0.772183	0.751315	0.711780	0.674972	0.640658	0.578704
4	0.854804	0.822702	0.792094	0.762895	0.735030	0.708425	0.683013	0.635518	0.592080	0.552291	0.482253
5	0.821927	0.783526	0.747258	0.712986	0.680583	0.649931	0.620921	0.567427	0.519369	0.476113	0.401878
6	0.790315	0.746215	0.704961	0.666342	0.630170	0.596267	0.564474	0.506631	0.455587	0.410442	0.334898
7	0.759918	0.710681	0.665057	0.622750	0.583490	0.547034	0.513158	0.452349	0.399637	0.353830	0.279082
8	0.730690	0.676839	0.627412	0.582009	0.540269	0.501866	0.466507	0.403883	0.350559	0.305025	0.232568
9	0.702587	0.644609	0.591898	0.543934	0.500249	0.460428	0.424098	0.360610	0.307508	0.262953	0.193807
10	0.675564	0.613913	0.558395	0.508349	0.463193	0.422411	0.385543	0.321973	0.269744	0.226684	0.161506
11	0.649581	0.584679	0.526788	0.475093	0.428883	0.387533	0.350494	0.287476	0.236617	0.195417	0.134588
12	0.624597	0.556837	0.496969	0.444012	0.397114	0.355535	0.318631	0.256675	0.207559	0.168463	0.112157
13	0.600574	0.530321	0.468839	0.414964	0.367698	0.326179	0.289664	0.229174	0.182069	0.145227	0.093464
14	0.577475	0.505068	0.442301	0.387817	0.340461	0.299246	0.263331	0.204620	0.159710	0.125195	0.077887
15	0.555265	0.481017	0.417265	0.362446	0.315242	0.274538	0.239392	0.182696	0.140096	0.107927	0.064905
16	0.533908	0.458112	0.393646	0.338735	0.291890	0.251870	0.217629	0.163122	0.122892	0.093041	0.054088
17	0.513373	0.436297	0.371364	0.316574	0.270269	0.231073	0.197845	0.145644	0.107800	0.080207	0.045073
18	0.493628	0.415521	0.350344	0.295864	0.250249	0.211994	0.179859	0.130040	0.094561	0.069144	0.037561
19	0.474642	0.395734	0.330513	0.276508	0.231712	0.194490	0.163508	0.116107	0.082948	0.059607	0.031301
20	0.456387	0.376889	0.311805	0.258419	0.214548	0.178431	0.148644	0.103667	0.072762	0.051385	0.026084

TABLE 2		Present Value of an Annuity of $1									
n	4%	5%	6%	7%	8%	9%	10%	12%	14%	16%	20%
1	0.961538	0.952381	0.943396	0.934579	0.925926	0.917431	0.909091	0.892857	0.877193	0.862069	0.833333
2	1.886095	1.859410	1.833393	1.808018	1.783265	1.759111	1.735537	1.690051	1.646661	1.605232	1.527778
3	2.775091	2.723248	2.673012	2.624316	2.577097	2.531295	2.486852	2.401831	2.321632	2.245890	2.106481
4	3.629895	3.545951	3.465106	3.387211	3.312127	3.239720	3.169865	3.037349	2.913712	2.798181	2.588735
5	4.451822	4.329477	4.212364	4.100197	3.992710	3.889651	3.790787	3.604776	3.433081	3.274294	2.990612
6	5.242137	5.075692	4.917324	4.766540	4.622880	4.485919	4.355261	4.111407	3.888668	3.684736	3.325510
7	6.002055	5.786373	5.582381	5.389289	5.206370	5.032953	4.868419	4.563757	4.288305	4.038565	3.604592
8	6.732745	6.463213	6.209794	5.971299	5.746639	5.534819	5.334926	4.967640	4.638864	4.343591	3.837160
9	7.435332	7.107822	6.801692	6.515232	6.246888	5.995247	5.759024	5.328250	4.946372	4.606544	4.030967
10	8.110896	7.721735	7.360087	7.023582	6.710081	6.417658	6.144567	5.650223	5.216116	4.833227	4.192472
11	8.760477	8.306414	7.886875	7.498674	7.138964	6.805191	6.495061	5.937699	5.452733	5.028644	4.327060
12	9.385074	8.863252	8.383844	7.942686	7.536078	7.160725	6.813692	6.194374	5.660292	5.197107	4.439217
13	9.985648	9.393573	8.852683	8.357651	7.903776	7.486904	7.103356	6.423548	5.842362	5.342334	4.532681
14	10.563123	9.898641	9.294984	8.745468	8.244237	7.786150	7.366687	6.628168	6.002072	5.467529	4.610567
15	11.118387	10.379658	9.712249	9.107914	8.559479	8.060688	7.606080	6.810864	6.142168	5.575456	4.675473
16	11.652296	10.837770	10.105895	9.446649	8.851369	8.312558	7.823709	6.973986	6.265060	5.668497	4.729561
17	12.165669	11.274066	10.477260	9.763223	9.121638	8.543631	8.021553	7.119630	6.372859	5.748704	4.774634
18	12.659297	11.689587	10.827603	10.059087	9.371887	8.755625	8.201412	7.249670	6.467420	5.817848	4.812195
19	13.133939	12.085321	11.158116	10.335595	9.603599	8.905115	8.364920	7.365777	6.550369	5.877455	4.843496
20	13.590326	12.462210	11.469921	10.594014	9.818147	9.128546	8.513564	7.469444	6.623131	5.928841	4.869580

A step-by-step audio-narrated series of slides is provided on the text website at www.mhhe.com/edmonds2011.

SELF-STUDY REVIEW PROBLEM

The CFO of Advo Corporation is considering two investment opportunities. The expected future cash inflows for each opportunity follow:

	Year 1	Year 2	Year 3	Year 4
Project 1	$144,000	$147,000	$160,000	$178,000
Project 2	204,000	199,000	114,000	112,000

Both investments require an initial payment of $400,000. Advo's desired rate of return is 16 percent.

Required

a. Compute the net present value of each project. Which project should Advo adopt based on the net present value approach?

b. Use the incremental revenue summation method to compute the payback period for each project. Which project should Advo adopt based on the payback approach?

Solution to Requirement a

Project 1

	Cash Inflows		Table Factor*		Present Value
Year 1	$144,000	×	0.862069	=	$124,138
Year 2	147,000	×	0.743163	=	109,245
Year 3	160,000	×	0.640658	=	102,505
Year 4	178,000	×	0.552291	=	98,308
PV of cash inflows					434,196
Cost of investment					(400,000)
Net present value					$ 34,196

*Table 1, n = 1 through 4, r = 16%

Project 2

	Cash Inflows		Table Factor*		Present Value
Year 1	$204,000	×	0.862069	=	$175,862
Year 2	199,000	×	0.743163	=	147,889
Year 3	114,000	×	0.640658	=	73,035
Year 4	112,000	×	0.552291	=	61,857
PV of cash inflows					458,643
Cost of investment					(400,000)
Net present value					$ 58,643

*Table 1, n = 1 through 4, r = 16%

Advo should adopt Project 2 since it has a greater net present value.

Solution to Requirement b

Cash Inflows	Project 1	Project 2
Year 1	$144,000	$204,000
Year 2	147,000	199,000
Total	$291,000	$403,000

By the end of the second year, Project 2's cash inflows have more than paid for the cost of the investment. In contrast, Project 1 still falls short of investment recovery by $109,000 ($400,000 − $291,000). Advo should adopt Project 2 since it has a shorter payback period.

KEY TERMS

Accumulated conversion factor 447
Annuity 447
Capital investments 444
Cost of capital 445
Incremental revenue 451
Internal rate of return 450

Minimum rate of return 445
Net present value 449
Ordinary annuity 448
Payback method 458
Postaudit 461
Present value index 454
Present value table 446

Recovery of investment 460
Single-payment (lump-sum) 446
Time value of money 444
Unadjusted rate of return 449
Working capital 451

QUESTIONS

1. What is a capital investment? How does it differ from an investment in stocks or bonds?

2. What are three reasons that cash is worth more today than cash to be received in the future?

3. "A dollar today is worth more than a dollar in the future." "The present value of a future dollar is worth less than one dollar." Are these two statements synonymous? Explain.

4. Define the term *return on investment.* How is the return normally expressed? Give an example of a capital investment return.

5. How does a company establish its minimum acceptable rate of return on investments?

6. If you wanted to have $500,000 one year from today and desired to earn a 10 percent return, what amount would you need to invest today? Which amount has more value, the amount today or the $500,000 a year from today?

7. Why are present value tables frequently used to convert future values to present values?

8. Define the term *annuity.* What is one example of an annuity receipt?

9. How can present value "what-if" analysis be enhanced by using software programs?

10. Receiving $100,000 per year for five years is equivalent to investing what amount today at 14 percent? Provide a mathematical formula to solve this problem, assuming use of a present value annuity table to convert the future cash flows to their present value equivalents. Provide the expression for the Excel spreadsheet function that would perform the present value conversion.

11. Maria Espinosa borrowed $15,000 from the bank and agreed to repay the loan at 8 percent annual interest over four years, making payments of $4,529 per year. Because part of the bank's payment from Ms. Espinosa is a recovery of the original investment, what assumption must the bank make to earn its desired 8 percent compounded annual return?

12. Two investment opportunities have positive net present values. Investment A's net present value amounts to $40,000 while B's is only $30,000. Does this mean that A is the better investment opportunity? Explain.

13. What criteria determine whether a project is acceptable under the net present value method?

14. Does the net present value method provide a measure of the rate of return on capital investments?

15. Which is the best capital investment evaluation technique for ranking investment opportunities?

16. Paul Henderson is a manager for Spark Company. He tells you that his company always maximizes profitability by accepting the investment opportunity with the highest internal rate of return. Explain to Mr. Henderson how his company may improve profitability by sometimes selecting investment opportunities with lower internal rates of return.

17. What is the relationship between desired rate of return and internal rate of return?

18. What typical cash inflow and outflow items are associated with capital investments?

19. "I always go for the investment with the shortest payback period." Is this a sound strategy? Why or why not?

20. "The payback method cannot be used if the cash inflows occur in unequal patterns." Do you agree or disagree? Explain.

21. What are the advantages and disadvantages associated with the unadjusted rate of return method for evaluating capital investments?

22. How do capital investments affect profitability?

23. What is a postaudit? How is it useful in capital budgeting?

MULTIPLE-CHOICE QUESTIONS

Multiple-choice questions are provided on the text website at www.mhhe.com/edmonds2011.

EXERCISES—SERIES A

All applicable Exercises in Series A are available with McGraw-Hill's *Connect Accounting.*

Exercise 10-1A   *Identifying cash inflows and outflows*   LO 1, 5

Required

Indicate which of the following items will result in cash inflows and which will result in cash outflows. The first one is shown as an example.

Item	Type of Cash Flow
a. Initial investment	Outflow
b. Salvage values	
c. Recovery of working capital	
d. Incremental expenses	
e. Working capital commitments	
f. Cost savings	
g. Incremental revenue	

LO 1, 2

Exercise 10-2A   *Determining the present value of a lump-sum future cash receipt*

Stan Sweeney turned 20 years old today. His grandfather had established a trust fund that will pay him $80,000 on his next birthday. However, Stan needs money today to start his college education, and his father is willing to help. Mr. Sweeney has agreed to give Stan the present value of the $80,000 future cash inflow, assuming a 10 percent rate of return.

Required

a. Use a present value table to determine the amount of cash that Stan Sweeney's father should give him.

b. Use an algebraic formula to prove that the present value of the trust fund (the amount of cash computed in Requirement *a*) is equal to its $80,000 future value.

LO 1, 2

Exercise 10-3A   *Determining the present value of a lump-sum future cash receipt*

Marsha Bittner expects to receive a $600,000 cash benefit when she retires five years from today. Ms. Bittner's employer has offered an early retirement incentive by agreeing to pay her $360,000 today if she agrees to retire immediately. Ms. Bittner desires to earn a rate of return of 12 percent.

Required

a. Assuming that the retirement benefit is the only consideration in making the retirement decision, should Ms. Bittner accept her employer's offer?

b. Identify the factors that cause the present value of the retirement benefit to be less than $600,000.

LO 1, 2

Exercise 10-4A   *Determining the present value of an annuity*

The dean of the School of Natural Science is trying to decide whether to purchase a copy machine to place in the lobby of the building. The machine would add to student convenience, but the dean feels compelled to earn an 8 percent return on the investment of funds. Estimates of cash inflows from copy machines that have been placed in other university buildings indicate that the copy machine would probably produce incremental cash inflows of approximately $15,000 per year. The machine is expected to have a three-year useful life with a zero salvage value.

Required

a. Use Present Value Table 1 in the Appendix to determine the maximum amount of cash the dean should be willing to pay for a copy machine.

b. Use Present Value Table 2 in the Appendix to determine the maximum amount of cash the dean should be willing to pay for a copy machine.

c. Explain the consistency or lack of consistency in the answers to Requirements *a* and *b*.

LO 3

Exercise 10-5A   *Determining net present value*

Metro Shuttle Company is considering investing in two new vans that are expected to generate combined cash inflows of $28,000 per year. The vans' combined purchase price is $91,000. The expected life and salvage value of each are four years and $21,000, respectively. Metro Shuttle has an average cost of capital of 14 percent.

Required

a. Calculate the net present value of the investment opportunity.

b. Indicate whether the investment opportunity is expected to earn a return that is above or below the cost of capital and whether it should be accepted.

Exercise 10-6A   *Determining net present value*   LO 3

Dimitry Chernitsky is seeking part-time employment while he attends school. He is considering purchasing technical equipment that will enable him to start a small training services company that will offer tutorial services over the Internet. Dimitry expects demand for the service to grow rapidly in the first two years of operation as customers learn about the availability of the Internet assistance. Thereafter, he expects demand to stabilize. The following table presents the expected cash flows.

Year of Operation	Cash Inflow	Cash Outflow
2012	$13,500	$ 9,000
2013	19,500	12,000
2014	21,000	12,600
2015	21,000	12,600

In addition to these cash flows, Mr. Chernitsky expects to pay $21,000 for the equipment. He also expects to pay $3,600 for a major overhaul and updating of the equipment at the end of the second year of operation. The equipment is expected to have a $1,500 salvage value and a four-year useful life. Mr. Chernitsky desires to earn a rate of return of 8 percent.

Required

(Round computations to the nearest whole penny.)

a. Calculate the net present value of the investment opportunity.

b. Indicate whether the investment opportunity is expected to earn a return that is above or below the desired rate of return and whether it should be accepted.

Exercise 10-7A   *Using the present value index*   LO 3, 6

Alonso Company has a choice of two investment alternatives. The present value of cash inflows and outflows for the first alternative is $90,000 and $84,000, respectively. The present value of cash inflows and outflows for the second alternative is $220,000 and $213,000, respectively.

Required

a. Calculate the net present value of each investment opportunity.

b. Calculate the present value index for each investment opportunity.

c. Indicate which investment will produce the higher rate of return.

Exercise 10-8A   *Determining the internal rate of return*   LO 4

Irving Manufacturing Company has an opportunity to purchase some technologically advanced equipment that will reduce the company's cash outflow for operating expenses by $1,280,000 per year. The cost of the equipment is $6,186,530.56. Irving expects it to have a 10-year useful life and a zero salvage value. The company has established an investment opportunity hurdle rate of 15 percent and uses the straight-line method for depreciation.

Required

a. Calculate the internal rate of return of the investment opportunity.

b. Indicate whether the investment opportunity should be accepted.

Exercise 10-9A   *Using the internal rate of return to compare investment   LO 4, 6
opportunities*

Hulsey and Wright (H&W) is a partnership that owns a small company. It is considering two alternative investment opportunities. The first investment opportunity will have a five-year useful life, will cost $9,335.16, and will generate expected cash inflows of $2,400 per year. The second investment is expected to have a useful life of three years, will cost $6,217.13, and will generate expected cash inflows of $2,500 per year. Assume that H&W has the funds available to accept only one of the opportunities.

Required

a. Calculate the internal rate of return of each investment opportunity.

b. Based on the internal rates of return, which opportunity should H&W select?

c. Discuss other factors that H&W should consider in the investment decision.

LO 1, 2, 5, 6

Exercise 10-10A *Determining the cash flow annuity with income tax considerations*

To open a new store, Alpha Tire Company plans to invest $240,000 in equipment expected to have a four-year useful life and no salvage value. Alpha expects the new store to generate annual cash revenues of $315,000 and to incur annual cash operating expenses of $195,000. Alpha's average income tax rate is 30 percent. The company uses straight-line depreciation.

Required

Determine the expected annual net cash inflow from operations for each of the first four years after Alpha opens the new store.

LO 9

Exercise 10-11A *Evaluating discounted cash flow techniques*

Rita Hendrix is angry with Bill Shaw. He is behind schedule developing supporting material for tomorrow's capital budget committee meeting. When she approached him about his apparent lacka-daisical attitude in general and his tardiness in particular, he responded, "I don't see why we do this stuff in the first place. It's all a bunch of estimates. Who knows what future cash flows will really be? I certainly don't. I've been doing this job for five years, and no one has ever checked to see if I even came close at these guesses. I've been waiting for marketing to provide the estimated cash inflows on the projects being considered tomorrow. But, if you want my report now, I'll have it in a couple of hours. I can make up the marketing data as well as they can."

Required

Does Mr. Shaw have a point? Is there something wrong with the company's capital budgeting system? Write a brief response explaining how to improve the investment evaluation system.

LO 7

Exercise 10-12A *Determining the payback period*

Sky Airline Company is considering expanding its territory. The company has the opportunity to purchase one of two different used airplanes. The first airplane is expected to cost $18,000,000; it will enable the company to increase its annual cash inflow by $6,000,000 per year. The plane is expected to have a useful life of five years and no salvage value. The second plane costs $36,000,000; it will enable the company to increase annual cash flow by $9,000,000 per year. This plane has an eight-year useful life and a zero salvage value.

Required

a. Determine the payback period for each investment alternative and identify the alternative Sky should accept if the decision is based on the payback approach.

b. Discuss the shortcomings of using the payback method to evaluate investment opportunities.

LO 5, 7

Exercise 10-13A *Determining the payback period with uneven cash flows*

Melton Company has an opportunity to purchase a forklift to use in its heavy equipment rental business. The forklift would be leased on an annual basis during its first two years of operation. Thereafter, it would be leased to the general public on demand. Melton would sell it at the end of the fifth year of its useful life. The expected cash inflows and outflows follow.

Year	Nature of Item	Cash Inflow	Cash Outflow
2012	Purchase price		$72,000
2012	Revenue	$30,000	
2013	Revenue	30,000	
2014	Revenue	21,000	
2014	Major overhaul		9,000
2015	Revenue	18,000	
2016	Revenue	14,400	
2016	Salvage value	9,600	

Required

a. Determine the payback period using the accumulated cash flows approach.

b. Determine the payback period using the average cash flows approach.

Exercise 10-14A   *Determining the unadjusted rate of return*

LO 8

Lilly Painting Company is considering whether to purchase a new spray paint machine that costs $4,000. The machine is expected to save labor, increasing net income by $600 per year. The effective life of the machine is 15 years according to the manufacturer's estimate.

Required

a. Determine the unadjusted rate of return based on the average cost of the investment.

b. What is the predominant shortcoming of using the unadjusted rate of return to evaluate investment opportunities?

Exercise 10-15A   *Computing the payback period and unadjusted rate of return for the same investment opportunity*

LO 7, 8

Foy Rentals can purchase a van that costs $60,000; it has an expected useful life of three years and no salvage value. Foy uses straight-line depreciation. Expected revenue is $30,000 per year. Assume that depreciation is the only expense associated with this investment.

Required

a. Determine the payback period.

b. Determine the unadjusted rate of return based on the average cost of the investment.

PROBLEMS—SERIES A

**All Problems in Series A are available with McGraw-Hill's
*Connect Accounting.***

Problem 10-16A   *Using present value techniques to evaluate alternative investment opportunities*

LO 3, 5, 6

Fast Delivery is a small company that transports business packages between New York and Chicago. It operates a fleet of small vans that moves packages to and from a central depot within each city and uses a common carrier to deliver the packages between the depots in the two cities. Fast Delivery recently acquired approximately $6 million of cash capital from its owners, and its president, Don Keenon, is trying to identify the most profitable way to invest these funds.

Clarence Roy, the company's operations manager, believes that the money should be used to expand the fleet of city vans at a cost of $720,000. He argues that more vans would enable the company to expand its services into new markets, thereby increasing the revenue base. More specifically, he expects cash inflows to increase by $280,000 per year. The additional vans are expected to have an average useful life of four years and a combined salvage value of $100,000. Operating the vans will require additional working capital of $40,000, which will be recovered at the end of the fourth year.

In contrast, Patricia Lipa, the company's chief accountant, believes that the funds should be used to purchase large trucks to deliver the packages between the depots in the two cities. The conversion process would produce continuing improvement in operating savings with reductions in cash outflows as the following:

Year 1	Year 2	Year 3	Year 4
$160,000	$320,000	$400,000	$440,000

The large trucks are expected to cost $800,000 and to have a four-year useful life and a $80,000 salvage value. In addition to the purchase price of the trucks, up-front training costs are expected to amount to $16,000. Fast Delivery's management has established a 16 percent desired rate of return.

Required

a. Determine the net present value of the two investment alternatives.

b. Calculate the present value index for each alternative.

c. Indicate which investment alternative you would recommend. Explain your choice.

Problem 10-17A *Using the payback period and unadjusted rate of return to evaluate alternative investment opportunities*

Louis Gallo owns a small retail ice cream parlor. He is considering expanding the business and has identified two attractive alternatives. One involves purchasing a machine that would enable Mr. Gallo to offer frozen yogurt to customers. The machine would cost $8,100 and has an expected useful life of three years with no salvage value. Additional annual cash revenues and cash operating expenses associated with selling yogurt are expected to be $5,940 and $900, respectively.

Alternatively, Mr. Gallo could purchase for $10,080 the equipment necessary to serve cappuccino. That equipment has an expected useful life of four years and no salvage value. Additional annual cash revenues and cash operating expenses associated with selling cappuccino are expected to be $8,280 and $2,430, respectively.

Income before taxes earned by the ice cream parlor is taxed at an effective rate of 20 percent.

Required

a. Determine the payback period and unadjusted rate of return (use average investment) for each alternative.

b. Indicate which investment alternative you would recommend. Explain your choice.

Problem 10-18A *Using net present value and internal rate of return to evaluate investment opportunities*

Veronica Tanner, the president of Tanner Enterprises, is considering two investment opportunities. Because of limited resources, she will be able to invest in only one of them. Project A is to purchase a machine that will enable factory automation; the machine is expected to have a useful life of four years and no salvage value. Project B supports a training program that will improve the skills of employees operating the current equipment. Initial cash expenditures for Project A are $100,000 and for Project B are $40,000. The annual expected cash inflows are $31,487 for Project A and $13,169 for Project B. Both investments are expected to provide cash flow benefits for the next four years. Tanner Enterprise's cost of capital is 8 percent.

Required

a. Compute the net present value of each project. Which project should be adopted based on the net present value approach?

b. Compute the approximate internal rate of return of each project. Which one should be adopted based on the internal rate of return approach?

c. Compare the net present value approach with the internal rate of return approach. Which method is better in the given circumstances? Why?

Problem 10-19A *Using net present value and payback period to evaluate investment opportunities*

Bruce Graham saved $250,000 during the 25 years that he worked for a major corporation. Now he has retired at the age of 50 and has begun to draw a comfortable pension check every month. He wants to ensure the financial security of his retirement by investing his savings wisely and is currently considering two investment opportunities. Both investments require an initial payment of $187,500. The following table presents the estimated cash inflows for the two alternatives.

	Year 1	Year 2	Year 3	Year 4
Opportunity #1	$ 55,625	$ 58,750	$78,750	$101,250
Opportunity #2	102,500	108,750	17,500	15,000

Mr. Graham decides to use his past average return on mutual fund investments as the discount rate; it is 8 percent.

Required

a. Compute the net present value of each opportunity. Which should Mr. Graham adopt based on the net present value approach?

b. Compute the payback period for each project. Which should Mr. Graham adopt based on the payback approach?

c. Compare the net present value approach with the payback approach. Which method is better in the given circumstances?

Problem 10-20A *Effects of straight-line versus accelerated depreciation on an investment decision*

Zito Electronics is considering investing in manufacturing equipment expected to cost $184,000. The equipment has an estimated useful life of four years and a salvage value of $24,000. It is expected to produce incremental cash revenues of $96,000 per year. Zito has an effective income tax rate of 30 percent and a desired rate of return of 12 percent.

Required

a. Determine the net present value and the present value index of the investment, assuming that Zito uses straight-line depreciation for financial and income tax reporting.

b. Determine the net present value and the present value index of the investment, assuming that Zito uses double-declining-balance depreciation for financial and income tax reporting.

c. Why do the net present values computed in Requirements *a* and *b* differ?

d. Determine the payback period and unadjusted rate of return (use average investment), assuming that Zito uses straight-line depreciation.

e. Determine the payback period and unadjusted rate of return (use average investment), assuming that Zito uses double-declining-balance depreciation. (*Note:* Use average annual cash flow when computing the payback period and average annual income when determining the unadjusted rate of return.)

f. Why are there no differences in the payback periods or unadjusted rates of return computed in Requirements *d* and *e*?

Problem 10-21A *Applying the net present value approach with and without tax considerations*

Paxton Kingsley, the chief executive officer of Kingsley Corporation, has assembled his top advisers to evaluate an investment opportunity. The advisers expect the company to pay $150,000 cash at the beginning of the investment and the cash inflow for each of the following four years to be the following.

Year 1	Year 2	Year 3	Year 4
$84,000	$96,000	$120,000	$184,000

Mr. Kingsley agrees with his advisers that the company should use the discount rate (required rate of return) of 12 percent to compute net present value to evaluate the viability of the proposed project.

Required

a. Compute the net present value of the proposed project. Should Mr. Kingsley approve the project?

b. Wilma Pate, one of the advisers, is wary of the cash flow forecast and she points out that the advisers failed to consider that the depreciation on equipment used in this project will be tax deductible. The depreciation is expected to be $80,000 per year for the four-year period. The company's income tax rate is 30 percent per year. Use this information to revise the company's expected cash flow from this project.

c. Compute the net present value of the project based on the revised cash flow forecast. Should Mr. Kingsley approve the project?

LO 4, 8

Problem 10-22A *Comparing internal rate of return with unadjusted rate of return*

Walker Auto Repair, Inc., is evaluating a project to purchase equipment that will not only expand the company's capacity but also improve the quality of its repair services. The board of directors requires all capital investments to meet or exceed the minimum requirement of a 10 percent rate of return. However, the board has not clearly defined the rate of return. The president and controller are pondering two different rates of return: unadjusted rate of return and internal rate of return. The equipment, which costs $100,000, has a life expectancy of five years. The increased net profit per year will be approximately $7,000, and the increased cash inflow per year will be approximately $27,700.

Required

a. If it uses the unadjusted rate of return (use average investment) to evaluate this project, should the company invest in the equipment?

b. If it uses the internal rate of return to evaluate this project, should the company invest in the equipment?

c. Which method is better for this capital investment decision?

LO 9

Problem 10-23A *Postaudit evaluation*

Ernest Jones is reviewing his company's investment in a cement plant. The company paid $15,000,000 five years ago to acquire the plant. Now top management is considering an opportunity to sell it. The president wants to know whether the plant has met original expectations before he decides its fate. The company's discount rate for present value computations is 8 percent. Expected and actual cash flows follow.

	Year 1	Year 2	Year 3	Year 4	Year 5
Expected	$3,300,000	$4,920,000	$4,560,000	$4,980,000	$4,200,000
Actual	2,700,000	3,060,000	4,920,000	3,900,000	3,600,000

Required

a. Compute the net present value of the expected cash flows as of the beginning of the investment.

b. Compute the net present value of the actual cash flows as of the beginning of the investment.

c. What do you conclude from this postaudit?

EXERCISES—SERIES B

LO 1, 5

Exercise 10-1B *Identifying cash inflows and outflows*

Required

Barry Nance is considering whether to invest in a dump truck. Mr. Nance would hire a driver and use the truck to haul trash for customers. He wants to use present value techniques to evaluate the investment opportunity. List sources of potential cash inflows and cash outflows Mr. Nance could expect if he invests in the truck.

LO 1, 2

Exercise 10-2B *Determining the present value of a lump-sum future cash receipt*

One year from today Bernice Smyth is scheduled to receive a $60,000 payment from a trust fund her father established. She wants to buy a car today but does not have the money. A friend has agreed to give Bernice the present value of the $60,000 today if she agrees to give him the full $60,000 when she collects it one year from now. They agree that 8 percent reflects a fair discount rate.

Required

a. You have been asked to determine the present value of the future cash flow. Use a present value table to determine the amount of cash that Bernice's friend should give her.

b. Use an algebraic formula to verify the result you determined in Requirement *a*.

Exercise 10-3B *Determining the present value of a lump-sum future cash receipt*   LO 1, 2

Cornelius Toran has a terminal illness. His doctors have estimated his remaining life expectancy as three years. Cornelius has a $1,000,000 life insurance policy but no close relative to list as the beneficiary. He is considering canceling the policy because he needs the money he is currently paying for the premiums to buy medical supplies. A wealthy close friend has advised Cornelius not to cancel the policy. The friend has proposed instead giving Cornelius $500,000 to use for his medical needs while keeping the policy in force. In exchange, Cornelius would designate the friend as the policy beneficiary. Cornelius is reluctant to take the $500,000 because he believes that his friend is offering charity. His friend has tried to convince Cornelius that the offer is a legitimate business deal.

Required

a. Determine the present value of the $1,000,000 life insurance benefit. Assume a 10 percent discount rate.
b. Assuming 10 percent represents a fair rate of return, is Cornelius' friend offering charity or is he seeking to profit financially from Cornelius' misfortune?

Exercise 10-4B *Determining the present value of an annuity*   LO 1, 2

Julia Rainy is considering whether to install a drink machine at the gas station she owns. Julia is convinced that providing a drink machine at the station would increase customer convenience. However, she is not convinced that buying the machine would be a profitable investment. Friends who have installed drink machines at their stations have estimated that she could expect to receive net cash inflows of approximately $4,000 per year from the machine. Julia believes that she should earn 10 percent on her investments. The drink machine is expected to have a two-year life and zero salvage value.

Required

a. Use Present Value Table 1 to determine the maximum amount of cash Julia should be willing to pay for a drink machine.
b. Use Present Value Table 2 to determine the maximum amount of cash Julia should be willing to pay for a drink machine.
c. Explain the consistency or lack of consistency in the answers to Requirement *a* versus Requirement *b*.

Exercise 10-5B *Determining the net present value*   LO 3

Rafael Ortega, manager of the Pena Music Hall, is considering the opportunity to expand the company's concession revenues. Specifically, she is considering whether to install a popcorn machine. Based on market research, she believes that the machine could produce incremental cash inflows of $2,400 per year. The purchase price of the machine is $7,500. It is expected to have a useful life of three years and a $1,500 salvage value. Ms. Ortega has established a desired rate of return of 16 percent.

Required

a. Calculate the net present value of the investment opportunity.
b. Should the company buy the popcorn machine?

Exercise 10-6B *Determining the net present value*   LO 3

Howard Parmer has decided to start a small delivery business to help support himself while attending school. Mr. Parmer expects demand for delivery services to grow steadily as customers discover their availability. Annual cash outflows are expected to increase only slightly because many of the business operating costs are fixed. Cash inflows and outflows expected from operating the delivery business follow:

Year of Operation	Cash Inflow	Cash Outflow
2012	$6,800	$3,200
2013	7,600	3,600
2014	8,400	3,840
2015	9,200	4,000

The used delivery van Mr. Parmer plans to buy is expected to cost $13,200. It has an expected useful life of four years and a salvage value of $2,400. At the end of 2013, Mr. Parmer expects to pay additional costs of approximately $540 for maintenance and new tires. Mr. Parmer's desired rate of return is 12 percent.

Required

(Round computations to the nearest whole penny.)

a. Calculate the net present value of the investment opportunity.

b. Indicate whether the investment opportunity is expected to earn a return above or below the desired rate of return. Should Mr. Parmer start the delivery business?

LO 3

Exercise 10-7B *Using the present value index*

Two alternative investment opportunities are available to Claude Reyna, president of Reyna Enterprises. For the first alternative, the present value of cash inflows is $133,000, and the present value of cash outflows is $127,000. For the second alternative, the present value of cash inflows is $230,000, and the present value of cash outflows is $223,000.

Required

a. Calculate the net present value of each investment opportunity.

b. Calculate the present value index for each investment opportunity.

c. Indicate which investment will produce the higher rate of return.

LO 4

Exercise 10-8B *Determining the internal rate of return*

Sam Eatmon, CFO of Chaiston Enterprises, is evaluating an opportunity to invest in additional manufacturing equipment that will enable the company to increase its net cash inflows by $150,000 per year. The equipment costs $448,591.80. It is expected to have a five-year useful life and a zero salvage value. Chaiston's cost of capital is 18 percent.

Required

a. Calculate the internal rate of return of the investment opportunity.

b. Indicate whether Chaiston should purchase the equipment.

LO 4, 6

Exercise 10-9B *Using the internal rate of return to compare investment opportunities*

Yvonne Tower has two alternative investment opportunities to evaluate. The first opportunity would cost $149,512.23 and generate expected cash inflows of $21,000 per year for 17 years. The second opportunity would cost $136,909.44 and generate expected cash inflows of $18,000 per year for 15 years. Ms. Tower has sufficient funds available to accept only one opportunity.

Required

a. Calculate the internal rate of return of each investment opportunity.

b. Based on the internal rate of return criteria, which opportunity should Ms. Tower select?

c. Identify two other evaluation techniques Ms. Tower could use to compare the investment opportunities.

LO 1, 2, 5

Exercise 10-10B *Determining a cash flow annuity with income tax considerations*

Jay Welch is considering whether to invest in a computer game machine that he would place in a hotel his brother owns. The machine would cost $14,000 and has an expected useful life of three years and a salvage value of $2,000. Mr. Welch estimates the machine would generate revenue of $7,000 per year and cost $1,200 per year to operate. He uses the straight-line method for depreciation. His income tax rate is 30 percent.

Required

What amount of net cash inflow from operations would Mr. Welch expect for the first year if he invests in the machine?

Exercise 10-11B   *Evaluating discounted cash flow techniques*   LO 9

Four years ago Jeanne Nolen decided to invest in a project. At that time she had projected annual net cash inflows would be $54,000. Over its expected four-year useful life, the project had produced significantly higher cash inflows than anticipated. The actual average annual cash inflow from the project was $63,000. Nolen breathed a sigh of relief. She always worried that projects would not live up to expectations. To avoid this potential disappointment she tried always to underestimate the projected cash inflows of potential investments. She commented, "I prefer pleasant rather than unpleasant surprises." Indeed, no investment approved by Ms. Nolen had ever failed a postaudit review. Her investments consistently exceeded expectations.

Required

Explain the purpose of a postaudit and comment on Ms. Nolen's investment record.

Exercise 10-12B   *Determining the payback period*   LO 7

The management team at Rawden Manufacturing Company has decided to modernize the manufacturing facility. The company can replace an existing, outdated machine with one of two technologically advanced machines. One replacement machine would cost $50,000. Management estimates that it would reduce cash outflows for manufacturing expenses by $20,000 per year. This machine is expected to have an eight-year useful life and a $1,250 salvage value. The other replacement machine would cost $63,000 and would reduce annual cash outflows by an estimated $22,500. This machine has an expected 10-year useful life and an $6,250 salvage value.

Required

a. Determine the payback period for each investment alternative and identify which replacement machine Rawden should buy if it bases the decision on the payback approach.
b. Discuss the shortcomings of the payback method of evaluating investment opportunities.

Exercise 10-13B   *Determining the payback period with uneven cash flows*   LO 5, 7

Cascade Snowmobile Company is considering whether to invest in a particular new snowmobile model. The model is top-of-the-line equipment for which Cascade expects high demand during the first year it is available for rent. However, as the snowmobile ages, it will become less desirable and its rental revenues are expected to decline. The expected cash inflows and outflows follow.

Year	Nature of Cash Flow	Cash Inflow	Cash Outflow
2013	Purchase price	—	$35,000
2013	Revenue	$20,000	—
2014	Revenue	15,000	—
2015	Revenue	13,750	—
2016	Major overhaul	—	5,000
2017	Revenue	7,500	—
2018	Revenue	5,000	—
2019	Salvage value	4,000	—

Required

a. Determine the payback period using the accumulated cash flows approach.
b. Determine the payback period using the average cash flows approach.

Exercise 10-14B   *Determining the unadjusted rate of return*   LO 8

Intercity Shuttle Service, Inc., is considering whether to purchase an additional shuttle van. The van would cost $36,000 and have a zero salvage value. It would enable the company to increase net income by $6,030 per year. The manufacturer estimates the van's effective life as five years.

Required

a. Determine the unadjusted rate of return based on the average cost of the investment.
b. What is the shortcoming of using the unadjusted rate of return to evaluate investment opportunities?

LO 7, 8

Exercise 10-15B   *Computing the payback period and unadjusted rate of return for the same investment opportunity*

Gunter Marina (Guntersville) rents pontoon boats to customers. It has the opportunity to purchase an additional pontoon boat for $30,000; it has an expected useful life of four years and no salvage value. Guntersville uses straight-line depreciation. Expected rental revenue for the boat is $10,000 per year.

Required

a. Determine the payback period.

b. Determine the unadjusted rate of return based on the average cost of the investment.

c. Assume that the company's desired rate of return is 30 percent. Should Guntersville purchase the additional boat?

PROBLEMS—SERIES B

LO 3, 5, 6

Problem 10-16B   *Using present value techniques to evaluate alternative investment opportunities*

Porter Automobile Repair, Inc., currently has three repair shops in Boston. Vincent Porter, the president and chief executive officer, is facing a pleasant dilemma: the business has continued to grow rapidly and major shareholders are arguing about different ways to capture more business opportunities. The company requires a 12 percent rate of return for its investment projects and uses the straight-line method of depreciation for all fixed assets.

One group of shareholders wants to open another shop in a newly developed suburban community. This project would require an initial investment of $480,000 to acquire all the necessary equipment, which has a useful life of five years with a salvage value of $160,000. Once the shop begins to operate, another $120,000 of working capital would be required; it would be recovered at the end of the fifth year. The expected net cash inflow from the new shop follows.

Year 1	Year 2	Year 3	Year 4	Year 5
$48,000	$96,000	$152,000	$192,000	$240,000

A second group of shareholders prefers to invest $400,000 to acquire new computerized diagnostic equipment for the existing shops. The equipment is expected to have a useful life of five years with a salvage value of $80,000. Using this state-of-the-art equipment, mechanics would be able to pinpoint automobile problems more quickly and accurately. Consequently, it would allow the existing shops to increase their service capacity and revenue by $120,000 per year. The company would need to train mechanics to use the equipment, which would cost $40,000 at the beginning of the first year.

Required

a. Determine the net present value of the two investment alternatives.

b. Calculate the present value index for each alternative.

c. Indicate which investment alternative you would recommend. Explain your choice.

LO 7, 8

Problem 10-17B   *Using the payback period and unadjusted rate of return to evaluate alternative investment opportunities*

Jessica and Victor Services is planning a new business venture. With $100,000 of available funds to invest, it is investigating two options. One is to acquire an exclusive contract to operate vending machines in civic and recreation centers in a small suburban city for four years. The contract requires the firm to pay the city $40,000 cash at the beginning. The firm expects the cash revenue from the operation to be $50,000 per year and the cash expenses to be $28,000 per year.

The second option is to operate a printing shop in an office complex. This option would require the company to spend $72,000 for printing equipment that has a useful life of four years with a zero salvage value. The cash revenue is expected to be $85,000 per year and cash expenses are expected to be $47,000 per year. The firm uses the straight-line method of depreciation. Its effective income tax rate is expected to be 20 percent.

Required

a. Determine the payback period and unadjusted rate of return (use average investment) for each alternative.

b. Indicate which investment alternative you would recommend. Explain your choice.

Problem 10-18B *Using net present value and internal rate of return to evaluate investment opportunities*   LO 3, 4, 5, 6

Kerry Wood's rich uncle gave him $60,000 cash as a gift for his 40th birthday. Unlike his spoiled cousins who spend money carelessly, Mr. Wood wants to invest the money for his future retirement. After an extensive search, he is considering one of two investment opportunities. Project 1 would require an immediate cash payment of $52,800; Project 2 needs only a $24,000 cash payment at the beginning. The expected cash inflows are $17,280 per year for Project 1 and $8,400 per year for Project 2. Both projects are expected to provide cash flow benefits for the next four years. Mr. Wood found that the interest rate for a four-year certificate of deposit is about 7 percent. He decided that this is his required rate of return.

Required

a. Compute the net present value of each project. Which project should Mr. Wood adopt based on the net present value approach?

b. Compute the approximate internal rate of return of each project. Which project should Mr. Wood adopt based on the internal rate of return approach?

c. Compare the net present value approach with the internal rate of return approach. Which method is better in the given circumstances?

Problem 10-19B *Using net present value and payback period to evaluate investment opportunities*   LO 3, 6, 7

Margaret Hubbard just won a lottery and received a cash award of $800,000 net of tax. She is 61 years old and would like to retire in four years. Weighing this important fact, she has found two possible investments, both of which require an immediate cash payment of $640,000. The expected cash inflows from the two investment opportunities are as follows.

	Year 1	Year 2	Year 3	Year 4
Opportunity A	$364,800	$208,000	$118,400	$134,400
Opportunity B	91,200	107,200	236,800	540,800

Ms. Hubbard decided that her required rate of return should be 10 percent.

Required

a. Compute the net present value of each opportunity. Which should Ms. Hubbard choose based on the net present value approach?

b. Compute the payback period for each opportunity. Which should Ms. Hubbard choose based on the payback approach?

c. Compare the net present value approach with the payback approach. Which method is better in the given circumstances?

Problem 10-20B *Effects of straight-line versus accelerated depreciation on an investment decision*   LO 3, 6, 7, 8

Pacific Steel Company decided to spend $160,000 to purchase new state-of-the-art equipment for its manufacturing plant. The equipment has a five-year useful life and a salvage value of $40,000. It is expected to generate additional cash revenue of $64,000 per year. Pacific Steel required rate of return is 10 percent; its effective income tax rate is 25 percent.

Required

a. Determine the net present value and the present value index of the investment, assuming that Pacific Steel uses straight-line depreciation for financial and income tax reporting.

b. Determine the net present value and the present value index of the investment, assuming that Pacific Steel uses double-declining-balance depreciation for financial and income tax reporting.

c. Why are there differences in the net present values computed in Requirements *a* and *b*?

d. Determine the payback period and unadjusted rate of return (use average investment), assuming that Pacific Steel uses straight-line depreciation.

e. Determine the payback period and unadjusted rate of return (use average investment), assuming that Pacific Steel uses double-declining-balance depreciation. (*Note:* Use average annual cash flow when computing the payback period and average annual income when computing the unadjusted rate of return.)

f. Why are there no differences in the payback period or unadjusted rate of return computed in Requirements *d* and *e*?

LO 3, 5, 6

Problem 10-21B   *Applying the net present value approach with and without tax considerations*

Luther Currie, the president of Luther's Moving Services, Inc., is planning to spend $625,000 for new trucks. He expects the trucks to increase the company's cash inflow as follows.

Year 1	Year 2	Year 3	Year 4
$163,500	$178,215	$194,255	$211,735

The company's policy stipulates that all investments must earn a minimum rate of return of 10 percent.

Required

a. Compute the net present value of the proposed purchase. Should Mr. Currie purchase the trucks?

b. Cheryl Percy, the controller, is wary of the cash flow forecast and points out that Mr. Currie failed to consider that the depreciation on trucks used in this project will be tax deductible. The depreciation is expected to be $150,000 per year for the four-year period. The company's income tax rate is 30 percent per year. Use this information to revise the company's expected cash flow from this purchase.

c. Compute the net present value of the purchase based on the revised cash flow forecast. Should Mr. Currie purchase the trucks?

LO 4, 8

Problem 10-22B   *Comparing internal rate of return with unadjusted rate of return*

Ledlow Corporation faces stiff market competition. Top management is considering the replacement of its current production facility. The board of directors requires all capital investments to meet or exceed a 9 percent rate of return. However, the board has not clearly defined the rate of return. The president and controller are pondering two different rates of return: unadjusted rate of return and internal rate of return. To purchase a new facility with a life expectancy of four years, the company must pay $90,000. The increased net profit per year resulting from improved conditions would be approximately $10,000; the increased cash inflow per year would be approximately $27,500.

Required

a. If it uses the unadjusted rate of return (use average investment) to evaluate this project, should the company invest in the new facility?

b. If it uses the internal rate of return to evaluate this project, should the company invest in the new facility?

c. Which method is better for this capital investment decision?

LO 9

Problem 10-23B   *Postaudit evaluation*

Max Baldwin is wondering whether he made the right decision four years ago. As the president of Baldwin Health Care Services, he acquired a hospital specializing in elder care with an initial cash investment of $2,800,000. Mr. Baldwin would like to know whether the hospital's financial performance has met the original investment objective. The company's discount rate (required rate of return) for present value computations is 14 percent. Expected and actual cash flows follow.

	Year 1	Year 2	Year 3	Year 4
Expected	$920,000	$960,000	$1,000,000	$1,200,000
Actual	800,000	760,000	1,280,000	1,400,000

Required

a. Compute the net present value of the expected cash flows as of the beginning of the investment.

b. Compute the net present value of the actual cash flows as of the beginning of the investment.

c. What do you conclude from this postaudit?

ANALYZE, THINK, COMMUNICATE

ATC 10-1   Business Application Case   *Home remodeling decision*

Karen and Steve Catrow want to replace the windows in the older house they purchased recently. The company they have talked to about doing the work claims that new windows will reduce the couple's heating and cooling costs by around 30 percent. The Catrows have heard from real estate agents that they will get back 70 percent of the cost of the new windows when they sell their house. The new windows will cost $30,000.

The heating and cooling costs for the Catrows' house average around $5,000 per year, and they expect to stay in this house for 10 years. To pay for the windows they would have to withdraw the money from a mutual fund that has earned an average annual return of 3 percent over the past few years.

Required

a. From a financial planning perspective alone, determine whether or not the Catrows should purchase the replacement windows. Show supporting computations.

b. (Requirement *b* can only be solved with Excel, or similar software, or with a financial calculator.) Karen and Steve are not sure their mutual fund will continue to earn 3 percent annually over the next 10 years; therefore, they want to know the minimum return their fund would need to earn to make the new windows financially acceptable. Compute the internal rate of return for the replacement windows.

c. Identify some of the nonfinancial factors the couple may wish to consider in addition to the financial aspects of the decision above.

ATC 10-2   Group Assignment   *Net present value*

Espada Real Estate Investment Company (EREIC) purchases new apartment complexes, establishes a stable group of residents, and then sells the complexes to apartment management companies. The average holding time is three years. EREIC is currently investigating two alternatives.

1. EREIC can purchase Harding Properties for $4,500,000. The complex is expected to produce net cash inflows of $360,000, $502,500, and $865,000 for the first, second, and third years of operation, respectively. The market value of the complex at the end of the third year is expected to be $5,175,000.

2. EREIC can purchase Summit Apartments for $3,450,000. The complex is expected to produce net cash inflows of $290,000, $435,000, and $600,000 for the first, second, and third years of operation, respectively. The market value of the complex at the end of the third year is expected to be $4,050,000.

EREIC has a desired rate of return of 12 percent.

Required

a. Divide the class into groups of four or five students per group and then divide the groups into two sections. Assign Task 1 to the first section and Task 2 to the second section.

Group Tasks

   (1) Calculate the net present value and the present value index for Harding Properties.

   (2) Calculate the net present value and the present value index for Summit Apartments.

b. Have a spokesperson from one group in the first section report the amounts calculated by the group. Make sure that all groups in the section have the same result. Repeat the process for the second section. Have the class as a whole select the investment opportunity that EREIC should accept given that the objective is to produce the higher rate of return.

c. Assume that EREIC has $4,500,000 to invest and that any funds not invested in real estate properties must be invested in a certificate of deposit earning a 5 percent return. Would this information alter the decision made in Requirement *b*?

d. This requirement is independent of Requirement *c*. Assume there is a 10 percent chance that the Harding project will be annexed by the city of Hoover, which has an outstanding school district. The annexation would likely increase net cash flows by $37,500 per year and would increase the market value at the end of year 3 by $300,000. Would this information change the decision reached in Requirement *b*?

ATC 10-3   Research Assignment   *Capital Expenditures at the Archer Daniels Midland Company*

Obtain Archer Daniels Midland Company's (ADM) Form 10-Ks for the fiscal year ending on June 30, 2006 and 2009. To obtain the Form 10-Ks you can use either the EDGAR system following the instructions in Appendix A, or it can be found under the "Investor Relations" link on the company's website at www.admworld.com/naen. Read the "General Development of Business" under the "Item I. Business" section of the 2006 10-K, and the Statement of Cash Flows and Note 15 of the 2009 10-K.

Required

a. What major plant expansions did ADM announce during 2006? How much does ADM estimate these expansions will cost?

b. How much did ADM spend on investing activities in its 2009 and 2008 fiscal years?

c. Where did ADM get the cash used to make these investments?

d. How much of ADM's investments in new property, plant, and equipment was related to its "corn processing" segment in 2009 and 2008?

ATC 10-4   Writing Assignment   *Limitations of capital investment techniques*

Webb Publishing Company is evaluating two investment opportunities. One is to purchase an Internet company with the capacity to open new marketing channels through which Webb can sell its books. This opportunity offers a high potential for growth but involves significant risk. Indeed, losses are projected for the first three years of operation. The second opportunity is to purchase a printing company that would enable Webb to better control costs by printing its own books. The potential savings are clearly predictable but would make a significant change in the company's long-term profitability.

Required

Write a response discussing the usefulness of capital investment techniques (net present value, internal rate of return, payback, and unadjusted rate of return) in making a choice between these two alternative investment opportunities. Your response should discuss the strengths and weaknesses of capital budgeting techniques in general. Furthermore, it should include a comparison between techniques based on the time value of money versus those that are not.

ATC 10-5   Ethical Dilemma   *Postaudit*

Gaines Company recently initiated a postaudit program. To motivate employees to take the program seriously, Gaines established a bonus program. Managers receive a bonus equal to 10 percent of the amount by which actual net present value exceeds the projected net present value. Victor Holt, manager of the North Western Division, had an investment proposal on his desk when the new system was implemented. The investment opportunity required a $250,000 initial cash outflow and was expected to return cash inflows of $90,000 per year for the next five years. Gaines' desired rate of return is 10 percent. Mr. Holt immediately reduced the estimated cash inflows to $70,000 per year and recommended accepting the project.

Required

a. Assume that actual cash inflows turn out to be $91,000 per year. Determine the amount of Mr. Holt's bonus if the original computation of net present value were based on $90,000 versus $70,000.

b. Is Mr. Holt's behavior in violation of any of the standards of ethical conduct in Exhibit 1.15 of Chapter 1?

c. Speculate about the long-term effect the bonus plan is likely to have on the company.

d. Recommend how to compensate managers in a way that discourages gamesmanship.

ATC 10-6   Spreadsheet Assignment   *Using Excel*

Kilby Company is considering the purchase of new automated manufacturing equipment that would cost $150,000. The equipment would save $42,500 in labor costs per year over its six-year life. At the end of the fourth year, the equipment would require an overhaul that would cost $25,000. The equipment would have a $7,500 salvage value at the end of its life. Kilby's cost of capital is 12 percent.

Required

a. Prepare a spreadsheet similar to the one following to calculate net present value, the present value index, and the internal rate of return.

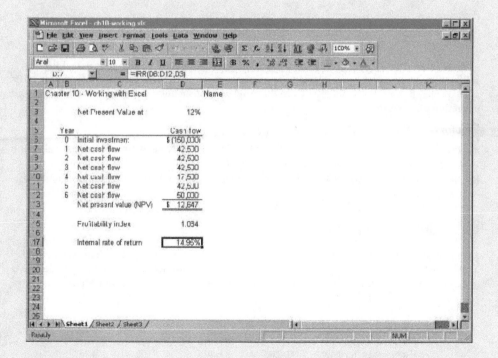

Spreadsheet Tips

Spreadsheets have built-in financial functions that make net present value and internal rate of return calculations very easy. The formats of these formulas are as follows.

1. *Net Present Value:* =NPV(rate,value1,value2,value3 . . . value29) where up to 29 values are allowed. The values must be at the end of the period, and each period must be equal in time (one year, for example). The formula is =NPV(D3,D7,D8,D9,D10,D11,D12) + D6.

2. *Internal Rate of Return:* =IRR (values,guess) where *values* is the range that includes the cash flows (D6 to D12) and *guess* is an estimate of the rate. Use the cost of capital as the guess.

3. *Percentage:* Rather than entering 12% in the formulas, refer to cell D3. This will allow you to change the rate and see the effect on the NPV and present value index.

4. *Present Value Index:* You must construct a formula because no built-in function calculates it.

ATC 10-7   Spreadsheet Assignment   *Mastering Excel*

ASAP Delivery is a small company that transports business packages between San Francisco and Los Angeles. It operates a fleet of small vans that moves packages to and from a central depot within each city and uses a common carrier to deliver the packages between the depots in the two cities. ASAP recently acquired approximately $4 million of cash capital from its owners, and its president, Alex Cade, is trying to identify the most profitable way to invest these funds.

Phil Duvall, the company's operations manager, believes that the money should be used to expand the fleet of city vans at a cost of $3,600,000. He argues that more vans would enable the company to expand its services into new markets, thereby increasing the revenue base. More specifically, he expects cash inflows to increase by $1,400,000 per year. The additional vans are expected to have an average useful life of four years and a combined salvage value of $500,000. Operating the vans will require additional working capital of $200,000, which will be recovered at the end of the fourth year.

In contrast, Amber Gomez, the company's chief accountant, believes that the funds should be used to purchase large trucks to deliver the packages between the depots in the two cities. The conversion process would produce continuing improvement in operating savings with reductions in cash outflows as the following:

Year 1	Year 2	Year 3	Year 4
$800,000	$1,600,000	$2,000,000	$2,200,000

The large trucks are expected to cost $4,000,000 and to have a four-year useful life and a $400,000 salvage value. In addition to the purchase price of the trucks, up-front training costs are expected to amount to $80,000. ASAP Delivery's management has established a 16 percent desired rate of return.

Required

a. Prepare a spreadsheet similar to the preceding one that calculates the net present value and the present value index for the two investments.

b. Include formulas in your spreadsheet to calculate the internal rate of return for each investment alternative.

COMPREHENSIVE PROBLEM

Magnificent Modems, Inc. (MMI), has several capital investment opportunities. The term, expected annual cash inflows, and the cost of each opportunity are outlined in the following table. MMI has established a desired rate of return of 16 percent for these investment opportunities.

Opportunity	A	B	C	D
Investment term	4 years	5 years	3 years	5 years
Expected cash inflow	$ 6,000	$ 5,000	$ 8,000	$ 4,800
Cost of investment	$16,000	$15,000	$18,000	$16,000

Required

a. Compute the net present value of each investment opportunity manually using the present value tables. Record your answers in the following table. The results for Investment Opportunity A have been recorded in the table as an example.

Opportunity	A	B	C	D
Cash inflow	$6,000.00	$5,000.00	$8,000.00	$4,800.00
Times present value factor	2.798181			
Present value of cash flows	$16,789.09			
Minus cost of investment	($16,000.00)	($15,000.00)	($18,000.00)	($16,000.00)
Net present value	$789.09			

b. Use Excel spreadsheet software or a financial calculator to determine the net present value and the internal rate of return for each investment opportunity. Record the results in the following table. The results for investment Opportunity A have been recorded in the following table as an example. Note that the manual computation yields the same net present value amounts as the financial function routines of Excel or a financial calculator.

Opportunity	A	B	C	D
Net present value	$789.09			
Internal rate of return	18.45%			

692

APPENDIX A

Accessing the EDGAR Database through the Internet

Successful business managers need many different skills, including communication, interpersonal, computer, and analytical. Most business students become very aware of the data analysis skills used in accounting, but they may not be as aware of the importance of "data-finding" skills. There are many sources of accounting and financial data. The more sources you are able to use, the better.

One very important source of accounting information is the EDGAR database. Others are probably available at your school through the library or business school network. Your accounting instructor will be able to identify these for you and make suggestions regarding their use. By making the effort to learn to use electronic databases, you will enhance your abilities as a future manager and your marketability as a business graduate.

These instructions assume that you know how to access and use an Internet browser. Follow the instructions to retrieve data from the Securities and Exchange Commission's EDGAR database. Be aware that the SEC may have changed its interface since this appendix was written. Accordingly, be prepared for slight differences between the following instructions and what appears on your computer screen. Take comfort in the fact that changes are normally designed to simplify user access. If you encounter a conflict between the following instructions and the instructions provided in the SEC interface, remember that the SEC interface is more current and should take precedence over the following instructions.

Most companies provide links to their SEC filings from their corporate website. These links are often simpler to use and provide more choices regarding file formats than SEC's EDGAR site. On company websites, links to their SEC filings are usually found under one of the following links: "Investor Relations," "Company Info," or "About Us."

1. Connect to the EDGAR database through the following address: **http://www.sec.gov/.**

2. After the SEC homepage appears, under the heading **Filings and Forms,** click on **Search for Company Filings.**

3. On the screen that appears, click on **Company or Fund Name. . . .**

4. On the screen that appears, enter the name of the company whose file you wish to retrieve and click on the **Find Companies** button.

5. The following screen will present a list of companies that have the same, or similar, names to the one you entered. Identify the company you want and click on the CIK number beside it.

6. Enter the SEC form number that you want to retrieve in the window titled **Filling Type** that appears in the upper left portion of the screen. For example, if you want Form 10-K, which will usually be the case, enter **10-K** and click on the **Search** button.

7. A list of the forms you requested will be presented, along with the date they were filed. Click on the **Document** button next to the file you wish to retrieve.

8. You will be presented with a list of documents from which to select; usually you will want to choose the file **form10k.htm.**

9. Once the 10-K has been retrieved, you can search it online or save it on your computer.

10. Often the 10-K will have a table of contents that can help locate the part of the report you need. The financial statements are seldom located at the beginning of the Form 10-K. They are usually in either Section 8 or Section 15.

GLOSSARY

absolute amounts   Dollar totals reported on financial statements; using them in financial analysis comparisons can be misleading because they do not reflect materiality levels of the underlying companies. *p. 589*

absorption (full) costing   Reporting method in which all product costs, including fixed manufacturing costs, are initially capitalized in inventory and then expensed when goods are sold. (Contrast with *variable costing*.) *p. 500*

accounts receivable turnover   Financial ratio that measures how quickly accounts receivable are converted to cash; computed by dividing net credit sales by average net accounts receivable. *p. 595*

accrual accounting   Accounting system that recognizes revenues when earned and expenses when incurred regardless of when the related cash is exchanged.

accumulated conversion factor   Factor used to convert a series of future cash flows into their present value equivalent when applied to cash flows of equal amounts spread over equal interval time periods; this factor can be computed by adding the individual single factors applicable to each period. *p. 47*

acid-test ratio   See *quick ratio*. *p. 595*

activities   Measures an organization undertakes to accomplish its mission. *p. 207*

activity base   Factor that causes changes in total variable cost; usually some measure of volume when used to explain cost behavior. *p. 65*

activity-based cost drivers   Measures of activities that cause costs to be incurred, such as number of setups, percentage of use, and pounds of material delivered; using such measures as allocation bases can improve the accuracy of cost allocations in business environments where overhead costs are not driven by volume. *p. 205*

activity-based costing (ABC)   A two-stage cost allocation process. First, costs associated with specific business activities are allocated or assigned to activity cost pools. Second, these pooled costs are allocated to designated cost objects by using a variety of appropriate cost drivers. The cost drivers chosen for each cost pool are those that most accurately reflect the demand placed on that cost pool by the cost object. *p. 207*

activity-based management (ABM)   Managing organization activities to add the greatest value by developing products that satisfy the needs of the organization's customers. *p. 23*

activity centers   Cost centers composed of operating activities with similar characteristics; pooling indirect costs into activity centers reduces record-keeping costs by allowing allocations based on a common cost driver for each center. *p. 207*

allocation   Process of dividing a total cost into parts and assigning the parts to the relevant cost objects. *p. 153*

allocation base   The factor used as the base for cost allocation; when possible, a driver of the allocated cost. *p. 155*

allocation rate   The mathematical factor used to allocate or assign costs to a cost object, determined by dividing the total cost to be allocated by the appropriate cost driver or allocation base. *p. 155*

annuity   Series of equal cash flows received or paid over equal time intervals at a constant rate of return. *p. 447*

applied fixed cost   Total cost determined by multiplying the predetermined overhead rate times the actual volume of production. *p. 356*

applied overhead   Amount of overhead costs assigned during the period to work in process using a predetermined overhead rate. *p. 491*

appraisal costs   Costs of identifying nonconforming products produced regardless of prevention cost expenditures. *p. 216*

asset turnover ratio   A measure of revenue dollars generated by the assets invested; calculated as net sales divided by average total assets. *p. 600*

average cost (per unit)   The total cost of making products divided by the total number of products made. *p. 26*

average days to collect receivables (average collection period)   Measure of how quickly, on average, a business collects its accounts receivable; calculated as 365 divided by the accounts receivable turnover. *p. 596*

average days to sell inventory (average days in inventory)   Measure of how quickly, on average, a business sells its inventory; calculated as 365 divided by the inventory turnover ratio. *p. 596*

avoidable costs   Potential future costs an organization can circumvent by choosing a particular course of action. To be avoidable, costs must differ among decision alternatives. For example, if materials cost for two different products is the same for each product, materials cost could not be avoided by choosing to produce one product instead of the other. The materials cost would therefore not be an avoidable cost. *p. 257*

balanced scorecard   A management evaluation tool that uses both financial and nonfinancial measures to assess how well an organization is meeting its objectives. *p. 412*

batch-level activities   Actions taken (e.g., materials handling, production setups) to produce groups of products, the cost of which is fixed regardless of the number of units produced in a batch. *p. 209*

batch-level costs   The costs associated with producing a batch of products, most accurately allocated using cost drivers that measure activity levels. For example, the cost of setting up a press to print 500 copies of an engraved invitation is a batch-level cost. Classifying costs as batch-level is context sensitive. The postage to mail a single product would be classified as a unit-level cost. In contrast, the postage to mail a large number of products in a single shipment would be classified as a batch-level cost. *p. 257*

benchmarking   Identifying best practices used by world-class competitors in a given industry. *p. 24*

694   Glossary

best practices   Identifiable procedures used by world-class companies. *p. 24*

book value per share   An accounting measure of a share of common stock, computed by dividing total stockholders' equity less preferred rights by the number of common shares outstanding. *p. 602*

bottleneck   A constraint that limits a company's capacity to produce or sell its products, such as a piece of equipment that cannot produce enough component parts to fully occupy employees in the assembly department. *p. 270*

break-even point   Sales volume at which total revenue equals total cost; can be expressed in units or sales dollars. *p. 108*

budgeting   Form of planning that formalizes a company's goals and objectives in financial terms. *p. 304*

budget slack   Difference between inflated and realistic standards. *p. 360*

by-products   Products that share common inputs with other joint products but have insignificant market values relative to the other joint products.

capital budget   Budget detailing the company's plans to invest in operational assets, new products, or lines of business for the coming year; influences many of the operating budgets and is a formal part of the master budget. *p. 308*

capital budgeting   Financial planning for the intermediate time range involving decisions such as whether to buy or lease equipment, purchase additional assets, or increase operating expenses to stimulate sales. *p. 306*

capital investments   Purchases of operational assets involving a long-term commitment of funds that can be critically important to the company's ultimate success; costs normally recovered through using the assets. *p. 444*

cash budget   A budget detailing expected future cash receipts and payments. *p. 313*

cash inflows   Cash receipts including cash generated from operating activities such as cash revenues or collections of accounts receivable; cash collected from investing activities such as selling investments; and cash collected from financing activities such as borrowing money or issuing stock. *p. 636*

cash outflows   Cash disbursements including cash paid for operating activities such as cash expenses or payments to settle accounts payable; cash paid for investing activities such as buying investments; and cash paid for financing activities such as repaying long-term debt or purchasing treasury stock. *p. 636*

certified suppliers   Suppliers who have demonstrated reliability by providing the buyer with quality goods and services at desirable prices, usually in accord with strict delivery specifications; frequently offer the buyer preferred customer status in exchange for guaranteed purchase quantities and prompt payment schedules. *p. 262*

common costs   Costs that are incurred to support more than one cost object but cannot be traced to any specific object. *p. 154*

companywide allocation rate   Factor based on a single measure of volume, such as direct labor-hours, used to allocate all overhead cost to the company's products or other cost objects. *p. 204*

constraints   Conditions that limit a business's ability to satisfy the demand for its products. *p. 270*

continuous improvement   An ongoing process through which employees learn to eliminate waste, reduce response time, minimize defects, and simplify the design and delivery of products and services to customers; a feature of total quality management (TQM). *p. 24*

contribution margin   The difference between sales revenue and variable cost; the amount available to pay for fixed cost and thereafter to provide a profit. *p. 61*

contribution margin per unit   The sales price per unit minus the variable cost per unit. *p. 109*

contribution margin ratio   The contribution margin per unit divided by the sales price per unit; can be used in cost-volume-profit analysis to calculate in dollars the break-even sales volume or the level of sales required to attain a desired profit. *p. 110*

controllable costs   Costs that can be influenced by a particular manager's decisions and actions. *p. 154*

controllability concept   Evaluating managerial performance based only on revenue and costs under the manager's direct control. *p. 404*

cost   Measure of resources used to acquire an asset or to produce revenue.

cost accumulation   Measuring the cost of a particular object by combining many individual costs into a single total cost. *p. 152*

cost allocation   Process of dividing a total cost into parts and assigning the parts to relevant objects. *pp. 12, 153*

cost averaging   Measuring the cost per unit of a product or service by dividing the total production cost by the total activity base to which the cost pertains; average cost is often more relevant to pricing, performance evaluation, and control than actual cost. *p. 66*

cost-based transfer price   Transfer price based on the historical or standard cost incurred by the supplying segment. *p. 416*

cost behavior   How a cost changes (increase, decrease, remain constant) relative to changes in some measure of activity (e.g., the behavior of raw materials cost is to increase as the number of units of product made increases). *p. 54*

cost center   A responsibility center that incurs costs but does not generate revenue. *p. 401*

cost driver   Any factor, usually a volume measure, that causes cost to be incurred; sometimes described as *activity base* or *allocation base*. Changes in cost drivers, such as labor-hours or machine-hours, cause corresponding changes in cost. *p. 152*

cost objects   Items for which managers need to measure cost; can be products, processes, departments, services, activities, and so on. *p. 150*

cost of capital   Return paid to investors and creditors for supplying assets (capital); usually represents a company's minimum rate of return. *p. 445*

cost per equivalent unit   Unit cost of product determined by dividing total production costs by the number of equivalent whole units; used to allocate product costs between processing departments (amount of ending inventory and amount of costs transferred to the subsequent department). *p. 550*

cost per unit of input   Cost of material, labor, or overhead for one unit; determined by multiplying the price paid for one unit of material, labor, or overhead input by the usage of that input for one unit of product or service.

cost-plus pricing   Strategy that sets the selling price at cost plus a markup equal to a percentage of the cost. *p. 112*

cost pool   A collection of costs organized around a common cost driver. The cost pool, as opposed to individual costs, is allocated to cost objects using the common cost driver, thereby promoting efficiency in the allocation process. *p. 165*

cost structure   The relative proportion of a company's variable and fixed costs to total cost. The percentage change in net income a company experiences for a given percentage change in sales volume is directly related to the company's cost structure. The greater a company's percentage of fixed to total costs, the more its net income will fluctuate with changes in sales. *p. 59*

cost tracing   Assigning specific costs to the objects that cause their incurrence. *p. 153*

cost-volume-profit (CVP) analysis   Management tool that reflects the interrelationships among sales prices, volume, fixed costs, and variable costs; used in determining the break-even point or the most profitable combination of these variables. *p. 107*

current ratio (working capital ratio)   Measure of liquidity; calculated by dividing current assets by current liabilities. *p. 594*

decentralization   Delegating authority and responsibility for business segment operation to lower-level managers. *p. 400*

deferral transactions   Accounting transactions in which cash payments or receipts occur before the related expense or revenue is recognized.

differential costs   Costs that differ among alternative business opportunities; usually relevant for decision making. Some differential costs, however, are not relevant. For example, although depreciation may differ between the alternatives, it is an unavoidable sunk cost and is therefore not relevant for decision making. *p. 259*

differential revenue   Revenues that are relevant to decision-making because they differ among alternative courses of action. *p. 256*

direct cost   Cost that is easily traceable to a cost object and for which it is economically feasible to do so. *p. 153*

direct labor   Wages paid to production workers whose efforts can be easily and conveniently traced to products. *p. 9*

direct method   (1) Allocation method that allocates service center costs directly to operating department cost pools; does not account for any relationships among service centers. (2) Method of reporting cash flows from operating activities on the statement of cash flows that shows individual categories of cash receipts from and cash payments for major activities (collections from customers, payments to suppliers, etc.). *pp. 171, 638*

direct raw materials   Costs of raw materials used to make products that can be easily and conveniently traced to those products. *p. 9*

dividend yield   Ratio for comparing stock dividends paid relative to the market price; calculated as dividends per share divided by market price per share. *p. 603*

downstream costs   Costs incurred after the manufacturing process is complete, such as delivery costs and sales commissions. *pp. 14, 214*

earnings per share   Measure of the value of a share of common stock based on company earnings; calculated as net income available to common stockholders divided by the average number of outstanding common shares. *p. 602*

economies of scale   Reducing the unit cost of production by increasing an operation's size. Increasing size usually increases the volume of activity, reducing the per unit fixed cost and resulting in a lower total production cost.

efficient market hypothesis   The proposition that creditors and investors evaluate the underlying substance of business events regardless of how those events are reported in financial reports.

equation method   Cost-volume-profit analysis technique that uses the algebraic relationship among sales, variable costs, fixed costs, and desired net income before taxes to solve for required sales volume. *p. 108*

equipment replacement decisions   Deciding whether to replace existing equipment with newer equipment based on comparing the avoidable costs of keeping the old or purchasing new equipment to determine which choice is more profitable. *p. 266*

equivalent whole units   A quantity of partially completed goods expressed as an equivalent number of fully completed goods. *p. 549*

expense transactions   Business events that decrease assets or increase liabilities in order to produce revenue in the course of operating a business.

external failure costs   Costs resulting from delivering defective goods to customers. *p. 216*

facility-level activities   Actions taken (e.g., insuring the facility, providing plant maintenance, employing a company president) that benefit the production process as a whole. *p. 211*

facility-level costs   Costs incurred to support the whole company or a segment thereof, not related to any specific product, batch, or unit of production or service and unavoidable unless the entire company or segment is eliminated; they are so indirect that any allocation of facility-level costs is necessarily arbitrary. *p. 211*

failure costs   Costs resulting from producing or providing nonconforming products or services. *p. 316*

favorable variance   Variance indicating that actual costs are less than standard costs or actual sales exceed budgeted sales. *p. 351*

financial accounting   Branch of accounting focused on the business information needs of external users (creditors, investors, governmental agencies, financial analysts, etc.); its objective is to classify and record business events and transactions to produce external financial reports (income statement, balance sheet, statement of cash flows, and statement of changes in equity). *p. 2*

Financial Accounting Standards Board (FASB)   Private, independent standard-setting body established by the accounting profession that has been delegated the authority by the SEC to establish most of the accounting rules and regulations for public financial reporting. *p. 5*

financing activities Cash inflows and outflows from transactions with investors and creditors (except interest), including cash receipts from issuing stock, borrowing activities, and cash disbursements to pay dividends. *p. 639*

finished goods Completed products resulting from the manufacturing process; measured by the accumulated cost of raw materials, labor, and overhead. *p. 6*

Finished Goods Inventory Asset account used to accumulate the product costs (direct materials, direct labor, and overhead) associated with completed products that have not yet been sold. *p. 486*

first-in, first-out (FIFO) method Means of computing equivalent units in a process cost system that accounts for the degree of completion of both beginning and ending inventories; more complex than the weighted average method, and used when greater accuracy is desired.

fixed cost Cost that remains constant in total regardless of changes in the volume of activity; per unit amount varies inversely with changes in the volume of activity. *p. 550*

fixed cost spending variance The difference between the *actual* fixed manufacturing overhead costs and the *budgeted* fixed manufacturing overhead costs. *p. 356*

fixed cost volume variance The difference between the *budgeted* fixed manufacturing overhead costs and the *applied* fixed manufacturing overhead costs. *p. 350*

flexible budgets Budgets that show expected revenues and costs at a variety of different activity levels. *p. 350*

flexible budget variances Differences between budgets based on standard amounts at the actual level of activity and actual results; caused by differences between standard unit cost and actual unit cost at the volume of activity achieved.

full costing See *absorption costing. p. 500*

generally accepted accounting principles (GAAP) Rules and practices that accountants agree to follow in financial reports prepared for public distribution. *p. 5*

high-low method Method of estimating the fixed and variable components of a mixed cost; the variable cost per unit is the difference between the total cost at the high- and low-volume points divided by the difference between the corresponding high and low volumes. The fixed cost component is determined by subtracting the variable cost from the total cost at either the high- or low-volume level. *p. 68*

horizontal analysis Financial analysis technique of comparing amounts of the same item over several time periods. *p. 589*

hybrid costing systems Cost systems that blend some features of a job-order costing system with some features of a process costing system. *p. 538*

ideal standard A measure of the highest level of efficiency attainable; assumes all input factors interact perfectly under ideal or optimum conditions. *p. 358*

incremental revenue Additional cash inflows from operating activities generated by using an additional capital asset. *p. 451*

indirect cost Cost that either cannot be easily traced to a cost object or for which it is not economically feasible to do so. See also *overhead. pp. 11, 153*

indirect method Method of reporting cash flows from operating activities on the statement of cash flows that starts with the net income from the income statement, followed by adjustments necessary to convert accrual-based net income to a cash-basis equivalent. *p. 638*

information overload Condition where so much information is presented that it confuses the user of the information. *p. 588*

interdepartmental service Service performed by one service department for the benefit of another service department. *p. 172*

internal failure costs Costs incurred to correct defects before goods reach the customer. *p. 216*

internal rate of return Rate at which the present value of an investment's future cash inflows equals the cash outflows required to acquire the investment; the rate that produces a net present value of zero. *p. 450*

inventory holding costs Costs associated with acquiring and retaining inventory including cost of storage space; lost, stolen, or damaged merchandise; insurance; personnel and management costs; and interest. *p. 14*

inventory turnover A measure of sales volume relative to inventory levels; calculated as the cost of goods sold divided by average inventory. *p. 598*

investing activities Cash inflows and outflows associated with buying or selling long-term assets and cash inflows and outflows associated with lending activities (loans to others— cash outflows; collecting loans to others—cash inflows). *p. 639*

investment center Type of responsibility center for which revenue, expense, and capital investments can be measured. *p. 401*

job cost sheet Record used in a job-order costing system to accumulate the materials, labor, and overhead costs of a job during production; at job completion, it summarizes all costs that were incurred to complete that job; also known as a *job-order cost sheet* or *job record. p. 538*

job-order costing system System in which costs are traced to products that are produced individually (e.g., custom-designed building) or in batches (e.g., an order for 100 wedding invitations); used to determine the costs of distinct, one-of-a-kind products. *p. 536*

joint costs Common costs incurred in the process of making two or more products. *p. 165*

joint products Separate products derived from common inputs. *p. 165*

just in time (JIT) Inventory management system that minimizes the amount of inventory on hand by avoiding inventory acquisition until products are demanded by customers, therefore eliminating the need to store inventory. The system reduces inventory holding costs including financing, warehouse storage, supervision, theft, damage, and obsolescence. It can also eliminate opportunity costs such as lost revenue due to the lack of availability of inventory. *p. 14*

labor efficiency variance Standard cost variance that indicates how the actual amount of direct labor used differs from the standard amount required.

labor price variance Standard cost variance that indicates how the actual pay rate for direct labor differs from the standard pay rate. *p. 365*

lax standards Easily attainable goals that can be reached with minimal effort. *p. 358*

least-squares regression A technique used to draw a line through a data set by minimizing the sum of the squared deviations between the line and the points in the data set. *p. 72*

liquidity ratios Measures of a company's capacity to pay short-term debt. *p. 593*

low-ball pricing Supplier practice of pricing a product below competitors' prices to attract customers and then raising the price once customers depend on the supplier for the product. *p. 262*

making the numbers Expression that indicates marketing managers attained the planned master budget sales volume. *p. 352*

management by exception The philosophy of focusing management attention and resources only on those operations where performance deviates significantly from expectations. *pp. 357, 403*

managerial accounting Branch of accounting focused on the information needs of managers and others working within the business. Its objective is to gather and report information that adds value to the business. Managerial accounting information is not regulated or reported to the public. *p. 2*

manufacturing overhead Production costs that cannot be easily or economically traced directly to products. *p. 11*

Manufacturing Overhead account Temporary account used during an accounting period to accumulate the actual overhead costs incurred and the amount of overhead applied to production. A debit balance in the account at the end of the period means overhead has been underapplied and a credit balance means overhead has been overapplied. The account is closed at year-end in an adjusting entry to the Work in Process and Finished Goods Inventory accounts and the Cost of Goods Sold account. If the balance is insignificant, it is closed only to Cost of Goods Sold. *p. 491*

margin Ratio that measures control of operating expenses relative to sales; computed as operating income divided by sales. Along with *turnover*, a component of return on investment. *p. 401*

margin of safety Difference between break-even sales and budgeted sales expressed in units, dollars, or as a percentage; the amount by which actual sales can fall below budgeted sales before incurring losses. *p. 119*

market-based transfer price Transfer price based on the external market price less any cost savings; it offers the closest approximation to an arm's-length price possible for intersegment transactions. *p. 413*

master budget The combination of the numerous separate but interdependent departmental budgets that detail a wide range of operating and financing plans including sales, production, manufacturing expenses, and administrative expenses. See also *static budget*. *p. 308*

material variance A variance sufficiently significant that its investigation could influence decision making. *p. 359*

materiality The point at which knowledge of information would influence a user's decision; can be measured in absolute, percentage, quantitative, or qualitative terms. *p. 589*

materials price variance Standard cost variance that indicates how the actual price paid for raw materials differs from the standard price for the materials. *p. 363*

materials quantity variance Standard cost variance that indicates the actual amount of raw materials used to make products differs from the standard amount required.

materials requisition form A form, either paper or electronic, used to request the materials needed for a specified job. The accounting department summarizes all materials requisitioned for a job on a job cost sheet. *p. 538*

minimum rate of return Minimum rate of profitability required for a company to accept an investment opportunity; also called *desired rate of return, required rate of return, hurdle rate, cutoff rate,* and *discount rate. p. 445*

mixed costs (semivariable costs) Costs that have both fixed and variable components. *p. 64*

multiple regression analysis A statistical tool that permits analysis of how a number of independent variables simultaneously affect a dependent variable.

negotiated transfer price Transfer price established through mutual agreement of the selling and buying segments. *p. 416*

net margin Profitability ratio that measures the percentage of sales dollars resulting in profit; calculated as net income divided by net sales. *p. 599*

net present value Capital budgeting evaluation technique in which future cash flows are discounted, using a desired rate of return, to their present value equivalents and then the cost of the investment is subtracted from the present value equivalents to determine the net present value. A zero or positive net present value (present value of cash inflows equals or exceeds the present value of cash outflows) means the investment opportunity provides an acceptable rate of return. *p. 449*

noncash investing and financing activities Certain business transactions, usually long-term, that do not involve cash, such as exchanging stock for land or purchasing property by using debt; reported separately on the statement of cash flows. *p. 640*

nonvalue-added activities Tasks undertaken that do not contribute to a product's ability to satisfy customer needs. *p. 15*

operating activities Cash inflows from and outflows for routine, everyday business operations, normally resulting from revenue and expense transactions including interest.

operating budgets Departmental budgets that become a part of the company's master budget; typically include a sales budget, an inventory purchases budget, a selling and administrative expense budget, and a cash budget. *p. 638*

operating departments Departments that perform tasks directly related to accomplishing the organization's objectives. (Contrast with *service departments*.) *p. 170*

operating leverage Cost structure condition that produces a proportionately larger percentage change in net income for a given percentage change in revenue; measured by dividing the contribution margin by net income. The higher the proportion of fixed cost to total costs, the greater the operating leverage. *p. 56*

operations budgeting Short-range planning activities such as the development and implementation of the master budget. *p. 306*

opportunity cost Cost of lost opportunities such as revenue forgone because of insufficient inventory. *pp. 15, 254*

ordinary annuity   Annuity in which cash flows occur at the end of each accounting period. *p. 448*

outsourcing   Buying goods and services from an outside company rather than producing them internally. *p. 260*

overapplied or underapplied overhead   The difference between the amount of overhead costs actually incurred and the amount of overhead costs allocated to work in process. *p. 491*

overhead   Costs associated with producing products or providing services that cannot be traced directly to those products or services in a cost-effective manner; includes indirect costs such as indirect materials, indirect labor, utilities, rent, depreciation on manufacturing facilities and equipment, and planning, design, and setup costs related to the product or service. *p. 6*

overhead costs   Indirect costs of operating a business that cannot be directly traced to a product, department, process, or service, such as depreciation. *p. 153*

participative budgeting   Technique in which upper-level managers involve subordinates in setting budget objectives, thereby encouraging employee cooperation and support in attaining the company's goals. *p. 308*

payback method   Capital budgeting evaluation technique in which the length of time necessary to recover the initial net investment through incremental revenue or cost savings is determined; the shorter the period, the better the investment opportunity. *p. 458*

percentage analysis   Financial analysis technique of comparing numerical relationships between two different financial statement items to draw conclusions; circumvents difficulties caused by differing materiality levels. *p. 590*

period costs   General, selling, and administrative costs that are expensed in the period in which the economic sacrifice is incurred. (Contrast with *product costs*.) *p. 10*

perpetual (continuous) budgeting   Maintaining a budget that always reflects plans for the coming 12 months by adding a new monthly budget to the end as the current month's expires; keeps management constantly involved in the budget process to allow timely recognition of changing conditions. *p. 306*

postaudit   After-the-fact evaluation of an investment project; the capital budgeting techniques employed in originally deciding to accept the project are used to calculate the results of the project using actual data; provides feedback regarding whether the expected results were actually achieved. *p. 461*

practical standard   A measure of efficiency in which the ideal standard has been modified to allow for normal tolerable inefficiencies. *p. 358*

predetermined overhead rate   Allocation rate calculated before actual costs or activity are known; determined by dividing the estimated overhead costs for the coming period by some measure of estimated total production activity for the period, such as the number of labor-hours or machine-hours. The base should relate rationally to overhead use. The rate is used throughout the accounting period to allocate overhead costs to work in process inventory based on actual production activity. *pp. 356, 490*

present value index   Present value of cash inflows divided by the present value of cash outflows. Higher index numbers indicate higher rates of return. *p. 454*

present value table   Matrix of factors to use in converting future values into their present value equivalents; composed of columns that represent alternative rates of return and rows that represent alternative time periods. *p. 446*

prestige pricing   Strategy that sets the selling price at a premium (more than average markup above cost) under the assumption that customers will pay more for the product because of its prestigious brand name, media attention, or some other reason that has piqued the interest of the public. *p. 112*

prevention costs   Costs incurred to avoid making nonconforming products. *p. 216*

price-earnings ratio   Measure that reflects the values of different stocks in terms of earnings; calculated as market price per share divided by earnings (net income) per share. *p. 602*

pro forma financial statements   Budgeted financial statements that reflect the master budget plans. *p. 308*

process costing system   System in which costs are distributed evenly across total production of homogeneous products, such as chemicals, foods, or paints; the average cost per unit is determined by dividing the total product costs of each production department by the number of units of product made in that department during the accounting period. The total costs in the last production department include all costs incurred in preceding departments so that the unit cost determined for the last department reflects the final unit cost of the product. *p. 536*

product costs   All costs related to obtaining or manufacturing a product intended for sale to customers; accumulated in inventory accounts and expensed as cost of goods sold at the point of sale. For a manufacturing company, product costs are direct materials, direct labor, and manufacturing overhead. (Contrast with *period costs*.) *p. 5*

product costing   Classifying and accumulating the costs of individual inputs (materials, labor, and overhead) to determine the cost of making a product or providing a service. *p. 5*

product-level activities   Actions taken (e.g., holding inventory, developmental engineering) that support a specific product or product line. *p. 210*

product-level costs   Costs incurred to support specific products or services; allocated based on the extent to which they sustain the product or service, and avoidable by eliminating the product line or type of service. *p. 257*

productive assets   Assets used to operate the business. May also be called *long-term assets*.

profit center   Responsibility center for which both revenues and costs can be identified. *p. 401*

profitability ratios   Measures of a company's capacity to generate earnings. *p. 599*

qualitative characteristics   Features of information such as company reputation, employee welfare, and customer satisfaction that cannot be quantified but may be relevant to decision making. *p. 256*

quality   The degree to which products or services conform to their design specifications. *p. 216*

quality cost report   Accounting report that typically lists the company's quality costs both in absolute dollars and as a percentage of total quality cost. *p. 218*

quantitative characteristics Features of information that can be mathematically measured, such as the dollar amounts of revenues and expenses, often relevant to decision making. *p. 256*

quick ratio (acid-test ratio) Measure of immediate debt-paying ability; calculated by dividing highly liquid assets (cash, receivables, and marketable securities) by current liabilities. *p. 592*

ratio analysis Same as *percentage analysis. p. 592*

raw materials Physical commodities (e.g., wood, metal, paint) transformed into products through the manufacturing process. *p. 9*

Raw Materials Inventory Asset account used to accumulate the costs of materials (such as lumber, metals, paints, chemicals) that will be used to make the company's products. *p. 486*

reciprocal method Allocation method that uses simultaneous linear equations to account for two-way relationships among service centers (service centers both provide services to and receive services from other service centers); the resultant cost distributions are difficult to interpret. *p. 175*

reciprocal relationships Two-way relationships in which departments provide services to and receive services from one another. *p. 175*

recovery of investment Recovery of the funds used to acquire the original investment. *p. 460*

reengineering Business practices companies design to improve competitiveness in world markets by eliminating or minimizing waste, errors, and costs in production and delivery systems. *p. 24*

regression analysis See *least-squares regression. p. 73*

relaxing the constraints Opening bottlenecks that limit the profitable operations of a business. *p. 271*

relevant costs Future-oriented costs that differ among alternative business decisions; also known as *avoidable costs. p. 254*

relevant information Decision-making information about costs, cost savings, or revenues that: (1) is future-oriented and (2) differs among the available alternatives; decision specific (information relevant to one decision may not be relevant to another decision). *Relevant costs* are also called *avoidable* or *incremental costs* and *relevant revenues* are also called *differential* or *incremental revenues. p. 254*

relevant range Range of activity over which the definitions of fixed and variable costs are valid. *p. 65*

residual income Performance measure that evaluates managers based on how well they maximize the dollar value of earnings above some targeted level of earnings. *p. 409*

responsibility accounting Performance evaluation system in which accountability for results is assigned to a segment manager of the business based on the amount of control or influence the manager has over those results. *p. 398*

responsibility center Identifiable part of an organization where control over revenues or expenses can be assigned. *p. 400*

responsibility reports Performance reports for the various company responsibility centers that highlight controllable items; show variances between budgeted and actual controllable items. *p. 401*

retained earnings Portion of stockholders' equity that represents the amount of net income kept in the business since inception (revenues minus expenses and distributions for all accounting periods). *p. 656*

return on assets The ratio of net income divided by average total assets. See also *return on investment. p. 600*

return on equity Profitability measure based on earnings a company generates relative to its stockholders' equity; calculated as net income divided by average stockholders' equity. *p. 601*

return on investment Profitability measure based on earnings a company generates relative to its asset base; calculated as net income divided by average total assets. ROI can be viewed as the product of net margin and asset turnover. Also called *return on assets* or *earning power. pp. 405, 600*

revenue transactions Business events that increase assets or decrease liabilities by providing services or products to customers in the course of operating a business.

R Square (R²) statistic The R^2 Statistic represents the percentage of change in a dependent variable that is explained by a change in an independent variable. *p. 73*

sales price variance Variance attributable to the actual sales price differing from the standard sales price; calculated as the difference between actual sales revenue and flexible budget sales revenue (the standard sales price per unit times the actual number of units sold). *p. 354*

sales volume variance Variance attributable to the actual volume of sales differing from the budgeted volume of sales; calculated as the difference between the static budget (standard sales price times standard level of activity) and the flexible budget (standard sales price times actual level of activity). *p. 352*

Sarbanes-Oxley Act of 2002 A federal law that regulates corporate governance. *p. 21*

scattergraph Method of estimating the variable and fixed components of a mixed cost by plotting cost data on a graph and visually drawing a regression line through the data points so that the total distance between the points and the line is minimized. *p. 69*

schedule of cost of goods manufactured and sold Internal accounting report that summarizes the manufacturing product costs for the period; its result, cost of goods sold, is reported as a single line item on the company's income statement. *p. 499*

Securities and Exchange Commission (SEC) Government agency authorized by Congress to regulate financial reporting practices of public companies; requires companies that issue securities to the public to file audited financial statements with the government annually. *p. 5*

segment Component part of an organization that is designated as a reporting entity. *p. 263*

selling, general, and administrative costs (SG&A) All costs not associated with obtaining or manufacturing a product; sometimes called *period costs* because they are normally expensed in the period in which the economic sacrifice is incurred. *p. 5*

semivariable costs See *mixed costs. p. 54*

sensitivity analysis Spreadsheet tool used to answer "what-if" questions to assess the sensitivity of profits to simultaneous changes in fixed cost, variable cost, and sales volume. *p. 121*

service departments Departments such as quality control, repair and maintenance, personnel, and accounting that provide support to other departments. (Contrast with *operating departments*.) *p. 170*

single-payment (lump-sum)   A one-time future cash flow that can be converted to its present value using a conversion factor. *p. 446*

solvency ratios   Measures of a company's capacity to pay long-term debt. *p. 597*

special order decisions   Deciding whether to accept orders from customers who offer to buy goods or services at prices significantly below selling prices regular customers pay. If the order's differential revenues exceed its avoidable costs, the order should be accepted unless qualitative factors, such as the order's effect on the existing customer base, could lead to unfavorable consequences. *p. 258*

split-off point   Stage in the production process where products made from common inputs become separate and identifiable. *p. 165*

standards   Budgeted per-unit selling prices or costs that are based on anticipated circumstances; multiplying the per-unit standards for cost and quantity produces the per-unit standard cost. *p. 358*

start-up (setup) costs   Costs of activities performed to prepare to make a different product or batch of products, such as resetting machinery, changing the production configuration, and conducting inspection. *p. 205*

statement of cash flows   The financial statement that classifies and reports a company's sources and uses of cash during an accounting period. *p. 636*

static budget   A budget based solely on the planned level of activity, such as the master budget; not adjusted for changes in activity volume. *p. 350*

step method   Two-step allocation method that accounts for one-way interdepartmental service center relationships by allocating costs from service centers to service centers as well as from service centers to operating departments; does not account for reciprocal relationships between service centers. *p. 173*

strategic cost management   Newer techniques managers can use to more accurately measure and control costs; implemented as a response to the complex modern automated business environment. These strategies include eliminating nonvalue-added activities, designing more efficient manufacturing processes, and developing more effective ways, like activity-based costing, to trace overhead costs to cost objects. *p. 216*

strategic planning   Long-range planning activities such as defining the scope of the business, determining which products to develop, deciding whether to discontinue a business segment, and determining which market niche would be most profitable. *p. 306*

suboptimization   Condition in which the best interests of the organization as a whole are in conflict with managers' own self-interests. *p. 409*

sunk costs   Costs that have been previously incurred; not relevant for decision making. For example, in an equipment replacement decision, the cost paid for the existing machine presently in use is a nonavoidable sunk cost because it has already been incurred. *p. 254*

T-account method   Technique for determining the cash inflows and outflows for the period by analyzing changes in balance sheet accounts from the beginning to the end of the period; infers the period's transactions from income statement and other data.

target pricing (target costing)   Strategy that sets the selling price by determining the price at which a product that will satisfy market demands will sell and then developing that product at a cost that results in a profit. *pp. 112, 214*

theory of constraints (TOC)   A management practice used to increase profitability by identifying bottlenecks or resource limitations that restrict operations and then removing them by relaxing the constraints. *p. 271*

time value of money   The concept that the present value of one dollar to be exchanged in the future is less than one dollar because of interest, risk, and inflation factors. *p. 444*

times interest earned   Ratio that measures a company's ability to make its interest payments; calculated by dividing the amount of earnings available for interest payments (net income before interest and income taxes) by the amount of the interest payments. *p. 497*

total quality management (TQM)   Management strategy that focuses on (1) continuous systematic problem-solving by personnel at all levels of the organization to eliminate waste, defects, and nonvalue-added activities; and (2) managing quality costs in a manner that leads to the highest level of customer satisfaction. *pp. 24, 218*

transferred-in costs   Costs transferred from one department to the next; combined with the materials, labor, and overhead costs incurred in the subsequent department so that when goods are complete, the total product cost of all departments is transferred to the Finished Goods Inventory account. *p. 537*

transfer price   Price at which products or services are transferred between divisions or other segments of an organization. *p. 413*

trend analysis   Study of business performance over a period of time. *p. 589*

turnover   Measure of sales in relation to operating assets; calculated as sales divided by operating assets. Along with *margin*, a component of return on investment. *p. 407*

turnover of assets ratio   See *asset turnover ratio. p. 407*

unadjusted rate of return (simple rate of return)   Measure of profitability computed by dividing the average incremental increase in annual net income by the average cost of the original investment (original cost divided by 2); does not account for the *time value of money. p. 449*

unfavorable variance   Variance indicating that actual costs exceed standard costs or actual sales are less than budgeted sales. *p. 351*

unit-level activities   Actions taken (e.g., using direct materials or direct labor) each time a unit of product is produced. *p. 208*

unit-level costs   Costs incurred with each unit of product made or single service performed; exhibit variable cost behavior; avoidable by not producing the unit of product or providing the service. Similarly, unit-level costs increase with each additional product produced or service provided. *p. 257*

upstream costs   Costs incurred before beginning the manufacturing process, such as research and development costs. *pp. 13, 214*

value-added activity   Any part of business operations that contributes to a product's ability to satisfy customer needs. *p. 24*

value-added principle   The benefits attained (value added) from a process should exceed the cost of the process. *p. 5*

value chain Linked sequence of activities that create value for the customer. *p. 24*

variable cost Cost that in total changes in direct proportion to changes in volume of activity; remains constant per unit regardless of changes in activity volume. *p. 54*

variable cost volume variance The difference between a variable cost calculated at the planned volume of activity and the same variable cost calculated at the actual volume of activity. *p. 352*

variable costing Costing method in which only variable manufacturing costs are capitalized in inventory; all fixed costs, including fixed manufacturing overhead, are expensed in the period incurred. On a variable costing income statement, all variable costs are subtracted from revenue to determine contribution margin, then all fixed costs are subtracted from the contribution margin to determine net income. Under variable costing, production volume has no effect on the amount of net income. (Contrast with *absorption costing*.) *p. 501*

variances Differences between standard (budgeted) and actual amounts. *p. 351*

vertical analysis Financial analysis technique of comparing items within financial statements to significant totals. *p. 592*

vertical integration Maintaining control over the entire continuum of business activity from production to selling, such as a company owning both a grocery store and a farm. *p. 262*

visual fit line Line drawn by visual inspection on a scatter-graph of data points to minimize the total distance between the data points and the line; used to estimate fixed and variable cost. *p. 70*

volume-based cost drivers Measures of volume such as labor-hours, machine-hours, or quantities of materials that are highly correlated with unit-level overhead cost; serve as appropriate bases for allocating unit-level overhead costs. *p. 204*

voluntary costs Discretionary quality costs incurred for prevention and appraisal activities. *p. 216*

weighted average method Means of computing equivalent units in a process cost system that accounts for the degree of completion of ending inventory only; ignores the state of completion of items in beginning inventory, accounting for them as if complete. *p. 550*

Work in Process Inventory Asset account used to accumulate the product costs (direct materials, direct labor, and overhead) associated with incomplete products that have been started but are not yet completed. *p. 486*

work ticket Mechanism (paper or electronic) used to accumulate the time spent on a job by each employee; sometimes called a *time card*. It is sent to the accounting department where wage rates are recorded and labor costs determined. The amount of labor costs for each ticket is summarized on the appropriate job-order cost sheet. *p. 538*

working capital A measure of the adequacy of short-term assets; computed as current assets minus current liabilities. *pp. 451, 594*

working capital ratio See *current ratio*. *p. 594*